Essays on Turkish Literature and History

Essays on Turkish Literature and History

By

Barbara Flemming

BRILL

LEIDEN | BOSTON

Cover illustration: Detail of 'Diez A fol. 70, p. 13 'Unterhaltung vor dem Mausoleum von Ġāzān Ḫān. Courtesy of STAATSBIBLIOTHEK ZU BERLIN – Preussischer Kulturbesitz, Orientabteilung, Diez A fol 70, p. 13.

Library of Congress Cataloging-in-Publication Data

Names: Flemming, Barbara.
Title: Essays on Turkish literature and history / by Barbara Flemming.
Description: Leiden ; Boston : Brill, 2018. | Includes bibliographical references and index.
Identifiers: LCCN 2017036761 (print) | LCCN 2017037118 (ebook) | ISBN 9789004355767 (E-book) | ISBN 9789004293106 (hardback : alk. paper)
Subjects: LCSH: Turkish literature--History and criticism. | Turkey--Civilization.
Classification: LCC PL206 (ebook) | LCC PL206 .F54 2017 (print) | DDC 894/.3509--dc23
LC record available at https://lccn.loc.gov/2017036761

Typeface for the Latin, Greek, and Cyrillic scripts: "Brill". See and download: brill.com/brill-typeface.

ISBN 978-90-04-29310-6 (hardback)
ISBN 978-90-04-35576-7 (e-book)

This book is printed on acid-free paper and produced in a sustainable manner.

For Sibylle Duda

Contents

Preface IX
List of Original Publications XIII

1 Faḫrī's Ḫusrev u Şīrīn from the year 1367: A Turkish mes̱nevī from the Emirate period 1

2 Turkish Manuscripts in the Staatsbibliothek 35

3 Şerīf, Sultan Ġavrī and the "Persians" 47

4 Some Remarks on Turkish Prose before the Tanẓīmāt Period 60

5 A *Ġazel* by Ḥasan oġlï (Unknown Poems in the *Dīvān* of Sultan Ġavrī) 73

6 The Pre-Wahhābī *Fitna* in Ottoman Cairo: 1711 78

7 From the Evening Talks of Sultan Ġavrī 88

8 Ḥālet Efendi's Second Audience with Napoleon 96

9 Literary Activities in Mamluk Halls and Barracks 105

10 Languages of Turkish Poets 117

11 Karl Süssheim 1877-1947: On his Hundredth Birthday, June 21st 1878/1978 131

12 Three Turkish Chroniclers in Ottoman Cairo 139

13 Literature in the Days of the Alphabet Change 148

14 The *Cāmiʿ ül-meknūnāt*: A Source of ʿĀlī from the Time of Sultan Süleymān 169

15 Two Turkish Bible Manuscripts in Leiden as Middle-Ottoman Linguistic Monuments 183

16 Romantic Emigrants in the Empire of Abdülhamid 190

17 *Ṣāḥib-qırān* and Mahdī: Turkish Expectations of the End of Time in the First Decade of the Rule of Süleymān 203

18 Political Genealogies in the Sixteenth Century 226

19 A Sixteenth-Century Turkish Apology for Islam: The *Gurbetname-i Sultan Cem* 239

20 Glimpses of Turkish Saints: Another Look at Lamiʿi and Ottoman Biographers 253

21 Public Opinion under Sultan Süleymân 276

22 Notes on ʿAruż in Turkish collections 285

23 The Sultan's Prayer before Battle 317

24 Re-reading the Story of the Religious "Fitna" of 1711 331

25 The Poem in the Chronicle: The Use of Poetry in Early Ottoman Historiography 344

26 ʿĀşıḳpaşazāde's View of Women 352

27 Female Participation in Earlier Islamic Mysticism (9th to 16th Century) 375

28 Goethe and Diez in the year 1790 423

29 On the Çırçıp: Yesterday and Today 448

Publications 469
Index 481

Preface

One justification for presenting this volume in English is the old "reason for writing", *sebeb-i teʾlif*, the topos "friends wanted me to publish this book," reinforced by online messages such as "someone just searched for your paper," and "researchers were not able to read your paper because you had not uploaded a copy." These twenty-nine essays, several of them updated, are made available as a varied account of fifty years of scholarship. Ever since my first report on work in the Westdeutsche Bibliothek in Marburg, I have been fortunate to live in the vicinity of great manuscript collections. Those holdings include unique manuscripts which were subsequently described and thereby opened up to research for generations of scholars.

The material is arranged in order of publication. Chronologically, it progresses as follows. The opening chapter introduces the reader to the culture of a Turkish principality in the Maeander estuary in the fourteenth century. I enlarged the text to depict the Aydınoğulları court from which the first Anatolian Turkish *Khusrev u Shirin* emerged that helped revise our conception of the literary period preceding Old Ottoman Literature.

A consensus implies that scholars perceive the Anatolian lands ruled by Seljuqs, Mamluks, Ilkhans and Turkmen princes not so much as independent territories in a non-Ottoman Anatolia, but as a preformation of the Ottoman Empire and by extension, the Turkish Republic. Accordingly, "Pre-Ottoman" figures as a "sub-discipline" in the *Comité International des Études Pré-Ottomanes et Ottomanes* that is now celebrating thirty years of existence.

Received wisdom has judged that Islamic mystical texts accord a privileged place to women. My chapter on "Female Participation" questions that judgment, and the not inconsiderable female presence in early Ottoman history is presented in the ʿĀşıḳpaşazāde chapter.

In a small series of essays I treated Turkish literature in Mamluk Egypt and Syria. They record, you might say, the progress of a Turkologist's contribution to early stages of what is now a large-scale international Mamluk research project. A little gem of old Azeri poetry (Hasan oglu) survived in a Mamluk manuscript. However unappealing to some scholars the Ottoman conquest of Egypt may have been – some called it a "final death knell" introducing "a life in apathy" – Cairo's Turkish and Arabic chroniclers, sometimes writing in both languages, had colourful information about social life in Ottoman Egypt.

In 1977, in my inaugural lecture at Leiden University, I spoke of Ottoman poets talking and writing in at least two different languages at a time when law forbade the use of other languages than Turkish. It could not be imagined then that Kurdish, Zaza, and Arabic would be considered Living Languages in Turkey today.

In the "supplications" (*tazarruʿ*) of Ottoman rulers before important battles with Christian enemies, concepts of the highest value to the Ottomans were brought forward. From Kosovo I (1389), I reviewed prayers spoken before major pitched battles down to 1448 (and 1596). Nationalist hindsight has assigned historical inevitability to such battles, especially to that of Koçhisar (today a *mahalle* in Mardin province). Just over five centuries ago, in May 1516, Safawid troops, consisting mostly of Turkmen tribesmen, were defeated by an Ottoman army of janissaries and Kurdish auxiliaries. Because this victory sealed the incorporation of the region of Diyarbekir into the Ottoman Empire, Koçhisar became an example of how Republican Turkish historiography entailed a *telos*, an endpoint from which history took its sense; thus at Koçhisar, the "unity of Turkey" was safeguarded, and the "Sunna of Anatolia triumphed over the Shiʿa of Iran."

Soon after this event, in Sultan Süleyman's age, catastrophes were visited on the population of "Rum": harvests failed, plagues and famine continued, an earthquake occurred. I examined the then almost universal expectation of the imminent end of all things, of the Last Day, expressed in Mevlana ʿIsa's *Cāmiʿ ül-meknunat*, the "Collector of the Concealed." My purpose was to define eschatology's function as an alternative narrative of suffering and loss. Three of my essays relate to the *Cāmī ül-meknūnāt*. The first (no. 14) has to do with the rediscovery of the work. The second (no. 17) mostly relates happenings and prophecies, and the third (no. 21) concerns the author and his milleniarist message.

Applying the criterion of attestation in order to draw a picture of what sixteenth-century Ottomans thought of early Anatolian shaykhs, we encounter a certain confusion caused by the close social interaction of established Islam and heterodox dervishes, while a sense of the holiness of Anatolia pervades Lamiʿi's biographies.

When a sixteenth-century Muslim Turk entered into a debate with a Christian, he did well to fortify himself by the *Gurbetname*, a story of how the captive Prince Jem defeated the Pope in a "discussion of faith." Next to the so-called "transcription texts" (in non-Turkish scripts), Turkish texts written in the Arabic script by non-Turkish scribes (an Ottoman Jew and a Pole) were linguistic sources for Middle Ottoman; the short paper sparked a Bible Project that was not to disappear from view for quite some time. A hint of early Wahhabism, or a touch of neo-Hanbalism, continued to attract attention to an incident in Cairo in 1711, where a *talib* from Syria preached against saint-worship and was accused of being a Muʿtazilite.

A widely shared view of Ottoman prose before the nineteenth century being either "simple" or "medium" or "elaborate," dependent on the circles for whom it was intended, left room for debate about intention, subject matter and stylistic level. Moreover, an Ottoman historiographer could make subversive poetical insertions in his prose narrative, treating events as they might have happened; lyrics could serve as an antidote to reasons of state demanding victory stories, and political genealogies demonstrated the legitimacy of rulers.

In the Goethe-Diez essay, the year 1790 appealed to me for several reasons. Taking notice of little-known details of Goethe's life during his journey to the outer reaches of the Holy Roman Empire, I looked into Diez's biography and suggested a revision of his place in Turkish studies.

In 1804, when Halet Efendi had his secret audience with Napoleon, his Sultan, barely three years after the invasion of Egypt, was not eager to recognize Napoleon as French Emperor and King of Italy. Halet Efendi's worries about court factions at home were justified; soon after his return, by 1806, the Ottomans were again at war with Russia.

In 1886, the German novelist Helene Böhlau, married to the newly-converted Omar al Rashid, settled in a quiet corner of the Ottoman capital; the idyll was recorded by a Turkish Muslim of Swedish origin, Ali Nuri (Dilmeç) (no. 16). In 1903, Karl Süssheim began his long sojourns in the Ottoman Empire. Süssheim, who narrowly escaped Nazi persecution to Turkey in 1941, is now by common consent a great collector and diarist; included in these pages is the beginning of what became decades of Süssheim studies by Jan Schmidt, myself and others.

It is generally acknowledged that abandoning the "old script" (Ottoman-Arabic) in 1928 was perhaps the greatest sacrifice made by Atatürk's educated followers. My original text was published in 1981; I incorporated further material.

For the last essay in this volume, I take both the long view and a micro-perspective. An accident in 2007 in which workers drowned in the Çırçıp river made me go backward from the present to the 1516 battle of Koçhisar.

All chapters are edited versions. Spelling and transcription are idiosyncretic and bear witness to stages in the history of transcribing Arabic, Persian, and Turkish, showing variations according to time and place.

Obviously, all the research covered in this volume has gone through a period of transition from books and journals to newspapers and the Internet. The footnote, that former "landmark in the history of civilization", now includes links to Web pages that are ephemeral and unstable. The Web's impact has been immense, and the study of textual data has progressed considerably. From the nineteen-eighties, the environment of Leiden University stimulated the search for ways to share knowledge through digital technology: students took part in an attempted corpus-based concordance of canonical Modern Turkish Poetry and textual criticism of Yunus Emre; to gain access to this renowned poet it is necessary to draw on literary tools such as old Turkish anthologies of poetry that served specific purposes (no. 22). A big desideratum remains: the Arabographic Optical Character Recognition applied to Ottoman manuscripts. Much toil went into a bi-directional dictionary project with Thijs Rault, who designed a word processing application that I am using to this day.

This book has been years in the making, and I am grateful to several people for their confident support and encouragement. Thank you to Dr. Sibylle Duda for being alongside every step of the way. I wish to thank Dr. Jan Schmidt for being my advocate from the start. For translating from the Polish at an early stage, I am grateful to my sister Dr. Dagmar Flemming.

Twenty-one of the chapters were originally published in German. With funding generously provided by an unnamed friend, they have been translated into English by John O'Kane, who was brought on board by Bernd Radtke. Thank you to John O'Kane for translating meticulously. Thank you to Professor Bernd Radtke for tireless support in general and for patiently processing my revisions to his Mac. Thank you to my nephew Christian Flemming for steering my venerable Word Perfect 5.1 through the ocean of Word and Windows. Thank you to Sibylle Duda for preparing the index. Thanks to Professor Karin Rührdanz for generous help with Ilkhanid manuscripts.

I have been heartened by the readiness of the Brill publishing house to undertake the publishing of this book. Thank you to Dr. Maurits van den Boogert for editing and publishing with great erudition and indefatigable patience. Thanks to Franca de Kort for thoughtfully taking care of publishing and illustration. Thanks to Peter Buschman for unflagging help at the printing stage.

The Hague, 19th May 2017

List of Original Publications

1. "Fahrī's Husrev u Šīrīn vom Jahre 1367. Eine vergessene türkische Dichtung aus der Emiratszeit", *Zeitschrift der Deutschen Morgenländischen Gesellschaft* 115 (1965), pp. 36-64.
2. "Türkische Handschriften der Staatsbibliothek", *Forschungen und Fortschritte der Katalogisierung der orientalischen Handschriften in Deutschland*, Wiesbaden 1966, pp. 1-9 (Forschungsbericht 10 der Deutschen Forschungsgemeinschaft).
3. "Šerīf, Sultan Ğavrī und die "Perser", *Der Islam* 45 (1969), pp. 81-93.
4. "Bemerkungen zur türkischen Prosa vor der Tanzīmāt-Zeit", *Der Islam* 50 (1973), pp. 157-167.
5. "Ein Gazel von Hasan oğlu (Unbekannte Gedichte im Divan von Sultan Gavrī)", with Turkish translation, *I. Türk Dili Bilimsel Kurultayına Sunulan Bildiriler 1972*, Ankara 1975, pp. 331-341.
6. "Die vorwahhabitische *fitna* im osmanischen Kairo 1711", *İsmail Hakkı Uzunçarşılı Armağanı*, Istanbul 1975, pp. 55-65.
7. "Aus den Nachtgesprächen Sultan Ğaurīs", in H. Franke, W. Heissig, W. Treue (eds.), *Folia rara Wolfgang Voigt LXV. diem natalem celebranti ab amicis et catalogorum codicum orientalium conscribendorum collegis dedicata*, Wiesbaden 1976, pp. 22-28.
8. "Hālet Efendis zweite Audienz bei Napoleon", in *Rocznik Orientalistyczny* 37 (1976), pp. 129-136.
9. "Literary Activities in Mamluk Halls and Barracks", in M. Rosen-Ayalon (ed.), *Studies in Memory of Gaston Wiet*, Jerusalem 1977, pp. 249-260.
10. *Die Sprachen der türkischen Dichter*, Leiden 1977. 28 pp.
11. "Karl Süßheim 1878-1947", in *Der Islam* 56 (1979), pp. 1-8.
12. "Drei türkische Chronisten im osmanischen Kairo", in I. Ševčenko en F.E. Sysyn (ed.), *Eucharisterion. Essays presented to Omeljan Pritsak on his Sixtieth Birthday. Harvard Ukrainian Studies* (Cambridge, Mass.) III/IV (1979-1980), pp. 228-235.
13. "Literatur im Zeichen des Alphabetwechsels", in *Anatolica* 8 (1981), pp. 133-157.
14. "Der Ğāmī ül-meknūnāt. Eine Quelle ʿĀlīs aus der Zeit Sultan Süleymāns", in H.R. Römer and A. Noth (eds.), *Studien zur Geschichte und Kultur des Vorderen Orients. Festschrift für Bertold Spuler zum siebzigsten Geburtstag*, Leiden 1981, pp. 79-92.
15. "Zwei türkische Bibelhandschriften in Leiden als mittelosmanische Sprachdenkmäler", Claudia Römer (ed.), *Wiener Zeitschrift für die Kunde des Morgenlandes. Festschrift Andreas Tietze zum 70. Geburtstag gewidmet von seinen Freunden und Schülern*, 76 (1986), pp. 111-118.
16. "Romantische Auswanderer im Reich ʿAbdülhamids", G. Schubert (red.), *Türkische Miszellen. Robert Anhegger Festschrift*, Istanbul 1987, pp. 131-143.

17. "Sāhib-Kirān und Mahdī. Türkische Endzeiterwartungen im ersten Jahrzehnt der Regierung Süleymāns", Gy. Kara (ed.), *Between the Danube and the Caucasus*, Budapest 1987, pp. 43-62.
18. "Political genealogies in the sixteenth century", *Osmanlı Araştırmaları. Journal of Ottoman Studies* VII-VII (1988), pp. 123-137.
19. "A Sixteenth-Century Turkish Apology for Islam: the *Gurbetname-i Sultan Cem*", *Byzantinische Forschungen* XVI (Amsterdam 1991), pp. 105-121.
20. "Glimpses of Turkish Saints: Another Look at Lāmiʿī and Ottoman Biographers", M.E. Subtelny (ed.), *Annemarie Schimmel Festschrift. Essays presented to Annemarie Schimmel on the occasion of her retirement from Harvard University, Journal of Turkish Studies* 18, Harvard University 1994, pp. 59-73.
21. "Public Opinion under Sultan Süleymân", H. İnalcık and C. Kafadar (eds.), *Süleymân the Second and His Time*, Istanbul 1994, pp. 49-57.
22. "Notes on ʿAruż in Turkish Collections", B. Utas and L. Johanson (eds.), *Arabic prosody and its Applications in Muslim Poetry*, Uppsala 1994, pp. 61-80 (Swedish Research Institute in Istanbul, Transactions Vol. 5).
23. "The Sultan's Prayer Before Battle", C. Heywood and C. Imber (eds.), *Studies in Ottoman History in Honour of Professor V.L. Ménage*, Istanbul 1994, pp. 63-75.
24. "Re-reading the Story of the Religious "Fitna" of 1711", I. Hauenschild, C. Schönig and P. Zieme (eds.), *Scripta Ottomanica et Res Altaicae. Festschrift für Barbara Kellner-Heinkele zu ihrem 60. Geburtstag*, Wiesbaden 2002, pp. 79-93.
25. "The poem in the chronicle: The use of poetry in early Ottoman historiography", Ugo Marazzi (ed.), *Turcica et Islamica. Studi in memoria di Aldo Gallotta*, Naples 2003, pp. 175-184.
26. ʿĀşıḳpaşazādes Blick auf Frauen", S. Prätor & Chr. K. Neumann (eds.), *Frauen, Bilder und Gelehrte. Studien zu Gesellschaft und Künsten im Osmanischen Reich. Festschrift Hans Georg Majer*, Istanbul, 2002, pp. 69-96.
27. "Teilhabe von Frauen an der älteren islamischen Mystik (9. bis 16. Jahrhundert)". *WZKM* 93 (2003), pp. 35-94.
28. "Goethe und Diez im Jahre 1790", Hendrik Fenz and P. Kappert (ed.), *Turkologie für das 21. Jahrhundert – Herausforderung zwischen Tradition und Moderne*, Wiesbaden 2007, pp. 129-148.
29. "Am Çırçıp: Einst und jetzt", Hendrik Fenz (ed.), *Strukturelle Zwänge – Persönliche Freiheiten. Osmanen, Türken, Muslime: Reflexionen zu gesellschaftlichen Umbrüchen. Gedenkband zu Ehren Petra Kapperts*, Berlin/New York 2009, pp. 145-167.

CHAPTER 1

Faḫrī's Ḫusrev u Şīrīn from the year 1367: A Turkish mes̱nevī from the Emirate period*

1 Scholarly Life at the Court of the Aydınoğulları

Among the numerous princes of the Emirate or Beylik Period who fostered the arts, the dynasty of the Aydınoğulları occupies a prominent position.[1] This *ġāzī* emirate, which owed its existence to the Turkish thrust westward during the last third of the 13th century and which from the start lay outside the traditional Seljuk state frontier,[2] came to acquire considerable wealth especially by means of its naval achievements. Early on, the Aydınoğulları began to employ the treasures taken from the Byzantines and Franks "on the path of God" for religious purposes and for the cultivation of the arts and sciences. Soon after the Turkish conquest of the western marches (*uc*), the Mevlevīye had established strong links to the house of Aydın, even before it had achieved independence. Intent on winning the Turkomans and enticing them away from their heterodox, quasi-shamanistic *babas*, Ulu ʿĀrif Çelebī (1312-1320) repeatedly sojourned in the marches. He visited the newly conquered Birgi (Pyrgion)[3] as early as 1304 and 1308, during the lifetime of his father Sultan Veled (d. 1312).[4] While many architectural monuments of the Aydınoğulları have been preserved, the written works produced at their court are not all known and reliably classified.

Within the framework of the present preliminary study, which will focus on a Turkish work that was composed in the Aydın Emirate and until 1965 remained unknown, special interest is due to the position of Turkish at the

* Translated by John O'Kane.

1 I. Mélikoff, art. "Aydın-oghlu", *EI²* (1960), 763. The scholarly discussion on the historical setting has since been continued and summed up in Cemal Kafadar, *Between Two Worlds. The Construction of the Ottoman State*, Berkeley and Los Angeles, 1995, and Elizabeth A. Zachariadou, *Studies in Pre-Ottoman Turkey and the Ottomans*, London 2007.

2 For the widespread notion that the Ottoman dynasty at the end of the thirteenth century entered upon the inheritance of the Seljuks see Colin Imber, "The Ottoman dynastic myth", *Turcica* XIX (1987), p. 321.

3 *Shams al-Dīn Aḥmad-e Aflākī. The Feats of the Knowers of God (Manāqeb al-ʿārefīn). Translated from the Persian by John O'Kane*, Leiden-Boston-Köln 2002, p. 663.

4 Paul Wittek, *Das Fürstentum Mentesche*, Istanbul 1934, pp. 37 and 61-63; my *Landschaftsgeschichte von Pamphylien, Pisidien und Lykien im Spätmittelalter*, Wiesbaden 1964.

 | DOI 10.1163/9789004355767_002

courts of Birgi, Tire and Ayasoluġ (Ephesus, modern Selçuk)[5] and to the works preserved in this language. But in order to judge the extent and relative importance of these beginnings of a Turkish national literature, it is appropriate to take a look at the scholarly activity and level of education at the courts of the princes.

The generous and enthusiastic sponsorship accorded to orthodox Islamic religion and education on the part of the Aydınoğulları begins with the first prince of the dynasty, the "Sultan of the warriors for the faith", Mubārizeddīn Muḥammed Beg (1308-1334). This prince, in an effort to serve his religion not only with the sword but to engage himself more deeply in its doctrines, brought well-known religious scholars to his court as teachers, had Traditions from the Prophet explained to him, and may also have endeavored to learn Arabic in the company of his teacher Ibn Melek (see below). Along with his construction of an important mosque, Muḥammed Beg founded the first *medrese* of Aydın ili in Birgi. His sister, Sulṭān Şāh Ḫatun (d. 1310), established another *medrese* in the same town. Later on, *medreses* were created in Tire, namely the Ibn Melek Medrese founded by Süleymānşāh (d. 1349), the third son of Muḥammed Beg, and a "private" foundation, the ʿAlī Ḫān or Orta Medrese, which was built in 1354 by the Sheykh Ḥāccī ʿAlīḫān b. Muḥammed. Finally, the Ottoman registers mention an *ʿimāret* with *medrese* which a certain Yaḫşı Beg founded in Tire during the Emirate Period. Where the *medreses* of Sulṭān Şāh Ḫatun in Birgi and of Yaḫşı Beg in Tire were located is not known; unfortunately today the other three buildings are in ruin.[6]

These institutions were provided with ample endowments. Muḥammed Beg donated considerable properties to his *medrese* in Birgi – an entire village, fields, olive and pomegranate groves, and a water-mill. The professors and students were allocated "official lodgings" and "hostels", *süknā ve yurd*, on Bozdağ (Mt Tmolos), the summer residence of the prince. Fixed amounts were provided for their salaries; in the Ottoman register that lists these endowments 25 (*aqçes*) per day were allocated to a professor and 7 (*aqçes*) to one student (or all students?).[7] On the way to an audience with Muḥammed Beg, the professor of Birgi, dressed in gold-embroidered garments, rode to the residence on a sprightly mule, accompanied on his left and right by slaves and servants, while

5 Franz Taeschner, "Aya Solūk", *EI*² I (1960), 777f.

6 Himmet Akın, *Aydın oğulları tarihi hakkında bir araştırma*, Istanbul 1946, pp. 111, 143-44, 170 and 199.

7 Akın, pp. 37, 137, 143, 147 and 160.

the students walked ahead of him.[8] Naturally, the kadi of Birgi also had a well-endowed post; the usufruct of a whole village was established for him.[9]

The teaching activity of judges and theologians, as well as of physicians, made it indispensable to set up libraries. Here as well, the prince dispensed the money required for the copying of the necessary books (one could scarcely think of buying books). This basic collection of works in the library was at the disposition of whoever was professor in the *medrese* at a given moment.[10] Additional books were of course assembled in the usual way through donations by the religious scholars who were active there.[11] Scribes would have been put to work copying books that were needed to complete the library collection, and were probably even sent out to large libraries. Beyond that, calligraphers were at work who produced splendid manuscripts, especially of the Koran, in case a copy was to be donated to a newly built mosque. Thus the calligrapher Muḥammad b. Muḥammad b. Ibrāhīm b. al- Mudarrisī (?) produced a precious gilded Koran on Ṣafer 727/December 1326 for Muḥammed Beg's great mosque in Birgi (built 712/1312),[12] and the latter's youngest son, ʿĪsā Beg (1360-1390), donated thirty large fascicles (*cuz'*) of the Koran[13] to his famous mosque built in 1375 in Ayasoluġ. For the daily recitation of the Koran Muḥammed Beg had an entire flock of Koran readers, and his granddaughter, ʿAzīze Melek Ḫatun, the daughter of Umur Beg (1334-1348), founded a *dār al-ḥuffāẓ*[14] for the recitation of the Koran. We cannot here enter into the rich endowments by the same princely family for *zawiye*s or *tekkes* of dervish orders such as the Mevlevīs mentioned earlier.

Some names are known of the religious scholars, physicians and craftsmen who at the court of the Aydınoğulları enjoyed such favorable material circumstances as well as, in accordance with each person's rank, the respect of the princes. Among the earliest is the artist Muẓaffaraddīn b. ʿAbdalvāḥid b. Sulaymān al-Ġarbī who in 722/1322 made the magnificent pulpit of the great mosque in Birgi.[15] One of the personalities that Ibn Baṭṭūṭa met in 1333

8 H.A.R. Gibb (transl.), *The Travels of Ibn Baṭṭūṭa, A.D. 1325-1354*, Cambridge 1962, II, p. 438.

9 Akın, p. 139.

10 Akın, pp. 143 and 147.

11 For practical details see Franz Rosenthal, *The Technique and Approach of Muslim Scholarship*, Rome 1947, p. 10.

12 Akın, p. 111.

13 Professor Süheyl Ünver saw the 3rd *cuz'* in the home of Ekrem Ayverdi, the architectural historian. Cf. A. Süheyl Ünver, "İlimler tarihimizde Aydınoğlu İsā Beyle şahsına ait mecmuanın ehemmiyeti hakkında," in: *T.T.K. Belleten* XXIV/95 (1960), p. 451.

14 Akın, p. 138.

15 Akın, pp. 37 and 107.

at the court of Aydın was the Jewish personal physician of Muḥammed Beg; the North-African scholar does not record his name, perhaps on purpose because he was annoyed that greater honor was shown to this doctor than to the Koran-readers.[16] The *faqīh* al-Ḫvārizmī, who actually belonged to the Menteşe court at Milas, was temporarily residing in Ayasoluġ.[17] Muḥyīddīn, who was Ibn Baṭṭūṭa's host, appears as professor (*mudarris*) at the *medrese* in Birgi.[18] Ibn Melek or Ibn Firişte, apparently the father of the famous *faqīh* ʿIzzaddīn ʿAbdallaṭīf b. Firişte,[19] was the kadi of Birgi and teacher of Aydınoğlu Muḥammed Beg himself. His son, Firişte-oğlu or Ibn Melek, taught for many years at the *medrese* of Tire. Bahādur b. Sayfaddīn al-Bayṭār (a veterinarian?) built a mosque (*mascid*) in Tire in 739/1338.[20] Şihābaddīn Aḥmad as-Sīvāsī al-Ayā̱sulūġī, a well-known religious scholar who was originally a freedman of a burger of Sivas, taught at the court of ʿĪsā Beg.[21] Under ʿĪsā Beg, a highly cultured prince who had certainly already learned Arabic and Persian in his youth, scholarly activity in general flourished once again. He occupied himself with almanacs and with religious and philosophical questions, as well as poetry and medicine, as can be seeen in the private miscellany manuscript (*el mecmuası*) of ʿĪsā Beg to which A. Süheyl Ünver devoted a study.[22] He summoned the most illustrious scholar of the time to his court, the physician and theologian from Konya, Ḫiżr b. ʿAlī b. al-Ḫaṭṭāb, called Ḥāccī Paşa, who had studied in Cairo and later practised there as head doctor of a hospital.[23]

The scholarly activity in the *medreses* in Aydın ili embraced the chief fields of Islamic science. Almost all of them are dealt with in the surviving handbook-like works which were written – in the Arabic language of course – in the form of commentaries, glosses on commentaries or treatises on individual subjects, by the theologians, jurists and medical doctors who taught there and which in part remained popular with later generations. Among these in the field of interpretation of the Koran was the above-mentioned Aḥmed

16 Ibn Baṭṭūṭa, C. Defrémery, and B.R., Sanguinetti, (ed. and transl.), *Voyages d'Ibn Batoutah*, Paris 1877, II, p. 305; Gibb, II, p. 443.

17 Ibn Baṭṭūṭa, II, pp. 279 f.; Gibb, II, p.429.

18 Ibn Baṭṭūṭa, II, pp. 296 f.; Gibb, II, pp. 438 f.

19 Cf. GAL, S II, p. 315; and Akın pp. 37, 96 (ftn. 472) and 111. And now Ö.F. Akün, *EI*², II, p. 923, s.v.

20 Akın, pp. 37 and 116.

21 Hellmut Ritter, "Ayasofya kütüphânesinde tefsir ilmine âit arapça yazmalar", in: *Türkiyat Mecmuası* VII-VIII, cüz II, 1945, p. 59, no. 48.

22 Ünver, "İlimler", pp. 452-55. The miscellany is preserved in the Ahmed Necib Paşa Library in Tire.

23 Cf. art. "Hâcî Paşa" in *İA*, V, pp. 28-30, by Abdülhak Adnan Adıvar.

as-Sīvāsī's commentary, *'Uyūn at-tafāsīr lil-fuḍalā' as-samāsīr*, known as the "*Tafsīr-i Şayḫ*",[24] as well as Ḥāccī Paşa's *Şarḥ Ṭavāli' al-anvār*, a commentary on the work of al-Bayḍāvī (d. 1286).[25] Commentaries on the *Ḥadīs̱* were provided by Ibn Melek (the son) whose chief fields were *fiqh* and *uṣūl al-fiqh*[26] but who also wrote on *taṣavvuf*,[27] as did Ḥāccī Paşa (commentary on the *Lavāmi' al-anvār* by al-Cīlī Şayd̲ala [d. 1100]).[28] In addition, the latter taught some branches of Islamic philosophy, wrote glosses to the commentary on logic by the kadi of Konya, Sirācaddīn Maḥmūd al-Urmavī (d. 1283),[29] and commented on the "Art of Disputation", the *Risāla fī ādāb al-baḥs̱* by Şamsaddīn Muḥammad as-Samarqandī (from the end of the 13th century).[30] Ḥāccī Paşa accomplished his major achievements in the area of medicine to which he had devoted himself in Egypt after a serious illness. Having composed two medical works in Cairo in 1369, he wrote his major work in this field in 1381 in Ayasoluġ, the *Şifā' al-asqām va davā' al-ālām* (*The Healing of Illnesses and the Remedy for Pains*) which is dedicated to 'Īsā Beg. In this work Ḥāccī Paşa bases himself on Galen, Ibn Sīnā and a series of other sources, but evaluates some observations of his own and summarizes in four *maqāla*s the knowledge of his time with regard to theoretical and applied medicine, nutrition, remedies and illnesses. The popularity of the book is attested by the particularly numerous surviving manuscripts – in Turkey, Egypt, Persia and India.[31] A similar presentation of the subject is found in his *Kitāb as-sa'āda val-iqbāl murattab 'alā arba'at aqvāl* which is also known as the *Kumm al-Calālī*; its content depends to a great extent on the *Şifā'*.[32] Finally, we may also mention a small medical treatise by him entitled *Kitāb al-musammā*.[33]

---

24 See ftn. 21 above.

25 GAL, I, p. 416, S, I, p. 743, no. 5; Mükrimin Halil Yınanç, *Düsturnamei Enverî*, Türk tarih encümeni külliyatı no. 15,, Istanbul 1929, p. 16, ftns. 1,5; Ünver, "İlimler", p. 449.

26 GAL, S I, p. 614c; S, I, p. 620; S I, p. 658, II(?), p. 191, S II, p. 263.

27 Muḥammed Mecdī's *Şaqā'iq-i nu'mānīye* (edition of Taşköprüzāde, Istanbul 1269/1852), p. 66; GAL S, II, p. 315.

28 GAL, S I, p. 775.

29 GAL I, p. 467. On the kadi's political activity in Konya cf. my *Pamphylien*, p. 41, ftn. 7, and p. 49, ftn. 2.

30 On as-Samarqandī's work see GAL I, p. 468, S I, p. 849; on the commentary see art. "Hâcî Paşa", *İA*, p. 28.

31 Art. "Hâcî Paşa", *İA*, pp. 28 f.; GAL, S II, p. 326.

32 GAL, S II, p. 326, no. 3; "Hâcî Paşa", *İA*, p. 29; Ünver, "İlimler", p. 448, following Ms. Manisa, no. 1788, Defter of the Veliyüddin Library, p. 145, no. 2536.

33 "Hâcî Paşa", *İA*, p. 29.

At the court of ʿĪsā Beg, who, as mentioned, was familiar with both classical Islamic languages, scholars also wrote in Persian. Yūsuf b. Muḥammad b. Ibrāhīm an-Nūrī translated for him under the title *Kaşf al-asrār ʿalā lisān aṭ-ṭuyūr val-azhār*[34] the religious reflections of ʿIzzaddīn b. Ġānim al-Vāʿiẓ (d. probably 678/1269): the *Kaşf al-asrār ʿan ḥikam aṭ-ṭuyūr val-azhār*.[35] Whether the famous Turkish poet Aḥmedī, Tāceddīn Ibrāhīm b. Ḫiżr (d. 815/1412-13), also wrote two Persian works for ʿĪsā Beg has not yet been sufficiently clarified. Here we may mention the two recently rediscovered writings: *Badāyiʿ as-siḥr fī ṣanāyiʿ aş-şiʿr* presents a reworking of the treatise on rhetoric *Ḥadāʾiq as-siḥr fī daqāʾiq aş-şiʿr* by Raşīdaddīn Vaṭvāṭ (d. 578/1182).[36] Although from the descriptions of the unique manuscript in Konya[37] dated Ramażān 835/May 1432 no mention of a patron emerges, it is assumed that Aḥmedī wrote for a certain Macdaddavla val-milla ʿĪsā Beg who is mentioned in Part II of the same manuscript.[38] The second newly discovered work of Aḥmedī entitled *Mirqāt-i adab* is one of the earliest rhymed dictionaries written in Anatolia and deals with Arabic and Persian. While it was not possible to ascertain a dedication in the Istanbul copy,[39] the Konya manuscript mentions Macdaddavla val-milla ʿĪsā Beg who commissioned the work, whereas the book was said to be written for his son Ḥamza Beg.[40] If this ʿĪsā Beg is really the Aydınoğlu as was declared with certainty when the Konya manuscript was discovered,[41] it would be desirable to examine two points. First, the honorific *laqab* of this prince is always attested as Faḫr add-avla va d-dīn.[42] Second, convincing evidence must be presented for the existence of a son named Ḥamza. While in fact three children

34 Yınanç, *Düsturnāme*, p. 16, ftn. 1,6. Described by Ahmed Ateş, "Hicrî VI.-VIII. (XII.-XIV.) asırlarda Anadolu'da Farsça eserler", in: *Türkiyat Mecmuası* VII-VIII, cüz II/194, 1945, p. 127, no. 35 (Ms.: Veliyüddin, no. 1630). Cf. also the Arabic Ms. in *Une liste des manuscrits choisis parmi les bibliothèques de Bursa*, Istanbul 1951, p. 18, no. 80, II.

35 GAL I, pp. 450 f.; S I, p. 808.

36 Ahmed Ateş, "Raşīd al-Dīn Vaṭvāṭ'ın eserlerin bâzı yazma nüshaları", in *Tarih Dergisi* 10 (1959), ftn. 2; on the treatise itself ibidem, pp. 15 f.

37 Ms. Konya, Müze no. 2540/1; Nihat Çetin, "Ahmedî'nin bilinmeyen bir kaç eseri", in *Tarih Dergisi* II/3-4 (1952), pp. 103 f.; Ahmed Ateş, "Konya kütüphanelerinde bulunan bazı mühim yazmalar", in *T.T.K. Belleten* XVI (1952), pp. 115 f., no. 63.

38 Ateş, "Konya yazmaları", p. 116.

39 Ms. of the library of the Türk Dili ve Edebiyatı Bölümü, no. 3923; Ali Alparslan, "Ahmedî'nin yeni bulunan bir eseri. 'Mirkat-i edeb'", in *Türk Dili ve Edebiyatı Dergisi* 10 (1960), p. 36.

40 Konya, Müze no. 2540/2. Çetin, p. 105. Ateş, "Konya yazmaları", p. 117, no. 6(?)

41 Çetin, p. 105; Ateş, "Konya yazmaları", pp. 116 f.

42 Akın, pp. 115 and 119; confirmed by the works mentioned here – cf. Ateş, "Farsça eserler", p. 127, concerning the *Kaşf al-asrār* – and the dedication repeated below on p. 57.

of ʿĪsā Beg are confirmed with certainty,[43] even in Akın's richly documented study a Ḥamza only seems to appear in the genealogical table.[44] So much for these two Persian writings of Aḥmedī who, as is known, lived at the court of Germiyan.

Against the backdrop of the busy scientific and literary activity in Arabic and occasionally also in the Persian language[45] in this Turkish *ġāzī* emirate, the number of Turkish works to be discussed now, which were produced at the instigation of the same princes of Aydın, will look rather modest. If the Turkish religious scholars of that period handled Arabic with such mastery, this had to do with the fact that – along with the fundamental supremacy of the Arabic language in classical Islamic studies – since the end of the 13th century close and friendly relations existed between the Turks of Anatolia and the Mamluk state, the result of which, in the intellectual domain, consisted not merely of a one-sided influence but of a lively intellectual exchange.[46] At the same time, however, the renowned *ʿulemāʾ* of Aydın ili spoke and also wrote in their Turkish mother tongue when this was necessary for the instruction of laymen; this was the case with both Ḥāccī Paşa, whose *Tashīl* will be discussed below, as well as with the professor Muḥyīddīn, whom Muḥammed Beg commissioned to write a Turkish commentary on the *ḥadīs̱* texts that were recorded by Ibn Baṭṭūṭa.[47] The objections raised against using Turkish for scientific purposes apparently did not exist for the domain of literature, not even for the religious-ethical literature of Islam, nor for medicine which, after all, belonged to the "foreign sciences".

Muḥammed Beg b. Aydın, the founder of *medrese*s in his principality, is also the initiator of the first Turkish translations in his region. He had an unknown author translate the collection of tales of the prophets, *Qiṣaṣ al-anbiyāʾ*, from Arabic into Turkish.[48] He may also have commissioned the translation of the

---

43 Mūsā, Umur II (Akın, p. 78), and a daughter, Ḥafṣa (Akın, p. 61).

44 Akın, p. 202. Ḫalīl Edhem, *Düvel-i islāmīye*, Istanbul 1927, p. 280; M. Fuad Köprülüzade, in *Türkiyat Mecmuası* II (1928), p. 9 ("Ḥamza Beg sought refuge with the Ottomans", without giving a source reference).

45 Presumably also produced in Aydın ili is the short *Risāla-i Calālīya* preserved in the Ms. Rağıp Paşa no. 670 (dated 763/1362), which an unknown author wrote in Persian for Çelebi Muẓaffaraddīn Mūsā Beg (ʿĪsā's son Mūsā?) and which is provided with a marginal note by the kadi of Aydın in the year 770/1369 (Ateş, "Farsça eserler", pp 131 f.).

46 For some examples see Flemming, *Pamphylien*, p. 119.

47 Ibn Baṭṭūṭa, II, p. 301; Gibb, II, p. 441.

48 We may mention the following Mss.: Türk Dil Kurumu Ktph. no. 1776-6037 (*XIII. Asırdan günümüze kadar kitaplardan toplanmış: Tanıklariyle Tarama Sözlüğü*, I/XVI). In Bursa: Kurşunluoğlu Tarih no.1 (Muharrem Ergin, "Bursa kitaplıklarındaki Türkçe yazmalar

Persian prose work by Farīdaddīn ʿAṭṭār (d. circa 617/1220), *Tad̲kirat al-avliyāʾ*, which was presumably undertaken by the same unknown author.[49] For the "King of the Emirs", Mubārizeddevle veddīn, who is thought to be Muḥammad Beg, a collection of medical treatises under the title, *Tuḥfe-i Mubārizī*, was translated into Turkish.[50]

Muḥammed's son and successor, Umur Beg (1334-1348), also had a medical book composed, a Turkish version of the collection of remedies which an unknown author wrote for him, the *Cāmiʿ mufradāt al-adviya val-aġdiya* (GAL, I, p. 492, and S, I, p. 897) by Ibn al-Bayṭār (d. 646/1248) under the title *Mufredāt-i ṭibb*.[51]

A certain Mesʿūd or Qul Mesʿūd dedicated to Umur Beg – presumably while the latter's father was still alive, circa 1330[52] – a Turkish translation of the book of fables, *Kalīla va Dimna*.[53]

In 751/1350 Mesʿūd b. Aḥmed, Ḫoca Mesʿūd, began working on the Turkish romance, *Kenz el-bedāyiʿ* or *Süheyl ü Nevbahār*, of which his nephew ʿIzzeddīn

arasında", in *Türk Dili ve Edebiyatı Dergisi* IV (1950), p. 131). Yınanç, *Düsturname*, p. 16, ftn. 1,1 and Köprülüzāde, in *EI* IV, p. 1013, mention a Ms. Ulu Câmi (no. 21). In Kayseri: Umumî Ktph. (Yınanç, *Düsturname*, loc.cit.). Cf. also İsmail Hakkı Uzunçarşılı, *Anadolu Beylikleri ve Akkoyunlu, Karakoyunlu Devletleri*, Ankara 1937, p. 81.

49 Manuscripts that according to their type belong together, in Istanbul: Mihrişah (Süleymaniye) no. 166, Veliyüddin no. 1643 and Bayezid Umumî no. 3286 (Hellmut Ritter, "Philologika XIV. Farīduddīn ʿAṭṭār, II", in *Oriens* 11 [1958], pp. 70 f.); in Bursa: Müze Kitaplığı no. E 53/218 (Ergin, p. 111; *Manuscripts choisis Bursa*, p. 61, no. 25)

50 Edgar Blochet, *Bibliothèque Nationale. Catalogue des manuscrits turcs*, Paris 1932-1933, I, p. 70, no. 171. According to Ünver, "İlimler", p. 451, Mesud Koman published the work on the basis of the Ms. Koyunoğlu.

51 F.N. Kutluk, in *Türk Tıb Tarihi Arşivi*, Yıl 3, sayı 112, Istanbul 1939, pp. 116-17 (cited from Akın, p. XV, ftn. 19); two manuscripts in Bursa: Müze no. E 83/217 (Ergin, p. 112; *Manuscrits choisis Bursa*, p. 61, no. 24) and Haraççıoğlu no.1119 (Ergin, p. 121; *Manuscrits choisis Bursa*, p. 31, no. 205). In Istanbul: Fatih no. 3635 (*Tanıklariyle Tarama Sözlüğü* I/XVII); Fehmi Edhem Karatay, *Topkapı Sarayı Müzesi Kütüphanesi Türkçe yazmalar kataloğu*, Istanbul 1961, I, pp. 571 f., nos. 1764-1765 (Revan Köşkü no. 1669 and Ahmed III no. 2113; on this see Ünver, "İlimler", p. 451); Ün. T. 1204 (GAL, I, p. 492). In Edirne: autograph in the Selimiye Library (Ünver, p. 451).

52 Köprülüzāde, *Araştırmalar*, p. 189.

53 Manuscripts: Lâleli Ktph. (now Süleymaniye), no.1897 (dated 895/1490) and Bodleian Library (Hermann Ethé, *Catalogue of the Persian, Turkish, Hindûstânî and Pushtû manuscripts in the Bodleian Library, Part II*, Oxford 1930, p. 1182, no. 2088). – An edition of three chapters and a study of the work: Ananiasz Zajączkowski, *Studja nad j≈ezykiem staroosmańskim. I. Morceaux choisis de la traduction turque-anatolienne de Calila et Dimna*, Kraków 1934.

Aḥmed had already written a thousand verses.[54] Whether this work of Mesʿūd b. Aḥmed and his *Ferhengnāme* (an abridged translation of Saʿdī's *Bostān*)[55] – both without a dedication – belong to the circle around the Aydınoğulları has been discussed in connection with the debate about identifying this author with the previously mentioned Qul Mesʿūd.[56] Since it was decided that Qul Mesʿūd and Mesʿūd b. Aḥmed were two different authors, the latter having been identified with Masʿūd b. Aḥmad b. Ṣādī[57] who in 746/1345 dedicated a Persian work, the *Tarcamat al-lālī(layālī?) va tadkirat al-maʿālī*, to a Vizier Abū Ṭālib,[58] there is no compelling reason to assume that the *Süheyl ü Nevbahār* and the *Ferhengnāme* were produced at the court of Aydın.[59] On the other hand, one may well suppose that Mesʿūd b. Aḥmed resided in the neighboring Germiyan[60] where his student Şeyḫoğlu Muṣṭafā lived.[61] Neither Turkish nor Arabic/Persian writings from the circle around Ḫiżr Beg (1348 up to circa 1360) have become known. A draft of a peace treaty, preserved in the Greek language,[62] bears the name and title of this prince who was forced to conclude a peace with the Latins that was unfavorable for the emirate.

Up until 1961 no Turkish work had been discovered that was associated with the name of the sponsor of Persian and Arabic works, Faḫreddīn ʿĪsā Beg. However, one may assume that both medical works that Ḥāccī Paşa wrote in Turkish belong to the period of ʿĪsā Beg. There are two translations or

54 J.H. Mordtmann based his first edition Mordtmann (*Suheil und Nevbehâr. Romantisches Gedicht des Mesʿûd b. Aḥmed*, Hannover 1925) on the Berlin Ms. or. fol. 3060. In 1926 a second manuscript was found in Çankırı by Ahmet Talat (Onay), whose relative Dehri Dilçin inherited it; his son Cem Dilçin based his second edition, *Süheyl ü Nev-Bahār. İnceleme – Metin – Sözlük*, Ankara 1991, on the Berlin (M) and Dilçin (D) manuscripts.

55 Four manuscripts have been mentioned: 1) Millet Ktph. Divanlar no.300 (basis of the printed edition of Veled Çelebi and Kilisli Rifat, have been mentioned: *Ferhengnāme-i Saʿdī tercümesi*, Istanbul 1342/1923-24. 2) Copenhagen: A.F. Mehren, *Codices persici, turcici, hindustanici* (*Codices orientales Bibliothecae Regiae Havniensis, Pars Tertia*), Copenhagen 1857, p. 59, no. XX. 3) Ms. in the possession of Muallim İsmail Hikmet Bey. 4) Part of the miscellany manuscript Manisa, Muradiye, Türkçe no.1856 (Köprülüzade, *Araştırmalar*, pp. 175-77).

56 For a survey of the relevant literature see Tahsin Banguoğlu, *Altosmanische Sprachstudien zu Süheyl ü Nevbahār*, Breslau 1938, pp. 9-11.

57 Rifat Bey Kilisli in *Türkiyat Mecmuası* II, p. 408; Köprülüzade, *Araştırmalar*, p. 190.

58 Manuscript Ayasofya no. 940, according to Banguoğlu, pp. 10 f.

59 Franz Taeschner, "Die osmanische Literatur", in *Handbuch der Orientalistik*, Bd. V, 1 Turkologie, Leiden-Köln 1963, p. 274, upholds this assumption.

60 Cf. Banguoğlu, pp. 11 f.

61 Cf. J. Deny, art. "Shaikhzāde" (1.) in *EI* IV (1934), pp. 303 f.; Taeschner, "Literatur", p. 274.

62 See Elizabeth A. Zachariadou, in *Byzantinische Zeitschrift* 55 (1962), pp. 254-65.

adaptations of Ḥāccī Paşa's above-mentioned *Kitāb as-saʿāda*. Concerning one of these compendia, entitled the *Muntaḫab aş-Şifāʾ*, it is occasionally said that it is dedicated to Muḥammed Beg of Aydın.[63] But since it is clearly a translation of the *Kitāb as-saʿāda*, which for its part has been recognized as a reworking of the *Şifāʾ* which was only written in 1381,[64] this attribution cannot be correct.[65] The short therapeutical handbook of the same author which is preserved in numerous widespread manuscripts, The *Tashīl aş-şifāʾ*[66] turns out to be a somewhat altered translation of the same *Kitāb as-saʿāda* with some theoretical and difficult passages left out. According to A. Adnan Adıvar, it cannot stand up to comparison with the Arabic original and has been translated in so hasty a manner that one would suppose a different translator had been involved if Ḥāccī Paşa himself had not written an apologetic preface emphasizing the importance of Arabic as a language for science.[67] And yet in the middle of the 15th century the *Tashīl* was still praised by a Turkish doctor, Sabuncuoğlu Şerefeddīn, as the "beginning and gateway of medical art" and held up as a model.[68]

---

63 Uzunçarşılı, *Beylikler*, p. 80: *Aydınoğlu namınadır* (which prince?). Manuscripts: Heinrich L. Fleischer, *Catalogus codicum manuscriptorum orientalium Bibliothecae Regiae Dresdensis*, Leipzig 1831, p. 7, no. 51 (without dedication); Wilhelm Pertsch, *Die orientalischen Handschriften der Herzoglichen Biblothek zu Gotha, II. Die türkischen Handschriften*, Vienna 1864, p. 98, nos. 112-113 (without dedication); Blochet, II, p. 69, no.1340 (without dedication), differing recension without dedication Blochet, I, p. 69, no. 170. GAL, II, p. 233 cites Istanbul, Ün. Yıldız Tıp no. 877. Additional manuscripts: Tire, İbn Melek Library, Manisa, Muradiye Library, several Istanbul libraries (according to GAL, S II, p. 326) and Konya, Ms. Müze no. 2832. 31. 2. E (Ünver, "İlimler", p. 449). Karatay, *Yazmalar*, I, p. 569, no. 1757 (Hazine, no. 545): *Aydınoğlu Meḥmed Beye ithaf olunmuş*. Autograph in the Topkapı Sarayı Ahmed III according to Ünver, p. 449.

64 Hâcı Paşa/*İA*, V, p. 29.

65 Already Süheyl Ünver, *Selçuk Tababeti*, Ankara 1940, p. 38, ftn. 3, expressed doubts in this regard.

66 Manuscripts: Fleischer, *Dresden*, p. 7, no. 52; H.L. Fleischer, *Codices arabici, persici, turcici*, in *Catalogus librorum manuscriptorum qui in bibliotheca senatoria civitatis Lipsiensis adservantur*, Grimma 1838, no. CCLXVIII; Pertsch, *Gotha*, p. 97, nos. 110-111; Gustav Flügel, *Die arabischen, persischen und türkischen Handschriften der k.-k. Hofbibliothek zu Wien*, Vienna 1865-1867, II, p. 536, no. 14; Wilhelm Pertsch, *Verzeichniss der türkischen Handschriften* (*Die Handschriften-Verzeichnisse der Königlichen Bibliothek zu Berlin*, Berlin 1889, p. 296, no. 280; Blochet, I, p. 69, no. 169, II, p. 217, no. 1271; Istanbul, Veliyüddin, no. 2490 and Süleymaniye, no. 849, according to *Tanıklariyle Tarama Sözlüğü* II/XV and Fatih, no. 3546, according to Vecihe Kılıcoğlu, *Cerrahiye-i İlḫaniye* (Ank. Ün. Dil ve Tarih-Coğrafya Fak. Yayınları no. 97), Ankara 1956, p. 80. According to Abdulhakk Adnan, *La Science chez les Turcs Ottomans*, Paris 1939, p. 16, the *Tashīl* was translated into German by Hans Bart.

67 Hâcî Paşa/*İA*, V, p. 29.

68 Kılıcoğlu, pp. 17 and 22.

At least five works were translated into the Turkish of Rūm at the court of the first Aydın princes Muḥammad and Umur, translations which today present valuable evidence regarding this language in the 14th century.[69] ʿĪsā Beg, whose interest in Arabic and Persian we have mentioned, was also committed to Turkish. Acquainted with this language on a much higher level of literary sophistication than formerly believed among "pre Ottoman" Turks (see Section VII below), ʿĪsā Beg commissioned his court poet Faḫreddīn Yaʿqūb to compose for himself and his circle of courtiers a long Turkish *mes̱nevī* based on the Persian romance *Ḫusrav u Şīrīn* by Niẓāmī (d. 1213/4). Of Faḫrī's work a single manuscript has survived. To this we shall now turn.

II The Berlin Manuscript Hs. or. Quart 1069

The single known manuscript Hs. or. quart 1069 belonged to the manuscript collection of Professor Karl Süssheim which the West German State library, Marburg, acquired from the scholar's widow toward the end of 1960. The manuscript was first described by me in December 1961/February 1962 during the process of cataloging Turkish manuscripts.[70] When the holdings of the State Library, Marburg, were relocated to West Berlin in the late 1970s, the manuscript became part of the Staatsbibliothek – Preussischer Kulturbesitz. From 1992 it has been preserved in Berlin in the reunited Staatsbibliothek zu Berlin – Preussischer Kulturbesitz.

The manuscript was rebound in violet cardboard with leather backing. Yellowish glazed paper without watermark. There is damage by bookworms, which towards the end of the manuscript have caused losses of text in the lower lines. The manuscript has been restored – with loss of text due to the overlap from pasting over – and rebound in random order. There are 168 folios, numbered with black ink after restoration but folio 58 has been skipped, from folio 118 there is another numbering that begins with 111.

The size of the paper is 250x165 mm, writing on each page is 195x130 mm. There are 15 lines to the page. The original catchwords are missing; sporadically catchwords have been added erroneously. The text has gold-ruled margins and in the middle two gold lines indicating the division between hemistichs. At the end are blue and gold decorative dots. The headings, which have been written in another, coarser hand and often do not accord with the text, are alternately blue with gold vocalization or gold and red with blue vocalization. On 42 pages

69 Cf. Ergin, p. 131, on the *Qiṣaṣ al-anbiyāʾ*: *14. asır Türkçesinin çok mükemmel bir örneğidir.*

70 Catalogue entry: *Türkische Handschriften. Teil 1.* Wiesbaden 1968, p. 324-325, No. 422.

blank spaces have been left for miniatures, none of which have been executed. The free spaces are in part defaced by practice pen strokes and scrawls.

The manuscript is not dated. It is written in black ink in a clear, professional *nesẖī*, fully vowelled, and would appear to have been copied in the early 16th century.[71] The scribe, who is not mentioned by name, in some places appears to have been wavering between different spelling conventions. He "apparently did not wish to mar the appearance of his work by crossing out his frequent errors, and his vowelling is as often as not capricious. One may presume, also, that he regarded many of the difficulties in the text merely as archaisms or dialectical peculiarities, and made no further effort to understand them."[72]

In 1974 I published the first edition of ms. Hs. or. quart 1069 in photocopy, with a transcription of the 4683 *mes̱nevī* verses and an introduction[73] discussing the work from a comparative point of view, as "a piece of literature rather than a linguist's source book" (Walsh). My transcription was marred by errors, the philological condition of the manuscript requiring more emendation and conjecture than I could manage; at least order has been restored to the folios as a basis for further research.

III Faẖreddīn Yaʿqūb b. Muḥammed, Known as Faẖrī

The following information about the author is taken from the manuscript. No reference to him has yet been found in other writings. The Turkish author, who repeatedly refers to himself by his *maẖlas*, Faẖrī, at the end mentions his name and hints at the country of his origin:

kemīne qul bu Faẖreddīn laqablu Verse 4673
bu illü yoq Mıṣırlu yā Ḥaleblü
adı Yaʿqūb özi ibn-i Muḥammed
şehini isteyen dāyim muẖalled

71 It is to some extent similar to the ductus of the Pressburg *Iskendernāme* manuscript from 991/1486 in plate XVI of Josef Blaškovi¸c (ed.), *Arabische, türkische und persische Handschriften der Universitätsbibliothek in Bratislava*, Bratislava 1961.

72 John R. Walsh in his valuable review of my *Faẖrīs Ḫusrev u Şīrīn* (see the next footnote) in WZKM 67 (1975), p. 331; hereafter cited as Walsh, review.

73 *Faẖrīs Ḫusrev u S˘īrīn: eine türkische Dichtung von 1367.* Wiesbaden, 1974. Extracts of the introduction, translated by Vanessa Karam, have been published as "Old Anatolian Turkish poetry in its relationship to the Persian tradion", in Lars Johansen and Christiane Bulut (eds.), *Turkic-Iranian Contact Areas*, Wiesbaden 2006, pp. 49-68.

"This lowly slave, with the honorific Faḫreddīn, is a native of this country, he is neither from Egypt nor from Aleppo; his name is Yaʿqūb, he is the son of Muḥammed; evermore wishing lasting life to his king."

Faḫrī makes a point of being a true son of this newly conquered land, the region of Aydın which had in fact only become Turkish by the end of the 13th century.[74] His complaints in verse 489 – *zī Türkmenlik* – besides being a formula for "ineptitude" may be taken as an indication that Faḫrī was a Turkoman. The few words that Faḫrī says here and there regarding himself are of a personal nature and do not allow any conclusions to be drawn about his external life, for instance about his study career and profession. In the introduction he says:

ne soyum var ne gücüm var ne mālum　　　Verse 210

"I have neither (noble) family nor power (strength) nor property."

The following couplet at the end of the work seems to indicate a Sufi attitude to life:

çu ʿömrüñ dünyede yarım nefesdür　　　Verse 4666
saña bir loqma vü bir ḫırqa bes dür

"Since your life in the world is only half a moment (breath), a single morsel and a patched frock are sufficient for you."

In another passage he expresses his relation to God thus:

elin dut Faḫrīnüñ dermānla <döndür>　　　Verse 2446
bu dünyādan anı īmānla göndür
günāhı var yazılar ṭopraġınca
vebāli var aġaçlar yapraġınca
hīç eylükden yaña tedbīri yoqdur
velī ṭāʿatda kim taqṣīri çoqdur
günāhı çoġısa ʿafvuñ daḫı çoq
s̱evābı yoġısa aña ṭañuñ yoq

74 On the history of the Aydınoğulları see I. Mélikoff, art. "Aydın-oghlı", EI^2 (1960), with bibliography.

> Hold Faḫrī's hand, give him a cure to mend his ways; with Faith lead him away from this world. He has sins as the plains have earth; he has transgressions as the leaves have trees. As for striving after the good, his designs are nil, but in obedience his remissness is great. Greater than the number of his sins is Your forgiveness; if his merit is lacking, this is of no concern to You.[75]

For favors granted him Faḫrī thanks the House of Aydın and especially his patron ʿĪsā Beg to whom he repeatedly pledges loyalty and with whom he actually did have a closer relationship:

> çu ʿāmm iken ėdindi ben qulın ḫāṣṣ Verse 183
>
> "He has made me, his slave, a commoner, his courtier."

One of the favors which Faḫrī received was the right to derive his pen name from "Faḫr ad-davla va d-dīn", ʿĪsā Beg's honorific (mentioned above).[76]

If on one occasion, out of modesty, Faḫrī denies that his poetry possesses color and fragrance,

> benüm şiʿrümde yoqdur rengi ne bū, Verse 147

when he is invited to translate Niẓāmī, we may either assume he had already composed other poetry, or this may refer to the work we have before us.

In one passage Faḫrī speaks about a direct observation of his own. Where Niẓāmī at the end of the story of Farhād declares that he has not himself seen the pomegranate tree that grew from Farhād's axe handle but has read about it in a manuscript:

---

75 For *ṭañı yoq* see *Tarama Sözlüğü* II *C-D*, pp. 1000-1001 "*ḍañı yok, ṭañı yok*)*: İḥtiyācı yok, önem verdiği yok* (?). For the theme "God has no need of the service and worship of His bondsmen," "God's "lack of need" (*istiġnā*), see Hellmut Ritter, *The Ocean of the Soul. Man, the World and God in the Stories of Farīd al-Dīn ʿAṭṭār, translated by John O' Kane with Editorial Assistance of Bernd Radtke*, Leiden 2003, pp. 567-571; see also Bernd Radtke, *Weltgeschichte und Weltbeschreibung im mittelalterlichen Islam*. Beirut 1992, citing aṭ-Ṭabarī's World History.

76 "It was the prerogative of the patron to grant this honour, which implied a specially close relationship to the sovereign." J.T.P. de Bruijn, "The name of the poet in classical Persian poetry", Charles Melville (ed.), *Proceedings of the Third European Conference of Iranian Studies* Part 2, Wiesbaden 1999, p. 46-47.

Niẓāmī gar nadīd ān nār bun-rā
bi-daftar dar chunīn ḫvānd īn suḫan-rā[77]

Faḫrī points to a local phenomenon

söze kim iki ṭanuq ola ayıq — Verses 3445-3448
inanur qāżī-yi Islām bayıq
bu nār aġacını görmiş iñen çoq
Çalabuñ qudretine hīç şek yoq
quru ṭaşı kireçde gördi özüm
ki bitti (!) çibuġı hem vėrdi üzüm
gören kişi çibuġı yüce ṭamı
bilür kim sözi gėrçekdür Niẓāmī

"The kadi of Islam will surely believe a statement for which there are two rational witnesses. Lots of people have seen this pomegranate tree; there is no doubt whatsoever regarding God's omnipotence. I myself have seen, in limestone deposits, an ordinary stone whose trunk (vine) grew and even brought forth grapes. Whoever sees the trunk and the (pillarless) high roof (of heaven), knows that what Niẓāmī says is true."

Faḫrī is surely thinking of the famous calcareous springs in Pamukkale near Denizli where one can see petrified plants of every kind.[78]

In the epilogue Faḫrī touches on old age and its signs:

çun elli geçdi açılmadı gözüñ — Verses 4657-4659
bu bėş günde ne ḥāṣıl ėde özüñ
sen oġlanlıq zamānın çun geçürdüñ
yigitlik kārivānın çun geçürdüñ
ṭoluñuñ qara iken şöylekim qīr
qarışdı qaraya aq olduñ oş pīr

"After fifty years have gone by, your eyes have not yet opened; what do you want to achieve during these five days, now that you have put your boyhood behind you and you have let the caravan of youth pass by? Though

77 *Ḫusrav u Şīrīn*/Dastgirdī, p. 262, l. 9.

78 I am indebted to Andreas Tietze for information and comments on this and many other passages.

your temples were once as black as pitch, white is mixing with black and now you are old."[79]

Faḫrī had three sons, Muḥammed, Aḥmed and Maḥmūd who, to his great sorrow, all died before him:

zemāne urdı saña bir qaç gez dāġ Verses 4661-4665
içüñde qomadı ḥasret odı yaġ
oġullar ölümi kesdi gücüñ hem
birisi zaḫmına olmadı merhem
Muḥammed diyü aġladuñ biraz gün
ururduñ göke āh Aḥmed diyü ün
bu gez Maḥmūdıla ḫoş eglenürken
ṣoñumda qala diyü öglenürken
seʿādet qılmadı baḫtıla yārī
aradan gitdi vėrdi saña zārī

"Destiny has several times inflicted wounds on you; in your inmost being the fire of suffering has left no remaining oil. The death of your sons has completely sapped your strength, there was no balm for the pain from a single one of them. All day long you wept over Muḥammed, you let your voice echo up to the heavens with sighs for Aḥmed. Then when you consoled yourself with Maḥmūd and comforted yourself with the thought that he would live beyond your end, luck did not assist you with a stroke of good fortune; [it (luck) passed you by and] gave you (only) lamentation."

If we attempt to place him in relation to contemporaries, we may well assume that Faḫrī, as a courtier – *ḫāṣṣ* – of ʿĪsā Beg, came into contact with the physician and theologian Ḥāccī Paşa, mentioned above.

A connection between Faḫrī and the "circle" of men of letters at the court of Germiyan is conceivable. Consider, for example, that Ḥāccī Paşa for his part was an acquaintance or even a friend of the poet Aḥmedī (see above); they had been in Egypt together. It remains to examine in the future whether Aḥmedī's rival, the *nişancı* and treasurer of the Germiyan prince, Şeyḫoġlu Muṣṭafā (born circa 1340)[80], knew our Faḫrī who may have been roughly the same age as Şeyḫoġlu's teacher, Ḫoca Mesʿūd. In his *Kenz ül-küberā'*, a mirror for

79 For the topos of age in Sanā'ī see J.T.P. de Bruijn, *Of Piety and Poetry*, pp. 30-31.
80 Kathleen Burrill, "Sheykh-oghlu", *EI* IX (1997), 418-419.

princes-cum-*tezkire* of poets Şeyḫoğlu cites poetry from contemporary poets, including one "Ḫāṣṣ", about whom nothing is known.[81]

IV Reasons for Writing, and Date of the Book

The impulse for composing the work came from ʿĪsā Beg who had Faḫrī recite to him Niẓāmī's epic in Persian:

şeh-i Aydınlaruñ yėgi vü faḫrı — Verses 128-129
işāret qıldı ben qula ki Faḫrī
oqıġıl Ḫusrev[82] u Şīrīn kitābın
işitlüm (sic) Ḫusrev Şīrīn ʿitābın

"The best and the pride of the kings of Aydın instructed me, the slave Faḫrī: 'Recite the book of Ḫusrev and Şīrīn! We want to hear the reproaches that Ḫusrev and Şīrīn made one another (or the things they said to one another).'"[83]

When the recitation turned out to be satisfactory and the prince had dispensed much praise, his great men consulted with him:

ḫavāṣṣ-i devleti aʿyān-i leşker — Verses 137-140
qamusı mihter ü bihter ü server
dėdiler şehriyāra kāmu-gāra

81 Kemal Yavuz, (ed.) *Şeyhoğlu Kenzü'l-Küberâ ve Mehekkü'l-Ulemâ*, Ankara 1991, p. 14. The single surviving manuscript, formerly in Mehmet Fuat Köprülü's private library, was preserved in the vault of the Yapı ve Kredi Bankası. For his edition, the manuscript being inaccessible, Professor Yavuz had recourse to photographs.

82 If the usual transcription Ḫusrev is employed here, this is with a certain hesitation since using the suffix *Ḫusravlıq* in fact indicates a velarized pronunciation. However, since in older Ottoman orthography it occasionally happens that a velarized ending is attached to a word we know to be palatal, this ending *-lıq*, which only occurs once, did not appear to be decisive enough. In Şeyḫī in the corresponding verse one finds *ḫusrevlik* (Timurtaş, *Şeyhī*, p. 30, verse 809).

83 A. Tietze: "Apparently [by *ʿitāb*] is meant simply "the things they said". Likewise, *maʿnī* [in line 4 of the next Turkish quotation] and words like *cevāb* were at the time used in a very general sense to mean something like 'story." In this epic, of course, the lovers do reproach one another and sometimes have their court singers express their expostulations (*muʿātaba*); for Şīrīn's reproach (*ʿitāb*) see Faḫrī's verses 2819-2857.

bu maʿnī olsayıdı āşikārā
ki bize daẖı ḥaẓẓ olaydı vāfir
budur biz cümlemizde meyl-i ẖāṭir
ki geçmiş işleri hem añlayavuz
biraz ʿibret dutuban ḍañlayavuz

"The officials of his state, the dignitaries of the army, all great, good and outstanding men, spoke to the sovereign of fair fortune: would that this literary theme (*maʿnā*[84]) were manifest, so that abundant pleasure would come to us, too! This is our unanimous wish: that we may understand past deeds, that in drawing lessons, we may wonder a little."

As a result, ʿĪsā Beg commissioned Faẖrī to translate the work into Turkish:

ki öldiyse Niẓāmī aña cān ol Verses 145-146
anuñ şīrīn sözine tercümān ol
ʿAcemden ḥāṣıl ėtdi ol s̱enālar
nola ger Türk eren qıla duʿālar

"Since Niẓāmī is dead, you become life for him; you be the interpreter of his sweet words! He has won praise among the Persians. How would it be if Turkish men uttered prayers (for him or for you)?"

Faẖrī protested his reluctance to embark on such a task. But despite his "humble protestations of inadequacy for the task assigned him,"[85] he does not share the view of many of his contemporaries and especially of literati in the 16th century (see below, Section VII) that Turkish was not suitable for all higher forms of literature because of its rough and sparse character:[86] We mention only the apologies which the author of *Süheyl ü Nevbahār*, Mesʿūd b. Aḥmed, makes in this respect.[87] An exception to the rule is Şeyẖ Aḥmed Gülşehrī, an important poet who was, it must be said, completely forgotten in the 15th and 16th centuries. While he wrote *Türk dilince daẖı Tāzīden laṭīf,*[88] Faẖrī also used his mother tongue in full self-confidence:

84 De Bruijn, *Of Piety*, p. 10.
85 Discussed in Walsh, review, p. 332-3.
86 Examples are found in Meḥmed Fūʾād Köprülüzade, *Millī edebiyāt cereyānınıñ ilk mübeşşirleri ve Dīvān-ı̈ Türkī-i basīṭ,* Istanbul 1928, pp. 10-15.
87 Suheil/Mordtmann, pp. 370-72; Köprülü, *Mübeşşirler*, ftn. 12.
88 Köprülü, *Mübeşşirler*, p. 12, cites Gülşehrī's adaptation (717/1317-18) of the *Manṭiq aṭ-ṭayr* by Farīdaddīn ʿAṭṭār.

şeker gibi bu Türkī dilce Verse 230

"...in this Turkish language as sweet as sugar."

His doubts about translating Niẓāmī are rather to do with the latter's special power of expression and out of fear of not doing justice to Niẓāmī's poetic greatness:

dėdüm şāha quluñ ḥaddı degül bu Verses 147-150
benüm şiʿrümde yoqdur reng ne bū
ki ol ulu sözine medḫal ėdem
veyā bir müşkilin anuñ ḥal(l) ėdem
ki şiʿri ḍoludur dürlü ʿibārāt
laṭāyifdür serāser istiʿārāt
ulularuñ ʿitābından aġladum
şehüme qarşu vālih şöyle qaldum

"I said to the king: 'This surpasses the range (of powers) of your servant. In my poetry there is neither (enough) color nor fragrance to be able to meddle in the words of that great one or to explain a difficult passage among them. For his poetry is full of all kinds of expressions; from one end to the other there are subtle remarks and metaphors.' I wept at the reproaches of the great and I stood completely at a loss before my king."

– But when ʿĪsā Beg persisted in his wish, Faḫrī carried out the commission:

gücüm yėtdükçe oldum tercümānı Verse 200
Niẓāmīnüñ ki şā<u>d</u> olsun revānı

"To the full extent of my power, I became the interpreter of Niẓāmī, may his spirit be happy!"

– He several times devotes verses to the memory of his model, as when alluding to his origin, he writes:

Niẓāmīdür qamu söz ehli faḫrı Verses 488-489
inanmazsañ aña nėtsün bu Faḫrī
zihī terk-i edeb bu tercümānlik
zihī aqduqluġ u zī Türkmenlik

"Niẓāmī is the pride of all artists with words. If you do not believe him, what can Faḫrī do? Oh what presumption is this translation work! Oh what inadequacy! Oh what Turkmen behavior!"

And another time he again voices his doubts about undertaking such a demanding task:

benüm ḥaddum degüldi bu kitāba Verse 431
qılam medḫal düşem dürlü ʿitāba

"I am not up to tackling such a book and exposing myself to all kinds of criticism."

With this work ʿĪsā Beg intended to establish a monument to himself for future generations:

bu maʿnī dārı olmaz hīç vīrān Verse 159

"This edifice of expression will never be derelict"[89]

(ö)lümden ṣoñra bizi ėdeler yād Verses 160-161
revānumuzı añup qılalar şād
(ci)hān durduqça adumuz qalısar
qalursa mālumuz yadlar alısar

"So that after death people remember us, recollect our soul and wish it happiness. As long as the world remains, our name will endure; if our property remains (i.e. if we leave behind property), strangers will take it."

– Maḥmūd of Ġazna (999-1030) provides him with an example of the transitoriness of all imperial dominion, and the power of poetry to confer immortality:

(bil)ür mi kimse ṣorġıl ḫāṣṣe ʿāme Verse 172
es̱er andan beġayr ez Şāhnāme

"Ask high and low.
Does anyone know a trace of him other than the *Şāhnāme*?"

eger Şāhnāme olmasaydı mevcūd Verse 174
ne Firdevsī añılurdı ne Maḥmūd

89 Walsh, review, p. 332.

"If it were not for the *Şāhnāme*, people would remember neither Firdavsī nor Maḥmūd."

– Faḫrī takes this occasion to praise his prince:

baña Firdevsi dėmek ger yaramaz Verse 207
şehüm Maḥmūd aña dur begler Āyāz

"Though it is improper to call me Firdavsī, none the less my King is Maḥmūd, for him his Begs are Āyāz (Maḥmūd's favorite)."

Finally, he has hopes that his book will enjoy a certain popularity:
ümīḏüm var ki bu defter oqına Verse 187
eger kāmil eger ebter oqına

"My hope is that this book – be it perfect or useless
– will come to be read."

Çalab dutsun hemīşe ol eri şāḏ Verse 191
ki qıla Faḫrīyi bir ḫayr-ıla yāḏ

"May God ever preserve in happiness the person who remembers Faḫrī with a benediction."

Date of the book

Faḫrī mentions dates at two points in his work. First, a date in chronogram, Verse 227, in the *qaṣīda*;

begüm yoqdur (ki) devrüñde qaçar rā
(ne haẓfı) kim degül(dür) saṭr bī-şīn

My lord, in your reign (*devr*) *rı* is not lacking (*devr* is not lacking its *r*), which yields *rā* without its *elif* (1) and its value thereby reduced to 199; nor is there curtailment for *saṭr* (269) is not without *şīn* (300)." This produces 769.[90]

Second, at the end, by using three calendars, Faḫrī indicates, without mentioning the year, that he finished his work on the 9th Receb/12 March:

90 Discussed in Walsh, review, p. 332-3.

yeñi yıl başı Ferverdīn-i Nevrūz	Verses 4678-4681
ki olmış idi güneş ʿālem-efrūz
Receb ayı doquzında seḥergāh
quzı burcında ol seyyāre yā şāh
ʿalem urmışdı kim bitdi bu defter
Ḥaqqa minnet qomadı bunı ebter
on ikinci güni Āzār māhuñ
tamām ėtdüm duʿāsın pādişāhuñ

"At the beginning of the New Year, Farvardīn of Navrūz, when the sun became the world-illuminator, on the morning of the 9th of Racab, that planet, oh King, planted his banner in the sign of the lamb (Aries) when this book was finished. Thanks to God, for (He) did not leave it unfinished. On the 12th day of March (Āẕār) I completed the prayer on behalf of the sovereign."

This yields 9th Receb 768/12 March 1367.[91]

Thus a year must be sought when the mentioned days of the month, which originate from three different calendars, coincide, with ʿĪsā Beg of Aydın's period of rule serving as a clue. In fact the first of Farvardīn 289 of the Calālī era, according to the Julian calendar, falls on the 12th of March 1367, which in turn – allowing for the difference of one day – corresponds to the 9th of Racab 768.[92]

V Structure of the Work

Faḫrī, like his model Niẓāmī, begins with praise of God:[93]

ḫudāvendā çu bismillāh diyü ben	Verse 1

91 Professor Paul Wittek solved the problem in a communication on 20 October, 1965: "Der 9. reğ. 768 ist tatsächlich = 12. 3. 1367 – nach der im 12.-15. Jhdt. in Rūm gebräuchlichen 15er Zählung. Siehe vorläufig Kraelitz, Urk. S. 83 Anm. 3 (und auch schon Hammer *GOR* III 621a)".

92 *Wüstenfeld-Mahlersche Vergleichungs-Tabellen*, neu bearbeitet von Bertold Spuler, Wiesbaden 1961, p. 39. According to p. 17 in the same work, 11 March 367 = 9 Racab 768. The trivial difference should not raise doubts about the corresponding equivalent given above. Regarding such problems, cf. Bertold Spuler, "Con amore", in *Der Islam* 38 (1962), pp. 154-60.

93 For the introductory sections see my Faḫrī edition; J.T.P. de Bruijn, *Of Piety*, pp. 186-188.

söze başlarvanın şükrüñ diyü ben

Right at the beginning there are lacunae. A few verses – 14 to 25 – lead up to the prayer (*münācāt*) which runs from verse 26 to 49 and is followed by the eulogy (*naʿt*) to Muḥammad, verses 92 to 127[94];

Praise of the prince and his family goes from verse 213 to 277 and verses 213 to 235 are written in the form of a *qaṣīda* rhyming in *-īn*. The tale of Ḫusrev begins with verse 278:

eyitdi ol söz eyden bilge üstād̲ Verse 278
ki dutmışdı çoq eski dāsitān yād̲

Compare the beginning in Niẓāmī (Dastgirdī's edition, p. 40):

çunīn guft ān suḫangū-yi kohan-zād
ke būdiş dāstānhā-yi kohan-yād

Faḫrī's narrative, on the whole, follows the plot in Niẓāmī and includes the whole Ferhād story which is set off from the plot by a new introduction and again contains a brief dedication to ʿĪsā. The Ferhād story contains original additions by Faḫrī.

Faḫrī and his princely patron apparently considered it to some extent a shortcoming that Niẓāmī, in the interest of his plot, only marginally touches upon Behrām Çūbīn's rebellion, the fall and murder of Hormuzd, and Ḫusrev's flight to Rūm and his final clash with Behrām. To fill in this background, the part of the *Şāhnāme* that deals with these subjects and that Niẓāmī used as a source is drawn upon:

şeker gibi bu Türkī dilce düz(dük) Verse 230
senüñçün qıṣṣa-i Pervīz ü Şīrīn
ʿAcem dilince düzen düzdi ʿısqın
ne cengin z̲ikr qıldı vü ne ṣulḥın
şehüm buyurdı Firdevsī sözinden Verse 232
yėtürem naẓmını maṭbūʿ-i Şīrīn
qıluban şekrini şehdile memzūc Verse 233
yėdürem ḫalqa şīrīn ḥavż-i Şīrīn

...

94 Here also something must be lost. The *sebeb-i teʾlīf* begins with verse 128 and contains three Persian verses (131-133).

> çu buyurdı şāhum Firdevsī şiʿrin — Verse 235
> qıluban tercüme ḫoş resm-i taẓmīn
> (here the qaṣīda ends)
> Niẓāmī naẓmına memzūc ėderven — Verse 236
> çu gendüzüme borc ėtdüm öderven

> "In this Turkish language as sweet as sugar we composed for you the story of Parvīz and Şīrīn. The one who wrote in Persian (only) treated his love; he mentioned neither his deeds in war nor his deeds in peace. My King ordered that I should take the poetry from Firdevsī's words about Şīrīn's nature, adding honey to her sugar, and feed the people with the sweet (fountain of Şīrīn)... In accordance with my King's command, I translated Firdavsī's poem in the pleasant form of a *tażmīn* (words interpolated from another poet): I mix it into Niẓāmī's poem, (and) since I have borrowed (something) for myself, I give back what I owe."

Accordingly, Faḫrī inserts in the suitable places almost the whole of the Behrām novel from the *Şāhnāme*, and at the end, when describing the death of Ḫusrev Parvīz, again goes back to Firdavsī and then, following Niẓāmī, concludes with the letter of the Prophet Muḥammad to Parvīz. The book ends with a concluding passage of 36 couplets, 4648-4683, from which we have cited above.

Thus, Faḫrī's free rendering appears as an adaptation of Niẓāmī's *Ḫusrav u Şīrīn*, in which long passages from the *Şāhnāme* of Firdavsī have been introduced. The meter is that of Niẓāmī's epic, namely *mefāʿīlün mefāʿīlün feʿūlün*: *hezec*, in which the selected verses from the *Şāhnāme* (originally composed in *mutaqārib*) are also recast. From the standpoint of the work's unity, one may regret that Faḫrī undertook to work in as an addition the tale of Behrām which Niẓāmī no doubt intentionally did not include in his romance. Excessively long interpolations, especially some of the exchanges in dialogue and letters, threaten the internal balance of the underlying poetic work, and a series of Sassanian heroes are rather abruptly brought onto the stage and then whisked away. But one must remember that the manuscript in question is incomplete; thence some "linking passages" between the texts of Niẓāmī and Firdavsī may have been lost. In any case the two works taken as models have only been imperfectly adapted to one another; an external sign of this is the fact that the painter, Ḫusrev's companion, is called Şavur in the Niẓāmī section and Şapur in the section from Firdavsī.

In total the *mes̱nevī*, as it appears in the manuscript Hs. or. quart 1069, consists of 4683 couplets. Of these around 3060 beyts are to be apportioned to Niẓāmī and Faḫrī himself, and around 1620 are adapted from the *Şāhnāme*. The work in its original form when it was completed would have contained several hundred more couplets – which we can assume on the basis of the above-cited verses of folio 168b (Verse 4677). The existing lacunae are of two kinds; on the one hand, entire folios are missing regarding which it is to be feared that they were lost during the rather clumsy attempts at restoration when many folios were bound out of order. On the other hand, there are lacunae within the text where the narrative suddenly jumps ahead a little. Such abridgements, in any case where they occur at the expense of the text's coherence, should be blamed on the scribe who seems occasionally to have made the work on this long *mes̱nevī* easier for himself.[95]

VI The Dedication to ʿĪsā Beg of Aydın and His House

Faḫrī glorifies his patron, the Aydınoğlu ʿĪsā Beg, in several passages of his work. At the beginning of his poem he sings the praises of ʿĪsā Beg's father and brothers. ʿĪsā Beg, as is known, was the youngest son of the most important Aydınoğlu, the "Sultan of the warriors for the faith", Mubārizeddīn Muḥammed Beg who has been mentioned earlier. Faḫrī writes about him:

ḫuḏāvendā cihān-ġāzī vü server Verses 240-247
ṣaf-ārā ṣaf-şiken ṣaf-sāz u ṣaf-der
şeh-i ūcāt sulṭān-i sevāḥil
seḫī vü bende-perver dāḏ u ʿādil
Mubāriz Ġāzī Meḥmed[96] Beg bin Aydın
ki andan oldı bu uc ili aydın
mesācid yapdı vu yıqdı delim dayr
elinden geldi çoq iḥsān ögüş ḫayr
sevāḥil kāfiristānidi cümle
açıldı serbeser çoq qıldı ḥamle
Firenk ü Alanos süyi sağışsuz
şehinşāh iline dutdı qamu yüz
ėrişdiler ,qamunuñ içi pür kīn
qamusın qırdı sulṭān-i selāṭīn
qılıcından amān bulmadı biri Verse 247
ki dönüb iline varubdı diri

95 On such practices cf. H. Ritter, "Philologika x", *Der Islam* 25 (1939), p. 146.
96 This reading is required by the meter, even though "Muḥammed" is vocalized in the text.

> "The sovereign, world-scale warrior for the faith and commander, ornament and breaker of the battle ranks, former of the ranks and smasher of the ranks, King of the borderlands, Sultan of the coasts,[97] generous and concerned for his subjects, moderate and just: Mubāriz(eddīn) Ġāzī Muḥammed Beg b. Aydın, through whom these marches became illuminated. He built mosques and demolished many a monastery,[98] from his hand came many good deeds, and welfare. The coasts were completely infidel territory; they were conquered from one end to the other, he made many an attack. The countless armies of the Franks and Alans all turned against the land of the King of Kings. They drew near, the heart of each and every one filled with malice; (but) the Sultan of Sultans destroyed them all. Not one found mercy before his sword so as to return alive to his country."

"Alanos" refers to the auxiliary corps made up of Alans and Wallachs which the emperor Andronikos II Palaiologos had engaged in 1300 in order to recover part of Western Asia Minor; in 1302 the co-emperor Michael IX led these people, ten thousand men with their wives and children, in a campaign which ended in defeat and plundering of the Byzantine countryside.[99]

When Enverī, a hundred years later, writes about Umur Beg, he describes Muḥammed Beg in similar, though fewer verses.[100]

The initial childlessness of Muḥammed Beg, which Enverī later referred to, is likewise mentioned by Faḫrī.

Çalabdan neẕr ü qurbānile ol şāh — Verses 250-251
oġul dilerdi tā kim qādir Allāh
aña vėrdi bėş oġul u cuvānbaḫt
beşidaḫı yaraşur binmege taḫt

97 On this title cf. Flemming, *Pamphylien*, p. 90, with bibliography.

98 On the survival of the Christian population as *ẕimmī*s and the bishoprics in Birgi and Ayasoluġ cf. Akın, p. 41, with bibliography.

99 See Georg Ostrogorsky, *Geschichte des byzantinischen Staates*, Munich 1949 {new ed. 1990}, p. 353; Irène Mélikoff-Sayar, *Le Destān d'Umur Pacha* (*Düstürnāme-i Enverī*), Paris 1954, p. 47, l. 33 sq. (*Alanos u Rūm u Sırf eyledi cenk*) "Alains, Grecs, Serbes, ils lui firent la guerre." "Alanos" may also refer to the mercenaries, also eventually defeated, of the Catalan Company under Roger de Flor (Ostrogorsky, p. 353-354; Claude Cahen, *Pre-Ottoman Turkey*, London 1968, p. 306; Wittek, *Mentesche*, p. 43. Communication by the late Professor Paul Wittek, 7 November, 1965.

100 Mélikoff, *Destan*, p. 47.

"With vows and sacrifice that King beseeched God for a son until almighty God bestowed on him five fine sons, all worthy to ascend the throne." Actually, in accordance with tradition all brothers of the House of Aydın took part in the government. Three of Muḥammed's sons in succession ruled the emirate, i.e. firstly Umur; when he was killed in 1348, Ḫiżr, the eldest, followed – who had originally stood down in favor of Umur. Both had no male progeny. The other two brothers died early, Ibrāhīm Bahādur in 1348 and Sulaymānşāh a year later. Then around 1360, ʿĪsā, the youngest brother, came to power. After the restoration brought about by Timur, ʿĪsā Beg's two sons, Mūsā and Umur II, succeeded one another (1402-1403), after which rule passed to Cunayd (1403-1425), in whom Akın sees a son of Ibrāhīm Bahādur, i.e. their cousin.[101] Faḫrī devotes two couplets to each of ʿĪsā Beg's four brothers who were already dead in his time.

Naturally, Faḫrī's eulogy to his prince and patron, ʿĪsā Beg of Aydın, is the richest in language. The *qaṣīda* mentioned earlier, an encomium in conventional style, begins with the *laqab* of the prince:

zihī ferḫunde faḫr-u devlet ü dīn, Verse 213

which is later repeated:

şeh-i ferḫunde faḫr-u devlet ü dīn Verse 262

and

yegāne faḫr-i mülk ü devlet ü dīn Verse 2931

Making use of the honorific name Faḫr addavla vaddīn which is documented for this prince (see above), he admires in him the usual noble qualities of an exemplary Muslim ruler. Faḫrī calls him "Ruler of the rulers of the world" (*ḫudāvend-i ḫudāvendān-i ʿālem*: verse 261), "king" or "sovereign of the world" (*şāh-i cihān*: verse 143, and compares him to Rustam, the hero of the Persian saga, and to Maḥmūd of Ġazna (see above). Although he accords him, somewhat incidentally, the title "warrior for the faith" (*ġāzī*; verse 143), above all Faḫrī praises the Aydınoğlu as a peaceful prince –

zamānında ne miḥnet var ne qīn Verse 266
qılıçsuz görmez oldı kimse bir qın

101 Akın, pp. 68-77.

"In his time there is neither oppression nor suffering, no one any longer sees a sheath without its sword (a drawn sword)" – and commends his charitable activity:

cihān durduqça dursun devletile Verse 277
ki ẖalqı ḍoyurur çoq niʿmetile

"As long as the world exists, may he prosper since he lavishes many gifts on the people." As far as the actual extent of ʿĪsā Beg's power is concerned, Faẖrī limits himself to traditional, somewhat vague expressions such as:

qamu şāhlar başına uzadur tāc Verse 267

"Over the heads of all kings he holds forth crowns" (i.e. he crowns them), or:

güneş gibi yüzini görmekiçün Verse 214
şehinşāhlar derildi mis̱l-i Parvīn

"In order to see his sun-like face supreme kings have gathered like the Pleiades." However, the blessing invoked at the end is simple:

ẖudāvendā anı pāyende qılġıl Verse 4672
anı şāh ẖalqı aña bende qılġıl

"Lord, let him persist; make him the King, and the people his servants!"

ʿĪsā Beg, who at the time maintained friendly relations with the Ottomans, still had more than twenty years before the following words that Faẖrī put in his mouth would be fulfilled:

qalursa mālumuz yadlar alısar Verse 161

"If we leave behind property, strangers will take it." After 1390, when the Ottoman ruler Bāyezīd I had annexed the emirate, ʿĪsā Beg lost his castles and the right to strike coins and have his name mentioned in the Friday *ẖuṭba*. He lived in Tire where he died before 1400. Once Bāyezīd had occupied his country, he only retained the administration of a few towns and the usufruct of the pious foundations endowed by his dynasty, in whose old residence, Birgi, his *türbe* was built which is no longer preserved.[102]

102 Akın, pp. 108 f.

After the Ottoman defeat at Ankara ʿĪsā's sons regained their land, but the people of Aydın suffered severely from the ferocity of the new overlord Timur. He seems to have divided Aydın between Umur II and Mūsā, but after a civil war Cunayd remained as sole ruler of Aydın. He was in Ayasoluġ[103] where the "rebel" Börklüce Mustafa was executed in 1416.[104] The last Aydınoğlu Cunayd[105] fought the Ottoman sultan Murād II, who only in 1425 could call himself the sole ruler of Western Anatolia.

VII Faḫrī's Position within Turkish Language and Literature

Faḫrī wrote in Old Anatolian Turkish. Contrary to earlier assumptions, Walsh has shown that Faḫrī handled quantitative metrics *ʿarūż* successfully. Regarding these "as the unique vehicle for poetry of this nature, {Faḫrī} would not lightly have lapsed into an accentual scansion. Given the license allowed in the treatment of Turkish vowels, this simple *hezec* metre could have presented no serious difficulty; and the fact that he was prepared to extend it by *ziḥāf* (vowel reduction) to Persian words, also, must be taken as an indication of his concern for correctness in this respect..."[106]

Within the framework of Turkish *mes̱nevī* poetry of the 14th century, Faḫrī's *Ḫusrev u Şīrīn* translation should be chronologically placed after Mesʿūd b. Aḥmed's above-mentioned *Ferhengnāme* and his narrative poem *Süheyl ü Nevbahār*. It is almost contemporary with Meddāḥ Yūsuf's *Varqa ve Gülşāh* (written in 1368-69) and can be described as a precursor to Şeyḫoğlu's *Ḫurşīdnāme* (completed in 1387; and also composed in the *hezec* meter), as well as having chronologically preceded Aḥmedī's large *Iskendernāme* (finished in 1390) which likewise in its poetry took its point of departure from Firdavsī and Niẓāmī.

With his adaptation of the Behrām Çūbīn epic, Faḫrī along with Aḥmedī belongs among the oldest Turkish translators of Firdavsī. Complete translations of the *Şāhnāme* were only undertaken a hundred years later; in 854/1450-51, under Murād I, an unknown author produced a translation in prose, regarding the completion of which a reference in fact exists[107] though it

103 Colin Imber, *The Ottoman Empire 1300-1481*, Istanbul 1990, p. 63.

104 Imber, *Ottoman Empire*, p. 85

105 I. Mélikoff, "Djunayd, EI II (1965), pp. 599-600. Imber, *Ottoman Empire*, pp. 42, 63, 106, 146.

106 Walsh, review, p. 333.

107 Blochet, II, p. 220, under no. 1279.

is only partly preserved.[108] The poet Şerīf from Āmid (d. circa 920/1514 in Egypt, see Qanısavh no. 3 in this volume) wrote his *Şāhnāme* translation in verse which he dedicated to the Mamluk Sultan al-Ġavrī (ruled 1498-1515).[109]

Among the old Turkish translations of Niẓāmī's *Ḫusrav u Şīrīn* known to us up until now, Faḫrī's free rendering chronologically occupies second place. The oldest discovered Turkish version, as is known, was composed by Quṭb in 1342 at the court of the Golden Horde and is preserved in a single manuscript in Paris[110] which has been published in transcription and facsimile, with a glossary, by Ananiasz Zajączkowski.[111]

Twenty-five years later – to summarize what has been said above – at the court of the Aydınoğlu ʿĪsā Beg there appeared, as the earliest known Anatolian-Turkish translation and adaptation, the work of Faḫreddīn Yaʿqūb b. Muḥammed, preserved in the Berlin manuscript.

Between 824/1421 and 834/1428-29, more than fifty years later, the *mes̱nevī Ḫusrev u Şīrīn* by Şeyḫī, Yūsuf Sinān, was finished, comprising 6944 beyt in the *hezec* metre with many interpolated *qaṣīda*s and 26 *ġazel*s dedicated to the Ottoman Sultan Murād II. Many manuscripts are witness to the popularity of the work, which, in contrast to its source, ends with the marriage of the main figure king Ḫusrev to Şīrīn – not his death – and with the discourse of Ḫusrev with the sage Buzurg Umīd (this fact led two Ottoman poets to compose continuations). It is available in transcription in the critical edition by Faruk Timurtaş.[112]

In Faḫrī's *mes̱nevī* the Turkish vocabulary is considerably greater than in Şeyḫī's; the style seems simpler and the translation shines through everywhere,

---

108 Karatay, II, p. 58, no. 2154 (Hazine no. 1518). The preceding manuscript, Hazine no. 1116, appears to belong to it as well.

109 The oldest manuscript – dated 903/1498 – is in Upsala: C.J. Tornberg, *Codices orientales bibliothecae Regiae Universitatis Lundensis*, Lund 1850-53, p. 92, no. 147. For additional manuscripts cf. Karatay, II, pp. 58 f., nos. 2155-2158; Süleymaniye, Damad İbrahim Paşa, no. 983 (*Tanıklariyle Tarama Sözlüğü* I/XVIII); Charles Rieu, *Catalogue of the Turkish Manuscripts in the British Museum*, London 1888, p. 152, no. 1126; Flügel, I, p. 495, no. 504; Vienna, Nationalbibliothek, no. 2111, according to David Eugene Smith (ed.), *Firdausī-Celebration 935 – 1935, Adresses delivered...at Columbia University...*, New York 1936, p. 93. – The *Şāhnāme* translations of the 16th and 17th centuries will not be considered here.

110 Blochet, I, p. 133, no. 312.

111 Edition and study: Ananiasz Zajączkowski, *Najstarsza wersja turecka Ḫusräv-u-Šīrīn Quṭba*, I. Text, II. Facsimile, III. Glossary, Warsaw, 1958-1961.

112 Timurtaş, Ş*eyhî*. Compare also the facsimile edition of the Paris manuscript, Bibliothèque nationale. A.F. Turc 322 by Ananiasz Zajączkowski, *Poemat Irański Ḫusrev-u-Šīrīn w wersji osmańsko-tureckiej Seyḫī*, Warsaw 1963.

although original touches are not lacking. A few verses set side by side will make this clear.

Faḫrī verse 1615	Şeyḫī verse 3373
süci içdüm ve içdüñ bile bayıq	çü nūş-ı bādede ḫoşyār olasın
ne maʿnīdür ben esrükin sen ayıq	niçün ben mest ü sen hūş-yār olasın
Faḫrī verse 359	Şeyḫī verse 914
Niẓāmīden dutaruz yād̲ bunı	naṣīḥat loqması olur gelū-gīr
ki ögüt quşınuñ acıdur üni	qo efsūnı göñül efsāneye gir
Faḫrī verse 3061	Şeyḫī verse 4399
quyu ger olsa yolda kim geçerdi	V'eger öñinde olsa bürke vü çāh
saqınmamaqdan içine uçardı	düşerdi bilmez idi sapıda rāh
Faḫrī verse 3414	Şeyḫī verse 4904
çu işitdi anuñ Ferhād̲ sözin	çü Ferhād ol kelāmı gūş qıldı
bıraqdı qayadan ḍaġ gibi özin	Sanasın zehr-i qātil nūş qıldī

Şeyḫī handles his model with much greater freedom, occasionally abridging Niẓāmī, inserting passages from the Behrām Çūbīn tale (a hint at his forerunner)[113] as well as his own original poetry, and succeeds in bringing everything together in a unified whole. Faḫrī's text is a more literal translation which retains much detail in the excerpts from the *Şāhnāme* and in the blending of the two original works only achieves a limited degree of success. The production of a *mes̲nevī* was a time-consuming task,[114] and Faḫrī did not quite succeed in blending his two Persian originals, for Ḫusrav's companion Şavur/Şapur, see above).

Was the physician and poet in Kütahya familiar with the work of his predecessor who was in fact close to him in place as well in time? Here and there in Şeyḫī's more artistic and polished work – which also follows the Şāhnāme for a while – we come across passages that bear a striking resemblance to verses of Faḫrī. A few examples are presented here, allowing for similarities deriving from the originals which both authors translated.

Faḫrī verse 1405	Şeyḫī verse 2833
melik Şīrīne baqardı nihānī	Melik gözlerdi Şīrīni nihānī
ki ol avdan ne ola armaġānı	ki ol avdan ne olur armaġānı

113 My Faḫrī edition; introduction, p. 201.

114 İmail E. Erünsal, *The Life and Works of Tâcî-zâde Ca'fer Çelebi, with a Critical Edition of his Dîvân*, Istanbul 1983, LII.

Faḫrī verse 1557	Şeyḫī verse 3287
çu güneş şīşesi ṭaşa ḍoqundı	çü gündüz şīşesi toqındı taşa
cihān qarardı çünkim şīşe ṣındı	Gice biñ biñ götürdi şīşe başa
Faḫrī verse 3182	Şeyḫī verse 4599
şu resme qaqıdı Ferhāda Pervīz	şu resme qaqıdı Ferhāda Pervīz
dilerdi boynına ura qılıç tīz	ki dökmek diledi qanın yire tīz
Faḫrī verse 3470	Şeyḫī verse 4979
Cihānı yaqdı feryād eylemekden	Cihānı yaqdı feryād eylemekden
añıla ʿāşıqı yāḏ eylemekden	Muvāfiq yārını yād eylemekden
Faḫrī verse 3477	Şeyḫī verse 4988
gerekmezdi anı öldürmek öñdin	Gerekmez idi öldürmek sitemden
çu öldürdüñ nice olasın ġamgīn	Çün öldürdüñ ne ḥāṣıl bunca ġamdan
Faḫrī verse 3478	Şeyḫī verse 4989
yėgil qayġusın çun qanın içdüñ	Yi qayġusını kim qanın sen içdüñ
yadırġama çu anuñla gey içdüñ	Tozın çek Āb-ı ḥāyvānın sen içdüñ

The recovery of Faḫrī's Ḫusrev u Şīrīn gave Turkish studies new insights into subjects connected with the Emirate or Beylik period, where "Anatolian Turkish[115] developed into a literary idiom, perceptibly different from the language of traditional song and story."[116]

The notion of an "unsophisticated atmosphere of pre-Ottoman Anatolia"[117] has been called into question. "The assurance with which [Faḫrī] treats Niẓamī's masterpiece – compressing the involuted imagery in order to maintain the narrative flow, and even expanding the original in certain places by translations from the Şāhnāme of Firdevsī – betokens a much higher level of literary sophistication among the Anatolian Turks than the few relics that have come down to us would indicate. Independently of his source, he introduces tropes and conceits which poets of a much later age would not disdain, and which, no doubt, he expected to be noticed and appreciated by the circle for

115 For the issue of the origin of Old Anatolian Turkish see Gönül A. Tekin, "Othmanlı", in *EI* VIII (1995), p. 212.

116 Walsh, review, p. 331.

117 See John R. Walsh, "Yunus Emre and Divan Poetry", *Journal of Turkish Studies* 7 (1983) (Orhan Şaik Gökyay Armağanı), pp. 453-464, especially p. 460.

which he was writing."[118] By translating, adapting and imitating Persian works there was "imported the notion of polite literature into a society the focal centre of which was in hesitant transition from camp to court."[119]

Şeyḫoğlu has a similar place in the development of the Turkish language as a literary vehicle in the 14th century. "Said to have complained (fashionably) about the unsuitability of Turkish as a vehicle for poetry, he nevertheless stressed the importance of producing works in that language and is praised for the style that he accomplished."[120]

Yaʿqūb II's (1387-1428) court of Germiyan "was adorned with ... poets like Aḥmedī, his brother Ḥamzavī, Aḥmed-i Dāʿī, and above all Şeyḫī, who in his qaṣīdas celebrated the virtues of his patron. All these poets and scholars were to move on to the court of the ʿOthmānlı sultans and there contribute to the development of classical poetry".[121] As the emirates receded in memory, many of their poets and scholars had become assimilated into the Ottoman Empire.

Şeyḫī (born 771/137, died ca. 834/1431) is a case in point. The fame of this poet, who wrote for the powerful Ottoman ruler Murād II and is also esteemed as the author of a *dīvān* and the satirical *Ḫarnāme*[122] – soon eclipsed that of the earlier men of letters of the Emirate period. While Aḥmedī, one of the greatest among them, never quite went out of fashion, poets like Ḫoca Mesʿūd and Şeyḫoğlu, and others including our Faḫrī[123] along with Yūsuf Meddāḥ and Tutmacı virtually sank into oblivion.

Striking similarities lead us to believe that a relationship existed between Faḫrī and Şeyḫī. The latter's work, the first Ottoman version of this theme, in style and technique outmatched that of his predecessor Faḫrī. To this day, Şeyḫī is regarded as "the most prominent of the early poets to emerge from Anatolia,"[124] and his *Ḫusrev u Şīrīn* is praised as the first of the romantic poems of Turkey.[125]

Even so, from the sixteenth century onwards it became a habit to disparage the poetry of pre-Ottoman and early Ottoman writers. "A grievous defect" was

118 Walsh, review, p. 331.

119 Walsh, review, p. 332.

120 Burrill, "Sheykh-oghlu", p. 419.

121 Mélikoff, "Germiyan"; Gönül Alpay Tekin, "Othmanlı. III. Literature. (a) Until 1600, *EI*, VII, Leiden 1995, 211.

122 Jan Schmidt, *A Catalogue of the Turkish Manuscripts in the John Rylands Library at Manchster*, Leiden/Boston 2011, pp. 54-56, no. 16 [2].

123 Faḫrī is mentioned by A.T. Karamustafa, "Early Turkish Islamic literature up to the Ottomans", *EI* X (2000), 716.

124 Erünsal, *Life and Works*, lii.

125 Gülşen Çulhaoğlu, "Şeyhi'nin Hüsrev ü Şirin Mesnevisindeki Aşk ilişkileri." Master Thesis Bilkent University, Ankara, July 2001. http://thesis bilkent.edu.tr/000206.1 pdf; access 24 February 2011.

seen in Kemālpaşazāde's endeavour to make his work both in language and phraseology as Turkish as possible."[126] The "homely language of the earlier Turkish writers" was considered "insipid".[127] Even Şeyḫī was criticized for paying scant attention to the rules of eloquence (*feṣāḥat*) and for employing archaic words...[128] "When Ali Nihat Tarlan observes that the language of Şeyḫī was inadequate to the themes which he treated he does no more than echo the plaints of the early Ottomans themselves",[129] for his imperfect handling of prosody (*ʿarūż*), and last not least, for "only translating".

For the earlier period, to sum up, a *mes̱nevī* such as Faḫrī's has helped to widen the circle of appreciation for the works of Persian literature in pre-Ottoman Anatolia.[130] Early *mes̱nevīs* such as his, therefore, are now considered to "mark significant stages in the development of an aesthetic awareness and discrimination that was ultimately to blossom into the refinements and elegancies of Ottoman divan literature."[131]

---

126 Gibb, *HOP* III, p. 13.

127 G.M. Meredith-Owens, *Meşāʿir üş-Şuʿarā or Tez̲kere of ʿĀşıḳ Çelebi*, London 1971, p. XIV.

128 Tācīzāde Caʿfer Çelebi in Erünsal, *The Life and Works*, pp. liii, Lxxxi.

129 John R. Walsh, "Yunus Emre and Divan Poetry", *Journal of Turkish Studies* 7 (1983) (*Orhan Şaik Gökyay Armağanı II*), p. 456.

130 Varying Walsh, "Yunus Emre and Divan Poetry", p. 455.

131 Walsh, review, p. 331. Kemalpaşazade "abandoned the exaggerated Turkicism of his early years and adopted the Persianised dialect which experience has shown to be the fittest medium for Ottoman poetry of the Iranian school", Gibb, *HOP* III, p. 127.

CHAPTER 2

Turkish Manuscripts in the Staatsbibliothek*

The intention of the present paper[1] is, with the help of a few concrete examples, to give some insight into the work that has gone on in cataloguing Turkish manuscripts. But to begin with I would like briefly to say something more general about my own work.

During the three years of my full-time employment in cataloguing, I worked on manuscripts belonging to the collections of what was formerly the Preußische Staatsbibliothek which is now the Staatsbibliothek zu Berlin – Preußischer Kulturbesitz, specifically on manuscripts in Marburg and in the Tübingen Depot of the Staatsbibliothek. In Marburg, moreover, I described almost one half of the Süssheim Collection which was purchased in 1960 by the Staatsbibliothek (then the Westdeutsche Bibliothek). These manuscripts were acquired between circa 1890 and 1960, i.e. since the time that Turkish manuscripts of the Preußische Staatsbibliothek had been described (1889) in an almost 600-page catalogue volume (the sixth) in the large series *Handschriften-Verzeichnisse der Königlichen Bibliothek zu Berlin*.

During the seventy-six years that have elapsed since the appearance of Pertsch's catalogue of Turkish manuscripts, scholars have naturally been busy with a number of manuscripts that were acquired in the meantime. Some treasures of the collection have been published – I will only mention Ms. or. fol. 3060, *Suheyl ü Nevbehâr*, edited in facsimile by Johann Heinrich Mordtmann in 1925; and Ms. or. quart 1975, Qıvāmī (unicum), in a facsimile edition by Franz Babinger in 1955 – or due to scholarship have returned to life via other paths, as for example the attractive old copy of Yazıcıoğlu's *Oğuznāme*, Ms. or. quart 1823. There is already a whole literature around this manuscript. It rendered crucial services in the case of H.W. Duda's translation of Ibn Bībī's Persian history of the Seljuks and may still hope to appear in its own edition and scholarly presentation.

In this "catalogueless" period, a number of manuscripts became known, at least by name, thanks to Franz Babinger who went through the uncatalogued holdings in Berlin and utilized, among others, Johann Heinrich Mordtmann's

* Translated by John O'Kane.

1 This essay had its origin in a paper presented on March 5th 1965 at a Conference of the Deutsche Forschungsgemeinschaft (*German Research Foundation*) concerning ongoing work on the Union Catalogue of Oriental Manuscripts in German Collections. Published in German in 1966, the translated paper has been partially updated and expanded.

 | DOI 10.1163/9789004355767_003

preliminary manuscript descriptions for his *Geschichtsschreiber der Osmanen und ihre Werke* (Leipzig 1927). J.H. Mordtmann had also described his father's manuscript collection in 1925 in *Der Islam*. In this way, up to 1927, these studies – though of necessity limited to the domain of history – were useful for finding new acquisitions. But with this date published information ended regarding manuscript materials even in this well-cultivated field. For potential users there were at best the accession registers of the Preußische Staatsbibliothek. Unexplored ground was opened up to scholarship when in 1960 the Süssheim collection of three hundred and thirty-eight manuscripts mainly in Turkish, was purchased (on Karl Süssheim see below).

I directed my attention predominantly to historical works and related subjects such as geographers, though I also described other manuscripts; in a moment I will mention an example from among these which belongs in the category of Turkish literary history. Works in Turkish range in date from Old Anatolian Turkish of the fourteenth century to Middle and Modern Ottoman, including some items from the Republic of Turkey.[2] I have seen dated manuscripts from the fifteenth century, but none from the fourteenth. In some Turkish manuscripts the Arabic script survived its replacement by the Latin alphabet; one case will be discussed below. From this long period, Turkish manuscripts can be singled out that bring about deeper insight and help to boost research in Turkish studies.

In this regard it is fortunate that in addition to the "classic" catalogues (Flügel, Rieu, Pertsch) we are able to draw on modern Turkish catalogues which have appeared since 1943. These are often indispensable for identifying Turkish manuscripts.[3] In the past individual scholars have explored manuscript holdings that were not catalogued.[4] To sum up, few greater services

2 Of the Turkish section (XIII) of the German Catalogue Project (Verzeichnis der orientalischen Handschriften in Deutschland, VOHD) the following volumes were published, Barbara Flemming, *Türkische Handschriften Teil 1*, Wiesbaden 1968 (VOHD XIII, 1), Manfred Götz, *Türkische Handschriften Teil 2*, Wiesbaden 1968 (VOHD XIII, 2), Hanna Sohrweide, *Türkische Handschriften und einige ... persische und arabische Werke*, Wiesbaden 1974 (VOHD XIII, 3), Manfred Götz, *Türkische Handschriften*, Wiesbaden 1979 (VOHD XIII, 4), and Hanna Sohrweide, *Türkische Handschriften Teil 5*, Wiesbaden 1981 (VOHD XIII, 5). *Türkische Handschriften*, the last volume prepared by the late Hanna Sohrweide, is as yet unpublished, but see below, page 486.

3 For a detailed history see E. Birnbaum, "Turkish Manuscripts: Cataloguing since 1920 und Manuscripts still uncatalogued. Part 5: Turkey and Cyprus", in *JAOS* 104 (1984), 468-472; Günay Kut, "Some aspects of the cataloguing of Turkish manuscripts", *Manuscripts of the Middle East* 3 (1988), 60-68; see also my review of the "Union Catalogue of Manuscripts in Turkey: Türkiye Yazmaları Toplu Kataloğu (TÜYATOK)," *Manuscripts of the Middle East* 1 (1986), 109-110.

4 Examples are given in Jan Schmidt, *A Catalogue of the Turkish Manuscripts in the John Rylands University Library at Manchester*, Leiden-Boston 2011, p. 3-4.

could be rendered to Turkish scholarship than the proper cataloguing and describing of these manuscripts. Not only do they provide useful bibliographical tools, but they also serve as a means of advancing and widening Turkish studies in general.[5]

As in other fields where cataloguing advances, here too works come to light which have remained unknown to scholars; writings which were only known by name actually take on shape, and finally the editing of rare works is facilitated thanks to additional copies – to mention only the most important possibilities. To give an indication on this occasion of the fascinating side of cataloguing, I have chosen the following five examples from among acquisitions that fall within what could be called the "unrecorded" time span, i.e. since 1927.

My oldest example is Faḫrī.

1) In the history of Turkish literature Niẓāmī's famous Persian *ma̱snavī* romance, *Ḫosraw u Şīrīn,* plays an important role as a literary model. Originally dedicated to three Turkish princes (Atabegs of Azerbaijan, 1180/81), this romantic epic, for the first time, as far as we know, found a Turkish adaptor within the Golden Horde in 1342. In Turkish Anatolia, Niẓāmī's work inspired no less than nineteen translations and adaptations. Considered the earliest in this series is the *Ḫusrev-Şīrīn* romance by Şeyḫī, dedicated to the Ottoman Sultan Murād II between 1421 and 1428/9. Given the literary pre-eminence that Şeyḫī enjoyed as the first *Ḫusrev u Şīrīn* adaptor, the surprise was great when in 1961 during my first examination of the Süssheim Collection a Turkish adaptation of the same theme, but sixty years older, came to light, dedicated to a prince of Aydın, written years before an Ottoman sultan could call himself the ruler of Western Anatolia, as described in the first essay of this collection.

All cataloguers share the thrill of chancing upon unknown or hardly known texts. Mention might be made of the series of rare manuscripts from the early and later Ottoman periods. In passing, we may note that the fragment of a chronicle – Hs. or. oct. 1142, Bostān, a manuscript from 1591 – had survived concealed inside an envelope.

2) Over recent years scholarship has focused on "the Muslim discovery of Europe" (Bernard Lewis) and the use of Christian sources by Muslim history writers. In the Ottoman domain profitable use has been made of the results of

5 Jan Schmidt, *Catalogue of Turkish Manuscripts in the Library of Leiden University* and other Collections in the Netherlands, volumes I-III, Leiden 2000-2006. Volume II, Leiden 2002, pp. XII-XIII contains a list of TÜYATOK and other Turkish manuscript catalogues.

modern manuscript cataloguing in Turkey. How the German cataloguing project can also contribute to clearing up specific questions is illustrated by the example of a Turkish "History of the Franks".

In the middle of the seventeenth century, before the heavy defeats in Hungary, educated Ottomans began to occupy themselves seriously with conditions in the West. An especially "open-minded" individual in this respect was the well-known Turkish polyhistor, Kātib Çelebi, also known to us as Ḥāccī Ḫalīfa (d. 1657), who made use of western sources including atlases.

When in 1959 on the occasion of the 300th anniversary of his death a collection of works on Kātib Çelebi was published in Ankara, in it[6] three writings were also described in which the Turkish scholar dealt with the Christian West. In this way a step was taken to clear up various errors which until then had obscured this area of Kātib Çelebi's work, but the three works remained difficult to consult since the only known manuscripts were owned privately in Konya and the texts had only partially been published and then in an inaccessible publication.

The Staatsbibliothek possesses one of the three existing works. It is entitled *Guidance of the Perplexed to the History of the Greeks, Romans and Christians* (*Irşād al-ḥayārā ilā tāriḫ al-Yunān va'l-Rūm va'l-Naṣārā*). Kātib Çelebi wrote this treatise in 1654 with the declared intention of waking Muslims from their ignorance about the forms of religion, government and administration of their Western opponents; it is based on Christian sources. To be sure, the work, by way of clearly distancing itself from Christian doctrines, begins with a formulation of the orthodox Islamic position: "Praise without end to the One whose holy being transcends a trinity and is too sublime and holy to be possibly described by the attribute of paternity."

The remarkable small volume was first made known in an article that Süssheim's friend Mesud Koman published in May 1945 in the monthly journal of the Konya People's House (*Konya Halkevi aylık kültür dergisi*). Koman based himself on a manuscript belonging to the well-known collector İzzet Koyunluoğlu of Konya.[7] Although scholars in Turkey in the Kātib Çelebi memorial volume, noted earlier, take notice of the existence of the inaccessible article by M. Koman, seemingly the work in question by Kātib Çelebi took long to attract the attention of researchers, since even in 1962 Bernard Lewis does not

6 Kâtip Çelebi. *Hayatı ve eserleri hakkında incelemeler*, Ankara 1957 (T.T.K. Yayınlarından VII, 33), pp. 54-57.

7 The article was not accessible to me. On April 7th 1965 I was able to look at the Koyunluoğlu manuscript thanks to the friendly permission of its owner in Konya. It is not dated but should be younger than the above-mentioned manuscript (also undated) of the Staatsbibliothek.

mention the *Irşād* in his essay on Christian sources referred to in Muslim history works.[8] The Staatsbibliothek now possesses, under the shelf mark Hs. or. oct. 866, a good exemplar of this history of the Franks from the Süßheim Collection. This manuscript – perhaps the only copy outside Turkey – will help make the small work of Kātib Çelebi accessible through scholarly effort.

3) Rarity value can also be claimed for a Nābī manuscript which likewise comes from the Süßheim Collection. It contains a *mes̱nevī* poem by the famous Turkish poet Yūsuf Nābī (d. 1712) which describes the circumcision celebration held by Sultan Meḥmed IV in 1675 for two of his sons, i.e. the poem is a *sūrnāme*. In 1934 and 1936 the Swiss scholar Ludwig Forrer spent time in Istanbul to study manuscripts. He recognized the *Sūrnāme* in a collective manuscript of the University Library and referred to it in an article that appeared in 1942 in *Der Islam*. In the meantime Agâh Sırrı Levend had discovered the *Sūrnāme* in the same Istanbul manuscript; in 1944 he published it in transcription.[9] Thus if until today there was only the one Istanbul manuscript, having been discovered twice, now it is possible to use the manuscript which Süßheim had earlier recognized and acquired, Hs. or. quart 1080, for comparison in preparing a text edition.

4) A large, weighty manuscript volume consisting of 486 folios lies before us in the Ms. or. quart 1977 of the Staatsbibliothek that was acquired in 1935. It is a good, dated (1855) and signed copy of the report that ʿAbdurraḥīm Muḥibb Efendi, Turkish Grand Ambassador to Napoleon, sent to the Porte, and bears the title *Sefāretnāme*. To be more precise, it is chiefly a compilation of the correspondence of the ambassador with the Grand Vizier and Foreign Minister (*Reʾīs ül-küttāb*), supplemented by minutes of his direct negotiations with the representatives of the European powers, translations of notes received from other ambassadors and his own observations. Muḥibb Efendi was dispatched to Napoleon in 1806 with congratulations and remained in France until 1811. There are two reasons for presenting this manuscript here; one is its content: along with much politics it reports in a matter-of-fact way on receptions and balls, conditions in Spain and the new "utensils called *telġrāflar*". Secondly, it is strange that up to today (1966) apparently only one manuscript of this report has been described, namely the one in the Austrian National Library, Vienna, Flügel II 316 no. 1145. We learn of the existence of a copy in Ankara from Enver

8 Bernard Lewis, "The Use by Muslim Historians of Non-Muslim Sources", in *Historians of the Middle East*, London 1962, p. 185.

9 Agâh Sırrı Levend, *Nabi'nin Surnâmesi*, Istanbul 1944.

Ziya Karal, but without any details.[10] Samples from Muḥibb Efendi's work are provided in French translation in a small book by Bertrand Bareilles published in Paris in 1920. The author writes in the preface that for his purpose he made use of a manuscript that was for sale "in a case made of red morocco" whose second part was incomplete. What can have become of this manuscript? In my 1966 essay I expressed the (premature) view that the Berlin manuscript was "very rare". Four years later Faik Reşit Unat's (completed and edited by Bekir Sıtkı Baykal), *Osmanlı Sefirleri ve Sefaretnameleri*, Ankara 1968, appeared, in which several manuscripts were described. Petra Kappert, who planned an edition of the *Sefāretnāme*, published an article;[11] Stéphane Yérasimos translated the work,[12] and Suraiya Faroqhi again drew attention to it.[13]

5) The Staatsbibliothek possesses a collection of modern Turkish manuscripts in Arabic script which are posterior to the law prohibiting its use. Four such volumes, from the pen of Dr. Rıza Nur, were acquired by the library in 1934-1935; they presumably came from Alexandria (Egypt) where the author was living at the time.

Personal remarks throughout the manuscripts helped to characterize the author, about whom very little could be found at the time. Why this was the case soon became clear, for the person writing was a bitter and vociferous opponent of Atatürk. Rıza Nur's works have become much better known and more accessible than in 1965 when I delivered my lecture. The following is merely an attempt to chart some of the developments.

Dr. Rıza Nur was born in Sinop in 1879, the son of a shoemaker. He trained as an army doctor and graduated from the Military Medical Academy in 1903 with a medical degree and the rank of captain (*tabip yüzbaşı*). He joined the Society for Union and Progress (*Ittiḥād ve Teraqqī*). After an assistantship he became a teacher at the Military Academy in Gülhane. After the revolution in 1908 he

10 According to a bibliographical note in E. Ziya Karal, *Osmanlı Tarihi* V2 (1961), p. 76, the Dil ve Tarih-Coğrafya Faculty of Ankara University possesses a manuscript. Karal summarizes the instructions given to Muḥibb Efendi (kept in the Başvekâlet Arşivi), in *Osmanlı Tarihi* VII (1956), p. 318, and VIII (1962), p. 165.

11 Petra Kappert, "Muḥibb Efendis Paris-Bericht. Die Französische Revolution aus der Sicht eines osmanischen Diplomaten," *Der Islam* 55 (1978), 93-98.

12 Stéphane Yérasimos, *Alî Efendi et Abdürrahman Efendi. Deux ottomans à Paris sous le Directoire et l'Empire, Relations d'ambassade*, translated with commentary, Paris 1998.

13 Suraiya Faroqhi, "Materielle Kultur und – zuweilen – gesellschaftlicher Wert. Das Europabild in den Berichten osmanischer Gesandter des XVIII. Jahrhunderts," Hendrik Fenz (ed.), *Strukturelle Zwänge – Persönliche Freiheiten. Osmanen, Türken, Muslime: Reflexionen zu gesellschaftlichen Umbrüchen. Gedenkband zu Ehren Petra Kapperts*, Berlin/New York 2009, 97-99.

was elected deputy (the youngest) for Sinop and entered the Ottoman Parliament. But he soon left the Society for Union and Progress and in 1911 became one of the founders of the Liberal opposition Freedom and Concord (or Liberty and Conciliation) party (*Ḥürriyet ve I'tilāf*). Once in power, the Liberals were overthrown by the Unionists; Rıza Nur was arrested several times and finally exiled. He lived in Paris, returning to Istanbul when the Unionists lost power in 1918, and by 1920 had firmly aligned himself with the Nationalist Movement under Mustafa Kemal.[14] As a member of parliament for Sinop and minister for education, he represented the Ankara government from 1920 to 1922 in the negotiations leading to the agreements with Soviet Russia and Soviet Ukraine, deputizing for İsmet (İnönü, 1884-1973) as foreign minister in 1922.[15] As minister of health he proposed the motion separating the caliphate from the sultanate. His career was at its height when, as İsmet's assistant in the Turkish peace delegation at Lausanne, he helped negotiate the favorable peace settlement for Turkey. But he soon voiced criticism on government politics during the second term of the National Assembly (August 1923-1927) and was forced to leave the country in 1926.[16]

In Paris, "writing in embittered exile" (Mango), Rıza Nur composed a large number of political and historical writings. He published, in French and Turkish, the *Revue de Turcologie* (*Türk Bilik Revüsü*) which he had founded in Paris but issued in Alexandria between 1931 and 1937. Eight volumes appeared until 1937. He apparently attended the 18th Congress of Orientalists in Leiden 1931 together with Reşit Saffet (Atabinen, 1884-1965).

On 27 January 1933 Rıza Nur left Marseilles and moved to Alexandria (Egypt). There he had transcripts made of his works. When the copies were completed and bound, on 12 March 1935, he decided "to send them to Europe and hide them in safe places. On the day on which I have done that I shall find complete peace."[17] Rıza Nur offered his manuscripts to four great European libraries, on condition that they were not made available to readers until 1960.

After Atatürk's death Rıza Nur came home to Turkey. He ended his career as a veteran intellectual and politician, living in Sülün Palas, Şehit Muhtar Caddesi, Taksim, Istanbul, surrounded by a circle of disciples. He edited the

14 F. Ahmad and D.A. Rustow, "Ḥürriyet we İ'tilāf Firḳası", *EI* III (1971), 594-595.

15 Stefanos Yerasimos, *Türk-Sovjet İlişkileri. Ekim Devriminden Millî Mücadele'ye*, Istanbul 1979, passim.

16 Andrew Mango, *Atatürk*, London 1999, pp. 363-4, 553; Erik Jan Zürcher, *Unionist Factor*, Leiden 1984, p. 52, with earlier literature. "Riza Nur" in Wikipedia. org/wiki/Riza_Nur, 11 March 2011.

17 Jan Schmidt, *Catalogue of Turkish Manuscripts in the Library of Leiden University, Volume Two*, Leiden 2002, p. 314.

weekly journal *Tanrıdağ*, which "daringly called for a return to Ottomanism."[18] When he died on 8 September, 1942, at sixty-three, a series of obituaries were written and commemorative speeches held by his friends and adherents;[19] they were collected and published in a booklet in 1962.[20] He was laid to rest in the Merkez Efendi cemetery.

When Dr. Cavid Orhan Tütengil (born 1921) was sent in 1963 to London to do research, Dr. Rıza Nur's manuscripts had recently become accessible in the British Museum. Tütengil, who taught sociology at Istanbul University, had written a prize-winning doctoral thesis on Montesquieu and published two books on Ziya Gökalp (1876-1924), the theoretician of the Turkist movement. In the summer of 1963, Tütengil more or less stumbled across the handwritten works of Dr. Rıza Nur. Astonished by these records of the recent past, he decided to draw attention to them, beginning with Rıza Nur's draft for the establishment of a pan-Turkist and Islamist political party.[21] Tütengil's three articles from 1963/1964 and specimens of the storm of protest in the Turkish press were collected in a small book dated 23 October 1964.[22]

When my paper was presented, in 1965, to Western observers Rıza Nur's rejection of Kemalism and propagation of a return to the caliphate seemed like an oddity. Before that time it was widely taken for granted that Turkism (merging with pan-Turkism) and Islamism were hardly reconcilable. Turkism was seen as "marked by neglect or hostility toward Islam."[23] By contrast, a new trend toward a synthesis, an "Islamic Turkishness," appeared in the writings of Rıza Nur, adding an Islamic ingredient to Pan-Turkism.[24]

Meanwhile, the publishing house Altındağ (a society under this name had been envisaged by Rıza Nur) produced a first edition of Rıza Nur's memoirs

---

18 Jacob Landau, *Radical Poltics in Modern Turkey*, Leiden 1974, pp. 193-195.

19 Jacob Landau, *Pan-Turkism in Turkey. A Study in Irredentism*, London 1981, pp. 88f. and 107, note 245. According to Landau, pp. p. 93 f., a group of Pan-Turkist adherents "appears to have been taken over by Hüseyn Nihal Atsız (1905-1975)".

20 Ziya Yücel İlhan (ed.), *Sevenlerinin kalemiyle Dr. Rıza Nur*, Istanbul 1962.

21 Such a party was "patently impossible" at the time, cf. Landau, *Radical Politics*, p. 188, and idem, *Pan-Turkism*, pp. 94 and 107, note 242. Necmettin Erbakan's (d. 2011) Milli Nizam Partisi was founded in January 1970.

22 Cavit Orhan Tütengil, *Doktor Rıza Nur üzerine üç yazı – yankılar – belgeler*, Ankara 1965. Cf. also *Varlık Yıllığı* 1965, Istanbul 1964, pp. 123-26.

23 Şerif Mardin, "Islam in 19th and 20th century Turkey", in Erik-Jan Zürcher (ed.) *Turkey in the Twentieth Century*, Berlin 2008, p. 461; Landau, *Radical Politics*, p. 193, remarked that "'Turanist' nationalists, in the nineteen-thirties "gave Islam a secondary place."

24 Landau, *Radical Politics*, pp. 192, 194, Şerif Mardin, op. cit., refers to the periodical *Tanrıdağ* without mentioning Rıza Nur.

(*Hayat ve Hatıratım*) in three volumes from microfilms brought from London. Rıza Nur's handwriting was transcribed into the modern script, with the usual "phonetic" spelling of foreign words (*Dayka* for Rıza Nur's German teacher at the Military Academy, Dr. Georg Deycke Pasha (1865-1938); *zergut* for "very good"). The blunt language of the memoirs hardly needed "Turkification" or "simplification" (as discussed below in chapter 13).

In their Preface (*Takdim*) the publishers said that no alterations had been made; only a slight cutting of offensive words had taken place as a precaution against the "Atatürk Law." The government nevertheless banned at least volume three of the memoirs because of derogatory and offensive remarks (*argoya varan ifadeler*) about Atatürk and İsmet İnönü, but by then the "Atatürk Law" had lost its effectiveness.[25] The publishers pointed out that the writings of Rıza Nur, whom they compared to Mehmed Akif, had their relevance as records for the future historian. This was in 1967-1969.

Ten years later, on 7 December 1979, Dr. Cavit Orhan Tütengil, professor and chairman of the Institute of Sociology of the University of Istanbul, columnist of the newspaper *Cumhuriyet*, was shot dead in Levent, Istanbul, on the way to university.[26]

For the present volume I have added the following list of **Rıza Nur's works** mainly to take account of recent publications

- *History of Turkey, Türk tarihi*, illustrated, with maps, considered as his main achievement by the author. Vols. I-XII were first published in Istanbul, 1924-1926, and issued. Vol. XII was printed but immediately withdrawn. Vol XIII, which was completed in manuscript, was suppressed by an order from Atatürk (it contains the author's condemnation of the alphabet change, proclaims Pan-Turkism, and rejects *Anadolucuk* as not viable). Vol XIV was completed in manuscript in 1931. The last two volumes are in Berlin, Ms. or. quart 1933.
- A shortened version of the *Türk tàriḫi, Abrégé Türk Tarihi*, completed by Rıza Nur around the beginning of 1930. Berlin, Staatsbibliothek, Ms. or. quart 1935.
- *Hayat ve Hatıratım Ma vie et mes mémoires*. "My Life and Memoirs".

25 Law No. 5816, passed in 1951, made it a criminal offence to insult Atatürk's memory; see A. Feroz Ahmad, *The Turkish Experiment in Democracy 1950-1975*, London 1977, pp. 43, 372. In 1968 I bought volumes one and two in a provincial bookshop.

26 http://www.en.wikipedia.org/wiki/List of assassinated people from Turkey, retrieved 14 June 2009. Cf. wikipedia.org/wiki/Cavit_Orhan_Tütengil, retrieved on 7 March 2011.

First edition Altındağ, I-III, Istanbul, 1967-1969 (based on the London manuscript).

Another edition: İşaret Yayınları, I-III, Istanbul 1992. Abdurrahman Dilipak (ed.), *Rıza Nur Kendini Anlatıyor*, Istanbul, İşaret (not seen).

– Draft for the establishment of a Pan-Turk, Islamist party, the *Türkçü* Party; a synthesis of extreme nationalism, pan-Turkism, anti-communism, and Islamism, including the re-establishment of the caliphate, restoring the previous status of dervish orders, abolition of women's emancipation, and bringing back the Arabic script. Only "racially pure Turks" should occupy posts as officers, civil servants and teachers. Written in Paris in August 1929. Published in *Hayat ve Hatıratım*, Altındağ, pp. 9-27.
– *A History of Armenia, Ermeni tárīhi*

Berlin, Staatsbibliothek, Ms. or. quart 1934.

– "Letters from Vienna" *Viyāna mektūbları* from 1908

Eight letters describing art treasures and cultural institutions in Vienna; the author argues that students should be sent to Vienna rather than to Germany.

Berlin, Staatsbibliothek, Ms. or. quart 2005/2.

– A serial of newspaper articles printed in *Akşam* on the parliamentary elections in the Sancak Sinop 1919 *1919 meclis-i meb'ūs̱ānı intiḫābı 1919*

Berlin, Staatsbibliothek, Ms or. quart 2005/3.

– "Pan-Hellenism is dying at Haymana" *Panelenizm Haymanada can veriyor*

Newspaper article published in *Hakimiyet-i Milliye*. Berlin, Staatsbibliothek, Ms. or. quart 2005/8.

– *Sinobda Rıżā Nūr kütübḫānesi*

History of the people's library, illustrated with photographs and sketches of the ground plan, which Rıza Nur founded in 1921 in Sinop as a religious endowment, with the author's *vāsiyetnāme*.

Berlin, Staatsbibliothek, Ms. or. quart 2005/9.

– *Paçi ile Ançi. Millī roman*, a "national novel" about a Pasha family from the times of Abdülhamid to the Second Constitution; one personage, Nūrī, is a thinly disguised Rıza Nur. Written in Genoa in 1914.

Berlin, Staatsbibliothek, Ms. or. quart 2005/4.

• • •

Manuscripts mentioned in this essay

Staatsbibliothek in Berlin – Preussischer Kulturbesitz

Ms. or. fol. 3060, *Süheyl ve Nevbahār* by Mesʿūd b. Aḥmed. Catalogue entry; W. Pertsch, *Verzeichniss der türkischen Handschriften der Königlichen Bibliothek zu Berlin,* Berlin 1889.

Ms. or. quart 1975, *Fetḥ-nāme-i Sulṭān Meḥmed* by Qıvāmī. Catalogue entry: B. Flemming, *Türkische Handschriften. Teil 1.* Wiesbaden 1968, 99-100 Nr. 122.

Ms. or. quart 1823, *Oġuznāme* by Yazıcıoğlu ʿAlī. Catalogue entry: Flemming 77 Nr. 101.

Ms. or. quart 1933, *Türk tarihi* by Rıza Nur. Catalogue entry: Flemming 174-175, Nr. 215.

Ms. or. quart 1935, *Abrégé Türk Tarihi* by Rıza Nur. Catalogue entry: Flemming 176-177, nr. 216.

Ms. or. quart 1934, *History of Armenia* by Rıza Nur. Catalogue entry: Flemming 97 Nr. 121.

Ms. or. quart 1977, *Sefāretnāme* by Muḥibb Efendi. Catalogue entry: Flemming 180-182 Nr. 220.

Ms. or. quart 2005, collective manuscript by Rıza Nur. Catalogue entry: Flemming 170-174 Nr. 214.

Hs. or. quart 1069, *Ḫusrev u Şīrīn* by Faḫrī. Catalogue entry: Flemming 324-325, No. 422.

Hs. or. quart 1080, *Sūrnāme* by Nābī. Catalogue entry: Flemming 137 Nr. 169.

Hs. or. oct. 1142, *Ġazavāt-ı Sulṭān Süleymān* by Bostān. Catalogue entry: Flemming 112 Nr. 138.

Hs. or. oct. 866, *Irşād el-ḥayārā ilā tārīḫ el-Yūnān ve n-Naṣārā* by Kātib Çelebi. Catalogue entry: Flemming 94-95 Nr. 117.

London, British Library

Or. 12.588 *Birinci Şiir Kitabına Dercedilmemiş olan şiirlerim*. Published in the Altındağ edition pp. 9, 25.

Or. 12.589 *Türkiye'nin yeni başdan iḥyāsı ve firqa programı.* Rıza Nur's draft for the establishment of the Pan-Turk party mentioned earlier. Published.

Or. 12.590 *Şi'irlerim ve Nesir ve Makalelerimden Birkaçı,* contains *Cehennemde Celse* (opera in two acts), *Topal Osman* (by Riza Nur), *Ziya Paşanın zafernāmesi, Vasiyetnāmem* "my testament", dated Alexandria, 17 January 1936. Published in Altındağ I, 18-21, 21-25, 28-32, 33-36, 36-42.

Or. 12.591 Rıza Nur's autobiography *Hayat ve Hatıratım.* Published.

Leiden, University Library

Cod. Or. 6694a *Türkiye'nin yeni başdan iḥyāsı ve firqa programı* by Rıza Nur; Catalogue entry: Jan Schmidt, *Catalogue of Turkish Manuscripts in the Library of Leiden University,* volume II, Leiden 2002, pp. 307-310.

Cod. Or. 6694b *Şi'irlerim ve neṡir maqālelerimden bir qaçı.* Collection of Rıza Nur's poems and prose writings, including the libretto for the opera *Cehennemde celse.* Catalogue entry: Schmidt II, 310-314.

Cod. Or. 6694c *Ḥayāt ve ḫāṭirātım.* Catalogue entry: Schmidt II, pp. 314-315.

Cod. Or. 10.805 *Türkiyenin yeni baştan iḥyasī ve firka programı.* Catalogue entry: Schmidt II, p. 442.

Paris, Bibliothèque nationale

No publication on Rıza Nur's MSS has come to my knowledge.

Vienna, Österreichische Nationalbibliothek

Muḥibb Efendi, *Sefāretnāme.* Cod. 1145. Catalogue entry: Flügel II, p. 316 No. 1145.

CHAPTER 3

Şerīf, Sultan Ġavrī and the "Persians"*

Already Elias John Wilkinson Gibb understood that the first translator of the complete *Şāhnāme* into Turkish verse, of whom he only knew the *maḫlaṣ* Şerīf, most probably was not an Ottoman because he had dedicated his work to a Mamluk sultan. In the meantime we have come to know, on the basis of the original draft, both the name of the author of the free Turkish rendition – Ḥuseyn b. Ḥasan (see below) – and the dates of composition of his work, and also to know that he was a descendant of the Prophet, but as to a more exact origin of Şerīf and his circumstances in life, we are still pretty much groping in the dark.[1] When considering the origin of our Turkish *şerīf* Ḥuseyn, account must be taken of the fact that before and during his lifetime Turkish and especially the Oġuz element was strongly represented not only in Rūm but also in Mamluk Egypt and Syria as well as in Persia, in Persian ʿIrāq and in the area of Diyārbakr. As members of powerful, often largely independent tribal groups disliked by the sedentary population who blamed all possible evils on these "Turkoman shepherds",[2] the Turkomans were viewed as coarse and uncivilized, as people who "never took up a book",[3] which did not hinder individual persons from having become assimilated into society.[4] "Vigorous Turks", abandoning the path of warlike valour, had settled down in Persian ʿIrāq for instance, had become landed proprietors,[5] emirs, religious scholars and even *qāżīs*,[6] and married into indigenous families. Through ties of this kind their progeny could become descendants of the Prophet, as appears to be the case with the famous Turkish poet Nesīmī, concerning whom there is much that speaks in favor of his originally having been from Baghdad. This *seyyid*, as is known, was executed in Aleppo (between 1417 and 1421) because of his hereti-

* Translated by John O'Kane.

1 HOP II, p. 391; on the history of the scholarship cf. Zajączkowski, Isfandiar, pp. 49-58; ŠN/Z, pp. 6-22. See now: Kristof D'hulster, "'Sitting with Ottomans and Standing with Persians': The Šāhnāme-yi Türkī as a Highlight of Mamluk Court Culture" in U. Vermeulen en K. D'hulster (eds.). *Egypt and Syria in the Fatimid, Ayyubid and Mamluk Eras VI*, Leuven 2010, pp. 229-256.

2 Ibn T VI, p. 416; P III, p. 79.

3 Ibn T VII, p. 262; P V, p. 172. Cf. Schimmel, p. 356, where this remark that was expressly applied to the Turkomans is transferred to the Mamluks in general.

4 One should picture circumstances to be similar to those in Rūm; cf. Pamphylien, pp. 38-40; Sohrweide pp. 108, 116, 120, 135 and 173.

5 Minorsky, Land Reforms, p. 456, based on Fażlullāh b. Rūzbihān, circa 1488-89.

6 Popper, Notes II, p. 9.

 | DOI 10.1163/9789004355767_004

cal teachings.[7] In 1448-9 we meet with another Turkish descendant of the Prophet in Egypt where he ended up after leaving his home in Baghdad, having been one of the distinguished Turks in that city.[8] Whoever held an administrative post in Aleppo had to know Turkish, and it was taken amiss if a functionary, such as a second chamberlain who had been posted there before 855/1451-2, used expressions of the village population and "did not know one complete phrase in Turkish".[9] In Iran as well the earlier Turkish element had become strengthened when, after the victory of the Aqqoyunlu over the Qaraqoyunlu and later in the wake of the Qızılbaş movement in the Ottoman Empire, numerous tribal groups withdrew into that country.[10] In the Ṣafavīya in Ardabil, which since the time of Shaykh Junayd (1429-1447) found its support predominantly among Turkish tribes, Turkish ethnic traditions and the Turkish language came to enjoy a special advantage. The "circle" around the Mamluk Sultan Ġavrī must also be seen against the background of close Turkish-Iranian interrelations. Our Şerīf, a servant of the Sultan of many years standing as he calls himself,[11] belonged to this circle. According to ʿOM who clearly bases himself on Eyyūbī (see below), Şerīf is an Āmidī, i.e. originally comes from a chief city of the Aqqoyunlu who from the Egyptian viewpoint belonged to the *bilād al-ʿAjam*.[12] Knowledge of this broadly conceived term ʿAjam helps in understanding a remark by Ibn Iyās that Sultan Ġavrī had an inclination for the *abnāʾ al-ʿAjam*[13] which revealed itself in his choice of his intimate courtiers. Let us consider some of the personalities we meet with in Ibn Iyās: there is the highly-reputed musician Nāṣiraddīn Muḥammad b. Qıjıq, "a pleasant, convivial personality". He was a virtuoso at playing the pandora,[14] a great connoisseur of music and master of all the singers and musicians of Cairo. When he died on 18 Ramażān 920/6 November 1514, a magnificent funeral was organized on his behalf.[15] Our Şerīf was clearly on friendly terms with this musician who had access to the Sultan's private apartments. In his additions to the Turkish *Şāhnāme* he dedicates an enthusiastic eulogy to him, describes him as possessing, apart from his musical capacities, a thorough expertise in "all" tongues, i.e. in the three Islamic languages, and mentions that Qıjıqzāde, as he calls him,

---

7 Gölpınarlı, Nesîmî, p. 207.

8 Ibn T VII, p. 318; P V, p. 206. Another such case: Ibn V, p. 195, cited in Popper, Notes II, p. 19.

9 Ibn T VII, p. 361; P V, p. 235.

10 Sümer, Avşarlar, pp. 472 ff.

11 ŠN/Z, pp. 52 and 51.(?)

12 Ibn Iyās III, p. 167.

13 Ibn Iyās V, p. 86.

14 For a description of this stringed instrument see Farmer, pp. 10, 32, 62 and 116.

15 Ibn Iyās IV, p. 401. On his good relations with the Sultan cf. Ibn Iyās IV, pp. 124, 321 and 326.

originates from Aleppo. The friendly relationship between him and Şerīf finds expression in a Turkish strophic poem in which Şerīf along with the musician, whom he here refers to as Qıjıqoğlu, wishes the Sultan's recovery from an illness.[16] The name of the musician in fact gives an indication of Turkish descent. When we hear that the artist originally comes from Syria, we are reminded that before he became sultan, Ġavrī for a period of twelve years or so had held high posts in this Mamluk province, for example that of grand chamberlain of Aleppo, and that for a while he was in charge of the prefectures of Tarsus and Malatya. Indeed, Şerīf also says that Ġavrī knows all the districts of Syria: *bilür Şām ėlinüñ bir bir diyārın*.[17] Some other figures of Ġavrī's court are not presented by Ibn Iyās in such a positive light as Qıjıqzāde. Al-Ḫvāja Ibrāhīm al-Samarqandī belonged to the closest circle around the Sultan; he originally came from Medina, had travelled throughout the regions of Persia into the Land of Rūm, and had a mastery of Turkish.[18] He and the *qāżī* Şarafaddīn Yūnus al-ʿĀdilī[19], whom Ibn Iyās also designated as al-Ḫvāja, often appear as *ḫāṣṣekī* of the Sultan; included as well in this inner circle was the court jester who was greatly appreciated and esteemed by Ġavrī and whom Ibn Iyās calls al-ʿAjamī al-Şanqajī[20] or Sanqaşī.[21] Ibn Iyās judged very negatively the fact that after Sultan Ġavrī's death in Aleppo these three endeavored to win the favor of his enemy, the Ottoman Sultan Selīm I.[22] Another court functionary of Sultan Ġavrī was a *Rūmī al-jins* by the name of ʿAbdallaṭīf who died in 1511.[23] From the *Nafāʾis al-majālis al-sulṭānīya* by Ḥusayn b. Muḥammad al-Ḥusaynī[24] who describes the gatherings that regularly took place from 1505 and in which not only religious scholars but also musicians like Qıjıqzāde, for example, participated and recited "in every language",[25] still more biographical material certainly comes to light.[26] But consideration of the information provided by

16 Dīvān, 85b. See no. 7 in this volume.

17 ŠN/Z, p. 45.

18 Ibn Iyās V, p. 141.

19 Laoust, Gouverneurs, pp. 136 f. and 144; Ibn Ṭūlūn II, p. 15.

20 Perhaps for *şaqajı? mużḥik* in Ibn Iyās IV, p. 482.

21 Ibn Iyās, see Index.

22 Ibn Iyās V, p. 82. A relevant illustrative example is Kristof D'hulster, "Caught Between Aspiration and Anxiety, Praise and Exhortation: An Arabic Literary Offering to the Ottoman Sultan Selīm I", *Journal of Arabic Literature* 44 (2013), pp. 181-239.

23 Ibn Iyās IV, p. 245.

24 Ed. ʿAbdalwahhāb ʿAẓẓām, Cairo 1941; cf. GAL II, p. 21. Unfortunately the edition was not available to me. Zajączkowski, Traduction, offers some quotations from the text.

25 ŠN/Z, p. 260.

26 Cf. Awad; ŠN/Z, p. 20.

Ibn Iyās[27] also gives the impression that by the words *abnāʾ al-ʿAjam* toward whom Ġavrī was inclined Ibn Iyās may not have meant exclusively Persians but possibly also Turks from ʿAjam (which, as said, was a broader term at the time). This impression is reinforced when one reads further in Ibn Iyās: "and perhaps the fact that he [Ġavrī] was inclined to the sect of the Nasīmīya was to be ascribed to his inclination for the company of Persians".[28] By Nasīmīya/Nesīmīye are clearly meant the followers of the already mentioned important Ḥurūfī and Ṣūfī poet Seyyid ʿImadeddīn Nesīmī whose teachings and poetry, as we know, had made a strong impression in particular in Egypt and Syria.[29] He had in fact also written poems in Persian but he is first and foremost known as a Turkish poet. He was appreciated as such by Ġavrī as well, who included in his Turkish *dīvān* a poem by Nesīmī for which he wrote a *naẓīre*.[30] On the basis of what has so far been said, one may draw the conclusion that by the *abnāʾ al-ʿAjam* at Ġavrī's court personalities from the Turkish-Persian domain are meant and in fact possibly Turks (from ʿAjam) rather than Persians.[31]

Ġavrī himself, who, as Şerīf puts it, was constantly in the company of Rūmīs and Persians (*oturmış Rūmile ḍurmış ʿAjemle*),[32] wrote poetry in Arabic and Turkish, occasionally also in Turkish-Persian; in any case he knew Persian (Şerīf in politeness maintains that he knew it better than a Persian)[33] but he lets it be understood that his understanding of the *Şāhnāme* would be considerably facilitated by a translation in Turkish.[34] When in Rabīʿ I 917/May-June 1511 a message from Şāh Ismāʿīl written in Persian arrives at the court in Cairo, it must be translated. One of the *abnāʾ al-ʿAjam* is brought in order to "read" it, i.e. to translate it (presumably into Turkish), and this is actually carried out by a *şerīf* by the name of Shaykh Ḥusayn.[35] I consider it possible that we have before us our *Şāhnāme* translator, Ḥüseyn b. Ḥasan b. Muḥammed el-Ḥuseynī el-Ḥanafī, called Şerīf. Let us examine in chronological order what we know about him together with our conjecture.

27 The influence of the *qāżīs* from the al-Ajā family, who under Ġavrī and his predecessors played an important role, should also be examined.

28 Ibn Iyās v, p. 86.

29 Gölpınarlı, Nesîmî, p. 207.

30 Dīvān, 57a and 58a.

31 Cf. Schimmel's remark, p. 378, regarding Ṣūfīs from the Turkish-Iranian zone.

32 ŠN/Z, p. 45.

33 ŠN/Z, p. 51.

34 ŠN/Z, pp. 49 and 51.

35 Ibn Iyās IV, p. 221. The *Gulistān* specialist, Badraddīn Maḥmūd al-Sarāyī (d. 1399) had to perform the same service for Sultan Barqūq in March 1394 (Ibn T V, p. 562; cf. Ibn T VI, p. 142, and P II, p. 103).

Şerīf, according to ʿOM, is meant to have been an intimate (*muqarreb*) of the Ottoman prince Jem. The prince had arrived in Cairo in Şaʿbān 886/September-October 1481 and from there set out for the Hijaz with the pilgrimage caravan in Muḥarram 887/February-March 1482. Although in the literature available to me there is no indication of his meeting Şerīf (who is not mentioned among Jem's intimates), it cannot be excluded that the two were acquainted with one another; in fact they may have met in the Mamluk state or perhaps during the pilgrimage.[36] Ġavrī, who as Qaytbay's *mamlūk* received his first more important appointment around the time of Jem's visit (as inspector of Upper Egypt), was familiar with the poetry of the Ottoman prince. This is attested by a *ġazel* of Jem that Ġavrī included in his own collection of poetry.[37] For this period we know nothing about Şerīf. His glance back at the Mamluk Sultans who preceded his patron Ġavrī begins with the year 900/1494-5, i.e. toward the end of Qaytbay's rule to whom he devotes an obituary.[38] Ġavrī at the very beginning of his rule in 1501 commissions the *şerīf* Ḥüseyn b. Ḥasan, whose literary talents he has heard about,[39] to translate the Persian *Şāhnāme* into Turkish verse. Şerīf, who is "not a man for the tournament field",[40] but by contrast wields an eloquent pen,[41] devotes himself summer and winter[42] to the great task which in his words no one before him had yet taken upon himself.[43] Thus he evidently has no knowledge of an allegedly complete prose translation that is supposed to have been produced for the Ottoman Sultan Murād II (1421-1451).[44] Even earlier in 1367, in West-Anatolian Ayasolug, Faḫreddīn Yaʿqūb had put into some 1,620 Turkish verses the novel of Behrām Çūbīn from the *Şāhnāme* for his Ḫusrev-Şīrīn poem based on Niẓāmī. In so doing, he chose to change the meter of the original to *hezej*.[45] Şerīf likewise does the same[46] and also points out that it was Niẓāmī who formed the Ḫusrev-tale into a poem.[47] In "this Turkish language", *bu türkī dili*, Şerīf is to compose poetry "in the dervish man-

36 For instance, Ḥasan b. Maḥmūd Bayatī (cf. GOW, p. 31) met Jem in Mecca.

37 Dīvān, 65b.

38 ŠN/Z, pp. 38 f.

39 ŠN/Z, p. 51.

40 ŠN/Z, p. 269.

41 ŠN/Z, p. 53.

42 ŠN/Z, p. 255.

43 ŠN/Z, p. 52.

44 V.L. Ménage in *EI2*, p. 921.

45 Faḫrī, pp. 54 f. See no. 1 in this volume.

46 ŠN/Z, pp. 14 and 53; Zajączkowski, Isfandiar, pp. 55 f.

47 ŠN/Z, p. 204.

ner", *dervīşāne*, so his patron has given him to understand,[48] and not without humor does Şerīf round off the panegyrical parts of his *Şāhnāme* with the image of the gnat that buzzes around the restless Sultan at night[49] or with a graphic depiction of the dusty *meydān* before its exemplary restoration by Ġavrī.[50]

That Şerīf is identical with Şarīf Ḥusayn who is apostrophized as a Persian shaykh by Ibn Iyās is a supposition and will be discussed in greater detail below. That he was one of "Ġavrī's Persians" who could be Iranians or Turks, should not be in any doubt, just as there can be no question about his having complete mastery of the Persian language and that he wrote poetry in Turkish. This justifies the conjecture that it may here be a matter of a Turk from a Persian region who grew up bilingually. In his congratulatory poem to Sultan Ġavrī, Şerīf remarks that his speech is "after the Turkish fashion": *türkanedür sözüñ Şerīf.*[51] For his part, Ġavrī exhorts his court poet: "Strive in writing, Şerīf, so that Şīrīn becomes honey, if like Ġavrī you wish to dominate Egypt with [your] name" (*Sözüñi jehd eyle kim şehd ola Şīrīn ėy Şerīf* / *Ġavrī gibi Mıṣr ėlin ḍutmaq dilerseñ ad ile*).[52] In another passage, he reminds him that Şerīf's words [only] attained honor because of Ġavrī's speech: *Şerīfüñ sözleri buldı şeref Ġavrī kelāmından.*[53] In another *ġazel* of Ġavrī it says: "What makes his words burning is that Şerīf like Ġavrī wants his name to be very famous in the world:"

> sözlerini sūz-nāk eyledügi budur Şerīf
> Ġavrī gibi ister adı ola 'ālemde 'alam.[54]

When Şerīf had been working for about two years on his *Şāhnāme* translation, in Ḏūlḥijja 908/the year beginning 28 May 1503, due to death, the office of shaykh of the Ṣūfīs became free in the much-respected mosque of Sultan Mu'ayyad Şayḫ (completed in 1419) by the Zuwayla Gate in northern Cairo. Ibn Iyās, who emphasizes that for a long time this post had been hereditary in the distinguished Arab *qāżī* family al-Dayrī, reports that the Sultan appointed the

48 That is to say, Şerīf is not to write "in the royal manner", *şāhāne*: ŠN/Z, p. 52; Zajączkowski, Isfandiar, p. 56.

49 ŠN/Z, p. 263.

50 ŠN/Z, p. 266.

51 Dīvān, 86b.

52 Dīvān, 85a.

53 Dīvān, 84a.

54 Dīvān, 83b.

Ḥanafī shaykh Ḥusayn Şarīf, "a Persian", to the position.[55] The chronicler is clearly preoccupied by this set-back for the Dayrīs[56] and reports the event once again under a different date.[57] On this occasion he does not waste many words on the new shaykh but notes that he is "now" in office. The part of his chronicle that covers 1503 Ibn Iyās concluded in 1508,[58] while the volume dealing with 1508 was finished in 1516[59] which thereby provides us with the year 1516 as the *terminus ad quem* for Shaykh Ḥusayn's time in office. For the reasons dealt with above and in view of the fact that our Şerīf ended his work in the Mu'ayyad Mosque (see below), I consider it possible that this Ḥusayn Şarīf is the same person as our *Şāhnāme* translator.

As Shaykh of the Mu'ayyadīye, Ḥusayn Şarīf simultaneously held the office of Professor of Ḥanafī law; the post, which paid 550 silver half-dirhems per month, is described as a respectable half-day activity (the professor met with his students in the afternoon) and took for granted other sources of income, for instance from service at the court.[60] Such could well be the case with our Şerīf.

At the beginning of Şa'bān 913/6 December 1507, Şerīf finished the first part of his *Şāhnāme* translation inside the *qubba* of the Emir Yaşbek.[61] As is known, this was one of the favorite residences of Sultan Ġavrī. The edifice which the powerful minister of Qaytbay had built as a pious foundation in Maṭarīya by Cairo and, among other things, provided with a preacher (it is not his grave),[62] from around 1470, even while the emir was still alive, had already served Sultan Qaytbay as a destination; one camped in the surroundings and in the building itself receptions were held, as for instance in Ramażān 886/October-November 1481 for the above-mentioned Ottoman prince Jem.[63] After the visits by Sultans among the successors to Qaytbay had become more rare, Ġavrī once more took up the tradition of these excursions to Maṭarīya; he had a house

55 Ibn Iyās IV, p. 54.

56 On the "customary hostility" between religious scholars of Arab and of Persian descent cf. Ibn T VI, pp. 793 f.; P IV, p. 171. Regarding animosity between Egyptians and religious scholars from Rūm see Ibn T VI, p. 852; P IV, p. 214.

57 Ibn Iyās IV, p. 135, under Jumādā I 914/the year beginning 28 August 1508. The death is mentioned still a third time: Ibn Iyās V, p. 93.

58 Ibn Iyās IV, Introduction, p. 7.

59 Ibn Iyās IV, Introduction, p. 8.

60 Popper, Notes II, pp. 119-121.

61 ŠN/Z, pp. 103 and 425.

62 He is buried in a *türbe* by the Zāviye Kuhnabūş. There is also another *qubba* that he had built; cf. Ibn Iyās III, p. 168.

63 Ibn Iyās III, p. 182.

built by Yaşbek's *qubba* and spent much time there; he made use of the place for convalescence, for walks and processions, as well as occasionally for splendid banquets with singers and musicians. If Şerīf felt like a *mülāzim*[64] at Ġavrī's court, it is reasonable to conclude that he was obliged to accompany his lord on such excursions. Indeed, Ġavrī manifestly entertained special respect for Emir Yaşbek who had been killed in Ruhā (Urfa) by the Aqqoyunlu in 1480 (and whose brother was an emir of the first rank in Ġavrī's service): in Ġavrī's collection of Turkish poetry a Turkish lament for Yaşbek's death[65] is found along with two Turkish poems by Yaşbek himself,[66] and in another of his Turkish poems Ġavrī calls the deceased the ʿAzīz-i Mıṣr alluding to the tale of Yūsuf and Zulayḫa.[67] A study of the cultural activity of the great emir Yaşbek, who for many years displayed prudence while occupying the highest state offices and whose death was sincerely mourned in Egypt,[68] would help establish greater differentiation in the often still too one-sided judgement regarding the Mamluk aristocracy. Although there are voices that appreciate the patronage of the Mamluk rulers,[69] apparently among Turcologists the tendency of the Arabic sources has been adopted in that it is maintained that most of the Mamluks had "no education".[70] The basis for this conclusion on the part of the "Arab-inclined" chroniclers, who were indifferent to the Turkish literature of the Mamluks, was the ability to write Arabic and a flawless pronunciation of that language,[71] i.e. criteria that should have been rather alien to Turcology which to a large extent has in fact deprecated Arabization. More recently with regard to the late Mamluk period, under the influence of Arab voices any cultural interests have been flatly denied to both Sultans and emirs.[72] Here are a few preliminary points concerning Yaşbek min Mahdī based on the secondary sources available to me: the great secretary of state, *al-dawādār al-kabīr*, com-

64 ŠN/Z, p. 51.

65 Dīvān, 70a-b. Unfortunately it is incomplete.

66 Dīvān, 43a and 45a.

67 Dīvān, 69b.

68 Ibn Iyās III, p. 168.

69 For example, Zajączkowski, Bulġat IX; Popper, Notes I, p. 5; Farmer, p. 86.

70 János Eckmann in *Fundamenta* II, p. 297.

71 As Bertold Spuler in *Der Islam* 40 (1965), p. 245, explains, the Arabs' criticism of the faulty Arabic pronunciation of the Turks was not accompanied by an attempt "to amaze the world at large by learning Turkish and its correct pronunciation"; already Ibn Taġrībirdī felt himself obliged to compose a work of his own due to the incorrect way Arabs wrote Turkish names (Ibn T P I, XIX).

72 Schimmel, p. 356. On the other hand, cf. GAL II, Introduction.

posed a work in Arabic, the *Şajarat an-nasab aş-şarīf an-nabawī*;[73] the *qāżī* and envoy Şamseddīn Muḥammad b. Maḥmūd, known as Ibn Aja, dedicated to him a work entitled *Tārīḫ al-Amīr Yaşbek aẓ-Ẓāhirī* or the *Riḥla*,[74] and Muḥammad al-Qudsī al-Şarīf apparently dedicated to him his *Duwal al-islām aş-şarīfa*.[75] He was a passionate collector of books which he acquired through purchase or "by dictation";[76] in this way he had the huge biographical dictionary of al-Ṣafadī copied for his library.[77] Moreover, that he also did not forget Turkish literature is attested by his own above-mentioned poems as well as the beautiful copy of the *Ġarībnāme* by ʿĀşıq Paşa that he had made for himself.[78]

But to return to Şerīf. On 2 Ḏūlḥijja 916/2 March 1511 he finished his *Şāhnāme* translation;[79] he wrote out a fair copy of the text himself[80] and this he did in the mosque of the deceased Sultan Muʾayyad in Cairo which seems to confirm our previous assumption that Şerīf was the Shaykh at this mosque. The voluminous book was adorned with miniatures and presented to the Mamluk Sultan who had it provided with his *ex-libris*. Bursalı M. Ṭāhir informs us that Şerīf received a gold piece for every couplet.[81] His source for this appears to be the Turkish prose translation of the *Şāhnāme* from the pen of the Ottoman poet Eyyūbī. Eyyūbī knew Şerīf's work which in the meantime had ended up in the library of Sultan Süleymān.[82] Therein the promise of Sultan Maḥmūd of Ġazna to Firdawsī is reported: *bu Şāhnāme neqadar biñ beyt gelürse ... aña her beyt başına bir altun vėrem*[83] – it seems probable that Eyyūbī was influenced by this in his ideas regarding Şerīf's recompense. Eyyūbī, who for Sultan Süleymān

73 GAL II, p. 72.

74 GAL II, p. 42, S II, p. 41; new research by Muṣṭafā Jawād (unavailable to me) is reviewed by G. Endress in *Oriens* 18-19 (1967), pp. 518 f. According to ḍawʾ X, p. 43, Ibn Ajā transposed the *Futūḥ al-Şām* of al-Wāqidī into twelve thousand Turkish verses.

75 GAL S II, pp. 51 f.: "dedicated to al-Malik (!) al-Ašraf Jišbek (!) ad-Dawādārī".

76 Żawʾ X, p. 274.

77 Cf. volume I of the text edition by Hellmut Ritter, *al-Wāfī bil-wafayāt*, Istanbul 1931, Introduction. An illuminated manuscript commissioned by Yashbek min Mahdi is *Risalat ar-riyāḍ al-qudsiyya*, Cod. Mixt 1420 in the Austrian National Library in Vienna, described by Dorothea Duda, *Islamische Handschriften II. Teil 1. Die Handschriften in arabischer Sprache. Textband*, Vienna 1992, pp. 238-239.

78 Ms. Istanbul, Lâleli 1752, according to *İA* I, p. 705.

79 ŠN/Z, p. 279.

80 ŠN/Z, p. 255.

81 ʿOM II, p. 256.

82 Possibly through Ḫādim Süleymān Paşa, governor of Egypt from 1524 to 1534, who was the first to carry off the so-called "Egyptian treasure" to the Porte.

83 ŠN/Z, p. 248.

wrote an account in verse of the deeds of this ruler,[84] clearly refers to our Şerīf as Şerīfī-yi Āmidī[85] which, as long as Eyyūbī's *Şāhnāme* translation does not come to light,[86] is our only basis for the assumption that Şerīf was originally from Āmid/Diyārbakr.[87] Şerīfī (sic), Bursalı Ṭāhir continues, was a gifted poet who possessed mastery over the three Islamic languages.[88] As mentioned above, in addition to his great *Şāhnāme* translation a Turkish poem by Şerīf has come to light in Sultan Ġavrī's collection of poems.

That the "Persian *şerīf*" Shaykh Ḥusayn, whom we believe we can identify as our *Şāhnāme* translator, in May/June 1511 translated an official letter in Persian for Ġavrī, has been alluded to in the opening of this essay. After Ġavrī's death changes came about in the occupancy of the office of Shaykh of the Mu'ayyadīya whose incumbent we would maintain had been the "*Şāhnāme* Şerīf".[89] Was Şerīf still in office when in January/February 1517 during the raging street battles in Cairo a group of Ottomans climbed into the minarets of his mosque and from there shot at the Mamluks?[90] Or, as Bursalı Ṭāhir writes, had he already died in Cairo in 920/the year beginning 26 February 1514?[91] Ali Emiri's conjectures that Şerīf settled in Istanbul where he dedicated a work on *beyān* and *bedī'* to Sinān Paşa and is meant to have died in 930/1523-4,[92] have clearly not been verified up until now.

In conclusion, I wish to say a few words about Şerīf's patron, Sultan Ġavrī. We read in Şerīf's *Şāhnāme* translation that Ġavrī knows the art of poetry and of *mu'ammā*, and has written *tevḥīd*, "professions of the divine oneness", as well as eulogies of the Prophet, which are so beautiful the hearer would lose his self-control.[93] Ibn Iyās remarks that Ġavrī wrote in Turkish.[94] In 1938 Mohammad Awad pointed out that the above-mentioned *Nafā'is al-majālis*

84 Anhegger.

85 'OM III, pp. 9 f.

86 Bursalı M. Ṭāhir, 'OM, op. cit., mentions its size as being three good-sized volumes; in the literature available to me I find no reference to a manuscript of the work.

87 Ali Emiri holds the same view on his origin: cf. Divanlar I, p. 212.

88 'OM II, p. 256.

89 Yaḥyā b. al-Tāj was replaced in January/February 1520 by "an ignorant, unknown Persian or an Ottoman" whose name is not even given: Ibn Iyās V, p. 319; two names are mentioned for June 1520: Ibn Iyās V, p. 337; from July/August 1522 al-Shaykh Ibrāhīm is the occupant of the office of shaykh.

90 Ibn Iyās V, p. 151.

91 'Om II, p. 256; Divanlar I, p. 212, no. 92, incorrectly cites: 950 AH.

92 Cf. 'OM II, p. 257; Divanlar I, p. 212

93 SN/Z, p. 47.

94 Ibn Iyās V, p. 87.

contains a Turkish song by Ġavrī and that the history of Aleppo by al-Ṭabbāḫ contains an additional song as well as four Arabic compositions by the Sultan.[95] In *Fundamenta* II mention is made of five Turkish poems.[96] János Eckmann has published three lines of a *mulammaʿ* and four lines of a purely Turkish poem,[97] while Ananiasz Zajączkowski has edited and commented on thirteen Turkish and Arabic *muwaşşaḥ*.[98] The religious poems of Ġavrī, which Şerīf praised so highly and which clearly until now have not been known to scholars, are found in a small collective manuscript from the library of Sultan Ġavrī.[99] On folios 2b up to 87b the manuscript contains Turkish poems under the heading: *dīwān mawlānā al-malik al-aşraf Qanṣawh Ġavrī ʿazza naṣruhū wa-ḫallada mulkuhū*. This Turkish collection of Ġavrī, which one may rightly call his *dīvān*, consists of a *qaṣīda* section with *tevḥīd*, *naʿt*, *munājāt* and *naṣīḥa* as well as over sixty *ġazel*s and six *rubāʾīs*; *ġazel*s by other poets are also included as models for *naẓīres*. According to my preliminary examination, the manuscript, which is not entirely complete, contains more than 550 Turkish couplets (rarely alternating with Arabic and once with a Persian verse), to which I shall return (see chapter 5 in this volume).

Abbreviations

Alderson	A.D. Alderson, *The Structure of the Ottoman Dynasty*, Oxford 1956.
Anhegger	R. Anhegger, "Eyyûbî'nin menakıb-i Sultan Süleyman'ı", *Tarih Dergisi* I (1950), pp. 117-138.
Awad	M. Awad, "Sultan al-Ghawrī. His place in literature and learning (three books written under his patronage). *Actes du XXe Congrès International des Orientalistes*, Bruxelles 1938, Louvain 1940, pp. 321f.

95 Awad, p. 322.

96 See bibliographical information given by János Eckmann in *Fundamenta* II, p. 300.

97 *Fundamenta* II, p. 300.

98 Zajączkowski, Muvaşşaḥ.

99 Ms. or oct. 3744 of the Staatsbibliothek, here cited as Dīvān. The manuscript is described by Manfred Götz in the *Verzeichnis der orientalischen Handschriften in Deutschland, Türkische Handschriften*. It also appears in the *Katalog der Malereien der persischen, indischen und türkischen Handschriften der Staatsbibliothek* was in preparation at the time of writing. I am grateful to the Staatsbibliothek, and especially to the library's director, Dr. Wolfgang Voigt, for permission to quote from the manuscript.

BSOAS	*Bulletin of the School of Oriental and African Studies*, London.
Dau'	as-Sakhāwī, *ad-Dau' al-lami` li-ahl al-qarn at-tāsi`*, 14 volumes, Cairo 1354/1935-6.
Dīvān	Ms. or. oct. 3744 of the Staatsbibliothek zu Berlin Preussischer Kulturbesitz.
Divaṇlar	*Istanbul Kitaplıkları Türkçe yazma divanlar kataloğu*, 3 vols., Istanbul 1947-1965.
Fakhrī	B. Flemming, „Fakhrī's Husrev u Sirin vom Jahre 1367", *ZDMG* 115 (1965), pp. 36-64.
Farmer	H.G. Farmer, *Islam*, Leipzig [without date] (*Musikgeschichte in Bildern. Vol. III: Musik des Mittelalters und der Renaissance*).
Fundamenta II	*Philosophiae Turcicae Fundamenta II*, Wiesbaden 1964.
GAL	C. Brockelmann, *Geschichte der arabischen Literatur*, vol. I. II Weimar-Berlin, 1898-1902; 2nd ed. Leiden 1943-1949 and *Suppl.* I-III, Leiden 1937-1942.
GOW	F. Babinger, Die Geschichtsschreiber der Osmanen und ihre Werke, Leipzig 1927.
Gölpınarlı, Nesîmî	A. Gölpınarlı, "Nesîmî" in *¤slam Ansiklopedisi* IX.
HOP	E.J.W. Gibb, *A History of Ottoman Poetry*, 6 vols., London 1900-1909.
Ibn Iyās	*Die Chronik des Ibn Ijās* ed. by P. Kahle, M. Mustafa and M. Sobernheim, 3 volumes, Istanbul 1931-1936, indices by A. Schimmel, Istanbul 1945.
Ibn T	Ibn Taġrībirdī, *an-Nujūm as-Zāhira fī mulūk Misr wa l-Qāhira*, ed. W. Popper, volumes V-VIII, Berkeley 1909-1936.
Ibn Tūlūn	*The Chronicle of Ibn Tulun, Mufakahat-ul-Khillan fī hawadith-iz-zaman*, ed. M. Mostafa, vol. II, Cairo 1964.
Laoust, Gouverneurs	H. Laoust, *Les Gouverneurs de Damas sous les Mamlouks et les premiers Ottomans*, Damascus 1952.
Minorsky, Land Reforms	V. Minorsky, «The Aq-qoyunlu and Land Reforms (Turkmenica, 11), *BSOAS* XVII 3 (1955), pp. 449-462. *41 (1965), pp. 95-223.*
`OM	Bursalı Mehmed Tāhir, *`Osmanlı müellifleri*, 3 vols., Istanbul 1334-1343.
P	*History of Egypt. Translated from the Arabic Annals of Abu l-Mahâsin Ibn Taghrî Birdî* by W. Popper, Berkeley and Los Angeles 1955-1960.

Pamphylien	B. Flemming, *Landschaftsgeschichte von Pamphylien, Pisidien und Lykien im Spätmittelalter*, Wiesbaden 1964.
Popper, Notes	W. Popper, *Egypt and Syria under the Circassian Sultans*, 2 volumes, Berkeley and Los Angeles 1955-1957.
RO	*Rocznik Orientalistyczny*, Warsaw.
Schimmel	A. Schimmel, "Some glimpses of the religious life in Egypt during the later Mamlūūk period", *Islamic Studies* (Rawalpindi) IV (1965), pp. 353-392.
Sohrweide	H. Sohrweide, "Der Sieg der Safawiden in Persien und seine Rückwirkungen auf die Schiiten Anatoliens im 16. Jahrhundert", *Der Islam* 41 (1965), pp. 95-223.
Sümer, Avşarlar	F. Sümer, „Avşarlara dâir", *Köprülü Armağanı*, Istanbul 1953, pp. 453-478.
ŠN/Z	A. Zajaczkowski, *Turecka wersja Šāhnāme z Egiptu Mameluckiego*, Warsaw 1965.
TDAY	*Türk Dili Araştırmaları Yıllığı*, Ankara.
TTS	*Tanıklariyle Tarama Sözlüğü*, vols. I-IV, Istanbul 1943-1957.
Zajaczkowski, Bulgat	A. Zajaczkowski, *Vocabulaire arabe-kiptchak de l'époque de l'État Mamelouk*, I, Warsaw 1958.
Zajaczkowski, Isfendiar	A. Zajaczkowski, „Historia Isfandiara podlug tureckiej wersji `Šāh-nāme' z Egiptu Mameluckiego", *RO* XXVIII, 1 (1964), pp. 49-90.
Zajaczkowski, Muvaššah	A. Zajaczkowski, „Poezje stroficzne muvaššah mameluckiego sultana Qansūh (Qansav) Gavrī: *RO* XXVII, 2 (1964), pp. 63-89.
Zajaczkowski, Traduction	A. Zajaczkowski, „La plus ancienne traduction turque (en vers) du Šāh-nāme de l'état Mamelouk d'Egypte (XV-XVIe siècles), *TDAY Belleten* 1966, Ankara 1967, pp. 51-63.

CHAPTER 4

Some Remarks on Turkish Prose before the Tanẓīmāt Period*

Turkish prose literature during the time span from roughly 1300 to 1830 has recently entered more fully the field of vision of scholarship that deals with language history and stylistic criticism. Scholarship has been gradually freeing itself from the authority that E.J.W. Gibb (1857-1901), through his evaluation of older Turkish literature, exercised on his contemporaries and successors.[1] One seems only lately to have become aware of the extent to which the great British expert on Turkish poetry was influenced by the Turkish literary criticism of his day, which in turn based its standards of judgement on French literature.[2] Progressive Turkish literary critics of the Tanẓīmāt period dismissed Turkish artistic prose (*dīvān* prose) as being hopelessly submerged in foreign influence and on occasion they went so far as to maintain that the older prose, in its totality, had transformed itself from its simple beginnings as a national language into a bombastic foreign tongue. In their wake, and in particular in the wake of Gibb, scholarship adopted the view that Ottoman artistic prose, at the high point of its development, was no longer actually Turkish; due to the overly cultivated artificiality of a Veysī (d. 1628) or Nergisī (d. 1635), the language had become utterly bogged down.[3] Yet there are also the non-bombastic domains of the older prose; and one has paid attention to them primarily out of an interest in their Turkish vocabulary but also partly in the desire to study specific Turkish, and especially Ottoman, modes of appropriating the conventions of classical Islamic literature. This has been considerably facilitated by new discoveries and the publication of text editions thanks to which large parts of a rich literature that had fallen into oblivion have once again been made accessible. Franz Taeschner[4] has undertaken useful preliminary studies that pave

* Translated by John O'Kane.

1 E.J.W. Gibb, *A History of Ottoman Poetry. 1900-1909.* (Vols. II-VI posthumously published by E.G. Browne), reprint 1958.

2 J. Stewart-Robinson, "The Tezkere Genre in Islam", in *JNES* XXIII (1964), p. 58.

3 One customarily speaks of "a dead end", *çıkmaz*, e.g. Björkman in *Phil. Turc. Fundamenta* II, p. 444; A.S. Levend, *Türk Dilinde Gelişme ve Sadeleşme Evreleri*, 1960, p. 78; Fahir İz, *Eski Türk edebiyatında Nesir* I, İstanbul 1964, p. X; Idem in *TDAY Belleten* 1967 (1968), p. 123. – The remarks that follow are from my review of Fahir İz (see here fn. 16).

4 F. Taeschner, "Die osmanische Literatur." In *Handbuch der Orientalistik* V. Altaistik, 1. Abschn. Turkologie, 1963, pp. 250-335 ("Altrumtürkische und altosmanische Prosaliteratur",

the way for a coherent presentation of West-Turkish prose literature.[5] Of course, here too it was necessary to set limits based on subject matter. Still, one cannot exclude everything which is intended for a special purpose and therefore is not autonomous, "pure" literature.[6] There is indeed an extensive narrative literature but, in fact, in the period from roughly 1300 to the middle of the 19th century history writing and biography,[7] as well as a quite diverse range of religious writings and secular didactic works, also constitute major forms of literary prose.[8] Writings one would call "technical", for instance juridical texts, should only be taken into consideration to the extent that they contribute to our understanding of literary works and how these are conditioned by their environment.

When great attention is paid to the older prose, especially from the perspective of language history, there is an immediate link with present-day issues, for example with regard to the movement for linguistic purification. Agâh Sırrı Levend, in his book dealing with "the phases of development and simplification of the Turkish language" – it first appeared in 1949, was republished in a revised form in 1960 and in 1972 was again expanded in a 3rd edition – emphasizes how simple Turkish (identified with the everyday language) has kept itself alive in works intended for ordinary people and in part even in works of the *dīvān* literature.[9] According to Levend, two kinds of prose coexisted alongside one another: the simple and natural, linguistically pure Turkish, on the one hand, and artistic prose on the other, the latter having formed in the 15th century and become so swamped by foreign influence in the 16th and 17th centuries that it ceased to be Turkish.[10] Levend also points out that individual

---

[hochosmanische] Kunstprosa, wissenschaftliche Literatur und [späte] Prosaliteratur: pp. 281-84, 307-18, 329-35). Cf. also the relevant sections in A. Bombaci, *La Letteratura Turca*, 1969, and Walther Björkman, "Die altosmanische Literatur" and "Die klassisch-osmanische Literatur" in *Phil. Turc. Fundamenta* (1964), pp. 403-65.

5 This Gibb thought to be superfluous since the few prose works with artistic ambition that he was acquainted with were, in his view, undeniably composed according to the rules of poetry: *HOP* I, p. v.

6 A. Bombaci speaks of a corresponding demarcation in *Phil. Turc. Fundamenta* II (1964), p. XI.

7 J.R. Walsh perhaps went too far when he maintained that the historical-biographical literary genre is in fact the only worthwhile vehicle for "creative" prose writing (his inverted commas) (in *Historians of the Middle East*, 1964², p. 198).

8 See Bombaci's summaries in *Fundamenta* II (1964), pp. LXIV-LXX; Idem, *La Littérature Turque*, 1968, p. 273; Idem, *Letteratura Turca*, 1969, p. 321.

9 Levend, *Evreler*, p. 12.

10 Ibidem, p. 21.

authors, depending on their purpose, made use of both these forms of prose separately or together in the same work (for instance: a florid introduction followed by a relatively simple main text).[11] As a designation for these two kinds of prose, which at times appear to be two different languages, Levend suggests "Turkish" and "Ottoman".[12] One can conceive of this as a resumption of the old formal division of prose into *ʿārī* "naked", unadorned, and *musaccaʿ* "with rhyme", embellished,[13] but now with a more historical linguistic emphasis. If in this case we have an attempt to offer proof of the unbroken continuity of Turkish[14] on the basis of a two-part division of prose, Fahir İz suggested a three-part division of older prose in the same endeavor. İz intended to make available in his large anthology that would consist of six volumes not only specimens of poetry but of old prose as well, in three volumes for each,[15] of which the first appeared in 1964.[16] In the preface to his book, which was conceived as a supplement to his planned history of older Turkish literature, Fahir İz divided the prose (*nesir, düzyazı*) of the Anatolian Turks into simple prose (*sade nesir*), middle prose (*orta nesir*) and embellished or ornamented prose (*süslü nesir*).[17] Simple prose, as is clear from its name, is unembellished and based on the everyday language. In middle prose, elements of the everyday language are to a limited extent combined with rhetorical artistic devices from the Arabic and Persian languages. By contrast, embellished prose employs all

11 Ibidem, p. 71.

12 Ibidem, pp. 12 f.

13 Theory and practice of Arabic artistic prose is dealt with by Johann Fück, *Arabiya*, 1950, pp. 80-85; there, following Qudāma b. Jaʿfar, he distinguishes the low (*sakhīf*) from the high (*jazl*) style. On the Persians and Turks taking this over cf. E.G. Browne, *Lit. Hist.* II, Introduction, and F. Taeschner in *Hdb. Or.*, pp. 307 f.

14 An assessment that focuses on vocabulary is available by Şerafettin Turan who stresses that Ibn Kemāl also accorded ample space to pure Turkish words, especially those of the older stage of the language. Turan provides a useful glossary to *Defter VII*, pp. 595 f. (see here fn. 59), which by employing a macron also indicates the older writing of the long Turkish vowels.

15 The first volume contains narrative writing in the broadest sense, including early Ottoman chronicles. The second volume was to devote a third of its space to historians and also to contain biographies, official writings like *fetḥnāmes*, as well as books on *aḫlāq* and *siyāset*. The third volume was meant to offer notes, a glossary, facsimiles and the bibliography.

16 Fahir İz, *Eski Türk edebiyatında Nesir. XIV. yüzyıl ortasına kadar yazmalardan seçilmiş metinler*, I, İstanbul 1964, pp. XX and 653. The second volume had not yet been published at the time of writing.

17 İz, *Nesir* I, pp. V-XVII, in the sequence *sade – süslü – orta*. On ʿAkif Paşa (1787-1848) and his *orta türkçe* (*qaba – orta – faṣīḥ*) cf. F. Taeschner in *Hdb. Or.* pp. 333 ff.

the devices of adorned language that *dīvān* poetry[18] had made available and was therefore, in the sense of Arabic literary theory, also an acknowledged component of it. This three-part division, in the first year of its appearance, was taken over into the *Philologiae Turcicae Fundamenta* where Alessio Bombaci speaks of "simple prose", "medium or intermediate prose"[19] and "stylistically elaborated prose". Fahir İz based his three-part division of old Anatolian-Turkish and Ottoman prose chiefly upon linguistic criteria. In this way he confronted the reproach that had never been silenced since the Tanẓīmāt period, that simple Turkish prose at some time in the Ottoman past had been utterly submerged in the influence of Arabic-Persian artistic prose. In his choice of texts as well as in his preface, İz aimed to demonstrate the continuity of the national language throughout the ages in the form of simple and intermediate Turkish prose. The article he later published on the history writers of the 17th century also served this purpose.[20] In 1970 Fahir İz explained his standpoint in *The Cambridge History of Islam* II, Cambridge 1970, pp. 692 f.: *Pure prose, ornamented prose, middle prose*.

In surveys of Turkish literature an empirically worked out division of prose into periods is scarcely discernible. In the wake of Gibb, a quite static picture has been sketched, set to the key note of "Persianization", and attempts at defining periods have depended, for the most part, on the period divisions for poetry.[21] The assessment of particular writers is at times based on an incomplete state of knowledge which in the meantime has been altered in part through text editions and monograph studies.[22] It is hoped that, as gaps in our knowledge come to be filled in, scholarship of a kind that deals with specifically literary questions will be increasingly pursued.

In that regard, the philological research of recent decades has accomplished no small amount of preliminary work. The Old Anatolian-Turkish literary language, the forerunner of the Ottoman literary language, has been worked out along with its own particular norms for writing,[23] as well as its grammatical,

18 Described by Alessio Bombaci, "The Turkic Literatures. Introductory Notes on the History and Style." In *Phil. Turc. Fundamenta* II (1964), pp. XXIX-XXXIV, XLI-XLIV, LXVII.

19 Ibidem, pp. XLVI and XLVIII.

20 Fahir İz, "Eski Düzyazının Gelişimi: XVII. Yüzyılda Halk Dili ile Yazılmış bir Tarih Kitabı: Hüseyin Tûgî, Vak'a-i Sultan Osman Han". In TDAY *Belleten* 1967 (1968), pp. 119-64.

21 Cf. Gibb's four periods in *HOP* I with remarks on this by Bombaci and Björkman in *Fundamenta* II, pp. XLIV and 438.

22 The state of research on older Ottoman history writing was appraised by Halil İnalcık and V.L. Ménage in *Historians of the Middle East*, 1964.

23 For instance, written indication of long vowels in the older period and complete vocalization in the succeeding period. Today when for technical reasons to do with printing

and especially its lexical, peculiarities.[24] The result of this research must also be exploited for the domain of high Ottoman Turkish where at times there appears to be uncertainty as to whether particular Turkish language features stem from the everyday language of authors or are archaisms from the older literary language.[25] This will have its effects on the stylistic assessment of Ottoman prose whose genres, due to the uneven state of research, are treated with varying degrees of intensity. Available to us for the epic genres of oral tradition are the authoritative studies of Pertev Naili Boratav who has also dealt with the genre of the literary story, *ḥikāye*,[26] which as an overarching genre (poetry and prose together) has also been studied by A.S. Levend.[27]

The *Tażarruʿnāme* by Sinān Paşa is considered a unique masterpiece of religious artistic prose.[28] With regard to the *fetḥnāme*s, it has been shown how excellently suited artistic prose was for propaganda and polemic.[29] The works of celebrated stylists of the 16th century such as Lāmiʿī with his *ʿIbretnümā* dated 1525/26, Tācīzāde Caʿfer Çelebi (d. 1515), Kemālpaşazāde (d. 1534), ʿAlī Çelebi (d. 1543/44), Celālzāde Muṣṭafā (d. 1567) and the biographers of the poets, ʿĀşıq Çelebi (d. 1571) and Ḥasan Çelebi (d. 1603), have been unevenly investigated and therefore assessed with a corresponding degree of variability. Thus the last two mentioned, whom Gibb appreciated as sources but criticized as writers,[30] are viewed by those who know them well as the best *munşīs* of

vocalization is abandoned (see İz, *Nesir* I, 1964, Timurtaş, *Osmanlıca Grameri* 1964, pp. 322 F. and Kreutel, *Chrestomathie* 1965 for a few old Ottoman specimens), the texts present an appearance quite different from the original, and vocalization has a "negative" effect which makes reading them more difficult; cf. V.L. Ménage in BSOAS XXIX (1966), p. 167.

24 Mecdut Mansuroğlu, "Das Altosmanische", in *Fundamenta* I (1959), pp. 161-82. The literary language during the period of transition to Ottoman Turkish is described by Faruk K. Timurtaş, "Şeyhî ve çağdaşlarının eserleri üzerinde gramer araştırmaları", in TDAY *Belleten* 1960 and 1961.

25 Cf. the lists of "deviations" in Levend, *Evreler*, pp. 25-33, 51-60, and İz, *Nesir* I, pp. XVII-XXI; passim in Kreutel, *Chrestomathie* 1965. H. İnalcık in TTK *Belleten* XXIX (1965), p. 673, quite rightly stresses the need for a special study on the historical development of Ottoman Turkish orthography.

26 P.N. Boratav, "L'épopée et la '*ḥikāye*'" and "Le conte et la légende", in *Phil. Turc. Fundamenta* II (1964), pp. 11-66; Idem, "The narrative genres of Turkish literature and folklore", s.v. *Ḥikāya* in EI2 III (1971), pp. 373-75.

27 A.S. Levend, "Divan Edebiyatında Hikâye", in TDAY *Belleten* 1967 (1968), pp. 71-117.

28 Cf. Hasibe Mazıoğlu, article "Sinan Paşa" in İA X (1967), pp. 666-70.

29 G.L. Lewis, "The Utility of Ottoman Fetḥnāmes", in *Historians of the Middle East*, pp. 192-96.

30 "Very laboured and highly artificial" (ʿĀşıq); "Unfortunately turgid in the extreme; meaningless verbosity and endless rodomontade..." (Ḥasan Çelebi), HOP III, pp. 8 and 199.

their time.[31] As examples for the 17th century when important works were composed in an intermediate style, in the domain of artistic prose the polished products of Veysī (d. 1628), who also wrote simply as his *Ḫvābnāme* shows, and Nergisī (d. 1635) continued to elicit disapproval from modern critics; it was somewhat surprising that Fahir İz was of the opinion that the *Nevādir-i Süheylī* by Aḥmed b. Hemdem, written 1626-28, stood only at the beginning of excessive verbal ornateness.[32] Andreas Tietze saw in the Cretan ʿAlī ʿAzīz Efendi a forerunner of modern Turkish prose literature. In his study of the *Muḫayyelāt-i ledünn ü ilāhī* (written 1796-97) that concentrates primarily on questions of subject matter and literary motifs, Tietze also deals with ʿAzīz Efendi's conception of style which, as he maintains, is still completely aligned with the standards of the congenial, witty, cultivated *çelebi*, the embodiment of the high-Ottoman ideal of lifestyle and education.[33] Descriptions of style like this are rare. Recently, by way of trial, scholars have answered the question as to what intentions authors pursued with their variety of styles by assigning an author to a particular stylistic category. The author who employs the simple style wants to communicate specific facts as clearly as possible (e.g. to write a reference work); the form of expression is only a means to an end; he wants to teach or edify the reader.[34] Another author combines communicating valuable knowledge with agreeable entertainment; a third writer makes it his priority to deploy his artistic repertoire, i.e. a *müselsel* and *müseccaʿ* prose. It is clear that the medieval concepts of style, the *humile – medium – sublime/tumidum*, and their sought after purpose in each case, is here in part derived from the old texts and in part projected onto them.[35] There is only one difficulty: the older Turkish authors cannot easily be confined to a single category of style. In the works of many writers one comes across passages in embellished as well as in simple prose.[36] For this reason, Halil İnalcık asks whether the

31 Meredith-Owens, in any case, preferred by far the style of ʿĀşıq Çelebi to the "lifeless and tasteless" style of Ḥasan Çelebi, whereas J. Stewart-Robinson has praised the latter's *Teẕkere* as the best example of artistic prose: "The Ottoman Biographies of Poets", in *JNES* XXIV (1965), p. 65, fn. 62.

32 İz, *Nesir* I, p. 360

33 A. Tietze, "ʿAzīz Efendis *Muhayyelât*", in *Oriens* I (1948), pp. 248-329.

34 Cf. Levend, *Evreler*, p. 21.

35 French models influenced the division of stylistic levels which the literary critic Recāʾīzāde Maḥmūd Ekrem (1847-1914) adopted for his period: *ʿādī* or *sāde*, *müzeyyen*, and *ʿālī*; cf. Levend, *Evreler*, p. 87. Kathleen R.F. Burrill, "A Nineteenth-Century Master of Turkish Literature: Notes on Recaizade Mehmut Ekrem (1847-1914) and His Literature Course", *Harvard Ukrainian Studies* Vol. III/IV Part I (1980), pp. 124-137.

36 G.M. Meredith-Owens in *JRAS* 1965, p. 138.

prose of Kātib Çelebi (d. 1657), of Fındıqlılı Meḥmed (d. 1723) or Qoçı Beg (d. 1650) is simple prose or intermediate prose between *inşāʾ*[37] and the everyday language.[38] The answers proposed have sometimes sounded rather forced; an author has only composed his introduction in ornamented prose, whereas the essential part of his work is in the simple style. This cannot be maintained in the case of many authors. Ḫvāca Saʿded-dīn (d. 1599) has totally "simple" passages in his history work which is taken as a model of historical artistic prose; the same can be said of the *Künh ül-aḫbār* by ʿĀlī (d. 1600) which, on the contrary, is taken to be simple but contains polished sections in artistic prose.[39] ʿĀşıq Çelebi, so writes his editor, is one moment colorful and pompous and the next moment simple, vivid and natural; he has a rich supply of idiomatic expressions and makes use of *inşāʾ* for humorous purposes.[40]

To what extent is such a mode of writing determined by literary taste? The question leads us back to Arabic literary criticism to which Turks as well as Persians were bound and which in poetry thoroughly separated the conventions of form and content of the individual genres.[41] In the case of prose, it is necessary to establish who the authorities of literary criticism were with respect to whom the Turks oriented themselves, since they already found before them a classical demarcation of the kinds of style; and in accordance with this, for "the representation of stories, anecdotes and jokes...which are set among the ordinary people" the low style was literary.[42] In any case, ʿĀşıq Çelebi is obviously pleased by the freedom conferred on him by prose:

> "It is true that prose is a deep sea upon which the reed pen's ship reaches the shore with every breeze, and a wide realm, the length and breadth of which (*ėnine uzunına*) the quill's steed speeds across easily and effortlessly to alight at the desired campsite. Her broad domain is too extensive to be measured by the ell of poetry's metres. She is a banquet where it is easy to partake of fruits of every kind, and a wine jug from which it is easy to drink with every manner of cup. It is impossible for the robe of honor

37 Cf. H.R. Roemer's article "Inšāʾ" in *EI*² III (1971), pp. 1241-44. Johanna Buri-Gütermann, "Der Satzbau der osmanischen Urkunden aus der Zeit von Meḥmed Fātiḥ bis Süleymān I. Qānūnī", Phil. Diss., Vienna 1970.

38 In *TTK Belleten* XXIX (1965), p. 674.

39 A most helpful map of the territory of ʿĀlī's themes, style and public is Jan Schmidt, Pure Water for Thirsty Muslims. A Study of Mustafa ʿĀlī of Gallipoli's Künhü l-Aḫbār, Leiden 1992, pp. 209-277.

40 G.M. Meredith-Owen (ed.), *Meşāʿir üş-şuʿarā or Tezkere of ʿĀşık Çelebi*, 1971, pp. xiv and xv.

41 G.E. von Grunebaum, *Kritik und Dichtkunst*, Wiesbaden 1955, p. 11.

42 Fück, *Arabiya*, p. 80.

of expressions (*ʿibārāt*) and metaphors (*istiʿārāt*) not to fit her physical form (*ḫilqat*), and impossible for the purse of her rendition (*edā*ʾ) not to contain the glittering gems of fantastical ideas (*taḫayyülāt*). Should the pure gold of speech of perfect content not keep its promise, nonetheless alongside it are found jewels of prolixity without their being prolix (*taṭvīl-i bilā-ṭāʾil*), and as high as effort's sums of cash may be, there are still the impoverished (*fuqarā*ʾ, "underdeveloped") among the written sections which call for an outlay of expenses."[43]

Apparently, the last sentence means that in prose what is not absolutely correct is offset by beautiful embellishment and that, conversely, despite all an author's efforts barren sections will still remain.[44] ʿĀşıq Çelebi had preceded the remarks translated above with his fundamental view supported by the Koran and the Hadith that prose, compared with poetry, is a more reliable "witness" (*şāhid*).[45] Prose and poetry are both parts of speech, *kelām*. Both fall into a higher and a lower category of style; in the case of prose, he calls this *aʿlā* "highest" and *ednā* "lowest"; regarding the latter, he has nothing further to say in this passage.

For the practical purpose of the history of literature, scholarship has for some time now adopted the aesthetic judgements of the biographers of poets regarding poetry of all kinds. It has been acknowledged that the *teẕkire*s can help us become acquainted with the criteria of Ottoman literary criticism;[46] they make it clear, for instance, that what mattered in poetry was to attain the Turkish tone (*edāʾ-i türkī*) of Rūm and as much as possible not to compose poetry in the manner of the Persians.[47] The task is rendered difficult, just as in the case of older Arabic literary criticism, by the fact that aesthetic literary conceptions which form the basis of practical judgements are only communicated incidentally and at random.[48]

---

43 *Meşāʿir*, ed. Meredith-Owens, folio 7b.

44 This appears to be in agreement with ʿĀşıq's view that one should judge verses on the basis of the successful ones among them, even if they are only a few among many...; see his judgement about a controversial prolific writer which H. Sohrweide cites in "Dichter und Gelehrte aus dem Osten im osmanischen Reich (1453-1600)", *Der Islam* 46 (1970), p. 291.

45 Regarding a preference for prose over poetry he could refer to al-Bāqillānī; cf. Renate Jacobi, "Dichtung und Lüge", in *Der Islam* 49 (1972), p. 91.

46 J. Stewart-Robinson, "Teẕkere Genre", pp. 58 and 65; Idem, "Biographies", pp. 57, 60, 72 f.; H. Sohrweide, "Dichter und Gelehrte", pp. 289 and 292.

47 H. Sohrweide, "Dichter und Gelehrte", pp. 292-95,

48 Cf. G.E. von Grunebaum, *Kritik und Dichtkunst*, pp. 89 f.

Certain relative standards regarding prose have been derived from the way biographers of poets judge one another and how in turn other men of letters judge them. Thus Laṭīfī is characterized by conciseness and lack of mannerism in the eyes of ʿĀlī who finds fault with Ḥasan Çelebi for "much ornament and little significance".[49]

Given the nature of scholarship's interests, it was inevitable that prose literature in particular would come to be strongly viewed under its aspects of cultural and social history. One was and is inclined to see the stylistic level of a work as determined by the circle of persons for whom it was intended (with regard to poetry, Gibb believed the poets only wrote for themselves or for one another, since their language was incomprehensible to the vast majority of the people; in any case, not for the public whom they ignored completely).[50] When it comes to prose, it was meant to be the public[51] who determined an author's style; the upper classes are imagined as the target group of the artificial *dīvān* style, whereas the simple folk are thought to be the recipients of simple prose.[52] Taeschner speaks of three groups in life from which writers originated and for which they wrote.[53] J.R. Walsh believes that as a genre history writing, like every other literary medium, was governed by fixed conventions which were imposed on it more by the public's temperament than by the demands of its subject matter.[54] The widespread fact that an author writes for his particular class is not useful for a description of his style. This is evident, for instance, in cases where authors continually change their stylistic category. Consequently, one extended the class of addressees and maintained that while authors like Kātib Çelebi (d. 1657), Naʿīma (d. 1716), Rāşid (1735) and ʿĀṣim (d. 1819) wrote in an intermediate to simple style, they did not write "exclusively for the ordinary folk".[55] It is clear that literature cannot be considered in isolation from its social circumstances but one should not jump to conclusions about literature solely

49 G.M. Meredith-Owens, *Meşāʿir*, p. xvii.

50 *HOP* III, p. 350; similarly Taeschner, *Hdb. Or.*, p. 298.

51 An overview of social groups in Ottoman society, based on what the *tez̲keres* tell us, is presented by J. Stewart-Robinson, "Biographies", pp. 59-69. F. İz announced an edition of Faqīrī's satirical description of the classes and types in the Ottoman Empire; cf. his article "Faḳīrī" in *EI*² (1965), p. 758.

52 Levend, *Evreler*, pp. 12 and 76; Björkman in *Fundamenta*, II, p. 439; İz, *Nesir* I, p. 360.

53 In *Hdb. Or.*, p. 289: 1) dervishdom, 2) the broad popular masses grouped around the Janissary corps, and 3) the Sultan's court with its following.

54 In *Historians of the Middle East*, p. 198.

55 Levend, *Evreler*, p. 22.

on that basis. The traditional bipartite scheme which goes back to the Arabs[56] cannot be employed in the case of many works which address themselves to high and low alike (*ḫāṣṣ u ʿāmm*), i.e. to society as a whole.

In view of the frequent shift in stylistic level, the question should also be posed as to what literary purpose has led the author to such a variable treatment of his subject matter. As an underlying basis there is the well-known fact that, as in the European Middle Ages,[57] the entirely simple, natural mode of expression devoid of "art" was considered to be *ʿārī* "naked" and was judged negatively. In the case of a specimen of prose that is ornamented with every possible artistic device, scholarship is inclined to assume that the author has only chosen his particular subject matter as "a pretext" to exhibit his artistic skill and erudition.[58] The legitimate purpose of displaying art is hereby overshadowed in advance by the idea of empty verbal bombast, in support of which, of course, the Arabic theory of literature has made its contribution from the beginning.[59]

Kemālpaşazāde puts the following challenge in the mouth of Sultan Bāyezīd II: the proposed Ottoman history that needs to be written "in order to be generally useful for high and low should, in the manner of Turkish diction, be clear in its expression and information; neither should effort be devoted to the empty clichés of politeness used in *inşāʾ* nor care be given to rhetorical showing-off, but the concern should be for clear observation and composition; and to render this service he has deemed worthy this worthless servant."[60] In this way, the philologist, poet and historian, Ibn Kemāl, could have described his own prose style which without a doubt was never meant to be "low", any more than it was meant to be "bombastic".[61] Certainly, Ibn Kemāl considers his style

56 The high style "is characteristic of the educated classes…"; the low style is used by the ordinary people and by the educated "in their dealings with the people because the latter do not understand the high style"; Johann Fück, *Arabiya*, p. 80.

57 Examples are given in Franz Quadlbauer, *Die antike Theorie der genera dicendi im lateinischen Mittelalter*, 1962, p. 155.

58 On literary prose narrative in this sense generally: Levend, "Hikāye", pp. 91-93.

59 Cf. Fück, *Arabiya*, p. 82 (Qudāma on prose) or Renate Jacobi in *Der Islam* 49 (1972), p. 89 (Qudāma on poetry).

60 *İbn-i Kemāl. Tevârih-i Âl-i Osman. I. Defter.* Ed. Ş. Turan, Ankara 1970, text, p. 37. Commentary on this passage: *İbn Kemāl. Tevârih-i Âl-i Osman. VII. Defter* (*Tenkidli transkripsiyon*). *Hazırlıyan* Dr. Şerafettin Turan, Ankara 1957, p. L.

61 Ş. Turan, while appreciating Ibn Kemāl's Turkish vocabulary, thinks that his artistic prose, saturated as it is with Arabic and Persian words, has to a certain extent got the better of him and so he has in fact acted contrary to the Sultan's command about rhetorical embellishment (Ş. Turan, *Defter VII*, p. L).

to be appropriate for Turkish diction, but in his language he makes extensive use of parallelism in phrases and rhymed prose (gerunds, rhyming forms in the aorist, perfect and the vocative) and he adds spice to his text by interpolating Turkish idioms, proverbs and (quite simple) verses. Another famous stylist of the 16th century, Muṣṭafā b. Celāl, called Qoca Nişāncı, in his *Ṭabaqāt ül-memālik* (written in 964/1556-1557), in which he draws on his experiences as an active statesman of many years standing, condemns the foolishness of certain unnamed authors who dared to portray the era of Sultan Süleymān on the basis of oral sources or even sheer hearsay. He especially criticizes the vain torrent of verbiage of a commissioned work in Persian verses, referred to as a *şāhnāme*, from the pen of Fetḥullāh ʿĀrif Çelebi.[62] Celālzāde Muṣṭafā ironically praises the style of Fetḥullāh ʿĀrif which is brilliant but has nothing authentic to express.[63] Obviously, Celālzāde Muṣṭafā intends not only to display his own polished chancellery style but also to make use of it especially in the nuanced communication of his own judgements. This brings us to the themes treated in prefaces, among which are found the concern for immortalization, the question of the utility of history and in general the use of literature as *ʿibret*:[64] That one gives the public at large a reason for writing which is as objective as possible does not exclude the wish to parade one's skill as a writer; yet how to proceed here should not be summarily decided but should be examined in the case of each author.

The words of ʿĀşıq Çelebi cited above show that this Turkish author enjoyed the freedom of prose not least because of the scope it allowed for the imagination. It allows him the choice between two levels of style and offers him great leeway in choosing his subjects; at the same time he does not have to be afraid of saying something inappropriate concerning "stature". He changes his levels of style: one would like to find out what "the instinctive feeling" is that tells him when he should pass from the one to the other.[65] Does it have to do with the quality of the subject he is dealing with? What ʿĀşıq Çelebi says about the women who write poetry is, in some passages, in the style he himself designates as "the lowest". This may be ʿĀşıq Çelebi's individual touch. But when reading so many "simple" passages in Ottoman prose works of high literary

62 On him see H. Sohrweide, "Dichter und Gelehrte", pp. 269 and 290 ff. There Persian critics find fault with ʿĀrif's manner of expression.

63 *Ṭabaqāt ül-memālik*, manuscript in the Staatsbibliothek Preußischer Kulturbesitz, Ms. or. quart 1961, folio 8b. Ḫvāca Saʿded-dīn proceeds in a similar manner with the much-praised Idrīs Bidlīsī: see J.R. Walsh in *Historians of the Middle East*, p. 199, ftn. 5.

64 Cf. Peter Freimark, *Das Vorwort als literarische Form in der arabischen Literatur*. Diss. Münster 1967.

65 G.M. Meredith-Owens, *Meşāʿir*, p. xiv.

quality, one may well wonder whether it is possible to speak of a general concept of style which is aligned with the subject matter being treated. An examination in this regard, which should include any formulated intention of the author, will focus not only on a literary intention that pervades the book as a whole but on one that is also recognizable even in the smaller units. With a view to the entire work one can naturally explain a change in the level of style by noting that too much artificiality becomes boring in the long run and that too simple a language appears trivial and off-putting: *variatio delectat*. But this is not adequate to describe the tension which Ibn Kemāl, for instance, creates between the stately tone of a sumptuous, richly flowing rhymed prose made up of Arabic, Persian and Turkish elements and a simple, at times austere Turkish tone. Clearly, it is not only a matter of a formal device but also of a conception of style to do with content.

As in the *fetḥnāme*s, the florid sections, in which the politics of an enemy prince are portrayed as the result of Satanic inspiration, certainly serve purposes of persuasion and propaganda; reasons of state shine through when the massacre of high-ranking prisoners after a battle is justified in mellifluous periods; pure panegyric is lavished upon the princes of a ruling house, be they ever so small, and especially bestowed upon the Sultan;[66] and this is entirely inspired by the *inşā*ʾ style which also determines the polemics between the warring rulers from one chapter to the next. One switches to a simple, factual Turkish tone when direct speech or, similarly, the contents of written messages is reported.[67] In the case of ʿAlī ʿAzīz Efendi, Tietze notes "an alternation" of style "between pompous rococo and – when reporting persons' speech – imitation of the simple language of the people".[68] A shift to the simple style in Ibn Kemāl may signal a change in milieu, for example when he recounts a miracle of the House of ʿOs̱mān in the plain tone of Turkish legend, where, of course, it may well be a matter of directly adopting a different literary genre (*menāqibnāme*).[69] Troop deployments and military events can be represented simply and concisely or with solemnity and long-windedness. In both cases, attention should be paid to the connection between intention, subject matter and stylistic level.

66 *İbn Kemāl, Defter* VII*, Transkr.*, pp. 8 f., 346, 361 and 548 ff.

67 For example, *İbn Kemāl, Defter* VII*, Transkr.*, pp. 324, 390 ff., 394; Ḫvāca Saʿded-dīn also proceeds like this.

68 Tietze, *Muhayyelât*, p. 251.

69 *İbn Kemāl, Defter* VII*, Transkr.*, pp. 394 ff.

In this way one will more fully do justice to the peculiar character of Turkish prose, i.e. its "adaptability",[70] which especially reveals itself in the literary tale and history writing – rather than by means of the strong emphasis on vocabulary that has prevailed up until now. The preceding remarks are intended simply to serve as a stimulus for discussion about Turkish prose once again from the stylistic side; a broader basis of texts now permits us to examine connections between subject matter and the concept of style and, by means of comparative studies, to work out how in his time an individual author set his own tone. In so doing, we will come closer to establishing a framework of periods for prose writing. Muslim Turkish writers had their classicistic norms on the basis of which they strove, as Ottoman statements attest, to attain the greatness of the Arabs and the Persians and where possible to surpass them.[71] How during this process of assimilation means of expression were found for individual characteristics and specific conditions of life is recognizable in literature, and prose in particular offers interesting materials which illustrate this.

70 Tietze, *Muhayyelât*, p. 313.
71 Sohrweide, "Dichter und Gelehrte", pp. 263 and 295-98.

CHAPTER 5

A *Ġazel* by Ḥasan oġlï (Unknown Poems in the *Dīvān* of Sultan Ġavrī)*

In a general sense the subject of this lecture is a collection of poems and in particular one Turkish poem which to my knowledge is unknown. Sultan Ġavrī's collection of poems is a good example of the close ties within the Turkish literatures, which Maḥmūd al-Kāşgarī had already documented so impressively and which modern scholarship rightly emphasizes.[1]

A colorful but also rather elusive personality of the older history of Turkish literature is Şayḫ ʿIzzed-dīn Pūr-i Ḥasan Asfarāʾinī, who is thought to have come from Asfarāyin in Khorasan and according to one view lived at the end of the 13th/beginning of the 14th century or according to another around 1400. While it has been said that the Shaykh used the Turkish form of his name Ḥasan oġlï for his Turkish poems, whereas he signed his Persian poems Pūr-i Ḥasan, what is clear is that from his apparently abundant literary production, up until now, no more than one Persian *ġazel* and one Turkish poem have come to light. Nonetheless, the Shaykh, on the testimony of the old *taẕkire*s, occupies a place of honor as the first Āzerī poet.[2]

The Turkish poem bearing the *taḫalluṣ* Ḥasan oġlï, which according to general consensus belongs to Şayḫ ʿIzzed-dīn Asfarāʾinī, has been preserved in an appendix to Sayf-i Sarāyī's Turkish translation of Saʿdī's *Gulistān*, which was completed in Egypt in 1391 and has survived in a single manuscript written in that country.[3] This seven-line poem owes its preservation to the fact that Sayf-i Sarāyī composed a parallel poem, a *naẓīre*, which was based on it. Thus

* Translated by John O'Kane.

1 Cf. A. Bodrogligeti, "A Collection of Turkish poems from the 14th Century", in *AOH* XVI (1963), pp. 245-311; A. Bombaci in *Phil. Turc. Fundamenta* II (1964), p. XX; Idem, *Storia della Lettera turca* (Milan, 1969), p. 126.

2 M.F. Köprülü, article Âzerî in *İA* II (1944), p. 129: "ilk âzerî klasik şairi"; T. Gandjeï in *Oriens* 8 (1955), p. 297; A. Bodrogligeti, *A Fourteenth Century Turkic Translation of Saʿdī's Gulistān* (?) (1969), p. 17; cf. the information collected by Hofman, *Survey* I vol. 3 (1969), pp. 191 f.; and especially A. Caferoğlu in *Fundamenta*, II, p. 636.

3 The view that this is Sayf's own autograph copy has been abandoned. Cf. A.F. Karamanlıoğlu, "Seyf-i Sarâyî'nin Gülistān Tercümesi'nin Dil Husûsiyetleri", in *TM* XV (1968), p. 82. Bodrogligeti and Karamanlıoğlu point out that from folio 186a on the ductus changes. Is it the script of Maḥmūd al-Gulistānī who after 1393 placed a small poem at the beginning of the manuscript (*li-kātibihī al-ʿānī Maḥmūd al-Kulistānī*) which is reproduced in F.N. Uzluk, *Gülistan Tercümesi* (1954), facsimile, p. 1/text, p. XI?

 | DOI 10.1163/9789004355767_006

Ḥasan oğlï's poem, which is structured around the rhetorical figure *su'āl/ cevāb*,[4] has been saved thanks to the mediation of an Egyptian Turkish manuscript.

I have recalled this well-known fact because I wish to present another Turkish poem, a *ġazel* bearing the *taḫalluṣ* Ḥasan oğlï, which has likewise been preserved by an Egyptian Turkish mediator.

The mediator in this case is the Mamluk sultan, Qanïṣav al-Ġavrī (1501-1516), who wrote poetry in the Turkish language himself and for the sake of his *naẓīre* compositions recorded poems by older poets and contemporaries from his immediate surroundings as well as from far-off regions. It was in this way that a *ġazel* of a certain Ḥasan oğlï also came to be included in Ġavrī's poetry manuscript. The poem is composed entirely in the Old Anatolian Turkish literary language as it is known for the 14th and 15th centuries in Anatolia, and as it had kept itself alive in the Mamluk state – indeed, longer than it did in the Ottoman Empire. Here is the poem in question, composed in the Anatolian Turkish literary idiom:

1 nicesin gel ėy yüzi ağum benüm
sen eritdüñ odlara yağum benüm
2 and içerem senden artuq sevmeyem
senüñile ḫoş geçer çağum benüm
3 ḥüsn içinde saña mānend olmaya
aṣlï yüce güñli alçağum benüm
4 al elümi ėreyim maqsüduma
qoma yürekde yana dāğum benüm
5 sen raqībe sirrüñi fāş eyledüñ
anuñile oldï şiltağum benüm
6 qïşladum qapuñda itlerüñile
oldï küyuñ oşda yaylağum benüm
7 ben ölicek yolïna gömüñ beni
baqa ḍursun yāra tobrağum benüm
8 tobrağumdan bite ḥasretle ağaç
qïla zārī cümle yaprağum benüm
9 bu Ḥasan oğlï senüñ bendeñdurur
anï redd étme yüzi ağum benüm
(fāʿilātün fāʿilātün fāʿilün, ramal)

4 Facsimile, Uzluk, pp. 366. Bodrogligeti discusses the poem: "A Collection of Turkish Poems from the 14th Century", in *AOH* XVI (1963), pp. 245-311; ed. Bodrogligeti, *Turkic Translation*, p. 185; and translation by Bombaci, *Storia* (1969), pp. 209 f.

The question now arises whether this can be a poem by Ḥasan oġlï Asfarāʾīnī. From the viewpoint of subject matter, a declaration of love and love's lament with skillfully woven-in literary motifs (e.g. being buried on the beloved's pathway), the two poems have features in common, though the latter poem certainly has less mystical undertones and more of a panegyric character (*aṣlï yüce*, line 3).

On the other hand, both these poems that bear the author's name Ḥasan oġlï differ noticeably from one another in terms of language. The poem of Ḥasan oġlï preserved in the *Gulistān* manuscript is composed in the 13-century literary language often designated as Khwarezmian with its East-Turkish writing tradition already showing signs of Oġuz influence.[5] The Ḥasan oġlï poem transmitted by Ġavrī follows, as does the whole manuscript in which it is found, the Old Anatolian Turkish tradition of writing (*kāf* for *ñ*); typical Āzerī features such as *nūn kāf* for *ñ*, *ḫ* instead of *q*, and *men*,[6] are absent but of course may have been removed by subsequent copyists.[7]

In line 5 it seems to me that the word *şiltaq* "quarrel, fight" somewhat falls outside the domain of the Old Anatolian Turkish literary language.[8] It deserves to be emphasized that the poem of Ḥasan oġlï recorded by Ġavrī is written in very pure Turkish in contrast to the poem in the *Gulistān bi't-türkī* which is saturated with loan-words and foreign vocabulary.

One should in fact examine whether the *ġazel* transmitted by Ġavrī can be acknowledged as the second tangible Turkish poem of the early Āzerī poet Ḥasan oġlï. In any case, whether the examination – the result of which could of course be that there was more than one poet named Ḥasan oġlï – turns out

5 Bodrogligeti, *Turkic Translation*, pp. 20, 22 and 27. Karamanlıoğlu, "Dil Husûsiyetleri", p. 75, speaks of "Kıpçak Türkçesi" with regard to the *Gülistān* translation.

6 Concerning Azarbaijani in general: A. Caferoğlu and G. Doerfer in *Fundamenta* I (1959), pp. 280-307.

7 On a certain interchangeability regarding the terms "Old Ottoman" and "Old Azerbaijani" literature cf. A. Caferoğlu and G. Doerfer in *Fundamenta* I, p. 282.

8 It is perhaps no coincidence that *şiltaq* happens to appear in the *dīvān*s of both Turkmen poets (or Āzerī poets, if one prefers), Qāḍī Burhāned-dīn and Nesīmī. The only early occurrence of the word cited in *Tarama, Sözlüğü* II (1953), p. 865, is taken from the *dīvān* of Qāḍī Burhāned-dīn: "*yarin yine bizim ile şıltağı ne imiş*"; on the Nesīmī verse see the next footnote. The word *şiltaq* is explained as a loan-word from West Middle-Mongolian (G. Doerfer, *Mongolische Elemente im Neupersischen* [1963], pp. 358 ff., no. 236; with no reference to Doerfer, M. Räsänen, *Versuch eines etymologischen Wörterbuches der Türksprachen* (1969), s.v. *sylta, šïlta, šiltä*), while Doerfer, op. cit., p. 359, shows that it could be a matter of "dissimulation" from Turkish tïltag "cause". Osman Nedim Tuna now gives a different explanation: "Osmanlıcada Moğolca ödünç kelimeler", in *Türkiyat Mecmuası* XVII (1972), pp. 241 f., no. 46.

positive or negative for Şayḫ ʿIzzed-dīn Asfarāʾinī, once again we are dealing with the fact that Turkish poetry was appreciated and preserved in circles receptive to it in Egypt and Syria at the end of the 14th century, and even toward the outgoing 15th and early 16th centuries; earlier findings have shown that works created in distant places could be found in these circles.

As is known, connective lines have been traced from Ḥasan oġlï to Nesīmī[9] with whom we already move into closer proximity to the Mamluks. Qanïṣav al-Ġavrī also included a poem by Nesīmī (d. 1404 in Aleppo) in his collection for the purpose of composing a parallel poem based on it, which I have not been able to find, however, in the printed Nesīmī *Dīvān* at my disposal. The poem begins (*ramal*):

ėy Mesīḥā-dem kim ola vėrmeye cān sizlere
ben vėrürem cān ü göñül müft ü meccān sizlere
(8 bayts)

In the case of Ḥasan oġlï's *ġazel*, a poem that is still problematic as far as its authorship is concerned, has been singled out of the *naẓīre* models in Sultan Ġavrī's collection. But one should also study the Turkish poems unknown until now – their authorship is perfectly clear – that were composed by Yaşbek min Mahdī, the famous minister of Sultan Qaytbay. There is an elegy, a *mersiye*, on behalf of Yaşbek (d. 1480 in Ruhā/Urfa) which unfortunately is incomplete at the end and in which the deceased himself speaks:

benem ol Yaşbek-i server ki Mehdī-yi zamānidüm
ten olmışdi qamu leşker olara cümle cānidüm.

Ġavrī's own poems, whose authorship (due to the *taḫalluṣ* Ġavrī) is likewise clear, also deserve attention. A brief word on this subject: Ġavrī when he was sultan, had the poems collected together in calligraphical form at the beginning of a small volume. Their content is both religious and worldly. The designation *Dīvān of Sultan Ġavrī* on the ornamented title-pages should perhaps not be taken all too literally since as a collection it is rather small to qualify as a *dīvān* – on the other hand, the manuscript contains lacunae of a still undetermined extent, especially at the end. Eighty of the poems are by Ġavrī himself

9 Who according to Navāʾī wrote poetry in Türkmenī and Rūmī. The following is a verse by him in which *şiltaq* appears: "göñlümi eliyle aldï şimdi cān ister gözüñ / bunca şiltaqï nedendür ʿāsïq-i şeydā ilen". The verse is cited by Hüseyin Kâzım Kadri, *Türk Lûgati* III (1943), p. 271, who explains *şiltaq* as an Āzerī word.

and along with these are twenty-nine poems by other poets such as the previously mentioned Ḥasan oġlï, Nesīmī, Yaşbek and others as well. Some of Ġavrī's poems certainly date from the time when he was still a Mamluk emir; in others he lets it be known that he is the Sultan.

The rediscovery of the Turkish *Dīvān* of Sultan Ġavrī in the contemporary Berlin manuscript MS. or. oct. 3744 of the Staatsbibliothek Preussi scher Kulturbesitz may be hailed as a welcome gain for the history of Turkish literature.[10]

The existence of a Turkish *Dīvān* of Sultan Ġavrī was known from information handed down by the Gülşenīye, the Cairene branch of the Ḫalvetīye. The rediscoverer of Kāşgarī, ʿAlī Emīrī Efendi (1857-1924), succeeded after much effort in acquiring a manuscript of the year 1909 with Arabic poems by Ġavrī among which was a single Turkish poem; this is the manuscript Millet Ali Emiri Arabî 4639.[11]

János Eckmann has been able to identify other single Turkish poems by Ġavrī in Istanbul manuscripts, poems on which Ananiasz Zajączkowski has also worked.[12]

---

10 The manuscript is described by Manfred Götz, *Türkische Handschriften*, Teil 2 (1968), pp. 207 f., no. 304, where the Sultan is not yet recognized as the author and compiler, see article 3 in this volume. – The miniature on the manuscript's frontispiece is described in *Illuminierte islamische Handschriften*, by Ivan Stchoukine, Barbara Flemming, Paul Luft, and Hanna Sohrweide (1971), p. 281, no. 111.

11 The one Turkish *ġazel* it contains in modernized spelling on pp. 8-9 begins: *Müstedām olġïl hemīşe ėy güzel ḫānim benim* (sic). The poem is not found in the Berlin MS.

12 Cf. J. Eckmann in *Fundamenta* II (1964), pp. 299 f., with bibliographical information. Other manuscripts with single Turkish poems by Ġavrī: Ayasofya 2047 (*muvaşşaḥāt*), Ayasofya 3313 (Arabic: *ʿUqūd al-jawharīya*), and Bağdat Köşkü 138 (*al-Qaṣāʾid al-rabbānīya*...). Cf. A. Zajączkowski, "Poezje stroficzne muvaššaḥ mameluckiego sultana Qānṣūh (Qansav) Ġavrī", in *RO* XXVII (1964), pp. 82-86.

CHAPTER 6

The Pre-Wahhābī *Fitna* in Ottoman Cairo: 1711*

In his *History of Egypt*, the scholar and chronicler ʿAbd ar-Raḥmān al-Ǧabartī (born 1167/the year beginning 29 October 1753; died 1825 or early 1826) describes the short-lived uprising that a preacher (*vāʿiẓ*) had unleashed in Cairo when he argued against the cult of graves and belief in posthumous miracles of saints.[1] Al-Ǧabartī was associated with al-Azhar which opposed the preacher. Although himself a critic of excessive veneration of saints in his own era,[2] al-Ǧabartī seems to distance himself from this *fitna* by noting that the preacher was from Rūm and the majority of his followers were Turks. He then introduces a poem in which Ḥasan al-Ḥiǧāzī, a contemporary of the *fitna* (d. 1718/19), castigates the erroneous doctrine of the preacher[3] and accuses him of incitement to civil unrest.[4]

In 1831 Hammer, following the Turkish source which is the subject to be treated in this essay, offered a brief retelling of the same event.[5] Ignaz Goldziher appreciated the teachings of the "religiously zealous young man" from the Muʾayyad Mosque as being a characteristic expression of the monotheistic reaction in Islam before the outbreak of the Wahhābī movement.[6]

Maḥmūd aş-Şarqāwī uses al-Ǧabartī's account, which he presents in detail, in order to criticize the narrowness of intellectual life in Egypt in the eighteenth century. He sees the preacher in question as a bold spirit in the midst of a conservative environment moulded by al-Azhar and hostile to reform.[7]

* Translated by John O'Kane.

1 *ʿAjāʾib al-āthtār fī t-tarājim wa l-akhbār* II, pp. 48-50.

2 Examples of this are given in Gamal el-Din el-Shayyal, "Some Aspects of Intellectual and Social Life in Eighteenth-century Egypt", in P.M. Holt (ed.), *Political and Social Change in Modern Egypt*, London 1968, pp. 129-31.

3 3 Elsewhere this author as well makes fun of inappropriate veneration of saints; cf. el-Shayyal, p. 131, and Gabriel Baer, "Fellah and Townsman in Ottoman Egypt", in *Asian and African Studies* 8 (1972), pp. 241 and 244.

4 "He [i.e. the preacher] whipped up the troops against us (!)"; in al-Ǧabartī II, p. 49; I2, p. 134.

5 Joseph von Hammer, *Geschichte des Osmanischen Reiches*, vol. VII, Pesth 1831 (reprint, Graz 1963), pp. 168 f.

6 Ignaz Goldziher, *Muhammedanische Studien* II, Halle 1890, pp. 370 f. He bases himself on Hammer's brief account, refers to the detailed description in al-Ǧabartī and finally cites ʿAlī Paşa Mubārak, *al-Ḫiṭaṭ al-ǧadīda* V, p. 130.

7 Maḥmūd aş-Şarqāwī, *Miṣr fīʾl-qarn aṯ-ṯāmin ʿaşr*, Cairo 19572, I, pp. 97 ff. Aş-Şarqāwī also knows Hammer's version in translation.

 | DOI 10.1163/9789004355767_007

H.A.R. Gibb and Harold Bowen, who devote a footnote to the event, classify it like Goldziher as a pre-Wahhābī current; they think that public opinion in Egypt was clearly against the preacher and on the side of the shaykhs who defended the cult of graves and veneration of saints.[8] The editors of the new annotated text edition of al-Ǧabartī provide the passage that concerns us with a footnote in which the teaching of the reform-minded preacher is justified.[9] Bayard Dodge in his book on al-Azhar follows aş-Şarqāwī; he as well uses the event to illustrate the conservative state of thinking in al-Azhar at that time.[10]

In 1968 Gamal el-Din el-Shayyal once again dealt with the event in detail following al-Ǧabartī. He described the teaching of the unknown preacher from Rūm as a new and bold attempt to eliminate innovations (*bida'*) which had made their way into Islam; in so doing, the preacher was a precursor of the famous revivalist Muḥammad b. 'Abd al-Wahhāb; like the latter he too had tried to confront the evil not only with words but "by force". El-Shayyal saw in this case the first reform movement that Egypt experienced in the eighteenth century. He explained the brief duration and lack of success of the revolt by noting that Egyptian society was not yet ready to accept such a movement.[11]

In view of the diverse interpretations that the reform sermon of the preacher has been subjected to since al-Ǧabartī, it seems appropriate to enlarge the basis of sources for this historical event. For this purpose the Turkish source rediscovered by Hammer is particularly suited since it describes the event in significantly greater detail than al-Ǧabartī.

It is clear that al-Ǧabartī who was born in 1753/54 cannot be a primary source for an event of the year 1711. He himself indicates in his preface some of the sources he used.[12] Regarding Arabic[13] and Turkish[14] history writing in

8 H.A.R. Gibb and Harold Bowen, *Islamic Society and the West*, vol. I, *Islamic Society in the Eighteenth Century*, Part II, Oxford 1957, p. 160, fn. 1.

9 Ḥasan Muḥammad Ǧawhar, 'Abd al-Fattāḥ as-Saranǧāwī, as-Sayyid Ibrāhīm Sālim (eds.), *'Aǧā'ib al-āṯār fī t-tarāǧim wa l-aḫbār*, vol I (1958), p. 132. The editors base themselves on the Koranic commentary of the Baghdad scholar al-Ālūsī (d. 1854), *Rūḥ al-ma'ānī*, according to which only the pure – and they are the angels – have access to the Well-guarded Tablet (*al-lawḥ al-maḥfūẓ*; see below)).

10 Bayard Dodge, *Al-Azhar*, 1961, p. 82.

11 El-Shayyal (see here fn. 2), pp. 126-29.

12 Cf. Aḥmad Ṭarabayn, *at-Ta'rīḫ wa'l-mu'arriḫūn al-'Arab fi'l-'aṣr al-ḥadīṯ*, Damascus 1970, pp. 66-74.

13 P.M. Holt, "Ottoman Egypt (1517-1798): An account of Arabic historical sources", in P.M. Holt (ed.), *Political and Social change...* (see here fn. 2), pp. 3-12.

14 Stanford J. Shaw, "Turkish source-materials for Egyptian history", in P.M. Holt (ed.), *Political and Social Change...* (see here fn. 2), pp. 28-48.

Ottoman Egypt we are now much better informed thanks to P.M. Holt and Stanford Shaw.

The source that Hammer drew on is the Turkish *Tȧrīḫ Mıṣr* by Muḥammad b. Yūsuf al-Ḥallāq (here abbreviated as Ibn ül-Ḥallāq).[15] Before considering this chronicle in connection with the religious-historical aspect of the *fitna*, let us make a few remarks about the background to the occurrence: the theater of the event is Cairo in the year 1711, in particular the Mosque of Sultan Mu'ayyad at the city wall not far from the Zuwayla Gate which supports both minarets of the mosque and is called *demür qapu* "Iron Gate" by the Turks. Here spectacular executions were carried out, as for instance that of the last Mamluk Sultan, Ṭumanbay, in 1517. The gate was considered the place of residence of the Mutawallī or Quṭb, an invisible saint, and for this reason was a hub of attraction for the faithful. It enjoyed high favor chiefly among Ṣūfīs. Here the founder of the Gülşenīye order, Ibrāhīm Gülşenī, resided from morning to evening with his gaze fixed on the *qıbla*. This shaykh had been allotted his *hüğre* in the Mu'ayyad Mosque[16] by Sultan Qanıṣav al-Ġawrī himself (1501-1516). From the time of its completion (1418), professors of religious dogma, law and other disciplines were employed in the mosque;[17] from the beginning a shaykh of the Ṣūfīs was also on hand. In the 17th century the mosque had fallen into disrepair; the Ottoman governor Aḥmed Paşa (1689-1691) had restored it.[18] The founder of the mosque, Sultan al-Malik al-Mu'ayyad aş-Şayḫ al-Maḥmūdī lies buried in his mosque under a cupola together with his son who died (1420) before him. His tomb is considered to be a place where prayers are answered,[19] indeed wishes are fulfilled for a person who every Sabbath (*sebt*) from the first prayer on performs prayers there in perfect sincerity (*iḫlāṣ*).[20]

Sultan Selīm I had let Ibrāhīm Gülşenī remain in the Mu'ayyadīya, and the garrison troops in Egypt, and the Janissaries and the Sipāhīs, were loyally

15 See my contribution to the First International Turcological Congress in Istanbul 1973. For bibliographical information, see article 24 in this volume.

16 *Ādāb-i ziyāret-i qubūr*, Ms. or. oct. 1608 of the Staatsbibliothek Preußischer Kulturbesitz, fol. 89a. Cf. Hanna Sohrweide, *Türkische Handschriften* 3, Wiesbaden 1974, no. 193.

17 Cf. William Popper, *Egypt and Syria under the Circassian Sultans. Systematic Notes II*, Berkeley and Los Angeles 1957, pp. 118-23. The *Ādāb-i ziyāret* adds from which regions the foundation's properties came: fol. 71a.

18 Al-Ğabartī II, p. 24.

19 *müsteğāb ed-du'ā*: *Ādāb-i ziyāret*, fols. 71a-72a.

20 Ibid. fol. 72a. The grave of Sitt Nafīsa and the *mesğid-i Mūsā* were also *müsteğāb ed-du'ā* (on the Synagogue of Moses in Cairo cf. Heribert Busse in *Der Islam* 42 (1966), pp. 119 and 142.

attached to him.[21] Under Sultan Süleymān a *zāviye* of his own was built for him.[22] Alongside these dervish orders worked the Mevlevīye for whom a first *zāviye* was built in the 16th century.[23] As is known, the Bektāşīs also had their establishments in Cairo, e.g. on the Muqaṭṭam mountain.[24]

Along with these *tekyes*, which were a thorn in the eye of the reforming preacher, also mentioned in connection with the *fitna* were: the al-Azhar Mosque, the tomb of Imam Şāfiʿī (d. 820), a splendid mausoleum from 1211 that was a well-known pilgrimage site with a wooden catafalque; the law court of Cairo: the house of the Ottoman Chief Judge; the Diwan of the Ottoman governor in the Citadel of Cairo which also served as a Court of Appeals.[25]

When in what follows the events of the *fitna* are reported according to the account of Muḥammad b. Yūsuf al-Ḥallāq,[26] a Turkish chronicle that has not yet been used with regard to the *fitna* will be mentioned in passing, that of ʿAbdülkerīm b. ʿAbdurraḥmān.[27] This compiler in long passages presents the same description as Ibn ül-Ḥallāq but in addition expresses his own divergent point of view.

In Ramażān 1123/the year beginning 13 October 1711, people gathered in the Muʾayyad Mosque for prayers. With a group of friends a theology student, *sūḫte*,[28] sat down in the mosque's rooms for prayer and with his companions read out a treatise by Birgili Meḥmed Efendi.[29]Around this group there soon formed an ever growing circle of listeners. After a while, the *sūḫte* ascended to the preacher's seat and gave a sermon which was so moving that more and more persons were attracted and the large mosque, its balustrades and even in part its courtyard filled up with people.

The preacher's teaching consisted of six points:

21 *Ādāb-i ziyāret*, fols. 93b-94a.

22 Ibid. fol. 101b.

23 Ibid. fol. 126b; see Sohrweide, op. cit., no. 193.

24 Cf. M. Fuad Köprülü, "Mısır'da Bektaşilik", in *TM* VI (1939), pp. 13-40.

25 Cf. Gibb and Bowen I, Part II (see here fn. 8), pp. 91 and 129.

26 Following the Ms. of the Austrian National Library in Vienna, H.O. 37 (Flügel II, p. 161, no. 936), fols. 243b-248a, compared with Ms. Istanbul, Üniversite T. Y. 628, fols. 296a-301a, and Stockholm, Royal Library, no. 75 (Riedel, p. 49).

27 See article 24 in this volume.

28 Ibn ül-Ḥallāq does not give his place of origin.

29 Muhammad Birgewī (Birgiwi, Birgeli, died 1573), the influential Hanafi scholar and puritan, is known for his manual of ethics and advice, *aṭ-Ṭarīqa al-Muḥammadīya*, and for a popular work on *ʿilm-i hal* composed in 970/1562-3.

1. "The miracles of saints end with their death; the miracles reported after their death are invalid and unfounded. Whatever is said in the *Ṭabaqāt* by Shaykh ʿAbd al-Wahhāb aş-Şaʿrāwī[30] about the miracles of saints is invalid and unfounded."[31]
2. (No one has access to the Well-guarded Tablet, *al-lawḥ al-maḥfūẓ*).

   "Not a single person from among the prophets and saints had access to the Well-guarded Tablet, not even our Prophet. Since our Prophet had no access to it, how could one of the saints have access to it?"[32]

3. (The cult of graves is unbelief, *kufr*).

   "It is necessary to destroy all the decoration on tombs of saints and an act like [lighting] the candles and candelabra and lamps that burn there is not allowed but forbidden by law. Whoever kisses coffins and thresholds is an infidel. Nor is it permitted to erect cupolas and edifices over graves; in fact it is necessary to tear these down."[33]

4. (Dervish cloisters should be transformed into *medreses*).

   "And the *tekye*s built for a band of dervishes, Gülşenī and Mevlevī and Bektāşī and whatever they may be called, should be abolished and the dervishes who stay there should be removed and in their place should be students of religious science. The *tekye*s should be transformed into *medreses*."[34]

5. (Visiting the grave of Imam Şāfiʿī and others while performing public prayers is legally forbidden).

   "To visit the grave of Imam Şāfiʿī and others while publicly performing *ḏikr* and ritual prayer in groups during the nights leading up to Saturday is legally forbidden."[35]

30 ʿAbd al-Wahhāb aş-Şaʿrānī (Şaʿrāwī; d. 1565), the well-known Egyptian mystic, who wrote *at-Ṭabaqāt al-kubrā* (= *Lawāqiḥ al-anwār*); cf. GAL II, p. 338.

31 This whole passage is lacking in al-Ğabartī.

32 In al-Ğabartī's description the preacher only attacks aş-Şaʿrānī over this point.

33 Al-Ğabartī here mentions the custom of the Egyptians, *ahl Miṣr*, to pray at graves.

34 This point is combined by al-Ğabartī with point 3; "it is not allowed to erect cupolas over the graves of saints or to build dervish cloisters (*at-takāyā*), and these are to be torn down."

35 Missing in al-Ğabartī.

6. (Noisy *d̲ikr* at the Zuwayla Gate is legally forbidden).

> "Further, during the nights of Ramażān it is legally forbidden for a crowd of ignorant fools made up of groups from around the Iron Gate to cry out and jump about until midnight with the slogan 'We are performing *d̲ikr*'.[36]

Hindering the persons mentioned is incumbent as a religious duty on the Judge and on others because it constitutes 'preventing what is reprehensible'. If they neglect to do this, they become sinners."

So much for what Ibn ül-Ḫallāq tells us up to this point; ʿAbdülkerīm writes disapprovingly that the preacher incited the people to abolish the *tekye*s and to expel the dervishes living in them: *tekyeleriñ ibṭālı... ve içinde sākın ışıqları çıqarmasına ḫalqı taḥrīż eder idi* "and he uttered many similar threats and sayings of the Muʿtazilites"... *ve buña beñzer niçe terhībāt ve Muʿtezileniñ aqvālı īrād eder idi*.[37]

The sequel according to Ibn ül-Ḫallāq:

> After that the preacher's followers drove off the groups around the Zuwayla Gate with wooden clubs.[38] The theses of the preacher were reported to the religious scholars of al-Azhar[39] who summarized their own doctrinal view in a *fetva* and had it signed by two shaykhs, Aḥmad an-Nafrāwī[40] and Aḥmad al-Ḫalīfī.[41]According to the *fetva*, the teaching of the shaykhs at al-Azhar was as follows:

---

36 Ms. Vienna fol. 244a: *ve Ramażān gėcelerinde Demürqapuda olan ğemʿīyetler ẕikr ėdevüz dėyü niṣf-i leyle degin bir alay ğāhiller bağırup sıçradıqları ḥarāmdır*. Al-Ğabartī only says: "He also mentioned that the dervishes (*al-fuqarāʾ*) stayed at the Zuwayla Gate during the nights of Ramażān."

37 Ms. İstanbul, Süleymaniye, Hekimoğlu Ali Paşa no. 705, fol. 148a.

38 38 Al-Ğabartī adds: "They pulled down the cloth and the balls that had been hung up and they cried: 'Where are the saints?'" Cf. el-Shayyal, p. 127.

39 39 The informants in Ibn ül-Ḫallāq are simply "some people" (*bir qaç ādem*), whereas ʿAbdülkerīm calls them approvingly "some people of the Sunna" (Süleymaniye, Hekimoğlu Ali Paşa, fol. 148a.

40 40 The shaykh and mufti, Aḥmad an-Nafrāwī, was *raʾīs* of the Mālikite *mad̲hab*; cf. al-Ğabartī II2, p. 41. Three years before this *fitna* he had stood as a candidate for the office of rector at the al-Azhar, supported by troops armed with muskets; in the tumult ten men were left dead on the spot; he himself was put under house arrest. Cf. Dodge, *Al-Azhar*, p. 83, following al-Ğabartī. The shaykh died from the plague at the age of eighty-two in 1125/the year beginning 28 January 1713; al-Ğabartī I1, pp. 183 f.

41 41 The shaykh and mufti, Aḥmad al-Ḫalīfī, died at the age of sixty-six on the 15th of Ṣafer 1127/19th of February 1715; al-Ğabartī I1, p. 184; II, pp. 41, 122 and 252.

> (Regarding point 1) "The miracles of the saints are reality. They do not stop with death since after the saints' departure the occurrence of miracles is possible. Thus whoever says the miracles of the saints come to an end is a Mu'tazilite."[42]
>
> (Regarding point 2) "It is not allowed to say that the prophets[43] had no access to the Well-guarded Tablet. Especially when it comes to our Prophet, such words are an impropriety; to utter these words is not allowed, and whoever says this publicly deserves to be chastised (*ta'zīr*).[44]If he does not come to his senses, he will be killed."
>
> (Regarding point 4) "To change the character of the *tekye*s and to make them into *medrese*s is not permitted because this contradicts the instructions of the [original] founder, and these are just as unalterable as the wording of divine law."[45]

As for theses 3, 5 and 6 of the preacher, no comment was explicitly given.

When the *fetva* was brought to the preacher, after citing the Koranic passage 47:7 he led his numerous congregation, that was loyally devoted to him, before the Turkish Chief Judge[46] to demand that the two al-Azhar shaykhs be summoned to hold a public debate with him about their *fetva*. The judge declared he was prepared to do so the following day but refused to issue a written judgement to the demonstrators regarding the invalidity of the al-Azhar *fetva* though he had declared it invalid by word of mouth. His justification for this was that the notaries were no longer on hand. The crowd attacked the interpreter and forced the Chief Judge's deputy (*nā'ib*) to produce a letter of confirmation.

On the next day the crowd was infuriated because their preacher had disappeared. There was suspicion that the Chief Judge had intervened. The crowd went to him with a large mass of people and compelled him to come with them before the governor.[47] Here as well the wishes of the excited crowd were at first consented to; the Pasha wrote out an order by means of which the al-

---

42 42 Treated more briefly in al-Ğabartī, in particular without the final accusation.

43 43 Al-Ğabartī attributes to the al-Azhar shaykhs the following assertion that goes even further: it is not allowed to deny that the saints (!) have access to the Well-guarded Tablet.

44 44 This could mean the death penalty: cf. Ahmet Mumcu, *Osmanlı Devletinde Siyaseten Katl*, Ankara 1963, pp. 47-51.

45 45 This passage is missing in al-Ğabartī.

46 46 The Chief Judge (called "Judge of the Army" *qāżī 'asker* after the first bearer of the office) had jurisdiction over Cairo, Old Cairo and Būlāq, as well as a *nā'ib* for each of these three cities. His name is not given (Paşmakçızāde?); his interpreter was named 'Abduh.

47 Velī Paşa was the Ottoman governor of Egypt from Thursday, the 20th of Reğeb 1123/3rd of September 1711 until Monday, the 6th of Şevvāl 1123/15th of October 1714.

Azhar shaykhs should be forced to appear. The preacher also turned up again and continued with his teaching; on the following day the debate was meant to take place.

In the meantime, however, the governor wrote to the two Mamluk chiefs of the city[48] and accused them of having instigated the whole affair simply to stir up a new tumult (a great insurrection had recently been suppressed) and once again to overthrow an Ottoman governor. Before the Sultan's honor as well as his own were insulted, he would rather set out for Istanbul with the judge while there was still time.

The two city chiefs – this time really not involved in the matter as it seems – immediately convoked the commanders of the military corps;[49] the Aġa of the Janissaries[50] had the Mu'ayyad Mosque searched; the preacher kept himself hidden, while a part of his supporters escaped and the others were given a beating.

After a couple of days, people heard that in Būlāq the preacher had secretly been placed on a ship headed for Syria via Damietta and he had gone to Jerusalem.

In comparison with al-Ǧabartī, the Turkish source surveyed here offers more statements and terms to do with religious dogma and thus more insight into the bitterly conducted polemic. The preacher employs *takfīr* and denunciation, he speaks of the *zandaqa* of the Azharites; the *'ulamā'*, for their part, denounce him – as a Mu'tazilite[51] – and, as far as his thesis concerning the absolute inaccessibility of the *lawḥ maḥfūẓ*, they focus on a crime punishable by death: blasphemy against the Prophet. The demands of the preacher about ritual practices, namely religious reform and the abolishment of the cult of graves, they pass over in silence. This was to do with the forbearance of orthodoxy which had already accepted in silence many a *bid'a* – and the cult of graves was just that. But it was also a result of the amalgamation of the class of religious scholars with Sufism.

48 Qayṭās Beg (Faqārīya) and Ibrāhīm Beg held the office of Şayḫ al-balad, chief/commander of the city.

49 The seven military corps were: the Janissaries, 'Azabs, Çavuş, Müteferriqa, Göñüllü, Tüfenkçi, and the Circassians.

50 'Alī Beg who died on the 2nd of Şevvāl 1123/the 13th of November 1711.

51 A part of the Mu'tazilites, the theological school that flourished during the 8th-10th centuries, took up a position against miracles. The polemic against them concluded with the first systematic credo, the so-called *Fiqh Akbar II* (10th cent.), which in the spirit of al-Aş'arī affirms that not only the miracles of the Prophet but the miracles of the saints as well are reality (*ḥaqq*).

In the sphere of efforts at reform, the religious element is mixed up with a political-social element. The *ʿulamāʾ*, who have become a rich aristocracy with hereditary offices and unassailable wealth, have the tendency to interpret the content of religious dogma in accordance with their own interests. They belonged to Ṣūfī orders themselves (aş-Şaʿrānī was a member in as many as twenty-six of them) and they derived material benefits – from the cult of saints and visits to graves.[52]

As for the preacher's congregation which was later brought to its senses by means of beatings and banishment, its enthusiasm for the "upright religion"[53]and its attacks against the dervishes scarcely accord with the usual image of the masses who believe in miracles, and the Pasha is also of the opinion that: *kendü fiʿlleri değildir bunları taḥrīk eder vardur* "These are not their own actions; someone has put them up to it." The authorities sought out the preacher's supporters in the military corps (*oğaq*). One may gather more or less directly from Ibn ül-Ḥallāq,[54] a contemporary of the event, what ʿAbdülkerīm[55] suggests and at a later date Ğabartī so definitely expresses: that the preacher and his supporters in their majority were Turks. Gamal el-Din el-Shayyal in his article that we previously cited asks about the spiritual origin of the preacher. Was he influenced by Ibn Taymīya as was the case with Ibn ʿAbd al-Wahhāb,[56] or was his movement a spontaneous reaction against impious innovations which he beheld in Egypt?[57] While this question cannot be answered on the basis of al-Ğabartī's account, Ibn ül-Ḥallāq gives us a clear indication: the *vāʿiẓ* wrote a commentary on Birgili Meḥmed Efendi (see here fn. 29). Ibn ül-Ḥallāq gives us a clear indication: the *vāʿiẓ* wrote a commentary on Birgili Mehmed Efendi (fn. 29). He was apparently inspired by the latter, whose student Qādızāde (d. 1635) and his followers (Qādızādeliler), vocal critics of innovation and corruption, had initiated a popular rebellion in the middle of the sixteenth

52 Cf. el-Shayyal, p. 127.

53 *her kimki dīn-ı qavīme* (Ms. İst. Ün. *ḥaqqa*) *intişār ėderse bizimle maʿen gelsün*: Ibn ül-Ḥallāq, Vienna fol. 245b.

54 Ms. Wien fol. 244b: The preacher to his followers: "Muslims! The religious scholars of your province, the sons of Arabs, *evlād-i ʿArab*, have given you a *fetva*..."; cf. İst. Üni. T. Y. 628, fol. 298a (with *ādem* instead of *müsülmānlar*).

55 ʿAbdülkerīm contains the earliest mention that the preacher came from Rūm: *mezkūruñ* (Velī Paşa is meant) *zamānında bir vāʿiẓ Rūmdan geldi Müʾeyyed Ğāmiʿinde ḥalqa vaʿẓ ėder idi* (Süleymaniye, Hekimoğlu Ali Paşa no. 705, fol. 147b).

56 El-Shayyal, pp. 128 f.

57 Already in the late 17th century the Egyptian *ʿālim* aş-Şirbīnī had levelled sharp criticism against the practices of the dervishes: G. Baer, "Fellah and Townsman" (see here fn. 3), pp. 242-46.

century.[58] The preacher at the Mu'ayyadīya is apparently to be included in that Turkish puritanical movement. Thirty years after the failed reform attempt at the Mu'ayyadīya, in the Arabian peninsula the struggle of the Wahhābīs began which was primarily aimed against the cult of graves; the founder of the movement did not deny the miracles of saints. At al-Azhar the shaykh al-Bāǧūrī (d. 1860) still affirmed the miracles of saints and in particular those of deceased saints... But voices for reform were raised regarding this as well as beholding the *lawḥ maḥfūẓ* (see here fn. 9), and the thesis of the preacher of 1711 concerning the limits of miracles of the saints would be taken over even by al-Azhar two centuries later due to ongoing reform.

Thus it is that we also learn, not from al-Ǧabartī but from Ibn ül-Ḥallāq, that the preacher in the Mu'ayyadīya was a *sūḫte/softa* and that along with his desire for true religion and the purification of worship he was concerned about the concrete needs of the severely beset group of theological students that he belonged to.[59] It was not his wish, as Hammer incorrectly translates, that the dervishes should be required to pursue studies.[60] Rather his view was that, instead of these dervishes, *softa*s like himself (the chronicler speaks of *ṭālib-i ʿilm*) who needed study places and then later often had to wait for years before being assigned a position, once the *tekye*s were abolished should occupy those buildings and use them as *medrese*s. Consequently, the chronicle of Ibn ül-Ḥallāq proves to be a valuable source regarding the *fitna* in question because it not only illuminates more clearly the religious aspects of the conflict but also points to a social dimension to the uprising which even al-Ḥiǧāzī (see here fn. 3 and 4) and ʿAbdülkerīm (see the text that goes with fn. 37), who were contemporaries of the event, pass over in silence and presumably for this reason was no longer discernible for al-Ǧabartī.

---

58 İsmail Hakkı Uzunçarşılı, *Osmanlı Tarihi* III2/I, Ankara 1973, pp. 354-66; cf. Halil İnalcık, *The Ottoman Empire. The Classical Age 1300-1600*, London 1973, pp. 183-85.

59 As is known, young men from the cities and the countryside had living quarters in the *medreses*; due to lack of employment they formed unruly bands of *softas*; cf. Gibb and Bowen (see here fn. 8), p. 202.

60 "...the dervishes should study instead of dancing", as he puts it in *GOR* VII (see here fn. 5), p. 168.

CHAPTER 7

From the Evening Talks of Sultan Ġavrī*

If one imagines the widely drawn circle of princely poets and patrons of Turkish literature during the last decades of the 15th and first decades of the 16th century – stretching from the Timurid Ḥusayn Bayqara (1469-1506) in Herat and the Uzbek Şaybānī Ḫān (d. 1510) in Samarqand across Iran where the Ṣafavid Shah Ismāʿīl (d. 1524) composed Turkish poetry for his followers, up to the Ottoman Sultan Bāyezīd II (d. 1512) in Istanbul – the Mamluk Sultan Qanıṣav II Ġavrī (ruled 1501– 1516) who commissioned the translation of the *Şāhnāme* into Turkish surely ought not to be left out. He wrote poetry in Arabic and Persian and also collected and himself composed Turkish poems whose previously known small number[1] has been increased to eighty[2] thanks to the rediscovery of the collective manuscript Ms. or. oct. 3744 in the Staatsbibliothek Preußischer Kulturbesitz.[3] If this number of poems is insufficient to constitute a proper *dīvān* in the term's full sense (the manuscript is actually incomplete) – in any case, Ġavrī stands out as an exceptional figure among the crowned patrons of Turkish literature in his time.

Certainly he was one of the linguistically most proficient rulers; he once enumerated to one of his intimates the languages he had knowledge of: firstly Arabic, secondly the Persian language *lisān al-ʿajamī*, thirdly the Turkish language *lisān al-turkī*, fourthly Kurdish *al-kurdī*, fifthly Armenian *al-armanī*, sixthly Circassian *al-jarkasī*, seventhly Abkhazian and Ossetic (*Asī*).[4] On the *laylat al-qadr* (the night the Koran was sent down), in the year 910/the night from the 3rd to the 4th of March 1505, the Sultan remarked: it was indelibly fixed in his memory how during the time he grew up in Circassia (*bilād al-*

* Translated by John O'Kane.

1 János Eckmann, "Die kiptschakische Literatur", in *Philologiae Turcicae Fundamenta* II (1964), p. 300: "only five".

2 Manfred Götz, *Türkische Handschriften* 2, Wiesbaden 1958, p. 207, no. 304. The one miniature in the manuscript is described in Ivan Stchoukine et alii, *Illuminierte islamische Handschriften*, Wiesbaden 1971, p. 281, no. 111.

3 Cf. also my "Şerīf, Sultan Ġavrī and the 'Persians'", no. 3 in this volume.

4 *Nafāʾis*, p. 257. On this source see below ftn. 17. The Ms. is paginated. As for the sultan's Caucasian languages, Kristof D'hulster offered the following emendations: *awaza* (Abkhaz or Abaza), Ossetic and Ubykh (Northwest Caucasian language, closely related to Abkhaz and Abaza). In "'Sitting with Ottomans and Standing with Persians': The Šāhnāme-yi Türkī as a Highlight of Mamluk Court Culture" in U. Vermeulen en K. D'hulster (eds.). *Egypt and Syria in the Fatimid, Ayyubid and Mamluk Eras* VI, Leuven 2010, p. 251, note 55.

 | DOI 10.1163/9789004355767_008

Çarkas) on the *laylat al-qadr* "water ceased to flow and the air stopped moving".[5] As a music lover Ġavrī also occupied himself with music theory and as a poet with theoretical writings on prosody, *ʿarūż* he had works on this subject included in his Turkish collective manuscript.[6]

For his Turkish poetry he made use of the Turkish literary language which since around the end of the 14th century had established itself in the Mamluk state, namely Old Anatolian Turkish or Old Ottoman which together with literary and other cultural influences from Turkish Asia Minor had supplanted Kipchak Turkish that had also been in use earlier.

Ġavrī also found his literary models predominantly in the Ottoman Empire; the Divan poems that he included in his collection show him to be up to date though perhaps with a slight time-lag. He put together for himself a small anthology of the poems of ʿAdnī, i.e. Maḥmūd Paşa of the Fātiḥ period who was executed,[7] and selected fifty longer and shorter poems from the *dīvān* of the even more famous Aḥmed Paşa (d. 1497).[8] He also included in his own "*dīvān*" individual *ġazels* of Ottoman poets as models for his parallel poems (*nażīres*); one of these, which in Ġavrī's version contains readings that differ from the Ottoman manuscripts, comes from the Anatolian poet, Niżāmī.[9] He also adopted a *ġazel* by the Ottoman prince Ğem (1459-1495) who, after his revolt against his brother, resided in the Mamluk state from September 1481 to the spring of 1482 before setting out on his long odyssey in the Land of the Franks. It is conceivable that Ġavrī even met this Ottoman pretender to the throne whose daugher married the son of Sultan Qaytbay in 1496 and who left his mother behind in Egypt. The *ġazel* of Ğem that he chose displays a considerable number of variants – more Turkish vocabulary – when compared with the undated manuscript that forms the basis for the facsimile edition of Ğem's *dīvān*.[10]

5 *Nafāʾis*, p. 15.

6 Aḥmedī, *Risāla fī' l-ʿarūż*, fols. 144b–147a; and an additional *Risāle-i ʿarūż* is contained in fols. 147a–153a. Tourkhan Gandjeï, at the time of writing, was preparing an edition of the *Risāla fīʾl-ʿarūż* by Qāżī ʿAbdullāh (Munşī), of which a second copy is found in Dublin, Chester Beatty Turkish Ms. 473.

7 Part 6 of the manuscript Ms. or. oct. 3744.

8 Part 2 of the same manuscript. And two of his poems also occur in Ġavrī's "*dīvān*".

9 Edited by Fahir İz, *Eski Türk Edebiyatında Nazım* I, p. 183, on the basis of the Istanbul Mss.; in the latter 8 beyts, in Ġavrī 6. On the poet cf. Halûk İpekten, "Karamanlı Nizamî", in *Türkiyat Mecmuası* XIII (1958), pp. 63-78.

10 Fol. 65b: *ol fitne-i qıyāmet bir serv-qāmet anğaq* – İsmail Hikmet Ertaylan, *Sultan Cem*, İstanbul 1951.

Ġavrī's former master, Sultan Qaytbay (1468-1496), and the latter's minister, the highly educated grand *dawādār* Yaşbek min Mahdī, who was also Ġavrī's friend, must have been familiar with Ottoman court literature. But at the Mamluk courts one was steadfastly attached to a "dervish style" close to the ordinary people with the result that their Turkish literature was not characterized by the preciosity and exclusiveness that was associated with a "court style".[11]

But the later Mamluks were also open to literary developments in the Iranian region, especially if this complied with their preference for Ṣūfī poetry. Contemporaries observed a special inclination for "Persians" in Sultan Ġavrī,[12] around whom all sorts of Turks gathered who originally came from Iran where Twelver-Shiʿism had recently become the state religion. Ibrāhīm Gulşānī (d. 940/1534), the founder of the Gulşānīye, a branch of the Ḫalvetīye dervish order, lived in Cairo and was originally from Tabriz. Gulşānī, who was forced to flee Tabriz in fear of the Ṣafavids, and his dervishes were given special support by Sultan Ġavrī. He assigned Gulşānī the Mu'ayyad Mosque as a residence; it is no wonder his biographer mentions the Sultan with respect and in addition makes mention of the latter's trilingual *dīvān*.[13]

Also originally from Azerbaijan like Gulşānī is the *ġazel* of a certain Ḥasanoġlı in Ġavrī's collection, if it is true that we here have a second (in fact linguistically Ottomanized) Turkish poem by ʿIzzaddīn Asfarā'inī, Pūr-i Ḥasan, "the first Turkish Azerbaijani poet",[14] which would be the earliest known *ġazel* to be written down a hundred years later, it having likewise been transmitted by the Mamluks.

Here two intimi of Sultan Ġavrī should be mentioned who both clearly came from the Turkish-speaking region of Iran. One of them is Ḥusayn b. Muḥammad al-Ḥusaynī whom Ġavrī addressed as *yā Şarīf* and whom he appointed as Shaykh of the Ṣūfīs at his own *madrasa* on 7 Rabīʿ I 911/8 August 1505.[15] The other is Ḥusayn b. Ḥasan b. Muḥammad al-Ḥusaynī whose penname was Şerīf and who made a Turkish translation of the *Şāhnāme* for Ġavrī, working in the cupola of the above-mentioned Yaşbek min Mahdī and later in

11 Which Ulrich Haarmann, "Altun Ḫān und Čingiz Ḫān bei den ägyptischen Mamluken", in *Der Islam* 51 (1974), p. 4, refers to: "höfische Kunst" (court art) and "türkische Gelehrtendichtung" (Turkish learned poetry).

12 "Şerīf" (see above ftn. 3), p. 82.

13 M. Sobernheim/I. Kafesoğlu, article *Kansu* in *İA* VI, p. 164.

14 From my talk entitled "Hasan oğlunun bilinmiyen bir gazeli" that I gave at the first Türk Dili Bilimsel Kurultayı on 28/3/1972; in *Bilimsel Bildiriler 1972*, Ankara 1975, pp. 331-41 (no. 5 in this volume).

15 *Nafā'is*, p. 115.

the Mu'ayyadīya Mosque. In view of the latter place of work, I have proposed that he should be identified with the "Persian" Ḥusayn Şarīf who from 1503 or 1508 was Shaykh of the Mu'ayyad Mosque.[16]

The first named of these two *şerīfs* who were possibly related (uncle and nephew?), Ḥusayn b. Muḥammad, wrote in Arabic descriptions of gatherings that Sultan Ġavrī held between the 25th of February and the 28th of December 1505 mostly on Tuesday, Thursday and Saturday evenings in the Duhayşa, a vestibule of the citadel of Cairo or in another hall.[17] After the ritual prayer which was led by an imam whose name is given on each occasion, the Sultan would announce the subjects that he wished to speak about. This occurred mostly in the form of a question, to which he himself or one of those present would then address themselves in the form of an answer.[18] Religious subjects such as explanations of passages in the Koran or assessment of the Koran commentary of al-Zamaḫşarī might predominate but they often served as a starting point for more historical and literary questions. Whether during the Flood the entire earth had been covered with water? Which human being had first spoken Arabic? (Adam). Whether the Prophet had spoken Persian? (In the answer distinctions are made between the different meanings of *'ajam*). Whether the love that Zulayḫa felt for Yūsuf had been "unreal"-earthly or "real"-divine (*majāzī* or *ḥaqīqī*)? (The Sultan judged that it had at first been *majāzī* but then in view of Yūsuf's purity it became *ḥaqīqī*).[19] Many of the juridical questions and answers remind one of a test in the form of a quiz. And the participants were asked to solve outright riddles (*luġaz*).

With his "recorder of the minutes", Ḥusayn b. Muḥammad, Sultan Ġavrī was clearly pleased to discuss philological questions. One time Ḥusayn informed him: "Nowadays in times of war the kings of Fārs speak Turkish, in exercising their power of command *fahlawī* (dialect, popular speech) and in proclama-

16 "Şerīf" (no. 3 in this volume), p. 87.

17 Ḥusayn b. Muḥammad al-Ḥusaynī: *Nafā'is majālis al-sulṭānīya fī ḥaqā'iq asrār al-qur'ānīya*. Manuscript İstanbul, Topkapı Sarayı, III. Ahmet 2680. F.E. Karatay, *Topkapı Sarayī Müzesi Kütüphanesi Arapça Yazmalar Kataloğu* III, İstanbul 1966, p. 207, no. 5285. I am grateful to the Topkapı Sarayı Müzesi for having provided the microfilm which Dr. Petra Kappert was kind enough to deliver to me. Shortly before the present article went to press, I received a copy of the rare printed edition prepared by 'Abdalwahhāb 'Azẓām, Cairo 1941, through the friendliness of Prof. P.M. Holt in London.

18 Briefly characterized by M. Awad, "Sultan al-Ghawrī. His place in literature and learning (three books written under his patronage)", in *Actes du XXe Congrès International des Orientalistes, Bruxelles 1938*, Louvain 1940, pp. 321 f.

19 *Nafā'is*, pp. 77-78.

tions and gatherings *fārsī*."[20] When the Sultan while eating once asked what the word *al-falūdaǧ* was in Persian, the answer (*palūda*) led to an anecdote about al-Asmaʿī and the caliph Hārūn al-Rašīd,[21] which generally characterizes the style of these *maǧālis*.

On these occasions Ġavrī would now and then speak about the Timurids – there were in fact quite a few dignitaries from their courts who had ended up in Egypt.[22] In his poetry collection no Chagatay poem appears but Ḥusayn b. Muḥammad once recited for him, perhaps from memory, the following verse that comes from Ḥusayn Bayqara:[23]

vah nä ḥāletdür ki män her niçä körgüzsäm niyāz
ey büt-i bad-mihr sändän ẓāhir olmaz ġayr-i nāz

When in May 1505 the plague was raging in Cairo and the Sultan had lost his thirteen-year-old son, he asked Ḥusayn b. Muḥammad to compose a chronogram poem. It goes like this:

söylemeñ kim oġlı öldi ḥaẓret-i Sulṭān-i Mıṣr
bir mu'min ölmedi fī kull-i arẓ il-ʿāmira
mālik oldı küll-i dünyā bi l-ʿadālet atası
gitdi oġlı tā ki dutsun mülk-i dār il-āḫira
ʿaqıl menden ṣordı taʿrīḫ-i vefātın söyledim
yėtişür taʿrīḫuhu aʿlā l-quṣūr al-fāḫira

yėtişür "reaches" has the numerical value of 910; the son died on the 6th of Ḏū'l-qaʿda 910/the 10th of May 1505.

During the night of 16 Ǧumādā I 911/from the 14th to the 15th of October 1505, the Sultan broke up the gathering when news arrived of the fatal illness of the great polyhistor Ǧalāl al-Dīn al-Suyūṭī, and had the first surah of the Koran recited three times.[24]

When a gathering was held on the night of 5 Rabīʿ I 911/from the 5th to the 6th of August 1505 for an evening of posing riddles, simultaneously, as the

20 *Nafā'is*, pp. 258-59.

21 *Nafā'is*, pp. 253-54.

22 One of them was Ḥusayn b. Pīr Ḥāǧǧī Abū Bakr, a Shirazi Turk who had held the office of chancellor of the exchequer at the Timurid court in Herat and later in Egypt won the favor of Yaşbek: al-Saḫāwī, *aḍ-Ḍau' al-lāmiʿ* III, p. 139.

23 *Nafā'is*, p. 258. Cf. İsmail Hikmet Ertaylan, *Türk Edebiyatı Örnekleri* V, *Divan-i Sultan Hüseyin(?) Mirza Baykara "Hüseyinī"*, Istanbul 1946, p. 213.

24 *Nafā'is*, p. 187. Ibn Iyās gives a different date.

author remarks, the dam of the Nile was ceremonially breached which that year had reached the unusual height of twenty ells (*ḏirāʿ*) and ten "fingers" (*aṣābiʿ*).[25] Shortly thereafter, Ḥusayn notes the arrival of an emir (Sībay) who was formerly a rebel but was now repentant. Besides the participants who regularly appeared there were occasionally guests at the gatherings. Among these, on 23 Ǧumādā I 911/22 October 1505, were the Shaykhs Timurtaş and Şāhīn,[26] famous deputies (*ḫalīfe*s) of the important Ḫalvetīye shaykh ʿÖmer Rūşenī who was originally from Aydın and under Uzun Ḥasan was active in Tabriz (he died there in 892/1487). The shaykhs Tirmutaş and Şāhīn worked in Egypt to pave the way for the above-mentioned Ibrāhīm Gulşānī who, for his part, had been a disciple and successor of ʿÖmer Rūşenī. That Sultan Ġavrī invited the two shaykhs to one of his evening gatherings is an indication of his connection with the circle around Ibrāhīm Gulşānī.

In order to honour the Sultan, Ḥusayn b. Muḥammad placed a Turkish-Arabic *mulammaʿ* poem by Ġavrī at the end of his "minutes of the gatherings".[27]

The other *şerīf*, Ḥusayn b. Ḥasan, indicates his familiarity with the Sultan's gatherings when he expresses his admiration for them in his versified introduction to his Turkish version of the *Şāhnāme;* "in his (the Sultan's) circle all the annals, histories and tales are read once more; he constantly looks into Koran commentaries – what a Sultan who occupies himself with things like this!"[28] When one time his Sultan was sick, Şerīf joined together with the court musician Nāṣir al-Dīn Muḥammad b. Qığıq (d. 1514)[29] and wrote the following respectful-humorous strophic poem with the refrain "good health befits the Sultan":[30]

25 *Nafāʾis*, p. 111. Cf. William Popper, *The Cairo Nilometer. Studies in Ibn Taghrî Birdî's Chronicles of Egypt* I, Berkeley and Los Angeles 1951, p. 203 (from Ibn Iyās).

26 *Nafāʾis*, p. 194.

27 M. Awad had already referred to this poem in 1940. In the meantime it has also become known from two Istanbul manuscripts; J. Eckmann, "Kiptschakische Literatur" (as in fn. 1), p. 300, presents the beginning; A. Zajączkowski, "Poezje strofìczne muvaššaḥ mameluckiego sultana Qānṣūh (Qansav) Ġavrī", in *Rocznik Orientalistyczny* XXVII/2 (1964), pp. 78-79.

28 A. Zajączkowski, *Turecka wersja Šāhnāme z Egiptu Mameluckiego*, Warsaw 1965, p. 263.

29 "Şerīf" (no. 3 in this volume), , pp. 82 f.

30 Fols. 85b-87a of the manuscript Ms. or. oct. 3744 of the Staatsbibliothek Preußischer Kulturbesitz.

1 ẖoş oldı ẖoş Sulṭānumuz
Sulṭāna ṣıḥḥat yaraşur
yolına qurbān ğānumuz
Sulṭāna ṣıḥḥat yaraşur
2 ẖoş olmadı bir niğe gün
bağrumuza vurdi dögün
ẖoşdur biḥamdillāh bugün
Sulṭāna ṣıḥḥat yaraşur
3 ʿadluñdan ördek qazıla
uçup qonarlar bāzıla
derler bülend āvāzıla
Sulṭāna ṣıḥḥat yaraşur
4 sensin bugün bu Mıṣra ẖān
sensiz gerekmez ẖānümān
ėy şāh-i sulṭān-ı ğihān
Sulṭāna ṣıḥḥat yaraşur
5 sensiz ğiger olur kebāb
sensiz gözüm yaşı şarāb
sensiz bu milk olur ẖarāb
Sulṭāna ṣıḥḥat yaraşur
6 sen çekmegil derd ü elem
qo ben senüñ derdüñ derem
her laḥẓe göñülden dėrem
Sulṭāna ṣıḥḥat yaraşur
7 Mıṣr ėlinüñ sen ẖānısın
ʿāşıqlaruñ burhānısın
ʿāriflerüñ sulṭānısın
Sulṭāna ṣıḥḥat yaraşur
8 yėrde perī gökde melek
Ḥaqqdan ėder dün gün dilek
sulṭānumuz Ġavrī gerek
Sulṭāna ṣıḥḥat yaraşur
9 sensiz bu ʿālem ẖastedür
işler qamusı bestedür
dilde duʿā peyvestedür
Sulṭāna ṣıḥḥat yaraşur
10 tendür ğihān sen aña ğān
ğānsuz ğübbe degmez ğihān
budur bize vird-i zebān
Sulṭāna ṣıḥḥat yaraşur
11 ẕevq eyle sen ṣaġ u esen
quluñ Qığıq oğlıyla ben
ṣıḥḥat dilerüz tañridan
Sulṭāna ṣıḥḥat yaraşur
12 türkānedür sözüñ Şerīf
sözüñe kim olur ḥarīf
her dem dėgil kim yā laṭīf
Sulṭāna ṣıḥḥat yaraşur
13 devrān bizüm devrānumuz
Sulṭān Ġavrī ğānumuz
ṣaġ olsun sulṭānumuz
Sulṭāna ṣıḥḥat yaraşur

"1. Again it goes well with our Sultan; good health befits the Sultan (health becomes him, suits him); we wish to sacrifice our lives for him; the Sultan is entitled to good health. 2. How many days he didn't feel well; a brand was burned into our breast; God be praised, today it goes well with him again… 3. Due to his justice duck and goose fly together with the falcon and they alight together; with loud voice they proclaim: good health befits the Sultan. 4. Today you are Khan over Egypt; without you home and family are dispensable; oh Shah, Sultan of the world… 5. Without you the liver (from grief) becomes roast meat; without you tears of my eyes become wine; without you this state falls into ruin… 6. Do not suffer pain and grief; let me gather up your pain; every moment I speak about hearts… 7. You are Khan of Egypt; the proof of lovers, the Sultan of those who know… 8. As for the *peris* on earth and the angels in heaven, they beseech

God day and night: our Sultan must be Ġavrī… 9. Without you this world is sick, all things are tied up; on the tongue prayer is unremitting… 10. The world is a body, you are its soul; without soul the world is not worth a robe; this is our continued litany: good health befits the Sultan. 11. Amuse yourself in health and good cheer; your servant Qığıq oğlı and I ask God to bestow good health … 12. Your poetry, Şerīf, is in the Turkish manner; who is well acquainted with your poetry (who can rival it?)? Every moment go on saying: oh Kind One [God], the Sultan deserves good health. 13. This time is our time; Sultan Ġavrī is our soul; he should be healthy, our Sultan: good health befits the Sultan."

Both *şerīfs*, the one in Arabic with a few Turkish samples, the other in Turkish, cause to emerge the cultural and social background against which literature, in this case specifically Turkish literature, was produced and appreciated during the last decades of the Mamluk era. In the Arabic-writing chronicler of this period, Ibn Iyās, almost nothing of this finds expression; he reports from a different vantage point, which is not so close to the court, and treats a long time span, whereas the *Majālis*[31] cited here do not even cover an entire year and Şerīf's verses are occasional poetry.

31 The notes recorded under the title *al-Kawkab al-durrī fī masā'il al-Ġawrī* should be studied. Their first part has likewise been described on p. 322 of M. Awad's article cited above; and cf. Karatay, *Arapça Yazmalar* III, p. 169, no. 5184. How criticism was expressed in the literary gatherings at the court in Herat as well is dealt with by Irmgard Engelke: "'Alī Šīr Navā'ī als Kritiker der Verse des Sultans Ḥusain Bāiqarā", in UAJb 42 (1970), pp. 91-113.

CHAPTER 8

Ḥālet Efendi's Second Audience with Napoleon*

The Turkish Ambassador Meḥmed Saʿīd Ḥālet Efendi, who had been residing in Paris since September 22nd 1803, wrote a report to the Porte shortly after July 7th 1804 which has as its subject his second secret audience with Napoleon. His first secret audience with Napoleon Bonaparte, who at the time was First Consul, took place on February 26th 1804.[1] In the meantime – on May 18th 1804 – France had changed its form of government and Napoleon had been proclaimed hereditary Emperor of the French. His envoy in Istanbul, General Brune, had informed the Porte of this in June 1804, and a war of nerves had arisen in which France pressured the Porte formally to recognize the new title of Emperor, whereas Russia and England threatened to respond to such a step by breaking off their relations with the Ottoman Empire.[2]

Ḥālet Efendi was a man of great intelligence and eloquence, an administrative generalist with a literary education. He had risen to the ranks of the "bureau chiefs" (*ḫācegān*), and his career took another upward turn as he was appointed ambassador to France with the rank of *baş muḥāsib* (chief accountant).[3]

Ḥālet Efendi's report, entitled *Qāʾime*,[4] which will be discussed here, was entirely composed as an *aperçu de conversation*, thus making use of direct speech. The writer refers to himself in the third person singular with the conventional expression of debasement (*çāker*). The change of tone from plain and simple language to the florid rhetoric of the concluding observations makes the *qāʾime* a good specimen of the complexity and elegance of Ottoman Turkish prose. By his nonchalant speech the dragoman, "that person" (*mersūm*),

---

* Translated by John O'Kane.

1 Examined and published in abridged form in Enver Ziya Karal, *Halet Efendinin Paris Büyük Elçiliği (1802-1806)*, Istanbul 1940, pp. 57-63; and cf. Ercümend Kuran, *Avrupa'da Osmanlı İkamet Elçiliklerinin Kuruluşu ve İlk Elçilerin Siyasi Faâliyetleri* 1793-1821, Ankara 1968, p. 49.

2 Kuran, p. 50; Stanford J. Shaw, *Between Old and New. The Ottoman Empire under Sultan Selim III 1789-1807*, Cambridge, Mass. 1971, p. 332.

3 Ercümend Kuran, "Ḥālet Efendi," EI III (1971), p. 90-91, for Ottoman scribal culture and careers see Carter Vaughn Findley, *Bureaucratic Reform in the Ottoman Empire. The Sublime Porte, 1789-1922*, Princeton 1980; idem, *Ottoman Civil Officialdom. A Social History*, Princeton 1989.

4 The *qāʾime*, an official document written on one large, long sheet of paper (in this case 535 + 375 mm), is preserved in the Staatsbibliothek in Berlin – Preussischer Kulturbesitz, Hs. orient. 2370. Catalogue entry Flemming, p. 178, no. 218.1. The word *qāʾima* was later used for paper money in Turkey; see Roderick H. Davison, "Ḳāʾime" in EI IV, (1978), p. 460-461.

 | DOI 10.1163/9789004355767_009

is labelled a man of lower rank. The writer's own calm response and final remarks combine irony with subtle policy statements.

Ḥālet Efendi's second interview with Bonaparte was one station on the long diplomatic road from Napoleon's proclamation as Emperor to Ottoman recognition of that title. Ḥālet's second audience with Napoleon was connected to the first one of February in so far as Bonaparte had in the meantime sent a communication written in his own hand to Sultan Selīm III.[5] In response to this, the courier Istefanaki had delivered to the Turkish ambassador in Paris a sealed letter from the Sultan, apparently the one dated 27 Muḥarrem 1219/8 May 1804,[6] along with a second encoded copy of the letter for Ḥālet Efendi as well as additional papers containing instructions for the ambassador.

As earlier in the case of his predecessor Seyyid ʿAlī Efendi[7] and the ambassador extraordinary Ġālib Efendi,[8] to a great extent correspondence with the Porte apparently took place in code.[9] Ḥālet Efendi himself deciphered the documents he received and immediately submitted a note to the Foreign Minister Talleyrand (a copy of which Ḥālet sent to the Porte along with his report). An hour later the First Dragoman of the French legation, Antoine Franchini,[10] arrived and coolly announced to Ḥālet Efendi:

> A note from you which I have translated has reached Talleyrand. You have requested to meet secretly with Bonaparte. But his Excellency Talleyrand thought that no audience would be granted as long as a letter with recognition of the title of Emperor failed to appear.

5 Cf. Johann Wilhelm Zinkeisen, *Geschichte des osmanischen Reiches in Europa*, Siebenter Theil, Gotha 1863, VII, p. 362.

6 Kuran, p. 49. The Sultan's letter is in the Başbakanlık Arşivi under H. H. 35065; French translation in Baron de Testa, *Receuil des traités de la Porte Ottomane*..., Paris 1864-1911, II, p. 256 (cited from Kuran).

7 On him see İsmail Soysal, *Fransız İhtilâli ve Türk-Fransız Diplomasi Münasebetleri* (1789-1802), Ankara 1964, pp. 338 f.

8 Soysal, pp. 340 f.

9 The documents I-IV and VIII in Enver Ziya Karal, *Fransa-Mısır ve Osmanlı İmparatorluğu* (*1797-1802*), were encoded; cf. Soysal, p. 333, with reference to İ.H. Uzunçarşılı, "Âmedî Galib Efendi'nin murahhaslığı ve Paris'ten gönderdiği şifreli mektupları", in *Belleten* I (1937), pp. 357-410.

10 In 1802 the French chargé d'affaires in Istanbul, Pierre-Jean Marie Ruffin, had seen to it that his agent Franchini was appointed as secretary and translator in Ġālib Efendi's embassy to Paris (Shaw, *Between Old and New*, p. 280). About a month after the interview discussed here, Franchini delivered an expensive gift to Ḥālet Efendi from Napoleon: Karal, *Halet Efendi*, p. 24. For Ruffin the orientalist see "Goethe and Diez" in this volume, no. 28.

> Ṭaleyrana bir teẕkereñiz geldi terceme eyledim Bonaparteyi maḫfī görmek maṭlūb eylemişsiz derḥāl teẕkereñiz tercemesiyle Bonaparteye irsāl olundı ancaq Ṭaleyran cenābları taḫmīnim imparaṭorluġuñ taṣdīqnāmesi gelmeyince mülāqāta müsāʿade etmezler dėdi.

Ḥālet Efendi contented himself with a cool reply:

> I (His Majesty's servant) said: 'Let the note reach his Excellency Bonaparte first; if he responds in that way, I assume that we by then, explaining its necessity to his Excellency Talleyrand, will receive consent.' – I said not another word "

> çākerleri teẕkere Bonaparte cenāblarına varsun da ol vecihle cevāb vėrirler ise ol zamān iqtiżāsı Ṭaleyran cenāblarına ifāde ile müsāʿade taḥṣīl ėderiz ẓann ederim dėyüp āḫir söz söylemedim

In fact the invitation arrived by return post, and Talleyrand even wrote in his own hand that he [Bonaparte] would expect Ḥālet Efendi the morning of the following day, a Saturday, i.e. the 7th of July 1804, in his castle Saint-Cloud located an hour from Paris.[11] Ḥālet rode there alone in his coach and was received by a general and served refreshments. Ḥālet Efendi had assumed that he would speak Napoleon alone,[12] and had prepared himself accordingly. That Franchini would be there was a disappointment. Contrary to his expectations, he learned that Franchini was commissioned by His Majesty the Emperor to be their interpreter during the conversation, thus rendering superfluous the report he had previously prepared; he resigned himself to the inevitable and along with the dragoman entered the room in which Bonaparte, standing up with his hat in his hand, received him in a most cheerful manner.

> Franchini came and said: "This time His Majesty the Emperor has appointed me to translate your private interview.' This meant that the introductory notes which I had prepared had become useless and of no avail because that person would be privy to the interview; (however,)

11 Ms. SNQLY. *Senqlū nām saray* was the place where Ḥalet Efendi's letter of dismissal was written on 11 September; cf. Karal, *Halet Efendi*, p. 88. It was in Saint-Cloud that Bonaparte announced his assumption of the title Emperor.

12 The Phanariot dragomans had been excluded from the first interview, which then, in the absence of competent translators, had been conducted in Arabic; Karal, *Halet Efendi*, p. 60. For the Phanariot Greek community see Carter Findley, *Officialdom*, p. 73.

non-acceptance by your humble servant being impossible, I went into another room together with the dragoman (*tercümān*) Franchini. Bonaparte had stood up, hat in hand, and displayed the utmost cheerfulness; the inquiries after health etc. having been completed...

Frankini gelüp bu defʿa olan meclis-i ḫāṣṣıñızı tercemeye Imparāṭor cenābları beni meʾmūr ėtdiler dėyü ifāde ėtmekle...istiḥżār eyledigim muqaddemāt mersūmuñ vāqıf-i meclis olacağı cihetle lağv u hebā olmuş ise daḫı ṭaraf-i çākerīden ʿadem-i qabūlı mümkin olamamağla...tercümān Frankini ile berāber āḫir bir odaya varup Bonaparte şapqası elinde qıyāmen ḍurmuş ve kemāl-i beşāşet iẓhār ėderek istifsār-i ḥāl u ḫāṭir tekmīl olduqdan ṣoñra...

Ḥālet Efendi began the interview by delivering the sealed letter of the Sultan, asking Bonaparte to open the seal. He then read out the entire communication, paragraph by paragraph, so that Franchini could translate it literally.[13]

While that person translated, the expression of the concord and friendship with the French that had been handed down from His (the Sultan's) great ancestors filled him (Bonaparte) with extraordinary pleasure; he positively beamed with joy and gratitude. When it came to the passage: 'Thank God that in protecting our lands we never harbor any mistrust towards our friends', he asked for clarification. When I (your servant) said: 'There is no reason to mistrust anyone because of our lands; were there the slightest doubt on our part, by [the Sultan's] express command we would take appropriate security measures (we would not hesitate to enforce safeguards to protect our lands),[14] he (Bonaparte) [answered}: "But all means! Who can interfere in his national territory. Everyone does as he wishes in his own territory. Read on up to the end! There is something I want to say."

mersūm daḫı terceme ėderek Françaluile ecdād-ı ʿiẓāmımdan mevrūˇs olan müsālemet ve muṣāfāt taʿbīrinden beğāyet maḥẓuẓ olup bayağı iẓhār-i sürūr ve teşekkür eyledi baʿdehu elḥamdülillāh memālikimizi

13 Kuran, p. 49, fn. 11: *"bend bend okudu ve Fransa tercümanı Antoine Franchini bunları aynen tercüme etti."*

14 Kuran, pp. 49 f., notes that Selīm III, after his bitter experiences in the past, appreciated the friendship of the French but did not intend to fall out with England and Russia who since Bonaparte's Egyptian campaign had become his allies.

muḥāfaẓada dostlarımızdan aṣlā vesvesemiz yoqdur taʿbīrine geldikde tekrār suʾāl ėdüp çākerleri daḫı memālikimizi kimseden vesvese iqtiżā ėtmez ednā mertebe şübhemiz olsa ʿādetā esbāb-i muḥāfaẓaya ihtimām ederdik dėmek irāde buyurulur dėdigimde hay hay mülklerine kim qarışabilür her kes kendü mülkinde istedigi gibi eder hele oqu bitsün de söyleyecegim var.

In his response Napoleon firstly expressed that he felt great affection for Sultan Selīm III and followed his efforts at reform with sympathy.[15] Secondly, that France was not a neighbor of the Ottoman Empire and therefore they shared common interests:

> If one of your neighboring states should occupy however small a piece of your national territory, that would be so harmful to us that the resulting harm could not be compensated even were we to conquer a large country somewhere else.

> Hemcivārıñız olan düvelden biri mülküñüzden ednā bir yere müstevlī olsa bize olqadar mużırr olurki āḫir yerden biz bir büyük ülke ẓabṭ ėtsek andan olan żararımıza muʿādil olmaz.

Bonaparte warned emphatically against Russia that had recently got a foothold on Corfu and now intended to acquire a port and a fleet in the Mediterranean. Now if the neighbors of the Ottomans proceeded to expand their territories, he could hinder the Austrians but:

> After it has emerged that you are also not making it clear where you stand and are concerned about your defense, each will follow the path that serves his own interest. Precisely because they did not take account of this outcome of affairs, I maintain that the ministers of your state are not loyal.[16]

> lākin siz de ṭavr alup müdāfaʿa qaydında olmadığıñızı taḥqīq ėtdikden ṣoñra herkes kendü maṣlaḥatına elverecek ṣūrete sālik olur işte böyle

15 It is known that in 1795 Bonaparte proposed his dispatch to the *Porte* at the head of a military delegation; Karal, *Fransa-Mısır*, pp. 35 f., with earlier relevant literature.

16 During the year 1804, when official recognition was late in coming, General Brune in Istanbul expressed this view in ever more rude notes in which he finally accused the Ottoman ministers of venality; cf. *Zinkeisen*, VII, p. 377.

> şey'iñ encāmına diqqat ėtmedikleriyçün vükelā-yı devletiñize ṣādıq degildirler dėrem dėdi.

At this point Ḥālet Efendi declared that he had fulfilled his task of making known the friendly contents of the Sultan's letter; if it were permitted, however, he would like to give a reply, not on behalf of his country, but simply as it occurred to him. Bonaparte: "Please do so! It was not my intention to presume to pass judgement on you but in a friendly manner I wanted to alert you to the danger that is confronting you." Ḥālet Efendi:

> After the said Corfu had become one more republic[17] in this way, at the time it was most expedient for the Ottoman Empire to become its protector and for Moscow to stand as surety and guarantor for its protection. And since it is one of the points that served as a basis for mutual understanding in entering a general peace agreement, to change it would not only be contrary to the treaty but how can the Ottoman Empire now attempt to find reasons for changing this arrangement, given that you and we have friendship pacts with Russia?
>
> He [Bonaparte] understood the meaning concealed under these explanations and, after clearing his throat a bit, he replied: 'My intention when I went to Egypt was not to cause damage to Egypt in any way,[18] but I went there in order to reach India.[19] However, since you suddenly declared war and imprisoned our ambassador,[20] one could not risk once again dispatching an ambassador from here. I myself many times wrote letters to be sent everywhere there and in order to win over the people... I went to Syria. The entire population submitted to me. But at the time I was not able to make clear to your ministers in detail that my intention was to go to India – otherwise, neither would these things have happened, nor would it have been necessary for you to conclude such a pact with Russia and England.' Since this was no explanation that creatures endowed with reason could accept and, on the other hand, to reply with the truth

17 The Free State of the Seven United Islands was created in 1800. Cf. Karal, p. 45; Soysal, pp. 321 and 361, with earlier literature; Shaw, p. 270.

18 Bonaparte affirmed this in writing to Selīm III: Soysal, p. 322.

19 On Bonaparte's plan concerning an Indian campaign for which the Syrian expedition was meant to be a kind of rehearsal, cf. Soysal, pp. 269-73. On the other considerations which led to the French expedition to Egypt, cf. Karal, *Fransa-Mısır*, pp. 37 ff. and Shaw, pp. 254 f. The Turkish ambassador in Paris, ʿAlī Efendi, was deceived for a long time; Karal, *Fransa-Mısır*, p. 129; Soysal, pp. 212 ff.; Shaw, pp. 255 f.

20 Ruffin; on him see Soysal, pp. 351 f.

> ran the risk of provoking disputes, I was obliged to follow the path of ingeniousness"

And so Ḥālet Efendi explained that the affair of Egypt was "as if it had never happened" and everything would be facilitated, given that both sides were disposed to continue their friendship. But for this to succeed from now on it would be necessary to deal with matters of this kind with careful consideration and not to lend one's ear to the first opinions that come along.

Ḥālet Efendi indicated that Bonaparte might have based his view on false information when he warned against the Greeks in the earlier audience (without the presence of the Greek interpreter). Bonaparte insisted, however, that the Greeks were virtually auxiliary troops of the Russians. He praised the recently deceased Ottoman Grand Admiral, Ḥüseyn Paşa, who had been completely loyal to him and the Ottoman Empire,[21] and uttered words of regret for the death of Cezzār Paşa.

Ḥālet Efendi took the opportunity to inform Bonaparte that the Ottoman fleet would sail for ʿAkkā; "since this coincides with the naval movement of the Russians who are bringing soldiers and ships from the Black Sea for the defense of Corfu, I wish to tell you now so that those weaving intrigues cannot once again impute all kinds of reasons for this." Bonaparte: "'This causes me no fear, but it suits her [Russia] to occupy Corfu completely', and then turning to me with a smile, added: 'Isn't that so?'"

Bearing in mind his instructions to avoid everything that might have kindled "the fire of jealousy", Ḥālet Efendi preferred silence which Bonaparte supposedly interpreted as agreement and responded with praise for Ḥālet Efendi's talents, predicting that he had a splendid career ahead of him. Finally, Bonaparte asked – obviously thinking of his title of Emperor – whether Ḥālet Efendi had anything else to report. Ḥālet had to answer in the negative and was only able to refer to the fact that the complete sincerity of both sides emerged from the Sultan's letter... In the closing remarks of his report Ḥālet Efendi criticizes Bonaparte's negotiating style and then touches on something which had not been directly dealt with in the audience: the alleged or real split within leading Ottoman circles between a pro-French and a pro-Russian party. Whereas Ḥālet Efendi had not wanted to go into the role of the Greeks – in any case not in the presence of Franchini – here he intimates that Ottoman statesmen had among their following "riffraff" inclined to irresponsible talk and that traitors existed who were in the service of the French:

21 On him see Shaw, pp. 276 f.

Although he [Bonaparte] had not engaged his dragoman [Franchini] in the previous audience because of the latter's many friends in Istanbul, this time he had allowed him to be present. After having first said that his intention with regard to the Egyptian campaign had been to go to India, the next moment he maintained he could have gone to Syria and won over the people, which completely places this event in a ridiculous light. One exploits the gossip of a kind of riffraff and rabble from among the following of Ottoman statesmen in order to maintain that in their opinion from the viziers all the way down to the servants (*ḫademe*)[22] there is a division into one group which is loyal to them and the Ottoman Empire, while another group is inclined to Russia; but no names are revealed concerning who the latter group is meant to be. Certain indications, however, lead one to believe that their intention is to transform the evil in their heart into action and bring about an estrangement between the Ottoman Empire and Russia and England if with such common and unpleasant subjects, which are inappropriate for intercourse between countries, they can trouble the ear of the Ottoman government and deceive the Ottoman Empire, and that – although such talk has been current in the mouth of the French nation since the start of their republic – this does in part stem from a band of sycophants that they have taken into their service.

muqaddemki meclisde bizim tercümānıñ āsitānede dostı çoq déyü anı maḥrem etmemişken bu def'a maḥrem eylemesinden ve Mıṣıra gitmekden ġarazim Hinde gitmek idi dedikden ṣonra Şāma gidebildim ehāliyi celb eder idim söziyle bu qażīyeyi bütün bütün tezyīf eylemesinden ve ricāl-i devlet-i ʿalīyeye müteʿalliq baʿżı erāzil ve evbāş maqūlesiniñ ağızlarından alınma sözleri esās-i ittiḫāẕ ėderek vüzerādan ḫademeye varınca ʿindlerinde ikiye taqsīm ile bir ṭaqımı kendülere ve devlet-i ʿalīyeye ṣādıq ve bir ṭaqımı Rusyaluya māʾil olmak üzere söylemekden ve bunlar kimler olduqlarını ketm ṣūretiyle isim beyān ėtmediginden böyle rüsūm-i düvelden ḫāric qaba ve bārid zemīnler ile sāmiʿa-i salṭanat-i senīyeyi teḫdīş ėderek devlet-i ʿalīyeyi iġfāl ėdebilürler ise derūnlarında olan fesādı icrā ve Rusyalu ve İngilterelü ile devlet-i ʿalīye beyninde bir bürūdet ilqā ėtmek fikrinde olduqları ve bu maqūle sözler Fransa milleti ağzında ibtidā-yı cumhūriyetlerindenberü var ise daḫı biraz da istiḫdām

22 For several types of servants (*hademe*) found in – or just outside – government offices see Carter-Findley, *Officialdom*, pp. 58-59 and p. 219.

eyledikleri bir alay ḫavaneden neş'et ėtmiş oldığı ba'ż-ı qarā'inden iḥsās olunur.

The attitude of the Sublime Porte regarding the question of the title of Emperor, which was one of continued stalling, must have had an effect on Ḥālet Efendi's mission. In January 1805 he had to give up his activity as ambassador but he was allowed to remain in Paris[23] which he only left in September 1806. Given over entirely to conservative Islamic viewpoints, he considered it his duty to warn against everything European and to speak with irony about all the so-called achievements of the French Republic.[24] In his aversion to his host country precarious financial circumstances must also have played a role in making him experience more painfully the neglect in protocol and the impertinent talk he was exposed to in the audience he describes. Toward the end of his sojourn once again he came to be treated with greater consideration, and he was dismissed and sent back with an affable letter to Istanbul where a successful career did in fact await him.[25]

His successor, 'Abdurraḥīm Muḥibb Efendi, to begin with could have had an easier time of it since he did bring with him recognition of the title of Emperor. The Porte had decided to take this step under the influence of the Battle of Austerlitz (2 December 1805) and the Treaty of Pressburg (now Bratislava, 26 December 1805). But Muḥibb Efendi's inaugural visit on the 5th of June 1806 almost turned into a fiasco because of an oversight of the Ottoman chancellery and the unnecessary inflexibility of the ambassador – the title of "King of Italy" had been omitted and Muḥibb refused to add it on his own authority. Muḥibb Efendi provoked his sovereign's wrath but was able to remain in his post and from this vantage point recorded in extensive reports his diverse observations on institutions in France and facts of every kind.[26]

23 Zinkeisen, VII, p. 380; Karal, p. 80; Kuran, p. 51. His predecessor, 'Alī Efendi, was also unable to exercise his office for a while because of the Egyptian campaign.

24 Karal, pp. 32 ff. and 38 f.; Bernard Lewis, *The Emergence of Modern Turkey*, Oxford 1961, pp. 69, 103 and 128.

25 Under Maḥmūd II Ḥālet Efendi became enormously powerful, but the events leading to the outbreak of the Greek Revolution led to his downfall; accused of being the cause of the event, he was executed in 1822. Kuran, "Ḥālet Efendi", p. 93.

26 Cf. Faik Reşit Unat (ed. Bekir Sıtkı Baykal), *Osmanlı Sefirleri ve Sefaretnameleri*, Ankara 1968, with a description of the embassy narrative by Muḥibb Efendi (mentioned in the second essay of this volume, pp. XX-XX).

CHAPTER 9

Literary Activities in Mamluk Halls and Barracks

Anyone who studies the social context of Muslim literature produced and appreciated in Egypt and Syria under the Mamluks has to take into account not only "the streets and coffee-houses of Cairo",[1] but also the halls of the four Chief Justices,[2] the madrasas and ṣūfī fraternity houses (*khānqāh*) where other jurists and shaykhs lived,[3] and the great households of the Mamluks.[4] Here as well as in the Cadis' halls the sophistication of the entertainment depended on the degree of the owner's wealth, rank and education. If someday the Sultans' and the grand amīrs' collections and activities can be viewed as a whole, it will be seen that their halls, and also those of other amīrs of sufficient rank and income, were places where literature in the widest sense was appreciated.

The importance of the *awlād an-nās* as a link between the Mamluk class and the native culture of Egypt has been justly emphasized.[5] Children of great Mamluk amīrs were brought up in their fathers' households, and learned their reading and writing from domestic *kuttāb* and from scholars called in from the outside; here the immigrants from Turkish countries to be mentioned below found employment. As regards connections with the local literature, the

1 Irfan Shahid, "Arabic Literature," in *The Cambridge History of Islam* II (Cambridge, 1970), 667.

2 Ibn Taghrībirdī grew up in such a household: that of the Chief Ḥanafite Cadi, who was married to his sister. – On Cadis' halls see A. Schimmel, "Kalif und Kadi im spätmittelalterlichen Ägypten," *Die Welt des Islams* 25 (1942), 111.

3 Here erotic poetry and satire were composed by Cadis on top of their official work; book-collecting was a favourite pastime. See A. Schimmel, "Kalif und Kadi," 66-67, 98-99. We hear of sumptuous banquets with musical performances organized by the Confidential Secretary, the Scribe of the bureau of Mamluks, and the Prefect of Markets (*ibid.*, 76, 98 f., 108, where also poetry is mentioned which was inspired by a quarrel over ʿOmar b. al-Fāriḍ's orthodoxy).

4 On the magnificence of these households see W. Popper, *Egypt and Syria under the Circassian Sultans 1382-1468 A.D. Systematic Notes to Ibn Taghrî Birdî's Chronicles of Egypt* (Berkeley and Los Angeles, 1955), 5. U. Haarmann, "Alṭun Ḫān und Čingiz Ḫān bei den ägyptischen Mamluken," *Der Islam* 51 (1974), 5-7, cites a number of such households from the earlier Mamluk period.

5 D. Ayalon, *The Muslim City and the Mamluk Military Aristocracy* (Proceedings of the Israel Academy of Sciences and Humanities II, No. 14) (Jerusalem, 1967), 327 f.; U. Haarmann, "Alṭun Ḫān," 9; Kristof D'hulster and J. van Steenbergen. "Family Matters. The 'Family-In-Law Impulse' in Mamluk Marriage Policy", *Annales Islamologiques* 47 (2013), 61-82.

DOI 10.1163/9789004355767_010

case of Ibn ad-Dawādārī, who numbered contemporary Arab writers among his friends,[6] need not be an exception.

In investigating the biographical material it may be useful to draw a line between those reported qualities incumbent upon any exemplary ruler of Islam and those reported traits that are of a more personal nature. To the former may belong a respectful attitude towards descendants of the Prophet and scholars of Islam, and humility in the presence of Coran readers in deference to the Words of God; to the latter, the attitude shown toward music, play and jesting.

If it suited his taste, a great amīr or a Sultan would maintain a number of performers (or attend *samāʿ* gatherings like Sultan Muʾayyad Shaykh). Whereas Sultan Jaqmaq disapproved so strongly of this that in his days "the fortunes of players and singers were low"; his son Muḥammad was very fond of music "after the manner of the Ṣūfīs". We find this again in al-Ghawrī, who delighted in music and jesting. His court musician and jester are known.[7] While any conscientious ruler would continue his studies under scholars of repute, and invite learned men to his hall, the eminence of the visitors whom he could attract depended to some extent on his own education and special interests. Jaqmaq, for instance, was noted for his interest in, and good memory for, legal questions. But it is significant that it was Jaqmaq's son, the talented, well-educated Nāṣiraddīn Muḥammad, who attracted visitors of the greatest distinction to his father's hall.[8]

The latest records of formal gatherings in Mamluk times, where the names of visitors and the topics under discussion were taken down, seem to be the *Nafāʾis al-majālis as-Sulṭānīya* by Ḥusayn b. Muḥammad al-Ḥusaynī[9] and *al-*

6 One of them was Ibn Dāniyāl (d. 1310), the ophthalmologist and writer of shadow-plays. U. Haarmann, "Alṭun Ḫān," 16. The names of three more Arab poets who probably were acquaintances of Ibn ad-Dawādārī are given in U. Haarmann, ed., *Die Chronik des Ibn ad-Dawādārī. 8. Teil. Der Bericht über die frühen Mamluken* (Freiburg, 1971), 20.

7 "Šerīf, Sultan Ġavrī und die "Perser" (no. 3 in this volume).

8 Ibn Taghrībirdī, *an-Nujūm az-Zāhira fī mulūk Miṣr wa l-Qāhira* (ed. W. Popper) VIII (Berkeley, 1936), 291; as-Sakhāwī, *aḍ-Ḍawʿ al-lāmiʿ li-ahl al-qarn at-tāsiʿ* (Cairo, 1354/1935-6) VII, 211; A. Schimmel, "Kalif und Kadi," 69.

9 The rare printed edition by ʿAbdalwahhāb ʿAzzām (Cairo, 1941) is inaccessible to me. F.E. Karatay, *Topkapı Sarayı Müzesi Kütüphanesi Arapça Yazmalar Kataloğu* III (Istanbul, 1966), 207, No. 5285, describes a copy of this work (Ahmet III 2680), to which M. Awad has drawn attention as early as 1938: "Sultan al-Ghawrī. His place in literature and learning (three books written under his patronage)," in *Actes du XXe Congrès International des Orientalistes, Bruxelles, 1938* (Louvain, 1940), 321 f.

Kawkab ad-durrī fī masāʾil al-Ghawrī[10] (both in Arabic). Such "transactions", which were actually written by insiders, are a very promising field for further study.

A cursory glance at the surviving books – dedication copies or manuscripts commissioned for personal use – shows the predominance of Arabic in the upbringing and later reading of the educated Mamluk. The proportion of books in Turkish, the vernacular of the ruling class, is not high, even if we allow for losses of manuscripts. Arabic was primarily used for public written business, for most branches of literature, and even for recording themes of Turkish and Mongolian tradition.[11] While Turkish was the prevailing *spoken* language of "Mamluke officialdom",[12] and was indispensable for office-seekers,[13] especially in Syria,[14] as a written language it was used secondarily: chiefly for the edification and amusement of the Mamluk class. As such it underwent a change. It is known that the earlier Turkish literary idiom, Kipchak-Khwarazmian Turkish, was gradually replaced by the Turkish of the Oghuz (called Turkmen in the glossaries composed for Arabs) as a result of the growing linguistic, literary, and intellectual influences from Turkish Anatolia.

In continuation of an earlier Mamluk practice, in Circassian Mamluk circles jurists and officials (*kuttāb*) were often of Turkish origin. They came from places under Mamluk dominion like Āmid, or they immigrated from Iraq or Anatolia. Towards the end of the 15th century many Turks and Persians emigrated from Azerbayjan as a result of the rise of the Shiʿite Ṣafawids. As usual, jurists and *kuttāb*, who had obtained their first education in their home countries, liked to go to foreign madrasas for their advanced studies, and, combining this with the Pilgrimage often came to Syria and Egypt. Several remained there, at least temporarily, and found appointments under the amīrs as well as the Sultans, whereas the religious often settled in khānqāhs. The Mamluk chronicles tell us how, if these newcomers stayed in the service of the Sultan, they were supported and rewarded from the various revenues at the disposal of their employers and friends. We know how the well-known Badraddīn al-ʿAynī,

10 Part I, equally in Istanbul, Ahmet III 1377, was also described by M. Awad, *op. cit.*, 322. See also Karatay, *Arapça Yazmalar* III, 169, No. 5184.

11 After the pioneer study by M.F. Köprülü, followed by F. Sümer, U. Haarmann was the first scholar to discuss in an illuminating way the first-rate material on Turkish, Kurdish, and Mongolian folklore and ethnology which is contained in the annals of Ibn ad-Dawādārī: see his "Alṭun Ḫān," 9-31.

12 W. Popper, *op. cit.* (above, n. 4), 5.

13 Ibn Taghrībirdī, *an-Nujūm az-Zāhira* (ed. W. Popper) VII, 361.

14 On the long history of the Turkish language in Syria see the introduction to T. Halasi-Kun, "The Ottoman Elements in the Syrian Dialects, in *Archivum Ottomanicum* 1 (1969), 16-21.

one of these newcomers, gained Sultan Barsbay's favour by lecturing on history and related subjects and occasionally translating works into Turkish for him.[15] Yaʿqūb Shāh of Arzanjān, who studied in Tabriz and became Chief of the Chancellery of the Qaraqoyunlu ruler, later moved to Egypt, where the Grand Dawādār Yashbek min Mahdī found for him the posts of "host" (*mihmāndār*) and director of the foreign department of the Egyptian Chancellery.[16] I assume he is the compiler of an Arabic book on the history of the Dhūlqadir Turkmens and other Turkish states.[17] A Turk from Shiraz, Ḥusayn b. Pīr Ḥājjī Abū Bakr, who was educated in Herat where he held office as treasurer of the Timurid ruler, gained favour with the Grand Dawādār by means of his musical accomplishments, and was appointed to Yashbek's Dome.[18] Finally, there is the Sharīf Ḥusayn b. Ḥasan who was commissioned to compose the Turkish *Shāhnāma* version and was rewarded by being appointed, over the heads of the Dayrī family,[19] as Shaykh of the Ṣūfīs of the Mu'ayyad Mosque.

In Mamluk circles of Egypt and Syria the dervishes found an appreciative audience. Muṣṭafā b. ʿOmar aḍ-Ḍarīr, the blind Mawlawī author from Arzan ar-Rūm in Anatolia, illustrates this. He came to Cairo at the beginning of the Circassian period, and, irrespective of his self-confessed deficiency in learning, was obviously accepted because of his proficiency as a religious writer. He stayed in Egypt to complete his Turkish Biography of the Prophet Muḥammad for the Sultan (Barqūq), which is appreciated in Turkey to this day, and survives in numerous manuscripts. He composed other Turkish works in Egypt and Syria.[20]

If we do use the term "court literature"[21] for Turkish poetry and prose composed in the Mamluk halls, we should rather use it in its literal sense than with the connotation of refinement and esoterism. Typical examples of Turkish (and Arabic) religious poetry surviving from Mamluk libraries, for example the *Kitāb ad-Daʿwāt* (Revan 1727, mentioned below), copied for Sultan Qaytbay,

15 A. Schimmel, "Some Glimpses of the Religious Life in Egypt during the later Mamluk Period," in *Islamic Studies* (Rawalpindi) 7 (1965), 356 f.

16 *Ḍawʿ* (above, n. 8) x, 280, No. 1104.

17 Karatay, *Arapça Yazmalar* III, 475, No. 6186 = Ahmet III 3057.

18 *Ḍaw'* III, 139.

19 My "Šerīf," (no. 3 in this volume).

20 See A. Bombaci, *La Letteratura turca* (Florence, 1969), 211 f; Gottfried Hagen, "Some Considerations about the Terğüme-i Darīr ve Taqdimetü z-Zahīr based on Manuscripts in German Libraries", *Journal of Turkish Studies* 26/I (2002), Harvard University, pp. 323-337.

21 U. Haarmann distinguishes between esoteric court literature in Turkish ("Alṭun Ḫān," 4) and popular Turkish concepts in history writing, which gained admittance to Arab literature through the Arab language (*ibid.*, 36).

and this Sultan's own poems,[22] are obviously influenced by oral dervish literature, and are themselves meant to be read aloud. It is true that Sultan Ghawrī was personally interested in Ottoman court poetry, which he had copied for himself and to which he contributed some *naẓīras*, and has written sophisticated Arabic and "mixed" poetry; nevertheless he enjoyed poetry in the dervish style such as it was cultivated by Sherīf.[23]

According to general usage, copies were made not only by professional scribes and calligraphers, but also by occasional copyists, who may have been connected with the Sultans' and the grand amīrs' assemblies. Book collecting was an expensive pursuit and could become a passion; we hear that Jaqmaq, in his days as Sultan and even before, would acquire precious books and pay for them prices which exceeded the reasonable price.[24] Yashbek the Grand Dawādār was known to be a passionate book collector.[25]

From descriptions of surviving manuscripts a few names emerge of persons who transcribed manuscripts for Sultan Qaytbay:

- Muḥammad b. Ḥasan aṭ-Ṭayyibī al-Azharī, who in Dhū l-ḥijja 877/ May 1473 copied the two-volume Ḥadīth work entitled *Mashāriʿ al-ashwāq ilā maṣāriʿ al-ʿushshāq*;[26]
- Muḥammad b. Aḥmad al-Ḥasanī al-Farnawī *al-mukattib*, who transcribed an Arabic work on medicine, *Ġunyat al-labīb ʿinda ġaybat aṭ-ṭabīb*, in September 1483;[27]
- Ismāʿīl b. Qāsim al-Ḥanafī, who in April 1484 finished a beautifully executed calligraphic copy of an Arabic Biography of the Prophet Muḥammad;[28]
- Muḥammad b. Muḥammad b. ʿAlī, known as التندى, the copyist of at least two *juzʾ* of the History of the Prophets by al-Kisāʾī;[29]
- ʿAlī b. Aḥmad b. Amīr ʿAlī, who copied a *mejmūʿa* in Turkish, with which language he was apparently not quite familiar, in 1489/90;[30]

22 See J. Eckmann, "Die mamluk-kiptschakische Literatur," in *Philologiae Turcicae Fundamenta* II (Wiesbaden, 1964), 299.

23 My "Šerīf," (no. 3 in this volume).

24 Ibn Taghrībirdī, *an-Nujūm* VII, 247.

25 See my "Šerīf," (no. 3 in this volume).

26 Karatay, *Arapça Yazmalar* II, 242, No. 2995-2996 = Ahmet III 649/1-2.

27 Karatay, *Arapça Yazmalar* III, 848, No. 7333 = Ahmet III 2048.

28 Karatay, *Arapça Yazmalar* III, 427, No. 6032 = Ahmet III 2829.

29 *Juzʾ* I: Karatay, *Arapça Yazmalar* III, 408, No. 5974 = Ahmet III 2863/1; *juzʿ* IV: *ibid.*, No. 5976 = Ahmet III 2863/4.

30 F.E. Karatay, *Topkapı Sarayı Müzesi Kütüphanesi Türkçe Yazmalar Kataloğu* II (Istanbul, 1961), 88, No. 2253 = Koğuşlar, 950. A facsimile of the title page was reproduced by A.

- Aḥmad b. ʿAlī al-Fayyūmī, the teacher of the Mamluk Sanṭabay, copied two works in Arabic, one collection of Forty Ḥadīths,[31] and the *Tafsīr al-Jalālayn*.[32]

Among Sultan Ghawrī's scribes we find:

- Abū l-Faḍl Muḥammad al-Aʿraj, the copyist of two works in Arabic, one on medicine by Qaysūnīzāde,[33] dated 1506, the other a discussion of theological-ethical questions by al-Aqfahsī;[34]
- Muḥammad b. Aḥmad al-Maḥallī, who transcribed the work of a contemporary, *Nuzhat al-abṣār fī manāqib al-aimma al-arbaʿa al-akhyār*, by Ḥasan b. Ḥusayn b. Aḥmad b. aṭ-Ṭūlūnī (1428/9–after 1503).[35]

I hesitate to give three other names of Ghawrī's scribes:

- Aḥmad b. Ḥasan aṭ-Ṭūlūnī al-Miʿmār,[36] who is possibly to be identified with Sultan Ghawrī's Controller of Public Works, repeatedly mentioned by Ibn Iyās;
- Ḥamza ash-Sharafī, who is supposed to have copied some Sūras in Istanbul (!) in 1503/4;[37]
- ʿAbdalqādir b. Ibrāhīm ad-Dimashqī, for whose transcript a date long before Ghawrī's accession is given.[38]

It is no easy task to verify these occasional copyists in contemporary sources. For this there is a better chance in cases where the authors themselves gave their works to a patron. Among such works which were committed to writing by the authors themselves or at least commissioned by them we may mention

---

Zajączkowski, "Poezje stroficzne muvaššaḥ mameluckiego sultana Qānṣūh (Qansav) Ġavrī, in *Rocznik Orientalistyczny* 27/2 (1964), 88. Fols. 7b–28b were published by the same scholar: *Poezje stroficzne ʿĀšïq-Paša* (Warsaw, 1967).

31 Karatay, *Arapça Yazmalar* II, 288, No. 3132 = Ahmet III 360.

32 Karatay, *Arapça Yazmalar* II, 533, No. 2058 = Koğuşlar 605.

33 Karatay, *Arapça Yazmalar* III, 864, No. 7380 = Ahmet III 1952.

34 Karatay, *Arapça Yazmalar* III, 197, No. 5256 = Ahmet III 1621. It seems that the same person transcribed vols. III and IV of the *Jāmiʾ aṣ-ṣaḥīḥ* by al-Bukhārī: see Karatay, *Arapça Yazmalar* II, 29, No. 2264 and 30, No. 2265, where the name Abū l-Faḍl Muḥammad b. ʿAbd al-Wahhāb as-Sunbāṭī al-Aʿraj is given.

35 Istanbul, Süleymaniye, Fatih 4517; cf. GAL S II 39.

36 Karatay, *Arapça Yazmalar* III, 14, No. 4718 = Ahmet III 1452.

37 Karatay, *Arapça Yazmalar* I, 75, No. 265 = Revan, 18.

38 Karatay, *Arapça Yazmalar* III, 717, No. 6948 = Ahmet III 1396.

that of another protégé of the Grand Amīr Yashbek and of Sultan Qaytbay, the Cadi of the Army Shamsaddīn Muḥammad b. Maḥmūd b. Khalīl Ibn Ajā (1417-1476/7). In addition to a number of works in Arabic, Ibn Ajā did also compose a Turkish version of the *Futūḥ ash-Shām* by al-Wāqidī. Until F.E. Karatay identified and briefly described part II of this "Conquest of Syria",[39] as-Sakhāwī had been the only source for the existence of such a book of "twelve thousand Turkish verses".[40] This *juz'* II of the Turkish version is a beautifully executed copy, made for Sultan Qaytbay's library, who in Dhū l-ḥijja 895/beg. 16th October 1490 dedicated it to the library of the Dome which he had built on the outskirts of Cairo, near Pilgrims Lake (Birkat al-Ḥājj) and Siryaqaws.[41]

Among the autographs produced for Ghawrī there is an Arabic History of the Caliphs by ʿOmar b. Muḥammad b. Aḥmad al-Ḥanafī.[42]

The Sharīf Ḥusayn b. Ḥasan, who translated the *Shāhnāma* into Turkish verse, working first in the Dome of the Amīr Yaṣhbek, and later in the Mosque of Sultan Mu'ayyad, produced a fine autograph presentation copy for Sultan Ghawrī,[43] which was further decorated by miniatures.[44]

Before I end this paper, which is dedicated to the memory of Gaston Wiet, the great Mamluk scholar, I wish to call attention to a source of text reproduction apparently peculiar to the Mamluk institution.

Among the manuscripts of Mamluk origin we find a number of outwardly very similar volumes with ex libris in white ink on gold and blue and also with illuminated headpieces, usually written in large round characters. Some of them have the appearance of being copied by inexperienced hands, but others are in neat consistent Naskhī. They are all signed by Mamluks with their typical Turkish names, often with the name of their former owner and that of the Sultan to whom they owed service, and in several cases with that of the barracks where they were brought up.

Transcripts were made by members of the following barracks:

39 Karatay, *Türkçe Yazmalar* I, 164, No. 489 = Koğuşlar 883.

40 *Ḍaw'* X, 43; GAL II, 42; A. Schimmel, "Kalif und Kadi," 40 f.

41 I should like to thank the directors and staff of the Topkapı Sarayı Müzesi Kütüphanesi for their kindness, and Dr. Petra Kappert for bringing me a photograph of the title page and the last page of this MS, from which the above is taken.

42 Karatay, *Arapça Yazmalar* III, 436, No. 6058 = Ahmet III 2823.

43 Karatay, *Türkçe Yazmalar* II, 58, No. 2155 = Hazine 1519. A. Zajączkowski published parts of this work from this manuscript in his *Turecka wersja Šāh-nāme z Egiptu Mameluckiego* (Warsaw, 1965), and in *Rocznik Orientalistyczny*; see *Der Islam* 45 (1969), 175-177.

44 N. Atasoy, "1510 Tarihli Memlûk Şahnamesinin Minyatürleri," in *Sanat Tarihi Araştırmaları* II (Istanbul, 1969), 49-69.

- *al-Arbaʿīn*:[45] members were Rūḥī al-Mamlūk, named Qaraja, who wrote (and copied?) his Turkish *dīwān* of mostly religious poetry (London, British Museum, Or. 4128),[46] and al-Mamlūk Barsbay min Ṭuman Bay, who copied an Arabic *Qiṣṣat Mūsā* (Istanbul, Topkapı Sarayı, Bağdat Köşkü 41).[47]
- *al-Ḥawsh*:[48] al-Mamlūk Sanṭabay ash-Sharīfī, who describes himself as a pupil of the Shaykh Shihābaddīn Aḥmad al-Fayyūmī, copied a *Mukhtaṣar Sīrat an-Nabī* in Arabic, dated 1495 (Topkapı Sarayı Ahmet III 2796);[49] Tenibek min Tashbek copied a book of prayers in Arabic and Oghuz Turkish (Topkapı Sarayı, Revan Köşkü 1717).[50] Whereas these manuscripts were clearly copied for Sultan Qaytbay, a certain Shād Bek min Özdemir, a member of the same *ṭabaqa* (al-Ḥawsh), copied a collection of religious poems entitled *al-Qaṣāʾid ar-rabbānīya* in Arabic and Turkish for Sultan Qanısawh al-Ghawrī, who is the author of some of these poems (Topkapı Sarayı, Bağdat Köşkü 138).[51]
- *az-Zimāmīya*:[52] an anonymous *Kitāb ül-miʿrāj* was transcribed for Sultan Ghawrī's library by the Mamluk Qaḍābirdi min Ḫayrbek (Topkapı Sarayı, Koğuşlar 989);[53]
- *al-Ashrafīya*:[54] the Mamluk Jānmar[d] min Özdemür, al-Malikī al-Ashrafī, on the 10th Dhū l-qaʿda 915/19th February 1510 finished his transcript of an

45 According to D. Ayalon, *L'Esclavage du Mamelouk* (Jerusalem, 1951), this *ṭabaqa* is mentioned most rarely in the sources.

46 See G.M. Meredith-Owens, in *Oriens* 18-19 (1967), 497. By the kindness of the British Museum and of Prof. Meredith-Owens, I obtained a microfilm of this manuscript.

47 Karatay, *Arapça Yazmalar* III, 410, No. 5984. The colophon reads *katabahu al-Mamlūk Barsbay min Ṭuman Bay min ṭabaqa al-Arbaʿīn al-Malikī al-Ashrafī* (fol. 20a). While in Istanbul in 1968, I took notes of some of these colophons, on which systematic research should be done.

48 This *ṭabaqa* is mentioned frequently according to Ayalon, *Esclavage*, 12.

49 Karatay, *Arapça Yazmalar* III, 422, No. 6019. Colophon: *min kitābat al-Mamlūk Sanṭabay ash-Sharīfī min ṭabaqat al-Ḥawsh al-Malikī al-Ashrafī tilmīdh ash-Shaykh Shihābaddīn Aḥmad al-Fayyūmī* (61b).

50 On the Turkish poems see J. Eckmann, "Mamluk-kiptschakische Literatur," p. 299, with earlier literature. Described as an Arabic manuscript in Karatay, *Arapça Yazmalar* III, 282, No. 5550.

51 See Eckmann, "Mamluk-kiptschakische Literatur," 300. Compare Karatay, *Arapça Yazmalar* IV, 339, No. 8606, where the copyist is not mentioned.

52 Mentioned very frequently according to Ayalon, *Esclavage*, 12 (*ṭabaqat az-Zimām*); compare Popper, *op. cit.* (above, n. 4), I, 22.

53 Karatay, *Türkçe Yazmalar* II, 108, No. 2303.

54 Also mentioned quite frequently; see Ayalon, *Esclavage*, 12; compare Popper, *op. cit.* (above, n. 4), I, 22.

anonymous Arabic book entitled *aṭ-Ṭarīq al-maslūk fī siyāsat al-mulūk* (Topkapı Sarayı, Ahmet III 1608);[55] and the Mamluk Bektimur ar-Ramaḍānī, also al-Malikī al-Ashrafī, transcribed the *Kitāb Nūr al-ʿuyūn talḫīṣ siyar al-Amīn wa l-Maʾmūn* (?) (Topkapı Sarayı, Ahmet III 3032);[56] a member of the *ṭabaqa al-Ashrafīya al-kubrā*, apparently the same barracks, was the Mamluk Esenbay min Sudun, who transcribed the *Muqaddimat aṣ-ṣalāt* by Abū l-Layth as-Samarqandī with the Turkish interlinear translation by an unknown (Istanbul, Süleymaniye, Aya Sofya 1451);[57]

- *al-Mustajadda*:[58] the Mamluk Berdibek min اصابه al-Malikī al-Ashrafī transcribed an "anonymous" *Ādāb al-mulūk* in Arabic (Topkapı Sarayı, Bağdat Köşkü 91);[59]
- *as-Sunbulīya*:[60] the Mamluk Temür, al-Malikī al-Ashrafī, transcribed an "anonymous" *Nuzhat al-anām wa miṣbāh aẓ-ẓalām*, a collection of prayers in Arabic (Topkapı Sarayı, Bağdat Köşkü 88).[61]

In addition to this group of transcripts in which barrack membership is indicated, there is a greater series of manuscripts, copied also by Mamluks but without indication of their barracks, with the reservation that it may have been omitted in manuscript descriptions. I cite only two examples: the Mamluk Ayās al-Maḥmūdī al-Malikī aẓ-Ẓāhirī transcribed a *Mukhtaṣar Sīrat an-Nabī* for Sultan Jaqmaq (1438-1453) (Topkapı Sarayı, Revan Köşkü 1582);[62] and the Mamluk by the Muslim name of Manṣūr b. Yūsuf al-Malikī al-Ashrafī who transcribed *Miʾa kalima ... min kalām ... ʿAlī b. Abī Ṭālib*, in Arabic with Turkish paraphrase (Topkapı Sarayı, Bağdat Köşkü 122).[63]

With the exception of Revan 1727 and Ahmet III 1608, all volumes enumerated above have less than 100 folios; Or. 4128, Ahmet III 2796 and Revan 1582 consist of more than fifty folios, but the remainder contain only between 47

55 Karatay, *Arapça Yazmalar* III, 727, No. 6982, without the copyist's name.

56 Karatay, *Arapça Yazmalar* III, 424, No. 6025.

57 Eckmann, "Mamluk-kiptschakische Literatur," 301, with bibliography. Facsimile edition by A. Zajączkowski, *Le traité arabe Muḳaddima d'Abou-l-Lait as-Samarḳandī en version mamelouk-kiptchak* (Warsaw, 1962).

58 Rarely mentioned in the sources according to Ayalon, *Esclavage*, 12.

59 Karatay, *Arapça Yazmalar* III, 727, No. 6981, without the copyist's name.

60 This (from Karatay) is not found in Ayalon, *Esclavage*, 11-12.

61 Karatay, *Arapça Yazmalar* III, 320, No. 5674.

62 Karatay, *Arapça Yazmalar* III, 428, No. 6035.

63 Karatay, *Arapça Yazmalar* III, 708, No. 6922. Published from this manuscript by A. Zajączkowski, *Sto sentencyj i apoftegmatów arabskich Kalifa ʿAlīego w parafrazie Mamelucko-Tureckiej* (Warsaw, 1968), with a complete facsimile (fols. 1a–18a).

and 18 folios. In this group the small number of lines to the page (between seven and three) and the size of the script betray a tendency to fill up as much space as possible with the least quantity of writing. Whereas the scripts of the more bulky volumes tend to a calligraphic standard, in the other manuscripts we see more inexperienced hands, some neat, some cramped and rude. Section headings are often in red, blue, or white ink on gold. Most of these manuscripts have the characteristic circular, indented Mamluk medallion of the period.[64]

The fact that each of these transcripts was made by a different Mamluk, the unequal quality of the scripts as well as the rich decoration, all seem to suggest that most of these manuscripts belonged to a larger number of texts which might be called special school-exercises of the Mamluks,[65] in which emphasis was laid on standards of calligraphy. We have seen how one successful student (Sanṭabay) paid his respects to his teacher (Fayyūmī), from whom survive two manuscripts transcribed for Sultan Qaytbay (see above).

It is known that in the first stage of the student Mamluk's education teaching concentrated on religion in its theological and practical aspects (Coran, Shariʿa, prayers); the principal subject was the reading and writing of Arabic, in which, after the earliest stages, almost all instruction must have been carried on. Besides the eunuchs, in whose care were the *kuttābīs*, doctors of law and other scholars taught in the barracks,[66] Qaraja, with the pen name Rūḥī, the author (and scribe?) of Or. 4128 mentioned above, may have been among these teachers. Since teaching at the second (military) stage was done by soldiers, Turkish must have been used for oral instruction. In addition to the bulk of military textbooks and books on the veterinary art in Arabic,[67] a number of

64 Typical examples in print: Sultan Ghawrī's ex libris in *Rocznik Orientalistyczny* 23/1 (1959), p. 75; see also the editions quoted in nn. 57 (*Muqaddima*) and 43 (*Shāhnāma*).

65 Comparable to the exercises written by the Jeunes de Langues in eighteenth century Pera, analyzed by V.L. Ménage, "Another text of Uruč's Ottoman chronicle," in *Der Islam* 47 (1971), 276-277. F.E. Karatay's catalogue of the Arabic manuscripts in the Topkapı Sarayı Müzesi, an inexhaustible mine of information on the libraries of the later Mamluk Sultans, is tantalizingly reticent on the subject of colophons. I quote the numbers in his *Arapça Yazmalar* I–IV (1962-1969) of a few more manuscripts transcribed by what I take to be Mamluk graduates, all for Sultan Ghawrī's library: 251, 3141, 4772, 5403, 5557, 5610, 5644, 5675, 6926, and 8539 (with an improbable date). With the exception of one Coran copied "in awkward naskhī" (no. 251), these manuscripts all number an average of 25 folios and of 5 lines to the page.

66 Ayalon, *Esclavage*, 48, note 112.

67 On the first group see J.D. Latham & W.F. Paterson, *Saracen Archery* (London, 1970). Examples of veterinary books are the sumptuous *Kitāb az-zardaqa* in the University Library in Istanbul, A.Y. 4689, described by Fehmi Edhem [Karatay] and I. Stchoukine, *Les Manuscrits orientaux illustrés de la Bibliothèque de l'Université de Stamboul* (Paris, 1933), 49, No.

such books were written in Turkish. Surviving manuals in Turkish on these and other matters, such as legal handbooks, have been described by J. Eckmann.[68]

The subject matter of the manuscripts inspected above and in note 65 falls under the headings of Coran, religious prose, religious poetry in Arabic and Turkish, prayers, ethics, Biography of the Prophet Muḥammad, and History of the Prophets.

If our assumption is correct that, at least in Qaytbay's and Ghawrī's times, Mamluk graduates were required to write exercises which then became part of the Sultan's library, we still cannot say whether these were written at the end of the first stage of education, or whether they formed part of the coming-out formalities before manumission. If they were part of an examination, the question is also whether all student Mamluks or only the elite, the Royal Mamluks, were required to take it.

The fact that a considerable number of these manuscripts are described as "anonymous" works or "abridged versions" raises the question whether some of the student Mamluks were set tasks going beyond mere copying, such as producing shortened versions like the *Mukhtaṣar Sīrat an-Nabī* written for Sultan Jaqmaq (Revan 1582, mentioned above), or translating into Turkish. The short interlinear Turkish translation contained in the MS Bağdat Köşkü 123, which consists of sayings spoken by the Imām ʿAlī,[69] seems to have just the right size for an examination paper in cases where competence in written Turkish was required.

If we accept the evidence that there existed a practice with a two-fold purpose, to train Mamluks and to supplement the Sultans' libraries,[70] we can hardly expect to find the names of these young scribes, who were just beginning their careers, in the biographical sources of the period. Incidentally, there is at least one manuscript in which an amīr who has higher rank and a library of his own, has his barracks (az-Zimām) indicated in his ex libris.[71]

XLIII, Pl. XV (the name of the book's owner has not yet been read satisfactorily); another is the *Kitāb fī ʿilm al-bayṭara wa aḥwāl al-ḥayl*, copied for the library of the Grand Amīr Özdemir min Inal, mihmāndār of Sultan Ghawrī (Topkapı Sarayı, III Ahmet 1959, described by Karatay, *Arapça Yazmalar* III, 873, No. 7407).

68 J. Eckmann, "The Mamluk-Kipchak Literature," in *Central Asiatic Journal* 8 (1963), 304-319; idem, "Mamluk-kiptschakische Literatur," 300-304.

69 Karatay, *Arapça Yazmalar* III, 707, No. 6919; not mentioned by Eckmann "Mamluk-kiptschakische Literatur."

70 Compare Ménage, *Uruč*, 276.

71 On fol. 334b I read *wa kutiba bi-rasm al-janāb al-ʿālī Qānṣūh b. ʿAbdallāh min Yaġībaṣṭī al-Ḥāṣṣakī min ṭabaqa az-Zimām*; the date is the 15th Shaʿbān 879/25th December 1474. Karatay, *Arapça Yazmalar* III, 407, No. 5972 = III Ahmet 2861.

The preceding remarks are necessarily incomplete. At a time when the cultural achievement of Mamluk Egypt and Syria, an "Islamic Byzantium",[72] is being re-examined, the valuable material contained in books surviving from Mamluk libraries merits the attention of scholars.

Postscript note: I am most grateful to Professor P.M. Holt, London, for giving me a photocopy of ʿAbdalwahhāb ʿAzzām, *Majālis as-Sultān al-Ghawrī. Ṣafaḥāt min tảrīḫ Miṣr fī l-qarn al-ʿāshir al-hijrī* (Cairo, 1941), which contains a partial edition of the *Nafāʾis* (n. 9) and part I *Kawkab* (n. 10).

72 B. Lewis, "Egypt and Syria," in *The Cambridge History of Islam* I (Cambridge, 1970), 228.

CHAPTER 10

Languages of Turkish Poets*, **

In Eastern Anatolia, so the biographer of poets ʿĀşıq Çelebi informs us, there lived a teacher and companion of the D̲ūlqadir prince ʿAlī Beg b. Şehsuvār (d. 1522),[1] a certain Şükrī by name. When the Ottoman Sultan Selīm I (1512-1520) ascended the throne, Şükrī addressed him with a request to enter his service. His petition (*ʿarż-i ḥāl*), as far as the passages that interest us here, reads:

> Hear, oh falcon on the Lote Tree,
> My word that the heavens praise!
> I am the servant Şükrī, presently without office,
> An insignificant bondsman of the Sultan...
> I know Traditions and Koran commentary,
> Have studied jurisprudence and interpretation.
> (Am skilled in meter and rhyme,
> an expert in enigma and riddle).
> I am a poet. Behold, my work lies before you.
> I have composed *ġazel*s in six languages.
> In Turkish I write poems as fluently as Navāʾī,
> And do the same in Persian, like Bannāʾī.
> I speak Arabic and am a speaker of Kurdish...
> The Armenian language I know to perfection,
> And I am proficient as well in Indian.
> I was once a professor and a judge,
> And in past times also a preacher.

(Some description follows of how irresistible his preaching was).

> I know what a good horse is and a good dog,
> I am knowledgeable about falcons and hunting panthers.
> I draw a crooked bow and shoot a straight arrow;
> I speak my mind frankly and do not sell myself.

---

* Translated by John O'Kane.

** What follows is a revised translation of my inaugural oration as Professor Extraordinary at the Rijksuniversiteit Leiden, given in German, on 16 September 1977.

1 This detail comes from ʿĀlī: see F. Babinger, *Die Geschichtsschreiber der Osmanen und ihre Werke*, Leipzig 1927, p. 51.

 | DOI 10.1163/9789004355767_011

With Turks I'm a Turk, with Kurds a Kurd,
At home I'm a sheep, abroad I'm a wolf...
I also propose myself as a boon companion:
The friend who weeps I bring round to laughter.

Despite all these gifts of intelligence, he goes on to say, science has brought him no profit. Only through poetry has he made a name for himself. He is therefore ready to compose poetry about whatever the Sultan commands. This simple poem which the Ottoman ʿĀşıq Çelebi presents along with its element of Āzerī Turkish[2] in which Şükrī still wrote at that time,[3] in fact brought its author a high post in the Ottoman provincial administration and a position of trust at the court.[4]

Şükrī's request provides a good illustration of one possibility of Ottoman multilingualism in which Turkish, Persian, Arabic, Kurdish and Armenian were normal and only "Indian" stands out as unusual. We are accustomed to hear about "the three languages" which Turkish poets used during the 14th to the 16th century, i.e. at a time when Turkish and Turkish-speaking dynasties ruled the Near East from Asia Minor, Mesopotamia and Syria/Egypt across the Iranian plateau up to Western Central Asia and maintained various forms of contact among one another.

Being "cultivated" in that world was, practically speaking, a synonym for being bilingual or multilingual.[5] The ability of the educated to communicate effortlessly was impressive. On journeys as well as when accompanying commanders during war, they found the opportunity to exchange ideas with local people.[6] When the Ottoman government secretary for the Sultan's monogram (*nīşāncı*), Celālzāde Muṣṭafā, was in Tabriz with the Ottoman army in July 1534,

2 *Meşāʿir üş-Şuʿarā or Teẕkere of ʿĀşıḳ Çelebi*. Edited by G.M. Meredith-Owens, London 1971, fol. 249a-b. Compared with fol. 331 of the Vienna manuscript, Flügel II, p. 371, no. 1219, that Meredith-Owens refers to as T.

3 The very polemical *qaṣīda* with which Şükrī at a later time attempted to rouse Sultan Süleymān to wage Holy War against the Qızılbaş maintains a stately Ottoman Turkish throughout: ʿĀşıq Çelebi, op. cit.

4 He received a "fief" (*zeʿāmet*) in the region of Diyārbekr, became an intimate courtier of Selīm I whose Qızılbaş campaign he described and he accompanied Sultan Süleymān on his campaigns against Belgrade and Rhodes, without living long enough to participate in the latter's campaign against the Ṣafavids. ʿĀşıq Çelebi op. cit.; F. Babinger, *Geschichtsschreiber*, pp. 51 f.

5 U. Weinreich, *Sprachen in Kontakt. Ergebnisse und Probleme der Zweisprachigkeitsforschung*, München 1977, p. 105. Cf. Uriel Weinrich (1926-1967), *Languages in Contact. Findings and Problems*, New York 1953, The Hague 1963.

6 After the capture of Tabriz by the Ottomans in 1526 Taʿlīqīzāde conversed with notables of the

while conversing he presented some high-ranking local religious scholars with excerpts from a history work dealing with his era (i.e. the era of Sultan Süleymān) which he had written in Turkish, and had the satisfaction of receiving in return Persian verses of praise which he incorporated in his book.[7]

One could cite innumerable examples of non-Arab writers of that time, including many Turks, who dealt with specific subjects in Arabic, as well as examples of non-Persians who wrote in Persian. The reverse situation – non-Turks who wrote in Turkish – is without a doubt less common but can also be demonstrated. Here a multitude of factors play a role, in particular cultural dominance and the usefulness for an individual of mastering and employing a language. Just as in Christian Europe where in the Middle Ages and the Renaissance Latin was in international use,[8] there were always reasons that led individual authors to employ a language other than their mother tongue in order to communicate their ideas to the public.

For religious and scientific purposes it was common practice to employ Arabic which in the ranking order of the three Islamic languages – based ultimately on religion – occupied first place. Aside from the fact that it was the language of revelation and the Traditions from the Prophet, Arabic possessed a vocabulary that was indispensable for treating scientific subjects. We are here speaking of Middle Arabic, used by writers in the established disciplines in as "classical" a form as their *medrese* education made possible but which inevitably succumbed to a certain interference from an author's mother tongue. It brought considerable prestige to the person who mastered it. An example from the Ottoman court illustrates this point. The Persian religious scholar and physician Qazvīnī, by means of the elegance with which he presented his medical explanations in Arabic, amazed the physicians of the Porte who beheld "how Ibn Nubāta (d. 1014), the most correct of Arab men of elo-

---

city: J.R. Walsh, "The Historiography of Ottoman-Safavid Relations", in *Historians of the Middle East* (eds. B. Lewis and P.M. Holt), London 1964, p. 202.

7 *Ṭabaqāt ül-memālik*, manuscript of the Staatsbibliothek Preußischer Kulturbesitz, Ms. or. quart 1961, fol. 250b-251a. I owe my knowledge of this passage to the late Dr. Petra Kappert, who was then preparing her edition of the text, which appeared as *Geschichte Sultan Süleymān Kanūnīs von 1520 bis 1557 oder Ṭabaqāt ül-Memālik ve Derecāt ül-Mesālik von Celālzade Muṣṭafā genannt Ḳoca Nişāncı*, in Facsimile herausgegeben von Petra Kappert, Wiesbaden 1981.

8 Fundamental for our subject are: H.J. Chaytor, *From Script to Print. An Introduction to Medieval Vernacular Literature*, Cambridge 1952, especially Chapter III "Language and Nationality", and L. Forster, *The Poet's Tongues: Multilingualism in Literature*, Cambridge 1970.

quence, looked like a barbarian alongside this non-Arab" (wordplay with *ʿacam*).[9]

To the extent that the Turks were adherents of the Ḥanafi School of jurisprudence, in principle their language too might have profited from the dispensation according to which, in the last resort, the ritual prayer of a believer who did not know Arabic was also valid in Persian.[10] But with regard to this long-standing controversy, which ultimately went back to the issue of the Koran's untranslatable character, Sunnī theologians mostly held the viewpoint that the believer who did not master Arabic could all too easily come into conflict with the religious law. After being cautioned to that effect, the Aqqoyunlu ruler Uzun Ḥasan (ruled 1453-1478) on one occasion felt constrained to wash down some pages on which he had written his religious thoughts which in any case were not in Arabic but possibly in Turkish.[11] Whereas in pre-Ottoman Turkish Anatolia of the 14th century it seemed that Turkish could be used freely and without compunction not only for the "external" sciences but also for religious-ethical purposes,[12] in the 16th century two great Ottoman religious scholars endeavored to discourage the use of non-Arabic, i.e. Persian and especially Turkish, in Islamic ritual practice. Persian had won second place in the hierarchy of Islamic languages but not without a struggle, as the following hostile *ḥadīth* testifies: "The language most hated by Allāh is Persian, the language of the satans is Khūzī, that of the dwellers in Hell Bukhārī and that of the blessed in Paradise Arabic."[13]

---

9 ʿĀşıq Çelebi (see here fn. 2), fol. 246b, Ms. T 325b-326a. On Şāh Muḥammad Qazvīnī cf. H. Sohrweide, "Dichter und Gelehrte aus dem Osten im osmanischen Reich (1453-1600). Ein Beitrag zur türkisch-persischen Kulturgeschichte", in *Der Islam* 46 (1970), pp. 266 f. and passim.

10 R. Brunschvig, "Kemâl Pâshâzâde et le persan", in *Mélanges d'Orientalisme offerts à Henri Massé*, Teheran 1963, p. 59.

11 W. Hinz, *Irans Aufstieg zum Nationalstaat im fünfzehnten Jahrhundert*, Berlin/Leipzig 1936, pp. 119-20.

12 Cf. my "Faḫrīs Ḫusrev u Šīrīn vom Jahre 1367", the first chapter in this volume.

13 J. Fück, *Arabiya*, Berlin 1950, p. 112; cf. R. Brunschvig, "Kemâl Pâshâzâde", p. 56. When Hoca Neş'et (d. 1807-8) was asked whether Persian was indeed the language of hell, he replied: "If it is so, it were as well to learn it; one can never tell where one may go…", E.J.W. Gibb, *A History of Ottoman Poetry*, vol. IV, edited by E.G. Browne, London 1905, reprint 1967, pp. 214-215. "While the religious scholars' studies required mastery of Arabic, Ottoman scribal intellectuals needed to study Persian as well. Some of the pious would say of this: 'Whoever studies Persian pays half of his debt'", Carter Vaughn Findley, *Ottoman Civil Officialdom. A Social History*, Princeton 1989, p. 36f., in his assessment of Ottoman *adab*-culture.

Clearly alluding to this, the encyclopaedist Ṭaşköprüzāde Aḥmed Efendi (d. 1561), who for the most part wrote in Arabic, warned preachers against using Persian and non-Arabic (by which he obviously meant Turkish) in their sermons, both being "languages of the dwellers in Hell".[14] It is true that in a small text the Mufti Kemālpaşazāde (1468-1534) extolled, with religious arguments, the Persian language, but that was as far as he would go; he would not allow the use of any other language for ritual practice.[15] Both attempted to restrain the uncontrolled advance of their vernacular language and were also certainly concerned on behalf of Arabic as the language of religious scholars.

It may be that Kemālpaşazāde, who was called "the mufti of human beings and angels", had in mind a further attack on some very specific "dwellers in Hell", namely the Ṣafavids whom he himself had actually condemned as heretics in a well-known *fetwā*.[16] The latter did indeed make use of the vernaculars for their religious propaganda; not only Turkish among their Anatolian and Azerbaijani followers, but also Persian among their Persian adherents. They took as their authority the founder of their order, Shaykh Ṣafī, who had said that the lack of Arabic did not matter among speakers of Turkish, Tajik and Kurdish, as long as the heart understood the – Arabic – language of the Lord.[17]

As far as language was here brought into the religious-political struggle, it should be noted that in this case the Ottoman side did not in fact push forward the promotion of its own language. The Ottomans, having now become a great Islamic power, in an equal measure fostered Arabic as the language of Islamic ritual and theology, Persian as the esteemed language of poetry, while their own Ottoman Turkish became the official language throughout the vast Ottoman bureaucracy.

No language was suppressed – otherwise Şükrī whom we mentioned at the beginning would scarcely have boasted of his native language; but due to the higher social status that it conferred Ottoman Turkish in the long run pushed the non-Turkish local languages into the background.

In the past much has been said about the fact that political hostility toward the Ṣafavid state in no way diminished the aesthetic appreciation of educated

14 *Miftāḥ as-saʿāda*, translation by O. Rescher, Stuttgart 1934, pp. 62-63. A preacher should choose "the most excellent of languages", i.e. Arabic which is the language of Paradise; conversely, one should not use non-Arabic and Persian, both of which are the language of the dwellers in Hell, except in an extreme emergency" (in Rescher: "in this context [cf. 'both of which'!] obviously Turkish").

15 R. Brunschvig, "Kemâl Pâshâzâde", pp. 52-59.

16 Ibid., p. 64.

17 E. Glassen, *Die frühen Safawiden nach Qāżī Aḥmad Qumī*, Freiburg im Breisgau 1968, pp. 7-8.

Ottomans for the literary culture that found expression in the Persian language. Likewise, in the East the poet prince, Mīr ʿAlī Şīr Navāʾī (d. 1501), when he set up his "court of arbitration regarding the two languages" Turkish and Persian, paid a respectful tribute to Persian culture: in the realm of ideas and science the Persian was more subtle, and more penetrating in his thinking; the Turk, however, possessed the gift of quicker perception and a more pure and salubrious temperament.[18] When Navāʾī, faced with the arts and sciences, philosophy and men of letters among the Persians, deploys the loyalty, sincerity and straightforward honesty of the Turks, it makes one think of the apologetic voices that were once raised to promote the European vernaculars in opposition to Greek and Latin. The Germans too saw themselves and their language as rough and uncouth, and attempted to make up for it by referring to their steady character and loyalty.[19]

Navāʾī's appeal for the use of Turkish as a language for poetry is so impressive because he is the first to apply philological criteria to prove that his language is richer in morphological possibilities, is more expressive (thanks to a greater number of nuanced expressions), and is richer in homophony, and above all in vocabulary. It is clear that in his professed intention to encourage the poets of his homeland to use their Turkish mother tongue, overtones of affection play a role in his relationship with the language. Devereux' assessment of this attitude as linguistic "chauvinism"[20] loses its credibility through his own translation.[21] But it is noteworthy that precisely among the Eastern Turks, where at the time in question the Persian element is in fact described as culturally dominant, a state of awareness manifests itself which Uriel Weinreich has called "language loyalty", i.e. a sense of one's language being threatened that emerges from a situation of close linguistic contact and frustrated feelings of superiority.[22]

For the Western Turks a long road still lay ahead before a new idea, born in the European Romantic movement, would emerge, namely that an official language was to be seen as a national heritage, indeed the embodiment of a

18 Mīr ʿAlī Şīr Navāʾī, *Muḥākamat al-Luġatayn*, ed. E.M. Quatremère, *Chrestomathie en turk oriental contenant plusieurs ouvrages de l'émir Ali-Schir…*, Paris 1841, pp. 1-39. This text is reprinted in Devereux (see here fn. 20).

19 From among many possible examples I cite H. v. Hofmannsthal, *Wert und Ehre deutscher Sprache* (19271), pp. 146 and 179.

20 R. Devereux, *Muḥākamat al-Luğhatain by Mīr ʿAlī Shīr. Introduction, translation and notes*, Leiden 1966, p. IX.

21 As long as no critical text-edition and literal translation exist, one can best consult the Turkish translation by İ.R. Işıtman, *Muhakemet-ül-lûgateyn*, Ankara 1941.

22 U. Weinreich, *Sprachen in Kontakt* (see here ftn. 5), pp. 131-35.

people's soul, as a property well as worth fighting for; a property that needed purifying, a task of purism, and protection against purism – the cause of the anti-purist counter-movement. In the Turkish Republic which by law protects its citizens, for example, from Kurdish publications from abroad,[23] alongside the purists anti-purist voices have more recently made themselves heard which defend borrowed vocabulary as war booty from the glorious old days that has become indigenous, as a possession which one ought not to renounce any more than one would renounce a piece of the homeland.[24]

But let us return to the era of Sultan Selīm I, surnamed the Grim, before whom Şükrī could so unabashedly present himself as a Kurd. Like other sovereigns of his time Selīm enjoyed conversing about linguistic matters. He once said to Kemālpaşazāde who accompanied him on the campaign in Egypt: "It seems odd that Seyyidī ʿAlīzāde should write a commentary in Arabic on the *Gulistān* which is after all in Persian." "How should he do otherwise?", retorted the mullah. "He doesn't really know any Persian and why should he set out on an erroneous path by doing it other than in Arabic?" And so at the same time "he unmasked the commentator in a jocular way".[25] For his part the Egyptian Sultan Qanīṣawh al-Ġawrī, against whom Sultan Selīm had set out on campaign, as a born Circassian felt proud of the eight languages he mastered, liked to discuss in his evening conversations the question of the origin of language (Adam spoke Arabic in Paradise), and to inform himself about what was spoken and written at other courts. Having a sound grasp of Ottoman poetry and having himself composed poems in that language, at the same time he showed an interest in the Timurids and consequently also had something recited to him in Eastern Turkish: in this way a verse by Ḥusayn Bayqara (d. 1506) found its way into the Arabic minutes of his evening gatherings.[26]

---

23 According to law no. 6/7635 of 25/1/1967, "the import and distribution of printed matter, phonograph records, cassette tapes and suchlike in Kurdish is forbidden". *T.C. Resmî Gazete* of 14/2/1967.

24 "The words that our nation has conquered so as to dominate other nations not only by the power of the sword but also by the power of culture and the mind, she has phonetically and semantically Turkified and made use of them thus", E. Bayrakdaroğlu, cited by T. Yücel, *Dil Devrimi*, Istanbul 1968, p. 30. "From regions they entered with a sword in one hand and a firebrand in the other the Turkish armies did not take away with them words on some temporary basis or as a loan. They (the words) are a kind of 'war booty'. Whatever pleased them they added to their language – the way they added a beautiful princess to their harem", H.N. Zorlutuna, cited by Yücel, op. cit. – "To rob Turkish of those words which have become indigenous here is as false as to give away a piece of the fatherland", E. Bayrakdaroğlu, cited by Yücel, op. cit.

25 ʿĀşıq Çelebi, fol. 38a, 20-22; cf. Ms. T, fol. 46a.

26 Cf. my "From the Evening Talks of Ġavrī", no. 7 in this volume.

It is tempting to investigate the reality of the linguistic diversity as it is reflected in many contemporary sources. But before we turn to consider briefly the paths of reception of Turkish literature, we should visualize for ourselves how linguistic differences found expression in the narrative literature of these societies that were so interested in philological matters. Was the difficulty of communication between different peoples represented at all? In narrative literature as in *ġazel* poetry one finds brief remarks along the lines of: "I am a Turk and cannot speak Persian."[27]

If we consider the more historical sections in the *Shāhnāma* where Turks appear, we see that Firdawsī does no more than indicate the difference between *pahlavī*/*pahlavānī* and *turkī* (rarely *tūrī*), to bridge which interpreters (*tarcumān*) are employed.[28] Since in the *Shāhnāma* and in the epic poetry it has inspired many letters come to be written, scribes are continually engaged who are "also in the service of non-Muslim, even non-human rulers".[29] They read out letters and write answers without any language difficulties ever being indicated. Thus the Sassanian Shah and the Emperor of Byzantium can exchange friendly or irate letters, and in so doing it comes to pass that the Byzantine Emperor deciphers a letter from Chosroes Parvīz "written entirely in Pahlavī" without the help of a scribe.[30]

From authors who treat an imaginary world of fantastical history and vague topography we cannot expect any consistency in matters of language.[31] In the Turkish *ʿIsqnāme* (1397), the kings of India, Kashmir and China fight one another in complete understanding as far as language is concerned, they hasten from country to country and are never lost for an answer if someone asks them in a friendly manner: "Now brothers, where do you come from? What are you buying and selling here?"[32]

---

27 Cf. the *ġazel* written in Chagatay by Qaramanlı Niẓāmī (the first hemistich is in Persian): *Türk oğlanı men anglamanam didi ʿacem-ni*: "'I am a Turkish youth', he said, 'and do not understand Persian'" (O.F. Sertkaya in *TDED* XIX [1971], p. 173).

28 Kowalski has pointed out that the Turks in the *Shāhnāma* appear as one uniform hostile mass without distinction being made between nomads and sedentary people or entering into any linguistic differences; T. Kowalski, "Les Turcs dans le *Šāh-nāme*", in *RO* XV (1939-40), pp. 93-95 and 98.

29 F. Meier, *Die schöne Mahsatī*, Wiesbaden 1963, p. 71.

30 E.E. Bertel's (ed.), *Firdousī, Šāch-nāme*, vol. IX, Moscow 1971, pp. 88 f. – Similarly, the Emperor's offers to give his daughter in marriage to the Iranian king which are recounted in the *Shāhnāma* and later in the *Humāynāme* are not hindered by any linguistic obstacles.

31 H.J. Chaytor (see here fn. 8), p. 26.

32 S. Yüksel, *Mehmed. Işk-Nâme*, Ankara 1965, verse 5805; A. Tietze, "Meḥemmeds *Buch der Liebe*", in *Festschrift. O. Spies*, Wiesbaden 1967, p. 677.

In Turkish works with a historical background such as the *Düstūrnāme*, the epic poem about the naval hero Umur Pasha, things happen with somewhat more nuanced distinctions. As in the *chansons de geste*, the Turkish sea-*ġāzī*s and the Frankish knights call out greetings to one another or insults on the field of battle. One example from among many: a Frank, the son of the dauphin, introduces himself thus: "I am the son of Torfil. Now tell me what your name is."[33] Two infidel women fall in love with the Turkish hero of the story, the beautiful Despina whom he meets while hunting and the mistress of the castle at Thermopylae who offers him her thirteen strongholds. Without having to call for an interpreter, they declare their love to him and he makes it clear to them that he cannot love them because he must fight against his carnal soul, the *nafs*.[34] Here as well letters are understood without any problem; even a religious dispute can be conducted without any language barriers. The Franks begin the dispute: "You (Umur Beg) have one God, we have three".[35] Only on one occasion in the *Düstūrnāme* is attention also directed to differences of language when an envoy of the Catalans says something "in his language" *dilince*.[36]

But why this preoccupation with how language is treated in stories? The differences in treatment could give us help with making distinctions within narrative literature. Take for example the *Dānişmendnāme* whose prose version is dated round about 1360/61. Here one notices a significantly greater closeness to reality when it comes to language. There is frequent mention of Greek, *Rūm dili*;[37] the Greeks declare in the Rūm language that they would prefer to become Muslims rather than to die.[38] Language as an obstacle to understanding is portrayed in an episode in which a Greek sings something *Rūm dilince* that the hero does not understand.[39] The Turks use their knowledge of Greek for ruses in war: by passing themselves off as people from Trebizond, they overrun a fortress; they write letters in Greek and send a female spy in disguise who knows their language. Small scraps of phrases are quoted such as: *Titi miti sunb-i ḫar-i ʿĪsā*.[40] This rather realistic treatment of Greek in the *Dānişmendnāme* should be examined in terms of its function in the work's structure and could result in new perspectives concerning its dating.

33 I. Mélikoff-Sayar, *Le Destān d'Umūr Pacha*, Paris 1954, p. 121, verse 2241.

34 Ibid., verses 559 and 1802.

35 Ibidem, verse 2029.

36 Ibid., verse 1087.

37 I. Mélikoff, *La Geste de Melik Dānişmend*, vol. II, Paris 1960, p. 26

38 Ibid., p. 236.

39 See here fn. 37.

40 Ibid., pp. 250, 260-61 and 270. On the scraps of Greek cf. the editor, ibid., vol. I, pp. 184 f.

However, Turkish poets, generally speaking, did not learn Greek. All Turkish men of letters, before they made creative use of their own or a foreign language, were readers of Arabic and Persian. In the domain of poetry, the language they learned was Persian, even though – for the reasons already mentioned – it was kept out of the *medrese* and was taught rather in children's schools, in some dervish convents and (despite the general tendency) in a few *medreses*.[41] The first verses written were in this acquired Persian language. The mistakes that still appeared one had corrected by a competent teacher.[42] This is how the young poet was introduced to the common Islamic heritage of poetic themes and set phrases. The relatively limited subject matter and the fact of working with transnational forms and topoi facilitated for poets a fluent literary mastery of a language that was not their mother tongue. The models had become imprinted on their mind. Thus one can understand why Navā'ī remarked that it is easier for beginners to write in Persian: it has also been said of Renaissance poets that it was often easier for them to write Latin than their own vernacular.[43]

The active participation of both Western and Eastern Turkish writers in Persian literature is a subject in its own right which cannot be dealt with here. But let us mention one of the tools of the trade which facilitated the learning process for them: dictionaries and commentaries.[44] In the world of Persian and Turkish artistic poetry there existed, to quote Uriel Weinreich: "a constant need for synonyms, an onomastic low pressure area, as it were. Wherever synonyms originating from another language were available, they were gratefully adopted."[45]

41 F.R. Unat, *Türkiye Eğitim Sisteminin Gelişmesine Tarihi Bir Bakış*, Ankara 1964, pp. 6 and 9; H. İnalcık, *The Ottoman Empire. The Classical Age 1300-1600*, p. 201.

42 Ṣādiqī, who was born in 1532 in Tabriz and for three years studied treatises on the science of poetry (*şiir ilmi*) in his home city under Mīr Ṣun'ī from Nishapur, was a student of Fezā'ī from Hamadan and in his early youth had his poems corrected by Ḥāfiẓ Ṣābūnī: T. Gandjeï, "Sâdikî-i Afşar'in Türkçe şiirleri", in *TM* XVI (1971), p. 20.

43 L. Foster, *The Poet's Tongues*, p. 29.

44 The Western Turks appear to have especially distinguished themselves in this area. The following dictionaries may be mentioned: the *Luġat-i Ḥalīmī* compiled for Meḥmed II in 1477/78, the *Şāmil al-luġa* put together for the latter's son Bāyezīd II, the *Tuḥfe-i Şāhidī* from 1514/15, the well-known *Daqā'iq al-ḥaqā'iq* by Kemālpaşazāde, the *Luġat-i Ni'metullāh*, a *Tuḥfet es-senīye ilā'l-ḥażret al-Ḥasenīye* (*Luġat-i Deşīsīye*(?)) from 1580-83, the *Tuḥfe-i Vehbī*; as well as the special dictionaries for the *Shāhnāma*, the *Mešnevī* and *Waṣṣāf*. And Turks have written commentaries on 'Aṭṭār, Calāleddīn Rūmī, Sa'dī, and Ḥāfiẓ, among others. In the Azerbaijani domain one may mention the *Tuḥfe-i Ḥüsām* (see *Fundamenta* II, p. 635) and later the *Sanglaḥ* (which used Rūmī sources as well).

45 U. Weinreich, *Sprachen in Kontakt*, p. 82.

Moreover, the flow was not always simply from Persian into Turkish. Not only had a large quantity of Turkish words flowed into the Persian language since the time of the Īlkhāns,[46] but Turkish poetry, especially since the time of the Ṣafavids for the reasons already indicated, had also come to occupy a stronger position in people's awareness. Persians translated Turkish works into their own language, compiled dictionaries, wrote occasionally in Turkish themselves, and imitated certain Turkish poets in Persian.

To sum up, the poets still presented their first works in an acquired language to which, for the sake of their public and in order to be understood, they might also switch over permanently (to Arabic, Persian or as in Şükrī's case to Turkish). But many took delight in exploiting the resources of their mother tongue, exercising it for serious poetic creation while expressing allegiance to their acquired languages: an acknowledged achievement known as *imitatio* in European literature.[47]

And then there was a further possibility of multilingualism for Turkish poets in the time period we are speaking about. To make oneself understood to a public who lived spread out across immense regions from Central Asia to the near East and whose dialects had drifted apart, three dialects that served as literary languages were available: Old Anatolian-Turkish or Ottoman (called *türk*, *türkī* and in the Mamlūk state *türkmenī*); East-Turkish (called *türkī* and later *çagatāyī*); and thirdly, Āzerī which lay between the other two and was designated as *türkī* or *türkmenī*.

Likewise, within these three literary dialects, by a certain analogy to the language hierarchy discussed earlier, there was the most respected of the dialects: East (Middle) Turkish. How did this come about?

The originally religious stimulus that had spurred on the study of Arabic as a native or a foreign language (e.g. its vocabulary or its pronunciation) likewise came to benefit Turkish, on behalf of which one could also cite the *ḥadīth*: "Learn the language of the Turks, for their rule will be of long duration." Under the influence of Arab philological methods and certainly under the influence of the Arab endeavor to preserve the language's purity, Maḥmūd al-Kāşġarī, who in 1072 undertook to describe Turkish languages for the first time, also spoke of the "purest" and "most correct" among the Turkish languages.[48] Al-Kāşġarī clas-

46 G. Doerfer, *Türkische und mongolische Elemente im Neupersischen*, vols. II-IV, Wiesbaden 1965-1975.

47 L. Foster, *The Poet's Tongues*, p. 33.

48 Tuḫşī and Yaġma; B. Atalay (translation), *Divanü Lûgat-it-Türk Tercümesi*, I, Ankara 1939, p. 30; cf. A. Caferoğlu, *Türk Dili II*, Istanbul 1964, p. 35. – On the cited *ḥadīth* cf. B. Atalay, op. cit., p. XVII. Robert Dankoff in collaboration with James Kelly, *Maḥmūd el-Kāşġarī.*

sified his own East Middle Turkish literary language, Karakhanid, if not as the most correct, in any case as the finest and clearest Turkish. The Oguz, whose poetry, *şiʿr-i ġuzzī,* the Persian poet Manūchehrī in a frequently cited verse had placed on an equal footing with the *şiʿr-i türkī,*[49] al-Kāşġarī reproached because of their bilingualism which he said resulted from their having lived so long with the Persians and had led to their forgetting their own words and adopting foreign ones.[50] Since a series of Turkish grammars written after al-Kāşġarī's great pioneering description have not survived, we only once again meet with this linguistic judgment, which became the basis for establishing a hierarchy among the Turkish dialects,[51] in Ibn Muhannā[52] and in the Mamlūk glossaries. It appears to have become an axiom that the language of the Türkmen – which in the meantime is what the Oguz for the most part came to be called – was "not pure". As late as in 1759 the author of the *Sanglaḫ* criticizes the Western Oguz (the Turks of Rūm, i.e. the Ottomans) for their bilingualism, this time, however, not because of their contact with the Persians but because of their frequent "relations and intercourse" with the Arabs due to which they have "Arabized, corrupted and contracted certain of their words".[53] That many western Turcologists embraced comparable views should not be overlooked.[54]

In any case, the hierarchy in question was not so strict that it could hinder the "less pure" dialects from developing into literary languages. Turkish poets made use of the possibility of adopting suggestions from neighboring Turkish literatures. This inner-Turkish reception, as I would like to call the literary exchange between Eastern and Western Turks, between Azerbaijanis and Turkish-writing Mamlūks, still furnishes scholars with interesting research tasks.

Compendium of the Turkic Dialects (Dīwān Luġat at-Turk). Edited and Translated with Introduction and Indices, Harvard University Printing Office, 1982, Part 1, p. 70: "Learn the tongue of the Turks, for their reign will be long", and p. 84: "The most elegant [Turkish] is that of the Khaqani kings".

49 A. Bombaci, *La Letteratura Turca*, Milan 1969, p. 87

50 On polemics by Arabs eager to defend their language "against the foreign corrupting influences that living together with subjected peoples exerts on the language", see G. Flügel, *Die grammatischen Schulen der Araber*, Leipzig 1862, pp. 22 f.

51 Cf. R. Blachère, *Histoire de la Littérature arabe I*, Paris 1952, p. 70, on the hierarchy among the Arabic dialects.

52 G. Doerfer, "Woher stammte Ibn Muhannā?", in *Archaeologische Mitteilungen aus Iran*, New Series vol. 9 (1976), pp. 243-51.

53 G. Clauson, *Mahdī Khān al-Astarābādī. Sanglax. A Persian guide to the Turkish language*, London 1960, pp. 14-15.

54 On views of Westerners about the priority of Chagatay cf. A. Caferoğlu, "Çağatay Türkçesi ve Nevaî", in TDED II/3-4 (1948), especially pp. 144-46.

Of these the most obvious would be a description of the reception of Chagatay poetry among the Ottomans. For this purpose studies are already available in which the social determinants of immigration and change of language are dealt with among religious scholars and poets from the East who settled in the Ottoman Empire.[55] Material for the study of Ottoman reception is provided by recently published Chagatay poems that were penned by Ottomans,[56] texts which, as far as I can see, have not yet actually been subjected to questions of a specifically literary nature – perhaps because one imagines that such questions have already been answered with the shorthand phrase "influence of Chagatay poetry". But scholars are not so completely in agreement: this is shown by the centenarian dispute revolving around the question of whether the 15th-century Ottoman prince of poets, Aḥmed Paşa, had been under the influence of Navāʾī or not.[57] Assertions to that effect and counter-arguments will not advance matters as long as one does not apply methods involving criticism of style and motifs in an attempt to understand in what terms the Ottomans viewed Navāʾī (characteristically only him, as being the greatest), and in what way their poems, possibly conditioned by different expectations on the part of the public, differed from his. The strange fact that in this case a dialect suddenly became a literary fashion, a dialect which with its typical forms (future using *-GAy*) had actually not been popular in 14th-cen-

55 In 1964 A. Caferoğlu collected together in the *Philologiae Turcicae Fundamenta*, vol. II, pp. 640 f., those poets from Azerbaijan who moved to Turkey. Cf. now H. Sohrweide, *Dichter und Gelehrte aus dem Osten im osmanischen Reich* (see here fn. 9), pp. 263-302; E. Birnbaum, "The Ottomans and Chagatay Literature. An Early 16th-Century Mansucript of Navāʾī's Dīvān in Ottoman Orthography", in *CAJ* XX (1977), pp. 157-90. Birnbaum's designation of the Ottoman Empire as the "Land of Promise" is rather general; his anachronistic comparison (the era of Bāyazīd II!) with conditions in Seljuk Anatolia (p. 161) brings to mind earlier ideas of the Ottomans as rough pioneers of the Western frontier (cf. B. Lewis, *The Emergence of Modern Turkey*, London 1961, p. 325).

56 K. Erarslan edited in *TDED* XVI (1968) the Chagatay *ġazels* of Seydī ʿAlī Reʾīs; O.F. Sertkaya, "Osmanlı Şairlerinin Çağatayca Şiirleri IV", in *TDED* XXII (1977), pp. 169-89, contains details about four earlier articles on this subject by the same author.

57 M.F. Köprülü seemed to have written the final word on the matter in *İA* I, p. 190, but now O.F. Sertkaya in *TDED* XVIII (1970), pp. 133-34, has again been adamant in claiming that the *naẓīre* recorded by ʿĀşıq Çelebi (Meredith-Owens 36a, Ms. T 43b; cf. A.N. Tarlan, *Ahmed Paşa Divanı*, Istanbul 1966, p. 125, no. 4) is not a parallel poem.

tury Anatolia,[58] could be considered in connection with the other fact that the Ottomans Ottomanized their Chagatay texts.[59]

Conversely, it is apparent that among the Oguz and the East-Turks living in Iran, Herat and Samarqand – and certainly among the Mamlūks – Anatolian-Turkish literature was read and highly esteemed, indeed it even prompted a literary fashion in *ġazel* poetry.[60]

While volume II of the *Fundamenta*, published in 1964, is still considered authoritative regarding scholarship that deals with Turkish literature, nonetheless we see the Ottoman and Chagatay inventory which is conveniently arranged there as bearing fixed labels, some of which have perhaps become obsolete. Looking for Mamlūk Turkish literature in the Oguz language[61] and for the older Azerbaijani-Turkish literature, one finds oneself on shaky ground. There a Ṣādiqī Beg (see here ft. 42) – even in the index – is split into three persons and distributed over three domains of literature, and Nešātī, writing in Shiraz (called Nišāṭī on p. 670), is transferred to Khorasan on p. 369, while his translation of the Ṣafavid *Ṣafvat al-ṣafā* is left linguistically hovering between Chagatay and Azerbaijani.[62]

Areas like this in which our present state of knowledge is still incomplete are particularly attractive. The tasks that result for scholars – making available individual works when the situation regarding manuscripts is difficult,[63] working out interrelations between literature and the society which produces it, and the deciphering of aesthetic factors – continue to pose a challenge for the whole of research in the domain of Turkish literature.

---

58 One might recall Doerfer's thesis according to which the original Ottomans had spoken East-Oguz with *–GAy* having been borrowed early on: "Das Vorosmanische", in *TDAY-Belleten* 1976, pp. 85 and 100.

59 E. Birnbaum, op. cit., pp. 175 ff.

60 Fażlallāh b. Rūzbihān, the court ideologist of the Uzbek Khān Şaybānī, in his *Mihmānnāma-yi Buḫārā* lavished enthusiastic praise on Aḥmedī's *Iskendernāme* (ed. by M. Sutūda, Teheran 1962, p. 151). On Chagatay literature see H.F. Hofman, *Turkish Literature. A Bio-Bibliographical Survey*, Utrecht 1969. – The very borrowings Eckmann and Doerfer dismissed as "only literary" – J. Eckmann, *The Divan of Gadā'ī*, Bloomington 1971, and G. Doerfer, *Das Vorosmanische*, pp. 99, 116 and 142 – are in fact what is of interest in the context discussed here.

61 See my paper "Zum Stand der mamluk-türkischen Forschung" published in *Die Akten des 19. Deutschen Orientalistentags*, Freiburg 1975.

62 Apparently Neşātī is concealed in the "Bisāṭī" mentioned by Abdülbâki Gölpınarlı, *Mevlana Müzesi Yazmalar Kataloğu III*, Ankara 1972, pp. 430 f., no. 1172. On Neşātī as a writer see my article "Die Hamburger Handschrift von Yūsuf Meddāḥs *Varka vü Gülşāh*", in *Hungaro-Turcica. Studies in Honour of Julius Németh*, Budapest 1976, p. 272, ftn. 13.

63 E. Birnbaum speaks of the neglected state of Turkish manuscripts in Iran, op. cit., p. 171; and cf. ibid., p. 158.

CHAPTER 11

Karl Süssheim 1877-1947: On his Hundredth Birthday, June 21st 1878/1978*

When the field of Oriental Studies in Germany recalled its dead in the early years after the Second World War, among the obituaries the name of one man who had died two years after the war's end was missing: Karl Süssheim, formerly associate professor at the University of Munich. On the occasion of his hundredth birthday it is appropriate to remember this German Jewish scholar who from his youth was attached to the Islamic East and for whom Turkey offered a place of refuge during the last years of his life. Whereas Süssheim's activity as a teacher and researcher for a long time had already laid claim to praiseworthy mention in the annals of German Islamic Studies, only in recent years has it become absolutely clear what degree of recognition the Turkish branch of this discipline in particular owes him.[1]

Karl Süssheim was born on the 21st of January 1878 in Nürnberg. He was the second son of the merchant Sigmund Süssheim and his wife Clara née Morgenstern. His grandfather on his mother's side, David Morgenstern,[2] was a respected jurist in Fürth and the first Jewish Deputy in the Frankfurt National Assembly. While his brother Max Süssheim followed in the footsteps of his grandfather becoming a jurist and an important SPD member of the Bavarian Diet,[3] Karl Süssheim, who graduated from the humanistic *gymnasium* of his

---

* Translated by John O'Kane.

1 The remarks of Franz Babinger, "Ein Jahrhundert morgenländischer Studien an der Münchener Universität", in *ZDMG* 107 N. F. 32 (1957), pp. 267-68, scarcely do justice to Süssheim's personality. For numerous forms of help I wish to thank Dr. Hans Striedl (Munich), Dr. Peter Freimark, and especially Dr. Ingrid Belke of the Institute for the History of German Jews (Hamburg). And I must thank the Staatsbibliothek Preuβischer Kulturbesitz in Berlin for permission to work on the Süssheim Collection. I was provided with essential information by the following archives: the Stadtarchiv Nürnberg, the Landeshauptstadt München, the Archiv der Ludwig-Maximilians Universität, the Bayerische Hauptstaatsarchiv and its Abteilung IV-Kriegsarchiv, the Stadtarchiv Kronach and the Stadtarchiv Neumarkt in der Oberpfalz. I am sincerely grateful to their directors and employees. For advice regarding Süssheim's biography I am indebted to Professor Ömer Faruk Akün (Istanbul), Elisabeth Gombos (Freising), Professor Fritz Rudolf Kraus (Leiden), Professor Gershom Scholem (Jerusalem), Professor Bertold Spuler (Hamburg), Privatdozent Dr. Arslan Terzioğlu (Munich), and Professor Andreas Tietze (Vienna).

2 Born 1814 in Büchenbach by Erlangen, died 1882 in Fürth; see Ernest Hamburger, *Juden im öffentlichen Leben Deutschlands*, Tübingen 1968, pp. 212-13.

3 Born 1876, died 1933 in Nürnberg; see Hamburger, op. cit., pp. 536-37.

 | DOI 10.1163/9789004355767_012

native city, chose history as his field of work. After completing his military service he studied primarily history in Jena, Munich, Erlangen and above all in Berlin, as well as the natural sciences, philosophy and even medicine for one semester.[4] Süssheim's dissertation which, according to the archives of Berlin, Nürnberg and Vienna, he wrote under Max Lenz (1850-1932), extended from a depiction of the conflicts between Prussia and the imperial city of Nürnberg to a description of the situation in Franconia during the struggle between Prussia and Austria at the end of the 18th century. His thesis was accepted by the University of Berlin in 1902 under the title *Preußische Annexionsbestrebungen in Franken 1791-1797, ein Beitrag zur Biographie Hardenbergs.* A version that was expanded to 430 pages appeared in the same year with the title *Preußens Politik in Ansbach-Bayreuth 1791– 1806.*[5] In Süssheim's development his student period in Berlin, where he made friends with Turks, led to a shift in his field of study. He began to learn Arabic and Turkish in the Department for Oriental Languages where Karl Foy (1856-1907) taught the Turkish language and Martin Hartmann (1851-1919) dealt with the modern era in the Arabic and Turkish world. And Süssheim also directed his attention to the living Orient by going to Turkey to take up residence as a student after he had received his doctorate. For four years from the autumn of 1902 to 1906 he lived in Istanbul: he came to know the absolutist police and censorship controls of the late era of ʿAbdülḥamīd, when intellectuals suspected of being liberally-minded agitators were spied upon or sent into exile. He attached himself to scholars like the library director Ismāʿīl Sāʾib Efendi (Sencer), who was praised in so many obituaries, and became eagerly engrossed in studying the three Islamic languages. With his learned friend Debreli Ḥüseyn Efendi, an Albanian "transferred" to Istanbul, he wandered through the city speaking Arabic. Men like this must have made Süssheim aware of the widespread desire for liberty and the re-establishment of the Constitution of 1876.

Süssheim began as an Orientalist with a small work on the modern Turkish shadow theater; but as the subject of his research he chose Persian historiography, the study and understanding of which was making significant progress in those years. He took on the task of editing the chronicle *al-ʿUrāża fīʾl-ḥikāyat al-Salǧūqīya* (*The Gift from the History of the Seljuks*), written by Ibn al-Niẓām in 1311, secured the consent of the Turkish authorities and collated two manuscripts of the work, one in London and the other in Paris. But when difficulties arose with the Ministry of Education regarding printing, Süssheim travelled to

4 M.F. Nafiz [Uzluk], "Türk Tababet Tarihi ile Uğraşan Müsteşrikler: Prof. Dr. phil. Karl Süssheim", in *İstanbul Üniversitesi Tıb Tarihi Enstitüsü* no. 2, Istanbul 1937, pp. 1-4.

5 The book was reprinted in 1965 in Vaduz.

Cairo where he was able to publish the Persian text of his *ʿUrāża* with a Turkish introduction and a Turkish appendix through the Maʿārif printing works.

The outbreak of the Young Turk Revolution made a lasting impression on the thirty-year-old Süssheim who remained in Cairo from May to August 1908 where he was in contact with exiled opponents of the Sultan and entered into an enduring friendship with the fiery free spirit, Dr. ʿAbdullāh Ǧevdet (1869-1932). He saw how common hopes brought together the most dissimilar people when on the 23rd of July 1908 Sultan ʿAbdülḥamīd II once again convened Parliament and the Constitution (which had never formally been abolished) was brought back into effect. Süssheim did not easily abandon his reserve but the high spirits of those days also must have had an effect on him, especially when in August 1908, with political exiles who were returning home, he arrived by ship in Istanbul where after decades of oppression people enthusiastically welcomed the beginning of a better era. During these years Süssheim laid the foundation of his manuscript collection which today is in the possession of the Staatsbibliothek Preußischer Kulturbesitz. In 1909 Süssheim had his text of the *ʿUrāża* printed again with Brill in Leiden, adding an extensive historical introduction to his Cairo edition. It had not escaped his attention that the author of the *ʿUrāża* had made use of an earlier Seljuk chronicle, namely the *Rāḥat al-ṣudūr wa āyat al-surūr* by al- Rāwandī which Charles Schefer had recently rediscovered. What was merely a suspicion for him in 1908/09, namely that his *ʿUrāża* was dependent on the *Rāḥat al-ṣudūr*, he expressed with certainty in 1911, before Muḥammad Qazwīnī and, after him, Muḥammad Iqbāl disqualified the *ʿUrāża* as a simple reworking, indeed as a work of plagiarism. Today, when al- Rāwandī's dependent position in the Seljuk tradition is also well established, Ibn al-Niẓām is no longer judged so severely. But Süssheim came to devote more enduring attention to the anonymous Arabic manuscript in London that bears the double title *Zubdat al-tawārīḫ-Aḫbār al-dawlat al-Salǧūqīya.* Süssheim did not publish an edition that he had in fact prepared but first presented in 1911 the results of his extensive research on the sources of the work. With this small volume entitled *Prolegomena zu einer Ausgabe der im Britischen Museum zu London verwahrten "Chronik des Seldschuqischen Reiches"*, which still today possesses value for Seljuk historiography,[6] Karl Süssheim in July 1911 defended his postdoctoral thesis (Habilitation) at the University of Munich and was accepted into the Philosophy Faculty on 4/10/1911 as a

6 Cf. Claude Cahen, "The Historiography of the Seljuqid Period", in *Historians of the Middle East*, ed. Bernard Lewis and P.M. Holt, London 1962, pp. 69 f. Müderris M. Şerefeddīn Efendi took on the task of translating the Cairo edition of the text into Turkish. His translation began to appear in the *Millī Tetebbuʿlar Meǧmūʿası* but remained incomplete.

Privatdozent for the history of the Mohammadan peoples and the Turkish language. Moreover, on 14/12/1915 he was granted authorization to teach Persian and modern Arabic.[7] Motivated by his search for the author of the *Zubdat-Aḫbār*, Süssheim at that time collected an abundance of material on the genealogy of the ʿAlids which he did not publish. But Süssheim had not lost interest in questions of contemporary history since his experience connected with the Second Turkish Constitution of 1908. Along with his Ottoman friends Süssheim shared the disappointment that became widespread when the Young Turks began to make harsh use of the old weapons of censorship, surveillance and persecution against people who thought differently from themselves. Süssheim, who only still visited Turkey for short stays for his research, had earlier written two articles for Turkish newspapers in 1908/09 and also reported from London, where his Seljuk studies had taken him, for the Istanbul newspapers *Iqdām* (in Turkish) and *Şams* (in Persian). Invited by Hugo Grothe, he published a report in 1913 in which he presented a sober account of the situation of Turkish colleges and spoke out in favor of setting up a German Technical College in Istanbul.[8] And he also contributed to the collective volume *Die Balkanfrage* an outline of Turkish history which after some introductory commonplaces about earlier periods reveals once more his particular strength, i.e. contemporary history; as in the case of Martin Hartmann he did not refrain from criticizing the forces in Turkey that were hostile to progress. The outbreak of the First World War kept Süssheim busy in his modern field of work – up till then he had been involved in contributing to the *Encyclopaedia of Islam*, indeed fifty years later six of his articles were retained without alteration in the encyclopaedia's second edition. In addition to his teaching activity, he undertook translation work for the military postal surveillance in Munich, services rendered in an honorary capacity and for which he was awarded the "King Ludwig Cross" in August 1916.[9] He also was engaged once again as a journalist in 1917; he reported for the *München-Augsburger Abendzeitung* on the fall of Baghdad and the Ottoman grand vizier Ṭalʿat Pasha's visit to Munich. And Süssheim gave lectures on contemporary and earlier aspects of Turkish history in the Munich Oriental Society. At that time he produced his contribution to

---

7 A communication from Dr. Busley of the Bayerisches Hauptstaatsarchiv on 29/5/1978.

8 See Hugo Grothe, "Gedanken zur Errichtung einer deutschen Hochschule in der Türkei. Eine Sammlung von Gutachten", in *Beiträge zur Kenntnis des Orients. Jahrbuch des Deutschen Vorderasienkomitees*, ed. Hugo Grothe, vol. 10, Halle 1913, pp. 164-70. I am grateful to Dr. Heidrun Wurm (Hamburg) for this reference.

9 Communication from Dr. Busley, Bayerisches Hauptstaatsarchiv, on 29/5/1978, and from Dr. Heyl, ibid. Kriegsarchiv, on 12/6/1978.

the Festschrift for Fritz Hommel (1854-1936), which though curiously inadequate in its structure reveals a precise study of source materials. Hommel, moreover, had persistently opposed awarding Süssheim his postdoctoral qualification as lecturer (Habilitation). The analysis of the memoirs of the former grand vizier Küçük Saʿīd Paşa (1838-1914) which one expects from the essay's title breaks off after a few pages and goes on to present a biography of Saʿīd Paşa's father, thereby becoming in fact a study of the Tanẓīmāt Period. Having finally been appointed associate professor in 1919, in this post without tenure Süssheim taught the history of the Islamic peoples and the three Islamic languages from the winter semester 1919 until June 1933. To his ever small circle of students, among whom at one time Franz Babinger (1891-1967) also belonged, the young Gershom Scholem attached himself in 1920/21. He read texts of Ibn al-ʿArabī with him and remarked that Süssheim was the only person in the department who was able to pronounce Arabic with a correct accent.[10] And Hans Joachim Kissling, Fritz Rudolf Kraus, Bertold Spuler and Hans Striedl also followed the lectures of Süssheim who was a quiet man imbued with a strong sense of duty. Meanwhile, Süssheim maintained his Turkish connections through correspondence and offered helpful support to Turkish colleagues and students in Germany; this was also the basis to his friendship with Feridun Nafiz (Uzluk, 1902-1974) who came to Munich as a young doctor in 1932.[11]

Süssheim, who in his teaching position was dependent on financial contributions from his family, was hard hit by the currency devaluation of 1923/24. On top of that, it must have been depressing for him that antisemitism, closely linked to nationalism, was gaining ground in Munich and in his native city Nürnberg. His brother Max, member of the Bavarian Diet, who had served Nürnberg with distinction and was especially exposed to anti-Semitic hostility, provided him with a vivid illustration of this.[12] In the year of the first Jewish persecutions Süssheim already suffered severe blows: on 27/6/1933, on the basis of the "Law to Re-establish the Professional Civil Service" he was dismissed from the Bavarian State service;[13] during the same year his mother and his brother died. Süssheim, who was now fifty-five years old, was forbidden from entering the university and the State Library; yet there were library

10 Gershom Scholem, *Von Berlin nach Jerusalem. Jugenderinnerungen*, Frankfurt 1977, p. 208.

11 Arslan Terzioğlu, "Feridun Nafiz Uzluk", in *Nachrichtenblatt der Deutschen Gesellschaft für Geschichte der Medizin, Naturwissenschaft und Technik* e.V., Jg. 25 (1975).

12 Arnd Müller, *Geschichte der Juden in Nürnberg 1146– 1945*, Nürnberg 1968, pp. 192-93; G. Scholem, op. cit., pp. 172 f., and a communication by letter from Professor Scholem dated 22/1/1978.

13 Communication from Prof. Laetitia Boehm, Archiv der Universität München, on 6/4/1979; and from Dr. Busley, Bayerisches Hauptstaatsarchiv, on 29/5/1978.

employees who saw to it that he was still supplied with books. The "independent scholar" Süssheim, who had difficulty making ends meet for himself and his family (he had married late in life) by giving private lessons, during these years produced a richly documented study of the translation by the Turkish encyclopaedist Şānīzāde ʿAṭāʾullāh (d. 1826) in his *Miʿyār ül-eṭibbā* of a handbook by the Austrian physician Anton von Stoerck (1731-1803). He sent this work to Dr. Feridun Nafiz Uzluk who published it in the Archive of Medical History of the University of Istanbul. The state of the printed text made it clear that Süssheim had submitted his manuscript in the Turkish language and in fact in Arabic script. As late as 1938, one of Süssheim's best works, a penetrating monograph about his friend ʿAbdullāh Ǧevdet, provided with an abundance of bio-bibliographical information, appeared in the supplement volume of the *Encyclopaedia of Islam*. With dismay Süssheim's Turkish friends followed in the press how in 1935 a new wave of antisemitism reached its climax with the enactment of the "Nürnberg Laws", on the basis of which Jews unambiguously became citizens with fewer rights. In the summer of 1938, M. Mesʿud Koman, the director of the Library of the People's House in Konya, offered to present Süssheim's medical-historical monograph to the President of the Republic, Atatürk. At the time Süssheim declined, but by the beginning of 1939 he had decided to go to Turkey, no doubt impressed by the excesses of the "Kristallnacht" during which his bother's wife lost her life.[14] Now his friends M. Koman and F.N. Uzluk, with some difficulty but supported by the Minister of Education Hasan-Âli Yücel (1897– 1960; minister from 1938 to 1946), were successful in getting the University of Istanbul in November 1939 to declare its willingness to offer Süssheim a position, to begin with for two years.[15] On 19/6/1941 Süssheim announced to the authorities his intention to depart for Turkey with his wife and two daughters who were minors.[16] The sixty-three year old, who was only familiar with pre-Republican Turkey, was obliged to adjust to unaccustomed circumstances, especially in the Edebiyat Fakültesi: as an associate professor, he had formerly only been used to addressing a small number of students, while for years under the Nazi domination he had only given private lessons to single students such as Hans Striedl. Now suddenly having to deal with large

14 Arnd Müller, op. cit., p. 243.

15 "... from 1940 lecturer and professor on temporary contract to the University of Istanbul", as Horst Widmann puts it in, *Exil und Bildungshilfe. Die deutschsprachige akademische Emigration in die Türkei nach 1933*, Bern/Frankfurt 1973, p. 291.

16 Communication from Dr. Schattenhofer, Stadtarchiv München, on 14/2/1977, and Dr. Busley, Bayerisches Hauptstaatsarchiv, on 29/5/1978.

"classes" of young Turkish students was not easy for him.[17] He also cooperated in editing the *İslam Ansiklopedisi* which came to incorporate many of his *EI* articles in translation, and he produced a new version of his large article on Albania for the *İA*.

When with the German surrender in 1945 the National Socialist domination, which had driven him from his teaching post and caused him to flee his homeland, collapsed, for Süssheim this did not mean freedom from the conditions that made life difficult and a return to scholarly productivity in his field. After long years of material deprivation and emotional stress, on the 13th of January 1947 Karl Süssheim died in Istanbul, quietly and unnoticed, just as he had lived. He was buried in the Ashkenazi Cemetery in Ortaköy, not far from where he had resided in the Palanka Yokuşu.

Süssheim was clearly a born collector; he built up a stamp collection by means of careful purchases and, as already mentioned, over the years gathered together a valuable collection of Islamic printed works and in particular Turkish manuscripts. This collection, which is presently in the possession of the Staatsbibliothek Preußischer Kulturbesitz in Berlin, demonstrates Süssheim's sound judgement in acquiring numerous works that are almost or completely unknown. These works have unveiled new discoveries for Turcology in the research fields of both history and literature.[18]

An unexploited source for Turkish history, and in part for German history as well, is the preserved portion of the diary that Süssheim kept in Turkish (in Arabic script) from the time of his first trip to the Ottoman Empire up to his emigration to the Turkish Republic, and in Arabic during his final years.[19] The diary deserves attention simply as an achievement in its use of language and is particularly striking for its sober, consciously impersonal registration of facts. Moreover, as long as this diary has not been edited, it would be premature to attempt a comprehensive assessment of Süssheim's work. Those who knew him personally as a teacher praise his scholarly rigor and the thoroughness of his academic teaching; whoever reads his works recognizes the unflagging

17 Friendly communication from Professor F.R. Kraus, Oegstgeest.

18 Catalogued in: *Türkische Handschriften Teil I*. Beschrieben von Barbara Flemming, Wiesbaden 1968 (Verzeichnis der orientalischen Handschriften in Deutschland, vol. XIII, 1) with a brief remark on Süssheim, p. X; and *Türkische Handschriften und einige in den Handschriften enthaltene persische und arabische Werke*, beschrieben von Hanna Sohrweide, Wiesbaden 1974 (Verzeichnis der orientalischen Handschriften in Deutschland, vol. XIII, 3).

19 Out of twenty-one numbered notebooks twelve have been preserved; they deal with the years 1912-1916, 1917-1924 and 1936-1941. I am presently working on them with the view to publishing an article that will also contain a list of Süssheim's writings.

attention to detail in his research and what appears to be the inexhaustible factual knowledge of the "participating observer" in his contributions on contemporary history. To make use of this material, and especially of Süssheim's collections and his own notes, will be the best way to render thanks to the quiet, solitary scholar.

Afterword

As of 2016, of the Süssheim diaries

Part one (begun in 1902) is considered lost.

Part two (from 30-10-1903 to 30-8-1908) is kept in the Library of Congress, Washington DC, where Corry Guttstadt, author of *Die Türkei, die Juden und der Holocaust* (Hamburg 2008; *Turkey, the Jews and the Holocaust*, Cambridge University Press, 2013), rediscovered it.

Parts three (1908), four (1912), five (1914), and six (1915) are kept in the Staatsbibliothek zu Berlin, Preussischer Kulturbesitz.

Part seven (June 1916 to January 1917) is considered lost.

Parts eight (1917), nine (1917-1918), ten (1918), eleven, twelve, and thirteen (1924) are kept in the Staatsbibliothek zu Berlin.

Parts twenty (November 1936-1938, in Arabic) and twenty-one (1938-3 July 1940, in Arabic) are kept in the Staatsbibliothek zu Berlin.

On the deciphering and translating stage, see Jan Schmidt, The Joys of Philology. Studies in Ottoman Literature, History and Orientalism (1500-1923), Istanbul 2002, pp. 8-9. His work resulted in two articles:

Jan Schmidt, "The Importance of the Süssheim Papers for Modern Turkish History"; idem, "Süssheim and the Bavarian Postal Censorship", in both 1989 and republished in Schmidt, *Joys of Philology*, in addition to Barbara Flemming and Jan Schmidt, The Diary of Karl Süssheim (1878-1947), Orientalist between Munich and Istanbul, Stuttgart 2002.

Jan Schmidt provides an edition and translation of Part two of the diary in his forthcoming volume *The Orientalist Karl Süssheim meets the Young Turk Officer Isma'il Hakkı Bey: Two unexplored Sources from the Last Decade in the Reign of the Ottoman Sultan Abdülhamid II*.

CHAPTER 12

Three Turkish Chroniclers in Ottoman Cairo*

At the beginning of the investigation of historical sources on Ottoman Egypt stands Joseph von Hammer-Purgstall (1774-1856) who made use of Egyptian chronicles in his history of the Ottoman Empire and listed them together in a bibliographical appendix.[1] Significant advances have resulted from the contributions presented at a conference on the modern history of Egypt held in 1965 in London.[2]

The volume that contains these contributions offers the most reliable and up-to-date introduction dealing with the sources and state of research concerning the history of Egypt from the Ottoman conquest up to Napoleon's occupation. The most important basis of source-materials for studying the population structure, administration and system of land ownership consists of the five large complexes of archives in Cairo and Istanbul whose formation and content S.J. Shaw has summarized.[3] Shaw's research especially concentrates on financial and administrative organization, and on questions of land ownership. In this way the overall picture is enriched with regard to important aspects but, as Shaw himself noted, the underlying registers only provide the "bones of history, the bare outlines" which are filled out by decrees and edicts and finally by the various chronicles of that period.[4] These latter sources as well are described in connection with one another for the first time in the referred to work: the Arabic chronicles by P.M. Holt[5] and the Turkish ones by S.J. Shaw.[6] What follows below is some supplementary information regarding this complex of source-materials which I would like to dedicate to my teacher in Hamburg, Omeljan Pritsak, in memory of his stimulating lectures on the Mamluk Turks.

The utility for us of the Ottoman chronicles of Egypt lies in the fact that they endeavor to explain or to describe in terms of their impact on situations and events which only rather randomly, if at all, find expression in the archives.

* Translated by John O'Kane.

1 J. von Hammer, *Geschichte des Osmanischen Reiches*, IX, Pest 1833, pp. 194-96.

2 P.M. Holt (ed.), *Political and Social Change in Modern Egypt*, London 1968.

3 S.J. Shaw, "Turkish Source-Materials for Egyptian History", loc. cit., pp. 28-43.

4 Loc. cit., pp. 43-44.

5 P.M. Holt, "Ottoman Egypt (1517-1798): An Acccount of Arabic Historical Sources", loc. cit., pp. 3-12.

6 S.J. Shaw, "Other Turkish Sources", loc. cit., pp. 43-48.

 | DOI 10.1163/9789004355767_013

These Egyptian Ottoman authors tend to offer a broad depiction of economic-historical and socio-historical events but they are also clearly interested in intellectual-religious occurrences as well. Both these characteristics are illustrated by the description of two relatively small popular uprisings which – in the wake of a large-scale insurrection – agitated Cairo in the years 1711 and 1715, each for a completely different reason.

The first of these tumults arose from socio-religious causes. In Ramażān 1123/the year beginning 13 October 1711, a preacher speaking from the pulpit of the Muʾayyad Mosque inveighed against the belief in miracles by saints and the cult of graves, and argued that dervish lodges should be transformed into *medreses*. He was joined by an incensed crowd which, when two shaykhs of al-Azhar issued a *fetva* in opposition, took the initiative to appeal to the Turkish chief judge and the governor himself on behalf of their preacher. To prevent rioting the governor ostensibly gave in but then deployed the Janissaries: the preacher escaped and public order was reestablished. Apparently nothing in the situation of the theology students changed. Only in modern times has this tumult, which was based on the fanatically puritanical teachings of Birgili Meḥmed Efendi, been interpreted as Wahhābism *avant la lettre* or bold reformative thought. Less spectacular than this popular uprising, which I have described in greater detail in another article,[7] was the tumult that broke out four years later over the Egyptian copper coinage. In connection with the currency reform which took place under Aḥmed III (1703-1730), it was also decided to remove from circulation in Egypt the local basic currency unit, the silver *para* that was underweight and further debased by being clipped,[8] to mint new *paras* and establish their value in relation to the native and foreign gold and silver coins in use and at the same time to put into circulation newly minted copper coins. How the population reacted is described in the Turkish *Tārīḫ-i Miṣr* by Meḥmed b. Yūsuf el-Ḥallāq[9] in a manner which is typical for the mode of description of the chroniclers; we therefore present it here in translation:

"On the 4th of the mentioned month [Muḥarrem 1128/30 December 1715], the governor [ʿAbdī Paşa; arrived 3 Ẕīlḥicce 1126/10 December 1714, was relieved of his post 11 Şaʿbān 1129/21 July 1717] issued an order by means of all the notables: From now on no clipped *para* would any longer be valid. Instead, a new

7 See my "Pre-Wahhabi Fitna", no. 6 and no. 24 in this volume.

8 M. Akdağ, *Türkiye'nin İktisadî ve İctimaî Tarihi* II, Ankara 1971, p. 201.

9 Ms. of the Bibliothèque nationale, suppl. Turc 512, fols. 190 f., compared with Ms. H.O. 37 of the Österreichische Nationalbibliothek, fols. 271 f. (see below). The event is mentioned in J. von Hammer, *Geschichte des Osmanischen Reiches*, VII, Pest 1831, p. 170.

para had been minted and distributed to the 61 money changers down in the city. Consequently, the Aġa of the Janissaries together with the police commandant (*subaşı*) rode into the city, and they had [the following currency rates] announced:

1 ducat with chain-patterned rim (*zincirli altun*)	107 *paras*
1 ducat with *ṭuġra* (*ṭurreli altun*)	100 *paras*[10]
1 *şerīfī* gold piece	90 *paras*
1 silver florin (*riyāl*)	60 *paras*
1 lion florin (*aslanlı*)	45 *paras*

Business was to be carried out on this basis and in this way profit would accrue to the state treasury because salaries would be paid out accordingly.

In the mint a new copper coin with *ṭuġra* (*ṭurreli manqır*)[11] was struck and this as well was distributed to the money changers. At a rate of eight to one, it was to be made into the new *para* and distributed at this rate of exchange. The old copper coin was declared invalid. Whoever still had clipped *paras* and old copper coins should turn them in for payment (*getürilüb bayʿ eyleye*).

When one began to make this announcement, it was already the time of the afternoon prayers. For this reason the bazaar merchants refused in the short time available to accept the clipped *paras* and old copper coins with which most poor people wanted to pay for their daily sustenance. Consequently, most of the poor received nothing to eat.

On the next day, a Tuesday, the people in the whole of Cairo, *reʿāyā* and the poor, rose up. They bolted the door of the al-Azhar Mosque, closed all the shops in the city and in a state of general uproar headed for the citadel. There they appealed to the Paşa: 'We wish to do everything you command [in Arabic 'we hear and obey'], we only ask for one thing: the old copper coins should keep their usual value because if they are done away with, the poor will suffer great affliction.'

At that same moment, the Paşa ordered that the old copper coins should forthwith have their earlier value. The Aġa of the Janissaries and the police

10 A.C. Schaendlinger, *Osmanische Numismatik*, Braunschweig 1973, p. 61, on both gold coins. Cf. also İ. and C. Artuk, *İstanbul Arkeoloji Müzeleri Teşhirdeki İslamî Sikkeler Kataloğu*, II, Istanbul 1974, nos. 1759 and 1760.

11 On the function of the *manqır*, *manqūr* or "*pul*" as small change see M. Akdağ, loc. cit., pp. 195-97. *Mangır*s were willingly struck without the name of the Sultan and without a specific year; in this way they could remain in circulation when the Sultan changed: C. Ölçer, *Nakışlı Osmanlı Mangırları*, Istanbul 1975, pp. 69-70, has published four such anonymous *mangır*s from Egypt.

commandant rode down to the city together and had this announced. After that the shops opened and the disturbance subsided. Still on the same day, the Paşa paid in full the wages of the soldiers and pensioners (*oturaq ocaqlar*) in the way that had been announced, in fact mostly in new *paras*.

On the second day, the 6th of Muḥarrem, a Wednesday (1 January 1716), the notables of the *vilāyet* met together in the house of Ibrāhīm Beg, who is still the *defterdār*, to work out an estimate of the fixed prices (*narḫ*); they set a fixed price for every category (*ṣınıf*). On the next day, Thursday, they presented this to the Paşa.

After he had consulted on the matter for three days, on the 10th [text: 3rd] of the mentioned month the order went out to the Aġa of the Janissaries. The latter, following custom, rode out with the adjutants (*mülāzım*), the police commandant and the chief officer of the marketplace (*muḥtesib*), on the right and on the left a herald and between them a Coptic scribe who, holding a list (*qā'ime*) in his hand, dictated to the heralds the fixed price for every category. They proclaimed in accordance with what he said:

10 *batmans* of butter	30 *paras*
10 *batmans* of bee's honey	20 *paras*
1 *batman* of coffee	13 *paras*
1 *batman* of soap	5 *paras*

and so on, and that the exchange rate for the new *para* was ten copper coins. The Aġa of the Janissaries rode together with the police chief through Cairo and Būlāq, and everywhere he had this proclaimed. Afterwards they went back up to the citadel. The Paşa canceled the minting of copper coins with *ṭuġra* and had the coins locked up in the Treasury. Thus for some days the *para* was exchanged at a rate of 10 copper coins.

After that, on Friday the 22nd of Muḥarrem (17 January 1716), the notables of the *vilāyet* gathered in the house of the *defterdār*, Ibrāhīm Beg, and agreed that in fact the *para*, following the old *qānūn*, should be exchanged for eight copper coins. They decided thus, let the Paşa know of their decision and accordingly received a *buyruldı*. But thirty days had not gone by before the *para* was again exchanged for ten copper coins. At the same time, on the 24th of the said month, a Sunday (19 January 1716), the Aġa of the Janissaries, according to custom, rode with the adjutants through the city and had it proclaimed that the *para* was to be exchanged at a rate of not more than eight copper coins."

It was not the first time that the population, having suffered loss through the "annulment" (*ibṭāl*) of their old copper money, rose up in protest.[12] Rather,

12 M. Akdağ, loc. cit., p. 197.

what is remarkable in the event portrayed here is the retreat of the authorities who of course then won through in the question of parity.

It would be rewarding to examine together all the clashes to do with monetary standards, wages and prices which at regular intervals shook the large city of Cairo. With their ever recurrent reports of this kind and complaints about high prices and occasional food shortages the narrative sources supplement the other groups of sources such as administrative records and coins. Such reports contribute to establishing the relative value of the *para*, about which enough is still not known,[13] and also contribute to providing knowledge about the fixed market prices (*narḫ*) that in accordance with tradition were kept as low as possible.[14]

What follows here is intended to provide information on this area of sources and to serve as a supplement to the essays on source materials by P.M. Holt and S.J. Shaw that we referred to earlier. The history book, which Muḥammad b. Yūsuf al-Ḥallāq wrote under the title of *Tuḥfat al-aḥbāb bi-man malak Miṣr min al-mulūk wa n-nuwwāb* and completed in 1128/the year beginning 27/12/1715, has been overlooked by chance[15] and should be classified among the Arabic works of group B in Holt. This unpublished work is preserved in a unique manuscript in the Academy of Sciences in Leningrad and described as an autograph in the academy's catalogue.[16] It consists of an introduction and four chapters (*bāb*) in which are treated 1) the rulers of Egypt since the Flood, 2) the rulers since the conquest by ʿOmar b. al-Ḫaṭṭāb, 3) the Ayyubids and Mamluks, and 4) the Ottomans. The fourth and by far the longest part, with many marginal glosses, is also outwardly set apart from the rest of the text.

After the author had composed this Arabic history work – he writes: *bundan aqdem ʿarabī bir tàrīḫ bu minvāl üzere cemʿ eyledüm* – , he wrote at the request of "some friends" – *ve lākin baʿżı iḫvān muṭālaʿa eylediklerinde bir türkīsi olsa maʿqūl olurdı*[17] – a Turkish version as well which deals with the Ottoman period up to around 1717. The structure, as in the Arabic version, is chronologi-

13 S.J. Shaw, *The Financial and Administrative Organization and Development of Ottoman Egypt, 1517-1798*, p. xxii.

14 M. Akdağ, loc. cit., p. 372.

15 The manuscript mistakenly appears among the Turkish chronicles in Shaw, "Turkish Source-Materials", loc. cit., p. 45, ftn. 2.

16 V. Rosen, *Les Manuscrits Arabes de l'Institut des Langues Orientales*, St. Petersburg 1877, p. 30, no. 58 (and following this, GAL II, p. 198); A.I. Michajlova, *Katalog arabskich rukopisej Instituta narodov Azii*, Part 3, *Istorija*, Moscow 1965, p. 134, no. 92, signature B 1036. For her help with bibliographical information I am grateful to the late A.S. Tveritinova; and I must thank R.E. Emmerick of Hamburg University for obtaining a microfilm of the manuscript for me.

17 Paris, Bibliothèque nationale, suppl. Turc 512, fol. 1b.

cal and, as there not so annalistic but based rather on individual, precisely dated and clearly separated terms of office of the Ottoman governors of Egypt in Cairo. This work, judging by the number of manuscripts, enjoyed a certain diffusion, and the fact that J. von Hammer consulted it for his history of the Ottoman Empire[18] stimulated later scholars to occupy themselves with the work.[19]

About Meḥmed or, in Arabic, Muḥammad b. Yūsuf al-Ḥallāq we know little more than that he was competent in Arabic and Ottoman Turkish, and was familiar with the Turkish milieu in Egypt. In the appendix to Kātib Çelebi's *Kaşf aẓ-ẓunūn*, he is presented as the author of a Turkish history of Egypt in a large volume (*mucallid kabīr*) dated 1 Muharrem 1123, beginning 19/2/1711.[20] The question arises as to whether he is the same person as Ẕihnī Meḥmed, known as Berberzāde, who, it is recorded, died in Istanbul in 1715, concerning whom Bursalı ʿOsmān Ṭāhir reports that he wrote *bir cild-i kabīr Tárīḫ-i Miṣr el-Qāhire*.[21] That the author notes with a certain pride that he is a barber's son should not appear surprising: the barber's profession, which occupied a special position among the guilds,[22] assumed medical knowledge and likewise a certain clerical competence. Indeed, the esteemed chronicler of Damascus, Aḥmad al-Budayrī, who some decades after Meḥmed b. Yūsuf recorded events in his home city in Arabic (1741-1762), was a barber (*ḥallāq*).[23]

Meḥmed b. Yūsuf el-Ḥallāq, for the beginning of Part 4 of his chronicle of Egypt during the Ottoman period, draws on the respected Arabic work of Shaykh Aḥmad b. Zunbul ar-Rammāl[24] which has a tendency toward hero worship. In part he takes it over, i.e. translates it into Turkish. In the main section

18 He cites it as a "history by the son of Yusuf" (vol. VII, pp. 168 ff.) and considers it to be "the most detailed and estimable of all Ottoman histories of Egypt" (vol. IX, p. 194).

19 F. Babinger, *Die Geschichtsschreiber der Osmanen und ihre Werke*, Leipzig 1927, pp. 244 f. The work was consulted by E. Bulam in "XVII. Yüzyıldaki Mısır valileri", Mezuniyet tezi, Istanbul 1965. In an unpublished paper for the First International Congress of Turcology in Istanbul 1973, I reported on Meḥmed b. Yūsuf, ʿAbdülkerīm and Hacı Mahmud 4877.

20 Hacci Halifa, *Lexicon bibliographicum*, ed. G. Flügel, VI London 1852, p. 539, no. 14542.

21 Bursalı Meḥmed Ṭāhir, *ʿOsmānlı müʾellifleri*, III, Istanbul 1343/1924-25, p. 53. *Sālim teẕkiresi*, Istanbul 1315/1897-98, pp. 250 f.: Ẕihnī, *Berberzāde Meḥmed*; cf. J. von Hammer, *Geschichte der osmanischen Dichtkunst*, IV, Pest 1838, p. 83, "Sehini XI".

22 G. Baer, *Egyptian Guilds in Modern Times*, Jerusalem 1964, pp. 3, 49 ff., 63 and notes; Idem, *The Structure of Turkish Guilds*, Israel Academy of Sciences and Humanities, Jerusalem 1970.

23 G.M. Haddad, "The Interests of an Eighteenth Century Chronicler of Damascus", in *Der Islam* 38 (1963), pp. 258 and 271.

24 P.M. Holt, "Arabic Historical Sources", p. 5 f.

of his Ottoman chronicle, Meḥmed b. Yūsūf clearly uses reports that informed authorities have provided him with; here it would appear that his detailed knowledge is predominantly to do with a group of military persons within the seven corps stationed in Cairo. The relation of the Turkish edition to the Arabic text must still be examined in detail. Stylistically, Meḥmed b. Yūsuf stands in the tradition of the older Arabic and Turkish *tavārīḫ* of Egypt which were composed in a relatively simple language and in which extensive passages occur in direct speech.

At present six manuscripts of the Turkish *Tȧrīḫ-i Miṣr* by Meḥmed b. Yūsuf are known; these, ordered according to the last dated occurrence in each of them, are as follows:

Vienna, Österreichische Nationalbibliothek, H.O. 40a. A fragment that only includes the year 1122/beginning 2/3/1710.[25]

Stockholm, Royal Library, 75. This goes up to the year 1126/beginning 17/1/1714.[26]

Istanbul, Üniversite Kütüphanesi, T.Y. 628. A carefully written manuscript which goes up to the year 1127/beginning 7/1/1715.

Vienna, Österreichische Nationalbibliothek, H.O. 40b. A fragment from the year 1127/beginning 7/1/1715.[27]

Paris, Bibliothèque nationale, suppl. Turc 512. Goes up to the year 1128/beginning 27/12/1717.[28]

Vienna, Österreichische Nationalbibliothek, H.O. 37. Up to the year 1130/beginning 5/12/1717.[29]

The manuscripts have not yet been critically examined; the Paris manuscript has a more extensive introduction than the other manuscripts; an epilogue has been added to the Istanbul manuscript in which ʿAbdī Paşa is praised.

Very close to the two chronicles by Meḥmed b. Yūsuf el-Ḥallāq chronologically and in terms of content is the work of ʿAbdülkerīm b. ʿAbdurraḥmān, the *Tȧrīḫ-i Miṣr* which in the Turkish language treats events up until the 9th of Ṣafer 1128/3 February 1716. As he tells us himself, ʿAbdülkerīm was employed in

25 G. Flügel, *Die arabischen, persischen und türkischen Handschriften der k.k. Hofbibliothek zu Wien*, II, Vienna 1865, p. 162, no. 937.1.

26 W. Riedel, *Katalog över kungl. Bibliotekets orientaliska handskrifter*, Stockholm 1923, p. 39.

27 Flügel, loc. cit., II, p. 162, no. 937.2.

28 E. Blochet, *Bibliothèque nationale. Catalogue des manuscrits turcs*, I, Paris 1932, p. 378.

29 Flügel, loc. cit., II, p. 161, no. 936. Hammer (*GOR* IX, p. 194) considered this manuscript "very rare and not to be found in any European library or even in the libraries of Constantinople".

the Arabic Secretariat of the Treasury – *beytülmāl-i ḫaṣṣeniñ ʿarab kitābetinde* – of the Governor of Egypt, el-Ḥācc Meḥmed Paşa, who came to Cairo on the 14th of Rebīʿ II 1111/9 October 1699.[30] Under the protection of this Paşa he began his work but, as it clearly turned out, he did not come to dedicate it to him. As he writes in his introduction, there were indeed historical accounts in Arabic books about the Ottoman governors of Egypt but such works are rare in the Turkish language:

> ʿarabī kitāblarında bulunur ve illā türkī diliyle
> ʿala t-tertīb bulunması nādir.

For this reason he collected the events of the period of the Ottoman governors and translated them from Arabic into Turkish: *ʿarabī lisānından türkī lisānına terceme eyledüm.*

Even without a specific indication of his model, in my opinion there is no doubt that ʿAbdülkerīm made use of the history work of Meḥmed b. Yūsuf el-Ḥallāq as his textual source, possibly on occasion consulting the Arabic version. Here and there he writes out in full the Turkish version, though he often abridges it, but he also introduces changes when he expresses different opinions and considers various events from a different viewpoint.

The similarity between the two works led Shaw in some of his studies to cite the Istanbul manuscrit of the *Tārīḫ-i Miṣr* by ʿAbdülkerīm b. ʿAbdurraḥmān, Süleymaniye, Hekimoğlu Ali Paşa 705, as a work by "Ḥallāq". This error has been corrected in his bibliographical essay.[31] However, there the manuscript Süleymaniye, Hacı Mahmud Efendi 4877, is mistakenly cited as the *Tārīḫ-i Miṣr* by Abdülkerīm.

Contrary to what the catalogue leads one to expect,[32] this manuscript, which bears the title *Kitāb-i tevārīḫ-i Miṣr-i Qāhire ḫaṭṭ-i Ḥasan Paşa*, contains a different Egyptian chronicle which extends up to the year 1094/beginning 31/12/1682 and which still must be examined to confirm whether it is possibly a work by a certain Ḥasan Paşa.

The purpose of these notes can be no more than to encourage closer study of these unpublished Arabic and Turkish narrative sources from Ottoman

30 Süleymaniye, Hekimoğlu Ali Paşa 705. On the author see F. Berberoğulları, *Abdülkerim b. Abdurrahman*, Mezuniyet tezi, Istanbul 1973.

31 Shaw, "Turkish Source-Materials", loc. cit., p. 45, ftn. 3.

32 *İstanbul Kütüphaneleri Tarih-Coğrafya Yazmaları Katalogları – Türkçe Tarih Yazmaları*, 2. fasikül, Istanbul 1944, pp. 110 f., attributes it to ʿAbdülkerīm with the remark "müellifin adı yazılı değildir".

Egypt. The Arabic chronicle of Meḥmed b. Yūsuf el-Ḥallāq and his Turkish version that he based upon it are a mine of information on social history. The chronicle of ʿAbdülkerīm, while being dependent on Meḥmed b. Yūsuf in terms of content, presents a different assessment of many events. As for the Egyptian chronicle available in the manuscript Hacı Mahmud 4877, it still remains to examine its value as a source.

The study of these texts written in a provincial setting would also be rewarding for Turkish linguistic history. While Meḥmed b. Yūsuf as well as ʿAbdülkerīm make use of "simple prose" (*sade nesir*), ʿAbdülkerīm grants more space to Turkish than Meḥmed b. Yūsuf, whose Arabic expressions he frequently replaces with Turkish ones. In both texts colloquial forms and phrases appear which are reminiscent of Old Ottoman.

In the pragmatic manner usual in the field of Ottoman Studies, these important sources of information until now have only been accorded serious attention for their concluding sections. But it would also make good sense to study them as a whole as an indication of the historical awareness of these authors who were Ottomans or who wrote for an Ottoman audience.

The time during which they wrote was considered to be a dark period for Egypt as long as the relevant sources still remained inaccessible. G. Wiet spoke on behalf of many when, by way of confirming the view of P. Casanova, he stated that under the Ottomans life, all artistic and literary movement, was extinguished, indeed everything became submerged in dismal apathy.[33] At the same time, the assessment of the Mamluk era, this other "dark period" as it was called from the perspective of the nation-state, now took on brighter aspects. However, after closer study of the Ottoman period obliged historians to formulate a more nuanced judgment, the neighboring discipline of Islamic Art History, where only a while ago one heard the echo of Wiet's somber words,[34] is now also prepared to turn its attention to the Ottoman period[35] and to come to terms with the styles peculiar to it.[36]

33 G. Wiet, *Introduction à la littérature arabe*, Paris 1966, pp. 143-44, speaks of "the deathknell of a highly developed culture".

34 R. Ettinghausen in his introduction to the work cited here in ftn. 36 writes: "The final deathknell was probably the Ottoman conquest of Egypt..."

35 G. İnal, "Kahire'de yapılmış bir Hümayunname'nin minyatürleri", in *Belleten* 40 (1976), pp. 439-65.

36 D. James, *Arabic Painting*, Edinburgh-London 1978, p. 43.

CHAPTER 13

Literature in the Days of the Alphabet Change[*, **]

Between 1927 and 1928 almost all Turks gave up the Arabic alphabet which, with few exceptions and in the end in variously adapted forms, they had employed for several centuries. After nearly all the Turks in the Soviet Union adopted a Latin script in 1927 and 1928, that would only remain in use until 1938-1940,[1] Turkey as well took the same step which in this case would be of permanent effect, and whose fiftieth anniversary was in fact celebrated in 1978.

In the Turkish Republic, in the year of the Script Revolution (*Harf İnkilabı*, later *Harf Devrimi*), dissociation from the Ottoman Islamic heritage was already well advanced. At the beginning of 1928 the numerals in international use were adopted. Again in the same year the change of alphabet was meant to be the culmination of these measures that aimed at westernization and the promotion of modernity. The situation in the country was favorable for this radical intervention. The intimidating influence of the Independence Courts (*İstiklal Mahkemeleri*) which had only recently suspended their activity, continued to be felt, and the Law for the Maintenance of Peace and Order (*Takrir-i Sükûn*) allowed a strict supervision of the press from March 1925 to March 1929.

Political events since 1925 had exacerbated existing conflicts in literature; while a number of authors left the country voluntarily or under compulsion, many other writers came forward in support of Mustafa Kemal's national endeavors. It is not easy, therefore, to point out a defining current in Turkish literature on the eve of the alphabet change. The revolutionary measures of the First Republic should not obscure the fact that the impact of the change was not the same in poetry and in fiction. In fiction the transition from the old to the new era was less abrupt. Here the past still seemed present; it encompassed the production of living authors who represented several generations.[2]

* Translated by John O'Kane.

** Revised version of my earlier attempt to draw up an ordered account of "Literatur im Zeichen des Alphabetwechsels", which appeared in *Anatolica* 8 (1981), pp. 133-57.

1 Cf. H.W. Duda, "Die neue Lateinschrift in der Türkei", in *OLZ* 1929, column 442; *EI1* IV (1934), art. "Türken", p. 984; G. Wheeler, "Modernization in the Muslim East: The Role of Script and Language Reform", in *Asian Affairs, Journal of the Royal Central Asian Society*, 61 (1974), pp. 157-64; M. Alpay, *Harf Devriminin Kütüphanelerde Yansıması*, Istanbul 1976, pp. 82 f.; K. Hüttemann, "Zum 50. Jahrestag der Schriftreform in der Türkei", in *Materialia Turcica* 4 (1978), Bochum 1980, p. 56.

2 R. Mutluay used the concept of generations, *50 Yılın Türk Edebiyatı*, Istanbul 1973, and Idem, *100 Soruda Çağdaş Türk Edebiyatı "1908-1972"*, Istanbul 1973; cf. also A. Tietze, "The

 | DOI 10.1163/9789004355767_014

Out of fourteen million Turks the rural population did not constitute a readership at all;[3] the educated few (eight to ten percent) cherished their poets and prose writers whose work still bore the mark of the nineteenth century, especially the stifling era of Sultan Abdülhamid II.[4] Poets had greeted the Young Turk Revolution in 1908 with enthusiasm and had taken part in it in one way or the other. In the *Meşrutiyet*, or restoration of the constitutional regime, language reform had been a most vital topic. The idea of reforming the Arabic script had also been revived. The idea of adopting the Latin script began to be defended openly, but this met with almost universal opposition.

The alphabet change in the Republic has been told and retold; actual experiments with the Latin scripts began toward the end of 1927. Mustafa Kemal (Atatürk) initiated a nationwide campaign in August 1928, and on 3 November 1928, the National Assembly passed the law establishing the new Turkish script and prohibiting the use of the Arabic script in all public affairs after 1 December of the same year. The adoption of the Latin script marked the beginning of the most critical stage in the Turkish transformation.[5] Among the various aspects of social life that felt the impact of this change was literature.

In studies of literary history and the history of Turkey generally the "traumatic nature of the change" (Niyazi Berkes, referring to the Hat Law) in the literary production tends to be overshadowed by other aspects, such as the implementation of literacy and language reform.[6]

In the first instance, the introduction of the script did in fact serve to promote literacy among the Turkish population;[7] in forty thousand villages, which

---

Generation Rhythm in the Literature of Republican Turkey", in *Boğaziçi Üniversitesi Dergisi* 2 (1974), pp. 117-21.

3 H.W. Duda, "Das Druckwesen in der Türkei", in *Gutenberg-Jahrbuch*, Mainz 1935, pp. 226-42.

4 Mutluay, *50 Yıl*, p. 110; on censorship cf. Alpay, *Harf Devrimi*, pp. 31-32; Cevdet Kudret, *Abdülhamit Devrinde Sansür*, Istanbul 1977. On the continued life of achievements of the 19th century cf. Ş. Kurdakul, *Çağdaş Türk Edebiyatı. Meşrutiyet Dönemi*, Istanbul 1976, pp. 18-25. On the social origin of the writers ibidem, pp. 32 f.

5 On the history and course of events cf. B. Lewis, *The Emergence of Modern Turkey*, London and New York 1968, and the bibliography given there; Z. Korkmaz, *Cumhuriyet Döneminde Türk Dili*, Ankara 1974, pp. 51-58; S.N. Özerdim, *Yazı Devriminin Öyküsü*, Ankara 1978[2]; Alpay, *Harf Devrimi*, pp. 10-23; *Yazı Devrimi*, Ankara 1979 (Türk Dil Kurumu); A. Merdivenci, *Türk Yazı Devrimi ve Yurt Dışındaki Türklere Yansıması*, Istanbul 1980.

6 Niyazi Berkes, *The Development of Secularism in Turkey*, Montreal 1964, pp. 422, 475-76; Mutluay, *50 Yıl*, p. 418

7 On 29/8/1928 İsmet İnönü said that reforming the script was in order to promote literacy: H.W. Duda, "Die neue Lateinschrift in der Türkei. I. Historisches", in *OLZ* 1929, column 445; J. Deny and R. Marchand, *Petit Manuel de la Turquie nouvelle*, Paris 1933, p. 241; F.R. Atay,

for the most part had no schools, there lived more than 12.4 million people who did not know how to read and write. The common efforts to attain the primary goal of literacy with the help of the script change have had an undisputed success.[8] With the improvement of the school system, the establishment of compulsory school attendance and the inclusion of courses for adult education notable successes have been achieved. If the statistics on illiteracy still appear to be high today,[9] as is known, this is because individual parts of the country remain very unevenly developed and the eastern provinces increase the overall average of the illiteracy figures.[10]

The script revolution opened up the significance of the language problem[11] and provided the strongest impetus to the language reform that was already underway; *Osmanlıca, yeni yazı yaşayamazdı*: "Ottoman Turkish could not survive in the new script."[12] Now work to reform the language began in earnest; the Alphabet Commission, which had made preparations for the introduction of the Latin script, was transformed into a Language Commission and now began – in contrast to earlier phases – the state-supported language reform whose first moderate and not very successful phase came to an end in 1931 with the dissolution of the commission.[13] The further development of language

Çankaya. Atatürk'ün doğumundan ölümüne kadar, Istanbul 1969, p. 443; Y.K. Karaosmanoğlu, *Politikada 45 yıl*, Ankara 1968, p. 113; Alpay, *Harf Devrimi*, pp. 23 and 83. For a state-of-the-art update see Johann Strauss, "Literacy and the development of the primary and secondary educational system; the role of the alphabet and language reforms", E.J. Zürcher (ed.), *Turkey in the Twentieth Century*, Berlin 2008, pp. 479-516.

8 K. Steinhaus, *Soziologie der türkischen Revolution*, Frankfurt a.M. 1969, pp. 111-12; cf. the criticism by İ. Başgöz, "The Free Boarding (Leyli Meccani) Schools" in K.H. Karpat, *Social Change and Politics in Turkey*, Leiden 1973, p. 208, and the balance sheet provided in "Harf Devriminden 50 Yıl Sonra" in *Varlık Yıllığı 1979*, Istanbul 1979, pp. 137-40; Alpay, *Harf Devrimi*, p. 83. For an update on literacy rates see Johann Strauss, "Literacy", pp. 504-06.

9 On 24 March 1981, the European edition of *Milliyet Halk Gazetesi* printed the announcement of the Minister of Education, Hasan Sağlam, according to which a new campaign to promote literacy, based on directives from the National Security Council, had begun in the year 1981 marking the centenary of Atatürk's birth; 13 milion Turks were still unable to read and write; of these 6 million aged 12 to 44. According to the same announcement, out of 100 Turkish men 33 were illiterate, out of 100 women 66, and among those active in agricultural work 51 out of 100 were illiterate. Strauss, "Literacy", passim.

10 *Varlık Yıllığı 1979*, p. 138, for 1979 counts 3116 villages as without a school. Cf. A.N. Yücekök, *Türkiye'de Örgütlenmiş Dinin Sosyo-Ekonomik Taban (1946-1968)*, Ankara 1971, pp. 208 and passim. Cf. J. Kolars, "The integration of the village into the national life of Turkey", in Karpat, *Social Change*, pp. 182-202.

11 Mutluay, *Çağdaş Edebiyatı*, p. 335.

12 Atay, *Çankaya*, p. 467.

13 K. Steuerwald, *Untersuchungen zur türkischen Sprache der Gegenwart*, Berlin 1963, I, p. 16.

purification up to the stage of radical purism[14] has been studied in much greater detail than the diverse effects of this development on literature.[15]

Just as the earlier secular laws, the abolition of the Arabic script brought about a certain amount of revulsion and antagonism in the Muslim population. Almost all of it was kept out of the newspapers. When in August 1928 a cold spell with exceptional snowfall on the Black Sea coast seemed to the pious Muslims of Trebizond to be a sign of God's wrath over abandonment of the holy alphabet of the Koran and they streamed into the mosques, an American newspaper set the Turkish authorities in motion,[16] although the law regarding the alphabet change only came into effect on November 3rd 1928. In January 1928 a report appeared in newspapers according to which there had been arrests in Sivas of certain persons who attempted to inflame the population by maintaining that the new script would harm religion. The official denials which followed and the legal proceedings that were instituted against the responsible editor[17] shed some light on the final months of the *Takrir-i Sükûn*. The forbearance with which Istanbul's doormen, porters and gardeners submitted to these and other reforms seemed to be based on the belief that the new regime was only temporary anyway.[18] Assuming that independent actions only arose from a fraction of the population and that the grumbling of villagers against "the infidel script"[19] remained ineffective, one may describe the change-over as a complete success. It was to the credit of the personal commitment of Mustafa Kemal as well as the zeal of the urban intelligentsia who followed him into the countryside with chalk and a blackboard.[20]

---

14 Ibidem, pp. 54 f. and passim. Gy. Hazai, *Kurze Einführung in das Studium der türkischen Sprache*, Budapest 1978, pp. 105-07; Idem, "Die Spracherneuerung im Reformwerk Kemal Atatürks", in *Der Kemalismus und die moderne Türkei*, Berlin 1979, pp. 82-87 (Asien, Afrika, Lateinamerika 5).

15 A.S. Levend, *Türk Dilinde Gelişme ve Sadeleşme Evreleri*, 19723, treats language and literature up until 1928 in connection with one another, but afterwards only the language reform. The survey I attempt here of the effect of the script change on Turkish literature is not nearly complete. For valuable help with procuring relevant literature I must thank the late R. Anhegger, A.H. de Groot, the late P. Kappert, D. Koopman, M.B.B.M. Rault, the University of Leiden Library and the Vereniging ter Bevordering van de Belangen des Boekhandels, Amsterdam.

16 B.N. Şimşir, "Amerikan Belgelerinde Türk Yazı Devrimi", in *Belleten* XLIII (1979), pp. 134-35.

17 Duda, "Lateinschrift I", column 449.

18 E.L. Ives, First Secretary of the American Embassy, in October 1928, in Bilal N. Şimşir, *Türk Yazı Devrimi*, pp. 180-81.

19 A. Schimmel, "Islam in Turkey", in *Religion in the Middle East*, II, Cambridge 1969, p. 71.

20 Duda, "Lateinschrift I", columns 448 and 452; Steinhaus, *Soziologie*, p. 112; Alpay, *Harf*

The quickest to become accustomed to the new alphabet, as foreign observers noted, were those who previously could not read and write,[21] and "the mass of semi-educated".[22] Ordinary people appeared to be pleased that they could now spell out the words of a newspaper,[23] and in a play that was written five years later a whole village eagerly learns the new letters; even the old wet-nurse can read a book about the Gazi after two months of reading-exercises.[24] At the time of writing (1981) no other treatments of the alphabet change in literature had come to my knowledge.

If mention was made of a turning-point[25] in Turkish cultural life in the sense that the script change represented a crisis that shook society,[26] this referred to, first, the efforts made to educate the masses, second to forms of resistance against the new script which the educated had to overcome within themselves. By prohibiting the learning and printing of the Arabic script the authorities were intervening profoundly into the innermost being of the cultural elite.

Of course, learning the old script had been difficult – Ahmet Râsim speaks about this in his autobiography *Falaka* which appeared in 1927 – and certainly the Turkish version of the Roman letters was easy to learn. But the dissatisfaction was not the result of an objective analysis of the pros and cons of both alphabets but was bound up with the traditional, religiously rooted feeling of attachment to the Arabic script.[27] To give this up was felt to be a sacrifice by even the most loyal of Mustafa Kemal's comrades-in-arms. This was "the most disturbing of Atatürk's upheavals".[28] İsmail Habib (Sevük, 1892-1954) wrote shortly after Atatürk's death: "The educated of a whole nation, all at the same time, had to rush forth from the clarity of the accustomed script into the dark-

---

Devrimi, pp. 26-29; Şimşir, "Yazı Devrimi", p. 147 (on how the law was carried out in only two months).

21 Şimşir, "Yazı Devrimi", pp. 172, 176, and especially 195.

22 Duda, "Lateinschrift I", column 451.

23 Şimşir, "Yazı Devrimi", p. 176.

24 Halit Fahri (Ozansoy), *On Yılın Destanı*, reviewed by C.-U. Spuler, "Das türkische Drama der Gegenwart", in *Welt des Islams* XI (1968), pp. 16-17.

25 Mutluay, *50 Yıl*, p. 175.

26 Deny-Marchand, *Manuel* (see fn. 7), pp. 240-41; Mutluay, *50 Yıl*, p. 214; Şimşir, "Yazı Devrimi", p. 113, according to an American newspaper. J.H. Kramers, art. "Türken" in *EI*[1] IV (1934), p. 991.

27 Şimşir, "Yazı Devrimi", p. 180.

28 "The most disturbing of Atatürk's revolutions (*inkılaplar*) was the new script. In order to commit oneself to this ordeal (*çile*), it was necessary to accept the sacrifice as an honor." Atay, *Çankaya*, p. 443.

ness of the script to which they had to get accustomed."[29] Falih Rıfkı Atay (1894-1971), looking back in 1951, noted: "As a national minority of five to ten percent, we would make a sacrifice for coming generations...Our generations had to shoulder the whole burden. We had grown up with the old script. Every Turkish word was a picture for us. We read it not by spelling out each letter (*heceliyerek*) but by simply looking at it. We stood before the thankless task, which we would perhaps not be able to achieve up to the end of our life, of having to give up this picture and to replace it with a new one. We once had read, now we would spell..."[30] All Muslim Turks, the illiterate as well as the educated, were familiar with *one* book: the Koran, which in the smallest peasant hut had its place of honor and which one knew how to open and hold. Anyone picking up a book in Latin script for the first time must feel confused – the directions had been switched; the top was the bottom, left had become right.[31] People were aware of what an effort it required from now on to write from left to right in an unfamiliar script. This sacrifice could be demanded of civil servants: already from September 1928 all administrative correspondence, including in the Directorate of Religious Affairs, had to be carried out in the new script.[32] All public employees had to undergo tests regarding knowledge of the new alphabet.[33] Writers did not have to fear anything like this but difficulties also arose for their work, the history of which can only be written after an interval of time. It had been writers, who along with well-known religious scholars, had declared themselves against the Latin alphabet.[34] Now some were not satisfied with the method and the tempo of its introduction.[35] The greatest difficulties were presented by orthography which in the begin-

29 İsmail Habib (Sevük), *Atatürk İçin. Ölümünden sonra hatıralar ve Hayatındayken yazılanlar*, Istanbul 19395, p. 77.

30 Atay, *Çankaya*, p. 443. Cited verbatim in Alpay, *Harf Devrimi*, p. 26, and in "purified" form in Merdivenci, *Yazı Devrimi*, p. 136.

31 Alpay, *Harf Devrimi*, pp. 43-44. Permission to print the Koran was not given until 1874; Berkes, p. 195. It is worth remembering that the Turkish public had earlier shown little enthusiasm for books *printed* in Arabic *letters*. By contrast, lithographic printing, introduced in the 1830s, had been very popular: it reproduced the beauty of the handwritten Arabic script in a way which the type-face of the letterpress could not equal. See Günay Alpay Kut, "Maṭbaʿa. 2. In Turkey", *EI*[2] VI (1991), p. 799 and 803; Ekmeleddin İhsanoğlu and Hatice Aynur, "Yazmadan Basmaya Geçiş Osmanlı Basma Kitap Geleneğinin Doğuşu (1729-1848)", *Osmanlı Araştırmaları* XXII (2003), pp. 219-55.

32 Şimşir, "Yazı Devrimi", p. 212.

33 Ibidem, pp. 184 f.

34 Levend, *Evreler*, pp. 396 f.

35 Duda, "Lateinschrift I", column 451.

ning was uncertain and arbitrary. Some were disturbed by the pronunciation that had been adopted as the basis[36] and complained of the absence of an authoritative dictionary.[37] The Language Commission on occasion contravened its own rules,[38] and so it was no wonder that writers, too, chose their own paths to follow. İbnülemin Mahmud Kemal İnal (1870-1957), the writer and scholar, ignored the new spelling up to the end of his life and insisted that his books be published in his own peculiar spelling, the latter being his attempt to reproduce the historical way of writing Ottoman Turkish.[39]

How difficult bidding farewell to the old familiar script was even for the willing, is illustrated by such curiosities as the philological treatise on the word "pasha", which in July 1939 Hüseyin Hüsameddin (Yasar, 1870-1939) in the Turkish modernized *rik'a* style dedicated to the nation's president, Mustafa Kemal[40] who himself no longer used the Arabic script. Calligraphy was still practiced as an art[41] but the art of the chronogram, based on the Ebced, i.e. on Arabic script, was now finished. The great dates of the early Republic had been immortalized in the chronogram.[42]

Declared opponents of the secularist Republic out of principle retained the Arabic script; Rıza Nur (1879-1942) always used it in exile and railed against the alphabet change.[43] The "Bediüzzaman" Said Nursi (1873-1960) never learned the Latin script and insisted that the Arabic script be used for his works.[44] Many contented themselves by continuing to use the old script for private purposes such as correspondence, note taking and writing preliminary drafts.[45] One of the younger authors, the teacher of literature and later professor of literature, Ahmet Hamdi Tanpınar (1901-1962), retained the old script for his own

36 Şimşir, "Yazı Devrimi", pp. 175, 186-87 and 198.

37 Duda, "Lateinschrift I", column 450; Idem, "Lateinschrift II", in OLZ 1930, columns 400-13.

38 Duda, "Lateinschrift II", column 406.

39 F. İz, art. "İnal" in EI2, see below p. XX.

40 İ. Parmaksızoğlu, *Türkiye Yazmaları Toplu Kataloğu*, Ankara 1979, pp. 3-4, no. 2. Cf. the "Véritable" *Histoire d'Amasya* also composed around the same time in Arabic script by Osman Fevzi (Olcay, 1887-1973) with a photograph of Gazi Mustafa Kemal; described in B. Flemming, *Türkische Handschriften*, Wiesbaden 1968, p. 265, no. 335.

41 Cf. A. Alparslan, art. "Khaṭṭ in Turkey" in EI^2.

42 M. Mercanlıgil, *Ebced Hesabı*, Ankara 1960, with chronograms celebrating the signing of the Treaty of Lausanne and the reform concerning hats (p. 61).

43 Cf. vols. 13-14 of his *Türk tarihi*, described in Flemming, *Türkische Handschriften*, p. 175, no. 215. When after his return Rıza Nur began working as editor of a magazine, he appears to have accepted the alphabet.

44 C.-U Spuler, *Nurculuk*, Bonn 1973 (Studium zum Minderheitenproblem im Islam I), pp. 134 and 162.

45 Şimşir, *Yazı Devrimi*, pp. 196-97.

literary use.[46] The "Latin expert", who within the civil bureaucracy transcribed the memoranda and rough drafts of his fellow civil servants from the old to the new script,[47] was also to be found in the editorial offices of newspapers, to which many prominent authors still handed in their articles in the old script.[48] For the printing-presses which had to make the change-over from Arabic to Latin fonts we may turn to a contemporary writer, Orhan Pamuk. "In the background an electrical printing-press (*tipo makine*) with treadle (*sallama pedal*) was running with a pleasant sound; a hundred and ten years old, it had been manufactured in Leipzig by the Baumann Company. After printing in Hamburg for a quarter-century, it had been sold to Istanbul in 1910, during the period of freedom of the press under the second constitutional monarchy. After it had done its work there for forty-five years, in 1955, just as it was about to be sold off as scrap it had been shipped to Kars by train by Serdar Bey's late father."[49] Several printing-presses now converted from setting type by hand, which until then had been the norm, to mechanical type-setting, and the demand for this kind of printing machinery rose by leaps and bounds. Due to the inexperience of the type-setters, initially the outer form was imperfect and there was a plethora of typographical errors.[50] But the technique of printing was soon perfected[51] and the technical improvement as well as the simplification resulting from the smaller number of letters led to a reduction in printing costs. Indeed, it was the era of cheap books: the prices varied from 5 kuruş (10 Pfennig) to 5 TL (10 Marks); prices ranging from 50 kuruş to 3 TL for books that were mostly

46 His posthumously published novel, *Aydaki Kadın*, was written entirely in Arabic script; cf. G. Güven, "Ahmet Hamdi Tanpınar'ın Son Romanı", in *Journal of Turkish Studies* 3 (Cambridge, Mass. 1979), pp. 135-95, with photomechanical printing of parts of the manuscript.

47 Şimşir, *Yazı Devrimi*, p. 194.

48 Ibidem, p. 197.

49 Duda, "Druckwesen", pp. 240-42; Alpay, *Harf Devrimi*, pp. 36 f. Orhan Pamuk, *Kar*, Istanbul 2002, pp. 28-29. Cf. *Snow*, Translation by Maureen Freely, London 2004, p. 24; Christoph K. Neumann, *Schnee*, Munich 2005, p. 34.

50 Ibidem, p. 242; Şimşir, *Yazı Devrimi*, p. 165.

51 J. Stummvoll, "Das türkische Buchwesen 1928-1933", in *Börsenblatt für den Deutschen Buchhandel*, no. 190, 17 August 1935, p. 674. The type-setter (*mürettip*) and the proof-reader (*musahhih*) had already had to learn new techniques in the first years of the Republic when the Arabic script was still in use. This did not come about without some resistance, as the trained journalist M. Zekeriya (Sertel, 1890-1980) experienced when he wished to modernize his magazine *Resimli Ay*. The *mürettiphane ustaları* put up a struggle, and the *başmürettip* beseeched him not to make him a laughing-stock in the eyes of his colleagues; M.Z. Sertel, *Hatırladıklarım (1905-1950)*, Istanbul 1968, p. 128.

paperbacks were the rule, higher prices being the exception.[52] The book trade was still organized in very different ways; there were numerous bookshops in Istanbul, including foreign ones, compared with very few bookdealers in Ankara.[53] Ankara was also still far behind Istanbul as a place of publication; here on the eve of the script change governmental and semi-governmental publications were printed which were meant to make known the new regime and to introduce people to contemporary science and technology. The printing in 1927 of Mustafa Kemal's "Speech" (*Nutuk*)[54] before the Congress of the Republican People's Party may be considered the most important publishing event of that kind. In Istanbul, the center of the book business, over a hundred publishers brought out works of fiction and poetry (*belles-lettres*). At the same time, the publication of serious novels and short stories in the years 1926-1927 was relatively small; and so the serialized novel in magazines and newspapers remained an important literary form which had been used earlier by popular authors such as Ömer Seyfettin (1884-1920) and now was not spurned by established writers like Halide Edip (Adıvar, 1882-1964) and Reşat Nuri (Güntekin, 1889-1956). As a possible outlet for publishing for many authors – within the restrictions of the *Takrir-i Sükûn* – the press also continued to be an instrument of literary criticism; newspapers like *Vakit* and magazines like *Dergâh* (1921-1923), *Resimli Ay* (from 1924) and *Hayat* (from 1926) played an important role in the literary debates; the founding of *Meş'ale*, which we will deal with in greater detail, occurred in the year of the alphabet change.

In 1928, on the brink of the introduction of the new alphabet, the number of printed titles rose considerably;[55] with higher hopes in possible sales for works in the old script, publishers brought everything available onto the market. When this possibility disappeared on the 31st of December 1928, adaptation to the new methods of production was bound to cause the number of new publications to drop drastically. In the first half of the year 1929 the situation took on crisis proportions. Authors assumed publication of their books themselves since publishers could not cover their own costs,[56] and in the book trade smaller book production led to a shortage, while on the other hand there were

52 Ibidem, p. 673.

53 Ibidem, p. 674. Upon his arrival in Ankara in September 1933, J. Stummvoll found only one book-dealer on hand: Akba; "the former branch of Hachette was set up as a lending library on the premises of a hairdresser" (see ftn. 51 above).

54 For editions of the "Speech", see Erik Jan Zürcher, *The Unionist Factor*, Leiden 1984, p. 175.

55 1084 books in 1928 in the old script as compared with 887 in the year 1927: Alpay, *Harf Devrimi*, pp. 52-53. A list of printing-presses and publishing houses for 1928-1938, ordered according to cities, is also provided there, pp. 129-39.

56 Mutluay, *50 Yıl*, p. 418.

complaints about the aversion of the public who had not been able to acquire a taste for the new script.[57]

In short, Turkey's fiction writers, with the Depression falling hard on their heads, had to find ways to publish and had to come to terms with the new printing technique, with orthography, and – in the days of language reform – with their choice of words.[58]

The established prose authors among them, as we mentioned at the start, came from the Ottoman past and were moulded by the ideal of *L'art pour l'art* of "the New Literature", *Edebiyat-i Cedide* (1896-1901), and "the Dawn of the Future", *Fecr-i Âti*; they constituted the last rearguard of the Ottoman *Tanzimat* traditions. The period of Abdülhamid II had shaped the work of the elders even in terms of subject matter which, since authors had no freedom of movement, remained narrowly confined within the municipal boundaries of Istanbul. The young Yakup Kadri (Karaosmanoğlu, 1889-1974) broke new ground with subjects taken from his West-Anatolian homeland.[59] From these authors, who had experienced the Young Turk Revolution and the subsequent limitations imposed on writers' work, no transforming upheaval in literature was to be expected. Rather they continued their efforts to create "a national literature", *Millî Edebiyat*, into which the *Fecr-i Âti* movement had flowed. No great names of Turkish literature are involved in the production of 1928-1929, except possibly at the outermost fringes. The *Servet-i Fünun* author Halit Ziya (Uşaklıgil, 1866-1945), the most prolific novel writer of the pre-Republican period, lived in retirement in his country house in Yeşilköy; Hüseyin Cahit (Yalçın, 1874-1957) had recently returned from banishment in Anatolia; Cevat Şakir Kabaağaçlı (1886-1973) turned his place of banishment, Bodrum, into his permanent residence and emphasized this by means of his pen-name Halikarnas Balıkçısı ('Fisherman of Halicarnassus'). Memduh Şevket (Esendal, 1883-1952), a master of story-telling, lived in honorable banishment as ambassador in Teheran.[60] Refik Halit (Karay, 1888-1965), the narrator of the *Memleket hikayeleri*, had been expelled from the country in 1922 because of his opposition to the emerging Republic; he lived for fifteen years in Syria and Lebanon. These writers were not able to wield any influence from a distance. Only Halide

57 Newspapers and magazines did not sell because the population was simply not capable of reading them yet; Z. Sertel, *Hatırladıklarım*, p. 167; Alpay, *Harf Devrimi*, pp. 55 f.; Şimşir, *Türk Yazı Devrimi*, pp. 191-92.

58 For the language reform, see Geoffrey Lewis, *The Turkish Language Reform: A catastrophic Success*, Oxford 1999.

59 Cevdet Kudret, *Türk Edebiyatında Hikâye ve Roman. 1859-1959. II. Meşrutiyet'ten Cumhuriyet'e Kadar.* Istanbul 19672, p. 112.

60 Ibidem, pp. 373 and 402.

Edip, who, for political reasons, lived abroad since 1924, had attained world fame because even abroad people saw Turkish history in her books. Her connection with Turkey was not entirely broken off; in the decisive year 1928 – she was against the Latin script – her novel *Zeyno'nun Oğlu* could still be published as a book in the old script, after it had been partly printed as a serialized novel in 1926 and 1927. The background of this novel is provided by the revolt of the Kurds in 1925; the authoress especially contrasts the superficial Istanbul "*alafranga*" society that wants to modernize the East-Anatolian garrison city of Diyarbakır, with the national self-assurance of the Turkish heroes.[61] The patriotic book was well received, notwithstanding the negative publicity which the appearance of the second volume of Halide Edip's memoirs written in English – *The Turkish Ordeal* – unleashed in the Turkish press during the summer of 1928.[62] People remained grateful to the authoress for her epic of the Turkish struggle for freedom, *Ateşten Gömlek* (1922, in book form 1923), and this became one of the first works in Latin script when, already in October 1928, the newspaper *Vakit* printed parts of it in the new alphabet.[63]

Inside the country itself Yakup Kadri and Reşat Nuri enjoyed the greatest success in their efforts to produce a national novel. Yakup Kadri, who wrote enthusiastically in newspapers in the service of the script reform, still had published in the old script, as part of his historical cycle, *Sodom ve Gomore* in which he describes the defeatist milieu of Istanbul at the time of the Armistice (*Mütareke*).[64] What struck Turkish critics in it was the heaping up of Arabic, Persian, and even foreign words from French along with a remnant of "Neo-Hellenism" from the *Meşrutiyet* period.[65] The all-dominating subject of the year 1928 found as little expression in this book as it did in the novel *Yeşil Gece* which Reşat Nuri published in the old script in 1928. It is the first novel of social criticism by this writer who saw his sensitive novel *Çalıkuşu* come out in its fourth edition in 1928 and who in the same year published three other titles:

---

61 İ. Enginün, *Halide Edib Adıvar'ın Eserlerinde Doğu ve Batı Meselesi*, Istanbul 1978, pp. 226-43.

62 Enginün, *Adıvar*, p. 71. With the controversial passages toned down by the authoress herself, the work appeared in Turkish decades later (i.e. 1959-1960) in the magazine *Hayat* under the title *Millî mücadele hatırlardan parçalar* and as a book in 1962 with the title *Türk'ün Ateşle İmtihanı*; cf. Enginün, *Adıvar*, p. 43.

63 Enginün, *Adıvar*, p. 490.

64 For socio-economic conditions, including intellectuals and the press, during the Armistice era, see Nur Bilge Criss, *Istanbul under Allied Occupation 1918-1923*, Leiden 1999.

65 Kudret, *Roman II*, pp. 133, 135 and 137; cf. İ. Enginün, "Yakup Kadri Karaosmanoğlu'nun Sodom ve Gomore adlı romanında yabancılar", in *Journal of Turkish Studies* 3 (1979), pp. 111-24.

Leyla ile Mecnun and *Sönmüş Yıldızlar* (short stories; 2nd edition in old script) and the novel *Acımak*. Reşat Nuri, who around this time translated Emile Zola's novel *Vérité* (*Hakikat* appeared as a book in 1929), takes the secularization of the Turkish education system as an occasion to launch an appeal for deliverance from the "Green Night" of Islamic obscurantism. While in *Vérité* Zola transfers the Dreyfus affair to the French school system, Reşat Nuri sees a Dreyfus case in the arson committed in a *türbe*, for which an innocent teacher is blamed and arrested. After the liberation of İzmir from the Greeks, the obscurantists who have now become "Kemalists" denounce the hero who has returned from prison.[66]

Prose literature of the year 1928 includes no less than four titles by Aka Gündüz (pseudonym of Enis Avni, 1886-1958): *Odun Kokusu, Tank-Tango*, and the short stories *Hayatdan Hikayetler* and *Bir Şoförün Gizli Defteri*, manifestly all in the old script. Burhan Cahit (Morkaya, 1892-1949) was represented with three titles, *Hizmetçi Buhranı, Bizans Akşamları* and the widely read *Harp Dönüşü*. Ercüment Ekrem (Talu, 1888-1956) published the novel *Gemi Arslanı* and a volume of short stories under the title *Gün Doğmayınca*. *Ak Saçlı Genç Kız* by Mahmut Yesari (1895-1945) appeared, and his *Hınç* also came out in serial form in the newspaper *Milliyet*. Mehmet Rauf (1875-1931), one of the first contributors to *Servet-i Fünun*, in 1928 published the novel *Kan Damlası* in old script and one year later in Latin script the novel *Halâs* which was hailed as "the first great novel in the Turkish letters". The short story writer and poetess, Şükûfe Nihal, published a novel, *Renksiz Istırab*, and a volume of stories with the title *Tevekkülün Cezası*. The widely admired novelist Hüseyin Rahmi (Gürpınar, 1864-1944), who had not belonged to the *Edebiyat-ı Cedide*, continued in his popular novels – *Kokotlar Mektebi* and *Muhabbet Tılsımı* appeared in 1928 in the old script – to describe the transformed society of Istanbul. Hüseyin Rahmi's novels have been said to offer a panorama of Turkish urban society in a state of acute moral crisis.[67]

The low-priced reading material that Peyami Safa (1899-1961) provided under the pseudonym Server Bedi in old and new script contributed to the expansion of the reading public. He had caused a sensation in 1922 with his novel on life and manners *Sözde Kızlar* (in book form 1925) and in addition published two novels in 1928 under his real name, *Bir Akşamdı* and *Şimşek*.

These works selected here as samples from the production of the year 1928 do not occupy a prominent position in literary history. Similarly, in the following year stories like *Kırmızı ve Siyah* by Nahit Sırrı (Örik, 1894-1960) – Turkish

66 Kudret, *Roman II*, p. 318.

67 Berkes, p. 303.

wife throws herself from precipice along with European female rival – or the sentimental novel *İki Süngü Arasında* by Aka Gündüz do not offer any new developments. This is hack work, produced under conditions of post-*Takrir-i Sükûn*.[68] Fiction writers spent the thirties absorbing the material they would use in the forties; modernist fiction had to wait until Ahmed Hamdi Tanpınar's *Huzur* (1949) and his *Clock-Setting Institute* (*Saatleri Ayarlama Enstitüsü*).[69]

For poetry the key moment occurred in 1928. Here, too, the past reached into the present. That past included names of which the Turkish Republic was proud. Abdülhak Hamit (Tarhan, 1852-1937) was venerated as the greatest poet of the *Tanzimat* period. The extent of esteem in which Tevfik Fikret (1867-1915), the great poet of the *Servet-i Fünun*, was held is demonstrated by the fact that one of the first books printed in Latin script in 1928 was a small volume containing his poems *Tarih-i Kadim* and *Doksan Beşe Doğru*,[70] which had caused a sensation in 1909 with their rejection of Ottoman history and late-Ottoman anti-parliamentarianism. Two poets of flawless form exercised immense authority, Ahmet Haşim (1884-1933) and Yahya Kemal (Beyatlı, 1884-1958). The first published two volumes of essays in 1928 and then a second edition of his famous volume of poetry *Piyale*. Yahya Kemal, as a diplomat in Warsaw, Madrid and Lisbon, was too far removed from publishing possibilities and no poems by him appeared during the years 1926-1933.[71] Bound to the language, those who had been banished or were political emigrés could scarcely attract notice in Turkey; Rıza Tevfik (Bölükbaşı, 1868-1949) lived in Mecca and Amman, Mehmet Akif (Ersoy, 1873-1936), the poet who had composed the Republic's national anthem, lived in exile in Egypt.[72] Alongside the national subjects treated by a Mehmet Emin (Yurdakul, 1869-1944), the *Millî Şair*, new problems emerged after the founding of the Republic. Emancipation from quantitative meter, for which Mehmet Emin had paved the way, was taken further by the poets of the First World War period, especially by the five "syllable-counting" poets. Three of the latter, Orhan Seyfi (Orhon, 1890-1972), Faruk Nafiz (Çamlıbel, 1898-1973) and Yusuf Ziya (Ortaç, 1895-1967), in 1928 published poems in book form, Orhan Seyfi the volume of collected poems *Gönülden Sesler*, Faruk Nafiz

68 "A period of stagnation", Strauss, pp. 507-08.

69 Analysis and partial translation by Walter Feldman in Kemal Silay (ed.), *Anthology of Turkish Literature*, Bloomington, Indiana, 1996, pp. 384-90.

70 With a preface by Hasan-Âli (Yücel, 1867-1961) who contributed his own poem *Yeni Hayat* (from 1925).

71 Mutluay, *50 Yıl*, p. 178. In 1933 in the Öz Türk Matbaası there appeared a small volume of poems, reprinted from magazines, under the title *24 Şiir ve Leyla*.

72 The six books of his *Ṣafaḥāt* appeared in old script in the 2nd to 4th editions in 1928 in Istanbul.

Suda Halklar (in *aruz*) and Yusuf Ziya the volume *Yanardağ*. In 1928, a group of six lyric poets and one prose writer undertook to formulate a common literary program which they published in the volume *Yedi Meş'ale*.[73] And they had their magazine *Meş'ale* follow this program, bringing out a total of eight issues between July and October 1928.[74] But the effect of "The Seven Torches" was greatly surpassed by two other poets who, in the same year, emerged from opposite ends of the poetic spectrum, Necip Fazıl (Kısakürek, 1905-1983) and Nâzım Hikmet (Ran, 1902-1963), both of whose first poems had appeared during the Independence War. In 1928, when Nâzım Hikmet, on his return home from Russia, had his first volume of poems printed in Baku,[75] Necip Fazıl who had returned from Paris in 1926 published his most important volume of poetry, *Kaldırımlar*. Whereas the latter made effective use of modern poetic techniques to express at first bohemian subjects in the tradition of Baudelaire and later ever more intensely his mystical turning away from the changing society around him,[76] the Marxist Nâzım Hikmet completed his shift from national to social themes. This poet, the Turkish poet with the greatest international reputation in the twentieth century, met with an enthusiastic reception when in 1929 he published his first collection of poems in Turkey, *835 Satīr*. Here were the bold ideas, the complete renewal that the prose writers were still unable to achieve. Here the Turks could perceive the truly popular tone which was often so difficult for the language reformers to attain.[77] And here, as well, the upheaval that the introduction of the Latin script had brought about could be used in a positive way for poetry, because the new alphabet revolutionized the very look of a poem on the printed page.[78] As it was, poetry in Turkey could

---

73 *Yedi Mes'ale* appeared in 1928 in Istanbul in the Ahmet Halit Kütüphanesi as an *ortak kitap* consisting of 128 pages priced at 50 kuruş and manifestly in the old script. The authors were Sabri Esat (Siyavuşgil), Yaşar Nabi (Nayır), Cevdet Kudret (Solok), Vasfi Mahir (Kocatürk), Ziya Osman (Saba), Muammer Lütfi (Bahşi) and Kenan Hulusi (Koray).

74 In any case, the magazine *Meş'ale* began in the old script. O. Spies, *Die türkische Prosaliteratur der Gegenwart*, Leipzig 1943, pp. 13-14, and Idem, "Tendenzen und Strömungen in der türkischen Literatur der Gegenwart", in *Zeitschrift für Kulturaustausch* 12 (1962), p. 187, gives the impression that the group came together after the introduction of the Latin script.

75 *Güneşi İçenlerin Türküsü* (in the Latin script), Baku 1928. Printed "for the first time" in 1978 by the Osmanlı Matbaası, Istanbul, as no. 1 of the Ortam Yayınları.

76 N. Menemencioğlu, *The Penguin Book of Turkish Verse*, Harmondsworth 1978, pp. 20 and 52.

77 Z. Baytar, *Nâzım Hikmet Üzerine*, Istanbul 19782, p. 41; S. Sertel, *Roman Gibi* (*Anılar*), Istanbul 1969, p. 132.

78 N. Menemencioğlu, *Turkish Verse*, p. 52.

lay claim to a much more widespread impact than in the West. A factor that contributed to the exceptional popularity of the early poems of Nâzım Hikmet which he published in magazines such as *Resimli Ay* and also soon brought out in book form,[79] were gramophone records that reached a diverse public in coffee houses and restaurants.[80] Young readers were thrilled by this living antithesis to bourgeois poetry but the older generation as well, including the Gazi Mustafa Kemal himself,[81] admired the new world of his free rhythms and images. A clash with the previous luminaries of Turkish literary life was not long in coming. To begin with, Nâzım Hikmet's debate on poetry with individual *üstadlar* such as Ahmet Haşim, Orhan Seyfi, Hamdullah Suphi (Tanrıöver, 1885-1966) and Yakup Kadri threw the literary world into turmoil. Then he and his collaborators from *Resimli Ay* upset the wider public by what was truly an iconoclastic onslaught that led to even older uncontested "idols" (*put*) being knocked from their pedestals. Only Abdülhak Hamit, the *şair-i âzam* and *üstad-i evvel*, showed sympathy for this ruthless break with the predecessors, which he compared to his own breaking away from the Divan literature.[82] Abdülhak Hamit did not live to see the reprinting of his famous works, the historical tragedy in verse *Eşber* (1880) and the elegies *Ölü* and *Makber* (1885), which had been republished in 1341 *hicrî*/1922, i.e. before the founding of the Republic, by the printer Abdülaziz, the owner of the Halk Kütüphanesi.[83] The historical drama in verse *Turhan* was apparently only printed in 1916.[84]

The more readers the books of the older authors had, the more interesting is the question whether the works which they had published in the time of Abdülhamid, under the *Meşrutiyet* and during the Armistice, were reprinted in

---

79 *835 Satīr* appeared in 1929.

80 S. Sertel, *Roman Gibi*, p. 133; Z. Sertel, *Hatırladıklarım*, p. 157.

81 In 1939 İsmail Habib (Sevük) reports how he read one of Nâzım Hikmet's earliest poems in March 1923 to the Gazi Mustafa Kemal who listened with emotion; İsmail Habib, *Atatürk İçin*, pp. 33-34; he was also impressed by the later poems; Z. Sertel, *Hatırladıklarım*, pp. 158-59; cf. H.W. Brands, *Nazım Hikmet. In jenem Jahr 1941*. Neuwied 1963, pp. 123 and 125; cf. also M.F. Köprülü in EI¹ IV, p. 1032. Andrew Mango, *Atatürk*, London 1999, pp. 302, 500 and 521-22.

82 S. Sertel, *Roman Gibi*, pp. 144-45; Z. Sertel, *Hatırladıklarım*, pp. 164-65.

83 *Eşber* was censored and "printed with the permission of the High Inspectorate of Information"; see Petra de Bruijn, *The Two Worlds of Eşber. Western Orientated Verse Drama and Ottoman Turkish Poetry by ʿAbdülhakk Hamid (Tarhan)*, Leiden 1997, with special attention to the editions: pp. 122-34.

84 A curiosity is the edition of the dramatic poem *Ruhlar* by Abdülhak Hamit, published by A. Fischer Leipzig 1941 in Arabic script with the German translation (*Abhandlungen für die Kunde des Morgenlandes* XXVI, p. 4).

the first five years of the Republic in Arabic script, and secondly, whether, when and in what textual form they again appeared on the market in Latin script.[85]

Of course, to begin with not everything could be transcribed; thus the new alphabet automatically assumed a selective function. Further, the need for transcription may have been felt less in the case of more recent books which the reading public still possessed and which could be purchased without difficulty in bookshops. This trade in "old" books actually experienced a revival for a time.[86] But eventually the stocks of book-dealers had to run out. When in May 1939, eleven years after the alphabet change, the First Turkish Publication Congress met in Istanbul – representatives of the book trade also participated – questions were raised concerning new editions of modern Turkish authors whose works were only available in Arabic script. The delegates of the *Dil Tarih-Coğrafya Fakültesi*, Ankara, among them Pertev N. Boratav, proposed to re-edit the complete works of a series of outstanding modern Turkish authors from before the *Tanzimat* period up to the Republic in critical editions in Latin script, while offering in footnotes explanations of words that had become obsolete.[87] In fact, after the Second World War new editions of the works of significant modern authors did appear in Latin script.

With hindsight many found the government's efforts to provide new versions of near-contemporary works insufficient. It was imperative to provide the general reader with reprints in Latin script, say, of the *Türkçe Şiirleri* (first published in 1898) by the "National Poet" Mehmet Emin (Yurdakul), or of fiction such as *Çalıkuşu* (mentioned previously) and the other novels by Reşat Nuri. Indeed, in a ministerial report from the end of the 1960s criticism was levelled against government policy after 1928: "The fact that the works which constitute our national cultural treasure were not transposed into Turkish letters by the competent authorities after the adoption of the Turkish script has loosened the ties with these works for the generations who no longer have a bond with the old script." The Ministry of Education saw as the only path to follow the transposing of the national cultural treasure into the present-day

85 In November 1979, Sami N. Özerdim planned to carry out a study on which old handwritten and printed books were transcribed into the Turkish alphabet; S.N. Özerdim, *Yazı Devrimi* – "Türkçe Gazete" in *Varlık* 866 (Nov. 1979), p. 22.

86 Alpay, *Harf Devrimi*, p. 55.

87 T.C. Maarif Vekilliği, *Birinci Türk Neşriyat Kongresi. 1-5 Mayıs 1939. Raporlar, Teklifler, Müzakere Zabıtları.* (Ankara) 1939, p. 294; the list contains 18 names, eight from the *Tanzimat* period, five of the *Servet-i Fünun* and five authors born between the years 1864 and 1885.

script and language according to a defined plan. There was an awareness that "the number of those who know well our cultural works in the old script and can transpose them (*aktar-*) into the language of today is declining on a daily basis". Haste was therefore recommended, and the Ministry of Education contributed to this planned undertaking by setting up a "Commission for the Great Turkish Writers and Poets". Among other things, the commission was meant to compile anthologies of poets and writers whose works were not required to be published in their entirety, and issue them as memorial volumes (*Anma Kitabı*) on the hundredth birthday of great authors.[88] The planners clearly had in mind near-contemporary Turkish literature in Arabic script. This task had obviously not been foremost in their minds in the years of the alphabet change.

Government sponsorship was to be expected for the intense translation work by means of which one wanted to provide for the need to catch up on foreign literature, and for which generous grants were accorded for buying books from abroad.[89]

As far as Turkish literature is concerned, a bibliographical survey is not intended here.[90]

Just as it is not possible to ascertain which was the last book printed in Arabic script, likewise it cannot be ascertained with certainty which was the first literary work in the Latin script.[91] Transitional phenomena turned up.[92] In

88 Millî Eğitim Bakanlığı Büyük Yazarları ve Şairleri Komisyonu; cited from Ahmed Râsim, *Falaka*, Ankara 1969, Introduction. A large anthology intended for students presented texts in the old language: the series, edited by M. Kaplan, İ. Enginün and B. Emil, *Yeni Türk Edebiyatı Antolojisi*, Istanbul, I (1978), III (1979), was planned to contain ten volumes.

89 Stummvoll, "Buchwesen", p. 674; Idem, "Das türkische Buch- und Bibliothekwesen im Jahre 1935/36", in *Börsenblatt für den deutschen Buchhandel* 211, 10 September 1936, p. 785. Klaus Kreiser, "Übersetzen ins Türkische. Ein Kapitel aus der jüngeren Kulturgeschichte", in G. Schubert (ed.), *Türkische Miszellen. Robert Anhegger Festschrift*, Istanbul 1987, pp. 199-211.

90 In 1981 an assessment of book production between 1923 and 1928, according to year of publication, number of copies printed and contents, was not possible: S.N. Özerdim, *Elli Yılda Kitap (1923-1973)*, Ankara 1974, pp. 16 ff., 66 and 75. Jale Baysal, "Turkish Publishing Activities Before and After the New Alphabet", *Anatolica* VIII (1981), pp. 115-26; drama down to the abolishing of the Arabic script is recorded in T. Poyraz and N. Tuğrul, *Tiyatro Bibliyografyası (1859-1928)*, Ankara 1967; see also Strauss, "Literacy", passim.

91 Competing for the honor is the small volume published by Hasan-Âli Yücel in 1928 with the poems *Tarih-i Kadim* and *Doksan Beşe Doğru* by Tevfik Fikret and the volume of prose poems *Damla Damla* by Ruşen Eşref (Ünaydın, 1892-1959) that likewise appeared in 1928; *Halâs* by Mehmet Rauf was held to be the first novel in Latin script. Cf. İ. Arar, "Bizde Arap Harfleriyle Basılan Son Yeni Harflerde Basılan İlk Kitap Hangisidir", in *Kitap Belleten* II (1962), pp. 6-8.

92 The novel *Gönül Gibi* by Suat Derviş (1905-1972), published in Istanbul in 1928, was printed

the first list of books in Latin script[93] and in the *Türkiye Bibliyografyası* (which began as a separate work), at least ten to fifteen percent of books that were actually published are missing; a deficiency that was only rectified in 1934 when a law came into effect requiring that state authorities be provided with a copy of every publication (dépot légal).[94]

Many of the fears that were voiced on the occasion of introducing the Latin alphabet have long since been disproved. Access to the old cultural and intellectual heritage of their own people has not been blocked for the Turks but has been facilitated through transcription and transference, especially in the case of the major works of the Old and Classical Ottoman period. Prohibiting the Arabic script did have a severe effect in particular on philology and literary studies,[95] but scholarship quickly surmounted this crisis. It has been rightly maintained that the Turkish Republic has shown concern in an exemplary fashion for making accessible the cultural heritage preserved in manuscripts:[96] catalogues of manuscripts,[97] text editions and interpretations have appeared in great numbers. The Turkish system of scholarly transcription is increasingly being applied to Turkish texts outside Turkey as well.

On the other hand, the picture one finds of the modern literature that immediately preceded the alphabet change, is neither uniform nor easy to survey. A few examples:

---

in Arabic script but on the book cover some information is already given in roman script; Arar, "İlk Kitap", p. 6.

93 The first systematic book index entitled *Bibliyografya* was an ongoing bibliography which by means of reviews and summaries was intended to form taste and aesthetic judgement. Its first issue, published in 1931 by the government printing-press, covered the period from the introduction of the roman script up to October 1930; cf. Stummvoll, "Buchwesen", p. 672.

94 The first *Türkiye Bibliyografyası*, published in 1933, contains titles – without a description of the contents – from 1928 to 1933. On the content of both bibliographies cf. Stummvoll, "Buchwesen", pp. 672-73; Idem, "Buch- und Bibliothekwesen", pp. 784-85; Alpay, *Harf Devrimi*, pp. 53-54.

95 As examples we will only mention the extensive dictionary by Hüseyin Kâzim Kadri (d. 1934) and the edition of the *Seyāḥatnāme* of Evliyā Çelebi. The publication of the *Türk Lûgati* (vol. I, 1927; vol. II, 1928) had to break off in the midst of the letter *sīn* and could only be completed during 1943-1945. Volumes VII and VIII of the *Seyāḥatnāme* critically edited by Kilisli Rifat (Bilge) in Arabic script (1928) was only followed by volumes IX and X in Latin script during 1935-1938.

96 Özerdim, "Yazı Devrimi – Türkçe Gazete", p. 22, cited from Melih Cevdet Anday; Alpay, *Harf Devrimi*, pp. 61-63.

97 Hatice Aynur, "Türkiye'de Türkçe Yazma Eserlerinin Kataloglanması üzerine bir Değerlendirme 1989-2002", *Journal of Turkish Studies* 26/I (2002), pp. 37-52.

Poetry:

From 1945 onward much editorial care was bestowed on the near-contemporary poets. In the year 1945 İsmail Hami Danişmend published a third, posthumous edition of Abdülhak Hamit's *Eşber*. He transcribed the text into the new Turkish alphabet according to the rules as given in the *İmlâ Kılavuzu*, sometimes using older spellings, and provided it with a glossary.[98] Tevfik Fikret once again enjoyed affectionate attention; in 1945 *Rübab-i Şikeste*, edited by Mehmet Kaplan, and *Haluk'un Defteri*, edited by Halit Fahri Ozansoy, appeared; in 1946 *Şermin* was brought out in a second edition.

Fahri Uzun's edition of Tevfik Fikret's poems is characterized by its sensitivity to tradition. The editor attempts to rescue something of the magic of Fikret's language by juxtaposing the transcribed original text with its modern Turkish equivalent. Fahri Uzun's transcription, with its attempt to represent the *ʿayn* in various positions (*g*, *'*), harks back to the beginnings of the Latin alphabet for Turkish.[99] A. Özkırımlı, in his book on Tevfik Fikret, prints the poems either with numbered explanations of words at the bottom of the page or transcribed without notes with the modern Turkish versions offered by A. Kadir and Ceyhun Atuf Kansu "speaking in today's Turkish" (*günümüz Türkçeyle söyleyen*).[100]

A. Bezirci also used this method in his study of Ahmed Haşim, in which he prints the poems in the old language with a juxtaposed new version and glosses on obsolete words.[101]

In this way the originals were made available to the reader for comparison.

Prose:

Exemplary editions of prose texts in transcription that remain true to the original are the 1964 reprint of the first Turkish novel, Şemsettin Sami's *Taaşşuk-ı Tal'at ve Fitnat* (1872), prepared by Sedit Yüksel, and the 1969 reprint of Ahmet Rasim's *Falaka* (1927).

However, compared with the meticulous care lavished on the poetry of Abdülhak Hamit, Tevfik Fikret and Ahmet Haşim, prose texts in general are no

98 Analyzed by Petra de Bruijn, *Eşber*, pp. 123-25 and 134.

99 F. Uzun, *Rübâb-ī Şikeste ve Tevfik-Fikret'in bütün diğer eserleri*, Istanbul 19622. In 1928 Hasan-Âli (Yücel), in his publication *Tarihi Kadim* referred to above (see fn. 70), could still print passages in his footnotes in Arabic script if they were especially difficult to understand in Latin script.

100 A. Özkırımlı, *Tevfik Fikret*, Istanbul 1978.

101 A. Bezirci, *Ahmet Haşim. Şairliği ve Seçme Şiirleri. Araştırma/Eleştirme*, Istanbul 1967 (19793)

longer offered to the general reader in the original form of the language. In 1989, Carter V. Findley gave a revealing account of the editorial state of İbnülemin Mahmud Kemal İnal's works, which were then "greatly in need of careful editing".[102]

Nineteenth-century Turkish novelists' unofficial written language had once been "closer to earth under the influence of the popular literature".[103] To Berkes (p. 282), writing in 1964, Ahmed Midhat's Turkish was "comprehensible to a high-school boy even today". Now it was these authors' turn to be "simplified" (*sadeleştirilmiş*) in posthumous editions of their work. The popular novel *Mürebbiye* by Hüseyin Rahmi, first published in 1887 and then brought out in a second edition in 1927, had to wait for its third edition until 1954. In 1960 it came out in a fourth edition in "simplified" (*sadeleştirilmiş*) language.

With the general reader in mind, versions have been produced which are as easy as possible to follow. This is certainly true of numerous titles first published by Halide Edip and Yakup Kadri in the *Meşrutiyet* and *Mütareke* years.

Attempts have been made to "simplify" or improve the author's vocabulary and syntax. Abridgements have been made. The names of the abridgers and simplifiers are usually absent; Baha Dürder (b. 1912) and Abdullah Birkan may be considered exceptions.

After forty-three years Halide Edip's early novel *Yeni Turan* (1912; it had been reprinted in the Arabic script in 1924) reappeared in a third edition, prepared by the writer Baha Dürder in "simplified" language. It then came out in a fourth edition in 1973.

Another example is *Efruz Bey* or *Asilzadeler*, the ironical "fantasy novel" by Ömer Seyfettin (1884-1920). It is made up of seven stories. The first story appeared in the newspaper *Vakit* in 1919 and the remaining ones were published in 1926, well after the author's death.[104] Abdullah Birkan prepared a first, abridged edition in book form, which he provided with a glossary.

The early stories of the modern writer Halit Ziya (Uşaklıgil) were even *Türkçeleştirilmiş* "translated into Turkish",[105] and Memet Fuat had no com-

---

102 Carter Vaughn Findley, *Ottoman Civil Officialdom. A Social History*, Princeton 1898, p. 240.

103 The sociologist Niyazi Berkes (1908-1988), in 1964, referring to Sami, Ahmed Rasim, Hüseyin Rahmi and Hüseyin Cahit, p. 279.

104 For an analysis of the work see Kemal H. Karpat, "Social Environment and Literature: The Reflection of the Young Turk Era (1908-1918)", in Kemal Silay (ed.), *An Anthology of Turkish Literature*, Bloomington, Indiana, 1996, pp. 201 and 280-94

105 Kurdakul, *Meşrutiyet*, p. 63; Halit Ziya (Uşaklıgil), "in part simplified his text himself"; Mutluay, *Çağdaş Edebiyatı*, p. 127.

punction in calling modern Turkish versions of Tevfik Fikret's poems *çeviri* "translation".[106]

The public was and is largely dependent on the discretion of editors and publishing houses. They offer texts *sade dille* "in simple language" or *sadeleştirilmiş* "simplified", which are, by conventional standards, "improved".

Is it due to a higher estimation of poetry over prose that so many older prose works are printed "uncritically" in increasingly modernized versions, whereas lyric poetry is assured of meticulous editorial care?

The changes undertaken in literary works from one edition to the next, even in those written in the Latin script from the start, provide work for the philologist. A grave complication is that some authors are themselves in the habit of making numerous textual alterations and revisions on the occasion of different reprints.

But even where it is a matter of editorial interventions by a foreign hand, the phenomenon of text alteration is noteworthy, as is likewise the amazing occurrence that a younger contemporary cites an earlier modern author in a lexically "purified" form without acknowledging it, as happened with F.R. Atay's *Çankaya* (see p. 153 above and fn. 30).

All these interventions in the text, which come close to being a second editing – while the reader is unable to go back to the original – deserve closer examination in view of their effect on a literary work of art. All simplifications and abridgements are part of their period.

This is illustrated by the Turkish terms employed for the revision of older literature. *Aktarmak* which is used for "transference" from the old script into the new, implies the passing on of the same content from one form into another. *Sadeleştirilmek* or *arılaştırmak* assumes the existence of a language's identity which one can "simplify" or "purify". If one undertakes *Türkçeleştirmek* "translation into Turkish", then one is confronted with the demands of philological faithfulness. The question of script change here runs over into the more comprehensive problems of the development of the Turkish language as well as the development of modern literature.

---

106 Memet Fuat (Bengü), *Tevfik Fikret. Yaşamı. Sanatçı Kişiliği. Yapıtları*, s.l. 1979, p. 95.

CHAPTER 14

The *Cāmiʿ ül-meknūnāt*: A Source of ʿĀlī from the Time of Sultan Süleymān*

The historian of the Ottoman period is confronted with almost unlimited possibilities for research in the area of texts transmitted in manuscript form. For the 15th and 16th centuries in particular, though the situation has improved during the last few years,[1] a broad field still awaits scholarly study. Tursun Beg's *Tārīḫ-i Ebü l-Fetḥ* has recently been edited twice, namely in transcription[2] and in an annotated edition based on one manuscript,[3] the scholarly results of which complement one another. The section of the Ottoman history by the poet Bihiştī that deals with Bāyezīd II has been translated and printed as a manuscript copy.[4] Since the large work of Kemālpaşazāde has been at least partially edited, Ottoman historical research stands on a completely new footing.[5] The works of Tursun Beg, Bihiştī and Kemālpaşazāde have thus been made accessible to an appropriate, indeed even a literary-historical investigation. Rūḥī's work, which is now clearly separated from the accounts of Neşrī and the Oxford Anonymous,[6] still remains unedited. The Chronicle of Oruç, of which a translation of the section dealing with Bāyezīd II now exists, should

* Translated by John O'Kane.

1 For example, by comparison with the survey in H. İnalcık, "Mehmed the Conqueror and his time", in *Speculum* XXXV (1960), pp. 408-27. Cf. also H. İnalcık, "The Rise of Ottoman Historiography", and V.L. Ménage, "The Beginning of Ottoman Historiography", in B. Lewis and P.M. Holt (eds.), *Historians of the Middle East*, London 1962, pp. 152-67 and 168-79.

2 A.M. Tulum, *Tursun Bey. Târîh-i Ebü l-Feth*, Istanbul 1977.

3 H. İnalcık and R. Murphey, *The History of Mehmed the Conqueror by Tursun Beg*, Minneapolis-Chicago 1978.

4 B. Moser, *Die Chronik des Ahmed Sinân Čelebi genannt Bihi̧šti. Eine Quelle zur Geschichte des osmanischen Reiches unter Sultan Bâyezid II*, Munich 1980.

5 Defter I: ş. Turan (ed.), *Ibn-i Kemal. Tevârih-i Âl-i Osman. I. Defter*, Ankara 1970; Defter VII, Idem, *Ibn Kemal. Tevârih-i Âl-i Osman. VII*, Ankara 1954 (photomechanically printed with intro. and indices); Ankara 1957 (critical transcription). Cf. H. Reindl, *Männer um Bāyezīd. Eine prosopographische Studie über die Epoche Bāyezīds II.*, Diss. Munich 1980, with bibliography.

6 V.L. Ménage, "Edirne'li Rûhî'ye atfedilen Osmanlı Tarihinden iki parça", in *İsmail Hakkı Uzunçarşılı'ya Armacan*, Ankara 1976, pp. 311-33. Reindl, *Prosopographie*, pp. 7 f., indicates a date for his biography.

 | DOI 10.1163/9789004355767_015

be edited once again in view of the new research results.[7] It will only be possible to make systematic use of the work of Qıvāmī once the manuscript photomechanically printed in 1955[8] is provided with an introduction and indices. The edition of the *Ṭabaqāt ül-memālik* by Qoca Nişāncı is in the press,[9] whereas the Persian *Haşt Bihişt* of Idrīs Bidlīsī, that was eclipsed by Kemālpaşazāde, still remains unedited,[10] nor has Saʿdeddīn's *Tāc üt-tevārīḫ* been published in a critical edition. The lack of a complete scholarly edition of the *Künh ül-ahbar*, "Essence of Histories", by Muṣṭafā ʿĀlī (d. 1600) has been a great hindrance for research. But the years 1986-1992 represent a turning point in the history of ʿĀlī scholarship. It was in 1986 that Cornell Fleischer provided the first comprehensive biography of ʿĀlī; in 1987 Jan Schmidt's discovery of a crucial part of the "Essence"'s Preface to the 4th Pillar (*rukn*) appeared, and in 1992 Jan Schmidt published the first full-scale analysis of the "Essence".[11] These historical works – one could of course mention several others – were not written for their own sake; they serve, on the one hand, to guide the ruler directly or to remind him indirectly of his duties; they provide him with historical precedents for his action; on the other hand, their purpose is to make policies of the rulers understandable and to influence broad circles with regard to their behavior.[12] For this reason, also, they were written preferably in the Turkish language. Defeats

7 F. Babinger, *Die frühosmanischen Jahrbücher des Urudsch*, Hanover 1925. On this see V.L. Ménage, "On the recensions of Uruc's 'History of the Ottomans'", in *BSOAS* XXX (1967), pp. 314-22; Idem, "Another text of Uruç's Ottoman Chronicle", in *Der Islam* 47 (1971), pp. 273-77. R.F. Kreutel (translated, with commentary) *Der fromme Sultan Bayezid. Die Geschichte seiner Herrschaft nach den altosmanischen Chroniken des Oruç und des Anonymus Hanivaldanus.* Graz-Wien-Köln 1978. In *Prosopographie*, pp. 11-12, Reindl identifies as another Oruç manuscript the manuscript from the private library of Köprülü that is now in the possession of the Yapı ve Kredi Halk Kütüphanesi in Istanbul.

8 F. Babinger, *Fetihnâme-i Sultan Mehmed. Müellifi: Kıvâmî*, Istanbul 1955. Sait Gökçe, *Kivāmı und sein Fetihnāme*, Diss. Munich 1955, is not accessible to me.

9 In the meantime, P. Kappert (ed.), *Geschichte Sultan Süleymān Ḳānūnīs von 1520 bis 1557 oder Ṭabaḳāt ül-Memālik ve Derecāt ül-Mesālik*, Wiesbaden 1981, has been published.

10 B. Moser in *Bihišti*, pp. 7 and 42, announced that an edition by Irene Witzel of Part II of the *Haşt Bihişt* that deals with Bāyezīd II was ready to go to press.

11 Cornell H.Fleischer, *Bureaucrat and Intellectual in the Ottoman Empire. The Historian Mustafa Âli (1541-1600)*, Princeton 1986; Jan Schmidt, *Mustafa ʿAli's Künhü ʾl-ahbār and its Preface according to the Leiden Manuscript*, Istanbul 1987; Jan Schmidt, *Pure Water for Thirsty Muslims. A Study of Mustafa ʿĀlī of Gallipoli's Künhü l-Aḫbār*, Leiden 1992. The present essay appeared in 1981 (*Festschrift Spuler*, Leiden).

12 İnalcık, *Historiography*, p. 164; also G.L. Lewis, "The Utility of Ottoman Fetḥnāmes", in *Historians of the Middle East*, p. 193.

and other events that were disagreeable to the ruler and his house were omitted in this historical literature or smoothed over, without this being seen from a present-day viewpoint as in the category of outright "distortion" and "falsification".[13] Sultan Bāyezīd II's refusal to accept the history work *Haşt Bihişt* which he had commissioned Idrīs Bidlīsī to write, and the circumstances which finally led to Selīm I accepting it and paying out a reward,[14] would be well worth investigating in this connection. Editorial work on the *ġazavātnāme* has moved ahead[15] so that a literary-historical examination is now possible of this category of source that combined religious-epic folk tales with factual historical information about sultans of famous frontier begs.

There are, however, Ottoman texts of historical content in which it is not so much the actions of the sultan that occupy the foreground but the imminent intervention of God through dispatching the Mahdī as a harbinger of the end of the world. In the great history writers as well, who composed histories of the world and of the prophets such as (at least in concept) Neşrī or, at the end of the 16th century, ʿĀlī with his world history *Künh ül-aḫbār*, God's action from the beginning of the world up to the present in fact formed the framework of the narrative. But there also existed an apocalyptic understanding of history that aimed to unveil, on the basis of Koranic revelation and authenticated Traditions along with the support of knowledge of the constellations, something of the secrets of the approaching end of time. The end of the world could be known by means of signs and calculated with the help of chronology which therefore came to play an important role. Defeats and disasters did not basically have to be passed over in silence; rather they were examined in order to ascertain whether they were indeed omens (*ʿalāmet*). Here pity could be expressed for the wounded in the innumerable wars and hope of Paradise for the dead, indeed even criticism of the rulers which had also not been lacking in the old chronicles. An apocalyptic spirit of this kind pervades the historical poem *Cāmiʿ ül-meknūnāt* "*Compendium of Hidden Things*", or rather "Collector of the Concealed" which was written by Mevlānā ʿĪsā. His name did occur in the Leiden manuscript (see no. 17 in this volume), but his identity was only revealed when five folios of ʿĀlī's Preface to the 4th "Pillar" had been discovered

13 The dissertation of B. Moser makes accusations of this kind against the history writer Bihiştī.

14 V.L. Ménage, Art. "Bidlīsī", in *EI2*.

15 A. Gallotta, "Le Ġazavāt di Ḫayreddīn Barbarossa", in *Studi Magrebini* III, Naples 1970, pp. 79-160; H. İnalcık and M. Ocuz, *Gazavât-ı Sultân Murâd b. Mehemmed Hân. İzladi ve Varna Savaşları (1443-1444) Üzerinde Anonim Gazavâtnâme*, Ankara 1978.

in Leiden. Since then, the author of the *Cāmiʿ* has been recognized as "Mevlānā ʿĪsā of Hamid of laudable conduct" (Jan Schmidt) or as "the praiseworthy man of Hamid-ili" (C.H. Fleischer).

For a century and a half this work has been known by name; the history of its slow investigation casts a light on the problems of the field of Ottoman studies where the lack of critical editions has so greatly impeded the study of sources and their relation to one another.

Muṣṭafā ʿĀlī consulted the *Cāmiʿ ül-meknūnāt* for his history of the world and of the Ottomans, *Künh ül-aḫbār*,[16] for which, along with many other models, the work of Aḥmedī's brother (early 15th century), Mollā Ḥamzevī,[17] and the work *Dürr-i meknūn*[18] also served as sources. Later on Ṣolaqzāde (d. 1657-58), in his popular history, cited the *Cāmiʿ ül-meknūnāt*, in fact in almost the same words as ʿĀlī.[19] The *Cāmiʿ* seems to have escaped the attention of Kātib Çelebi (d. 1658).

Joseph von Hammer was the first European scholar who on the basis of Ṣolaqzāde spoke of the "Dschami ul-meknunat",[20] apparently without knowing the work itself. About ten years later, the Leiden University Library purchased from a member of the Genoese Testa family a "poetic miscellany" containing

16 *Künh ül-aḫbār* v (Istanbul 1277/1860-61), p. 94, l. 2 (the episode that involved eating yoghurt when Timur met Bāyezīd i) and *Künh* v, pp. 140, ll. 22 f.; Leiden Cod. Or. 288, fol. 78a, l. 4 (the betrayal of Müsā Çelebi by şaruca), cf. J.H. Mordtmann in *Der Islam* xiii (1923), p. 159; Hüseyin Nihal Atsız, *Âlî Bibliyografyası*, Istanbul 1968, p. 22.

17 *Künh* v, p. 94, l. 2, says: *ammā Cāmiʿ ül-meknünāt nām kitābda ve Aḥmedī qarındaşı Mollā Ḥamzanıñ taʾrīḫinde yazılmışdır ki...*; Leiden Cod. Or. 288, fol. 52b, l. 3 from bottom. The biography of Mollā Ḥamzevī is found in *Künh* v, pp. 125 f.; Leiden Cod. Or. 288, fol. 72a. Already Mordtmann had noticed that ʿĀlī does not mention a history work by Ḥamzevī (loc. cit.).

18 According to Mordtmann, loc. cit., p. 161, this is a work by Yazıcıoğlu Aḥmed Bīcān, who wrote under Meḥmed ii. Can it also have served as a source for ʿĀlī about the circumstances of Bāyezīd ii's dethronement (*Künh* Leiden Cod. Or. 288, fols. 293b-294a)? S. Tansel, *Sultan ii Bâyezit'in siyasî hayatı*, Istanbul 1966, pp. 302-03, does not enter into this question. V.L. Ménage for this reason raises the issue of whether ʿĀlī, here as well as elsewhere, mixes up his sources; see Ménage, "Edirne'li Rûhî", p. 314. For the *Dürr-I meknun* by Yazıcıoğlu Aḥmed Bīcān see the critical edition by Laban Kaptein, Asch 2007.

19 Ṣolaqzāde Meḥmed Hemdemī, *Taʾrīḫ*, Istanbul 1298/1881, p. 79, on the occasion of the Timur-Bāyezīd episode.

20 J. von Hammer, *Geschichte des Osmanischen Reiches* (gor) i, Pest 1827, p. 625 and p. 324, the latter being an extensive explanation (*Erläuterung*) to his rendering of a famous table talk between Timur and Bayezid I (*bir aqsaq ben ve bir kötürüm sen*); Hammer quotes "Solaqzade fol. 20 who is basing himself on the *Dschamiul-meknunat* and the history of Hamza, the brother of Ahmedi".

the *Cāmiʿ ül-meknūnāt*; it reached Leiden from Aleppo, together with other valuable manuscripts.[21] In 1865, P. de Jong and M.J. de Goeje described the work in this manuscript for the first time – without referring to Hammer.[22] When scholars in Turkey began to occupy themselves with the older Ottoman sources, unawareness of the Leiden catalogue and a misunderstanding of the above-mentioned quotation from ʿĀlī caused Necīb ʿĀṣım in 1910 to think that Ḥamzevī, the brother of Aḥmedī, was the author of the *Cāmiʿ ül-meknūnāt*.[23] Bursalı Meḥmed Ṭāhir spoke of an Ottoman history written partly in verse by an author with the *maḫlaṣ* Ḥamzevī and preserved in a manuscript of the private library of the well-known scholar İbnülemin Mahmud Kemal [İnal].[24] In the 1920s, when Ottoman Studies flourished, the *Cāmiʿ* just missed being properly elucidated when Friedrich Giese (in passing)[25] and – in greater detail – Johann Heinrich Mordtmann once again conflated the two separately mentioned sources of ʿĀlī into one "*djāmiʿ ül-meknūnāt* by Mollā Ḥamza, the brother of Aḥmedī"; Mordtmann added that "the *djāmiʿ ül-meknūnāt*" seems "otherwise not to be found anywhere."[26] Franz Babinger, on the other hand, was aware of the Leiden codex, knew that it was not a work by Ḥamzevī, and yet he still decided to search after this author and to ascribe to him a *Cāmiʿ ül-meknūnāt*.[27] Afterwards Babinger seems to have lost sight of the Leiden *Cāmiʿ*, which otherwise undoubtedly he would have classified among the works of the period of Süleymān. The summarizing description in Babinger's GOW, in this case helped an unknown "chronicle in verse by the brother of

21 R.P.A. Dozy, *Catalogus Codicum Orientalium Bibliothecae Academiae Lugduno Batavae*, Leiden 1851, pp. XVII-XVIII. On Gaspard Baron de Testa (born 27/8/1770 in Istanbul, and died there 16/4/1847; Minister Resident of the Netherlands in Constantinople) cf. *Nederland's Adelsboek* 45, The Hague 1952, p. 321 (bibliographical reference A.H. de Groot). Jan Schmidt, *Catalogue of Turkish Manuscripts in the Library of Leiden University, Volume Two*, Leiden 2002, pp. 80-81.

22 P. de Jong and M.J. de Goeje, *Catalogus Codicum Orientalium* III, Leiden 1865, p. 26, no. DCCCCXLIV

23 Necīb ʿĀṣım, "Os̱mānlı taʾrīḫ-nüvīsleri ve müverriḫleri", in *TʿOEM* I (1910), p. 46.

24 Bursalı Meḥmed Ṭāhir, *ʿOs̱mānlı Müellifleri* II, Istanbul 1333/1914-15, p. 74. – The identical remark appears in the new edition in Latin script by A.F. Yavuz and I. Özen, *Bursalı Mehmed Tahir Bey. Osmanlı Müellifleri* II, Istanbul 1972, p. 12.

25 F. Giese, "Einleitung zu meiner Textausgabe der altosmanischen anonymen Chroniken tewārīḫ-i āl-i ʿos̱mān", in *MOG* II (1925), p. 71.

26 J.H. Mordtmann, review of *MOG* I-II, in *Der Islam* 13 (1923), p. 159.

27 F. Babinger, *Die Geschichtsschreiber der Osmanen und ihre Werke*, Leipzig 1927, pp. 13-14, with reference to the manuscript of İbnülemin Mahmud Kemal [İnal].

Aḥmedī" to take on a shadow existence in the history of Turkish literature.[28] In the meantime, Osman Ferid Sağlam had announced that a manuscript of the *Cāmiʿ ül-meknūnāt* was found in his library,[29] and in 1954 Adnan Sadık Erzi took a careful look at the *Cāmiʿ* manuscript of İbnülemin Mahmud Kemal [İnal] for a study of Ottoman genealogy.[30] In 1976 Victor L. Ménage, with reference to Adnan Erzi, again brought up for discussion ʿĀlī's relation to his sources, including as well the *Cāmiʿ ül-meknūnāt*.[31] But even aside from its quality as a source for ʿĀlī, the *Cāmiʿ ül-meknūnāt*, of which apparently three manuscripts have by now been identified,[32] deserves to be appreciated for its own sake and, thanks to the Leiden Codex or. 1448 (I) Testa, we are in the fortunate position to be able to examine a manuscript of the work.[33]

By means of forms of address like *ėy paşa, ėy beşe, ėy piser, ėy yigit*, the author suggests public gatherings in which his work was read aloud. In conclusion he emphasizes the originality of his work: "I have studied prosody, but I am no poet; I make no great show of this trivial versification. My book is no translation from Persian or Arabic. After all, it is easy to put into rhymes a story that has already been recounted, be it from Arabic or be it from Persian. But to find something that has not been written and put it into verse, that is something difficult!" (fol. 134b). Mysteriously, he leaves the date of composition unclear; he once mentions 936/the year beginning 27/7/1533 (fol. 132b). For the year 960/beginning 18/12/1552 he predicts that "a great terror will befall the earth". In any case, the year of composition is after the siege of Vienna (autumn 1529) and presumably before 942/beginning 2/7/1535, the year of execution of

28 A. Bombaci, *La letteratura turca*, Milan 1969, p. 312: "Anche il fratello di Ahmedi, colui che celebrò Hamza, avrebbe composto una cronaca in versi, della quale non si sa nulla".

29 O.F. Sağlam, "Şimdiye kadar yayınlanmamış bazı kitabelerle meskukatın millî tarihe hizmetleri", in *IV. Türk Tarih Kongresi Ankara 1948*, Ankara 1952, pp. 173-74.

30 A.S. Erzi, "Akkoyunlu ve Karakoyunlu Tarihi Hakkında Araştırmalar", in *Belleten* 18 (1954), p. 200, ftn. 64.

31 Ménage, "Edirne'li Rûhî", p. 314.

32 L – Leiden University Library, Cod. 1448 I Testa from 1605; I – Private library of İbnülemin Mahmud Kemal [İnal], now in İstanbul Üniversitesi Kütüphanesi. S – Private library of Osman Ferid Sağlam; copy from the time of Aḥmed I; S = Ankara, Türk Tarih Kurumu, Y. 240, Part 4, dated 1012/year beginning 11 June 1603.

33 For a description of the Leiden manuscript Cod.Or 1448 I, see now Jan Schmidt, *Catalogue of Turkish Manuscripts in the Library of Leiden University, Volume Two*, Leiden 2002, pp. 83-87. Part II of Cod.Or 1448 is a chapter from the *Şemsiye* by Yazıcı Salahaddin, described in Jan Schmidt, *Catalogue of Turkish Manuscripts in the Library of Leiden University, Volume Two*, Leiden 2002, p. 86. For permission to use the Leiden manuscript I wish to thank the University Library, and especially the Custodian of Oriental Manuscripts, J.J. Witkam.

the Grand Vizier Ibrāhīm Paşa whom the author unhesitatingly praises as the Āṣaf of the Solomon-like Sultan. In the year 909/beginning 26/6/1503, the author himself personally experienced something of the distress that afflicted the Ottoman Empire at the time: "In the Land of Rūm there was much famine and epidemic; many died of starvation and were destroyed; those who did not die of hunger were carried off by the plague that like a sword cut down everything in its path. People called it the Great Plague – many eyes went blind with weeping. We too had our share of this to bear – what help is there? It is the Creator Who gives and takes away" (73b). After that a harsh winter followed and in the spring the rivers overflowed their banks and ravaged city and countryside. Then again in 915/beginning 21/4/1509, the well-known great earthquake destroyed the inner area of the city of Istanbul (Qosṭanṭinīye): "at the time countless signs became visible".[34]

The work consists of four parts: 1) a *mevlid* story about the ancestors and the birth of the Prophet, 2) a history of the Ottomans up to 1529, 3) a calendar section about the "old dates", and 4) an epilogue (*ḫātime*).

The first part begins with the light substance of the Prophet, *nūr-i Aḥmed*, describes the Creation and establishes the genealogical connection of the old prophets with Muḥammad through the Qurayş, via Noah, Ibrāhīm, Ismāʿīl and Isḥāq. The narration deals with the marriage of Hāşim in Medina, the birth of Şaybe and the attempted sacrifice of his son ʿAbdallāh down to Abraha, the elephant and the Ebābīl birds. The exceptionally favorable position of the heavenly bodies at the birth of the Prophet is described with precision; they are depicted with their "signs" by means of Koranic verses and Traditions. Here the first part ends (39b).

As *meclis-i dīger*, the second part is added, the history of the *mülūk-i ʿOsmāniyān*. The author bases himself on Aḥmedī:

Aḥmedī sābıqları ˇzikr eylemiş
āl-i ʿOs̱māna gelince söylemiş
āl-i ʿOsmānuñda nice beglerin
söylemiş neyleyüben nėtdüklerin
Ādem atadan dėmiş ʿOs̱māna dek
daḫı mādūnın Mīr Süleymān dek
anuñ adına Sikendernāmesin
ḫatm ėdüben anda sımış ḫāmesin
ėy ḫüdāyā tā ėrişince ecel

34 Treated in more detail in ni. 17, whiich paper, finished in 1979, appeared in *Between Danube and Caucasus*, Budapest, 1987.

bize daḫı söylemege vėr mecel
āl-i ʿOsmānuñ ġazāsın bīşümār
söyleyelüm diñlesün şeyḫ ü kibār (40a).

"Aḥmedī has mentioned those who lived earlier and discussed them up to the Ottomans; he recounted how many Begs there were among the Ottomans and what they did. From Father Adam he recounted up to ʿOsmān and then on down to Mīr Süleymān; when in the latter's name he completed his *Iskendernāme*, he broke his pen. God give us the strength, before the foreordained hour arrives, to narrate the countless *ġazā*s of the Ottomans. We want to speak of these, let the chiefs and nobles listen!"

Thus *ġazavāt*, as the author repeats on several occasions, are his concern and the work, with its chivalrous and in part novelesque treatment of this subject, is closely linked in terms of genre to the *ġazavātnāme*s. In fact, Aḥmedī had already given this title to the Ottoman section of his *Iskendernāme* and found a successor in the person of Tütünsüz Aḥmed Rıżvān who added to his *Iskendernāme* a rhymed history of the heroic deeds of the Ottomans at Kili, Aqkermān and Moton – he had himself taken part in this last conquest as a Sancak Beg under Bāyezīd II.[35] Also from the point of view of its orthography[36] and what for its time was a simple and seemingly old-fashioned language, the *Cāmiʿ ül-meknūnāt* is close to the *ġazavātnāmeler*; while the latter not infrequently alternate between prose and poetry, the author of the *Cāmiʿ* employs different meters – *remel* and *hezec* – and announces the transition from one to the other with headings like *baḥr-i dīger* (15a) and *bāz baḥr-i evvel āmed* (81a).

Yet the work is not really a *ġazavātnāme* but, with its emphasis on the imminent end of the world that emerges ever more strongly in the course of the narrative, it belongs rather to the area of apocalyptic or *melāḥim* writings.[37]

Here time and space are lacking for an examination of his sources. But the text suggests the assumption that the author took the historical material for his abridged Ottoman history from the various *Tevārīḫ-i āl-i ʿOsmān*, i.e. from ʿĀşıqpaşazāde, Oruç or anonymous writers. Just as he knew the "*Ġazavātnāme*" at the end of Aḥmedī's *Iskendernāme*, he had possibly also read other *ġazavātnāmeler* along with old almanacs (*taqvīm*) in which important events were

35 A.S. Levend, *Ġazavāt-nāmeler ve Mihaloclu Ali Bey'in Ġazavāt-nāmesi*, Ankara 1956, p. 2. Cf. İ. Ünver, "Ahmed Rıdvan'ın İskendernâmesindeki Osmanlı tarihi (Nusret-nâme-i Osmân) bölümü", in *Türkoloji Dergisi* 8 (1979), pp. 345-402.

36 Cf. Levend, *Ġazavāt-nāmeler*, p. 225; İnalcık-Ocuz, *Gazavât-ı Sultân Murâd*, p. 111.

37 J. Aguadé, *Messianismus zur Zeit der frühen Abbasiden: Das Kitāb al-Fitan des Nuʿaim ibn Ḥammād*, dissertation Tübingen 1979. Cf. no. 17 in this volume.

enumerated chronologically, as well as astrological *Aḥkām ve Iḫtiyārāt* that predicted the future.[38] Thus the following verses about a solar eclipse in the year 762/beginning 11/11/1360 – after the capture of Filibe – indicate an almanac as a source.

> hem bu yılda oldı der küll küsūf
> ʿārif oldurkim bular sırra vuqūf
> bir gece bir gün olur gey qarañu...(46a).

On the other hand, the astronomical-astrological *Iḫtiyārāt* tables, which have scarcely been examined for the 16th century, may well have played a part in suggesting his predictions to the author.

Digressions and novelesque embellishments in the style of the *ġazavāt-nāmeler* and even outright deviations from the historical materials known to us are undertaken by the author, surprisingly, especially for the time period he lived in himself. Here is not the place to delve further into this question, since without carrying out a comparative examination the nature of such interventions and the reasons behind them cannot be understood. Moreover, the Leiden manuscript in the section on the beginnings of the Ottomans in Māhān displays lacunae and corruptions. The history of the Ottomans begins with the family tree of the ruling house, which like the well-known dream in which Ertoñrul (written thus in the old-fashioned way in the Ms. for Ertogrul) is promised world dominion should be compared with the tradition in the Anonymous Chronicles. Recruitment of the Janissaries and registration of the infantry the author dates already to the period of Orḫan,

> Yeñiçeri dermek andan qaldı hem
> hem yaya yazmaq daḫı ėy bū l-kerem (44b).

The *Cāmiʿ* has in common with the *ġazavātnāmeler* the romantic transfiguration of the ruler and the claim to have first-hand information about him. Selīm I can be cited as an example, who, after his successful struggle for the throne is depicted in detail in the *Cāmiʿ ül-meknūnāt*, is portrayed above all as a proponent of justice, as a ruler who eliminated reprehensible innovation (*bidʿat*), oppression and heresy (*żalālet*) (81a). In this period, our author says, offering an original variant of the old topos of peace, such harmony reigned that "the sheep walked along with the wolf without strife and the mouse placed his head on the cat's paw:

38 Bombaci, *Letteratura turca*, p. 312.

qoyun urd ile yürür yoq savaşı
kedi pāyına mūşek qodı başı (81a).

Selīm I fell ill; supported by *fetvas*, he had conducted a just war against the Qızılbaş but at the end of his life he regretted three things: that "the Qızılbaş" still existed at his (Selīm's) end; that he had built no *ʿimāret*, and that, finally, he had not taken the field against the infidels:

dahı dīvāna gelmezsiz bilürem
velī üç nesne içün yaqıluram
biri bu ṣoñuma qaldı Qızılbaş
ikinci qomadum ṭaş üzre bir ṭaş
ʿimāret qılmadum cismüm yatağın
üçünci qılmadum küffāra aqın
müyesser olmadı ġazv u cihādum
egerçi söylenür dillerde adum (97a).

This is the style of the old *ġazavātnāmes*; from them the author of the *Cāmiʿ* also takes his inspiration for his treatment of Christian adversaries who are sometimes historically tangible but at times appear to originate from an epic repertoire, not dissimilar to the "souvenir collectif" of the still older epic *ġāzī*-tales from the period of the conquest of Anatolia by the Turks.[39]

The title *Qayṣer*, which was once the "name" of the Greek Emperor in general,[40] no longer occurs; behind *Tekūr* (62a) is concealed in the *Cāmiʿ* the last Emperor of Byzantium in 1453. For the Holy Roman Emperor the title *Çasār* is used, without mentioning a name (109b, 115b); *Qıral* is used for the kings of Hungary whose names are given as Laloş (Louis II) and Yanoş (John Zápolya). The title of the Pope in our text always appears as *Pōpa*; the Grand Master of the Order of the Knights of St John, who was allowed to withdraw from Rhodes in 1522, is here called *Māstūr meġāl* or simply *Meġāl*, and for nobles *Bān* and *Bānzāde* is used.[41] Several of the Christian adversaries are also mentioned by name, as was customary in the Ottoman *ġazavātnāmes*; besides the names of the Hungarian kings, *Qarloz*, Charles V, *Mīr* of Spain, appears, as well as his brother Ferdinand who is called *Feravuş*. In Albania war is being

39 Cf. I. Mélikoff, *La Geste de Melik Danişmend* I, Paris 1960, pp. 137-42. M. Labęcka-Loecherowa and T. Majda (translators), *Arif Ali. Daniszmendname*, Warsaw 1980.

40 B. Flemming, *Faḫrīs Ḫusrev u Şīrīn. Eine türkische Dichtung von 1367*, Wiesbaden 1974, p. 145.

41 İnalcık-Ocuz, *Gazavât-ı Sultân Murâd*, p. 108, ftn. 42.

waged against *Ḫāʾin Iskender*, George Kastriota, and his son *Ivan*, in Croatia against the *Derencil Bānı*, by whom is meant Trencsény Imre.[42] The people of the Ottoman state are unselfconsciously called *Türk*; among the opposing countries and peoples appear Hungary, Poland, Ruś (present-day Ukraine),[43] Czechs, Croats, *Nemçe* and *Alamān*, (Transylvanian) Saxony (*Ṣāṣ*), the Moscovite Empire of the Czars (*Mosqova*), Spain and Portugal. All kinds of place names occur that are worth examining, as in the report about the capture of Otranto.

It would be interesting to examine the extent to which the manners and customs of the Christian adversaries we come across in the epic *ġazā*-tales are based on topoi. While the non-Ottoman *Dānişmendnāme* in the version of circa 1360 at times revels in details, for instance when describing a Christian banquet with onions, garlic and of course pork and wine (but also *qabuqlu böcek ü sıçan kebābı*: grilled beetles and rats),[44] the Ottoman heroic tale of Varna depicts at length Biblical discussions of monks.[45] The author of the *Cāmiʿ* notes that the day of the capture of Rhodes, the 3rd of Ṣafer 929/23 December 1522, is considered by the Christians to be the birthday of Jesus, *mevlid-i ʿĪsā* (106b). And it is also known that the infidels regularly send legations to one another – the *Cāmiʿ* describes some of these before the battle of Mohács – and that they come together to consult. The Turks were aware that before 1444 the Christians had negotiated for "ten years long" in Rome,[46] and that the commanders of the Crusaders' army held consultations before Varna.[47] This subject acquires increasing importance for the author of the *Cāmiʿ ül-meknūnāt*: in his account the Princes of the Christians gather "in a place"; the Pope is meant to crown one of them so that he can march against the Turks as *Ṣāḥib-qırān*. The Pope does not consider anyone worthy of this; then the Mīr of Spain, Qarloz, demands the crown (116a); the strife that develops here is the prelude to the Sacco di Roma (see below). To the political fears of the infidels are added those of an eschatological nature: after the fall of Rhodes the Turks "heard" that the infidels believed that the wall that provided protection against Gog and Magog had now been demolished. "Two gates have been breached, one to the sea and one to the land; through the one the Turk can set out for Frengistān and through the other for Hungary and Russia"

42 Moser, *Bihişti*, p. 144.

43 O. Pritsak, "Das erste türkische-ukrainische Bündnis (1648)", in *Oriens* (1953), pp. 292-93.

44 Mélikoff, *Geste* II, p. 91.

45 İnalcık-Ocuz, *Gazavât-ı Sultân Murâd*, p. 72.

46 Ibidem, p. 109, according to a *Fetḥnāme*.

47 Ibidem, pp. 59-60 and 107.

(106b).[48] The Princes of Christendom are in agreement that the end of the world is at hand – the *Cāmiʿ* says this on more than one occasion.

In this situation the infidel *Benī Aṣfar*, over whom Charles V establishes himself as supreme commander, appeal to Lāt, Menāt and ʿUzza… Thus the tradition of the epic *ġāzī*-tales is once more conjured up in which the opponents of the Muslims have recourse to the old goddesses of Mecca. In this way the Christians swear oaths in the *Dānişmendnāme*[49] and hope to be saved by the three divinities,[50] and in the same way the Christians try to save themselves in the *ġazavātnāme* of Sūzī Çelebi.[51] Thus our anonymous author also has the young King of Hungary call upon Lāt, Menāt and ʿUzza against the Turks before the battle of Mohács; of course the author, given his knowledge of the eschatological Traditions, is aware that these old Arabian divinities "as omens" belong to the corpus of hadiths that deal with this subject.[52]

In contrast to these fruitless invocations of the infidels stand the pious prayers with which the *ġāzī*s turn to God. What was usual in the "pre-Ottoman" *Dānişmendnāme*[53] and in the early Ottoman *ġazavātnāmes*[54] is also taken up by the author of the *Cāmiʿ*, namely that Sultan Süleymān immerses himself in a long prayer (112a). But here as well his novel concern is apparent. The campaigns of Sultan Süleymān, of which the *Cāmiʿ* describes the first four, in fact surpassed everything experienced up until then. "Never", writes the author on the occasion of Mohács, "did such a *ġazā* take place, never was there such booty." But the victories are won at great expense; the author is not unaware of the distress of the wounded and the death of thousands, whether it be in open battle, on the march or during sieges like that of Rhodes which he vividly portrays. On the occasion of the siege of Belgrade that involved heavy losses, the author explains the five possible ways (he sees a parallel with the five times of prayer) to become a martyr for the faith (*şehīd*) according to the *şarīʿa*: firstly in battle, secondly on the pilgrimage, thirdly abroad (he cites the hadith: "He who dies in a foreign land dies as a *şehīd*), fourthly from the plague, and fifthly in the womb.

---

48 Cf. no. 17.

49 Mélikoff, *Geste* II, p. 40.

50 Ibidem, p. 102.

51 Levend, *Ġazavāt-nāmeler*, verses 326, 971 and 1726.

52 D.S. Attema, *De Mohammedaansche Opvattingen omtrent het tijdstip van den Jongsten Dag en zijn voortekenen*, Amsterdam 1942, p. 80; no. 17.

53 Cf. for example Mélikoff, *Geste* II, p. 106.

54 İnalcık-Ocuz, *Gazavât-i Sultân Murâd*, p. 58; Levend, *Ġazavāt-nāmeler*, verse 1040.

ne baẖt olakim şehīd ola ġazāda
qopısar yüzi aq yevm-i cezāda
ikinci Kaʿbe yolunda vefātı
bulan üçünci ġurbetde memātı

budur dördünci fevt olan vebādan
beşincisi şikem derd-i ʿanādan
şehādet beş durur beş vaqt namāza
muṭābıq düşdi emri bī-niyāza (99b).

The great quantity of their martyrs for the faith and the hardships of the campaigns and in particular the suffering on the retreat through the flooded countryside after the abandoned siege of Vienna,[55] suggested to the Turks as well that events on earth were moving toward their final end. In support of this, besides his knowledge of hadiths and astrology, the author's familiarity with events in Europe gives him a special credibility. He knows, in fact, that two years before the siege of Vienna the city of Rome was captured by troops of the Emperor. This and the famous plundering that ensued, the Sacco di Roma, is a sign for our author that the end of the world is drawing near. Indeed, the Koran already alluded to the fall of Rome – Rūm – by which the Second Rome, Byzantium, was meant. Hadiths had further elaborated on the prediction and shifted it into an ever more distant future. In addition, in sound Traditions since the 10th century the idea is also documented that the fall of the First Rome would precede the end of the world.[56] Mevlānā ʿĪsā also finds his views about the end of the world confirmed in most recent history, namely in the capture of Rīm – Rome in Italy – by the imperial army in 1527, which he describes, along with traits of a legendary character, as the result of the war between the Mīr of Spain, the King of France, and the Pope. The "Prince" of Spain, after having gained control of the Pope, laid claim to dominion over the world, i.e. *ṣāḥib-qırānī*; "to me", he says, "God has given the world" (*baña vėrdi ẖü ḏā dėdi cihānı*). But Sultan Süleymān – according to our author – will return and for his part assume dominion over the world.[57] The city of Rome will once again flourish; but then the Mahdī will capture it. With the advent of the latter, a happy final phase of the world will commence. Peace and abundance will reign and taxes, as in the case of chiliastic expectations, will no longer be lev-

55 Cf. K. Teply, *Türkische Sagen und Legenden um die Kaiserstadt Wien*, Wien-Köln-Graz 1980; no. 17 in this volume.

56 loc. cit.

57 loc. cit., pp. 12 f.

ied or only "in accordance with the law"; the Mahdī will be the seal of the saints, just as Muḥammad was the seal of the prophets. Of course, the author does not wish to commit himself regarding a fixed time but carries on with chronological speculations around a still further-off future by means of which the imminent eschatological expectation is once again mysteriously annulled. He has no doubt that God will send a *Ṣāḥib-qırān* before the collapse of the world and that four large constellations in the course of the ages will precede him. Consequently, this work, extending beyond the *ġazavāt* of the Ottomans as "a report about the past, the present and the future", as the author summarizes (135a), is a source for Ottoman history of a special kind which reveals to us that the age of Süleymān, not only among European contemporaries but among the Turks themselves, triggered eschatological expectations. Whether the work had a more widespread impact is not yet clear. Muṣṭafā ʿĀlī, who quotes from it, was also interested in the older *ġāzī*-literature and, when he resided in Anatolian Niksar in 1589, reworked the epic tale of Melik Dānişmend into an Ottoman "Ladder of Holy War", *Mirqāt ül-cihād*.[58] The period of Sultan Aḥmed I (1603-1617), as manuscripts show, brought a revival of interest in the *Cāmiʿ ül-meknūnāt* and also demand for the *Aḥvāl-i qiyāmet* (*The Circumstances of the Resurrection*) which transfer eschatological events completely into the unhistorical realm.[59] This literature has its worth for studying the mood of the time and for that reason possesses value as evidence especially where the authors themselves take the occasion to speak.

58 Mélikoff, *Geste* I, pp. 54 and 62 f.

59 B. Flemming, "Het einde der tijden bij de Turken in de zestiende eeuw", M.O.I. publication 1981.

CHAPTER 15

Two Turkish Bible Manuscripts in Leiden as Middle-Ottoman Linguistic Monuments*

Protestantism of the 17th century in its missionary zeal brought forth a number of great Bible translations. At the University of Leiden, which was founded in 1575, a project to translate the Bible into Arabic had also begun.[1] The Dutch orientalists were joined by Bohemian Protestants who were driven out of their homeland after 1620 and found refuge in the Republic of the Netherlands. Their most famous spokesman was Johannes Amos Comenius who spent his last years of life from 1656 to 1670 in Amsterdam. From apocalyptic forebodings and expectations to battles with the House of Habsburg which were meant to usher in the end of time, Comenius' endeavors aimed at winning over the Ottoman Turks to the cause of Protestantism. His success was meant to bring about the fall of the Habsburgs and Catholicism, make possible the return of the exiles to Bohemia and, finally, mark the start of the Second Coming of Christ. It is true that Comenius' Dutch friends scarcely shared his religious political premonitions. On the other hand, they were convinced, as was he, of the necessity of bringing Christianity close to the Turks by means of a complete translation of the Bible.[2]

During the preparations for this Leiden-sponsored Turkish Bible, scholars and educated laymen from different nations encountered one another. The translation and later the printing were to be financed in the Netherlands; translators were engaged whose work was to be examined and edited. Comenius was responsible for the general management of the project; in Leiden the well-known orientalist Jacobus Golius was in charge, and the actual translation work in Istanbul was under the direction of the latter's student Levinus Warner, 'resident' of the States General since 1655. The course of this remarkable undertaking has already been described at an earlier time[3] and

* Translated by John O'Kane.

1 The details of the project are found in T.H. Darlow and H.F. Moule, *Historical Catalogue of the printed editions of Holy Scripture in the Library of the British and Foreign Bible Society*, London 1903-1911, nos. 1612, 1642 and 1645.

2 M.E.H.N. Mout, "Calvinoturcisme in de zeventiende eeuw. Comenius, Leidse orientalisten en de Turkse bijbel", in *Tijdschrift voor Geschiedenis* 91 (1978), pp. 597-600.

3 A.A. Cooper, *The Story of the (Osmanli) Turkish Version with a brief account of related versions*, London 1901; F. Lyman MacCallum, "Kitabi Mukaddes'in Türkçe Tercümesine Dair", in *Tercüme* 3/13 (Ankara 1942), pp. 60-68; J. Deny, "A propos des traductions en Turc Osmanli des textes

 | DOI 10.1163/9789004355767_016

should only in part occupy us here. The translation did come about but could not be printed as planned because the men in charge of the undertaking died one after the other in quick succession.

What we will discuss here are the codices which form the foundation for this Leiden Turkish Bible. Warner gave the commission for the translation to two Ottoman subjects who resided in Istanbul, Ḫākī and ʿAlī Beg.

1) The four-volume Codex or. 391 of the Leiden University Library[4] consists of the rough translation which Yaḥyā b. Isḥāq, known as Ḫākī, completed in Istanbul in the year 1659. The manuscript is his autograph copy.

Ḫākī worked quickly; this is apparent when one notes that Warner only first became involved with the Bible project in 1658. His text was in fact written quickly with few corrections made by himself. That he was well-versed in Hebrew as well as Turkish is clear from all sorts of Hebrew glosses in his text. Due to this and from his name, it can be concluded that he was of Jewish descent. What was the first language he learned cannot be determined at present; possibly it was Turkish.

From the rough translation a fair copy was partly produced which, just as the first draft, ended up in Leiden after Warner's death with his manuscripts (Cod. 386 Warn.).

2) The four-volume Codex 390 of the Leiden University Library[5] consists of the rough translation which ʿAlī Beg, i.e. Albert Bobowski (Bobovius; 1610-1675), the well-known court interpreter for Sultan Meḥmed IV, produced in Istanbul between 1662 and 1664. This is also an autograph copy, and each of its fascicles is dated and provided with remarks by the translator. Much in the text has been corrected; one feels one sees how the author hesitates over certain words, crosses them out and begins again. ʿAlī Beg had mastered several languages including Latin. The actual mother tongue of the translator who was born in Lvov in Galicia was probably Polish.

A fair copy of ʿAlī Beg's text, even adorned with calligraphy, was also produced (Cod. 1101 Warn. and Cod. 1117a Warn.); both the rough translation and the fair copy were sent to Leiden.

The Leiden Turkish Bible, like many other Bible translations, was a collective undertaking. Since both translators to start with because of their different

religieux chrétiens", *Welt des Islam* IV (1956), pp. 32 and 36; Mout, "Calvinoturcisme", pp. 600-05. See now Hannah Neudecker, *The Turkish Bible Translation by Yaḥya bin 'Isḥak, also called Ḫaki* (1659), Leiden 1994.

4 M.J. de Goeje, *Catalogus Codicum Orientalium Bibliothecae Academiae Lugduno-Batavae*, Leiden 1873, 98 no. MMCCCCIII.

5 de Goeje, *Catalogus*, 98 no. MMCCV.

religious origin could not read and interpret the text in the same manner, it was necessary that a systematic effort be made in the final editing regarding the uniformity of the entire text. Here some questions remain unanswered. One would like to know whether ʿAlī Beg Bobowski already incorporated parts of Ḫākī's (reworked) text into his translation. The criteria for judging the translation had been established by Comenius; out of respect for the sacred text the translation should preferably be literal, though it should also remain true to the spirit of the original.[6] The first objections were raised by the co-translator ʿAlī Beg who checked the whole of Ḫākī's rough translation and added remarks in the margins. The best known of his glosses is: "Haki Scripturam Sacram in sermonem Turcicum ex Hebraico traduxit, non aperte nec plane, sed obscure et intricate, dum verbo verbum reddidit et hoc quoque male, sine constructione genuina, ut pene Turcicum Talmutum putes."[7] If the latter had to do with the question of literal fidelity, ʿAlī Beg had to put up with criticism regarding style. J. Golius examined his text and although he knew Turkish, judging it on philological grounds was a problem for him. None the less, in his view the Bobowski translation, concerning which he had been instructed by an Armenian from Damascus by the name of Şāhīn Qandī, was "inadequate, boorish and barbaric; no educated Turk would be able to read it". Thereafter no further advice was sought in the matter.[8]

The criticism Ḫākī was subjected to by ʿAlī Beg, and the latter was then subjected to by Şāhīn Qandī, can to some extent be relativized from a present-day point of view. A literal translation with simple Turkish words and phrases in the manner of an interlinear version like the one Ḫākī produced can be thought of as an aid to understanding the Hebrew and does not have to be taken as proof of the translator's incompetence. On the other hand, ʿAlī Beg, by using words from the lofty language of scholars, definitely strove to stylize his Turkish in the manner of the original and thereby to produce a biblical Turkish. If one takes account of the time and the circumstances in which they came about, both translations as the work of single individuals are quite considerable achievements.

6 Mout, "Calvinoturcisme", p. 603, based on letters of Comenius.

7 Cited in de Goeje, *Catalogus*, 98. Dr. J. Schmidt of Rotterdam collected for a seminar paper a complete series of remarks of ʿAlī Beg, in part about himself.

8 Johann Heinrich Hottinger from Zurich died on the way to Leiden where he had been appointed professor of theology; apparently he was meant to participate in the Bible project. W.M.C. Juynboll, *Zeventiende-eeuwsche Beoefenaars van het Arabisch in Nederland*, Utrecht 1931, pp. 209-10; Mout, "Clavinoturcisme", p. 604.

Likewise, the function of the Turkish Bible as an aspect of the undertaking merits attention. First and foremost the Bible translation was intended for the highest representatives of the Turkish government; but the effort on the part of the initiators to bring about conversion met with a secular interest on the Turkish side.[9] Comenius wanted to have the printed Turkish Bible presented to the Sultan and had already composed a dedication for this purpose.[10] The association of contemporary court and scholarly circles with Christians of various confessions, with or without the mediation of the omnipresent interpreters of the Porte, remains a fascinating subject for research.[11] It is known, for instance, that Hezārfenn enlisted the services of the indefatigable ʿAlī Beg Bobowski. Included among the latter's numerous acquaintances was Jakob Nagy de Harsány (1615-after 1677), who took lessons in Turkish[12] from ʿAlī Beg and collected material or a part of his *Colloquia familiaria turcico-latina* from the Ottoman court interpreter.[13] Jakob Nagy, who had studied in the Netherlands – he was briefly in Franeker and matriculated in Leiden in 1640[14] – knew J. Golius. With Warner, whom he may already have met in Leiden, he certainly had relations as representative of the Prince of Transylvania (Siebenbürgen) at the Porte. From Warner the connections then went back to Comenius through the Bohemian *emigré* circles in which the born-Hungarian had moved in the Netherlands.[15] Ḫākī whom we should perhaps imagine as being employed in an Ottoman chancellery, deserves to be more clearly embedded in this varied network of relations. All the writers of Turkish

9 H. Wurm, *Der osmanische Historiker Ḥüseyn b. Ǧaʿfer, genannt Hezārfenn, und die Istanbuler Gesellschaft in der zweiten Hälfte des 17. Jahrhunderts*, Freiburg 1971, pp. 50-52.

10 Mout, "Clavinoturcisme", p. 605; the dedication is also printed photomechanically in D. Zbavitel, *Die Orientalistik in der Tschechoslowakei*, Prague 1959, after p. 32.

11 Wurm, *Hezārfenn*, has done pioneering work in this area.

12 M. Blekastad, Comenius, Oslo – Prague 1970, p. 507, citing Szilágy, Ung. Rev. 1899, pp. 32 and 36.

13 G. Hazai, *Das Osmanisch-Türkische im XVII. Jahrhundert. Untersuchungen an den Transkriptionstexten von Jakab Nagy de Harsány*, Den Haag – Paris 1973, pp. 16-17; in his review of this work V.L. Ménage makes the sources it depends on clear in *BSOAS* 38 (1975), p. 162.

14 S.J. Fockema Andreae and Th. J. Meijer, *Album studiosorum Academiae Franekerensis (1585-1811, 1816-1844)* I, Franeker 1968, p. 117 (Jacobus Harzani, Ungarus, theol.; *Album Studiosorum Academiae Lugduno Batavae MDLXXV-MDCCCLXXV*, Den Haag 1875, pp. 315 and 355 (Jacobus N. Harsanyinus, Ungarus, and Jacobus Horsani Transylvanus). Cf. J. Zoványi, *Magyarországi Protestáns Egyháztörténeti Lexikon*, Budapest 1977, s.v. Harsányí Nagy Jakab [Erdély]. I am indebted for this reference and its translation to Dr. M.E.H.N. Mout of Leiden. Now also see Gábor Kármán, *A Seventeenth-Century Odyssey in East Central Europe. The Life of Jakab Harsányi Nagy*, Leiden 2016.

15 Mout, "Calvinoturcisme", p. 607.

mentioned here knew the Turkish of the capital Istanbul with its diverse, multilingual population. The dialect of this sizeable city, due to a continuous stream of immigrations from Rumeli, was greatly influenced by the Rumeli dialect.[16]

Our two versions of the Bible, with their differences in form and sometimes even in content, offer a favorable opportunity, without great expenditure, to undertake synchronous observations regarding the Turkish of Istanbul in the middle of the 17th century. For this purpose their character as unpolished drafts is even an advantage, as is the fact that the authors were not Ottoman scholars but educated laymen. Of course, three objections could be raised with regard to the Turkish Bible; firstly, that the mother tongue of the authors was not Turkish; secondly, that it was written in Arabic script; and thirdly, that it is a translation.

The effects of non-Turkish languages on Turkish, phenomena of interference in a bilingual situation,[17] have not escaped the notice of scholarship; scholars have devoted attention to "falsely pronounced" sounds as well as syntactical influences from non-Turkish languages in the Empire.[18] In the Bible autograph manuscripts we are concerned with a series of violations of the laws of Turkish phonetics and rules of grammar that are noticeable. But before one explains these as phenomena of interference which are to be "blamed" on the foreign mother tongue of the author, the colloquial speech of Istanbul should be taken into account as a factor. Ḫākī (and ʿAlī Beg as well) neglects in various ways Turkish vowel harmony; in palatal words he employs velarized consonants and vice versa; e.g. he writes *büyuk* and *öqsüz*. On the other hand, this could in part be due to slips in writing which the author himself would have wanted to correct: even an author whose mother tongue was Turkish could make many mistakes when writing quickly, as is demonstrated in the case of the interpreter ʿO̱smān Aġa.[19] When Ḫākī consistently writes the personal pronoun *oni* instead of *ani*, this may well reflect the spoken language. In the

16 A. Tietze, "Das Stambuler Türkisch des XVII. Jahrhunderts und die türkishen Dialekte der Balkanhalbinsel", in G. Káldy-Nagy (ed.), *Hungaro-Turcica. Studies in Honour of Julius Németh*, Budapest 1976, p. 340; Hazai, *Jakab Nagy*, p. 344.

17 U. Weinreich, *Sprachen in Kontakt. Ergebnisse und Probleme der Zweisprachigkeitsforschung*, München 1976, p. 29.

18 Cf. E. Prokosch, *Studien zur Grammatik des Osmanisch-Türkischen unter besonderer Berücksichtigung des Vulgärosmanisch-Türkischen*, Freiburg 1980, p. 14, and the important study by M. Mollova, "Parallel syntaxique entre la langue turque des Colloquia et celle des textes turcs transcrits et les parlers turcs balkaniques occidentaux, in WZKM 72 (1980), pp. 123-45.

19 R.F. Kreutel, *Die Autobiographie des Dolmetschers ʿO̱smān Aġa aus Temeschwar. Der Text des Londoner Autographen in normalisierter Rechtschreibung*, Cambridge-Hertford 1980, pp. I-XXVII.

morphology they adopt, Ḫākī and ʿAlī Beg oscillate between the various forms that can be used for the future. Both already use Ecek as a finite verb, but Ḫākī appears to prefer the optative; for the aorist he uses the older pronoun ending *siz* in contrast to ʿAlī's *siñiz*. Quite frequently, ignoring principles of Turkish word-order, Ḫākī employs inversion; ʿAlī Beg avoids it. John 14/4: *siz bilürsiz nereye giderim ve yolı daḫı bilürsiz* – Ḫākī; *siz nereye vardugumı* (with the Arabic letter *kāf*!) *bilürsiñiz hem yolı da bilürsiñiz* – ʿAlī Beg. It is worthwhile to compare the unusual grammatical features of both Bible translators with the peculiarities of ʿO̱smān Aġa's manuscript (decades younger) which have been described as phenomena of common speech, i.e. mistakes from the standpoint of the literary language.[20] For Ḫākī who had perhaps learned Turkish as his first language and for ʿAlī Beg who had learned it in his youth, Turkish was in any case the "dominant" language; this may be offered in response to the first objection. In this sense the somewhat younger Eremiya Çelebi Kömürciyan, the notary of the Armenian community in Istanbul and translator of parts of the Bible into Turkish, may also be considered as bilingual.[21]

How much less was the competence of authors who only lived for a time in the Ottoman Empire, or indeed of travelers who acquired a very limited knowledge of Turkish while their informants for the most part remain unknown.[22]

The usefulness of texts in the Ottoman in Arabic script, especially where the texts display violations of the conservative orthography, has already been pointed out in earlier scholarship.[23] Recently, it has been shown that the criteria developed on the basis of the *Colloquia familiaria* for the statistical study of texts in transcription can also be used for Turkish texts in Arabic script.[24] If up to now scholarship has had a preference for texts in transcription that were

20 The individual causes that can have prompted ʿO̱smān Aġa to make mistakes in writing and grammatical errors, in any case in his quickly written first draft, should be dealt with within the framework of interference studies.

21 E. Schütz, "Jeremia Čelebis türkische Werke (Zur Phonetik des Mittelosmanischen", in L. Ligeti (ed.), *Studia Turcica*, Budapest 1971, pp. 401-30. A.K. Sanjian and A. Tietze, *Eremya Chelebi Kömürjian's Armeno-Turkish poem "The Jewish Bride"*, Wiesbaden 1981.

22 On Megiser cf. M. Adamović, "Zu den Quellenbezügen Megisers", in *Materialia Turcica* 4 (1978), pp. 17-21, and H. Stein, "Zu Fragen der Lautbezeichnung in einem türkischen Transkriptionstext," in *RO* XL/2 (1979), pp. 51-64. For the 17th century cf. M. Kennessey, "A Turkish Grammar from the 17th Century", in *AOH* 28 (1974), p. 123.

23 J. Blaškovič, "Das Osmanisch-Türkische im 17. Jahrhundert im Donauraum", in G. Hazai and P. Zieme (eds.), *Sprache, Geschichte und Kultur der altaischen Völker*, XII. PIAC, Berlin 1974, pp. 125-38.

24 A. Gallotta, "16th Century Ottoman Turkish as represented in the Ghazavat-i Khayreddin Pasha", in *POF* 30 (1980), pp. 145-52.

written in non-Turkish alphabets, this took place, however, with an awareness of how defective those writing systems were and of the extent to which the inconsistencies of the authors and the mistakes of their copyists and printers could confuse the picture.[25]

One could reply to the third objection that many of the texts in transcription that have been studied up to now also consisted of translations.[26] Bible translations in other languages, besides their religious significance, have gladly been made use of for philological research because of their idioms and their wealth of concrete verbal elements. A few examples from 1 Corinthians, 9:

	Ḫākī	ʿAlī Beg
7	kim işler kendüniñ nafaqası içün kim bir baġ diker ve ḥāṣılından yemez ve kim bir qoyun yüder ve yemez o qoyunuñ südini	kendü ʿulūfesi ile cenge kim çıqar baġı kim diker de anuñ yemişinden yemeye yā süri kim güder ki anuñ südinden içmeye
8	ben bu qıṣṣaları söylerim ādem üzerine dīn dėmez o bu qıṣṣaları	ben bunı insān gibi mi söylerim tevrāt daḫı bu nesneleri demez mi
24	siz bilmez misiz ki onlarki segirdirler cerīde cümle eyü segirdir ammā biri yalñız şikārı alur segirdiñ ber vechle ki sikārı alasız	bilmez misiñiz ki qoşu ėdenler hepisi qoşu ėderler ammā biri ögdüli alur şöyle qoşu eyleñ ki gdüli alasız
26	ben imdi böyle segirdirim ki mechūl degil böyle cehd ėderim havada mücāhid gibi degil	pes ben böyle qoşarım ki nāmaʿlūm şe'ye olmaya ve böyle matraqçılıq ėderim ki havāya urmayam

The Turkish Bible translations, precisely dated as they are by means of the autograph manuscripts of Ḫākī and ʿAlī Beg, are indeed a rich source for the linguistic history of Middle-Turkish and deserve to be exploited to the full.

25 Tietze, "Stambuler Türkisch", p. 338; V.L. Ménage in *BSOAS* 38 (1975), p. 162, points to the printers as the source of the errors. Cf. also J. Németh, *Die türkische Sprache in Ungarn im siebzehnten Jahrhundert*, Budapest 1970, pp. 7-28. M. Adamović gives a list of inconsistencies, "Ein italienisch-türkisches Sprachbuch aus den Jahren 1525-1530", in *WZKM* 67 (1975), pp. 223-25.

26 As representatives of this one may cite J. Németh, *Türk. Sprache in Ungarn*, p. 25, and G. Hazai, *Jakab Nagy* (see above).

CHAPTER 16

Romantic Emigrants in the Empire of Abdülhamid*

A hundred years ago, in 1886, the philosopher Omar al Raschid from St. Petersburg and the journalist Ali Nuri Bey from Malmö crossed paths. The cause for this was a recent event, a scandal in Weimar society. Omar al Raschid, then still Friedrich Arnd, director of a geographical institute in Weimar, had abandoned his wife and three children in 1885, and had run off to Istanbul with Helene Böhlau, the daughter of the well-known publisher Hermann Böhlau. What these three persons had in common was their search for personal fulfilment in the Ottoman capital; they were, at one and the same time, emigrants and "Romantic exiles".[1]

Ali Nuri Bey (Dilmeç, 1859-1937), the "Viking" (Th. Herzl), was the first to come to Istanbul. Gunnar Jarring has devoted three articles to his biography.[2] Şahin Alpay provides a useful summary.[3] Ali Nuri was born in 1858 in Malmö as Knut Gustaf, the son of Maria Elisabeth Gernandt; his father was a well-off Malmö burgher. The tailor Knut Persson Noring, whom Maria Gernandt married, adopted Gustaf and brought him up. Gustaf was a gifted boy who early on became a book collector and tried his hand at being a political writer.

In 1879 he decided to emigrate to Turkey. He never explained his reasons for this. It is thought that it happened, on the one hand, out of his love for the

* Translated by John O'Kane.

1 On German emigration cf. R. Anhegger, "Almanların Türkiye'ye Göçü", in *Tarih ve Toplum* 4 (1985), pp. 201-07; Idem, "Die Entvölkerung Anatoliens im 19. Jahrhundert-Osmanische Gegenmassnahmen – Deutsche Siedlungspläne Anatoliens im 19. Jahrhundert – Kongress für Türkische Wirtschafts- und Sozialgeschichte (1071-1920), München, 4.– 8. August 1986." On Russian emigration in the first half of the 19th century see E.H. Carter, *The Romantic Exiles. A nineteenth-century portrait gallery*, reprint Harmondsworth 1968. For valuable references as well as photocopies, I wish to thank Dr. R. Bos of the Dutch Foreign Ministry Archives. For a bibliography of Helene Böhlau see www.de.wikipedia.org/wiki/Helene_Böhlau; retrieved 14 September 2011.

2 Gunnar Jarring, "Gustaf Noring – alias Ali Nouri – och hans turkiska Karl XII forskningar", in *Karolinska Förbundets årsbok* 1976, pp. 7-18; Idem, "Ali Nouri – alias Gustaf Noring – en viking i frack", in *Studie Kamraten* no. 3 (1982); Idem, "Bibliofilen Ali Nouris tänkar på upprättandet av ett turkiskt nationalbibliotek", in *Meddelanden*, Zeitschrift des Schwedischen Forschungsinstituts in Istanbul (p. 183) (quoted from Ş. Alpay).

3 Şahin Alpay, "Bir Osmanlı Vikingi. Herr Gustaf Noring ya da Ali Nuri Bey", in *Tarih ve Toplum* 1/3 (March 1984), pp. 230-33, with two photos. Şahin Alpay (b. 1944) completed his PhD at Stockholm University. The respected political scientist, columnist and author was arrested on July 27, 2016, over his alleged involvement in the 15 July coup attempt.

 | DOI 10.1163/9789004355767_017

country and, on the other, to expunge the stigma of his illegitimate birth. At first he worked for a foreign diplomat. He was introduced as a private tutor among high-ranking personalities in the Ottoman government. He became occupied with the project of an Ottoman national library which had been planned earlier by Münif Paşa (1828-1910);[4] he was allowed to work in the Sultan's library and in Turkey began studies on the Swedish king Charles XII concerning whom he had found a source. The library project would only attain realization much later.

Noring was also a businessman and had bold plans. He formed ties with Bethel Henry Strousberg (1823-1884) the Railway King and attempted to obtain money in Sweden for investment in the construction of the Baghdad railway, the building of which had been decided in 1899.

In 1884, when he was appointed to the Ottoman Ministry of Foreign Affairs, Gustaf Noring converted to Islam and adopted the name Ali Nuri. He married a princess named Hayriye bint Ayad.

A year later Friedrich Arnd came to Istanbul. Only a few reference works give information about him (pseudonym Arnd-Kürenberg).[5] He was born on the 3rd of July 1839 in St. Petersburg as a German Jew;[6] his mother originally came from Istanbul. He became an architect in Russia, then came to Germany as a stateless emigrant and studied philosophy in Leipzig and, according to his son, received a doctorate in philosophy.[7] Arnd was director of a geographical institute in Berlin. He had married in 1863;[8] the marriage produced two daughters and one son.

In the 1870s he moved with his family to Weimar where the running of the geographical institute there (apparently private) was transferred to him. During his youthful years, Arnd was attracted to drama in addition to philosophy. He drew on the contents of the saga of the Nibelungen, at that time a subject of Romantic research on the past, for the plot of his tragedy *Kriemhild* which around 1874 was performed in Weimar with mediocre success.

This was not surprising since in 1861 the great Nibelungen trilogy by Friedrich Hebbel (1813-1863) was staged to considerable acclaim in the Weimar court theater of the Grand Duke of Sachsen-Weimar. Not only that, two years later, in

4 Jale Baysal "Kütüphanecilik", *Cumhuriyet Dönemi Türkiye Ansiklopedisi* 5, p. 1306. See below.

5 *Neue deutsche Biographie*, II; *Deutsches Literatur-Lexikon. Biographisch-bibliographisches Handbuch. Begründet von Wilhelm Kosch*, 3rd ed. I, Bern/Munich [1968], p. 146.

6 The source for this is Th. Lessing; see ftn. 21.

7 H. Böhlau (al Raschid Bey), introduction to the 3rd edition of *Das hohe Ziel der Erkenntnis* (see below), p. XI.

8 On Helgoland because he had no papers in Germany, according to Ali Nuri; see below.

August 1876, Richard Wagner's (1813-1883) complete *Ring des Nibelungen* would radiate its powerful impact from Bayreuth. Arnd changed his subject matter; he now wrote a play called *Lebensstürme* which would be published in 1877 under the title *Nur Liebe berechtigt die Ehe* (*Love Alone Justifies Marriage*).

In the home of the book publisher and court printer Hermann Böhlau, who at the time was publishing the multivolume complete editions of the works of Luther and Goethe ("Sophienausgabe" 1887-1919), Arnd became acquainted with the eldest daughter of the family, Helene who was born in 1859. With criticism and encouragement he closely followed her development as a writer. In 1882 she made her literary début with a volume of short stories published by W. Hertz, Theodor Fontane's publisher, and quickly became known. In the meantime the relationship of the mentor to his pupil had evolved into a love which would determine the future life of both of them. To help the Arnds who were struggling with financial difficulties, Helene Böhlau asked the dramatist and poet Richard Voss (1851-1918) to use his influence with the Grand Duke so that Arnd might be provided with an annual stipend.

> But how Helene Böhlau spoke of this person who is entirely unknown to me: with an enthusiasm that was ecstatic, with a delight resembling rapture. According to her words, this Herr Arnd had to be a divinely gifted genius... The marvelous man was writing a mysterious work that would only be published after his death and he found himself in very unfavorable circumstances.

Voss' request for an honorarium was quite brusquely turned down.

Helene Böhlau moved to Berlin, occupying a modest furnished apartment on Dessauerstrasse. "To my astonishment", writes Voss, "the entire Arndt family followed her there: husband, wife and both daughters... She [Helene] said to me: her friend was also a poetic genius, a great dramatist who has written a tragedy of the Nibelungen, and she asked me to be present at a reading of this drama. Naturally, I was prepared to do so and promised that I would see to arranging a performance of the extraordinary work."

The evening of the reading turned out to be oppressive; Frau Arnd, "an enfeebled, piteous female figure...was so much under the influence of the work which in her judgement was sublime that she recited the entire long tragedy with a failing, tear-choked voice so that in general I found it difficult to understand... After the second act suddenly the poet himself entered, draped in a black cloak – a most peculiar apparition."

To Richard Voss "it became clear during the reading that Helene Böhlau, this fresh, healthy, splendid creature and great literary talent had fallen under an inescapable spell, a form of hypnosis. This was to extend even beyond the death of the man who later, when his wife refused to give him a divorce, went to Constantinople, became a Turk, adopted the fantastical name Al Rachid Bey and took Helene Böhlau as his second wife…"[9]

Voss could not have known that Frau Arnd at the time did finally make up her mind to separate from her husband so that he could marry Helene who became more and more indispensable to him. But a divorce in Germany was unthinkable. Consequently, it came about that Arnd at first went to Turkey alone.

When, after searching for a long time in Istanbul, he located his mother's elderly brother, a friend of Münif Paşa[10] (mentioned above) who even found him employment, he had Helene Böhlau join him. They were provided with letters of recommendation, including one from the aged Field Marshal Helmuth von Moltke (1800-1891). Helene Böhlau's Istanbul acquaintances asked Ali Nuri to intervene personally in what were now necessary official negotiations.

To Ali Nuri, Arnd seemed rather dubious – the philosophizing geographer, the mystic, "whom no one quite knew where he had come from nor how he had attained his prominent position". He had come to Turkey "where he believed that having multiple wives represented the norm and polygamy was nothing short of a cult" in order to become a Muslim and "under this flag to undertake a second marriage…" Chiefly to help Helene Böhlau, Ali Nuri supported Arnd's conversion to Islam and their marriage.

Decades later Ali Nuri described these events in all their details and his judgement about Arnd had finally become more moderate.[11]

One had to apply to the section dealing with religious affairs within the Ministry of Justice and present an explanation for one's wish to convert to Islam. The section for religious affairs issued a certificate regarding the request and passed the matter on to the Ministry of Foreign Affairs which informed the German Embassy, which in turn commissioned a dragoman to examine the case. Although strictly speaking he was stateless, Arnd was viewed as a subject

9 Richard Voss, *Aus meinem phantastischen Leben. Erinnerungen*, Stuttgart 1920, pp. 270-72.

10 Münif Paşa (1828-1910), the progressive writer, thinker and statesman, was three times appointed Minister of Education, 1877, 1878-1880, 1885-1891; in 1880 as Minister of Education he opened the Museum Çinili Köşk. On his biography cf. İsmail Habib Sevük, *Tanzimat Devri Edebiyatı*, Istanbul, no date, p. 181; B. Lewis, *Emergence of Modern Turkey*, pp. 421, 431 and 433; Sümer Atasoy, "Türkiye'de Müzecilik", *Cumhuriyet Dönemi Türkiye Ansiklopedisi* 6, p. 1459. Cf. also the Index of the same encyclopaedia. For the "reformer, westernizing statesman and founding father of Turkey's modern education system" see Andrew Mango, "Münif Pasha" in *EI* VII, p. 573.

11 Ali Nuri, *Helene Böhlau. Der Roman ihres Lebens*, Istanbul 1932.

of the German Empire and, in accordance with the capitulations in force, he came under the jurisdiction of the German Consulate.

The explanation for converting to Islam had to be repeated before the interpreter along with confirmation that the change of religion was voluntary and devoid of outside coercion or influence. After that the conversion was an accomplished fact. Circumcision, as Ali Nuri tells us, was not unavoidable: if the father who is responsible for this duty has neglected it in childhood, a Muslim can omit it at a later time.

Everything went according to wish; Baron von Testa, the First Dragoman of the German Embassy, issued the necessary certificate. In the Ministry of Foreign Affairs, the Under-Secretary Artin Efendi and Ohannes Aga who was all-powerful in the department helped to expedite the matter. The Director of the section for religious affairs, Siver Bey, a friend of Ali Nuri Bey, completed the official formalities.

To begin with he explained that the Ottomans had no interest whatsoever in engaging in proselytizing. Friedrich Arnd who presented himself as a German Protestant declared that he was not motivated to convert to Islam by any material interests (such as seeking employment). He maintained as the real reason his conviction, acquired from philosophical study, that Islam was the best religion. He had read the Koran in translation. He pronounced the formula for the profession of faith correctly and made a solemn declaration of his belief in Islam before witnesses. When asked, he proposed Omar al Raschid as his new name. Siver Bey brought the official formalities to a close by congratulating Omar Efendi.

After the formalities, Siver Bey expressed to Nuri Bey the conjecture that the new Muslim Omar al Raschid had originally been a Jew and consequently had changed his religion for the second time. His conjecture was based on the careful and measured way in which Arnd pronounced the formula for the profession of faith.

Ali Nuri who suspected that Omar al Raschid did not wish to separate legally from his first wife (to whom he had made over his property), now insisted, in the interest of Helene Böhlau, that he irrevocably divorce his wife. With his conversion to Islam Arnd's marriage was said to have become invalid, although it could formally be renewed in accordance with Islamic guidelines. After serious hesitation, Omar al Raschid wrote out the divorce letter to Frau Arnd in the presence of the imam; it was sent to her by the German postal service in Galata; Ali Nuri advised Helene always to keep a second copy of this document with her.

On the advice of Ali Nuri, the couple chose not to make Beyoğlu their fixed residence but to live in the Armenian neighborhood of Kumkapı. They rented the upper floor of a small, somewhat dilapidated wooden house with a garden on the old city wall. Their identity papers and birth certificate were translated and authenticated. After the imam had confirmed their residence with a certificate, their marriage contract was concluded before the same imam.[12]

Ottoman citizenship was not obtained by converting to Islam but had to be applied for. For this a five-year residence in Turkey was necessary. In exceptional cases the government could deviate from these procedures. And this also turned out successfully; Omar al Raschid became a Turkish citizen. Ali Nuri whose vacation came to an end – he sailed away on board a ship – was helpful to him in this respect as well.

Münif Paşa, the Minister of Cultural Affairs, "one of the men of power here, a remarkable man, around sixty years old, aristocratic, educated, simple in his habits, a truly distinguished person, was an envoy in Paris and Berlin, speaks excellent French and German, has translated much from Goethe and Heine", kept his word and obtained a post for Omar al Raschid in the Ministry of Education. Now and again he visited the couple "in his elegant coach with two *kavas* in attendance on horseback, and accompanied by his two daughters." Omar worked mornings at the ministry. It seems that there were difficulties with the salary as in the case of other civil servants as well. Omar al Raschid made good progress in the Turkish and Arabic languages.

He was a frequent guest in the "Indian cloister in Akssarai" whose "Scheich ül Reis" inspired him.[13] In Aksaray on the 15th of Rebi I 1304 (20th of September 1886) al Raschid began writing down his work *Das hohe Ziel der Erkenntnis* (*The Lofty Goal of Knowledge*) or *Aranada Upanishad, i.e. the doctrine of the storm's*

12 These kinds of contracts are dealt with by G. Engelschalk, "Ein *münakehat defteri* der Jahrhundertwende", IV. Internationaler Kongress für Türkische Wirtschafts- und Sozialgeschichte, München, 4.–8. August 1986. For the sea wall on the Marmara shore see Wolfgang Müller-Wiener, *Bildlexikon zur Topographie Istanbuls*, Tübingen 1977, pp. 312-19; for the Arnds' residence in Kumkapı see ibid. p. 317 (map showing the sea wall and the Armenian Patriarchal church). Gisela Engelschalk, "Ein Münakehat Defteri der Jahrhundertwende", *Osmanlı Araştırmaları Dergisi* 9 (1989), pp.323-30.

13 The "Indian cloister in Akssarai" must be identified with the Hindliler Tekkesi in Aksaray. This was a Nakshbendi lodge where traditionally Kadiri and Nakshbendi pilgrims from Central Asia stopped on their way to Mecca to obtain symbolic permission from the Caliph; they were received as guests in the dervish lodge (for the location see Müller-Wiener, op. cit., p. 254, with map). The political role of another dervish lodge, the Özbekler Tekkesi in Üsküdar, is described in Nur Bilge Criss, *Istanbul under Allied Occupation 1918-1923*, Leiden-Boston-Köln 1999, p. 103. www.tarihistan.org/haber/1105-islam-dünyasinin-dervislerinin-ugrak-yeri.istanbul.html; retrieved 14 September 2011.

end which he cast in an oriental form though it is not the work of an Indian as he claims in the introduction.

During these years, Helene Böhlau developed into an established author whose narrative talent, on the one hand, breathed new life into Weimar which since Goethe's time had become rather museum-like and, on the other hand, fought for the social rights of women. Today only her name still appears in most relevant reference works;[14] her novels and short stories, however, which were twice published together as her collected works[15] and were often reprinted individually as well, have not been available in bookshops for a long time. In 1940 she died at Widdersberg near Munich.

Helene Böhlau's own autobiographical novels *In frischem Wasser* (1881; written in Istanbul) and *Isebies* (1911) provide the basis for a description of her years with Omar al Raschid. The works were only in part composed with hindsight and in fact often describe events at the time they occurred, even if admittedly not as precise and objective biographies.

In these books she speaks with warmth of her happy years in Istanbul, the marvelous city. "Imagine", she has Dohrn (Arnd) write to Helene, "a city like a labyrinth, infinitely sprawling, with wooden houses and gardens and cypress groves, forests in the middle of the city, and immensely spread out over hills, a city without street numbers...without policemen..." She writes of the "wonderful Turkish people, of their strength, goodness and nobility". Here and there she sprinkles in a smattering of Turkish.

The first autobiographical novel ends with reflections about "marriage and everything connected with it". "Divorce entails no disgrace here, one does not have to fight with all one's force to obtain it. Each spouse is allowed to separate from the other legally... Discord is not allowed to persist. Marriage should not be a burden, an inescapable misery, an eternal chain for the persons involved... And despite this immense freedom, divorce is a great rarity." Helene Böhlau describes this problem of her life in *In frischem Wasser*, and her biographer Friedrich Zillmann in 1918 is concerned about whether, for all its art, "this at the least unnatural and rare subject is appropriate for a novel".[16]

---

14 M.H. Würzner, "Böhlau, Helene", *Moderne Encyclopedie van de Wereldliteratuur*, 2, Haarlem/Antwerpen 1980, p. 12. [But now also see Carol Diethe, *Towards Emancipation: German Women Writers of the Nineteenth Century*, New York 1998, esp. pp. 158-170.]

15 Consulted in the Public Reading Room of 's-Gravenhage: Helene Böhlau, *Gesammelte Werke*, 6 volumes, Berlin: Ullstein and Egon Fleischel 1914-1915.

16 Friedrich Zillmann, *Helene Böhlau. Ein Beitrag zu ihrer Würdigung*, Leipzig 1918, p. 82.

She describes the natural beauties of the city neighborhoods Kumkapı and Yedikule; for her Pera is the place for "all European stupidities". In Kumkapı they live door to door with Armenians.

The couple also knows other emigrants: Nuri, the Thuringian who, having become a Muslim, worked for the government tobacco monopoly that was set up in 1883 and who scarcely spoke any Turkish; as well as Ali Nuri's confidant, Abdülkadir Efendi, who was born in Bavaria.

After years in Istanbul, the al Raschids went back to Germany. Via correspondence they learn "that their family members considered their marriage as never having taken place...and that Frau Dohrn (Arnd) caused distress and anxiety to the Böhlaus." Frau Arnd attempted to reestablish her marriage through the law courts and after years of litigation in 1903/4 succeeded in having the marriage with Helene Böhlau declared invalid. A son was born to the al Raschids, Hermann Böhlau al Raschid Bey.

When the medical student Theodor Lessing (1872-1933) came to Munich in January 1895, the al Raschids had just settled in the artists' neighborhood Schwabing. In the strange bohemian world of Schwabing that has been described in numerous memoirs[17] where the "Kosmiker" (cosmics) gathered around Karl Wolfskehl (1869– 1948)[18] and the periodical *Simplicissimus* was published, a circle now formed around Omar al Raschid that along with various artists like Olly Weiss and Anna Spier also included Theodor Lessing and his friend Ludwig Klages (1872-1933), as well as the writer Franziska Gräfin zu Reventlow (1871-1918).[19] The al Raschids were friends with Paul Heyse (1830-1914).

The literary output of Helene Böhlau, who was at her peak, was not only a fulfilment of her own existence but a source of income for the family as well. In her best books she devotes her powers of expression as a writer to defending equal rights for women. In 1974 her book *Halbtier!* (1899) was held up as an expression of female civic protest;[20] her best book is nowadays considered to be her novel about artists in Munich, *Rangierbahnhof*.[21]

Theodor Lessing, the physician and philosopher, is a witness who after longstanding intimate acquaintance and in spite of personal enthusiasm, portrays

17 M. Winkler, *George-Kreis*, Stuttgart 1972.

18 F. Schonauer, *Stefan George*, Reinbek bei Hamburg 1960, p. 44; M. Winkler, *George-Kreis*, pp. 32 and 38-39.

19 In 1901 her son played with the little Omar al Raschid, known as das Bobbele; E. Reventlow (ed.), *Franziska Gräfin zu Reventlow. Tagebücher 1895-1910*, Munich-Vienna 1971, p. 199.

20 Hans Kaufmann and Silvia Schlenstedt, *Geschichte der deutschen Literatur vom Ausgang des 19. Jahrhunderts bis 1917*, Berlin 1974, p. 539.

21 Theodor Lessing who reviewed the novel considered it a work of "marvelous beauty".

his subject with objective detail so that on the basis of this source and the previously cited books a picture of al Raschid in fact begins to emerge. Whereas the description in Richard Voss is sarcastically colored and in Ali Nuri polemically inclined, Lessing depicts him as "a good-looking patriarchal figure with a greying beard", a Buddhist philosopher oriented toward Kant and Schopenhauer; he calls *Das hohe Ziel der Erkenntnis* "a wonderful fragment".[22]

"He was no human being but a god imprisoned in human form. From what distant star had this unique man come down to earth? Since human beings are incapable of making sense of such strangers other than in terms of the vanities and intentions they all understand…, consequently al Raschid's strangeness was exposed to all forms of misinterpretation and misunderstanding which, wrapped up in his mystery, he neither grasped nor even took notice of." When the whole circle around the "reflective, deeply expressive" al Raschid withdrew for some months in 1897 to the remote mountain village of Klausen (Chiusa) in South Tyrol, the events of 1885 threatened to repeat themselves between the master and a young female disciple. Lessing was able to prevent this from happening by his energetic intervention.[23]

Omar al Raschid retained something oriental in his clothing; he "never appeared other than in a burnous and tarboosh, with high boots, and wearing a yellow-gray cape".[24] He died on the 26th of January 1911 and is buried in Munich's Waldfriedhof.

Ali Nuri remained a Turk. He was appointed Ottoman consul general in Rotterdam. The purpose of this appointment was apparently to spy on the Young Turks living in exile in Europe. But through his contact with them Ali Nuri was won over to their cause. In the Sultan's palace suspicion was soon aroused. An article in the French-language newspapers of the capital by means of which Ali Nuri wished to show his loyalty and his fruitful activity in the Netherlands in a favorable light was forbidden by the newspaper censorship authorities.[25]

The satirical newspaper *Davul* proved to be his downfall. This French-language paper appeared fortnightly from 1900 and continued with interruptions up until the 31st of March 1909.[26] Since *Davul* was very effective at

22 Theodor Lessing, *Einmal und nie wieder*, first edition Prague 1935; unaltered reprint, Gütersloh 1969, with a foreword by Hans Mayer, pp. 364-65.

23 Lessing, *Einmal und nie wieder*, pp. 367-69.

24 Lessing, *Einmal und nie wieder*, p. 364.

25 Ministerie van Buitenlandse Zaken, The Hague, Archive Gezantschap Istanboel W 72-1920, B XI, no. 2, 1898-1917.

26 D. Akünal, "Jön Türk Gazeteleri", *Tanzimat'tan Cumhuriyet'e Türkiye Ansiklopedisi* 3 (1985), p. 852.

castigating social and political abuses – the Sultan himself was the subject of its keen political satire as was among others Emperor Wilhelm II and his visits to Turkey – through their ambassadors in Bern, Paris and Berlin the Ottoman government authorities attempted to find out where the paper was published. However, its place of publication remained unknown; even today doubts persist in the matter.[27]

Ali Nuri dismissed the charge levelled against him with an ironical reference to the place of publication as given in the newspaper: "Istanbul, *Hamidiye* printing-press"; the first issue of *Davul* appeared with a pseudo-*Hatt-i hümayun* suggesting that the Sultan himself had founded the newspaper.[28] For his part, Ali Nuri claimed that a personal, non-political court intrigue was responsible for the Ottoman ambassador in Paris, Münir Bey, having instituted legal proceedings against him as the editor of *Davul*.[29]

Ali Nuri put in a request for his dismissal as consul general;[30] "Mundji Bey" who had been waiting in The Hague for his exequatur since October 1900 would occupy Nuri's position in Rotterdam.[31]

In April 1901, the Turkish newspapers published a subpoena, according to which Ali Nuri Bey, the Turkish consul general in Rotterdam, was called upon to defend himself in a criminal trial against charges of seditious activities. On the 21st of May 1901, his name appeared on a list of persons for whom, by virtue of a higher order, a warrant of arrest had been issued by the public prosecutor of the court of appeal in Istanbul, a list that was published in all the newspapers of the capital. The charge was high treason and lese-majesty by means of violent attacks on the Sultan and his government in inflammatory newspapers and writings. If the accused did not present himself within fourteen days

27 In Dündar Akünal, "Yeni Osmanlılar'la Jön Türkler'in Ülke Dışında Çıkardıkları Gazeteler", in *Sosyalist Kültür Ansiklopedisi* 9 (1980), pp. 1296-99, "Daoul" appears as no. 15 with the place of publication indicated as "Paris", whereas Turgut Çeviker, "Tanzimat'tan Cumhuriyet'e Türk Karikatürü", *Tanzimat'tan Cumhuriyet'e Türkiye Ansiklopedisi* 4 (1985), pp. 1101-08, introduces a question mark for the place of publication.

28 Photo: Akünal in "Jön Türk Gazeteleri", *Tanzimat'tan...Ansik.*, p. 854.

29 Paul Fesch, *Constantinople aux derniers jours d'Adul-Hamid*, Paris, no date [1907], p. 349, mentions *Davul* among the "journaux Jeunes Turcs disparus", with a portrait of Münir Paşa (p. 81).

30 Ministerie van Buitenlandse Zaken, The Hague, letter 231/109. The letter from Pera dated the 12th of April 1901 announces that the Turkish Consul in Rotterdam "zijn ontslag had aangevraagd" (had handed in his resignation).

31 Ministerie van Buitenlandse Zaken, The Hague, Archive Gezantschap Istanboel W 72-1920, B XI, no. 2, 1898-1917.

before the criminal court in Istanbul, he would be sentenced *in absentia* and his possessions confiscated.

Ali Nuri did not present himself before the court. He was in fact condemned the same year to 101 years in prison, and then the sentence was increased in harshness to imprisonment in a fortress for life. At almost the same time, in the German Empire the satirical treatment of Emperor Wilhelm II's journey to Palestine (1898)[32] in *Simplicissimus* earned Frank Wedekind a sentence of seven months in prison because of lese-majesty; it was hardly a consolation for Ali Nuri that Wedekind's sentence was commuted to imprisonment in a fortress, followed by his release after five months in 1900.

Ali Nuri from now on publicly wrote for newspapers as a bitter opponent of Sultan Abdülhamid II. His book of 1903 contains primarily the caricatures of *Davul* that make fun of the goings-on in the Yıldız Palace.[33]

He travelled throughout Europe with his wife who supported him in his campaign. In 1902 he was obliged to auction off his book collection in Malmö. When in February 1903 advertisements appeared in Stockholm newspapers announcing a public lecture by Hayriye Hanim about the Turkish woman and life in the harem, the Swedish police authorities, for fear of diplomatic complications with the Porte, forbade her to speak.

On the 24th of February 1904, Theodor Herzl in Vienna records in his diary: "Yesterday I had a most curious visit: 'Ali Nouri Bey, ex-Consul Général de Turquie' it said on his visiting card, which he had first sent me in the N(eue) F(reie) Pr(esse). He is the husband of a Turkish princess who is giving lectures here on life in the harem. His good German surprised me. He explained that he is a Swede, came to Turkey as Strousberg's representative at the age of eighteen and became a Mohammadan. Today, as a forty-year-old man, he looks rather Turkish...with...a red beard and glasses...and his head sitting deeply embedded between his shoulders.

His proposal, which he laid out to me between the [morning] hours of 9:30 and 12:30 in my apartment, culminated in: we will sail up the Bosphorus with two cruisers, bombard Yıldız, put the Sultan to flight or capture him, replace him with another Sultan (Murad or Reschad), but before that form a provisional government which should give us the charter for Palestine. A novel or an adventure? ...Everything presented in a cool, quiet manner, like a proposal to

32 On the journey cf. Alex Carmel, *Die Siedlungen der württembergischen Templer in Palästina 1868-1918*, Stuttgart 1973, pp. 157-69; İlber Ortaylı, *Osmanlı Imparatorluğunda Alman Nüfusu*, Istanbul 1983, pp. 64-69.

33 For Ottoman cartoonists see Palmira Brummett, *Image and Imperialism in the Ottoman Revolutionary Press, 1908-1911*, New York 2000.

buy a load of grain. He wants to take part in the naval action himself and go ashore... They will fire into the air and no one will get hurt in the process."[34]

Theodor Herzl had serious objections, even when Ali Nuri visited him for a second time on the 4th of March 1904: "Once again the Bosphorus plan. But this is doubtlessly a highly intelligent conspirator and adventurer. A Viking in a frock-coat. Very nice how he wants to cover the two cruisers in the Dardanelles by placing merchant ships between them and the forts. A merchant captain is prepared to do that for 50 or 100 L. And he is already cutting telegraph wires in his imagination, etc." Th. Herzl asked a Swedish colonel about Ali Nuri Bey; he was told that the latter had been called "Nordling" (sic) in Sweden.[35] Herzl gave the plan careful consideration[36] but rejected it in April 1904 (he died the 3rd of July the same year).[37]

After the Young Turk Revolution Ali Nuri returned to Turkey in 1909. Little is known about his life after that. The book about Helene Böhlau that he published in 1931 does not in fact contain the biography announced in the title but presents in a lively manner his memories of the days of 1885. It is known that in 1934 he adopted the family name Dilmeç and that he died in Istanbul in 1937 at the age of sixty-nine.

Appendices

I *Works of Ali Nuri Bey*

Article in the Swedish newspaper *Framat* (*Forwards*). At the age of nineteen he had his first work consisting of eleven pages printed at his own expense in ten copies under the title *Några tänkar om orientaliska frågan*.

Ali Nuri's illustrated small work about Sultan Abdülhamid II in caricature appeared in 1903 in Swedish,[38] Danish[39] and German.[40] The French original could still not be

34 *Theodor Herzls Tagebücher 1895-1904*, III, Berlin 1923, pp. 568-69. R. Patai (ed.), *The Complete Diaries of Theodor Herzl*, IV, New York-London 1960, pp. 1614-15; Y. Kutluay, *Siyonizm ve Türkiye*, Konya 1967, pp. 282-85. H. Tanyu, *Tarih Boyunca Yahudiler ve Türkler*, 2nd edition, no date [1979], I, pp. 460-62, quoted by Y. Kutluay.

35 *Theodor Herzls Tagebücher 1895-1904*, III, Berlin 1923, p. 571; Patai, *Diaries*, p. 1617.

36 *Th. Herzls Tagebücher* III, p. 573; Patai, *Diaries*, p. 1619.

37 *Th. Herzls Tagebücher* III, pp. 574-75; Patai, *Diaries*, pp. 1619-21.

38 Ali Nuri Bey, *Abdul-Hamid i Karikatur. Interiorer från Yildiz-Kiosk i ord och bild*, Stockholm 1903, 111 pages.

39 Ali Nuri Bey, *Abdul-Hamid i Karikatur. Interiorer fra Yildiz-Kiosk i Billeder og Tekst*, Copenhagen 1903, 104 pages. Another edition: ibid. 1903.

40 Ali Nuri Bey, *Abdul-Hamid in Karikatur. Intimes aus Yildiz-Kiosk in Wort und Bild*, 1904, 120 pages.

published at the time. It was first published in 1931 in Kadıköy; the second edition appeared one year later.[41]

Unter dem Scepter des Sultans, Berlin 1905 (in one chapter this book deals with the Conference of Basel in 1897 which paved the way for Zionism).[42]

Ur gamla gömmor-En gard at det förflutna (*From old treasures-Honoring the past*) was published in twenty copies in Malmö at his own expense in 1902; it describes his pain at separation from his book collection.

Helene Böhlau (*Frau Omar al Raschid*). Der Roman ihres Lebens, von Ali Nuri, Istanbul: Druckerei Universum G.m.b.H., 1932.

II Works of Omar al Raschid Bey

Kriemhild (a tragedy; 1876).

Lebensstürme (1876), later under the title *Nur Liebe berechtigt die Ehe* (*Love Alone Justifies Marriage*).

Das hohe Ziel der Erkenntnis. Aranada Upanishad, published by Helene Böhlau al Raschid Bey, Munich: R. Piper 1922, with a preface dated June 1922 by the son of the author, Hermann Böhlau (al Raschid Bey).

41 Ali Nouri, *Abdul-Hamid en Caricature. Intérieurs de Yildiz-Kiosk*, Istanbul, Imprimerie des Banques Haim, Rozio & Cie., Imprimeurs-éditeurs 1932.

42 This book served as a source for Paul Fesch, *Constantinople aux derniers jours d'Abdul-Hamid*, Paris, no date [1907].

CHAPTER 17

Ṣāḥib-qırān and Mahdī: Turkish Expectations of the End of Time in the First Decade of the Rule of Süleymān*

In the beginning of the 16th century the population of Anatolia was frequently hard hit by natural catastrophes, plagues and famines. The effects of the great plague epidemic must have especially been felt in all regions. There was surely scant consolation in explaining the insecurity and mismanagement as due to the illness of the ageing Sultan Bāyezīd II and the failure of his viziers. His son Selīm I only pursued the heterodox Shīʿite Qızılbaş in Anatolia, who looked to the Persian Shah for their support, with all the more grim determination. It is astonishing how Selīm I was able to achieve his military goals, despite the casualties he sustained during his Qızılbaş persecutions: his troops had scarcely defeated the Persian Shah in 1514 and to some extent sealed off the frontier with Persia, when in August 1516 they engaged in the decisive battle against the Mamluks that made possible the Ottoman entry into Cairo in January 1517. But when Sultan Süleymān ascended the throne, there were at once uprisings among the Anatolian rural population who fought against a new land registration which the central government was undertaking after rounding off its Anatolian domains and due to a shortage of money. None the less, the almost yearly expeditions followed their course; in 1521 Belgrade was captured, in 1522 Rhodes fell after bitter fighting, in 1526 Hungarian military power was annihilated at Mohács and Hungary's capital Ofen (Buda) was occupied. Three years later the huge Ottoman army was at the gates of Vienna but then, when an early cold spell and difficulties in obtaining provisions forced the lifting of the siege, the army beat a sluggish retreat through the flooded countryside in rain and driving snow. The battered army was able quickly to replenish its numbers but now more clearly than before tension was perceptible between the smaller organized group who promoted military operations in its own interest and the unorganized masses who had to carry the burden of the campaigns.[1] If the latter defended themselves in a series of revolts and tribal uprisings that were characterized as religious uprisings, the disturbances were to a large extent the

* Translated by John O'Kane.

1 Gy. Káldy-Nagy, "Rural and Urban Life in the Age of Sultan Sulayman", in *Acta Orientalia Hungarica* 32 (1978), pp. 285-319. – The manuscript of the present essay was completed toward the end of 1979; a few additions were made at the time of printing.

 | DOI 10.1163/9789004355767_018

result of endless wars, whose costs had to be borne by those classes of the population who never had a share in the captured booty.[2] The dissatisfaction among the tax-paying population was considerable, but the insurgents were suppressed with such violence that they did not dare to engage in an armed uprising for a long time to come.[3] Where the leaders of the rural population appeared under the banner of the Qızılbaş Ṣafavīya, as had occurred earlier with Şāhqulı of Teke ili (1511-1512) and Shaykh Celāl from Bozoq (1519-1520), and was now the case with Qalender from the Bektaşi heartland around Kırşehir (1527-1528), the popular uprisings were still able to assume the form of large-scale revolts which, especially later when Ottoman princes took part in them, threatened the very existence of the ruling dynasty.[4]

The terrible fighting during persecution of the insurgents and the acts of violence and cruelty perpetrated in these wars, as from time immemorial in the Islamic world so too in the Ottoman Empire, provided a breeding ground for expectations that an even more terrible "upheaval" (*fitna*) was imminent, after which the end of the world would occur. Such views could be associated with the expectation that before the end of the world a decisive change for the better would once again take place. This would be the advent of the Kingdoms of Peace presided over by the Mahdī and ʿĪsā under whom Islam would spread across the whole world. Ideas like this, whose origins lie in the apocalyptic tradition of Daniel,[5] were also a known phenomenon in the West which, for its part, anticipated the ultimate triumph of Christianity.

In Islam the eschatological scheme, which had grown up historically and was therefore not free from contradictions and repetitions, in broad outline consisted of the following: After a chaotic period of *fitna* the Mahdī appears. He establishes a kingdom of peace which lasts for seven years. Rūm is conquered. Then there appears the figure ad-Daccāl, who corresponds to the Anti-Christ, and he seizes power for a short or a longer time. He is vanquished by Jesus (ʿĪsā) who descends from heaven in Damascus. ʿĪsā once again founds

2 Ibid., p. 288; cf. also F. Sümer, *Oğuzlar (Türkmenler). Tarihleri – Boy Teşkilâtı – Destanları*, Ankara 19722, p. 172.

3 Káldy-Nagy, op. cit.

4 H. Sohrweide, "Der Sieg der Ṣafaviden in Persien und seine Rückwirkungen auf die Schiiten Anatoliens im 16. Jahrhundert", in *Der Islam* 41 (1965), pp. 95-223; M. Akdağ, *Türkiye'nin İktisadî ve İçtimaî Tarihi*. II. *1453-1559*, Ankara 1971; M. Akdağ, *Türk Halkının Dirlik ve Düzenlik Kavgası*, Ankara 1975, passim.

5 D.B. Macdonald, art. *Malāḥim* in EI1; A. Abel, "Changements politiques et littérature apocalyptique dans le monde musulman", in *Studia Islamica* II (1954), pp. 23-24; J. den Heijer, "Malḥamat Dāniyāl and Christian Arabic Literature", in *Orientalia Christiana Analecta* 218 (1982), pp. 223-32.

a Kingdom of Peace. After that the apocalyptic harbingers Gog and Magog appear and the Final Hour occurs.[6]

The fall of Rūm belonged to the permanent repertoire of these accumulated Traditions. Originally Rūm had meant Constantinople.[7] But, in the course of time, as it became ever clearer that there was little chance of the city being captured by force of arms, Traditions began to circulate that predicted that Byzantium would continue to exist until the final hour. Alongside this not undisputed idea[8] there arose around the 10th century a new interpretation of the *ḥadīth* about Rūm – namely that the Eternal City in Italy would be conquered – which the imagination of Muslims, aided by descriptions of Rome by their old geographers, now furnished with all sorts of buildings, talismans and statues.[9]

Medieval Arabic writers readily made use of these ideas in the *malāḥim*-books in order to explain great events of the past or contemporary occurrences such as the coming to power of the ʿAbbāsids, the Crusades, the rise of the Mamluks and the conquests of the Turks, and occasionally they attempted to use these ideas in the service of political propaganda.[10] However confused and irrelevant later Muslim eschatological descriptions may at first seem from the historian's point of view,[11] as popular literature they represent a source of high value in so far as they help us "to understand the reaction of peoples themselves to the course of history".[12]

The Anatolian Turks also drew from eschatological sources of this kind. One of the oldest preserved works written in Anatolia and dedicated to the Seljuk Sultan ʿIzzeddīn Qılıç Arslan II (1156-1192) is a text of prophecy in the "Daniel

6 A summary of the subject is found in D.S. Attema, *De Mohammedaansche Opvattingen omtrent het tijdstip van den Jongsten Dag en zijn voortekenen*, Amsterdam 1942; cf. C. Snouck Hurgronje, "Der Mahdi (1885)", in *Verspreide Geschriften* I (1923), pp. 147-81; A. Abel, "Un hadith sur la prise de Rome dans la tradition eschatologique de l'Islam", in *Arabica* V (1958), pp. 1-14.

7 A.J. Wensinck, *A Handbook of Early Muhammadan Tradition*, Leiden 1927 (reprint 1971), s.v. *Hour*.

8 M. Canard, "Les expéditions des Arabes contre Constantinople dans l'histoire et dans la légende", in *JAS* CCVIII (1926), pp. 108-10; on other *ḥadīth*s ibid. pp. 106-07 and L. Massignon, "Textes prémonitoires et commentaires mystiques relatifs à la prise de Constantinople par les Turcs en 1453 (= 858 Hég.)" (sic), in *Oriens* 6 (1953), p. 11.

9 Abel, "Prise de Rome".

10 Abel, Signification apologétique, p. 535.(?)

11 Snouck, "Mahdi", p. 165: "Calculations and conjectures about the time of the Mahdi constantly found a sympathetic ear with a multitude of believers".

12 Abel, "Changements politiques", p. 43.

tradition".[13] In addition, astrology was enlisted in order to predict with precision the end of the world and to indicate peculiar positions of the heavenly bodies. A famous example of the agreement of Islamic and Christian thought regarding these subjects was the "Great Conjunction" of Şaʿbān 582/October 1186, in connection with which the astronomers had announced dangerous storms and an immense flood. This led both the above-named Seljuk Sultan as well as his Byzantine counterpart, Emperor Manuel Komnenos (1143-1180) to undertake costly protective measures. The ever-recurring idea of the end of the world also nourished itself on political reality; religious-social movements of chiliastic character already existed in the Seljuk state which was dangerously shaken around 1240 by the revolt of Bābā Isḥāq, the "Messenger of God" (*Rasūl Allāh*), who was inclined to Shiʿite views, and his followers who wore red caps. At the end of the Īlḫān period, a religiously particularly eager governor laid claim to absolute sovereignty and the status of Mahdī.[14]

A century later the bold Sufi shaykh Bedreddīn Maḥmūd (1358-1416) and his *ḫalīfe* Börklüce Muṣṭafā aroused expectations of the end of time,[15] even though Shaykh Bedreddīn himself was supposed to have been restrained in his comments about prognostic symptoms of the end of time.[16]

The tremendous event of the capture of Byzantium by the Ottoman Turks in 1453 stimulated renewed study of the relevant *ḥadīth* literature. After all, the fact had to be considered that the city once thought to be impregnable had now been conquered by the sword, whereas only at the end of time were the walls of the city – whose one side lies on the land and two other sides face the sea – meant to collapse before the *şahāda*- and *takbīr*-cries of seventy thousand of the Banū Isḥāq, i.e. the Arabs.[17] It was possible to ignore the eschatological aspects of the *ḥadīth* corpus as Qıvāmī does in his *Fetḥnāme* of 1488

---

13 Cf. Ch. Rieu, *Catalogue of the Persian Manuscripts in the British Museum*, London 1881, p. 852.

14 Cl. Cahen, art. "Babāʾī", *EI* second ed. I (1960), pp. 843-844; Timurtaş, the Governor of the Īlḫāns in Konya and for a time independent ruler (he fell in 1327), attempted to enlist the Mevlevī Order in support of his propaganda; cf. B. Flemming, *Landschaftsgeschichte von Pamphylien, Pisidien und Lykien im Spätmittelalter*, Wiesbaden 1964, pp. 74-76.

15 The anonymous chronicles, for example, have him say: "They call me the King Mahdī" (*baña melik Mehdī dėrler*) – see F. Giese, *Die altosmanischen anonymen Chroniken* I, Breslau 1922, p. 54; II, Leipzig 1925, p. 74.

16 H.J. Kissling, "Das Menāqybnāme Scheich Bedr ed-dīns, des Sohnes des Richters von Samavna", in *ZDMG* (1950), pp. 112-76; E. Werner, *Die Geburt einer Großmacht. Die Osmanen (1300-1481)*, Berlin 19722, p. 200.

17 See here ftn. 8; on the opinion of the Arab commentators that the Arabs – the Banū Ismāʿīl – are meant, cf. Canard, "Expéditions", p. 110; Attema, *Opvattingen*, pp. 92-93.

which only makes use of the description of the place in *ḥadīth*s: when the Turks draw near to the city of Koṣṭanṭinīye, they behold a fortress beyond all comparison", whose two sides turn their back to the sea while one side directs its breast to the land (*iki ṭarafı arqalarını baḥre vėrmiş ve bir ṭarafı sīnesini berrden yaña dutmış*).[18] The Old Ottoman anonymous chronicles, on the other hand, reshape the *ḥadīth*s in two respects; namely, it says here that the *ʿulemāʾ* report a prophecy according to which Constantinople would be conquered just once – *bir daḫı* – by the sword before the advent of the Daccāl: in this way account is taken of the conquest of 1453. But then when the Day of Judgement dawns "the sons of *Abū Isḥāq* will capture it with *tekbīr*". By means of this second alteration, the Arab Banū Isḥāq became the Turkish dervishes of the Isḥāqīye, "sons" of Abū Isḥāq Kāzerūnī (963-1034), who from the 14th to the 16th century were active as militant zealots of the faith.[19] For other Ottoman history writers the eschatological "sons of Isḥāq" provided a cause to search for a genealogical connection between them and the Turks. The debate between religious scholars that was thus kindled over the question as to which son of Noah the Turks are descended from, whether from Japheth, the blessed third son, or, through Esau (ʿĪsū), Isḥāq's son, from Shem,[20] in this way acquires an eschatological-ideological dimension which can only be hinted at here in passing. Suffice it to say that many early Ottoman chroniclers, including ʿĀşıqpaşazāde, the cited *Tevārīḫ-i āl-i ʿOsmān*, as well as the author of the *Cāmiʿ ül-meknūnāt* which will be discussed below, unambiguously decided in favor of Japheth as the traditional progenitor of the Oguz.[21]

18 F. Babinger (ed.), *Fetihname-i Sultan Mehmed*, Istanbul 1955, p. 61. On the same page Qıvāmī also cites the corresponding part of the *ḥadīth* in Arabic.

19 P. Wittek was the first to draw attention to this reinterpretation in the appendix to his translation of M. Fu'ad Köprülüzāde's article "Abū Isḥāq Kāzerūnī und die Isḥāqī-Derwische in Anatolien", in *Der Islam* XIX (1931), pp. 18 ff.; Appendix, pp. 25-26. Already earlier during the siege of Constantinople in 1422 it is transmitted that a man of God wanted to cause the city walls to collapse by means of cries of *takbīr*: *GOR* I, pp. 413 f.; K. Teply, *Türkische Sagen und Legenden um die Kaiserstadt Wien*, Vienna-Cologne-Graz 1980, p. 120, who points out the typological closeness to the miracle of Jericho.

20 ʿĪṣū is then identified with Qayı Ḫān, the progenitor of the Ottomans. For a discussion of the subject cf. A.S. Erzi in *Belleten* XVIII (1954), p. 200, and Ş. Turan (ed.), *İbn-i Kemāl. Tevarih-i Âl-i Osman*. Defter I, Ankara 1970, Introduction.

21 J.H. Mordtmann in his review of the MOG (cf. ftn. 24) showed that Muṣṭafā ʿĀlī considered Sultan Meḥmed II to be a descendant of ʿĪṣ b. Isḥāq (*Künh ül-aḫbār*, Defter V, pp. 251 ff.); cf. *Der Islam* XIII (1923), p. 163. How then can *GOR* I, p. 668, ftn. to p. 523, maintain that ʿĀlī denied the Turks' origin from Esau and rejected it as a "scandalous error"? Time and space is lacking to enter into this question here.

But the Ottoman chroniclers also take a Koranic passage as an indication of the conquest of Constantinople by their Sultan, calculating the numerical value of the letters in the words *baldatun ṭayyibatun* in 34:14 as the year of the city's conquest 857 AH.[22]

Likewise, the Ottoman Turks adopted the *ḥadīth* that much earlier had already been reinterpreted to refer to Rome in Italy by connecting it with the goal of their triumphal campaigns, *qızıl elma*, the "red" or "golden apple" which symbolized the far-off capitals of the Christian kingdoms, but especially Rome.[23] In the well-known prophecy that already referred to Rome, which Bartholomaeus Georgievits in fact heard from Christian subjects of the Ottoman Empire, there is talk of a twelve-year rule of that city by a future Turkish Padishah who will then be driven back by the sword of Christendom:[24] perhaps this is an echo of the traditional idea of temporary kingdoms that succeed one another shortly before the end of time.

The first decades of the 16th century, as mentioned at the beginning of this essay, were a time of religious unrest. At the start of Sultan Süleymān's period of rule adherents of the teachings of Bedreddīn of Samavna were still to be found in the Ottoman Empire.[25] While in the capital legal proceedings were instituted against a religious scholar because he judged Jesus to be a prophet of greater eminence than Muḥammad (1527),[26] Qalender, whom we have already

22 The Koranic verse originally refers to the Sabaeans; this is how it is still understood in the old Ottoman Koran translation by Muḥammed b. Ḥamza (beginning of the 15th cent.): *ildür hoş, dakı Çalapdur yarlıġayıcı*; A. Topaloğlu, *Muhammed bin Hamza. XV. Yüzyıl Başlarında Yapılmış Kur'an Tercümesi* I, Istanbul 1976, p. 347. On the use of the Koranic passage in the chronicles to indicate the conquest of 1453 cf. Giese, *Anonyme Chroniken* II, pp. 99 and 148; cf. also J.H. Mordtmann, art. *Constantinople* in EI1 (1913), p. 867. The *Cāmiʿ üt-tevāriḫ* (see below) also cites the Koranic passage as the date of the conquest: *fetḥe ta'rīḫdur hem bu kelām* (Ms. L, fol. 62a).

23 C. Göllner, *Turcica. Die europäischen Türkendrucke des XVI. Jahrhunderts. III. Die Türkenfrage in der öffentlichen Meinung Europas im 16. Jahrhundert*, Bukarest – Baden-Baden 1978, p. 341; R.F. Kreutel, *Im Reiche des goldenen Apfels. Des türkischen Weltenbummlers Evliyâ Çelebi denkwürdige Reise in das Giaurenland und in die Stadt und Festung Wien anno 1665*, Graz-Vienna-Cologne 1957, p. 11, with older literature; Teply, *Türkische Sagen*, pp. 34-73.

24 J.H. Mordtmann in: *Mitteilungen des Seminars für orientalische Sprachen*, V. Jahrgang, II. Abt. (1902), p. 167; A. Fischer, "'Qyzyl elma', die Stadt (das Land) der Sehnsucht der Osmanen", in ZDMG 74 (1920), pp. 170-71. In the West as well people believed that the Turk (1485) would rule in Rome; Göllner, *Turcica III*, p. 338; Telpy, op. cit.

25 H.J. Kissling, art. *Badr al-Dīn b. Kāḍī Samāwna*, in EI2.

26 The most detailed contemporary report comes from Qoca Nişāncı who was surely an eyewitness; see P. Kappert (ed.), *Geschichte Sultan Süleymān Kānūnī von 1520 bis 1557 oder*

referred to earlier, made his appearance in Anatolia. He is meant to have declared himself to be the Mahdī of time, similarly to his predecessors Şāhqulı and Celāl who were linked to what came to be the Ṣafavīya of the Twelver Shīʿites and had preached the approach of the end of time – whether they were operating as *ḫalīfe*s of the Persian Shah or themselves claimed to be the Mahdī.[27] The violent measures of persecution adopted by the Ottoman regime are an indication of how worried the central government was about the unrest among the rural population that was sympathetically oriented toward the ʿAlids.[28]

These Mahdīs of the Qızılbaş embraced extremist Shīʿite eschatological expectations[29] which were not shared by the Sunnis of the Ottoman Empire. In his *Selīmnāme* the Kurd Şükrī writes about Celāl of Bozoq: *ata bindi Mehdīyem dib urdı ad / kendüye uydurdı çoq ehl-i fesād*: "He mounted his horse and proclaimed himself to be the Mahdī; he gathered many rabble-rousers around him", and: *dediler bu fitne-i aḫir zamān / bir ʿalāmetdür qıyāmetden hemān*:[30] "People said this is the upheaval of the end of time; this is surely a sign of the Last Judgment." – but without the author letting himself be impressed by any of this.

In Sunni eschatology the Mahdī has a less fixed place than the Daccāl:[31] this is shown in the anonymous Turkish *Aḥvāl-i qıyāmet* (presumably written at the end of the 16th century) which depicts in simple language the apocalyptic events without providing further information about their date but with a prospect of the happy end of time under ʿĪsā. The end of the world begins with a change in the course of the heavenly bodies (the sun rises in the West). The "Gate of Remorse" is described. The birth of the Daccāl is indicated with precision, "on a Wednesday in the month of Rebīʿ ül-evvel" in the time of the Prophet Muḥammad when he moved from Mecca to Medina. On that occasion, by

Ṭabakāt ül-Memālik von Koca Nişāncı, Wiesbaden 1981, pp. 66-67, fols. 172b-175b; cf. *GOR* IV, pp. 69 f; H. İnalcık, *The Ottoman Empire. The Classical Age 1300-1600*, London 1973, p. 174.

27 Sohrweide, "Sieg" p. 178; B. Flemming, "Het einde der tijden bij de Turken in de 16de eeuw", in *M.O.I.* publicatie 7 (1981), pp. 92-93.

28 C.H. Imber, "The persecution of the Ottoman Shiʿites according to the *mühimme defterleri*, 1565-1585", in *Der Islam* 56 (1979), pp. 245-73.

29 Relevant bibliography in Flemming, "Einde", pp. 104-05.

30 Şükrī, *Selīmnāme*, manuscript H.O. 32 from 927/1521 in the Austrian National Library, Vienna (Flügel II, p. 229, no. 1007), fol. 62a.

31 D.B. Macdonald, art. *al-Mahdī* in *EI*1. In any case, the Berlin manuscript Ms or. oct. 878 begins with "the appearance of the Mahdī Muḥammed b. ʿAbdullāh"; so H. Sohrweide informs us: *Türkische Handschriften und einige in den Handschriften enthaltene persische und arabische Werke*, Wiesbaden 1974, p. 33, no. 41 (abbreviated as *Türkische Handschriften* III). Regarding the Mahdī's name see Attema, *Opvattingen*, p. 177.

means of a miracle of the Prophet, the Daccāl was transferred to a cave by the sea in Ṭabaristān.[32] He appears again on an enormous donkey to wage war near Kufa against the army of the God-fearing king Aḥmed b. ʿAbdullāh (an allusion to the Mahdī, who otherwise plays no role here, and to his activity in the Ḥicāz). Now ʿĪsā comes down from the heavens, kills the Daccāl and rules for the next forty years:[33] during this happy time "no one will be concerned with gold and silver because the world will be full of these metals and all things will be cheap" (*ucuzluq ola*).[34] After the death of ʿĪsā, Gog and Magog once more bring oppression and chaos, the "Beast of the Earth" (*dābbat al-arż*) appears, the angels weep over mankind, Isrāfīl's trumpet sounds, everything becomes empty, heaven and earth are filled with smoke, Muḥammad and then the other people rise from their graves, a cold wind sweeps away the human beings like butterflies and the final reckoning begins; the good enter Paradise and the bad enter Hell – which is depicted in great detail.

At present a general survey of the different currents in Turkish eschatological literature is not possible because the contents of unprinted works have as yet scarcely been studied. The various treatises dealing with the Mahdī and the "circumstances" of the Final Hour, *cefr* writings, *sāʿatnāme*s, and *melḥeme*s have clearly still not been examined in terms of their relationship with the older Islamic apocalyptic expectations.[35] Only the illustrations of some *cefr* books from the time of Sultan Meḥmed III (1595-1603) and the *Aḥvāl-i qıyāmet*[36] have been iconographically analyzed. Thus it has become well-known that a view of the city of Rome occurs in a Turkish *Terceme-i cefr el-cāmiʿ* produced after 1006/the year beginning 14 August 1596. Whereas the drawings of the city's buildings are from the artist's imagination or based on mosques in Istanbul, the inhabitants are depicted in European military costumes of the 16th century.[37] It is certain that this interesting miniature has a relationship

32 *Aḥvāl-i qıyāmet*, fols. 7-19 in the Leiden manuscript Cod. Or. 14349, described by Jan Schmidt, *Catalogue of Turkish Manuscripts in the Library of Leiden University. Volume Three*, Leiden 2006, pp. 404-406 with plate. Other manuscripts are kept in the Staatsbibliothek Preußischer Kulturbesitz in Ms or. 1596 and Ms or. oct. 928; see M. Götz, *Türkische Handschriften*, Part 2, Wiesbaden 1968, p. 165, no. 241 (abbreviated *Türkische Handschriften* II); H. Sohrweide, *Türkische Handschriften* III, p. 32, no. 40.

33 Attema, *Opvattingen*, p. 152, following al-Suyūṭī.

34 *Aḥvāl-i qıyāmet*, Cod. Or. 14349 Leiden, fol. 10b.

35 On this subject see D.B. Macdonald, art. *Djafr* and *Malāḥim* in *EI1*; T. Fahd, art. *Djafr* in *EI2*.

36 I. Stchoukine et al., *Illuminierte islamische Handschriften*, Wiesbaden 1971, p. 229, no. 85.

37 Fehmi Edhem [Karatay] and I. Stchoukine, *Les Manuscrits orientaux illustrés de la Bibliothèque de l'Université de Stamboul*, Paris 1933, p. 14, no. VI, unfortunately without an illustration. The illustrator of the Dublin manuscript of this work made it simpler for himself

with the prophecy of the fall of Rome that we have already referred to several times and which we will come back to again. It may be mentioned in passing that the breakdown of morals is another sign of the advent of the Final Judgment; this is illustrated in the above-mentioned *cefr* work by means of a genre scene in which a young man in the presence of appalled women and children extends his hand toward the headscarf of an unveiled young lady.[38]

Along with the experience of new large-scale wars and acts of violence – Lepanto, Cyprus, the war with Austria, and the outbreak of the Celālī uprisings in Anatolia – the approach of the millennium of the *hijra* (beginning on 19 October 1591) must have given an impetus to more intense concern with questions to do with the end of time. At that moment, on the basis of astrological calculations and appropriate Traditions, many circles still expected that the end of time was about to occur,[39] even though al-Suyūṭī, who enjoyed a high reputation with the Ottomans, had long ago established that Muḥammad's community would certainly exist for more than a thousand years (but not longer than 1500 years) and though the mufti Kemālpaşazāde (1468-1534), as a precaution, had translated the relevant treatise by al-Suyūṭī into Turkish.[40]

In view of the role that eschatological writings played in the late-medieval Arab world, the question inevitably arises as to what degree eschatological subjects among the Ottoman Turks were connected with political realities and became included in the disputes of their time. For example, the topos of the Kingdom of Peace[41] that arrives shortly before the end of time offered a starting point for voicing the desire for change in the prevailing order in the form of chiliastic expectations.

Likewise, a comparison with contemporary Western publicists dealing with the problem of the Turks, which for a long time has received the attention it deserves in scholarship, encourages one to pose questions of this kind. After all, people in the West were thoroughly convinced that the Turks were harbingers

by representing Medina instead of Rome and an uninhabited coast: V. Minorsky, *The Chester Beatty Library. A Catalogue of the Turkish Manuscripts and Miniatures*, Dublin 1958, p. 81.

38 Karatay-Stchoukine, *Manuscrits orientaux*, Plate VII, illustration 14.

39 Cf. N. Berkes, *The Development of Secularism in Turkey*, Montreal 1964, pp. 18-19; A.H. de Groot, *The Ottoman Empire and the Dutch Republic*, Leiden 1978, pp. 12, 19 and 48; E. Glassen, "Krisenbewußtsein und Heilserwartung in der islamischen Welt zu Beginn der Neuzeit", in *Die islamische Welt zwischen Mittelalter und Neuzeit. Festschrift für Hans Robert Römer*, Beirut 1979, pp. 167 and 169 f.

40 For a bibliography on the subject see Flemming, "Einde", pp. 100 and 106-07.

41 On its literary form, cf. B. Flemming, *Faḫrīs Ḫusrev u Sˇīrīn. Eine türkische Dichtung von 1367*, Wiesbaden 1974, pp. 72 f.

of the imminent end of the world. In recent studies attention has focused on how their emergence was exploited as a means of political-religious propaganda and polemic between Lutherans and Catholics,[42] what expectations groups that were socially disadvantaged and persecuted as heretics had regarding them,[43] and what apocalyptic ideas, nourished by astrology and the Daniel tradition, Western authors associated with the Turks[44] – all this well into the middle of the 17th century.[45] Naturally, the actual visions of the future held by the Turks themselves are not mentioned in such a context.

For this reason it is appropriate to discuss here a Turkish text which contains such a prophecy from the time of Sultan Süleymān. A certain ʿĪsā during the year of the first siege of Vienna (936/begins 5 September 1529) wrote a history of the world and the Ottomans in verse with the title *Cāmiʿ ül-meknūnāt* (*Compendium of Concealed Things*), of which three manuscripts have been identified up until now:

- Ankara, Library of the Türk Tarih Kurumu, Y. 240, Part 4, dated Receb 1012/begins 5 December 1603 (formerly in the possession of O.F. Sağlam): A.[46]
- Leiden University Cod.or. 1448, Part 1, dated mid-Ramażān 1013 (30 January–8 February 1605): L.[47]

42 Now see Göllner who offers a summary, *Turcica III*; as well as on the Lutheran equating of the "two arch enemies of Christ (zween Ertzfeinde Christi)", the Pope and the Turks, who were in turn equated with the Anti-Christ, and against whom resistance was not permitted because they have been sent as a punishment by God (Göllner, *Turcica III*, pp. 178-83). On the toleration that was forced upon the Reformation with regard to a common defense against the Turks see M.E.H.N. Mout, "Calvinoturcisme in de zeventiende eeuw", in *Tijdschrift voor Geschiedenis* 91 (1978), p. 584. Idem, "Turken in het nieuws. Beeldvorming en publieke opinie in de zestiende-eeuwse Nederlanden", in *Tijdschrift voor Geschiedenis* 97 (1984), pp. 362-81.

43 H.J. Kissling, "Türkenfurcht und Türkenhoffnung im 15. und 16. Jahrhundert. Zur Geschichte eines 'Komplexes'", in *Südost-Forschungen* XXIII (1964), pp. 1-18.

44 For Luther and Melanchthon the Day of Judgment was directly at hand, whereas Zwingli and Calvin saw it as drawing "near"; Göllner, *Turcica III*, p. 182; on astrology ibid., pp. 343 f.

45 For Comenius (1592-1670), who was living in the Netherlands as an exile, the renewed attack of the Turks in 1662 was the beginning of the fall of the Habsburgs; thereafter Christendom would unite in the reformed faith and then, as a preliminary stage of the end of the world, the conversion of the Turks would follow. For this purpose he brought into being the project of the Leiden Turkish Bible translation; see no. 15 in this volume.

46 I wish to thank the Library of the Türk Tarih Kurumu for providing me with a microfilm.

47 Described by Jan Schmidt, *Catalogue of Turkish Manuscripts in the Library of Leiden Uni-*

- Istanbul, Üniversite Kütüphanesi, I.E. 3263, formerly Ibnülemin Mahmud Kemal [İnal]: I.[48]

The manuscripts, though written at almost the same time, display differences of content and in some passages a different sequence in the contents. The quotations from the text which follow are based on L.

We may identify the author as the same Mevlānā ʿĪsā, compiler of a *Cāmiʿ ül-meknūnāt*, whom Muṣṭafā b. Aḥmed, known as ʿĀlī (1541-1600),[49] in the preface to *rükn* IV of his history of the world and the Ottomans, *Künh ül-aḫbār*, mentions as being among his sources along with the chroniclers Rūḥī Edrenevī and Neşrī, who "recorded events up to the era of Bāyezīd II in prose and verse in accordance with the demands of time".[50] This ʿĪsā, whose *Cāmiʿ ül-meknūnāt* ʿĀlī does indeed cite a few times,[51] introduces his name in the prophetic concluding part of his book:

> ḫilāf olmaya ʿĪsānuñ sözinde
> ḍoquz yüz daḫı otuz ḍoquzında (L 126b; A 152b)
>
> "ʿĪsā's words are true (should not be contradicted); in the nine hundred and thirty-fifth [year Sultan Süleymān will set out against Charles V; see below]."

The work is a *mesnevī* in the Old Ottoman language, composed in the meters *remel* and *hezec* with advance notice when the meter changes. First and

versity. Volume Two, Leiden 2002, pp. 83-87. Part II of Cod.Or. 1448 is a chapter from the *Şemsiye* by Yazıcı Salahaddin, described ibid. p. 86.

48 I wish to thank the İstanbul Üniversitesi Kütüphanesi for providing me with a microfilm. In particular, I am grateful to Prof. Adnan Sadık Erzi and Dr. Osman Sertkaya for their help.

49 Cf. A. Tietze, *Muṣṭafā ʿĀlī's Counsel for Sultans of 1581. Edition, translation, notes* I, Vienna 1979, p. 7 f., with a bibliography dealing with earlier works.

50 *...ve kitāb-i Cāmiʿ ül-meknūnāt müʾellifi Mevlānā ʿĪsā nām Hamidī-i hamīde-kirdār* ...in *Künhü l-Ahbār, rükn* IV, Leiden, Cod.or. 288, fol. 6a. Reference to this passage that occurs only in the Leiden manuscript, I owe to Jan Schmidt, whose study, *Mustafa ʿAli's Künhü ʾl-ahbār and its Preface according to the Leiden Manuscript*, Istanbul 1987 was then in the press (p. 8, p. 35 (text), p. 58-59 (translation) and p. 84 (plate fol. 6b)). For a description of Cod. Or. 288 see Jan Schmidt, *Catalogue of Turkish Manuscripts in the Library of Leiden University, Volume One*, Leiden 2000, pp. 54-56.

51 Atsız, *Âlî Bibliyografyası*, Istanbul 1968, p. 22; See my no. 14 in this volume. Jan Schmidt, *Pure Water for Thirsty Muslims. A Study of Mustafa ʿĀlī of Gallipoli's Künhü l-Aḫbār*, Leiden 1992, p. 41 no. 18 and p. 301 no. 11.

foremost, it is a descriptive compilation of military campaigns (*ġazavāt*) that presents the Ottomans as heroes of Holy War who have nearly conquered the whole world and will also dominate what still remains:

> kim nice dutdı cihānı serbeser
> başmaduq ayaqları qalmadı yėr
> qalanın daḫı başısar bī-gümān
> qılıncından düşmeni bulmaz āmān (L 40a: 12-13)

Beginning with the Prophet's light substance, *nūr-i Aḥmed*, the author establishes genealogical connections between the old prophets from Adam to Muḥammad and the Ottomans. Much attention goes to the actions and thought of the Christian opponents. Throughout the work like a red thread run the author's eschatological ideas for which he combines the Koran, Tradition and astrology, and bases himself on a learned friend, the Mīralay Murād Beg.

Thus, as to genre, the work belongs as much to the tradition of the *ġazavātnāmeler* as it does to that of the *malāḥim* of prophetic texts which in a religiously determined world of ideas could be used to express opinions and the desire for change. One does not expect from a work of this kind any new historical facts – in fact this one even contains historical errors – but it can give information about the relationship of the Ottomans to contemporary events around them.

At a time when printed books were busily manufactured and distributed in western Europe, the printing-press being of crucial importance for "literature on the Turks" – the area of influence of individual Turkish works, reproduced by copyists, remained very limited; the author of the *Cāmiʿ ül-meknūnāt* addresses his copyists urging them to make the effort to write with an attractive script (*gökçek ḫaṭṭıla*).[52] In these circumstances it is difficult to identify the audience; at best one goes by the narrative situation hinted at by addresses to the public – ėy *fetā, ėy yār, ėy qardeş, ėy ḫvāce* – and by the author's exhortations to himself to be brief and by his subject divisions. This along with the simple language and the prognostic nature of the contents points to a broad reading public for whom the so-called Old Ottoman anonymous chronicles were probably written as well. The author refers to the *Iskendernāme*, in which Aḥmedī deals with the earlier Ottomans up to Emir Süleymān, but he names no further sources, indeed in his conclusion he emphasizes that he is breaking

52 Cf. H. Sohrweide, "Autoren- und Schreibersorgen im Istanbul des 18. Jahrhunderts", in *Folia Rara Wolfgang Voigt* LXV. *diem natalem clebranti...dedicata*, Wiesbaden 1976, pp. 120-25.

new ground: "I've studied prosody but I'm not a poet; I make no boast of this insignificant poetry. That's why this book is not a translation from Arabic or Persian: it's easy to put into rhymes a story that has already been told whether it be from Arabic or from Persian. But to transpose something into poetry that hasn't been told, that's a difficult job" (*hezec*).

> ʿarūż oqıdum şāʿir degülem
> bu cüzʾī naẓmıla fāḫir degülem
> ʿacemden tercüme yāḫuᵛd ʿarabdan
> degüldür bu kitābum ol sebebden
> denilmiş qıṣṣayı naẓm etmek āsān
> ʿarabdan yā ʿacem dilinden ėy cān
> velī bir söz kim ol denilmemişdür
> bulub naẓm etmek anı müşkil işdür (L 134b: 8-11)

ʿĪsā experienced for himself the suffering of the population at the beginning of the 16th century which we referred to in the opening of this essay: in the year 909/begins 26 June 1503 "in the Ottoman Empire (in the Land of Rūm) there was much famine and epidemic disease; many starved to death and were destroyed; those who did not die of hunger were carried off by the plague which like a sword cut down everything in its path. People called it the Great Plague – many eyes went blind with weeping. We as well had our share of this to bear; what can one do? It is the Creator Who gives and takes away."

> oldı Rūm ilinde çok qaḥt u vebā (remel)
> niceler açın ölüp oldı hebā
> açdan ölmeyenleri ṭāʿūn dėrer
> ėrdügine ol qılıç gibi qırar
> dėdiler nās aña ṭāʿūn-i kebīr
> ağlamaqdan oldı çok gözler żarīr
> bize daḫı degdi ḥiṣṣe aradan
> neydelüm alan veren ol yaradan (L 73b: 1-4)

The winter that followed was very severe and in the spring floods caused widespread devastation.

The earthquake of 1509 which contemporaries called the "Little Resurrection" (*küçük qıyāmet*) was naturally not passed over in silence by an author like ʿĪsā who was oriented toward the hereafter. His description is as follows: "Now hear how great the tumult was; during the night of Friday a mighty earthquake took place. The interior of the City of Constantine was destroyed, old and young were buried under stones and wood. No minaret of *mescids* and mosques remained standing, and the castle walls collapsed in ruins. Numerous signs became visible, too many to count; for no one can oppose destiny when it strikes. Couriers were sent out for construction workers and for many engineers and master builders. Altogether they came to sixty thousand construction workers, oh Prince, and they rebuilt the interior fortress in three months. The [spring] New Year arrived and everything was once again bustling; that was when the year of the hijra 915 (!) arrived."

diñle imdi nice oldı velvele
cumʿa gėcesi olur gey zelzele
şehr-i Qoṣṭantīn içi olur ḫarāb
ḍaş ağaç altında qaldı şeyḫ şāb
qalʿenüñ dīvārı oldı tārümār
çoq ʿalāmet ẓāhir oldı bī-ʿaded
ėdemez gelse qażā bir kimse red
ṣaldılar ulaqları ırġād içün
çoq mühendis yapıcı ustād içün
cemʿ ėdüb altmış biñ ırġād ėy hümām
qalʿe-i üç ayda yapdılar tamām
ėrdi nevrūz geldi her şey cünbişe
girdi hicret hem ḍoquz yüz on beşe (L 74a)

The passage is typical of the narrative manner of ʿĪsā who compresses the facts together as much as possible – one may compare his version with that of Rūḥī who took an interest in the building works.[53] ʿĪsā is primarily concerned with the symbolic significance of the event.

Instead of a full description of its contents, we will here discuss how the author of the *Cāmiʿ ül-meknūnāt* treats Sultan Süleymān's first four military campaigns, namely the first Hungarian campaign of 1521 which ended with the capture of Belgrade, the siege and capture of Rhodes, the second Hungarian campaign that resulted in the battle of Mohács and the taking of Ofen, and finally the first "German" campaign that entailed the siege of Vienna in 1529. The young Sultan, after having suppressed the revolt of Cānberdi Ġazzālī, sends an envoy to the King of Hungary (Louis II) to confirm "whether the Czechs, Poles, Germans and Rús (Ukrainians) are still abiding by the treaties". The youthful, foolish king has the envoy's nose and ears cut off. With this rea-

53 Cf. V.L. Ménage, "Edirne'li Rûhî'ye atfedilen Osmanlı tarihinden iki parça", in *İsmail Hakkı Uzunçarşılı'ya Armağan*, Ankara 1976, pp. 322-27.

son for war Süleymān sets out and lays siege to Belgrade and captures it.[54] The author laments the heavy losses which the Turkish army sustains on this occasion and takes the opportunity to explain the five kinds of death for the faith which makes it possible for the *şehīd* to be resurrected with a white face on the Day of Retribution. In continuation of a *ġazā* of his father (sic!) Süleymān now lays siege to Rhodes. Here as well great difficulties occur; after seven months the besiegers are at the end of their tether and only prayer can still help them. The author has the Sultan say: "I will not leave here even if this goes on for ten years...otherwise with what sort of face will I return to the throne of Rūm?" (L 103a). The well-known accord is reached which permits the Grandmaster of the Order of the Knights of St. John, here referred to as "the King of Hell" and *Māstūr meġāl* or simply the *meġāl*, to withdraw freely, which occurred on 3 Ṣafar 929/23 December 1522, at the beginning of winter, the day "which the Christians call *mevlid-i ʿĪsā*" (L 106b: 3). The conquest has been successful in the end but there are ten thousand corpses to lament; *qamu maʿlūla çalındı manāṣib* "all war-wounded lost their ranks" i.e. all disabled cavalrymen (sipahis) lost their fiefs.[55] (L 106a). News of the fall of Rhodes unleashes consternation among the infidels who say: the wall of Ya'cūc and Ma'cūc has been made to collapse, now Ma'cūc has been set loose on us. "We heard that they said it is the work of providence, *taqdīr*: that no place remains where the tread of the Turks does not reach – *ki qalmaz Türk ayaġı başmaduq yėr*" (106b: 3). They lament: "Two gates have been breached, one to the sea and one to the land; through the one he can depart for Frengistān and through the other for Hungary and Russia." In the meantime, the author describes the revolt of Aḥmed Paşa in Egypt and the "death of the defeated Qızılbaş", Shah Ismāʿīl, who is supposed to have gone to Kerbala to die in the *türbe* of Ḥüseyn (Shah Ismāʿīl is buried in Ardabil); when this is reported to the Sultan, he contents himself with the remark that destiny overtakes the good as well as the bad, *alur bir bir eyüyi ger yamanı* (L 107a). Now the author again takes up the thread of conquests with the second Hungarian campaign, *ġazā-yı Budūn*.

54 Cf. A.C. Schaendlinger, *Die Feldzugstagebücher des ersten und zweiten ungarischen Feldzugs Süleymāns I.*, Vienna 1978, p. 48.

55 *Maʿlūl* (emendated from *Makhlūl*) is a term applied to soldiers wounded or disabled in action. The implication is that Sipahis, cavalrymen of the tax-exempt military class, who had become unfit for armed service and had failed to apply for a timar-fief lost their ranks and were "consequently reduced under the law to the status of (tax-paying) *reʿāyā* again." Cf. J. Káldy-Nagy, "The 'Strangers' (*Ecnebiler*) in the 16th century Ottoman Military Organization," in Gy. Kara, *Between the Danube and the Caucasus*, Budapest 1987, pp. 168-169, referring to H. Inalcık, *The Ottoman Empire. The Classical Age 1300-1600*, pp. 114-115.

The Sultan has it announced that he will go to Hungary and set out against Germany and Russia (L 107b). A messenger from the Emperor (*Çasār*) arrives. The latter is the father-in-law, *qayın atası*,[56] of the Hungarian king and he attempts to make excuses to Süleymān for the king's many mistakes; may the Sultan forgive him – if the Sultan wishes tribute (*ḫarāc*) or a province, he will receive it. These words were not acceptable; "what fault was there on the part of my envoy?" Süleymān must take revenge for his envoy's treatment. The envoy of *Çasār* departs without having accomplished his mission but not without having seen the immense Turkish army. The army arrives at Belgrade; the Sultan sends Balı Beg ahead as a scout (L 108b) and he crosses over the Sava. Behind him marches Ibrāhīm Paşa and then the Sultan; they pass through the Syrmian Plain and conquer Varadin (Peterwardein). When the envoy of the infidels arrives before King "Laloş", the king is terrified and faints. Supported as he is by Lāt and 'Uzza (L 109b: 3),[57] he is still able to appeal with success to his co-religionists to help him against the Turks who in the meantime have entered upon the Plain of Mohács. In contrast with the arrogance of the Hungarian king, the Sultan immerses himself in a long prayer: he fears harm could come to Islam if he should lose the battle (L 112a: 2). Then there rings out the *tekbīr* of the *ġāzī*s who fight heroically, and victory is attained; the plain is strewn with corpses. The death of the king in the swamp is reported (L 115b). The Sultan marches to Ofen which he finds "empty", and he occupies its throne. The author tells of the masses of prisoners. "There has never been such a *ġazā*, never such plundering", whole shiploads are removed, the city is burnt to the ground, only the castle is spared[58] – all this as a cautionary example (*'ibret*) for the infidels.

In the reports that now follow about the uprisings in Anatolia, Mevlānā 'Īsā's remarks display a conspicuous mixture of historicity and hearsay which must be approached with a degree of criticism. It begins with the "coming forth of the son of 'Alā' ed-devle". When the plain of Syrmia[59] had been conquered, the Sultan thought it would be a shame if the Turks did not hold on to this land. The inhabitants would not become obedient until Islam had taken firm root here. Therefore a beg and several *qāżī*s took it upon themselves to resettle several *il* of the Bozoqlu and to populate that land. But the latter would not agree

56 Mary, the sister of Charles V, was married to Louis II of Hungary while Louis' sister was the wife of Ferdinand of Austria.

57 On their eschatological function see Flemming, "*Ǧāmi'*", p. 90. (no. 14)

58 Cf. Schaendlinger, *Feldzugstagebücher*, pp. 86-87.

59 For Ottoman Syrmia see Bruce McGowan, *Sirem Sancağı Mufassal Tahrir Defteri*, Ankara 1983, pp. lvii-lxvi; for resettlement and "immigrants" p. lxi.

to be deported; they rebelled, killed the beg and the *qāżīs*, and found someone who was recognized as a descendant of the ʿAlāʾ ed-devle family. The evildoers flowed together like water and they became an entire army of rebels. Various begs, especially (Güzelce?) Qāsım Paşa, attacked the rebels... When the Sultan comes to Filibe (in May 1526), the suppression of the revolt is reported to him. If it is here apparently a matter of a peculiar version of the Bozoq revolt, then secondly the "coming forth of Celāl" is an already quite legendary portrayal of this famous rebellion,[60] after which at a later time great uprisings in Anatolia would be named. Celāl had come from the Dhū'lqadir region, had laid waste cities and areas of the countryside. When they heard that the Sultan was arriving, they fled in the direction of the region of the Qızılbaş. When Qızılbaşoğlu would not give them free passage, Celāl headed for Erzurum, fortified the city and entrenched himself there (the report goes no further). Thirdly, "The Death of Qalender-Şāh b. Bektaş" is described in such a way that the latter went "to Celāl"; the Sultan sends troops (*qul*) after him who are meant to fetch him back from there but they arrest him on the way. The dervishes (*ışıklar*) sacrifice themselves for their leader when they see he has been captured, form a considerable army in Anatolia and defeat five to ten thousand men with their begs.[61] The victorious dervishes go with their families to the shrine of Ḥāccī Bektaş or they flee, i.e. they go "to Celāl". The Sultan sends Ibrāhīm Paşa against them with an army; this takes place with the speed of lightning.[62] Before they can reach "Celāl", Qalender has been beheaded, and the women and children taken away. At this point Anatolia was stark-naked (*anadan oldı doġma*) but freed from *fitne*, and "no one rebelled against the Sultans again":

> fitneden qurtılub buldı ḫalāṣī
> daḫı bir kimse olmaz ḫāna ʿāṣī

And now the Paşa retook his place (in August 1527). This account of the Anatolian uprisings only presents to a limited extent episodes from what happened, but it contains informative indications of the image that ordinary people made of it for themselves. Different again is the "Vienna Campaign" (*ġazā-yı Beç*) in

60 On the Bozoq revolt cf. Sohrweide "Sieg", p. 174; there the spark was an insult to a Turkoman leader, whereas here the reason given was the planned deportation of entire tribal groups. On Celāl's revolt cf. Sohrweide, "Sieg", pp. 167-70.

61 What is meant here is the great victory of Qalender's supporters at Karaçayır north of Sivas on 8 June 1527.

62 On 22 June 1527. Previously Ibrāhīm Paşa had satisfied the Dhū'lqādir Turkomans and so separated them from Qalender's supporters; Sohrweide, "Sieg", p. 182.

which a romantically transfigured episode almost distracts from the serious events of the war.

The *ġazā* against Vienna[63] is justified by a request for help from "the Prince of Transylvania" (John Zápolya); an envoy must deliver the Sultan's threats to the "ruler of Germany" (Ferdinand I). The Turkish army sets out for Belgrade; the ruler of Transylvania comes to meet the Sultan; Ofen is occupied once again and John, *qıral Yanoş*, is solemnly crowned; there then follows a description of the Crown of Stephen. Now the army that is in good shape (*dinç*), sets out on an arduous march through marshlands up to the gates of Vienna. There in vain the attackers seek the king whom ʿĪsā calls *Feravuş*. The city is bombarded and land-mines are laid. Now there follows an episode in the style of the *ġazavātnāmeler* or of the old romantic *mes̱nevī*: a young nobleman, a *bānzāde*, falls into Turkish captivity and by means of his beauty and noble nature wins the goodwill of the Sultan. The historical person behind this youthful figure is the Silesian ensign Christoph von Zedlitz who "passed himself off as a native of Bohemia" and was much admired in his cuirass."[64] For the sake of this *bānzāde* and his family who send costly gifts and submit themselves to the Sultan, mercy was shown to the inhabitants of the fortress: *ḥiṣār ehline vėrdiler amānı* (L 125a: 10).[65] Winter sets in; still the Sultan wishes to leave nothing untried: "If I spare Ferdinand, I am no man; if I do not obtain his head; I am no hero":

> Feravuşı qorısam er degülem
> serin almazısam server degülem (L 125b: 3)

But then, because destiny has determined it this way, Süleymān gives the order for the return march. While advancing in snow and rain through the flooded and devastated region, the army suffers heavy losses; only in Ofen does it regain its strength. Having received rich gifts, King Yanoş(Zápolya) remains behind, and the Sultan with "innumerable captives" sets off for Rūm.

63 Cf. W.F.A. Behrnauer, *Sulaiman des Gesetzgebers (Kanūnī) Tagebuch auf seinem Feldzuge nach Wien im Jahre 935/6 d.H.=1529 n. Chr.*, Vienna 1858; F. Tauer, "Solimans Wiener Feldzug", in *Archiv Orientální* 24 (1954), pp. 507-63. A recent summary is presented by G. Düriegl (ed.), *Wien 1529. Die erste Türkenbelagerung*, Vienna-Cologne-Graz 1979 (for a special exhibition at the Historical Museum of the City of Vienna).

64 Quoted thus by J. von Hammer, *Wien's erste aufgehobene türkische Belagerung*, Pest 1829, p. 83, from a collection of documents in the Vienna municipal archives. Cf. L. Kupelwieser, *Die Kämpfe Österreichs mit den Osmanen vom Jahre 1526 bis 1537*, Vienna 1899, p. 59.

65 The official version was that the king was not in the fortress; cf. Hammer, *Wien's Belagerung*, p. 118; Behrnauer, *Tagebuch*, p. 27.

The nonetheless depressing result of the siege of Vienna is for ʿĪsā cause for political and chiliastic expectations. He predicts: "Later the Sultan will march against Vienna again. For the ruler of Spain, King Qarloz, after not having been put in his place by the army of Islam, will lay claim to being Lord of the Constellation (*ṣāḥib-qırān*), "Ruler of the World"[66], as well as Lord of India and King of Germany; he will call himself – and this too is an eschatological allusion – *Benī Aṣfār*, "Head of Christendom", and also claim rule over Persia, Rūm and Arabia. Sultan Süleymān shall hear of this; he will set out against Vienna like a raging lion and pursue Charles V, forcing him to flee; it shall cause him pain not to find him; he will wish to follow in the footsteps of the Possessor of the Two Horns [Alexander] and march until the Western Sea; people will say: it is winter, the cold season is upon us, which means time-off for frontier guards and farmers; thereupon he will turn back in felicity, for God has conferred victory on him; safe and sound, he will [once more] sit upon his throne. Let us also say in which year this sign [will occur]; ʿĪsā's words will countenance no contradiction (the verse has been cited above): in 939; in the eighth (938) he will set out on military campaign, in the ninth (939) he will cast his shadow over Rūm."

gėrü sulṭān gidiser ṣoñra Beçe
velī gitdigin eydem saña nice
meger Ispānya mīri mīr-i Qarloz
çün Islām ʿaskerile olmadı uz
qıla daʿvā ki ben ṣāḥib-qırānem
kuşād-i Hindū vü mīr-i Alamānem
Benī Esfar benem devrān benimdür
ʿAcem Rūm ʿArab zīr efkenimdür
eşidicek anı Sulṭān Süleymān
yürüye Beçe doġru şīr-i ġarrān
gelecegin bile Qarloz araya
yüzin döndür ẓulmāta yüriye
...
pes andan Qarlozuñ taẖtına vara
bulımaduġına incine yara

66 For *ṣāḥib-qırān* in the "hierarchy of sovereignty" see Cornell H.Fleischer, *Bureaucrat and Intellectual in the Ottoman Empire. The Historian Mustafa Âli (1541-1600)*, Princeton 1986, pp. 279-285. For Selīm I's prestige as "lord of the happy conjunction" see Jan Schmidt, *Pure Water for Thirsty Muslims. A Study of Mustafa ʿĀlī of Gallipoli's Künhü l-Aḫbār*, Leiden 1992, pp. 134 and 319.

dileye düşe Ẕū'lqarneyn izine
yüriye vara Maġrib deñizine
dėyeler qışa ėrişdük şitāya
icāzetdür akıncı rustāya
pes andan devletile ėde ʿavdet
vėrildi çünki ḥaqdan aña nuṣret
ėrişe taḫtına ṣaġ u selāmet
dėyelüm hem ne yılda bu ʿalāmet
ḫilāf olmaya ʿĪsānuñ sözinde
ḍoquz yüz daḫı otuz ḍoquzında
sekizinde gidiserdür ġazāya
ḍoquzında salısar Rūma sāye (L 126a/b)

One must ask whether the campaign of 939 (begins 3 August 1532) is here predicted *post eventum*. This is the campaign Turkish sources designate as "the German campaign against the King of Spain", and which primarily developed into the siege of Güns and vanguard skirmishes. The expedition to the Maġrib could be a prediction of the offensive in the Mediterranean and the capture of Tunis by the Ottoman admiral Ḫayreddīn Barbarossa in 1534. Then the work's date of composition would in reality be *after* 1532,[67] surely not after 942/1535-36, the year of execution of the grand vizier Ibāhīm Paşa whom the author unreservedly praises as the Āṣaf of the Solomon-like Sultan.

On the occasion of the siege of Vienna, for this very Ibrāhīm Paşa, who at the time was at the summit of his career, a eulogistic poem was composed in which Rome is mentioned: "Āṣaf, when the Poles, Germans, Russians and Czechs beheld your attack, they uttered (the chronogram): may he knock the Pope of Rome on the head!"[68]

The author of the *Cāmʿ ül-meknūnāt*, for his part, connects his chiliastic expectations to Rome which are as follows: There is a sign that the end of the world is near: the army of Islam will advance on Rome, penetrate into her churches, plunder all her treasures and then spread into France.

67 For similar adjustments on the Christian side cf. Göllner, *Turcica III*, p. 342. On the prophecies recorded by Evliyā Çelebi regarding the second siege of Vienna see Kreutel, *Reich des goldenen Apfels*, pp. 62 and 219 the talk was also about numerous "pseudo-prophecies fabricated with hindsight" by Evliyā; cf. also Teply, *Türkische Sagen*, pp. 16 ff. and passim.

68 *Asafā görüp hücumun Lih-ü Nemçe Rus u Çeh – didiler tarihüni "çak gele Rîmpâp üstüne"* (935 AH): in the Topkapı-Sarayı Archives, no. 12071, cited from M. Tayyib Gökbilgin, art. *İbrāhīm Paşa* in *İA* V, p. 915.

bu yılda hem işitgil bir ʿalāmet
yaqın olduqda dėrlerdi qıyāmet
varısar leşker-i Islām Rīme
ne Rīme Maġrib u Maşriq-i qadīme
kilisesine varub giriserler
qamu küffārı anda qırısarlar
uşadup pulların malın alalar
varub Franca iline ḍolalar

In addition, the author reports, on the basis of sound tradition (*ṣaḥīḥ isnād*), an event dated 934 (begins 27 September 1527): The Mīr of Spain had a clever vizier in the Land of the Franks (*Efrenc*) who, when the French did not wish to allow his troops to travel through on their way to Rome, employed trickery to bring about their passage. The army forces its way into the city of Rome and into the churches; "there they spared neither idols nor crosses" (*ne put qorlar içinde vü ne haç*) (L 128a: 2). In accordance with God's will, they plunder, rape and murder. The Mīr of Spain in this way brought the Pope under his control and laid claim to the Dominion of the Constellation (*daʿvā-yı ṣāḥib-qırānī*); God is said to have given him the world:

bañа vėrdi ḫuḏā dėdi cihānı (128a: 13).

The conquerors remain in Rome for twelve days. The author joins to his description of the Sacco di Roma (May 1527) the following prophecy: This city will quickly come to thrive once more and be filled with silver and gold. When the end of the world is near, God will fill it, and then the Mahdī will come and capture it:

yaqın olsa qıyāmet zer ḍolısar
pes ol malı varub Mehdī alısar (L 128b: 5).

The author anticipates the coming of the Mahdī: he cannot be described, nor can his era, but he will be young and seem lowly to the ignorant and be scorned; at his side as his viziers will be three prophets: ʿĪsā, Ilyās and Ḫıżır. He will be the Seal of the Saints as Muḥammad was the Seal of the Prophets. He will conquer the whole world and fill it with peace and tranquility; war and strife will cease. At the same time he will be shaykh and emir of the age, and the protector of religion. Those who were "Anti-Christs" (Daccāl) for the people, the stubborn who played and amused themselves, will be annihilated.

Islam will spread over all the earth: polytheism (*şirk*), doubt and the different religious confessions will disappear:

qamu bir dīn bir meẕheb olısar (L 129a: 6).

There will be three things in his community: mysticism, science and authoritative rule: *taṣavvuf*, *ʿilm* and *salṭanat*. Riches will be open on behalf of all needs; the "tithe" (*öşr*) and the "poll-tax" (*ḫarāc*) will be collected in accordance with the *şerīʿat*. The people will not be in want of anything; no one will have to rely on alms-tax (*zekāt*).[69]

This happy end of time, whose duration is cautiously calculated by the author's source of information Murād Beg, remains overshadowed by fear of the disorders (*fitan*) that are to be expected. The author knows, as we saw above, that the Christians also perceive the end of the world to be near. The Daccāl plays no role here and the descent of Jesus is also not mentioned.

Going by the contents of what is stated, at the end of the world one can only speak of a radical transformation in the purely religious domain: the sects and confessions, among which the author includes Christianity, disappear. But taxes continue to be levied, though now in accordance with law, and – a popular expectation – all things will be available in abundance (and so low prices are guaranteed). The author evidently imagines the existing powers as still on hand at the happy end of time,[70] without, however, abstaining from a bit of criticism of his own era when making this projection onto the future.

Thus the prophecies and the political arguments in the *Cāmiʿ ül-meknūnāt* form an interesting counterpart to the remarks which the "Turkish question" evoked in the public opinion of 16th-century Europe. On both sides mythical figures, the *Ṣāḥib-qırān* and the Last Emperor, symbolized the political claim to power over the terrestrial globe.[71] The Sunni Turks of that era thought this universal responsibility had been allotted to their Sultan, Süleymān the Lawgiver, whereas the Christian peoples saw in the Emperor Charles V the champion of the *orbis christianus*. On the basis of the personification of the antagonism between the Ottoman Empire and the Spanish monarchy that dominated

69 For the eschatological significance of the *daccālūn* cf. Attema, *Opvattingen*, p. 114; the cessation of *zakāt*, *cizye* and *ḫarāc* also belongs to the classic expectations at the end of time; Attema, op. cit., p. 106.

70 "Bringing about the ideal situation is purely a consequence of the expansion of the already existing powers of order, not in fact the consequence of a radical inner transformation of the ruling order": B. Töpfer, *Das kommende Reich des Friedens. Zur Entwicklung chiliastischer Zukunftshoffnungen im Hochmittelalter*, Berlin 1964, passim.

71 Göllner provides numerous instances of ideas about a Christian ruler who will conquer the whole world and defeat the Sultan, in *Turcica III*, p. 338 and passim.

the epoch,[72] one can explain the ever recurrent demand of the Sultan to pit himself on the open battlefield against the Emperor Charles V who himself expressed the same demand. Both hereby complied with widespread expectations as these are expressed for the Turkish side in the *Cāmiʿ ül-meknūnāt*. As a mythical designation, *ṣāḥib-qırān*, which ʿĪsā frequently employs, did not actually belong to the ceremonial titles of Sultan Süleymān in the architectural inscription of his mosque[73] but was used in inscriptions such as those found on the candelabra looted from Ofen's main church.[74] Opinions about the war aims of the Ottoman Sultans are also given expression by the author of the *Cāmiʿ ül-meknūnāt* in talks the Sultans have with themselves and other of their statements. It should not go unnoticed that the defeated opponent in the East, Shah Ismāʿīl, also linked his political claims to the same personification as *ṣāḥib-qırān*.[75] Let us say by way of summing up: the Ottomans too made use of eschatological literature in the heated disputes of their day and age. This literature, aside from a limited iconographical assessment, has up until now been neglected in the field of Ottoman Studies. And yet it has its value for investigating what one may call public opinion in the Ottoman Empire.[76] It can contribute to clarifying political history with occasional reports; but even precisely where one may speak of pure fiction, this literature is particularly informative about the mood of the age.

---

72 H.G. Yurdaydın, *Kanunî'nin Cülusu ve ilk seferleri*, Ankara 1961; M.T. Gökbilgin, "Kanunî Sultan Süleymanın Macaristan ve Avrupa Siyasetinin Sebep ve Âmilleri", in *Kanunî Armağanı*, Ankara 1970, pp. 5-40; Y. Öztuna, Kanunî'nin Türk ve Dünya Tarihindeki Yeri, ibid., pp. 41-46; Gy. Káldy-Nagy, "Suleimans Angriff auf Europa", in *Acta Orient. Hung.* 28 (1974), pp. 163-212; J. Matuz, "Der Verzicht Süleymāns des Prächtigen auf die Annexion Ungarns", in *Ungarn-Jahrbuch* 1974-5, pp. 38-46; P.F. Sugar, *Southeastern Europe under Ottoman Rule, 1354-1804*, Seattle-London 1977.

73 C. Çulpan, "İstanbul Süleymaniye Camii Kitabesi", in *Kanunî Armağanı*, Ankara 1970, pp. 291-99.

74 G. Fehér, "Kanunî Sultan Süleymān preisende Inschriften zweier [aus] Buda stammender Renaissance-Kunstgegenstände", in *Kanunî Armağanı*, pp. 203-06.

75 E. Glassen, *Die frühen Safawiden nach Qāżī Aḥmad Qumī*, Freiburg 1968, p. 200, and Glassen, "Krisenbewußtsein" (see ftn. 39), pp. 172 f.

76 To this same category belongs the manuscript Mixt. 471 of the Austrian National Library, described by J. Buri-Gütermann, "Ein Türke in Italien", in *ZDMG* 124 (1974), pp. 59-72.

CHAPTER 18

Political Genealogies in the Sixteenth Century

The political implications of the "Oghuzian theme" for all the Turkmen powers in the fifteenth century are by now a familiar theme. After the pioneer studies by Paul Wittek who pointed to a romantic revival of steppe traditions, while acknowledging the political aims which the Oghuzian tribal genealogy clearly served,[1] Halil İnalcık put the Ottoman interest in Oghuzian matters in the perspective of the fateful defeat of 1402. Struggling for the survival of their state, the Ottomans had to show themselves the equals of the Timurid Khans of the East, not only to escape the vassalage established by Timur, but also to claim supremacy over the Turkish principalities in Anatolia.[2]

John E. Woods, from another angle, made the claims on Oghuz lineage more comprehensible by showing that not only the Ottomans, but many competing Turkish dynasties found it necessary to invoke Oghuz genealogies in support of their claims to the loyalties of all the Oghuz Turkmens of Anatolia, Syria, Irak and Iran.[3] Recently Cornell H. Fleischer re-emphasized the significance of nomadic political notions for the Ottomans in the fifteenth century.[4]

Even in Mamluk society, where the sultan's or emir's household was held superior to the natural family,[5] there was a consciousness of the Djingizid Yasa,[6] and the stories of the Oghuzes and the Djingizids were highly valued for their mythical content. As early as the thirteenth century Arabic versions or revisions of Turkish and Mongol lore were copied and read in Mamluk circles.[7]

1 P. Wittek, *The Rise of the Ottoman Empire*, London, 1938, and especially the same author's "Yazıji'oghlu 'Alī on the Christian Turks of the Dobruja", *BSOAS* 14 (1952), 646-647.

2 H. İnalcık, "The Rise of Ottoman Historiography", in B. Lewis and P.M. Holt (eds.), *Historians of the Middle East*, London, 1962, 155-156.

3 J.E. Woods, *The Aqquyunlu. Clan, Confederation, Empire. A Study in 15th/9th century Turko-Iranian Politics*, Minneapolis & Chicago, 1976, p. 186.

4 C.H. Fleischer, *Bureaucrat and Intellectual in the Ottoman Empire. The Historian Muṣṭafa Āli (1541-1600)*, Princeton, 1986, p. 275, 277, note 8, and 288.

5 P.M. Holt, "The exalted lineage of Riḍwān Bey", reprinted in the author's *Studies in the History of the Near East*, London, 1973, p. 226.

6 Cf. the conflicting views of A.N. Poliak, "The Influence of Chingiz Khān's Yāsa", *BSOAS* 10 (1939/1942), p. 862-876; and D. Ayalon, "The great Yāṣa of Chingiz Khān", *Studia Islamica* 36 (1972), p. 146-158, and 38 (1973), p. 107-142.

7 M.F. Köprülü, *Türk Edebiyatında ilk mütesavvıflar*, 2nd ed., p. 213, and F. Sümer, *Oğuzlar (Türkmenler). Tarihleri, Boy Teşkilatı, Destanları*, 2nd ed., Ankara, 1972, p. 377-378; U. Haarmann, *Quellenstudien zur frühen Mamlukenzeit*, Freiburg, 1969, p. 73; U. Haarmann, "Altun Ḫān und Čingiz Ḫān bei den ägyptischen Mamluken", *Der Islam* 51 (1974), passim.

 | DOI 10.1163/9789004355767_019

What had medieval authors written about the Oghuz and Turkish ancestry? Maḥmūd al-Kāshgharī described it as early as 1077 in his encyclopaedic lexicon. It was he, too, who made it serve a political purpose by distinguishing the Oghuz tribe of Ḳinik, "to which our present sultans belong", referring to the Seldjuḳs.[8]

However, the political genealogies of the fifteenth century had their origin in the classical account of Oghuz history which had been written down and disseminated by the Ilkhanid minister Faḍl Allāh Rashīd al-Dīn (1247-1318) in his "Compendium of Histories". By claiming descent for Turks and Mongols alike from the biblical Japheth as well as from the Turkish national hero Oghuz, Rashīd al-Dīn had helped to consolidate the sultanate of Maḥmūd Ghāzān (Ilkhan from 1295 to 1304), who had been brought up as a Buddhist but had converted to Islam shortly before his accession. The union of Mongols and Turks under the first Muslim Ilkhan could thus be seen as the return to an ancient tradition in which Turks and Mongols were united under one ruler.

Oghuz had conquered the world, and had died at the age of a thousand years. According to Rashīd al-Dīn, the kings tracing their origin from Oghuz were the descendants of his six sons, the eldest of whom was Gün Khan, and whose eldest son was Ḳayı.[9] Rashīd al-Dīn saw sovereignty vested in the tribe of Ḳayı. Not only did he provide the first Ghaznawid with a Ḳayı pedigree, but he incorporated the Seldjuks, the Khwārizmshāhs and, significantly, the emerging Turkmen dynasties of the Anatolian marches: the Ḳaraman, the Eshref oghulları, "and others".[10] The Ottomans, whom he did not mention, always emphasized their Ḳayı descent.[11] At the turn of the fifteenth century, Timur had claimed to be reconstituting the empire of the Mongols under the auspices of Islam. The notion of Turks and Mongols joined under the rule of a single prince had also been brought forward by Timur's writers in justification of his policies.[12]

---

8 R. Dankoff, *Maḥmūd al-Kāšgarī. Compendium of the Turkish Dialects* (*Dīwān Lugāt at-Turk*), I, Harvard Printing Office, 1982, p. 82, 101-102.

9 K. Jahn, *Die Geschichte der Oguzen des Rašīd ad-Dīn*, Vienna, 1969, p. 44, 66-68; T. Baykara (ed.), *A Zeki Velidi Togan. Oğuz Destanı. Reşideddin Oğuznāmesi, Tercüme ve Tahlili*, Istanbul, 1972; F. Sümer, *Oğuzlar*, p. 210-211. For concepts of authority see O. Turan, "The Ideal of World Domination among the Medieval Turks", *Studia Islamica* IV (1955), p. 77 sq. Oghuz's six sons were Gün, Ay, Yıldız, Gök, Dağ, Deñiz. Gün's sons were Ḳayı, Bayat, Alka evli, Kara evli; Jahn, *Geschichte*, p. 45; Woods, *Aqquyunlu*, p. 188.

10 Jahn, *Geschichte*, p. 66-68.

11 M.F. Köprülü, "Osmanlı Imparatorluğu'nun Etnik Menşei Meseleleri", *Belleten* 7 (1943), p. 219-303.

12 M. Kafalı, "Timur", *Islam Ansiklopedisi*, 12 (1974), p. 336-346; Woods, *Aqquyunlu*, p. 189; Fleischer, *Bureaucrat and Intellectual*, p. 276.

A desire to discover continuity permeates the Ottoman restoration after Timur. This is seen in the Ottoman claim to be the successors of the Rūm Seldjuḳs.[13] But there was the Timur problem. Yazıdjıoghlu ʿAlī, writing for Murād II in 1423, tackled it head-on. The audacious passage runs as follows, "After his father, Ḳayı was Khanlar Khanı for a long time. And according to this custom the greatest pādishāh ... Sulṭān Murād Khan who is the most noble of the house of ʿOsman, is the most suitable and the most worthy of sovereignty of all the remaining clans (*uruḳ*) of the Oghuz Khans, yes, even of the clan of the Djingizid Khans, he is the highest in origin and "bone" (ancestry). Therefore it is fitting by holy law as by customary law that not only Turkish Khans but also Tatar Khans come to his Porte to salute and to serve him".[14]

In this way the actions of the Ottomans, their conquest of so many countries, their wars not only against unbelievers but also against fellow-Muslims, were no completely new departures, but were justified and had been foreseen in Oghuz Khan's testament and the prophesy pronounced by Ḳorḳut Ata. That "consummate soothsayer of the Oghuz" had said that in time to come the sovereignty would again light on the Ḳayı and none would take it from their hands until the end of time. This prophecy had found its way into the Book of Dede Ḳorḳut, where a later narrator had added, "This of which he spoke is the House of ʿOsman and behold it continues yet".[15] Later historians such as Rūḥī recalled this utterance.[16]

Ottoman writers were not the only ones who argued that Oghuzian rule was intended to be accomplished by one of their clan; rather, this claim had to be defended against the Ḳaraman and the Aḳḳoyunlu, who also stressed their affiliation with the Oghuz past by having genealogies constructed to prove their descent from the stock of Oghuz. Ottoman sultans emphasized this connection by naming their sons Ḳorḳud (Bāyezīd I and Bāyezīd II), and an Ottoman prince (Djem) named his second son Oghuz.

---

13 H. İnalcık, "Rise of Ottoman Historiography", p. 156; I. Beldiceanu-Steinherr, *Recherches sur les actes des regnes des sultans Osman, Orkhan et Murad I*, Munich, 1967, p. 64-74; Fleischer, *Bureaucrat and Intellectual*, p. 288.

14 Yazıdjıoghlu ʿAlī, *Tevārīkh-i āl-i Seldjūḳ*, Leiden University Library, Cod. 419 Warn., fol. 19b; cf. P. Wittek, "Yazıjıoghlu ʿAlī on the Christian Turks", p. 646.

15 G. Lewis, *The Book of Dede Korkut. Translated, with an Introduction and Notes*, Harmondsworth, 1974, p. 190; M. Ergin, *Dede Korkut Kitabı. Metin-Sözlük*, Ankara, 1964, p. 1; Turan, "Ideal of World Domination", p. 78.

16 H. İnalcık, "Rise of Ottoman Historiography", p. 156. J.R. Walsh, "The Historiography of Ottoman-Ṣafavid Relations in the sixteenth and seventeenth centuries", in Lewis and Holt, *Historians of the Middle East*, p. 198 note 4.

After the great events of the second half of the fifteenth century, Uzun Ḥasan's overthrow of the Ḳaraḳoyunlu and the Timurids, the collapse of the Golden Horde, and Mehmed Fātiḥ's awe-inspiring conquest of Constantinople, nomadic legitimizing principles began to lose persuasion; it could not be denied that elaborating the "middle links" was a task which wearied the genealogists, just as in contemporary Western Europe.[17] And yet genealogical controversy was a form of political argument, in an age where innovation often had to be disguised as a return to the past.[18]

The conceptions of the ruling houses of the Aḳḳoyunlu and Ottoman states underwent considerable modification as the basis of their power changed. The virtues of the mythical Oghuz ceased to form the basis for a universal appeal to the loyalties of all Oghuz Turkmens. In Persia Shāh Ismāʿīl imposed Shīʿism on a country which was still predominantly Sunni. He annihilated the Aḳḳoyunlu. The Khans of the Crimea had become Ottoman vassals. The Ottomans, abandoning the traditions of the marches, had assumed their new style as sultans of an empire in the traditions of the ancient Near-Eastern states. Their sultan, not content with the title *khalīfa*, claimed that he had acquired the dignity of Inheritor of the Great Caliphate by the will of God.[19] Such revolutionary doings of contemporaries called for a demonstration of their legitimacy. Genealogical links had to be established between contemporary rulers and ancient forerunners, and prophecies also played a part. Against an older and more "modest" lineage of the Ottomans a more elaborate and ambitious pedigree was now supplied.[20]

Japheth

As is well known, many Turkish, Mongolian and indeed European genealogies lay within the tradition of Japheth. The Muslims regarded him as the ancestor of the "white" race.[21] Among his descendants, besides the Turks, figured the

17 K. Thomas, *Religion and the Decline of Magic. Studies in Popular Beliefs in Sixteenth and Seventeenth-Century England*, Harmondsworth, 1971, p. 507 and passim.

18 I have dealt briefly with this subject in an unpublished paper entitled "In search of forefathers. Political functions of genealogy in Herat and Istanbul in the 16th century", "Workshop on Central Asian Studies", Utrecht, 16 December 1985.

19 H. İnalcık, *The Ottoman Empire. The Classical Age 1300-1600*, London, 1973, p. 3; idem, "The Ottomans and the Caliphate", *Cambridge History of Islam* I, p. 320-322; M.A. Cook, "Introduction", *A History of the Ottoman Empire to 1730*, Cambridge, 1976.

20 H. İnalcık, "Rise of Ottoman Historiography", p. 161.

21 A selection, in Turkish translation, from medieval Islamic sources concerned with Turkish origins has recently been published by R. Şeşen, *İslam Coğrafyacılarına göre Türkler ve Türk Ülkeleri*, Ankara 1985.

Gog and Magog. Like others before and after him Maḥmūd al-Kāshgharī considered *Türk* the son of Japheth, that is the grandson of Noah,[22] or he spoke of him as the son of Noah.[23] Rashīd al-Dīn stated that Noah, when he distributed the world among his sons, gave the East to his eldest son Japheth, whom he declared identical with the Khan whom the Turks named Uldjay (or Abuldja, Buldja), and whose son was Dib Yavku (Yabghu) Khan.[24]

The Ottomans, too, had at an early stage taken their place in this tradition. All Turks descended from Abuldja Khan who was Japheth himself (Yazıdjıoghlu) or Japheth's son (Neshrī). Abuldja's son was Dib Yakuy whose eldest son was Ḳara Khan, the father of Oghuz.[25] Neshrī gave "Buldjas" three sons, Türk, Oghuz, and Moghul. Again in Neshrī, Buldjas's successor was Dib takuy, who had four sons, the eldest of whom was Ḳara Khan, Oghuz's father.[26] The light of Islam shone on Oghuz; he lived in the time of the Prophet Abraham and believed in him.[27] All this has for a long time been known in Europe.[28]

In the fifteenth century there was a divergence between Ottoman genealogists over the parentage of Ertoghrul. Who was his father, Süleymān Shāh or Gündüz Alp? In the sixteenth century the discussion was closed; Süleymān Shāh was declared O͟smān's grandfather. But writers like Neshrī and Kemālpashazāde seem to have felt uneasy about this. The latter took the precaution of working backward from the present, not forward from Noah. He brushed aside the long list of names between Japheth and Ḳayı with their obvious discrepancies, surely for the reason that the Oghuz question was losing much of its former actuality.

---

22 Dankoff, *Maḥmūd al-Kāšgarī* I, p. 82; B. Atalay, *Divanü Lûgat-it-Türk Tercümesi* I, Ankara, 1939, p. 28.

23 Dankoff, *Maḥmūd al-Kāšgarī* I, p. 274; Atalay, *Tercüme* I, p. 350.

24 Jahn, *Geschichte*, p. 17. V.V. Barthold, *Four Studies on the History of Central Asia. III. A History of the Turkman People*, Leiden, 1962, p. 114-116. This was taken over by Neshrī and (directly from Rashīd al-Dīn) by Kemālpashazāde, who paraphrased it, with invectives against the Tatars; see the edition by Ş. Turan, *İbn-i Kemal. Tevārih-i Âl-i Osman. I. Defter*, Ankara, 1970, p. 201-204.

25 Yazıdjıoghlu ʿAlī, *Tevārīkh-i āl-i Seldjūḳ*, Leiden Cod. 419, fol. 7b.

26 For a list of Ottoman chroniclers following the Japhetic tradition see Turan, *İbn-i Kemal. I. Defter*, p. 21; cf. also p. 12-28, 44-45.

27 F. Taeschner (ed.), *Ǧihānnümā. Die altosmanische Chronik des Mevlānā Meḥemmed Neschrī*, I and II, Leipzig, 1951 and 1955; see below, notes 52-53.

28 V.L. Ménage, "The Beginnings of Ottoman historiography", B. Lewis and P.M. Holt, *Historians of the Middle East*, London, 1962, p. 179; J. Klaproth, *Abhandlung über die Sprache und Schrift der Uiguren*, reprint of the 1820 edition by W.-E. Scharlipp, Hamburg, 1985, p. 36-43.

At the time the *Ṣubḥat al-ahbār* was compiled (the original work was dedicated to Sultan Süleymān), the family tree followed the pattern Noah, Japheth, Ottomans, but the dubious (or by now less relevant) nature of the genealogical connection between Japheth, the Djingizids, and the Ottomans is marked by a line on fol. 7a-b, which fades out in the middle of the folio (*bu chizi Âl-i ʿOs̱māna chıḳar*).[29]

Djingiz Khan

In the sixteenth century the empire of the Great Mongols had left as its enduring legacy the intense genealogical pride of the Djingizids, although only the Timurid Moghuls could cherish realistic ambitions to extend their rule. The Secret History of the Mongols had also contained a prophecy: that the Khanate would pass to another branch than the descendants of Ögedei; a prophecy that had been fulfilled.[30]

Shaybānī Khan Uzbek (he became prominent about 1500, and died 1510 near Marw) had commissioned Faḍl Allāh b. Rūzbihān Khundjī to compose an impeccable Djingizid pedigree for him.[31]

Djingiz Khan's eldest son Djoči was the ancestor not only of the Shaybānids, rulers over the peoples that came to be called Uzbek, but also of the Crimean Khans. Their ruling house, the Giray (Kerey) family, was descended from Togay Timur, a younger son of Djoči. Although their state was now subordinate to the Ottoman Empire, they remained influential rulers, who laid claim to being the rightful heirs to the patrimony of the Golden Horde.[32] Sunni Muslims and Turkish-speaking, these Djingizid rulers had no reason to revise their illustrious lineage.

29 MS.A. F. 50 of the Austrian National Library, Flügel II 00 nr. 868. See the edition by K. Holter, *Rosenkranz der Weltgeschichte*, Graz, 1981. For an exhaustive description of the famous illustrated *Sübhat ül-ahbār* (A.F. 50) see Dorothea Duda, *Islamische Handschriften II Teil 2. Die Handschriften in türkisher Sprache. Textband*, pp. 27-44 and *Tafelband*, six colour plates (III-VIII) and 17 black and white photographs (*Abb.* 118-135). Vienna 2008. The unfinished line "leading to the Ottomans" mentioned above is in fol. 7a (*Abb.* 122).

30 J.A. Boyle, "Juvaynī and Rashīd al-Dīn as sources on the history of the Mongols", B. Lewis and P.M. Holt, *Historians of the Middle East*, London, 1962, p. 136.

31 U. Ott, *Transoxanien und Turkestan zu Beginn des 16. Jahrhunderts. Das Mihmān-nāme-yi Buḫārā des Faḍlallāh b. Rūzbihān Ḫunğī. Übersetzung und Kommentar*, Freiburg, 1974, p. 61-62.

32 M.E. Yapp, "The Golden Horde and its Successors", *Cambridge History of Islam* I, p. 495-502; H. İnalcık, "Giray", *EI*, 2nd ed.

A passage from the *Ta'rīkh-i Ṣāḥib Giray*, containing a personal account, illustrates this. "Travelling through the world, I came to Istanbul. I saw that mankind had gone out to watch the *khüdāvendigār* of the Ottoman dynasty, Sultan Süleymān Khan – may God make perpetual his sovereignty and eternal his government – mounting his horse to ride for pleasure. Next to the Padishah I saw a handsome young man of radiant beauty ..., thirty years old, with the crown of government on his head... he kept the Padishah company. I asked, 'Who is this young man?' and they said, 'He is of the family of Djingiz Khan, whose forefathers have been khans for seventy-two generations".[33] This was said of the Crimean Khan Ṣāḥib Giray Khan (1532-1551). Writing of Meḥmed Giray II (reigned 1577-1584), Muṣṭafā ʿĀlī put a mere "thirty or forty generations" between him and the world conqueror.[34] The place of the Djingizids, and of Timur, in genealogical works such as the *Ṣubḥat al-akhbār* deserves to be studied.

In Herat, at the other end of the Islamic world, historians like Khwāndamīr drew on the rich fund of the Turkish-Mongol tradition introduced by Rashīd al-Dīn and modified by Timur's historians.[35] There all genealogical discussion – in the seventeenth century to be summed up by Abū l-Ghāzī Bahādur Khan[36] – was conducted on the assumption of an unchanging, Japhetic, genealogical structure. Türk, with Oghuz, and Moghul were the substance of the Turkish raison d'etre in the political situation in which they found themselves in the sixteenth century, cut off from their old connections in the West and from world politics.[37] No ideological changes were needed as yet. Their opponent, emerging in the North-West, more important than Timur or even Djingiz Khan, was to be the Emperor of Russia, a King of the *Banū l-Aṣfar* who will be mentioned below.

33 T. Gökbilgin, *Tarih-i Sahib Giray Han*, Ankara, 1973, p. 19-20. For the Giray family in the 18th century see Barbara Kellner-Heinkele, *Aus den Aufzeichnungen des Saʿīd Giray Sultān*, PhD dissertation Hamburg 1975.

34 Fleischer, *Bureaucrat and Intellectual*, p. 277, note.

35 Ghiyāth al-Dīn Kwāndamīr, *Ḥabīb al-siyar fī akhbār afrad al-bashar*, ed. Dj. Humāʾī and M. Dabīr-Siyāḳī, Teheran, 1954, III, 4 sq.; Barthold, *Four Studies*, p. 115 sq.; Woods, *Aqquyunlu*, p. 24, 189.

36 Abū l-Ghāzī Bahādur Khan, *Shedjere-i Terākime*, ed. and transl. A.N. Kononov, *Rodoslovnaja Turkmen. Sočinenie Abu-l-Gazi*, Moscow, 1958.

37 B. Spuler, "Central Asia from the sixteenth century to the Russian conquests", *The Cambridge History of Islam*, I, p. 468-470.

ʿAlī b. Abī Ṭālib

In comparison with the audacity of Murad II's genealogical claims, the Ṣafavid mandate for sovereignty may have seemed less hubristic than it would be seen now. Coming from native Iranian stock, and speaking Azeri-Turkish, the Ṣafavids constructed a genealogy connecting them with the Prophet. Not only did they trace their descent from the seventh of the Twelver Imāms, Mūsā al-Kāẓim, but also, through him, the Shāh of Persia was descended from ʿAlī b. Abī Ṭālib and Fāṭima, the Prophet's daughter.[38] In this way their religious leadership was formally legitimized; Sheykh Ṣafī al-Dīn and his descendants were a truly holy family.[39] They set themselves completely apart from the Ottomans, relying upon heterodox Turkmen tribes in the Ottoman Empire, who saw in Shāh Ismāʿīl both their temporal ruler and their spiritual guide.

Being himself a branch of the tree of prophecy, a seed of the sheaves of saintship, belonging to the children of the Prophet of God and of Fatima the Resplendent,[40] Shāh Ismāʿīl might well brush aside the nomadic legitimizing principle, calling the descent from Djingiz Khan "a branch from the tree of unbelief".[41] Conscious of the religious force of his claims, the Ottomans at first did not refuse Ismāʿīl the title *sayyid*;[42] the forgery took some time to be exposed, and even after Ebūl-suʿūd's *fetvās* had left no doubt that the Ṣafavid lineage was fictitious,[43] this was seldom alluded to.[44]

---

38 For a summary see E.G. Browne, *A Literary History of Persia*, IV, Cambridge, 1924, 6th ed. 1969, p. 36-38; J.R. Walsh, "Ottoman-Ṣafavid relations", p. 202-203; H. Sohrweide, "Der Sieg der Ṣafaviden in Persien und seine Rückwirkungen auf die Schiiten Anatoliens im 16. Jahrhundert", *Der Islam* 41 (1965), p. 117-124; R.M. Savory, "Ṣafavid Persia", *The Cambridge History of Islam* I, Cambridge, 1970, p. 394-401; A. Allouche, *The Origins and Development of the Ottoman-Ṣafavid Conflict*, Berlin, 1983, p. 157-166.

39 Walsh, "Ottoman-Ṣafavid Relations", p. 203; Cf. P.M. Holt, "The Coming of the Funj", reprinted in P.M. Holt, *Studies in the History of the Near East*, London, 1973, p. 79; Fleischer, *Bureaucrat and Intellectual*, p. 274-275.

40 Cf. B. Lewis, *Islam from the Prophet Muḥammad to the Capture of Constantinople*, I New York/London 1974, p. 103.

41 Woods, *Aqquyunlu*, p. 182, 296.

42 J.R. Walsh, "Ottoman-Ṣafavid Relations", p. 208; A. Allouche, *Origins*, p. 77.

43 E. Eberhard, *Osmanische Polemik gegen die Ṣafawiden im 16. Jahrhundert nach arabischen Handschriften*, Freiburg, 1970, p. 165 f., 207; J.R. Walsh, "Ottoman-Ṣafavid Relations", p. 207-208.

44 H. Sohrweide, "Sieg der Ṣafaviden", p. 96; J.R. Walsh, "Ottoman-Ṣafavid Relations", p. 208.

Alexander

Shaybānī Khan's political hopes were sustained by prophecies gathered by his "court ideologue" Faḍl Allāh b. Rūzbihān. The Khan had among his books the Turkish *Iskendernāme*, written by the Anatolian poet Aḥmedī around 1390. In the manuscript which Shaybānī took with him on his campaigns, a piece of Persian verse had been found, which prophesied that a conqueror would come out of the steppe, with whom Shaybānī liked to identify himself.[45]

There were much older steppe traditions in connection with the arrival of Alexander of the "two horns" or "two kingdoms", *Dhū l-ḳarneyn*, in the lands of the Turks. Maḥmūd al-Kāshgharī quoted from them and linked the life-span of the ancestors of the Oghuz tribes to Alexander's expedition to Central Asia.[46] Kāshgharī's concern was with Alexander and the Turks, not with the Dhū l-ḳarneyn of Revelation (Koran, Sūras 18 and 21), who built a barrier against the warlike Gog and Magog, whom early Arabic exegetes had situated in the country of the then infidel Turks or even identified with the Turks.[47] Al-Kāshgharī, writing at a time when Turkish supremacy was recognized, demonstrated his independence from the older view, mentioning only that the language of Gog and Magog was "unknown because of the Barrier and the interposition of the mountains and the sea".[48]

Aḥmedī's epic poem *Iskendernāme* was widely read inside and outside Anatolia. Motifs from the Alexander legend, especially that conqueror's quest of the Water of Life and the discovery of that water by Khiḍr, had of course long been stock images of Persian and Turkish poetry, and rulers were pleased to be compared with Iskender.[49] Inevitably, Meḥmed the Conqueror, heir to the Oghuz and the Ghāzī tradition of the Ottomans, also exploited the fact that he

45 Ott, *Transoxanien*, p. 156; E. Birnbaum, "The Ottomans and Chagatay Literature. An Early 16th Century Manuscript of Navā'ī's Dīvān in Ottoman Orthography", *Central Asiatic Journal* 20 (1977), p. 163. The first complete edition of the *Iskendernāme* was published by İ. Ünver, *Aḥmedī. Iskender-nāme. İnceleme-Tipkibasim*, Ankara, 1983.

46 R. Dankoff, "The Alexander Romance in the Dīwān Lughāt at-Turk", *Humaniora Islamica* I (1973), p. 233-244; idem, *Maḥmūd al-Kāšgarī* I, p. 5.

47 R. Şeşen, "Eski Arablar'a Göre Türkler", *Türkiyat Mecmuası* 15 (1969), p. 11-36; for a spirited refutation of anti-Turkish hadiths see I. Cerrahoğlu, "Ye'cüc-Me'cüc ve Türkler", *İlâhiyat Fakültesi Dergisi* 20 (1975), p. 97-126.

48 Dankoff, *Maḥmūd al-Kāšgarī* I, p. 83.

49 E.J.W. Gibb, *A History of Ottoman Poetry*, I, 1900, 2nd ed. 1958, p. 284; T. Kortantamer, *Leben und Weltbild des altosmanischen Dichters Aḥmedī unter besonderer Berücksichtigung seines Diwans*, Freiburg, 1973, p. 17, 370, H. Özdemir. *Die altosmanischen Chroniken als Quelle zur türkischen Volkskunde*, Freiburg, 1975, p. 170-171.

was now also Caesar, Emperor of the Romans.[50] The title, *Ḳaysar-i Rūm*, was indeed used by Persian historians. But for an imperial precedent the Ottomans turned to Alexander.

Ṭursun Beg, one of Meḥmed Fātiḥ's historians, felt it appropriate to introduce this sultan's exceptional conquests with an evocation of Iskender. The opening line of his *Ta'rīkh-i Ebū l-Feth* is a quotation from Sūra 18: "And they will ask you of Dhū l-ḳarnayn, the two-horned. Say: I will recite to you an account of him". And the author proceeds, in his introduction, to hold Dhū l-ḳarneyn up as a model for imitation, showing that he had behaved in a perfectly Islamic manner.[51]

Neshrī scrutinized ancient traditions of the nomadic Turks with a view to extracting from them some justification of Turkish affiliations with Alexander. He stated in the first draft of his *Djihān-nümā*, "The nomadic Turks (*etrāk*) believe that Oghuz is that Dhū l-ḳarneyn of whom God speaks in His holy Book as the man who built a wall against Gog and Magog".[52] This was written in 1493. Sometime after 1512, Neshrī's oldest copyist modified this text as follows, "the nomadic Turks believed that Iskender Dhū l-ḳarneyn whom God mentions in His Revelation was perhaps this [Oghuz] and said so".[53] This was written under Selīm I, whom Faḍl Allāh b. Rūzbihān wanted to see as Dhū l-ḳarneyn and Caesar in Rūm, and who added the dominion of Persia to his own.[54] This is not the place to embark on a summary of Alexander and the Gog and Magog, who remained significant in Turkish historical writings for a long time.

50 J.H. Mordtmann in *Der Islam* 13 (1924), p. 165 note 2; J.R. Walsh, "Ottoman-Ṣafavid relations", p. 201; İnalcık, "Rise of the Ottoman Empire". p. 296-297. For a critical view of this Ottoman claim see Cook. "Introduction", p. 4.

51 A.M. Tulum, *Tursun Bey. Tarih-i Ebu'l-Feth*, Istanbul, 1977, p. 3 sq., 20; H. İnalcık and Rhoads Murphey, *The History of Mehmed the Conqueror by Tursun Beg*, Minneapolis & Chicago, 1978, p. 2b, 15b.

52 For Neshrī's draft, the manuscript Mz, dated February 1493, see V.L. Ménage, *Neshrī's History of the Ottomans. The Sources and Development of the Text*, Oxford, 1964, p. 20-30. For the text see F. Taeschner, *Ğihānnümā. Die altosmanische Chronik des Mevlānā Meḥemmed Neschrī* I, Leipzig, 1951, fol. 5a.

53 Text: F. Taeschner, *Ğihānnümā. Die altosmanische Chronik des Mevlānā Meḥemmed Neschrī* II, Leipzig, 1955, fol. 4-5. For the manuscript, Mn, see Ménage, *Neshrī's History*, p. 45-47.

54 For the text see E.G. Browne, *A Literary History of Persia*, IV, Cambridge, 1924, 2nd ed. 1969, p. 78-80; for the authorship of the poem in question see Ott, *Transoxanien*, p. 24.

Esau

Esau, ʿĪṣū, the son of the Prophet Isaac, and Jacob's elder brother, was the ancestor of the Rūm in the Arabic tradition. His designation *aṣfar* "yellow, red" was customarily applied to the Greeks, who were called *Banū l-Aṣfar* "Sons of the Red One" in Arabic traditions and poetry.[55] Maḥmūd al-Kāshgharī alluded to this when he drew a parallel between Turkish and Greek genealogical notions: "As the Turks were called by the name of their ancestor *Türk*, so the children of Rūm were called by the name of *Rūm*, the son of Esau, son of Isaac, son of Abraham, God's blessing be upon them".[56] This medieval tradition, which Muslims shared with the Jews who had identified Esau first with their enemy Edom (Obadiah 8-20) and then with Rome,[57] acquired new political significance after the conquest of Constantinople by the Ottoman Turks.

This triumph was hailed by Ottoman writers as the fulfilment of prophesies uttered by the Prophet. Muḥammad had foretold that that vast city, that lofty fortress, would be subdued by the exertions of his followers: "Verily Constantinople shall be captured. How excellent a commander shall be that commander, and how excellent an army shall be that army".[58] But there were also hadiths which made the fall of Constantinople a preamble to eschatology. In the end of days, before the advent of the Dadjdjāl, the sons of Isḥāḳ (or of Abū Iṣḥāḳ) would take the city with the call "God is most great". But were the Turks descendants of Isaac?[59]

The historian whom we know as the Oxford Anonymous or Pseudo-Rūḥī asserted that this was so. He showed O͟smān's father Ertoghrul to be descended, not from Japheth, but from Shem through Gök Alp b. Oghuz b. Ḳara Khan b. Dib Takuy Khan, "whose name in the Coptic tongue means Esau (ʿĪṣ), who is

55 I. Goldziher, "Aṣfar", *Encyclopaedia of Islam*, 2nd ed.

56 Dankoff, *Maḥmūd al-Kāšgarī* I, p. 82; Atalay, *Tercüme* I, p. 28. Cf. Atalay, *Tercüme* III, Ankara, 1941, p. 369; Dankoff, *Maḥmūd al-Kāšgarī* I, p.274; Atalay, *Tercüme* I, 351.

57 G.D. Cohen in A. Altmann (ed.), *Jewish Medieval and Renaissance Studies*, Cambridge, Mass., 1967, p. 20-21, 44-45.

58 M. Canard, "Les expéditions des Arabes contre Constantinople dans l'histoire et la légende", *Journal Asiatique* 218 (1926), p. 106. L. Massignon, "Textes prémonitoires et commentaires mystiques relatifs à la prise de Constantinople par les Turcs en 1453", *Oriens* 6 (1953), p. 11.

59 Medieval Arabic commentators had assumed that "sons of Isaac" designated *Arabs*; cf. Canard, "Les expéditions des Arabes", p. 110. For the Turks see J.H. Mordtmann in *Der Islam* 13 (1924), p. 163-164; P. Wittek, "Der Stammbaum der Osmanen", *Der Islam* 14 (1925), p. 99.

the son of the prophet Isaac".[60] The relevance of the "Semitic" genealogy could directly be understood in conjunction with the hadith just quoted.

Neshrī, at the very end of the fifteenth century, rejected the Esau pedigree "because Esau is the father of the Lesser or Second Rome" and a descendant of Shem, whereas, according to him, Oghuz, Türk and Moghul were all descended from Japheth, "just as the First Rome".[61] Neshrī also took exception to those who argued that the Seldjuks were descended from the Prophet Abraham.

With all this, he did not succeed in demolishing the new Esau genealogy of the Ottomans. Idris Bidlisi gave it his authority, though not omitting to mention the old Japhetic lineage of the Turks; he told the story of how Jacob deprived Esau of his birthright, whereupon Esau went to Turkestan and there became the ancestor of the Turks. "And most historians say that Ḳayı Khan who was famous in Turkestan is Esau (ʿĪs), whom they call ʿĪṣš in the Coptic language".[62] Kemālpashazāde, while disregarding the more obscure Oghuzian ancestors, could not avoid the Esau issue and seemed baffled by it.[63] Professing the Semitic Esau thesis – Kemālpashazāde checked on it in the Oxford Anonymous – meant putting an end to the hallowed tradition that the Turks were descendants of Japheth. On the other hand, a Semitic pedigree made Turks in some ways akin to Arabs. This is significant in view of the fact that the Ottomans had not chosen to adopt a genealogy linking them to the Ḳuraysh, the tribe of the Prophet.[64]

There remained a minority of critics. At the end of the sixteenth century, the learned Khwādja Saʿd el-Dīn pointed to the historians who connected the Ottomans with Japheth,[65] and his contemporary Muṣṭafā ʿĀlī, too, showed himself still aware of Neshrī's refutation of the Esau pedigree. Drawing on a

60 Wittek, "Stammbaum der Osmanen", p. 99f.; according to Ménage, *Neshrī's History*, p. 12, the relevant chapter "consists mostly of the story of how Jacob cheated Esau of his birthright, the relevance of which appears in a long genealogy (but without Ḳayı!) showing ʿOs̱mān's father Ertoghrul to be descended from Shem". – For the Esau tradition in Ebū l-Khayr-i Rūmī's *Saltuḳnāme* see A.S. Erzi, "Akkoyunlu ve Karakoyunlu Tarihi Hakkında Araştırmalar", *Belleten* 14 (1954) p. 192-202; especially p. 200.

61 Neshrī's text : Taeschner, *Ġihānnümā* I, p. 19, and II, p. 23; Erzi, "Akkoyunlu", p. 200.

62 M. Şükrü, *Osmanlı Devletinin Kuruluşu. Bitlisli İdris'in "Heşt Bihişt" adlı eserine göre tenkidî araştırma*, Ankara, 1934, p. 29; in the Turkish translation of Idrīs Bidlīsī's work which P. Wittek consulted in the Vienna manuscript, Esau is identified with Dib-takuy, who is the predecessor of Ḳayı Khan; Wittek, "Stammbaum", p. 95-96.

63 Turan, *İbn-i Kemal. I. Defter*, p. 21-22; 27-28.

64 Cook, "Introduction", p. 5.

65 Cf. Wittek, "Stammbaum", p. 97.

wide variety of written sources,[66] ʿĀlī tried to reconcile the conflicting views. Based on "trustworthy books", he offered the following solution: Esau was one step ahead in coming into the world, and that was why his descendants became kings on earth, whereas the offspring of Jacob became the prophets and messengers of God.[67] As descendants of Esau and thus of Isaac, the Ottoman rulers could now exploit not only the Oghuz myths, but also the Islamic tradition to their own advantage. Their ruling house was descended from Esau; the Turks were Japhetids like the Mongols, and the inhabitants of their empire, the people of Rūm, were of mixed origin.[68]

And there we may let the matter rest for the moment, knowing that there is much more in the *Künh* and other sources, which has yet to be sorted out and queried.

---

66 ʿĀlī mistakenly cites ʿĀshıḳpashazāde as identifying Uldja Khan with Esau, whereas in reality ʿĀshıḳpashazāde followed the Japhetic tradition; Wittek, "Stammbaum", p. 95-96, see also R.F. Kreutel, *Vom Hirtenzelt zur Hohen Pforte*, Graz-Vienna-Cologne, 1959, p. 10.

67 ʿĀlī, *Künhü l-akhbār*, Leiden, University Library, MS. orient 288, fol. 14b-15a.

68 ʿĀlī, *Künhü l-akhbār*, vol. I of the printed edition, p. 16. With thanks to Jan Schmidt, Den Haag, who was then preparing his study of the *Künhü l-akhbār*: *Pure Water for Thirsty Muslims. A Study of Mustafa ʿĀlī of Gallipoli's Künhü l-Aḫbār*, Leiden 1992. For details see no. 14 in this volume. The passage on the Rumis has been translated by C.H. Fleischer in his *Bureaucrat and intellectual*, p. 254.

CHAPTER 19

A Sixteenth-Century Turkish Apology for Islam: The *Gurbetname-i Sultan Cem*[*]

Background

Turkish perceptions of Western Christianity in the fifteenth and sixteenth centuries have been studied in a general way. It has long been held that as a rule Muslims did not see Christianity as a religious threat to Islam and that they showed little interest in and curiosity about what went on in Christian Europe, taking little trouble to inform themselves even about the languages spoken there.[1] It is true that the Ottoman government, the Porte, did have access to first-hand material; it made use of the knowledge of seamen, and employed secret agents, some of whose depositions have been preserved.[2] But as far as the Turkish public was concerned, its potential sources of information on the "House of War", *darülharb* were chronicles and heroic poems on military exploits, the *gazavatnames*.[3]

Their writers combined direct and hearsay evidence with older authorities, and for special subjects such as the history of Constantinople and the Hagia Sophia they derived their knowledge from Greek chronicles and legends which had been translated, with inevitable distortions.[4] One of the few detailed

---

* Contribution to the 19th Spring Symposium of Byzantine Studies, Birmingham, 24 March, 1985. I am grateful to J.T.P. de Bruijn, E. van Donzel and M.E.H.N. Mout for their help in shaping my ideas. My appreciation is extended also to Stephen Reinert, to whose paper the following is a continuation.

1 B. Lewis, *The Muslim Discovery of Europe* (New York, London 1982), 82, 142, 182. For European indifference on matters Islamic see C. Göllner, *Turcica III. Die Türkenfrage in der öffentlichen Meinung Europas im 16. Jahrhundert* (Bucarest, Baden-Baden, 1978), 201, 214.

2 One example is the report of the famous seaman Barak̦ (died in 1499), subject of a masterly study by V.L. Ménage, "The mission of an Ottoman secret agent in France in 1486", *JRAS* (1965), 112-132. Further material about Turkish map-making and geographical knowledge in Lewis, *Discovery*, 152f.

3 See for example I. Mélikoff, *Le Destàn d'Umūr Pacha* (Paris, 1954): A.S. Levend, *Ġazavāt-nāmeler ve Mihaloğlu Ali Bey' in Ġazavāt-nāmesi* (Ankara, 1956); I. Mélikoff, *La Geste de Melik Dānişmend* (Paris, 1960); H. İnalcık and M. Oğuz, *Gazavât-i Sultân Murâd b. Mehemmed Hân* (Ankara, 1978).

4 K. Süssheim (F. Taeschner), "Aya Sofya", *EI*², I (1960), 776-77; B. Lewis, "The Use by Muslim Historians of non-Muslim Sources", in B. Lewis and P.M. Holt, *Historians of the Middle East*

 | DOI 10.1163/9789004355767_020

accounts of Western lands is the remarkable itinerary of Prince Cem (1459-1495) who was dragged through France and Italy as a hostage of Christian powers. It is included in the biography of the Prince, the *Vakiât-i Sultan Cem*, written by one of his close companions.[5]

Within the Ottoman Empire large numbers of Christians, alongside Jews, continued to practise their religion as *zimmis*, protected taxpayers or "scriptural infidels". The Turks knew of the old division of Near Eastern Christianity into Greek Orthodox, Jacobite (Monophysite) and Nestorian Christians. Their Christian subjects were organized in three religious communities, *millet*: the Greek Orthodox, by far the great majority; the Armenian, Monophysite, *millet* which included besides Armenians all subjects of the Sultan not otherwise classified,[6] and the Jews.[7] Catholicism was the most foreign of them all; in the 15th century it was the religion of all the Franks, the enemies of Islam. When the *millets* were formed, almost its only adherents within the Empire were foreigners such as the Genoese citizens of Galata.[8]

In the early period of the Empire, when Islam had been preached in a rather broadminded way and in a familiar guise, absorption of Christians by conversion had been rapid. But as Ottoman orthodoxy strengthened its grip on its flock and the *millets* were more tightly organized, conversions were actively prevented by the *millet* leaders and soon all but ceased.[9] In the villages of the early Empire, Muslims and Christians, sharing the status of "taxpaying subjects", *reaya*, were often on good terms with each other. In the towns, however, there were marked divisions between the communities. Intercourse between

---

(London 1962), 184-85. For the attitudes of neighbouring peoples see S. Franklin, "Byzantine and Kievan Russia", *Byzantion*, 53 (1983), and E.M. Jeffreys, "The Attitude of Byzantine Chroniclers toward Ancient History", *Byzantion*, 49 (1979), 199-238.

5 Published by Mehmed Arif as a supplement to *Tarih-i Osmani Encümeni Mecmuası*, parts 22-25 (Istanbul, 1330 / 1911-1912). The work was used by the historian Sa'deddin, so that its contents were indirectly available to European historians; cf. Ménage, "Ottoman agent", 119. For a perceptive critique of the *Vakiât*, cf. N. Vatin, "A propos de l'exotisme dans les Vâḳi'at-i Sulṭân Cem: le regard porté sur l'Europe occidentale à la fin du xve siècle par un Turc Ottoman", *JA*, 272 (1984), 237-248.

6 H.A.R. Gibb and H. Bowen, *Islamic Society and the West. A study of the Impact of Western Civilization on Moslem Culture in the Near East*, I, II (London, New York, Toronto, 1957), 221. For historiography on the Orthodox church in the early Ottoman Empire see M. Philippides, "Patriarchal Chronicles of the Sixteenth Century", *GRBS*, 25 (1984), 87-94.

7 B. Braude and B. Lewis, *Christians and Jews in the Ottoman Empire. The Functioning of a plural society* (New York, London, 1982).

8 Gibb and Bowen, *Islamic Society*, 245.

9 Gibb and Bowen, *Islamic Society*, 256-258.

Muslims and infidels had more to do with practical matters, such as the payment of the "poll tax", *cizye*, than with religious differences.

If a religious debate did take place, the protagonists operated on familiar ground. Islam had from the start been engaged in debate with Jewish and Christian critics, and in the Koran itself Muhammad is enjoined to "argue" or "dispute" with the unbelievers (Sūra 3:61).[10] The Turks, too, had their share of religious debates, going back to the times of the Seldjuks, the Anatolian emirates, and the early Ottomans. Well-known examples are the discussions between an elderly *müderris* and Manuel II in Ankara, and between Mehmed II, the Conqueror (d. 1481), and Gennadius II Scholarius whom he had installed as patriarch.[11] Polemic literature was, it is true, aimed at the religious adversary, but in practice it was meant to strengthen one's own flock.[12] The average Muslim Turk knew no more about intricate theological concepts of his own religion than did the average *zimmi* about the subtle distinctions of Christian theology.

In the sixteenth century centres of Christianity in South-Eastern Europe were overrun by the Turks. Ranging far beyond the limits of Greek Orthodoxy, the victorious Muslims encountered, alongside Jews, a Christian population which was composed of Catholics, the foreign religion par excellence, and Protestants belonging to various denominations, Calvinist, Lutheran, or Unitarian. The spread of Islam northwards into Hungary during the high tide of Turkish conquests[13] caused anxiety to the churches, who tried to hold in and contain this current. The readiness of Christians to participate in public debates

---

10 J. Brugman, *Godsdienstgesprekken tussen Christenen en Moslims in de vroege Islam* (Leiden, 1970), 45; for the oldest disputes see ibid., 46-51, and S. Vryonis, Jr., *The Decline of Medieval Hellenism in Asia Minor and the Process of Islamization from the Eleventh through the Fifteenth Century* (Berkeley, Los Angeles, London, 1971), 422f.

11 E. Trapp (ed.), *Manuel II. Palaiologos. Dialoge mit einem "Perser"* (Vienna, 1966); A. Papadakis, "Gennadius II and Mehmet the Conqueror", *Byzantion*, 42 (1972), 88-106; A. Decei, "Patrik II. Gennadios Skolarius" un Fatih Sultan Mehmet için yazdığı ortodoks i'tikadnamesinin Türkçe metni", *Fatih ve Istanbul*, I (Istanbul, 1953), 98-116; Vryonis, *Decline*, 423-436; Göllner, *Türkenfrage*, 199-215; B. Flemming, "Turkse discussies omtrent het christendom", in *Historische betrekkingen tussen Moslims en Christenen*, ed. Sj. van Koningsveld (Nijmegen, 1982), 116, 118, 123.

12 Brugman, *Godsdienstgesprekken*, 61. Cf. the Turkish sermon reported by a Christian prisoner in the 1450's; the preacher pointed out the errors of the Unbelievers concerning the death of Jesus: "the *kaury* say that Jesus was... crucified. You must not believe that". B. Stolz (transl.), S. Soucek (commentary), *Konstantin Mihailović, Memoirs of a Janissary* (Ann Arbor, 1975), 18-19, 202.

13 P.F. Sugar, *Southeastern Europe under Ottoman Rule, 1354-1804* (Seattle, London, 1977), 50, with earlier literature.

arranged by the Ottomans can be seen in this light.[14] One of the best known was the debate held on Whitsunday May 1547 in the church of the Franciscans in Nagyvárad (Grosswardein, Oradea Mare); the protagonists being a Turkish scholar named Dervis Çelebi, as organizer of the debate, and a Turkish-speaking Catholic humanist, Bartholomeus Georgievits, who later had his account of the debate printed in Cracow.[15]

This renewed energy in Ottoman-Christian religious polemic may be correlated with the situation of heightened tension in the two camps. Strictly Sunni *ulema*, their numbers vastly strengthened through the recent Ottoman conquests in the Near East, closed ranks against heterodoxy in general and the threat of the heterodox Shīʿa of the *Kızılbaş* in particular,[16] while a sense of crisis pervaded the "Frankish" camp in the wake of the Reformation.[17]

The Gurbetname

Proclaiming their faith against the adherents of what they considered an earlier and incomplete form of God's revelation, Turkish debaters found it useful to refer to Christian beliefs, and needed information which indeed existed in an ancient body of literature, mostly Arabic.[18] But not everyone had access to such books and could read Arabic. Especially in their new provinces in Europe, in strongholds in an alien land with a fluid frontier zone,[19] many a Muslim Turk must have felt the need for some exegetical equipment ready for use in his own language. It is surely no accident that such an equipment was provided by an unnamed sixteenth-century Turk within the framework of his "Book of Exile of Prince Cem" *Gurbetname-i Sultan Cem*. This book begins with a biography of

14 Göllner, *Türkenfrage*, is the best comprehensive study. See M.E.H.N. Mout, "Calvinoturcisme in de zeventiende eeuw", *Tijdschrift voor Geschiedenis*, 91 (1978), 593-595; idem, "Turken in het nieuws. Beeldvorming en publieke opinie in de zestiende-eeuwse Nederlanden", *TvG*, 97 (1984), 362-381.

15 Göllner, *Türkenfrage*, 208, with reference to his own *Turcica. Die europäischen Türkendrucke des XVI. Jahrhunderts* (Bucharest, Leipzig, Baden-Baden, 1961-1968), Nr. 879. On Georgievits's contribution to Turkology see G. Hazai, "Zum balkanischen Hintergrund der osmanisch-türkischen Transkriptionstexte von Bartholomaeus Georgievits", *Studia Slavica Hung.*, 20 (1974), 71-106.

16 H. İnalcık, *The Ottoman Empire. The Classical Age 1300-1600* (London, 1973), 182-185, with earlier literature. For demographic developments Gibb and Bowen, *Islamic Society*, 232.

17 Göllner, *Türkenfrage*, 173-186; Mout, "Calvinoturcisme", 582-585.

18 Lewis, *Muslim Discovery*, 136, 175, 182, 184.

19 Cf. Gy. Káldy-Nagy, "Mādjār. The Ottoman Period", *EI*², V (1984), 1023.

the well-known Ottoman prince who lived for twelve years in Europe, becoming, during the last years of his life, an instrument of Christian rulers for their political plans. Their diplomatic activity around his person and the Ottoman counter-measures as revealed by the Turkish archives have been the object of profound historical research up to the present day.[20]

The *Gurbetname* has been known since 1911 when Mehmed Arif mentioned it in the introduction to his edition of the *Vakiât-i Sultan Cem* cited above. In 1927 F. Babinger suggested that its author might be Cem's trusted follower Haydar Çelebi.[21] In 1954 I.H. Danişmend printed the text from a manuscript, now in Paris, in a modern Turkish transcription.[22] H. İnalcık in 1979 again drew attention to it; within the scope of his enquiry, the *Gurbetname* was a "modified version" and in many ways "simply a copy" of the *Vakiât-i Sultan Cem* into which the author inserted, "quite awkwardly" a long controversy on Islam and Christianity.[23] This controversy will be dealt with here, and it will be shown that the unnamed author of the *Gurbetname* had a purpose of his own. Using the travels of the Prince as an introduction to a long debate between Prince Cem and Pope Innocent VIII, he wrote in fact a Turkish apology for Islam which deserves to be studied as such. "It was my wish", the author said, "to write a brief and clear record[24] of the adventures of Prince Cem whom God has taken into his mercy and whose sins are forgiven – may his grave be pleasant and may he make Paradise his dwelling – and of the words[25] which he

20 The classical study is L. Thuasne, *Djem-Sultan. Fils de Mohammed II, frère de Bayezid II* (1459-1495). *Etude sur la question d'Orient à la fin du XVe siècle* (Paris, 1892). Recent treatments are by K.M. Setton, *The Papacy and the Levant (1204-1571), II, The Fifteenth Century*, (Philadelphia, 1978), especially the chapter entitled "Innocent VIII, Jem Sultan, and the Crusade (1484-1490)"; and H. İnalcık, "A Case Study in Renaissance diplomacy. The Agreement between Innocent VIII and Bayezid II on Djem Sultan", *Journal of Turkish Studies*, 3 (1979), 209-230; Vatin, "Exotisme" (cf. note 5).

21 See note 5; F. Babinger, *Die Geschichtsschreiber der Osmanen und ihre Werke* (Leipzig, 1927), 32, mentions a manuscript in the Halis Efendi library, which is now in the Library of the University of Istanbul; cf. H. İnalcık, "Djem", *EI*², II (1965), 535.

22 I.H. Danişmend, "Gurbet-nâme-i Sultan Cem", *Fâtih ve Istanbul*, II, 3/6, (Istanbul, 1954), 211-270. The call number of the Paris manuscript is Suppl. Turc 1434. For information about this manuscript I am grateful to J. Schmidt, Den Haag. My special thanks are due to Professor Adnan Erzi, Ankara, who gave me his own handwritten copy of the Paris manuscript in 1980.

23 İnalcık, "Case Study", 209.

24 *müsvedde* "rough copy, draft".

25 *Kelimat.*

exchanged with the Pope of Rome[26] on the subject of religion, in order that the reader be overcome by compassion and remember him with blessings and delight his soul. If eloquence is absent here this is not for want of rhetorical figures; rather, it is due to the fear that (an embellished text) might not be useful because, being illiterate, the greater part of the folks of the Ottoman dominions might not understand our purpose. And its brevity is occasioned by the fear that, should I transgress the boundaries of actual fact, there might be a lack of acceptance..."[27]

These *kelimat* or "words" – we might also use the term *meclis-i kelam* "discussion",[28] being consciously aimed at ordinary people, are written in the straightforward Turkish which we know from other popular works from the early sixteenth century. The writer adapts his theme to the understanding of his readers or listeners, embroidering it with stories to keep alive their interest. The popular appeal is also served by the approving and admiring remarks with which the Pope invites the Prince to speak and comments on his utterances.

"The Pope saw that the late Prince was a commander of the word and a profoundly learned man. He began to question him on his knowledge and said, 'We hear that you confirm our religion; is that so?' Watch now how the late Prince answered and refuted him. He said, 'Yes, we affirm the religion of Jesus – peace be upon him – but not your religion which was invented by those 318 monks gathered in Nicea.[29] If you will listen and not be offended, shall I make an explicit declaration?' The Pope said, 'God forbid that I should be offended by you! You are my son, say what you wish'".[30] "When (the late Prince) had said this, the Pope showed himself very much inclined and obliged and said, 'It is certainly my wish. Could there be a more beautiful and praiseworthy discussion? I wish that our whole life would pass in scholarly discussions!'"[31]

The Prince, too, treated the Pope with politeness; Christians in the *Gurbetname* are not referred to as "infidels", but the Koranic term "Nazarenes", *Naṣārā*, is used. The author quotes from a number of Muslim and Christian sources, named (for example, Abū Yazīd al-Balkhī) and unnamed. It is certain that the *Gurbetname* was from the beginning a composite work. In addition, the text seems to have suffered from some revision, especially at the junction between the historical biography of Cem and the religious debate.[32]

---

26 *Rim-Papa*. The title of the Pope is not followed by any formula such as "God speed his soul to Hell" etc., cf. Lewis, *Muslim Discovery*, 148.

27 Danişmend, "Gurbet-nâme", 213.

28 Used by the author here and there; "argumentation" in Islamic theology is *ḥudjdja*.

29 Council of Nicaea 325 A.D.

30 Danişmend, "Gurbet-nâme", 228.

31 Danişmend, "Gurbet-nâme", 231.

32 Danişmend, "Gurbet-nâme", 212 and 249.

The Prince had entered Rome on 13 March, 1489, huge crowds gathering to see him ride through the city.[33] The *Gurbetname* follows the *Vakiât* in describing how Cem was received by Innocent VIII – named *Visenso* as in the *Vakiât* but not identified by name in the debate,[34] and how the Pope gave him honours. It relates, still from the same source, Cem's proud refusal to genuflect before the Pope and his scornful rejection of the belief that the Pope could remit sins.[35] Cem did have a series of encounters with the Pope, but the disputation which now follows in the *Gurbetname* does not resemble them. There is no indication of the surroundings in which the debate took place. While this may cast doubts on the author's claim to autopsy, it is not inconceivable that he did belong to Cem's retainers – he alludes to his remaining in Rome to settle some important matters for the Prince when he left for Naples, where he died on 22 February 1495[36] – and that he set out, in his old age, to picture the son of the Conqueror emerging, from his dealings with the Christian enemy, as an impressive spokesman of Islam. A prophecy that Sultan Süleyman (1520-1566) would conquer Rome[37] allows us to date the work before 1566, perhaps in the thirties or the forties of the sixteenth century.[38]

The Dialogue between Cem and the Pope

The Islamic apology of the *Gurbetname* unfolds gradually over the course of an unspecified number of encounters with the Pope, and it is often really a monologue delivered by Cem. The Pope opened the debate with the words quoted above; "do you confirm our religion?"

---

33 Setton, *Papacy* II, 407.

34 Danişmend, "Gurbet-nâme", 222.

35 Cf. Lewis, *Muslim Discovery*. 178, with reference to the *Vakiât*; Vatin, "Exotisme", 243.

36 Setton, *Papacy* II, 481-482. The Sultan's purpose had always been the elimination of his brother; cf. İnalcık, "Case Study", 213. See also B. Flemming, "Zwei türkische Herren von Avlona", *Der Islam*, 45 (1969), 310-316; H. Reindl, *Männer um Bayezid. Eine prosopographische Studie über die Epoche Sultan Bāyezīds* II. (1481-1512) (Berlin, 1983), 303-308.

37 Danişmend, "Gurbet-nâme", 227-228; İnalcık, "Case Study", 218. For actual Turkish plans to invade Italy in about 1480 see Lewis, *Muslim Discovery*, 32. According to the *Gurbetname*, a Venetian scholar had written in a history book that after 920/beg. 26 February 1514 an Ottoman called Süleyman would become Sultan, that he would make great conquests in Hungary as elsewhere, and that he would finally fit out a great fleet and would conquer Rome. For signs and portents read by the Venetians, this time in relation to the fall of Rome to the French on 31 December 1494, see Setton, *Papacy* II, 473.

38 After the siege of Vienna; for a Turkish prophecy connected with that event see article 14 in this volume.

Five Gospels

Cem, going far back in his answer, acknowledges five gospels, of which only one, the genuine *Incil* was authentic revelation;[39] the other four gospels by Matthew, Mark, Luke and John being the work of those four men. He conceded that there were blessed sayings of the prophet Jesus in them, but he deplored the process of *tahrif*, corrupting and falsifying the sacred text, especially through the confusion of tongues caused by translating it into countless languages. By contrast, nobody in the whole world was capable of translating the book of Islam, the Koran, and of altering or corrupting a single line of it.[40]

Cem proceeded to tell a story about Salmān the Persian, a companion of the Prophet, from the time when he was still a Zoroastrian and fire worshipper. While hunting on a mountain, Salmān met an old ascetic monk who converted him to Christianity and told him about the Authentic Gospel which foretold the coming of the Prophet Muḥammed. In line with a tendency in the *Gurbetname* to avoid a direct mentioning of names, the monk's name is not given; his appearance is an obvious allusion to the monk Baḥira, an early witness for Islam in Muslim tradition.[41] The monk implored Salmān the Persian not to follow the actual corrupted religion of the Christians, because they no longer kept the Mosaic Law and the law of the Authentic Gospel, eating pork, rejecting circumcision, changing their orientation in prayer, and deifying Jesus and Mary. All this they did under the influence of a wicked Jewish scholar, whose story Cem had in prospect. But he first changed the subject by suggesting a discussion about the textual promise concerning the prophet of Islam.

The Paraclete

The old monk had read in the Authentic Gospel that Aḥmad, the seal of prophets, would come, and he had found the same announcement in the gospels of John and Mark: The Paraclete, the spirit of God, my father shall send him in my

39 Cf. Koran, 5 : 46.

40 This is an extension of the meaning of the technical term *iʿdjāz*, which originally referred to the inimitability of the Koran in content and form, applied to "competition" with the Koran, not to altering or translating it; cf. G.E. von Grünebaum, "Iʿdjāz", *EI*², III (1971), 1018-1020.

41 He is a heretical monk in Christian polemics; cf. A. Abel, "Baḥīra", *EI*², I (1960), 922-923; E. van Donzel, *ʿEnbāqom. Anqaṣa amin (La porte de la foi). Apologie éthiopienne du christianisme contre l'Islam à partir du Coran* (Leiden, 1969). For Salmān al-Fārisī see G. Levi della Vida, s.v., *EI*.

name, and the Paraclete shall teach you everything... And "father" here meant not father but lord, master.[42]

Cem now turned his full attention to the intricate questions raised by the concept of the *faraḳlīṭā*, Paraclete. He offered four interpretations. At first he borrowed from *al-Tafsīr al-Kabīr*, the great commentary of the Koran by Fakhr al-Dīn al-Rāzī (1149-1209).[43] After translating this Arabic classic, Cem displayed the range of his knowledge by offering a supplement, heard from a former monk converted to Islam, which he reproduced in "Greek" with a Persian translation, which he in turn translated into Turkish. It said: "From the people of Āzer, that is from the sons of the Prophet Abraham, there shall come one worthy of the prophethood... he shall be the son of one 'Abdallāh, and his blessed name shall be Muḥammad... Whosoever shall have faith in him shall be the master of the world and of the hereafter").[44]

Corruption of Religious Practice and Belief

"The Pope now reminded him, 'We should like to hear that tale from you about the man who did damage to the Christian religion. You were kind enough to promise us this, so if you do not think me over-persistent, please explain it'. Wishing to gain the goodwill of the Pope, the late Prince at once began with his story". It ran as follows.

The Christian community had been persecuted by a learned, but wicked Jew. When he was too old to harass them, he decided to mislead the Christians and began by pretending that he had been temporarily blinded by Jesus. Again the *Gurbetname* expressly avoids mentioning a name, although there are many indirect references to Paul.[45] This Jew, then, taught the Christians to abandon

42 The *locus classicus* is Sura 61 : 6, where Muḥammad is announced; cf. R. Paret, *Der Koran. Kommentar und Konkordanz* (Stuttgart, 1979), 476-477. For this *topos* in Muslim polemics, cf. F. Sepmeijer, *Een weerlegging van het Christendom uit de 10e eeuw* (Kampen, 1985), 94, 121, with earlier literature. For "lord, master" cf. J.-M. Gaudeul, "The Correspondence between Leo and 'Umar. 'Umar's Letter re-discovered?", *Islamochristiana*, 10 (1984), 139-140.

43 C.G. Anawati, "Fakhr al-Dīn al-Rāzī", *EI²*, II (1965), 754. Cf. J.M. Gaudeul and R. Caspar, "Textes de la Tradition musulmane concernant le *taḥrîf* (falsification des Ecritures)", *Islamochristiana*, 6 (1980), 61-104.

44 Danişmend, "Gurbet-nâme", 231-232.

45 For traditional accusations against Paul, which may reflect hostile criticism of Paul by Christian theologians favourable to Peter, cf. R.A. Nicholson, *The Mathnawí of Jalálu'ddin Rúmî. Commentary* (London, 1936), 36-39, cf. W.M. Watt, "Ash-Shahrastani over de

the Sabbath and to worship on Sunday, and he also encouraged them to drink wine. Moreover, he perverted their belief in the Authentic Gospel, confusing the three leaders of early Christianity. This archdeceiver was completely grounded in philosophy, *ilm-i hikmet*. Interestingly, the author puts the following words into Cem's mouth: "In those times philosophy was different. Nowadays Muslim scholars have intervened in this;[46] our sheikhs have thoroughly investigated those passages[47] which might be harmful to the faith (*itikad*). Everyone who studies those passages knows this".[48]

And thus the Jewish scholar misrepresented Jesus to the three Christian leaders, Melkā, Nastūr, and Mar Yaʿḳūb. They had started out believing that Jesus was the slave of God, his messenger and his word, but this false teacher gave each of them a different creed to follow, and they submitted to him, though grudgingly. When the deceiver vanished – there was conflicting evidence about his death and its whereabouts, one source being the *Mathnawī* by Mevlānā Djalāl al-Dīn Rūmī (d. 1273)[49] – the Christian leaders met and were startled to see that their creeds differed; they began to repudiate and abhor one another, the point at issue being the figure of Jesus.

Melkā, the leader of the Greek Orthodox, believed in Jesus the son of God, his word, brought by Gabriel, conceived miraculously by Mary,[50] born, lived among men, then returned to his father and sat at his right hand. Nestorius spoke of three hypostases; he argued, as the deceiver had told him, that Jesus was the Light of Light, Son of God, had entered Mary as a ray of light, became flesh, was born, lived and returned to his origin. Mar. Yaʿḳūb, as the Jew had told him, believed that God had no son and did not use light as his son; he came himself into Mary, took the form of man and drove away Satan.

triniteitsleer", *Historische betrekkingen* (cf. note 11), (1982), 9-10; idem, "ash-Shahrastānī's Account of Christian Doctrine", *Islamochristiana*, 9 (1983) 247-259, esp. 251 f. For later developments cf. M. Ayoub, "Muslim Views of Christianity: Some modern Examples", *Islamochristiana*, 10 (1984), 57, 66-67.

46 *karışdı*.

47 *yerler*; Danişmend, "Gurbet-nâme", 235-236.

48 Danişmend, "Gurbet-nâme", 235-236.

49 In the *Mathnawī* the deceiver was the vizier of a Jewish king; after contriving his plot against the Christians, he "killed himself in seclusion"; cf. R.A. Nicholson (ed.), *The Mathnawí of Jelálu'ddín Rúmí* (London, 1925), 41 verse 662; R.A. Nicholson (transl.), *The Mathnawí of Jalálu'ddín Rúmí*, I-II (London, 1926), 38; idem, vol. VII, *Commentary* (London, 1936), 36-39. For the explanation given by Fakhr al-Dīn al-Rāzī (cf. above) of how the Christians came to err, cf. J. Jomier, "Unité de Dieu, Chrétiens et Coran selon Faḫr al-Dīn al-Rāzī", *Islamochristiana*, 6 (1980), 170-171.

50 For Muslim doctrines regarding Mary, cf. Koran 3 : 33 f.; 3 : 47, 66: 12.

With this meagre "Christology" the author of the *Gurbetname* would seem to confirm the saying that Ottomans felt that "Christians of all colours were much alike".[51] The author did display some familiarity with the Nicene Creed, but did not puzzle his readers with the Orthodox tenet that Jesus had two natures, one divine and one human, but only one person. As for the Nestorians and Jacobites, regarded as heretical by the Orthodox and thrown together, despite their disparity, in one *millet*, the author took little notice of them. Their distinguishing tenets[52] were reduced to the level of vague stereotypes and reminiscences.[53] It was enough to explain the seeds of disagreement between the Christians.

Early Christian History

After this survey of early Christianity Cem proposed to set forth the life-story of Jesus and the history of the early Christian empires. This body of information, taken from Muslim and (so it seems) Byzantine sources, would require a different scale of treatment than can be given here.

A Dialogue within the Dialogue

After another lacuna in the manuscript we find Cem taking up an old story as testimony to the truth of Islam:

> Our purpose in recording this story is to prove the weakness of the Christian religion; neither by reason nor by tradition[54] can its sayings be accepted as even resembling the divine word.[55]

Cem reproduced a polemic in which a learned Muslim, an Arab sheikh, refuted first a Christian called Beshīr, then a monk called in to help Beshīr, and finally the greatest monk at the emperor's court in Constantinople. The learned Muslim was a prisoner of the emperor; the Christians hoped to convert him; surrounded by great crowds he addressed the monks; they plotted to put him

51 Gibb and Bowen, *Islamic Society*, 233.

52 Cf. Sepmeijer, *Weerlegging*, 37-42, 109-111.

53 E.g., "light of light", taking up a conventional theme from Platonism.

54 *ne aklen ve ne naklen*.

55 Danişmend, "Gurbet-nâme", 247.

to death; finally, he recited the call to prayer in their great church and was set free by the emperor, a just man, who let him go back to his own country. It is easy to find features of Cem's life in this story; one is tempted to suspect that the author was inspired by this older debate.

When we consider the civility and even amiability of Cem's encounters with the Pope, it is surprising to observe the acrimony with which this Muslim sheikh attacked his enemies. Jesus was a prophet, not the son of God, and he could list weak points in the Christian doctrines to prove it. Either Jesus endured bodily suffering as a helpless man: then how could they call him God? Or his sufferings happened with his divine consent: then why did they curse the Jews? They said that Jesus was God or the son of God because he performed miracles: they should look in the Torah and the Histories of the Prophets, *Ḳıṣaṣ ül-Enbiyā'*, at the other prophets who had the power to work miracles – some also went up to heaven – and they should draw the conclusion that Jesus was a prophet like the others.[56] Jesus was created by God, without an earthly father: so was Adam who had no father and no mother, either. They had better worship Adam! Jesus was in need of cleansing: John the Baptist[57] cleansed and baptized him. How could they say that Jesus was holy, and John the Baptist was not! The monks were liars: they claimed powers to purify the water of baptism, knowing that, being sinners, they did not have these powers. Their divine redeemer had humiliated himself to a sojourn of nine months in a woman's womb:[58] and here their greatest monk disdained intercourse with women. As for prostrating oneself in front of the greatest monk: this was blasphemy, man ought to prostrate himself only before God.

After this, the Pope was mortified; the following question represented his last stand: "'My son, did not the Messiah say: there will not come a prophet after me?' The late Prince replied, 'Yes, this saying is true; but it refers to the prophets of the children of Israel;[59] there is no doubt about this, just as the pride of the two worlds, Muḥammad Muṣṭafā – may God commend and salute him – is the seal of the prophets'". Here ends the disputation, *meclis-i kelam*, in which, just as in later debates, the Prince had not yielded on a single point. The *Gurbetname* now proceeds to tell its own story of the death of the Prince.[60]

56 For the theme "Other prophets performed miracles" cf. Gaudeul, "Correspondence between Leo and 'Umar", 146-147.

57 Yaḥyā. For the creation of Adam cf. Gaudeul, "Correspondence between Leo and 'Umar", 146.

58 Cf. Gaudeul, "Correspondence between Leo and 'Umar", 144-145.

59 Koran, Sūra 3: 49.

60 İnalcık, "Case Study", 217.

This study, too, has almost reached its end. It has set out to trace the polemical equipment to which a sixteenth-century Turk might have had recourse in order to refute a Christian who took up the challenge, suggesting that the *Gurbetname* was indeed written for such a purpose. To be sure, it does seem a curious shortcoming that his author had so little to say about the contemporary Latin Church. Events in Rome, ostensibly witnessed by him, did not stimulate him to report more about Catholic beliefs and practices than the outrageous claim, copied from the *Vakiât*, of the Pope to forgive sins. The *Gurbetname's* mental world was Islamic, Turkish-speaking, with a knowledge of Persian and some Arabic, and, as far as Christianity was concerned, it was reasonably familiar with a Greek Orthodox Church whose theology was rooted in a remote age before the schism which split the "Melkites" into West and East.[61] This tradition had tended to shield the Turkish-speaking Muslims from information about, for example, the dispute about images, the filioque-clause, or the primacy of Rome.[62] Seen from this vantage-point, the Latin Christians in the West were dissenters from the Great Church, not to speak of the emerging Protestants.

Further questions, such as the relationship between the *Gurbetname* and later Ottoman Turkish writings on this theme[63][62a] go beyond this short survey. For example, the memoirs of Turkish prisoners returning from Christian lands in the seventeenth century might help us to understand their thoughts over Christianity such as they witnessed it.[64] The learned Katib Çelebi (died 1657), who used Western books, gave his scholarly description of Christian doctrines a less polemical edge than is to be expected from his defiant Koranic

61 Lewis, *Muslim Discovery*, 176. For the attitude of the Latins towards the Byzantines cf. R.W. Southern, *Western Society and the Church in the Middle Ages* (Harmondsworth, 1970), 82.

62 B. Lewis noted that even Katib Çelebi's list of Popes stopped in 1535; Muslim *Discovery*, 179.

63 62a When the Ottoman scholar Taʿlīkīzāde (died c. 1599) composed his *Şemāʾilnāme*, examples of the qualities distinguishing individual Ottomans, he became fascinated by Cem in Rome, embroidering its description and introducing additional dialogues. These are discussed in J. Buri-Gütermann, "Ein Türke in Italien. Aus einer unbekannten Handschrift der Nationalbibliothek Wien", ZDMG, 124 (1974), 59-72. A different Vienna manuscript has since been described in C. Woodhead, *Taʿlīḳīzāde's Şehnāme-i hümāyūn* (Berlin, 1983), 12.

64 Autobiographical accounts of former prisoners-of-war are I. Parmaksızoğlu, "Bir Türk kadısının esaret hatıraları", *Tarih Dergisi*, 5 (1953), 77 ff., and F. Kreutel, *Die Autobiographie des Dolmetschers ʿOsmān Aġa aus Temeschwar. Der Text des Londoner Autographen in normalisierter Rechtschreibung* (Cambridge-Hertford, 1980).

opening.[65] The great traveller Evliya Çelebi (died 1682) was much closer to the popular approach of the *Gurbetname*. When he was in Antioch he visited Mount Nakūra, where stood the sanctuary of Shemʿūn Ṣafā, who in Muslim lore represents the apostle Peter. According to him, Shemʿūn lived and died there, together with Ḥabīb en-Nedjdjār, "the Carpenter", an unnamed believer referred to in the Koran. In their sanctuary the Authentic Gospel, *ṣaḥīḥ Indjīl*, was preserved, written by Shemʿūn on a gazelle skin. Evliya pored over it and took from it the verse, *ayet*, which was also recorded in Salmān the Persian's story: that Muḥammad was the man about whom the Authentic Gospel says: "He shall be a prophet from the house of Āzer, he shall be without falsehood, he shall be born in Mecca... his name shall be Aḥmed... and his followers shall own the earth".[66]

This old prophecy runs through Muslim religious polemics of the nineteenth and twentieth century.[67] Quite recently the confident, combative spirit of the *Gurbetname* reappeared in a "Handbook for the (Muslim in) Exile", *Gurbetçinin El Kitabı*.[68] This book, and similar publications, provide an indication of the extent to which these polemics will take on the colour of the age in which they are written. Any history of Turkish Islam must take into account this development of religious apology.

65 Flemming, "Turkse discussies", 120.

66 Evliya Çelebi, *Seyahatname* III (Istanbul, 1928), 103; cf. the modernized version by Z. Danışman (Istanbul, 1972), 4, 298-300. On Ḥabīb an-Nadjdjār see *EI*² s.v.

67 Cf. the survey by Bursalı Mehmed Tahir, *Osmanlı Müellifleri* I (Istanbul 1333 / 1914-15), 247-48.

68 E. Sanay, *Gurbetçinin El Kitabı* (Ankara 1984), 74-80, quoting the prophecy concerning Muḥammad from the *Seyahatname*. The Handbook is publication nr. 238 of the Directorate of Religious Affairs of the Turkish Republic. For a recent international debate, the Dialogue arranged by Muʿammar al-Kadhdhāfī in Tripoli, Libya, in February 1976, see *Islamochristiana*, II (Rome, 1976) and V (Rome, 1979) 291 f. on the book by A.A. Aydın, *Islam-Hiristiyan Diyalogu ve Islam in Zaferi* ("The dialogue between Islam and Christianity and the victory of Islam") (Ankara, 1977).

CHAPTER 20

Glimpses of Turkish Saints: Another Look at Lamiʿi and Ottoman Biographers

Introduction

It is generally acknowledged that mystical writing reached a peak of attainment in Anatolia in the thirteenth century, and great masters of mystical thought and poetry such as Yahya as-Suhrawardi al-Maktul (d. 1191), Nacm ad-Din Daya Razi (1177-1256),[1] Baha'uddin Valad (d. 1231),[2] Calal ad-Din Rumi and his mystical friend Shams-i Tabrizi,[3] Muhyi ad-Din ibn al-ʿArabi,[4] Sadr ad-Din Konawi (Konevi, d. 1274),[5] and his pupil, the Sufi master Saʿd or Saʿid ad-Din Farghani,[6] the visiting scientist Kutb ad-Din Shirazi (1236-1311),[7] Fahr ad-Din ʿIraki (d. 1289),[8] can be cited as outstanding exponents of this achievement of Persianate culture.[9] Turkish culture, with vestiges of shamanism,[10] was alive in the sheykhs Baba Ilyas

1 Annemarie Schimmel, *Mystical Dimensions of Islam*, Chapel Hill, 1975, 257; J.T.P. de Bruijn, The Qalandariyāt in Persian Mystical Poetry, from Sanā'ī Onwards", in L. Lewisohn (ed.), *The Legacy of Medieval Persian Sufism*, London/New York 1992, 80; M.I. Waley, "A Kubrawī Manual of Sufism: The Fusūs al-ādāb of Yaḥyā Bākharzī", in Lewisohn, *Legacy*, 290-291.

2 Fritz Meier, *Baha-i Walad. Grundzüge seines Lebens und seiner Mystik*, Leiden 1989.

3 A. Schimmel, "Yusuf in Mawlana Rumi's Poetry", in Lewisohn, *Legacy*, 45-60; V. Holbrook, "Diverse Tastes in the Spiritual Life: Textual Play in the Diffusion of Rumi's Order", in Lewisohn, *Legacy*, 103.

4 William C. Chittick, *Ibn al-ʿArabi's Metaphysics of Imagination. The Sufi Path of Knowledge*, New York, 1989.

5 Gudrun Schubert, *Annäherungen. Der mystisch-philosophische Briefwechsel zwischen Ṣadr ud-Dīn-i Qōnawī und Naṣīr ud-Dīn-i Ṭūsī*, 2nd ed. Beirut 2011.

6 Chittick, "Spectrums of Islamic Thought", *Legacy*, 203-218; John T. Walbridge, "A Sufi Scientist of the Thirteenth Century: The Mystical Ideas and Practices of Qutb al-Din Shirazi", Lewisohn, *Legacy*, 326-327.

7 Walbridge, "A Sufi Scientist", Lewisohn, *Legacy*, 324 f.

8 W.C. Chittick and P.L. Wilson, *Fakhruddin ʿIraqi: Divine Flashes*, New York 1981; Chittick, "Spectrums of Islamic Thought", Lewisohn, *Legacy*, 207.

9 A. Ateş, "Hicrî VI-VIII./XI-XIV. asırlarda Anadolu'da Farsça eserler", *TM* VII-VIII (1945), 94ff; Schimmel, *Mystical Dimensions*, 315; L. Lewisohn, "Iranian Islam and Persianate Sufism", Lewisohn, *Legacy*, 25.

10 For a study of the Kalenders see Ahmet Yaşar Ocak, *Osmanlı İmparatorluğunda Marjinal Sûfîlik: Kalenderîler (XIV-XVII. Yüzyıllar)*, Ankara, 1992.

 | DOI 10.1163/9789004355767_021

and Baba Ishak, who were remembered in hagiography[11]. In the fourteenth century, as part of a broader advance in literary and religious standards, the writing of Arabic and Persian works continued. This is attested by Kadi Burhan ed-Din's eminent prose works written in Arabic[12], by the extensive works of the jurist and mystic Sheykh Bedr ed-Din of Samavna (executed as a rebel in 1416) including the *Waridat*; by the Persian prose written by Ahmad Ilahi,[13] by the historian Karim ad-Din Aksarayi (d. after 1320) and the hagiographers, Faridun b. Ahmad Sipahsalar,[14] Shams ad-Din Ahmad Aflaki[15] and ʿAziz b. Ardashir Astarabadi.[16] Also included is the Persian poetry composed by Sufi poets, not only Sultan Veled,[17] but also Sayf-i Farghani who composed a voluminous divan of mystical poetry containing two long reproachful kasides, called the "Tears of Anatolia", addressed to the Ilkhan Ghazan.[18] But in the course of the same century Turkish works, especially those concerned primarily with the aim of spiritual advice and exhortation, were increasingly compiled and circulated. Such works are: Sultan Veled's Turkish verses, Yunus Emre's *ilahis* and his *Risale*,[19] the long mesnevis by Gülshehri, ʿAshık Pasha (d. 1332) and his son Elvan Pasha (d. after 1358).[20] Among Ahmad

11 Ismail E. Erünsal and A. Yaşar Ocak have edited *Elvan Çelebi. Menâkibu'l-Kudsiyye fi Menâsibi'l Ünsiyye*, Istanbul, 1984, a Turkish mesnevi dated 760/1358-9.

12 William C. Chittick, "Sultan Burhan al-Din's Sufi Correspondence", in *WZKM* 73 (1981), 33-45.

13 According to Kasım Kufralı, "Molla İlâhî ve Kendisinden Sonraki Nakşbendîye Muhiti", *TDED* III (1948), 131, Ahmed Ilahi who wrote, in 1475/76, a Persian commentary of Sadr ad-Din Konawi's *Miftah al-ghaib* at the request of Sultan Mehmed II, in a *zawiye* in the port Edremit in Western Anatolia, is not identical with ʿAbdullah Ilahi as suggested by Chittick, "Burhan al-Din's Sufi Correspondence", 37.

14 Faridun b. Ahmad Sipahsalar, *Risala-yi Ahwal-i Mawlana*, ed. Sa'id Nafisi, Tehran 1325/1946. V.R. Holbrook, "Diverse Tastes in the Spiritual Life", 99, with more literature.

15 The author of the *Manakib al-ʿArifin*, edited by Tahsin Yazıcı, 1959-1961. John O'Kane (transl.), *The Feats of the Knowers of God: Manāqeb al-ʿārifīn*, Leiden, 2002. The work was begun in 718 and completed in the second redaction in 754/1353 (died in Konya in 761/1360). V.R. Holbrook, "Diverse Tastes in the Spiritual Life", Lewisohn, *Legacy*, 99 and 103-105.

16 *Bazm u razm*; summarized by H.H. Giesecke, *Das Werk des Aziz Ibn Ardaşir Astarabadi. Eine Quelle zur Geschichte des Spätmittelalters in Kleinasien*, Leipzig, 1940.

17 V.R. Holbrook, "Diverse Tastes in the Spiritual Life", Lewisohn, *Legacy*, 103, with literature.

18 A. Ateş, "Anadolu'nun Unutulmuş Büyük Bir Şairi: Sayf al-Dīn Muhammed al-Farġānī", *Belleten* XXII (1959), 415-456.

19 The most recent critical edition is Mustafa Tatçı, *Yunus Emre Divanı I-III*, Ankara, 1990, containing the divan and the *Risaletü n-Nushiyye*, accompanied by a full analysis.

20 For full information on Elvan Pasha (later entitled Chelebi) and his father see İ.E. Erünsal and A.Y. Ocak, *Elvan Çelebi. Menâkıbu'l-Kudsiyye fî Menâsıbi'l-Ünsiyye*, Istanbul, 1984, xxiii-lxix.

Yasawi's (Yesevi's, d. 1166) distant followers were the disciples of Barak Baba[21] who amazed the town-dwellers by their strange attire. Baba Ilyas, Haccı Bektash, and Emir Sultan (1368-1429) were Turkish saints from the east; the latter came to Bursa in the early years of Bayezid I.[22] Tapduk Emre who was Yunus Emre's spiritual leader[23] and to whom the Bektashis also lay claim, may have belonged to the Kalenders who were known for their contempt of outward forms of morality and religion. The Turkish works of Ahmed Fakih[24] and Sheyyad Hamza, or the *Kıssa-yi Yusuf* by an unknown 'Ali (13th century?), may have been recorded more for their moral content than for their literary merit. Kadi Burhan ed-Din's Turkish *Divan*[25] was preserved only in one copy in that prince's library, whereas countless copies circulated of Süleyman Çelebi's *Vesiletü n-necat*; Bedr ed-Din's son-in-law Eshrefoghlu Rumi (d. 1469),[26] the author of the *Müzekki n-nüfus* (completed 1448),[27] Nesimi the martyred poet (between 1404 and 1417),[28] are names provided by recent research.

To draw from this synchronic and diachronic mass a coherent picture of what sixteenth-century Ottomans would have thought of the early saints, we may turn to their biographers.[29] Did they remind the Ottomans that Karaman and the old province of Rum had possessed saintly men who could challenge comparison with their own? We may apply the criterion of attestation: if a 'pre-Ottoman' saint can be seen to exist in, say, Taşköprüzade's hagiographies, then that person was probably considered saintly in the Ottoman age as well. But when it comes to Ottoman biographers of poets and their arrangement of the lives of saints, what do they write about Nesimi? Why is Yunus Emre omitted by one and praised by

21 H. İnalcık, *The Ottoman Empire. The Classical Age*, London 1973, 186; s.v. EI new edition.

22 Cavid Baysun, "Emîr Sultan" in *İA*.

23 Schimmel, *Dimensions*, 329.

24 Fahir İz, "Ahmed, Fakih", in EI2 Supplement (1980), 50, with reference to the revision proposed by T. Gandjeï.

25 Ali Nihad Tarlan, "Kadı Burhaneddin'de Tasavvuf", *TDED* VIII (1958), 8-15 (commentary of the first ghazel).

26 William Hickman, "Eshrefoğlu Rumi: Fifteenth Century Anatolian Mystic Poet", PhD diss., Harvard University, 1972 (not seen).

27 For this work see M. Götz, *Türkische Handschriften Teil* 2, Wiesbaden, 1968 (VOHD XIII,2), 22 no. 28 and 101 no. 144, with earlier literature.

28 Kathleen R.F. Burrill, *The Quatrains of Nesimî. Fourteenth-Century Turkic Hurufi*, The Hague/Paris, 1972.

29 B. Kellner-Heinkele, "Osmanische Biographiensammlungen", *Anatolica* 6 (1977-1978), 171-194, covers classical biographies to the end of the eighteenth century; her study "The transmission history of a text of joint authorship", *Manuscripts of the Middle East* 3 (1988), 45-53, concerns a work written between 1744 and 1846. Barbara Kellner-Heinkele (ed.), *Devhat ül-Meşāyiḫ*, 2 volumes, Wiesbaden 2006 (Mustakimzade, Münib, Süleyman Faik)

another? Such questions, already asked by E.J.W. Gibb,[30] are easier to ask than to answer; and it may be instructive to look a little more closely into the complexities of Turkish saints commemorated by Taşköprüzade and his forerunner Lamiʿi. This paper presents glimpses which I offer as a small token of friendship and of deep appreciation and respect.

Taşköprü[lü]zade Ahmed

ʿIsam ed-Din Ahmed b. Mustafa, known as Taşköprüzade, was one of the great Ottoman scholars, who wrote an impressive number of theological and encyclopaedic works[31]. But it is for the "Peonies (Anemones) containing the scholars of the Ottoman Empire", *aş-Şaka'iku n-nuʿmaniya fi ʿulama'i d-dawlati l-ʿUthmaniya*,[32] that magnum opus to which he devoted most of his life, that he is rightly remembered. His language was still Arabic, the medium of scholarly writing, and because of this the "Peonies" are known principally through the Turkish translations which began to appear soon after Taşköprüzade had to conclude his work, in 1558, because of failing eyesight. Along with the Arabic original[33], these Turkish translations of Taşköprüzade, especially Edirneli Mecdi's *Hada'ik aş-Şaka'ik*,[34] and O. Rescher's German translation,[35] have been chosen for much distinguished research as a primary biographical source.[36]

30 *HOP* I, 392: "It is not easy to say why [Yazıcı oghlu Mehemmed] is omitted by ʿAshık [Chelebi] and [Kınalızade] Hasan Chelebi. These two biographers seem to have deliberately ignored most of the old religious poets; ʿAshiq Pasha is not so much as mentioned by either, while Suleymán, the author of the Birthsong, is referred to only by ʿAshiq Chelebi, and that in the most perfunctory manner" (Gibb).

31 *GAL* II 425-426; S II 633-634. My "Tashköprüzāde 2.", *EI* X (2000), pp. 351-352.

32 GOW 84. For the *Şaka'ik* and its continuations see R. Repp, "Some Observations on the Development of the Ottoman Learned Hierarchy", and B.G. Martin, "A Short History of the Khalwati Order of Dervishes", in N.R. Keddie, *Scholars, Saints, and Sufis*, London, 1972, 18-19 and 275.

33 A critical edition has been published by Ahmed Subhi Furat, *Eş-Şeka'iku n-Nu'maniye fi ʿUlema'i d-Devleti l-'Osmaniye*, Istanbul 1985.

34 Behcet Gönül, "Istanbul Kütüphanelerinde al-Şaka'ik al-Nu'maniya Tercüme ve Zeyilleri", 138, 151-152; Bekir Kütükoğlu, Art. Medjdi (d. 1591), in *EI2*.

35 Oskar Rescher, *Es-Saqa'iq en-No'manijje von Tasköprüzade. Mit Zusätzen und Anmerkungen aus dem Arabischen übersetzt*, Konstantinopel/Stuttgart 1927-1934. Reissue Osnabrück 1978. The translation is based mainly on the text of the "Peonies" printed on the margin of the 1310/1893 Cairo edition of Ibn Khallikan's *Wafayyāt al-ʿayān*, collated with several good manuscripts, with occasional recourse to Mecdi's Turkish translation.

36 See for example H.J. Kissling, "Aus der Geschichte des Chalvetijje-Ordens", *ZDMG* 103 (1953), 234. It is noteworthy that Erünsal and Ocak (*Elvan Çelebi*), writing before Furat's edition was

Taşköprüzade was born in 1495, in Bursa, and died in 1561, in Istanbul. The *Şaka'ik*, up to 965/1558, applies the *tabakat* or "class" principle, as was fitting for a book on about five hundred eminent scholars and dervish sheykhs. In terms of book division, these ten "classes" correspond to the reigns of ten Ottoman sultans, culminating in the reign of Sultan Süleyman. The relative inequality of the ten parts in Taşköprüzade is due, of course, to his material, but may also lead one to form an idea of the significance which holiness had for this author. Notable examples in a book on Ottoman personalities are the lives of 'Abdurrahman Cami, of Khwaca Baha' ad-Din Nakshband, of Muhammad Parsa, and of Khwaca 'Ubaydullah Ahrar, the Nakshbandi sheykh and effective ruler in Central Asia (1404-1490).[37] 'Ubaydullah Ahrar never came near the Ottoman Empire, but his luminous apparition in a battle had aided Sultan Mehmed II. Taşköprüzade's source materials still need investigating, and the extent to which Taşköprüzade is dependent on Lami'i's Turkish *Nafahat al-uns* is especially interesting. Taşköprüzade could make claims to comprehensiveness which Lami'i did not. One must suppose that his biographies of scholars were based in part at least on material gathered professionally during many years of *medrese* teaching, and as judge of Istanbul. As a boy he had visited the tomb of sheykh Elvan in a village near Amasya. When, however, he undertook the composition of a combined volume of the scholars and Sufis of the Ottoman Empire – adding the foreigners already referred to – he had to go back in time to a date well beyond his own birth and experience. His solution was to base part of his hagiographies on information transmitted in his own family; his father had told him many things that he had heard and seen; he knew that he had heard a certain name from his deceased father which he could not recall at the moment, or his uncle on his mother's side; the sons of people he described were his informants. He also recorded things "from the lips of Kemalpashazade himself"[38], and could use the *Terceme-i Nafahatu l-uns* of his compatriot Lami'i. In reading many of the pages on early Sufis in the *Şaka'ik*, it must be remembered that the author one is reading is really Lami'i. Taşköprüzade translates long passages from him almost word for word, obliquely acknowledging his debt to him in his obituary on Lami'i, whom he classes among the Sufi sheykhs under Selim I. In this way Taşköprüzade became not only the biographer of the scholars but also the hagiographer of the saints, presenting, as the late Behçet Necatigil wrote in 1945, a book containing the lives of Turkish scholars and sheykhs, for which

available, base their Taşköprüzade quotations on Mecdi's translation. Taşköprüzade does not say that 'Ashık Pasha came "from outside"; he was born in Kırşehir as the son of Mukhlis Baba who had already been born in the *bilad-i Karaman*.

37 Hamid Algar, "Ahrar," *EI2* Suppl. (1980), 50-52.

38 *HOP* II, 348.

Lamiʿi had laid the foundations with his *Terceme-i Nafahat*.[39] It is astonishing that the earlier book has been so consistently overlooked by Western specialists. For not only does it help to understand difficult passages of the Arabic text of Taşköprüzade,[40] it also presents readings from which Taşköprüzade started out and which he decided to change according to his own perceptions. These are of interest not merely in themselves, but because they help to detect changes in the historical tradition. Lamiʿi was a Nakshbendi sheykh, Taşköprüzade a member of the Khalweti order. These and other circumstances no doubt had some influence on the tone and content of some biographies. For example, their versions differ subtly as to the role of the Khalweti sheykh Chelebi Khalifa in the topical story of Karamanlı Mehmed Pasha's downfall and the triumph of Bayezid II,[41] and in Sheykh Vefa's biography. Taşköprüzade's short notices on Yunus Emre and Haccı Bektash quite clearly echo, but do not directly correspond to, two of the shortest notices at the end of Lamiʿi's 'sandwiched' chapter in the Turkish *Nafahat*. A sober, principled and hard-working author,[42] Taşköprüzade organizes his material with an Ottoman ʿalim's sense of career and promotion. He often changes Lamiʿi's direct speech to a more distant "it is related". Minor discrepancies aside (did Mavlana Tusi meet Sheykh Ilahi in Tabriz or in Kerman?), his strength is that he is so well connected and "knows all about anybody who was anybody". Some criticism has been levelled at Taşköprüzade by O. Rescher (1883-1972; his translation also serves as a memorial to this distinguished scholar) who, while praising the quality of Taşköprüzade's research and his moral integrity, takes exception to his dry expository manner and hesitates to put him next to the great spirits of the Islamic past.

Lamiʿi's Terceme

Lamiʿi's Turkish *Terceme-i Nafahat* cannot be accused of being dry; a characteristic at least of his additions is their rambling style and their unpredictability, passing from the lawful killing of a scorpion during ritual prayer to a discussion of essentials of Sufism. Its Persian model, ʿAbdurrahman Cami's *Nafahat al-uns min*

39 Behcet Gönül, "Istanbul Kütüphanelerinde al-Şaka'ik al-Nu'maniya Tercüme ve Zeyilleri", TM VII-VIII (1945), 136-137.

40 Occasional recourse to the *Terceme-i Nafahat* has given O. Rescher useful guidance for his translation of the *Şaka'ik*.

41 Martin, "Khalwati Order of Dervishes", 281-282, with earlier literature.

42 For a study of the author's introduction to the "Peonies" see M.T. Gökbilgin, "Taşköprü-zade ve ilmî görüşleri", *İslam Tetkikleri Dergisi* 6 (1976), 127-138. The continuation of this article, *İslam Tetkikleri Dergisi* 6 1976 (1977), 169-182, has not been accessible to me.

hadarat al-kuds[43] with its biographies of saintly poets (ending with Hafiz) and concluding chapter on holy women, dated 1496, is often cited for Persian saints, while less mention seems to have been made of his lives of Turkish saints. Lamiʿi's Turkish *Terceme-i Nafahat* has had a wide, if indirect, influence on Turkish letters. It appeared in two early letterpress editions published in 1270/1853-54 and 1289/1872. The latter is apparently still considered definitive and has been reissued with a preface by Süleyman Uludağ.[44] To my knowledge no attempt has so far been made to collate all the known manuscripts[45] or to elucidate the relationship between them. I am indebted to the ʿAmire edition of 1872[46] for the quotations from the *Terceme-i Nefahat* which follow.

Lamiʿi's translation was completed in June 1521,[47] entitled *Fütuhu l-mücahidin li-tervihi l-kulubi l-müshahidin* and dedicated to Sultan Süleyman who was about to conquer Belgrade. The work took Lamiʿi nine years. It became known under its shorter title *Terceme-i Nefahat al-üns*.

Mahmud b. ʿOsman with the pen-name Lamiʿi was born in 1472 in Bursa and died there in 1531. Because of his prominence, he has been comparatively well studied, and several surveys of his life and writings are available.[48] But biographical details are still coming to light, such as Lamiʿi's taking part in the campaign of Bayezid II in the Morea in 906/1500-01 where he witnessed a miracle.[49] A little-known work of his has been described,[50] and the list of his estate dated 15 Zilhicce 938/19 July 1532, recently discovered in the Bursa archives, shows that his own

43 Ed. Mahdi Tawhidipur, Tahran 1337 sh. For the importance of the work see A. Schimmel, *Mystical Dimensions*, 465.

44 The reissue dated Istanbul 1980, with a preface on Cami and Lamiʿi by Süleyman Uludağ, is based on the ʿAmire edition dated Istanbul 1289. Faruk Timurtas, *Klasik Osmanlıca*, p. 422, reproduced the passage on Yunus Emre, p. 691 from the 1270 edition.

45 37 MSS in Istanbul alone had been described in catalogues in *Istanbul yazmaları*, 6. fasikül, Istanbul 1946, no. 303; three were in the Ist. Üniv. Manuscripts are listed by Kut, *JNES*, 78; N. Tezcan 1979, 323-324, with a listing of microfilms in the Milli Ktph. in Ankara, 337-338; cf. my catalogue (VOHD XIII,1) no. 254, and M. Götz, *Türkische Handschriften*, Wiesbaden 1979 (VOHD XIII,4) no. 140.

46 Fahir İz, *Türk Edebiyatında Nesir. XIV. yüzyıldan XIX. yüzyıl ortasına kadar yazmalarden seçilmiş metinler I*, Istanbul 1964, 212-223, published the biographies of Sheykh Ilahi and of Lami'i's own teacher Seyyid Ahmed el-Bukhari from the MS Topkapı Sarayı, Revan 498.

47 M. Götz, *Türkische Handschriften*, Wiesbaden, 1979 (VOHD XIII, 4).

48 On Lami'i, see A. Karahan, "Lâmii" in *İA* VII (1957); Günay Kut Alpay, "Lami'i Chelebi and His Works", *JNES* 35 (1976); N. Tezcan, "Bursalı Lâmiî Çelebi", *Türkoloji Dergisi* VIII; E. Birnbaum, "The Ottomans and Chagatay Literature", *CAJ* 20 (1977), 166; my article in *EI* V (1986), 649-651.

49 H. Sohrweide, *Türkische Handschriften. Teil 5*, Wiesbaden, 1981, 20-21 (VOHD XIII,5).

50 H. Sohrweide, *Türkische Handschriften und einige in den Handschriften enthaltene persische und arabische Werke*, Wiesbaden, 1974, 246-247 no. 283 (VOHD XIII,3).

copy of his *Terceme* as well as the Persian *Nafahat* were in his possession at the time of his death[51].

Investigation is needed on the transformation which Cami's lives of saints underwent in the hands of his Turkish translator. Lamiʿi had translated Cami's biographies with his own intellectual authority, knowledge and an enthusiasm which led him to add lives of saints, including that of ʿAbdurrahman Cami himself. But his zeal was not satisfied. Not only did he feel that "this noble book should not entirely fail to mention the sheykhs of Rum", but "their number exceeded expression, and it was not easy to succeed in writing their lives". "After the Ottoman conquest alone, even a short description of their lives would fill volumes". Their austerity and their miraculous powers had to be described. With this in mind Lamiʿi produced substantial biographies in addition to those found in Cami's work, ending with biographical notices of varying length of Hamid b. Musa al-Kayseri, Haccı Bayram, Ak Shems ed-Din, Sheykh ʿAshık Pasha (under Orkhan), Ibrahim [Tannuri], Geyiklü Baba, Yazıcızade Mehmed, finishing with only the briefest information on Yunus Emre and Haccı Bektash.[52] This chapter he then sandwiched between the end of Cami's chapter on Sufi poets and the final chapter on saintly women.

Lamiʿi's Sources

It seems that no historian has as yet satisfactorily investigated the sources upon which Lamiʿi's additions depend. To cover the huge field which he had mapped out for himself, Lamiʿi relied mainly on his eyes and ears, his personal connections, and his books. He had recourse to Kemalpashazade's (d. 1534) History of the Ottoman Dynasty, showing his appreciation for the work of this first-rank historian[53] which was then quite new. No doubt he made use of documentary sources and inscriptions, in addition to Cami, but most of his material was collected in the way he describes: by being present at medreses, by going about asking questions, and by conversations with high officials and travelling Sufis. Immediately afterwards he may have written notes on what he had been told, resulting in a special kind of hagiography, combining the virtues and defects

51 İsmail E. Erünsal, "Türk Edebiyatı Tarihi Arşiv Kaynakları IV: Lami'i Çelebi'nin Terekesi", *JTS* 14 (1990), 179-194 (Fahir İz Armağanı I).

52 Behcet Gönül [Necatigil], "Iśtanbul Kütüphanelerinde al-Şaka'ik al-Nu'maniya Tercüme ve Zeyilleri", *TM* VII-VIII (1945), 137.

53 For Kemalpashazade's career see R. Repp, "Ottoman Learned Hierarchy" in Keddie, 28. Lami'i used it for his description of the conquest of Constantinople.

of the individual eye-witness, the mystic, and the historian. His talent for reproducing spoken language produced a fascinating work which does contain some puzzles. He may be proved wrong on points of detail. But because of his contemporary position he had access to sources of information lost to the biographers of the next generation. He made notes of the sayings of, to name a few, his revered teacher Seyyid Ahmed el-Bukhari (d. 922/1516-17); of sheykh Gevrelü Uzun Muslih ed-Din;[54] of Sheykh ʿAbdurrahim Mısırluoghlu;[55] of the grandson of ʿUbaydallah-i Ahrar[56]; the imam ʿAli Efendi who was Kadiʿasker to Sultan Bayezid II, and whose father had been a *mürid* of Haccı Bayram. Lamiʿi mentions the feud between Mevlana Habib al-ʿUmari and Sheykh Muhyi ed-Din, who was the Hünkar sheykh (sheykh of Sultan Bayezid II), a conflict finally settled by the "power of dervishdom". Hasan Beg, the Nishancı of Prince Shehinshah, the governor (*beg*) in Karaman, a sound and pious man, told Lamiʿi stories about Habib al-ʿUmari which circulated among the people. The late Tacizade Caʿfer Chelebi, Kadiʿasker of Anadolu under Selim I, told Lamiʿi an episode from the time when Prince Bayezid was governor (*beg*) of Rum and resided in Amasya, which is as follows: "My father Taci Beg was in the service of Prince Bayezid.[57] One day he gave my father three thousand *Akçe* and said, 'take them to Chelebi Khalife to spend on food for the derwishes and to do something in the matter of a wish which I have'". This wish, it appeared, was the downfall of Mehmed Pasha. Later Tacizade Caʿfer Chelebi talked to Mehmed Pasha's son who told him of a talisman which his father always wore, but not on that particular day. Caʿfer Chelebi continued, "And when my father (Taci Beg) brought Prince Bayezid the news (of Mehmed Pasha's downfall), Prince Bayezid changed colour with shame and said, 'By God, I am not one of those who rejoice in the misfortune of others... But this tyrant has relations with my brother Cem'.[58] Lamiʿi's account, whether regarded as fact or fact-based fiction, has the great merit of presenting those happenings as a contemporary saw them.

---

54 Sheykh Muslih ad-Din-i Tavil from the village Bakır Küresi near Kastamonu. Lami'i, *Terceme-i Nafahat*, 462, gives the date of his death 896/1490-91 in a chronogram; cf. Kufralı 133-134; TKZ 234.

55 TKZ 150. Kissling 216: he belonged to Ak Shems ed-Din's Bayramiye, flourished in Karahisar.

56 Kufralı, 135; on Ahrar see Hamid Algar s.v., EI2 Suppl. (1980), 50-52.

57 For his governorate see Petra Kappert, *Die osmanischen Prinzen und ihre Residenz Amasya im 15. und 16. Jahrhundert*, Istanbul, 1976, 54-55.

58 Lami'i, *Terceme-i Nafahat*, 580. Cf. Martin, "Khalwati Order of Dervishes", 281-282, where Taşköprüzade is quoted who mentions neither Taci Beg nor his son Tacizade Caʿfer Chelebi, the latter having been put to death in 1515 for allegedly turning the Janissaries against the sultan. V.L. Ménage, Art. "Djaʿfar Celebi" in EI.

Lamiʿi's Geographical Range

The geographical range of Lamiʿi's observations is very wide and includes Khorasan and Syria. The author's references to Khorasan[59] include the episode where Sheykh Ilahi, at a time of extreme distress and anxiety of mind, wanted to fling his books into the water or the fire. When Samarkand had been Timur's capital many artists had been forcibly taken there. Lamiʿi's grandfather had been carried off in this way. From 1457 Samarkand had been under the domination of Khwaca ʿUbaydullah-i Ahrar (died 1490) whose *mürid*, the Anatolian ʿAbdullah Ilahi, was to introduce the Nakshbandiya to Turkey[60]. In Bukhara Ilahi spent a year as a suppliant on the grave of Baha'uddin Nakshband. Once he, Ilahi, walked outside the city, saw tents surrounding it and asked what they were. The answer was, "Don't you know that the Uzbeks have besieged us for eight months, that these are their tents?" He said, "God knows best, and now, I, too, know it..." (Lamiʿi 464). In Herat Ilahi visited Mevlana Cami.

The information on Syria is incidental. Maghrebi went to Damascus; it was the birthplace of Ak Shems ed-Din. To Aleppo Ak Shems ed-Din went from Rum and returned (to Haccı Bayram) after a dream.

It was the Ottoman capital Istanbul which made the strongest appeal to the Turkish saints. Ak Shems ed-Din rose to prominence through his presence at the conquest.[61] Scholars and Sufis who sought quiet went to the Zeyrek Mosque and medrese, originally the Comnenian Pantokrator foundation of 1136, as a haven of refuge. Here Tusi had taught, and Ilahi had studied. The building had fallen into disrepair after the 'Courtyard of the Eight' (*Sahn-i Saman*) had been established, but Ilahi made it his home after he had been called to Istanbul. However, the throng of people attracted to his medrese alarmed him, and he accepted an invitation to Macedonia. In the case of sheykh ʿAli al-Khalveti it was the Court that was alarmed by the crowds which he attracted, and he was politely removed[62].

---

59 For a description of the people of Khurasan where *ta'lim* Sufism changed to *tarbiya* Sufism see Fritz Meier, "Hurasan und das Ende der klassischen Sufik", in *Atti del Convegno Internazionale sul tema La Persia nel Medioevo*, Rome, 1971, 545-570. See "Khurāsān and the End of Classical Sufism", Fritz Meier, *Essays on Islamic Piety and Mysticism*, trans. by John O'Kane with editorial assistance of Bernd Radtke, Leiden-Cologne 1999, pp. 189-219.

60 Hamid Algar, "Ahrār", EI Supplement 1-2, 1980, 50-52. I have not seen Mustafa Kara, "Molla Ilâhî: un précurseur de la Nakşibendiye en Anatolie", M. Gaborieu, A. Popovic and T. Zarcone (eds.), *Naqshbandis. Cheminements et situation actuelle d'un ordre mystique musulman*, Istanbul-Paris, 1990.

61 The Türbe of Ak Shemseddin was built there in 1463.

62 Lami'i 577. G.B. Martin, "Khalwati Order of Dervishes", 276-277.

Of Western Anatolian towns Bursa, where Lamiʿi was born, held an important place. Here were Bayezid Yıldırım's Great Mosque, the Green Mosque and the Green Mausoleum, where his grandfather the master calligrapher had taken part in the decoration. In Bursa where Maghrebi's successor was buried, Sheykh Hamid had preached for a while. Simav in Germiyan is linked with the life of ʿAbdullah Ilahi who was born here and returned after Khorasan; crowds flocked to his and Ahmed Bukhari's sermons; he left the town when he found the countryside plunged in disorder after the death of Mehmed II. In nearby Balıkesri Maghrebi's successor died.

Pervading Lamiʿi's Turkish *Nafahat* is a sense of the holiness of Anatolia; "if from those famous in each region only the noble names were given they would fill many volumes". Konya and Aksaray had produced great numbers of ʿulemȧ, and the sway of mysticism at Lamiʿi's time was still associated with these and other towns.[63] In Konya Lamiʿi had studied with Mevlana Habib al-ʿUmari when this itinerant sheykh stayed there[64]; Ibrahim as-Sarraf had also studied there. Aksaray was a "tower of saints" comparable to Baghdad; it was the burial place of Sheykh Hamid. Sivas was the birthplace of Ibrahim as-Sarraf, Laranda that of ʿÖmer Dede, Sheykh Rusheni,[65] who left his homeland to attach himself to the Akkoyunlu; he died in Tabriz.[66] His elder brother ʿAli al-Khalveti, whom Mehmed II did not want in Istanbul, was buried in Larende.[67] In Ankara Mevlana Habib al-ʿUmari had lived for a while, had visited the grave of its patron saint Haccı Bayram (d.1429) and had conversations with Ak Shems ed-Din.[68] Kayseri was the birthplace of Sheykh Hamid; the burial place of Ibrahim es-Sarraf; the town where Hamid and Haccı Bayram are said to have met.

Amasya, residence of princely governors, had traditions of heterodoxy and popular revolt[69] and was a nucleus of the Khalwati order. Lamiʿi mentions the

---

63 Cf. M. Balivet, "The Long-Lived Relations between Christians and Moslems in Central Anatolia: Dervishes, Papadhes, and country Folk", *Byzantinische Forschungen* XVI (1991), 313-322, with earlier literature. For urban and rural medreses see S. Faroqhi, "The Anatolian Town and its Place within the Administrative Structure of the Ottoman State (1500-1590)", *ibidem*, 236-238.

64 Lami'i 578.

65 Lami'i 576.

66 B.G. Martin, "A Short History of the Khalwati Order of Dervishes, in N.R. Keddie, *Scholars, Saints, and Sufis*, London, 1972, 278-279; A.Y. Ocak, *Kalender*, 204-205.

67 Lami'i 577.

68 Lami'i 578. For this founder of the Bayramiye see İnalcık, *Classical Age*, 191; Kissling, *Dissertationes*, passim.

69 B.G. Martin, "Short History of the Khalwati Order", 278-280.

mufti Pasha Chelebi, a brother of Ak Sheykh.[70] Iskilip was for a time the abode of Mevlana Habib al-ʿUmari. In Osmancık north of Amasya Ak Shems ed-Din was a müderris who left and came back and met the father of Imam ʿAli;[71] it was also a Bektashi settlement. Like Amasya, Tokat was an "urban island in the sea of a Turkish nomad population".[72] Chelebi Khalifa studied there with the Khalveti sheykh Tahiroghlu, a Turkmen who loved hunting and was uneducated (*ümmi*) to the extent that he said *heyz* when he meant *feyz*; but he possessed inner powers... He subjected Sheykh Chelebi to the harshest solitude (*khalvet*) and made him fast sitting in a hole dug in the ground.[73] The "province of the Turkmens" where Haccı Bektash was buried, where the nomads had their summer pastures between Kırşehir and Kayseri, was the setting for a mysticism of the uneducated which could all too easily slip over into heresy. This is reflected in Lamiʿi's notice on Haccı Bektash. Lamiʿi writes with some understanding of the Turkmens, in an age where sympathy for nomadic or semi-nomadis tribes, virtually a foreign race from the sedentarist point of view,[74] would have been exceptional.

Vardar Yeñicesi (Giannitsa) had grown into a flourishing centre of Islam thanks to the largesse of the conqueror of Macedonia, Evrenos Beg (d. 1417), the first Ottoman march-lord.[75] In Lamiʿi's time his descendant Evrenosoghlu Ahmed Beg (d. 1499) had added another mosque, charitable institutions and a medrese. The presence of a member of the court aristocracy in the Vardar valley – Evrenosoghlu Ahmed Beg was the resplendent commander whose obeisance to a *müderris* made the young Kemalpashazade embrace the career of *ʿilm*[76] – marks the cultural importance of the former frontier town Yeñice which continued into the sixteenth and seventeenth century. Evrenosoghlu Ahmed Beg had invited Sheykh Ilahi who settled there and wrote his works.[77] When he died in 1490/1 Ahmed Beg built a mosque over his tomb.

70 Lami'i 686.

71 Lami'i 685.

72 Martin, "Short History of the Khalwati Order", 279.

73 Lami'i 579.

74 For their relationship within the old frontier zone see Keith Hopwood, "Nomads or Bandits? The Pastoralist/Sedentarist Interface in Anatolia", *Byzantinische Forschungen* XVI (1991), 179-194.

75 Machiel Kiel, "Yenice Vardar – Vardar Yenicesi – a forgotten Turkish cultural centre in Macedonia of the 15th and 16th century", *Studia Byzantina et Neohellenica Neerlandica* 3, Leiden 1971, 300-329; Vasilis Demetriades, "The Tomb of Ghazi Evrenos Bey at Yenitsa and its inscription", *BSOAS* 39 (1976), 329-332.

76 HOP II, 348; V.L. Ménage, "Kemal Pasha-zade", *EI* IV (1978), 880.

77 For Ilahi's works see *ʿOm* I, 91 (for a note of caution see Kufralı 135 note 2); Mehmed Tahir who visited his grave mentions a commentary on the *Waridat* by Sheykh Bedr ed-Din;

The town of Gallipoli is incidentally mentioned in connection with the brothers Yazıcıoghlu[78] who spent their lives there, and with the visit of Haccı Bayram on his return from Edirne where he had had to submit to an interrogation by Sultan Murad II to prove his orthodoxy, which he duly did, accompanied by Ak Sheykh.[79]

By comparing Lamiʿi's exploration of Turkish saints in his *Terceme-i Nafahat* with that of Taşköprüzade, we are led to appreciate that there must have been a considerable give and take between the hagiographic and biographic genres. The following may illustrate this point.

The Yunus Emre Menakıb: Model and Imitation

Lamiʿi writes: "One of the people famous in Rum is Yunus Emre, may God bless his mystery. There are famous and well-known sayings by him. They are all accepted by the peoples (tribes, *tava'if*), and they are secrets of monotheism and modes of asceticism and symbols and signs from end to end. He is a follower of Tapduk Emre, may God bless his secret. They say that he brought wood for his sheykh on his back for many years, and that he never brought a crooked stick. Tapduk said: Yunus, it appears that among those sticks [which you bring] there is never a crooked one; he said, 'My master, into this gate nothing crooked fits'. He is buried near the place where the Kütahya River (Porsuk Çayı) flows into the Sakarya. And one of them is his excellence Haccı Bektash Veli, may his mystery be blessed. He is buried in the province of the Turkmens. He was a friend of God and a miracle-worker. At present [above his grave] is a soup kitchen and a place of pilgrimage. It is a famous and well-known place around which people of the world walk in procession. It must be said that in our way of talking the people who are considered his followers and the throngs at the blessed grave for the most part inexcusably graze on the pasture of libertinage (*ibaha*), having shaken off the yoke of Islam. But a consensus has been reached regarding his own soundness and his affiliation to this group".

---

a commentary on the *Miftah al-ghayb* by Konawi; Lami'i mentions *Zad al-muştakin, Nacat al-arwah*, and the Turkish *Meslekü t-talibin vü l'abidin* on which see M. Götz, *Türkische Handschriften Teil 2*, 44 no. 58-63. For Ilahi's Turkish *Esrar-name* see Götz *ibidem*, 42 no. 55-57.

78 Laban Kaptein, *Apocalypse and the Antichrist Dajjâl in Islam*, Asch, Privately published, 2011. First published in Dutch as a doctoral dissertation, Leiden 1997. Laban Kaptein (ed.), *Ahmed Bican Yazıcıoğlu, Dürr-i meknûn. Kritische Edition mit Kommentar*, Asch 2007.

79 Nefahat 686; H.J. Kissling, "Zum islamischen Heiligenwesen auf dem Balkan, vorab im thrakischen Raume", ZB 1 (1962), 49; quoted from H.J. Kissling, *Dissertationes Orientales et Balcanicae Collectae I. Das Derwischtum*, Munich, 1986, 281.

The *Şaka'ik* shares most data with its model. Taşköprüzade writes: (p. 20): "al-Hacc Bektash. And among the sheykhs of his time [Murad's I; Third class] there is the sheykh, the mystic al-Hacc Bektash. He belonged to the miracle-workers and holy men, and his noble grave is in the land (*bilad*) of the Turkmens. His grave is surmounted by a dome, and there is also a hermitage which is visited and where blessing is obtained and prayers are answered. But in our time some heretics (*malahida*) have, by mendacious attribution, taken their designation from him, although he doubtless is far from them. May God sanctify his secret". (p. 56) "To these [under Bayezid I; sub-chapter, Fourth class] belongs also the sheykh and mystic Tapduk Emre. He came from a village near the Sakarya River. He was a recluse and separated himself from the people. And he possessed the quality to lead and performed great miracles. May his secret be sanctified". (p. 57) "And to these belongs also the sheykh and mystic Yunus Emre. The deceased one belonged to the companions of sheykh Tapduk Emre and used to bring wood into the hermitage of his sheykh for a long time, without there ever being a crooked stick among it. And when his sheykh asked him about this, he answered: this gate does not deserve anything crooked[80]. He performed apparent miracles and had raptures and ecstatic trances. He also composed much poetry in the Turkish language, from which it is understood that he had attained a high station in the knowledge of God's unity and a great knowledge (*ma'rifa*) of the divine things. May his secret be sanctified".

'Ashık Chelebi devotes[81] a chapter to Yunus Emre; in the MSS British Library Or. 6434[82] and Vienna Nationalbibliothek H.O. 134[83] it runs:

> 'Yunus Emre is from the district Bolu in the province of Anadolu. He belongs to the mürids of Tapduk Dede. He belongs to the perfect men and precious gems of the world who are pulled by the hook of [divine] attraction from the world of earthly power to the world of the angels. Although he is illiterate, he belongs to those who read in the college of the divine, and to those who turn the pages of the book: "We have been given knowledge for an inheritance from the Living who dieth not"[84].

80 A. Schimmel, *Mystical Dimensions*, 329-330; Idem, *Wanderungen mit Yunus Emre*, Cologne, 1989, 25, 32.

81 Despite a preference for poets of his own generation; cf. P.K. Kappert in *Bibliotheca Orientalis* 5/6 (1975), 402.

82 Fol. 98b-99a in Or. 6434 in the British Museum edited in 1971 by G.M. Meredith-Owens, *Meşā'ir üş-Şu'arā or Tezkere of 'Āşık Çelebi*, London, 1971.

83 G. Flügel, *Die arabischen, persischen und türkischen Handschriften der Kaiserlich-Königlichen Hofbibliothek zu Wien*, Vienna, 1865-1867, II, 381 no. 1219, fol. 127a-b.

84 *HOP* I, 166.

He was of the "substitutes" (*abdal*) and pious who translated the language of the lip into the language of the heart, and of the companions of the secrets who with the voice of the invisible (*lisan-i gayb*) declare what is in the soul. It is related that every time he wanted to read his tongue did not turn to complete the letters of the alphabet, and the mirror of his heart was undulled by the opaqueness of inscriptions and lines". The poem which Yunus, according to 'Ashık Chelebi, pronounced spontaneously (*bedihaten*),[85] appears as

> nazar eyle ıtırı bāzār eyle götüri yaradılanı hoş gör yaradandan ötüri

> Look (favourably) upon the rose water (pelargonium)
> Fix a good price in putting an end to it.
> Tolerate the created (overlook its defects)
> On account of the Creator.

The second poem, which 'Ashık Chelebi designated as *sehl-i mümteni*ʿ (effortless beauty),[86] runs as follows,

> dimedüñmi sev beni derdüñe dermān olayın / sevdügimce artdı derdüm ya'nī dermān eyledi

> "Did you not say: Love me
> I will be a cure for your suffering
> Loving you increased my suffering
> That is to say, it cured it."

These two poems[87] which apparently delighted 'Ashık Chelebi deserve the status of other poems by Yunus Emre (the two poems published by the "Mühlbacher"[88] are now included in the corpus) with which they bear comparison.

---

85 A rhyming four-liner with the rhyme scheme a-a-b-a. For the comparisons with the market; (a lump bargain). "With God is the best bargain" (Rumi) and for commercial terminology found in the Koran see Schimmel, *Mystical Dimensions*, 321. In the mouth of the people this *beyt* has become, according to M. Tatçı, *Yunus Emre Divanı*, Ankara, 1991, 28, elif okuduk ötürü, bazar eyledik götürü / yaradılanı severüz yaradandan ötürü.

86 The rhyme scheme is a-x-x-a. The syllable scheme is 4+3 = 7. ce+artdı is crasis. Compare Tatçı, *Yunus Emre Divanı*, 1991, p. 28 and 109 no. 125, and Tatçı, *Tenkitli Metin*, no. 125: *Ben derdile âh iderdüm derdüm bana dermânımış.*

87 They were not found in the Yunus Emre manuscripts available to Mustafa Tatçı.

88 A new edition of these two poems, published by T. Tekin in *Erdem* 3 (1987), 367-387, followed by words of caution by A. Tietze, *Erdem* 5 (1989), 399 ff., has superseded the first edition by K. Foy which appeared in 1901.

Mecdi in his Turkish translation of the *Şaka'ik* relates that Yunus Emre (Class IV) was a native of the district (*sancak*) of Bolu, and that he was a disciple of a sheykh called Tapduk Emre who had settled in a hamlet near the river Sakarya, that he used to gather wood for him, but that he never brought a crooked stick because "Things crooked profit not in either world that I should bring such to your threshold". Mecdi says that from the words he uttered it was clear and manifest that he had a perfect knowledge of the Divine mysteries and held an exalted station in the perception of monotheism ... Yunus could not read or write but was deeply immersed in mysticism; from his sayings which were composed in the Turkish language (*lisan-i türkide*) and in the form of *varsağı* (*varsağı üslubında*), which Gibb translated as "ballad style"[89]. The following verses are then quoted, apparently as one poem,

> nazar eyle ıtırı bāzār eyle götüri
> yaradılanı hoş gör yaradandan ötüri
> dimedüñmi sev beni derdüñe dermān olayın
> sevdügimce artdı derdüm yaʿnī dermān eyledüñ

J.H. Mordtmann[90] translated this combined poem (the last word has been changed from eyledi to eyledüñ) tentatively thus:

> "Blicke scharf hin, mache den Handel in Bausch und Bogen.
> Das Geschöpf schaue wohlwollend an um des Schöpfers willen.
> Sprachst du nicht: liebe mich, deinem Schmerze will ich Heilmittel sein.
> Je mehr ich liebte, desto größer ward mein Schmerz, d.h. du hast Heilung gebracht".

Lamiʿi's 'Anatolian' chapter of the *Terceme-i Nefahat* offers us glimpses of three moments in the unfolding of the nascent Haccı Bektash and Yunus Emre hagiography: a negative response to the Bektashis on the part of the Sufis in Bursa, within six years of the revolt of Kalender (who claimed descent from Hacci Bektash); a judicious compromise in affirming the holy status of Hacci Bektash; and a certain confusion occasioned by the close social interaction of established Islam and heterodox dervishes within Turkish Islam. Lamiʿi's position in this controversy – that Hacci Bektash is saintly but his followers are not – has served as a fundamental statement of this difference. While Lamiʿi's sequence of saintly

89 *HOP* I, 166.

90 J. Mordtmann, "Türkisches. Zu Bd. IV, S. 230-277", *Mitteilungen des Seminars für orientalische Sprachen*, V. Jahrgang, II. Abt. (1902) 162-169.

persons – Yunus Emre, Tapduk Emre, Haccı Bektash – seems clear, the chronology is left open and the topography is vague: Yunus is not localized, Tapduk is buried near the confluence of the Kütahya and the Sakarya rivers; Haccı Bektash is buried "in the land of the Turkmens".

While the *Şaka'ik* text is a very close paraphrase in Arabic, it changes the sequence of saintly persons – Bektash, Tapduk, Yunus Emre – and separates them in two classes, antedating Haccı Bektash and putting Tapduk Emre and Yunus Emre together into the next reign. The topography is changed: Tapduk originated near the Sakarya. The only deletion in the *Şaka'ik* is Lami'i's description of the people who walk on the pastures of *ibaha*... In what we may term editorializing on the part of 'Ashık Chelebi, he declares that Yunus did not read ... Mecdi enlarges considerably on Taşköprüzade, localizing Yunus Emre, and adding the term "*varsağı* style" which was absorbed into Gibb's work of 1900[91]. J.H. Mordtmann's article quoted above is of interest here in suggesting how secure Mecdi's tradition became; it is a very thorough documentation of the growth of the Yunus "Junis Imre" (Amra)[92] tradition from Mecdi through Sa'deddin and Mustafa 'Ali, usefully pointing out the errors in J. von Hammer's Yunus Emre, and showing Tayyarzade Ahmed Ata's, Ahmed Vefik Paşa's and Barbier de Meynard's interdependence. After this digression into one case of "model and imitation" let us return to Lami'i's contemporaries.

Saints in Sehi Beg's *Tezkire*

Much scholarly work has already been done on the 'Eight Paradises' compiled by Sehi Beg (d. 1548), the first Ottoman *Tezkire* of poets completed in 945/1538-9. Günay Kut has edited the work and subjected its textual history to a complete investigation.[93] What we find in Sehi Beg, by contrast with Lami'i, are biographical sketches accompanied by selections from the poets' compositions. As biographies, they remain mostly external, with incidental information on pro-

91 *HOP* I, 166.

92 Mordtmann, "Türkisches", *MSOS* V, II (1902), quoting Flügel's manuscription in his catalogue, I, 636. Saïd Khorchid, "La deuxième composante du nom de Yûnus Emre" in *JAS* 1991, 233-238, has proposed an etymology of Yunus Emre's second name as an imperative of *amra-* "be in peace".

93 Günay Kut, *Heşt bihişt, the tezkire by Sehi Beg. An analysis of the first biographical work on Ottoman poets with a critical edition based on MS. Süleymaniye Library, Ayasofya, O. 3544*, Cambridge, Mass., 1978; Günay Kut, "Heşt Bihişt'in Yeni Bir Nüshası ve Bir Düzeltme, in *JTS* 7 (1984), 293-301.

fessional promotions and the dervish orders to which poets belonged.[94] Sehi's model is Nawa'i's *Macalisu n-nafa'is* with its short memoirs arranged in the *tabakat* or "class" pattern. Poets were grouped under particular periods of time in relation to the author's own age or generation[95]. For instance, Mevlana Shirazi, "someone who is reckoned among the sheykhs" receives a brief memoir as the writer of the "useful book entitled *Gulshan-i raz* full of subtleties...", his *vilaya* was obvious, and he was a holy man". The memoir on Lamiʿi concentrates on his Nakshbendi identity besides his being a poet and translator; the *Terceme-i Nafahatu l-uns* is not mentioned. To himself Sehi refers as a dervish (a poem on Mevlana Celaleddin Rumi has been found in his *Divan*). He does not reserve special space for saintly poets in his Tezkire. Chapter one is devoted to Sultan Süleyman, the second chapter to six sultans and princes who wrote poetry, the third to 26 or 28 statesmen, the fourth to 16 or 17 ʿulemȧ. The actual poets were classified in chapters five (33 deceased poets), six (57 living poets), seven (37 to 38 young poets and women), and eight (43 to 49 very young poets). Sehi Beg's treatment of Molla Sheykh Rusheni is apolitical; he lived a carefree life of earthly pleasures until he emigrated to Persia, where he was chastened and purified and eventually died near Tabriz; he had thousands of *mürids*, one of them being Sheykh Ibrahim Gülsheni in Egypt. His poetry was well known and showed his Sufi tendency; he addressed a reproachful kaside to himself.[96] Stylistic rather than religious considerations seem to have been a major factor in the making of Sehi Beg's anthology. Saints and their deeds he treats with respect, as is only to be expected, though how far this is conventional there is no means of telling.

Saints in Latifi's *Tezkire*

Despite the fact that Latifi (1491?-1582) devotes an introductory chapter of his *Tezkire* to saintly men and despite the fact that Latifi considered moral-spiritual value to be the raison d'être of poetry – the dervish or the dervish-minded member of the ʿulemȧ was the purveyor of these values, and poetry's primary purpose was to transmit a 'spiritually valuable message'[97] – no systematic study of saints and saintly men in Latifi's *Tezkire* (completed in 953/1546) has thus far

94 The pattern is discussed in Kut, *Heşt Bihişt*, 8-10.

95 J. Stewart-Robinson, "The Ottoman Biographies of Poets", *JNES* 24 (1965), 61.

96 *Nedjati Hüsnü Lugal and O. Reşer (trsl.), Sehi Bey's Tezkere. Türkische Dichterbiographien aus dem 16. Jahrh.*, Istanbul 1942, 49-50.

97 W.G. Andrews, Jr., "The Tezkere-i Su'ara of Latifi as a source for the Critical Evaluation of Ottoman Poetry", PhD dissertation at the University of Michigan, 1970, 123, 137-138.

been attempted. The study by W.G. Andrews expressly ignores the chapter on saints[98]. The edition currently in use, by Ahmed Cevdet, Istanbul 1314/1896-7, is almost a hundred years old. W.G. Andrews has traced the process of compilation and has shown that the final *Tezkire* passed through two recensions.[99] A future study might address itself to the way in which Latifi continued the series of saints which Lamiʿi provided. Latifi has recourse to Aflaki and to the *Terceme-i Nafahatu l-uns* (without citing Lamiʿi; he praises his work in a general way).[100]

Latifi expresses his conviction of the supreme importance of the saintly personages who either lived in Rum as their native country or acquired fame by pertaining to it (Rumilik); they were 'speakers of the truths of versification (*nazm*) and perfect in the subtleties of the sciences. Guided by this principle, he continued Lamiʿi's studies on the saints by describing

Mawlana Calal ed-Din Rumi who had lived under Sultan Ala' ad-Din of the house of Seljuk (Persian extracts)[101] (Lamiʿi 516)
Sultan Veled (*Rebabnama*, Persian extracts)[102] (Lamiʿi 525)
Sadr ad-Din Konawi (two Persian quatrains)[103] (Lamiʿi 632)
ʿAshık Pasha (d. 1333): Latifi has some additional information; the sheykh was rich and influential; he came from a place near the Persian border, settled in Kırşehir and made friends with Haccı Bektash[104]
Latifi's chapter "Elvan Shirazi" imparts a mosaic of citations, conflating the son of ʿAshık Pasha and the translator, for Murad II, of Mahmud Shabistari's *Gulshan-i raz*, and adding verse quotations; making him a Turkestanian whose family came from Shiraz and who flourished under Sultan Orkhan[105]

98 Andrews, "The Tezkere-i Su'ara of Latifi", 10, 15.

99 Andrews, Tezkere, has demonstrated that two major recensions survive in a large number of manuscripts, an old one completed in 953, and a new one completed after 980. O. Rescher translated the work (Tübingen 1950), referring to nine old MSS. For a new manuscript see Sabahattin Küçük, "Latifi tezkeresi (Tezkiretü'ş-şu'ara)nın Çorum nüshası", *TKA* 25 (1988), 49-54.

100 Latifi ed. Ahmed Cevdet, 290-294; [O. Rescher], *Türkische Dichterbiographien II: Latîfî's Tezkere*, Tübingen, 1950, reissue Osnabrück 1979; 234-237; *HOP* iii,25.

101 A. Cevdet 38, Rescher 30.

102 A. Cevdet 42, Rescher 32.

103 A. Cevdet 43; Rescher 33.

104 A. Cevdet 44; Rescher 33; Erünsal/Ocak lxv, lxvii dismiss the story of ʿAshık Pasha's Eastern origins.

105 A. Cevdet 46; Rescher 35. For a description of the Persian model, dated 1311, see Schimmel, *Mystical Dimensions*, 280-281. For the Turkish work see my *Türkische Handschriften* 286 no.

Sheyh Vefa (two *matla*ʿs in Turkish rhyming in -ūd, īr eylemez, and -işt) from Konya.[106] (Lamiʿi 559)
Sheyh Rusheni (died in Tabriz), ʿÖmer Dede (Lamiʿi 576)[107]
Sheyh ʿAbdullah Ilahi (*matla*ʿ)[108] (Lamiʿi 460)
Sheyh Seyyid Shems ed-Din Buhari[109] (Lamiʿi 465)
Sheyh Ibrahim Gulsheni[110]
Yazıcızade Mehmed[111]
Süleyman Chelebi[112]
Sheykh Bayezid (Commentary on Muhyi ad-Din, *matla*ʿ)[113]

This comes to a total of thirteen saints. It is not as poets, as Gibb observed, that these saintly personages are presented to the reader: ʿAshık Pasha's verse is somewhat rough and monotonous, but the poem is useful; Gülsheni's *Maʿnavi* of 40,000 couplets is a *nazire* to Rumi's Mathnawi, all in Persian; Ilahi wrote in Persian and Turkish, and Bukhari did not write much poetry of any kind. But it is as teachers and spiritual guides of Turkish Sufi writers that they are presented[114]. By grouping Sheyh Rusheni among the saints Latifi stresses his religious quality and his piety.

Other writers of religious poetry are consigned to the chapters on poets; Nesimi, of whom Latifi speaks warmly and whom he describes as a leader of the *abdals* (*malamis* in other MSS); and Sheykhi, an 'old poet', a holy man educated in Sufism in Persia, was a khalife of Hаccı Bayram, did not get around to instructing

366 (VOHD xiii,1); Götz, *Türk. Handschriften Teil 2* pp. 21 no. 24-25; with older literature. F. Şahiner, Şeyh Elvân-i Sirâzi, Gülşen-i Râz, DTCF, bitirme tezi, is quoted in Ismail Ünver, Mesnevi, p. 439, note 35.

106 A. Cevdet 47; Rescher 36.

107 A. Cevdet 48; Rescher 37. For Dede ʿÖmer Ruseni (1486) see Ocak, *Kalenderi*, 204-205; cf. B.G. Martin, "A Short History of the Khalwati Order of Dervishes, in N.R. Keddie, *Scholars, Saints, and Sufis*, London, 1972, 278-279.

108 A. Cevdet 50; Rescher 39; *HOP* II 373-374.

109 A. Cevdet 51; Rescher 40.

110 A. Cevdet 52; Rescher 40-41. See K. Kufralı, "Gülşenî" in *IA* IV 835-6; Martin, "History of the Khalwati Order"; M. van Bruinessen, "Religious Life in Diyarbekir: Islamic Learning and the Role of the Tariqats", in M. van Bruinessen and H. Boeschoten, *Evliya Çelebi in Diyarbekir*, Leiden 1988, 50. His hagiography, composed by Muhyi-yi Gülsheni, begun in 1569 and completed in 1604, was edited by Tahsin Yazıcı, *Muhyi-yi Gülşeni. Menakıb-i Ibrahim-i Gülşeni*, Ankara, 1982.

111 A. Cevdet 51; Rescher 41.

112 A. Cevdet 55; Rescher 42 and 310; Schimmel, *Mystical Dimensions*, 216-217.

113 A. Cevdet 58; Rescher 43-44.

114 *HOP* II, 374-375.

mürids and was spared the spell of wrong ideas. Turabi, a contemporary of Sheykhi, lived as a strange and holy ascetic. 'A type of impassioned poetry' was suitable to the nature of the common people.[115] Temenna'i's anti-social behaviour is condemned,[116] and Latifi tries to explain a heterodox and emotional type of sufism in terms of an intellectual orthodoxy...'[117] In taking up this matter, Latifi's *tezkire* becomes quite unlike Sehi's, with whom Latifi shares the royal poets in slightly different order, directing the reader's attention to Sultan Süleyman.[118] An entire chapter might be devoted to the geographical background of Latifi's memoirs, which is so much wider than Lami'i's as a result of the expansion of the Ottoman Empire.

Conclusion

It is a point of interest that the Ottoman biographers whom we have discussed were known to one another, and that the works of Lamiʿi, Sehi, Latifi and Taşköprüzade were all completed within a period of less than forty years. 'Ashık Chelebi[119] studied under Taşköprüzade. His *Tezkire* and that of Kınalızade Hasan Chelebi[120] as well as the biographical sections of Mustafa 'Ali's *Künhü l-ahbar* should be considered in this context because of their close connection. The several biographical works did not result from any single purpose, whether practical or literary. But their authors' personal associations and a degree of interdependence in the contents of some of the compilations has led us to recognize a lively interchange between the historical and biographical genres, including hagiography. We may well say that for the early mystics Taşköprüzade has absorbed Lamiʿi's *Terceme-i Nafahat*. Sehi shows little or no reliance on Lamiʿi; he applies a conventional form of biography in "classes", without special attention to saintly poets. Latifi has recourse to Lamiʿi, rewriting and drawing from other sources as well.

---

115 Andrews, Tezkere, 124-125.

116 *HOP* I, 383; Andrews, Tezkere, 68-69.

117 Andrews, Tezkere, 65.

118 (a) Süleyman tab. 1 Sehi (g) fasl 2 Latifi; (b) Murad II tab. 2 Sehi (a) fasl 2 Latifi; (c) Mehmed II tab. 2 Sehi (b) fasl 2 Latifi; (d) Bayezid II tab. 2 Sehi (c) fasl 2 Latifi; (e) Cem tab. 2 Sehi (d) fasl 2 Latifi; (f) Selim tab. 2 Sehi (f) fasl 2 Latifi; (g) Korkud tab. 2 Sehi (e) fasl 2 Latifi

119 A translation of this great and much-quoted writer is needed, to supplement the edition by G.M. Meredith-Owens, *Mesha'ir ül-shu'ara*, London, 1971.

120 İbrahim Kutluk (ed.), *Tezkiretü ş-şu'ara*, vol. 1 Ankara, 1978, vol. 2 Ankara 1981.

In the introduction the criterion of attestation has been brought forward in order to draw a picture of what sixteenth-century Ottomans would have thought of the early saints. Many of the old saints were attested by Lamiʿi, and, through him, by other biographers[121]. The major differences between later imitations and their models can be grouped into four types: deletion, variation, substitution, and addition. It is through such changes and through changes in sequence and evaluation, that we gain insights which contemporary Ottoman historians do not give us. When they turn to Anatolian history, they do not set out to convince their readers that the annals of Karaman, or the pious foundations established by the earlier rulers, deserved their attention, but rather to remind them that the Anatolians had sided with Timur and had committed acts of treason against the Holy War which the Ottomans were waging[122]. A study which reveals the extent to which the Anatolian wars affected the lives of almost every Turk, Ottoman subject or not, has yet to be written.

Raising this issue may mean to question those interpretations that stress harmony and "the Ottoman government's toleration and support of locally based foundations".[123] In any political sense, of course, the Anatolian principalities had lost the last vestiges of their independence in the seventies of the fifteenth century. The material rewards of the *ghaza* in Rumelia had attracted many of the ablest Anatolian soldiers, scholars, and saintly men to the West. The Ottoman governing class now had its centre in Istanbul. The Anatolian past was evaded; names of rulers and patrons were preferably suppressed, while acknowledging "pre-Ottoman" foundation inscriptions[124]. That a seyyid from Khorasan had founded Seydishehir deserved to be remembered in 1554, but, as the author bears witness, it was strongly suggested that the ruler of that country, the Eshrefoghlu, had opposed such a foundation at first[125]. One may well say that in the days when Taşköprüzade was writing, "pre-Ottoman" Turkish Anatolia, the rule of the Seljuks, Mongols and Emirates, which had given Islam so many famous names,

121 Information on Elvan Chelebi the Elder was available in the Christian West as early as 1490 through the "Mühlbacher" Georgius of Hungary. For Hans Dernschwam's account of his visit to Elvan Chelebi's grave see Semavi Eyice in *TM* XV (1968), 211-246, and Erünsal/Ocak, xxiii. The Mühlbacher's presentation of Islam has been analyzed by Heribert Busse, "Der Islam und seine Rolle in der Heilsgeschichte in Georg von Ungarns Türkentraktat", K. Röhrborn and H.W. Brands (eds.), *Scholia. Beiträge zur Turkologie*, Wiesbaden 1981, 22-37,

122 H. İnalcık, *The Ottoman Empire. The Classical Age 1300-1600*, 14.

123 S. Faroqhi, "The Anatolian Town and its Place within the Administrative Structure of the Ottoman State (1500-1590)", *Byzantinische Forschungen* XVI (1991), 242-243.

124 For a list see K. Kreiser, "Drei Stiftungsinschriften aus Istanbul", *Istanbuler Mitteilungen* 31 (1981), 193.

125 Cemâl Kurnaz (ed.), *Abdülkerim bin Şeyh Mûsâ. Makâlât-i Seyyid Hârûn*, Ankara, 1991.

was definitely a thing of the past. The revolt round Bedr ed-Din had become part of provincial non-conformity. But in its own way Karaman remained a challenge and a threat; in the struggle for the throne after Mehmed II's death all the saints of Karaman appeared in a dream to Bayezid's ally Chelebi Khalifa[126] and pleaded for Cem (as relayed by Taşköprüzade). At the end of the sixteenth century Mustafa 'Ali felt free to rediscover and rewrite the history of the Danishmendids, who had been rivals of the Seljuks in Anatolia.[127] Our biographers were perhaps not far enough removed from the struggle over Karaman to measure earlier achievements fairly. But a mystic of Lami'i's stature could hope to benefit his fellow Ottomans by the inspiration and example of the Anatolian saints.

126 Martin, "Khalwati Order of Dervishes", 281-282, dwells on Chelebi Khalifa's role of a magical practitioner.

127 Cornell H. Fleischer, *Bureaucrat and Intellectual in the Ottoman Empire*, Princeton, 1986, 132-133.

CHAPTER 21

Public Opinion under Sultan Süleymân*

The age of Sultan Süleymân has left its imprint on men's minds. Indeed, his government's political aims, as those of his father, grandfather and great-grandfather, were extraordinarily ambitious. The intention was a continuous Holy War and a continuous expansion of the *Dârü'l-İslâm*.[1] If Yavuz Selîm had been the first *Ḫâdimü 'l-ḥaremeyn*, if Bâyezîd II claimed to be *Eşrefü 's-selâṭîn*, if Meḥmed II had been the greatest *ġâzî*, Süleymân laid claim to the "Supreme Caliphate."[2]

The aim in view remained a universal Muslim empire and at the same time a true Frontier State. The means: a great central army developed out of the sultan's own household troops ready to die in the *ġazâ*. Other loyalties, to origin and region, to dervish orders, were subservient to this goal. Holy War was the uniting ideology. All were subjects of the Ottoman sultans,[3] the greatest of whom was Süleymân.

The splendour surrounding this sultan in history tempts us to idealize his reign as a true golden age. Yet Sultan Süleymân's popularity declined in the 1540's. Surely nobody in this conference is feeling an urge to prove Süleymân less than his reputation. But his reputation should be measured in contemporary Ottoman terms, not in ours. In order to adequately measure the ruler against the values of his own times, we need the narrative sources. In this paper, I shall try to point out one aspect of the age of Süleymân, of "public opinion" in the sense of opinion publicly held and expressed.

This was in the first place that of the central government. The sultan's historiographers made known the course of events in such a way as to "prevent misunderstanding and to forestall uninformed criticism."[4] But next to this, it

* This is a revised and slightly enlarged version of the paper read at the Conference on the Age of Süleymân the Magnificent, Princeton University, November 19-22, 1987. I wish to express my gratitude to Professors Eva Baer, Cornell Fleischer, Remke Kruk, Bernard Lewis, and Andreas Tietze for their encouragement and many helpful suggestions.

1 See H. İnalcık, *The Ottoman Empire. The Classical Age*, 1300-1600, (London, 1973) p. 6.

2 See further İnalcık, *Classical Age*, p. 57.

3 İnalcık, *Classical Age*, p. 80.

4 B. Lewis and Ch. Pellat, "Djarîda", El, 2nd ed., s.v.

 | DOI 10.1163/9789004355767_022

was possible for the educated to express their view, concealing their identity if necessary.[5]

The work which I shall discuss, written by an author who does give his name, belongs to a little-known genre of "public opinion," prophecy. Its writers were adepts of *reml* and of *cefr*, esoteric knowledge concerning the destinies of nations, in its apocalyptic aspects, a literature which is also known as *melâḥim*, eschatological expectations centring around natural calamities, great conjunctions and eclipses.

For the prophetic writers, in distinction from the later *naṣîḥatnâme* writers, the most insistent questions revolved around the perfection of man's soul, made most urgent by the expectation of the Mahdî. The *Câmi ᶜü'l-meknûnât*, "Collector of the Concealed", is such a book.

Its author, Mevlânâ ʿÎsâ, was born in about 879/1474-1475 (according to his own words) in Ḥamîd ili (according to Muṣṭafâ ʿÂlî).[6] He studied law and became a deputy judge. He may have been in some way affiliated to a dervish order; I have suggested the Ḫalvetîye.[7] He had studied *ʿarûż* and history, in which chronology and millenarian speculation attracted him.

The text is found in three manuscripts dating from the first years of the seventeenth century. They are:

> **Le**: Library of the University, Leiden, Cod. Or. 1448. Part I of a manuscript of two parts, dated 10-20 Ramazân 1013/February 1605. 13 lines to the page. It was first described in 1865.[8]

> **An**: Library of the Türk Tarih Kurumu, Ankara, Y. 240/4. Part six of a manuscript dated Receb 1012/beg. 11 June 1603. 15 lines to the page. First described by its former owner, Osman Ferid Sağlam.

---

5 The *Vâḳiʿât-i Sulṭân Cem* and the *Ġurbetnâme*, both describing the life and deeds of Prince Cem, remained anonymous, even in the time of Süleymân. Ş. Turan examined an anonymous work, the author of which was in the service of Prince Selîm (later Selîm II); J. Turan, *Kanunî'nin Oğlu Şehzâde Bayezid Vak'ası* (Ankara, 1961) p. 9.

6 C.H. Fleischer, *Bureaucrat and Intellectual in the Ottoman Empire. The Historian Mustafa Âli (1541-1600)* (Princeton, 1986) 247f.; J. Schmidt, *Muṣṭafâ ʿÂlî's Künhü'l-aḫbâr and its Preface according to the Leiden Manuscript* (Istanbul-Leiden, 1987) pp. 8, 35, 72.

7 Table Ronde "L'ordre des Bektachis" in Strasbourg, June 1986. On these matters see now Ahmet T. Karamustafa (ed.), *Vahidi's* Menakib-ı Hvoca-i Cihan ve Netice-i Can, *critical Edition and Analysis*, Cambridge MA, 1993. I thank Professor Karamustafa for putting his unpublished PhD thesis (McGill University, 1987) at my disposal.

8 P. de Jong and M.J. de Goeje, *Catalogus Codicum Orientalium Bibliothecae Academiae Lugduno Batavae* III (Leiden, 1865) 26 no. DCCCCXLIV. Jan Schmidt, *Catalogue of Turkish Manuscripts in the Library of Leiden University, Volume Two*, Leiden 2002, pp. 83-87.

Is: Library of the University, Istanbul, T. Y. 3263, formerly Ibnülemin Mahmud Kemal (Īnal). In the colophon Īsmaʿîl el-kâtib writes that he finished the "rough draft" (*tesvîd*) on Muḥarrem 1 of a year ending with six (the rest of the date has been cut off); probably late sixteenth or early seventeenth century. It consists of 150 folios, with 15 lines to the page. The manuscript has been rebound at least once.[9]

The manuscripts represent three recensions, a short one (Le), a longer one (An), and an even longer one (Is). Contrary to what I said in an earlier paper, I now think it possible that these recensions were made, in that order, by the author himself. In Le and An the work is dated 936/beg. 5 September 1529 and 940/beg. 23 July 1533; in Is 950/beg. 6 June 1543 is given as the final date.

The book is ostensibly a *ġazavât-nâme*, but its essential object is announcing the end of the world and preparing the initiated for this event. It is written as a *mes̱nevî* poem alternating between the metres *hezec* and *remel;* the form suggests that the text was to be read aloud to listeners who are addressed *iy fetâ* etc. In order to make the contents more accessible to his public, use is made, especially at the beginning, of fables and parables.

In the longest recension the work is divided into one hundred twenty-five (unnumbered) short chapters, of which the first forty-seven consist of a history of creation, of the *nûr-i Aḥmed*, "light of Muḥammad", and of the prophets. The nativity horoscope of the Prophet is set out in detail, because it helps in the recognition of the Mahdî.

Chapters forty-eight to ninety-five tell the history of the Ottomans from the legendary beginnings of the dynasty to the death of Selîm I. Chapters ninety-six to one hundred and twenty-three are mainly devoted to the reign of Sultan Süleymân.

Many passages of ʿÎsâ's poem deal with situations which were half-forgotten when he was writing, and with people who had long been dead. He had suffered during the great famine, followed by the plague, of 1503, and had witnessed the earthquake which in 915/beg. 21 April 1509 destroyed the inner city of Istanbul. Nearer to his own time were the revolt of the Mamluks in Syria and Egypt; the campaign of Rhodes; the conquest of Belgrade, Mohács, Pest, and the conquest and re-conquest of Buda.

Quite close to the author's old age – he was seventy-one when he wrote his final version – were the third Hungarian campaign, known as the "Raids in Germany", *ġazavât-i vilâyet-i Alâmân*, begun with the hope of conquering

---

9 For earlier literature see articles 14 and 17 in this volume. I thank the keepers of the Leiden, Ankara and Istanbul collections for putting microfilms of their manuscripts at my disposal.

Vienna but settling for the small fortress of Kösek (Güns, Köszeg); the peace with Ferdinand who agreed to pay an annual tribute, the campaigns against the Safavids and especially the Baghdad campaign; the raids on Corfu and Apulia (Körfüz and Pulya) under Luṭfî Paşa; Ḫayruddîn's conquests by sea; the secret pact with infidel France and the disappointment at the French betrayal; the campaign in Moldavia.

The end of ʿÎsâ's longest version takes us to the year of writing, 1543, when Ottoman campaigning led to the occupation of several fortresses in western Hungary, sc. Esztergom (Gran), Tata and Székesfehérvár (Istolni Belgrad, Stuhlweissenburg), before Süleymân started home with his army.[10]

What should ʿÎsâ write about his own time? With the world at war, with such catastrophes as the bloody civil war in Anatolia behind one, with such feats of piracy as the capture of Algiers and Tunis and such unexpected failures as Vienna, with the incessant moving of armies and ships from east to west as the situation demanded. The first twenty years of Süleymân's reign had been years of almost uninterrupted warfare and crisis.

The final battle had not yet been fought. Sultan Süleymân, with all his might, had not been able to lure either the Habsburg monarchs, Charles V and Ferdinand, or the Shah of Persia, Ṭahmâsb into open battle, to decide who was the "supreme ruler of all the world".[11] The term denoting this universalist aspiration was *ṣâḥib-ḳırân* "lord of an auspicious conjunction, invincible hero."[12] The Turkish author takes Charles V's aspirations seriously: he quotes him as asking the Pope for the crown and as announcing that he would go to the mountain of Ḳaf which forms the frontier of the terrestrial world (An 144a). Süleymân writes to Charles V: *çu ḳılduñ daʿvâ-i ṣâḥib-ḳırânî/ er iseñ ḳarşula saña varanı* (since you have claimed universal lordship, meet, if you are a man, him who is advancing towards you).

In those years Sultan Süleymân was *ṣâḥib-ḳırân* rather than *ḳânûnî*. Ebû's-suʿûd, as Şeyḫü'l-islâm (after 952/1545), was yet to undertake the great revision and compilation of the *ḳânûn* which earned Süleymân the title of "lawgiver."

ʿÎsâ's statements about Sultan Süleymân must be seen against the background of politic and religious expectations of his time. His *Câmiʿü 'l-meknûnât*

10 I gave an impression of this part in a paper entitled "Mevlânâ ʿÎsâ's view of Ottoman Hungary" at the 7th CIEPO Symposium in Pécs, 7-11 September 1986.

11 Stanford Shaw, *History of the Ottoman Empire and Modern Turkey*. I (Cambridge, 1976), p. 94.

12 C. Fleischer, "Royal Authority, Dynastic Cyclism, and Ibn Khaldûnism' in Sixteenth-Century Ottoman Letters", *Journal of Asian and African Studies* XVIII (1983), p. 206.

contains detailed statements concerning the end of the world, and some remarkable prognostications about the political future.

The world's life-span was seven thousand years; to the Imam Caʿfar aṣ-Ṣâdiḳ (d. 765) the author ascribes the statement that a thousand years had not yet passed and that forty-five years were left; to Aristotle the foretelling that there would be a flood once in seven thousand years (Is 66a/b).

The author discusses its date, which he locates in an obscure, but imminent future. The Mahdî, he suggests, would come soon. Born under the same constellation as the Prophet, he would be preceded by thirty perfect human beings, *aḳṭâb*, several of whom were Ḫalvetî sheykhs. ʿÎsâ affirms that the present sultan, Süleymân bin Selîm, was such a mighty *ġâzî* that he might well be the Mahdî himself, but he moderates this claim immediately by adding that at any rate he might be his chief paladin (*server*).

Towards the end of the Istanbul version, written in 1543, only seven years after the death of Maḳbûl Ibrâhîm Paşa, ʿÎsâ touches on the extraordinary power of the *serʿasker* of the sultan and the shock of his fall, after which Ayâs Paşa became Grand Vizier.

But in a prophetic passage, ostensibly written earlier, ʿÎsâ traces a picture of the Ottoman society to come. What did he see? A *pâdiṣâh* who would leave matters of state to his vizier; a lawlessness of the emîrs of the time, who would rob the *reʿâyâ* with impunity; a corruption among the kadis who would violate sacred law and substitute ruses for it; but then suddenly there would be a remedy: the killing of the vizier by the sultan, who would then reign as another Maḥmûd (of Ghazna) with his Ayâs...

Such statements – and the last one has all the appearances of a prophecy *ex eventu* – may reflect ʿÎsâ's opinion of the reigning sultan; but conclusions can only be drawn after a closer examination of his work. At the moment, one may only consider the treatment of certain key themes, where the author discusses not so much what happened but what people thought was happening to them and was going to happen.

I shall give four short illustrations of what may be called Mevlânâ ʿÎsâ's political convictions. The first concerns the succession to the throne. 1543 was a critical year. The aging Sultan Süleymân, his favorite having died, showed his preference for his youngest son and transferred the eldest to Amasya. People saw that there were troubles ahead, princes taking up arms against their brothers or against their father. For ʿÎsâ, who does not refer to this directly, the troubled years preceding the deposition of Bâyezîd II and Selîm's usurpation of the throne must have been living realities.

He depicts Selîm I as a just ruler who removed innovation, *bidʿat*, tyranny and corruption, *ḍalâlet*; in his time the sheep could walk with the wolf, the mouse could put its head on the cat's paw. ʿÎsâ imputes to the dying Selîm I an expression of regret on three accounts; that he died before the Ḳızılbaş, that he did not build an *ʿimâret* for himself, and that he did not wage Holy War.

It is surely no accident that Mevlânâ ʿÎsâ, who was of the same generation as Sultan Selîm I, pays special attention to Bâyezîd II's forced abdication, deposition and death. Early on in his work, ʿÎsâ gives a glancing hint, praising the times of ʿOs̱mân, "when fratricides did not yet exist."[13]

Not long after ʿÎsâ's writing the army was going to demand Süleymân's retirement to Demotika (Dimetoka): this would have reduced the *ṣâḥib-ḳırân* to the pitiable state of the aged Bâyezîd II.[14] Indeed, this precedent was what Prince Muṣṭafâ had in mind, as his letters (admittedly not until the early fifties) reveal.[15]

My second illustration bears on the issue of social order. Did people recognize that it was breaking down, and that the sultan's policies were responsible for it? Among modern historians there is a growing awareness that this breakdown began in the early years of the sixteenth century.[16]

Contemporary Ottoman historiographers, it has been suggested, were blinded to the more immediate social and economic causes of Anatolian unrest, which they preferred to attribute to religious causes, especially the "hideous Safavid doctrine."[17] This may be accounted for, not by lack of insight, but by their function, mentioned above, of presenting the course of events according to the opinion of the central government.

> "When the plain of Syrmia had been conquered", ʿÎsâ wrote, "the sultan said: feel ashamed as long as the Turks have not taken root here. The people of this country will not be obedient until Muslims have settled down here. In order to deport many tribes (*il*) from the Bozoḳlu and fill that country, a beg went and a number of kadis. These (tribes) were not willing to be deported; they rebelled, they slew the beg and also killed the kadis."

13 Here, as elsewhere, ʿÎsâ probably uses the Anonymous Chronicle as a source for his work; see my paper in Pécs.

14 Turan, *Şehzâde Bayezid Vakʿası*, p. 11.

15 A.D. Alderson, *The Structure of the Ottoman Dynasty* (Oxford, 1956); Turan, *Şehzâde Bayezîd Vakʿası*, p. 25.

16 M.A. Cook, *Population Pressure in Rural Anatolia 1450-1600* (Oxford, 1972) p. 32.

17 J.R. Walsh, "The Historiography of Ottoman-Safavid Relations in the Sixteenth and Seventeenth Centuries", B. Lewis and P.M. Holt, eds., *Historians of the Middle East*, 2nd ed., (London, 1964) pp. 206-209.

For Mevlânâ ʿÎsâ, deportation and forced resettlement, not Safavid doctrine, is the cause of the first great tribal disturbance. Here and elsewhere in the *Câmiʿü 'l-meknûnât* there is no lack of insight into social conditions and their causes. This would bear out the view that ʿÎsâ was not an official historian.

My third example concerns ʿÎsâ's treatment of booty, *ġanîmet*. Professor İnalcık[18] noted certain facts about the reservoirs of slave labour that were opened through the Turkish conquests in Christian lands. Soldiers could get cash out of prisoners from the slave-merchants who set up their markets at the end of a battle.[19] Mevlânâ ʿÎsâ often has occasion to write that after a successful siege or campaign the army took such a vast amount of booty and prisoners that they were "drowned" in them. The slave market actually plummeted after the battle of Mohács and the ensuing raids into Hungary. *Aḳıncıs* and *göñüllüs* carried off thousands of prisoners; "every poor man in the army got rich;" "one man took thirty to forty captives and sold them – it was unheard-of; but ten of them did not surpass the value of one, and there was nobody who would pay a hundred akçe for one, so that when everybody had his fill, they were not left in the army but put on the boats; they took *pencik* alive for the state treasury, amounting to 120.000 prisoners, compare this now with the 600.000 taken" (An 142b).[20]

My final illustration concerns the need for appointments. ʿÎsâ refers to survivors inheriting the positions of the dead. He observes the heavy losses of the Ottoman army during certain campaigns, especially after the sieges of Belgrade and Rhodes. Tens of thousands were dead or disabled, positions had to be refilled. After a Hungarian campaign two hundred (akçe?) were paid to each disabled soldier (*maḥrûc*) (Is 91).

Though he does not actually mention unemployment among the kadis, it is clear that Mevlânâ ʿÎsâ who had served as a substitute judge during thirty-five years, foresaw misery for his own profession. He warned that the Final Hour would be preceded by the portent (*ʿalâmet*) "humiliation of the learned": Judges and professors would be put to shame; when the flute or the violin would be played they would be alert, but they would pay no heed when Traditions and Commentaries on the Koran were read.

Mevlânâ ʿÎsâ's sources must have been diverse. He knew and cited Aḥmedî's *Iskender-nâme*; he had recourse to the *Tevârîḫ-i Âl-i ʿOsmân*. He displays a

18 H. İnalcık, Introductory Address to the Princeton Conference.

19 H. İnalcık, "Ghulâm" in EI, 2nd ed., s.v.

20 According to İnalcık, "Ghulâm:" "in the second half of the 9th/15th century the average price of a slave was 40-50 Venetian ducats"; Pakalın writes: "when there were many captives, their price fell to 125 akça" (*Tarih Deyimleri* II 766).

thorough knowledge of writings containing the wisdom of Aristotle and Caʿfar aṣ-Ṣâdiḳ. His profession must have given him access to works[21] and libraries where such works were kept.[22]

He discussed these matters with his three friends, two of whom were kadis. He does not say much about the judge Iştibzâde Aḥmed, whose companion he was during the reign of Sultan Bâyezîd II. He is more informative about another judge, Ḳâdî Muḥyîddîn, whose close friend he was between 1512 and 1520 and who was well versed in all the sciences and eminent in *cefr*. Mevlâna ʿÎsâ admired this learned kadi from the naval port of Gelibolu, whose full name was Meḥmed b. Ismaʿîl, Muḥyîddîn, with the nickname Kepecioğlı. For him ʿÎsâ made the final copy of his (Muḥyîddîn's) Turkish compilation concerning juridical questions, *mesâ'il*, entitled, tantalizingly, *Minhâc* (only the Istanbul manuscript contains this information). Mevlânâ ʿÎsâ admired Ḳâḍî Muḥyîddîn who practised, among other sciences, *cefr*. A third friend was the colonel (*mîra-lay*) Murâd Beg, an expert astronomer/astrologer.

These men may perhaps be regarded as the author's patrons. The book is not expressly dedicated to the reigning sultan. Did Sultan Süleymân actively try to influence public opinion through the prophetic writers? A *reml*-prophecy was presented to him after the execution of Prince Muṣṭafâ.[23] The *Rumûz-i Kunûz* of the Bayrâmî Şeyḫ Ibn ʿÎsâ Aḳḥiṣâri (died 1559/60) was completed under his reign.[24] What did he think of the Bayrâmî-Melâmetî Şeyḫ Pîr ʿAlî, who claimed to be the Mahdî? We hear of a conversation between the two men, in which the şeyḫ is said to have uttered, "my *pâdişah*, now to outward appearance you are the Mahdî..."[25] Again, some years later, Seyyid Loḳmân was to write that Süleymân had left behind şeyḫs of religious orders in his pious asceticism and had attained the degree of the perfect men, *aḳṭâb*...[26]

With regard to *ġazâ* ʿÎsâ speaks as an expansionist Ottoman: *ġazâ* is the sultans' duty; integration of the conquered lands is necessary. Vienna must be destroyed in the interest of a safe and prosperous Buda (Ist 90a); it had been

21 An example would be the Turkish version of the *Risâle-i sî faṣl* by Nasîraddîn Ṭûsî, described by M. Götz, *Türkische Handschriften*, (Wiesbaden 1979) (*VOHD* XIII, 4), 341 no. 355.

22 F. Sezgin, *Geschichte des arabischen Schrifttums* VII (Leiden, 1979) refers to many Arabic manuscripts in Turkish libraries.

23 Turan, *Şehzâde Bayezîd Vak'ası*, 25 note 2, quoting T. Gökbilgin.

24 M. Götz, *Türkische Handschriften*, Teil 4 (Wiesbaden, 1979) (*VOHD* XIII, 4), 353 no. 369; H. Sohrweide, *Türkische Handschriften*, Teil 5. (Wiesbaden, 1981) (*VOHD* XIII, 5), 275 no. 293.

25 Abdülbâkî (Gölpinarlı), *Melâmîlik ve Melâmîler* (Istanbul, 1931) with an anecdote of Sultan Süleymân setting free a Melâmî prisoner to ensure victory at Rhodes.

26 *Ḳiyâfetü 'l-İnsâniyye fî Şemâili 'l-ʿO̱smâniyye* (fascsimile, Istanbul, 1987), 48b.

necessary that the Akıncıs had turned Hungarian and Austrian lands into a desert; at least ʿÎsâ boasted that they had done so. After Mohács there was no Ottoman soldier who had not cut off five to ten heads; they used corpses as cushions for their own heads (An 142b). At the same time ʿÎsâ was interested in Christian affairs; he records, in the style of the *ġazavâtnâme*, the deliberations of their leaders; he describes the Sack of Rome; he welcomes the sultan's generosity in giving the Christians back one of their churches in Esztergom.

Perhaps the *Câmiʿü'l-meknûnât* was designed for instruction of a circle of friends, who may have had dervish (Ḫalvetîye? Melâmîye?) connections. By ʿÎsâ's time, suspicion had long turned against subversive Shîʿîs. The hold of the Sunnî establishment had tightened. The Ḳızılbaş were an abomination. But ʿÎsâ's chapter on the death of Shah İsmaʿîl is surprisingly mellow. The Ḳızılbaş finds his resting place in Kerbelâ, where he has built a canal.

With millenarian beliefs speculations sprang up that, pending the end of days, a good life on earth would come. In this mood it was possible to raise the question of the cost of the *ġazavât*, considering the terrible price in dead and wounded, but concluding that it was worth it.

The book's archaic Old Ottoman and the *mes̱nevî* form, which became anachronistic from the seventeenth century onwards, may have been responsible for its being neglected for some time. But it was not wholly forgotten, because Muṣṭafâ ʿÂlî quoted from the work in his *Künhü'l-aḫbâr*. Its semi-esoteric nature may have appealed to him. Through ʿÂlî, public (though not official) opinion under the sultans Murâd III and Meḥmed III remained in touch with Mevlânâ ʿÎsâ's *Câmiʿü'l-meknûnât*, three generations after Sultan Süleymân.

CHAPTER 22

Notes on ʿAruż in Turkish collections

Preliminary Remarks

The boundaries between alliterative, syllabic and rhythmic Turkish verse and ʿaruż metrics have been blurred from the earliest times, and patterns of ʿaruż feet were superimposed on rhythmic Turkish poetry at an early age.[1] Even the archaic poetical quotations contained in Mahmud al-Kashgari's *Diwan Lugat at-Turk* have been shown to be not syllabic folklore but varieties of ʿaruż with various degrees of irregularity.[2] The Khwarazmian poets Kutb[3] and Khwarazmi used old and new forms to meet the metre. Syllabic metres exerted an influence on the quantitative metre,[4] while inversion, graphic representation of closed and open syllables, and "graphic rhyme" were used to accommodate ʿaruż.[5] The redif was useful in difficulties with the choice of rhyme[6]. Syllabic verse forms appealed to the mystic poets who mediated between the court and folk literatures. Turkish sources dealing with ʿaruż and syllabic metres and the poetry composed by wandering mystics belong to tekke or minstrel (aşık or saz şairi) literature which is surveyed in a special issue of *Türk Dili*.[7]

1 T. Gandjeï, "Überblick über den vor- und frühislamischen türkischen Versbau", *Der Islam* 33 (1957), 142-146; I.V. Stebleva, *Razvitie Tjurkskich Poetičeskich form v XI Veke*, Moscow 1971, 285-298.

2 Stebleva, *Razvitie*, 290-298; A. Bodrogligeti, "A Collection of Turkish poems from the fi4th century", *AOH* 16 (1963), 266.

3 A. Zajączkowski, "Studia nad stylistiką i poetiką tureckiej wersji Husräv u Sirin Qutba" I, II *RO* XXV (1961), 31-92, and XXVII (1963); Bodrogligeti, "A Collection", 266.

4 T. Gandjeï, "Zur Metrik des Yusuf u Zulayha von Šayyad Hamza", *UAJb* 27 (1955), 204-208; A. Bombaci, "The Turkic Literatures. Introductory Notes on the History and Style", *PhTF* II (1964), xxvi.

5 S. Rymkiewicz, "Beitrag zur Entwicklung des Reims in der türkischen Kunstliteratur", *RO* XXVII (1963), 45-101.

6 Rymkiewicz, "Beitrag zur Entwicklung des Reims"; Stebleva, *Razvitie*, 294. For a description of full rhyme (the rhyming of Turkish with Arabic and Persian words was a 'mistake'), half rhyme (*yarım kafiye*), rich rhyme (long words), *cinaslı kafiye* "rhyme with word-play", *zengin kafiye* "rich rhyme" see Kathleen R.R. Burrill, *The Quatrains of Nesimî. Fourteenth-Century Turkic Hurufi*, The Hague-Paris 1972, 57-59. For the practical use of redif (all syllables subsequent to the rhyme vowel) see İsmail E. Erünsal, *The Life and Works of Tâcî-zâde Caʿfer Çelebi, with a Critical Edition of His Dîvân*, Istanbul 1983, CI.

7 A. Güzel, "Tekke Şiiri" *TD* 445-450 (June 1989), 251-454, especially 274-283. For folk poets using ʿaruz see C. Dilçin, "Divan Şiirinde Gazel", *TD* 415-417 (July-Sept. 1986), 117-119.

 | DOI 10.1163/9789004355767_023

Turkish poetry continued to build upon the foundation laid by Arabic and Persian theory and practice (Persian could be used for teaching prosody) and by the work of the Karakhanid poets,[8] Turkish poetry continued to build. Its two traditions, rhythmic and quantitative, combined to produce that flowering of prosodic skill which characterized fifteenth- and sixteenth century Turkish poetry in Central Asia, the Mamluk territories, and Anatolia. Turkish poetry did for a long time remain flexible in the application of the classical theories of Persian prosody,[9] but to the poets this seemed a struggle with their "narrow" language for which there was no dictionary to look up origins of words, a language which was "hard", "dry" or "cold",[10] especially if few Arabic and Persian words were used to enhance the smoothness of the prosodical forms. There is evidence to show that this was a "modesty formula" and a rhetorical exercise: the same poets would praise the Turkish language.[11] Some metres could be distinguished intuitively; Latifi's teacher Fani pointed out that in the hazac and the ramal the feet seemed to fall naturally[12], a fact which is also due to their closeness to the rhythm of the syllabic form 4+4+3[13]. Despite their age-old acquaintance with the ʿaruż, Turkish writers for a long time continued to apologize for the "inelegance and barbarity" of their compositions. Such seemingly modest disclaimers were often mere literary conventions. When Şeyyād Hamza, an early Anatolian religious poet, alleges that *ne ʿaruż bilür ol ne nahv u tasrīf / ne kāfiye redīf ne tecnīs-i tam* "he neither knows prosody nor syntax and declension, neither rhyme, repeated rhyme words nor compound harmonies", this may have been sincerely intended. But even accomplished poets would have us believe that their verses were composed in artless and unschooled language.[14] The fear of criticism of learned men was

8 Cf. Finn Thiesen, *A Manual of Classical Persian Prosody with Chapters on Urdu, Karakhanidic and Ottoman Prosody*, Wiesbaden 1982, 210-216; Wheeler M. Thackston, Jr., "Die Prosodie der "persifizierten" Sprachen: Türkisch und Urdu", in W. Heinrichs (ed.), *Neues Handbuch der Literaturwissenschaft. Band 5. Orientalisches Mittelalter*, Wiesbaden 1990, 420-421.

9 Walter G. Andrews, Jr., *An Introduction To Ottoman Poetry*, Minneapolis & Chicago 1976; Erünsal, *Life and Works of Tâcî-zâde Caʿfer Çelebi*, xcix-cv.

10 Sedit Yüksel, *Mehmed. Işk-Nâme*, Ankara 1965, 5; For Hoca Mesʿud's specific complaints regarding metrics see İ. Ünver, "Mesnevî", in *Türk Şiiri Özel Sayısı II (Divan Şiiri), TD* 415-417 (July-September 1986), 560-561; C. Dilçin, *Mesʿud bin Ahmed. Süheyl ü Nev-Bahar*, Ankara 1991, 133-135. For Şeyoğlu's reproaches against the Turkish language see H. Ayan, *Şeyhoğlu Mustafa. Hurşîd-Nâme (Hurşîd u Ferahşâd)*, Erzurum 1979, 11-13.

11 See Ünver, "Mesnevi", *TD* 458 , 558-563 and my no. 1, chapter VII (Fahri), in this volume.

12 W.G. Andrews, Jr., "The Tezkere-i Şuʿara of Latifi as a source for the Critical Evaluation of Ottoman Poetry", PhD dissertation at the University of Michigan, 1970, 82.

13 Dilçin, *Süheyl ü Nev-Bahar*, 135-6.

14 M.F. Köprülü, "La métrique ʿaruz", *PhTF* II, 254, quotes the example of Fuzuli.

always present; Hoca Mesʿud is dismayed by the difficulty of "squeezing" his language into the metre[15]. Within the prosodic rules that so pervaded poetic writing, mistakes were conceded beforehand to fault-finders even in the most high-flown introductions to divans.[16] No wonder that the need for instruction in the system of ʿaruż metrics was felt. Persian handbooks on poetics such as the *Muʿcam* by Şams-i Kays and the *Hadayık as-sihr* by Raşid ad-Din Vatvat were available, as was the *Talhis al-balaga* by Kazwini;[17] the list of manuscripts in Elmalı gives an impression of the range of reference works available even in a provincial Anatolian library.[18] I have listed Turkish ʿaruż manuals in appendix II of this article.

Distribution of epic metres

İsmail Ünver's useful survey of Anatolian Turkish mesnevis[19] lists the following short epic metres:

1. v---/v---/v-- mafāʿīlun mafāʿīlun faʿūlun [hazac 3]
2. --v/v-v-/v-- mafʿūlu mafāʿilun faʿūlun [hazac]
3. -v--/-v--/-v- fāʿilātun fāʿilātun fāʿilun [ramal 1]
4. vv--/vv--/vv- faʿilātun faʿilātun faʿilun [ramal 2]
   (-v--/v--/-- fāʿilātun faʿilātun faʿlun)
5. vv--/v-v-/vv- faʿilātun mafāʿilun faʿilun [hafīf]
   (-v--/v-v-/-- fāʿilātun mafāʿilun faʿlun)
6. vv-/-vv-/-v- muftaʿilun muftaʿilun fāʿilun [recez]
7. v--/v--/v--/v- faʿūlun faʿūlun faʿūlun faʿūl [mutakarib]

Ünver's documentation of published and unpublished Turkish mesnevis, divided into four groups – 1. didactic, a) religious, b) mystic, c) moral, d) encyclopaedic, 2. heroic, a) legendary, b) historic, 3. artistic narratives of love and adventure, 4. mesnevis describing people or events – makes few explicit connections with the metres in which they are written, and does not address the association of certain

15 Hoca Mesʿud's body almost "melted with shame"; for his fear of the anger of people with taste at the sight of incorrectness in composition see Dilçin, *Süheyl ü Nev-Bahar*, 134-135, and Ünver, "Mesnevi", 562-3.

16 Tahir Üzgör, *Türkçe Dîvân Dîbâceleri*, Ankara 1990, 124-126 (Revani, d. 1523).

17 Andrews, *Introduction To Ottoman Poetry*, 13.

18 TUYATOK II 07, 475-480 no. 1601-1612.

19 Ünver, "Mesnevî", 430-563; the following has been compared with the coding of the metres in Erünsal, *The Life and Works of Tâcî-zâde Caʿfer Çelebi*.

metres with genres as in Persian poetry.[20] Attention should be paid to mesnevis where a change in metre occurs, such as the *Risaletü n-Nushiyye* by Yunus Emre which begins in ramal, changes to prose and continues in hazac (*mafāʿilun mafāʿilun faʿūlun*).[21] Epic poems in syllabic metre were unusual in Divan literature; one of the few known examples is the topical *destan* by the sixteenth-century poet Meʿali, based on a line of eight syllables, with the rhyme type called *koşma*. Its theme is the appeal to sultans to redress wrongs, and the cry for help is contained in the refrain "Sultan, fly to our help" *yetiş Gazi Hünkar yetiş*.[22]

The *Shahnama* metre mutakarib, *faʿūlun faʿūlun faʿūlun faʿūl*, appears in the two didactic poems of Karakhanid literature, the long poem *Kutadgu Bilig* (which contains over two hundred quatrains) and the shorter *ʿAtebetü l-haka'ik*. This metre does not lend itself easily to Turkish poetry. In fourteenth-century Anatolia, Hoca Mesʿud chose the hard way by using the mutakarib successfully not only for his 5703 beyt romance *Süheyl u Nev-bahar* but also for his translation of Saʿdi's *Bustan* entitled *Ferheng-name-i Saʿdi Tercemesi*.

The great popularity of the ramal metre in the form *fāʿilātun fāʿilātun fāʿilun*, in Anatolian verse narratives has been attributed to its closeness to the rhythm of the syllabic form 4+4+3, and to the effect which the writings of Calal ad-Din Rumi and his son Sultan Valad had.[23] Şeyyad Hamza's *Yusuf u Zulayha* and Tursun Fakih's *Yemen'de Mukaffaʿ kalʿası destanı*, Gülşehri's *Mantıku t-tayr tercemesi*, ʿAşık Paşa's *Garib-name*, Yusuf Meddah's *Varka ve Gülşah*,[24] Süleyman Çelebi's *Vesiletü n-necat* (*Mevlid*),[25] Enveri's *Düsturname*[26] are all in ramal. It is noteworthy that Ahmedi wrote his long *Iskendername*[27] in this metre and not in the "more lively" hazac.

The hazac in the form *mafāʿilun mafāʿilun faʿūlun*, which also could be scanned to the syllabic rhythm 4+4+3, was preferred for narratives such as the first

---

20 J.T.P. de Bruijn, *Of Piety and Poetry*, Leiden 1983, 191. E.J.W. Gibb, *A History of Ottoman Poetry*, I, 1900, 107 f., tables epic and lyric metres together. Often the metres are connected to the names of poets rather than to specific works.

21 Mustafa Tatçı, *Yunus Emre Divanı. Risaletü'n-Nushiyye. Tenkitli Metin*, Ankara 1991.

22 Published by E. Ambros, *Candid penstrokes. The lyrics of Me'ali, an Ottoman poet of the 16th century* Berlin 1982, 149-155; see also A. Turgut Kut, "XVI. Divan Şairlerinden Me'ali'nin Hece Vezinli Bir Destanı", *Folklor ve Etnografya Araştırmaları* 1984, 311-321.

23 S. Yüksel, *Mehmed. Işk-Nâme*, Ankara 1965, 41. V. Rowe Holbrook, "Diverse Tastes in the Spiritual Life: Textual Play in the Diffusion of Rumi's Order", in L. Lewisohn, *The Legacy of Mediaeval Persian Sufism*, London/New York 1992, 99-120.

24 G.M. Smith, *Yusuf-i Meddah. Varqa ve Gülşah*, Leiden 1976.

25 Published by N. Pekolcay, *Süleyman Çelebi. Mevlid*, Istanbul 1980.

26 I. Melikoff-Sayar, *Le Destan d'Umur Pacha*, Paris 1954.

27 İ. Ünver, *Ahmedi. Iskender-name*, Ankara 1983.

Anatolian *Husrev u Şirin* by Fahri[28], Şeyhoglu Mustafa's *Hurşid-name*, Mehmed's *'Işk-name*, Ahmedi's *Cemşid ü Hurşid*,[29] Tutmacı's *Gül ü Husrev* and the well-known *Husrev u Şirin* by the fifteenth-century poet Şeyhi[30]. The other hazac metre --v/v-v-/v-- (*mafʿūlu mafāʿilun faʿūlun*), rhythmically congenial to Turkish, was used by Fuzuli for his *Leyla ve Mecnun* in the footsteps of Nizami[31].

The hafif, *faʿilātun mafāʿilun faʿilun* (*faʿlun*), the metre of Sultan Veled's *Ibtidanama*, was used by Elvan Çelebi for his mesnevi on the old mystics entitled *Menâkibu'l-Kudsiyye fi Menâsibi'l Ünsiyye*[32] and by Şeyhi in his satirical *Harname*.[33]

The tavil is very rare in Turkish poetry and appears late.[34]

Lyrics in the romances, that is gazels interspersed in mesnevis, have been studied by R. Dankoff.[35]

The metres most commonly used in Anatolian gazels and kasides have been tabulated several times. Walter G. Andrews, Jr. took stock of the more common rhythmical patterns,[36] and his picture of frequency of metres in five published Ottoman divans is,[37]

33.3%	ramal	fāʿilātun fāʿilātun fāʿilātun fāʿilā(tun) fāʿilun
19.4%	mużāriʿ	mafʿūlu fāʿilātu mafāʿilu fāʿilūn
16,6%	ramal	faʿilātun faʿilātun fāʿilātun fāʿilātun
16.5%	hazac	mafāʿilun mafāʿilun mafāʿilun mafāʿilun
5.4%	hazac	mafʿūlu mafāʿilu mafāʿilu mafāʿil (faʿūlun)
4.3%	muctass	mafāʿilun faʿilātun mafāʿilun faʿilun

28 B. Flemming, *Fahris Husrev u Šīrin. Eine türkische Dichtung von 1367*, Wiesbaden 1974; no. 1 in this volume.

29 Mehmet Akalın, *Ahmedî. Cemşid ü Hurşid*, Ankara 1975.

30 F.K. Timurtaşın *Şeyhî'nin Husrev ü Şîrin'i*, Istanbul 1963.

31 A. Bombaci in S. Huri (tr.), *Leyla and Mejnun*, London 1970, 85.

32 The mesnevi dated 760/1358-9 has been published by Ismail E. Erünsal and A. Yaşar Ocak *Elvan Çelebi. Menâkibu'l-Kudsiyye fi Menâsibi'l Ünsiyye*, Istanbul, 1984.

33 F.K. Timurtaş in *TDED* III 1949, 370-387, and *TDED* XI 1961, 99-108.

34 I. Pala, *Ansiklopedik Dîvân Şiiri Sözlüğü* I, Ankara 1989, 123.

35 R. Dankoff, "The Lyric in the Romance: The Use of Ghazals in Persian and Turkish Masnavis", *JNES* 43 (1984), 9-25; see also Dilçin, *Süheyl ü Nev-Bahar*, 136, Yüksel, *Iskname*, 3, 8, 41. Contents of structure of Hamidi's autobiographical mesnevi have been analyzed by M. Glünz, "Vom Paradies bis nach Bursa: Die Lebensbeschreibung des persisch-türkischen Dichters Hāmidī (9./15. jh.)", *Asiatische Studien* XLI (1982), 147-161. See also my "Poem in chronicle", no. 25 in this volume.

36 Andrews, *Introduction to Ottoman Poetry*, 30-32.

37 Andrews, *Introduction to Ottoman Poetry*, 27-29; "these numbers represent the results of a highly unscientific survey of the poems (a total of 2,395) in five published Ottoman divans" (Necati, Ahmed Paşa, Zati, Figani, and Baki).

3.3%	hafīf	faʿilātun mafāʿilun faʿilun (faʿlun)
1.3%	racaz	mustafʿilun mustafʿilun mustafʿilun mustafʿilun
0.8%	hazac	mafʿūlu mafāʿilun mafāʿil (faʿūlun)
0.6%	mużāriʿ	mafʿūlu fāʿilātun mafʿūlu fāʿilātūn
0.5%	mutakārib	faʿūlun faʿūlun faʿūlun faʿūl(un)
0.3%	racaz	muftaʿilun mafāʿilun muftaʿilun mafāʿilun
0.3%	hazac	mafʿūlu mafāʿīlun mafʿūlu mafāʿīlun

According to Erünsal, ramal 1 and 2, muzariʿ 1, and hazac account for most of the authors whose divans have been scrutinized. Full analyses of metrics and their exigencies in specific divans have been published by İsmail E. Erünsal in his edition of the divan by Taci-zade Caʿfer Çelebi and by Edith Ambros in her edition of Me'ali's poetry. Their analysis shows differences in the distribution of metres, Caʿfer Çelebi's metres being ramal 1 and 2, muzariʿ 1 and 2, hazac 1, 2, 3 and 5, muctass 1, hafif, and racaz,[38] and Me'ali's metres being (in his gazels, müfreds, and kitʿas) long variants of ramal, muzariʿ 1 and 2, 5 variants of hazac, hafif, mutakarib, muctass, munsarih, and sariʿ.[39]

Rhyme

Next to studies of the use of rhyme in Anatolian, Khwarazmian, and Chagatay mesnevis[40] and to redif in the mesnevi rhyme,[41] lyric rhyme in divans has been discussed by Andrews.[42] Kadi Burhan ed-Din's rhyme letters have been compiled by Muharrem Ergin in his publication of the *Divan*. The fifteen gazels interspersed in the *Süheyl ü Nevbahar* have pronouncedly Turkish rhymes, such as *virdi/girdi, dirdi, turdı, dürdi, yurdı, buyurdı, burdı*. The *redifli gazel* invited a nazire[43] and at the same time made it difficult to achieve a satisfactory "answer" to the long redifs which, for example, some contemporaries of Caʿfer Çelebi favoured.[44] Gazels in

38 Erünsal, *Life and Works of Tâcî-zâde Caʿfer Çelebi*, C.

39 Ambros, *Candid penstrokes. The lyrics of Me'ali*, 72-74.

40 Sedit Yüksel, *Mehmed. Işk-Nâme*, Ankara 1965, 43, Hüseyin Ayan, *Şeyhoğlu Mustafa. Hurşîd-Nâme*, Erzurum 1979, 102-107, and Dilçin, *Süheyl ü Nev-Bahar*, 141-149, discuss the use of rhyme in epic poems.

41 Such as *kar itdügin bildi hem/ şikar itdügin bildi hem* in Dilçin, *Süheyl ü Nev-Bahar*, 150.

42 Andrews, *Introduction to Ottoman Poetry*, 48-71.

43 Dilçin, "Divan Şiirinde Gazel", 90-92, 108-115, and Dilçin, *Süheyl ü Nev-Bahar*, 149.

44 Erünsal, *Life and Works of Tâcî-zâde Caʿfer Çelebi*, CI.

mesnevis[45] are also in the nazire form.[46] Andrews discussed the function of a redif where the finite verb is in the aorist mood (*elden gider* "[it] goes out of hand"), which means that every couplet will have a normal sentence order with the verb at the final position. In his perceptive analysis of a poem with this redif by Taşlıcalı Yahya, Andrews showed the emotional and social implications of the contrast between emphatic imperatives (*mey sun*! *aç gözüñ*! *kes dilüñ*!) and statements of fact (*elden gider*).[47]

Collections

The remainder of this paper will be devoted, without any claim to completeness, to anthologies (*mecmuʿa*) of poetry. The field is, of course, immensely wide. Whereas the "oevres complètes" of the great divan poets have been published, most of them by Turkish scholars,[48] lately Turkish research has also been directed to the prefatory texts, collections and anthologies which await detailed study. The turkologists' choice of single authors, their interest being in early representatives of Anatolian Turkish literature, has affected the study of these collections. Dealing with the material in collections is a severe test to editors and cataloguers. Names of poets have been listed, but research is now also needed on the purpose and arrangement of the 'miscellanies', most of which are still in manuscript[49]. Whereas in the last decades a great deal of information has appeared in new manuscript catalogues,[50] it must be said that there remain hundreds of unpublished collections which still need sifting[51]. Of the surviving old dated

45 Dankoff, "The Lyric in the Romance", 9-25.

46 Dilçin, "Divan Şiirinde Gazel", 95-98.

47 W.G. Andrews, *Poetry's Voice, Society's Song. Ottoman Lyric Poetry*, Seattle and London, 1985, 124-140.

48 A useful survey of this achievement, which had the incidental effect of canonizing the Turkish tradition to which these poets belonged, is Dilçin, "Divan Şiirinde Gazel", 246-247.

49 Ambros, *Candid Penstrokes. The lyrics of Me'ali*, XX, with bibliography.

50 See the review articles by Eleazar Birnbaum, "Turkish Manuscripts: Cataloguing Since 1960 and Manuscripts Still Uncatalogued", *JAOS* 103 (1982), 413-420 on the *VOHD*, the *TÜYATOK* and Günay Kut, *Tercüman Gazetesi Kütüphanesi Türkçe Yazmalar Kataloğu I.*, Istanbul 1989; see Günay Kut, "Some aspects of the cataloguing of Turkish manuscripts", *Manuscripts of the Middle East* 3 (1988), 60-68.

51 E. Birnbaum, "Turkish Manuscripts: Cataloguing Since 1960 and Manuscripts Still Uncatalogued. Part 2: Yugoslavia, Bulgaria, Romania", in *JAOS* 103 (1983), 515-532, part 3 idem, 691-707, part 4 in vol. 104 (1984), 303-314, part 5 (Turkey and Cyprus) in the same volume, 465-503, lists several collections.

nazire collections, none seem to be earlier than the fourteenth century. The most important fall in the fifteenth century, though many belong to the sixteenth century. The method of publishing a nazire collection is now associated with the name of Mustafa Canpolat, whose edition of the *Mecmūʿatü n-neẓāʾir* by ʿÖmer b. Mezīd suffices to show how useful complete editions of these collections would be.

Through the centuries Turkish anthologists have made efforts to elicit from literature what was of living value to them. The historian of literature sees a development of Turkish poetic traditions as part of medieval literature, reaching back to modest origins and achieving mounting confidence through continuous training in classical imitation, bringing about effective progress and continuous change. Andrews reopened the discussion by expressing a sense of the timelessness of Turkish divan poetry which, for him, embodied the tradition as itself a text[52]. What distinguished one poet's gazels from another's? For an answer we may look for the anthologists' feeling for their living literature and for the values and changes it embodied in anthologies of poetry. It was to meet more than one need that these anthologies were planned and produced; one was the concern for prosody, another was the need for texts to be used at religious gatherings.

Anthologies with Prosodic Concerns

Let us consider some anthologies with prosodic concerns. There is the small collection of Khwarazmian Turkish poetry of Mamluk/Khwarazmian provenance which Sayf-i Sarayi put together as an appendix to his prose work *Gülistan bi t-Türki*, extant in the MS. Leiden, University Library, Cod. Or. 1553[53]. The compiler laid down his concerns in a mesnevi (185v) in which he distinguished two basic features in a literary composition: the correlation between meaning and form (surat). By the latter the whole make-up of a poem is understood, i.e. the satisfaction of prosodic requirements (vazn) and the choice and application of suitably selected expressions (lafz). Sayf distinguishes poets in whose works surat and maʿni are in adequate relation to each other; the intensive cultivation of vazn at the expense of other features of the poem is emphasized. Metrics, pros-

52 Andrews, *Poetry's Voice, Society's Song*, 11.

53 Jan Schmidt, *Catalogue of Turkish Manuscripts in the Library of Leiden University*, vol. II, Leiden 2002. 124-127. It has been published and analyzed by A. Bodrogligeti, *A Fourteenth Century Turkish Translation of Saʿdi's Gulistān*, Budapest 1969, 179-188; see the same author's "Glosses on Sayf-i Sarāyī's Gülistān bi-t-türkī", *AOH* XIV (1962), 207-218; and his article "A Collection", 271-272.

ody and rhetoric qualities come first[54]. Sayf is "very consistent in meeting the requirements of quantitative prosody in the Turkish language".[55] Bodrogligeti showed that Sayf tended to respond to mystical poems by expressing a preference for earthly love[56]. Sayf's collection comprises poems by nine poets (Mevla Kazi Muhsin, Mevlana Ishak, Mevlana ʿImād Mevlevī, Ahmed Hoca as-Sarayi (a poet born in the territory of the Golden Horde), Hvarezmi (a kaside on sunrise, an eulogy on nature), ʿAbdulmecid, Toğlı Hoca, Hasanoğlı, and Sayf-i Sarayi's nazires on the poems of those eight as well as eleven poems by Sayf himself. The rubaʿi was written in answer to a poem by Mahmud Gulistani.[57]

The extensive anthology on Turkish poetry entitled *Mecmūʿatü n-naẓāʾir* compiled by ʿÖmer b. Mezīd dated 840/1437 and dedicated to Sultan Murad II is of Anatolian provenance.[58] The work is preserved in the Ms. London, School of Oriental and African Studies, no. 27,689, and has been published in 1982 by Mustafa Canpolat.[59] It is of special importance for our subject because of its metrical paradigms. It numbers 397 actual poems by eighty-four poets. ʿÖmer's favourite poet is Ahmedi, to whom even earlier writers are made to write nazires. In his preface ʿÖmer explains the notions underlying the selection of poems. He writes for enthusiasts and men of taste, and he includes poems which he likes best as well as those of sympathetic rulers, and also his own (in fact, the core of the collection are seventy poems by himself). He says that "in the realm of word-painting" and the "field of sweetness" skilful constructions and figures of speech (*sanayiʿ ve bedayiʿ*) run the risk of being lost. He makes it clear that he transcribed poetry which was recited: "I collected and listened" he writes (*cemʿ etdüm ve şemʿ etdüm*), his concern being to save this poetry from dispersion and obscurity.

ʿÖmer's anthology contains only poems in which the rhyme schemes and the metres of classical prosody are applied. He divides them into five chapters, headed, hazac (mafāʿilun mafāʿilun mafāʿilun mafāʿilun), hazac (mafāʿilun mafāʿilun faʿūlun), ramal (fāʿilātun fāʿilātun fāʿilātun fāʿilun), ramal (fāʿilātun fāʿilātun fāʿilun), mutakārib (faʿūlun faʿūlun faʿūlun faʿūl), with the mnemonic formula of the metre in a little verse.

54 Bodrogligeti, "A Collection", 253.

55 Bodrogligeti, "A Collection", 261.

56 Bodrogligeti, "A Collection", 259-261.

57 Bodrogligeti, "Glosses on Sayf-i Sarāyī's Gülistān bi-t-türkī", *AOH* XIV (1962), 207-218; *AOH* XIV (1962), 281.

58 C.S. Mundy, "Notes on Three Turkish Manuscripts", *BSOAS* CII (1948), 533-541, described the manuscript.

59 Mustafa Canpolat (ed.), *ʿÖmer bin Mezīd. Mecmūʿatü'n-Neẓāʾir*, Ankara, 1982. N. Pekolcay, *İslâmî Türk Edebiyatı*, Istanbul 1967, published photographs of the introduction (pl. 45); A.S. Levend, *Türk Edebiyatı Tarihi* I, 1973, 167; M. Canpolat, "Hassan'ın Şiirleri", *Ömer Asım Aksoy Armağanı*, Ankara 1978, 27-44; G. Kut, "Mukhtārāt in Turkish", *EI* VII, 531.

ʿÖmer points out that the full title of his work, *Mecmūʿatü n-naẓāʾir nüzhet-geh-i defātir ṣayal-zen-i havātır,* is written in sacʿ and can be scanned to two metres, for example mustafʿilun faʿūlun mustafʿilun faʿūlun or mafʿūlu fāʿilātun mafʿūlu fāʿilātun (ten tāni ten tenā ten ten ten tani ten tena ten).

Equally interesting is an anthology of nazires in the shape of a diwan put together for the Mamluk Sultan al-Malik al-Ashraf Kanisavh al-Gawri, who grew up under the influence of Sultan Kaytbay. It is extant in the manuscript Berlin, Ms. or. oct. 3744. This royal "pocket library"[60] which includes a miniature representing the ruler, was produced at a time when Turkish poetry flourished not only in Anatolia, but also in Egypt, where it developed a style which, compared with that of 'classical' writing, was something new and strange. The new manner was *dervişane*; music played a role in it, and it is not fortuitous that Gawri's manuscript contains a treatise in the defence of music which Kaytbay had also been fond of. There is no preface to this incomplete collection, which numbers 109 poems by some twenty-two poets and has no metrical paradigms, although the interest in prosody is apparent. The collection is followed by poems by ʿAdni, Ahmed Pasha and Ahmedi[61] and at the end the art of prosody is treated in didactic poems.

The poet Nazmī Mehmed Çelebi from Edirne (d. 1543-4), a clerk of the law-courts turned sipahi, wrote four volumes of poetry in a variety of metres in addition to compiling poetry written up to 1523-4 in his *Mecmūʿatü n-naẓāʾir* which survives in three manuscripts in Istanbul (Topkapı Sarayı Ahmed III 2644; Nuruosmaniye 4222, and Millet Library, Ali Emiri manzum 683 = I, and 684 = II), and Vienna H.O. 142[62]. The biographers Sehi Beg and Latifi knew this work as a collection of nazires composed by the poets of Rum under the title *Camiʿu n-naẓaʾir*. Latifi observed that it consisted of nazires composed by earlier poets of Rum up to 930/1523-24, arranged in alphabetical order and by metre, and that he invented new metres (including pointed and unpointed musammat) in composing a gazel to each of the verses ending in *elif* in the *Risale-i ʿaruż* by Vahīd-i Tabrizi.[63] Nazmi's anthology consists of 3,356 entire gazels by 243 poets,[64] among them 73 by Caʿfer Çelebi and 72 by Meʾali.[65]

---

60 I borrow the expression from J.T.P. de Bruijn, "Mukhtarat in Persian literature", *EI* VII, 529.

61 M. Götz, *Türkische Handschriften Teil 2,* Wiesbaden 1968, 210 no. 306; ibidem 212 no. 308, and 213 no. 309.

62 Under the title *Nazaʾirü l-eşʿār*, cf. Ambros, *Candid Penstrokes. The lyrics of Meʾali*, XX-XXI.

63 Günay Kut, *Hest bihişt, the tezkire by Sehi Beg. An analysis of the first biographical work on Ottoman poets with a critical edition based on MS. Süleymaniye Library, Ayasofya, O. 3544*, Cambridge, Mass., 1978, 305; Latifi ed. Ahmed Cevdet, Istanbul 1314/1896-7; [O. Rescher], *Türkische Dichterbiographien II: Latifi's Tezkere*, Tübingen 1950, 275-276.

64 M. Ergin, "Melihi" in *TDED* II (1947), 60; Levend, *Türk Edebiyatı Tarihi* I, 168, and G. Kut, "Mukhtarat".

65 Ambros, *Candid Penstrokes. The lyrics of Meʾali*, 64.

A precious manuscript preserved in the Topkapı Sarayı Müzesi Bağdat Köşkü 406 contains the collection by Pervāne b. ʿAbdullāh, a page in the household of Sultan Süleymān (*min gilmān-i beyt ul-hāssa fi sarāy al-ʿāmira as-sultāniya*), entitled *Cāmiʿu n-naẓā'ir*. This anthology is divided according to metres (*bahr*) and has short notices on the poets. The preface (fol. 1) is lost, but the colophon gives the purpose: ʿhe collected and classified these fine distichs and lovely gazels by poets from Ottoman towns (*bilād*) and fusahā from the Süleymanic lands'. Pervane selected eighty gazels by Caʿfer Çelebi. The date is given in fractions.[66] Royal gazels were later added in the margins.[67]

The *Zübdetü l-eşʿar* completed in 1614 by the professor, judge and poet Kafzade Feyzullah Efendi (Fa'izi; died 1621-2) is primarily an anthology of poetry, and only secondarily a dictionary of about five hundred poets. It consists not of full gazels but only of 'best' couplets; the arrangement is according to poets in alphabetical order (it has been ranged among the tezkires). Fa'izi quotes a larger number of lines from Haleti (a contemporary and a prominent member of the ʿulema) than from Baki, using the excuse that "...it is impossible for anyone to drink a fountain quite dry, however thirsty he may be"[68]. This work may be seen as the most successful anthology of the type which chose prosody as its priority. It is preserved in at least ten manuscripts (see appendix IV).

Hisālī of Budin (died 1651) compiled the undated *Meṭāliʿü n-naẓā'ir* in two volumes; it consists of matlaʿs (including the compiler's) grouped according to metres and rhymes. The autograph copy is preserved in Istanbul, MS. Nuruosmaniye 4252-4253[69].

The *Zübdetü l-eşʿar* inspired a sequel, the *Zeyl-i Zübdetü l-eşʿar* by Seyrekzade Mehmed ʿAsim (d. 1675), which consists of citations from poets who lived between 1622 and 1675[70], and a sequel to the sequel,

> compiled by Belig Seyyid Ismaʿil from Bursa (d. 1729), entitled *Nuhbetü l-Asar li zeyl-i Zübdetü l-eşʿar* and dedicated in 1726 to Damad Ibrahim Paşa. The material is again arranged alphabetically according to the poets. The autograph is preserved in the Library of the University of Istanbul, TY 1182[71].

66 I saw the date (963/beg. 16 Nov. 1555) but did not have time to copy the text and apply the principles developed by H. Ritter, "Philologika XII. Datierung durch Brüche", *Oriens* 1 (1958), 237-247. The date 968/beg. 22 Sept. 1560 is given by G. Kut, "Mukhtarat" 531, and Levend, *Türk Edebiyatı Tarihi* I, 168.

67 M. Ergin, "Câmi'ü l-Meâni'deki Türkçe Şiirler", *TDED* III (1949), no. 3-4, 539-569, esp. 540.

68 Gibb, *HOP* III, 140-141, 203-4, 223, 233.

69 G. Kut, "Mukhtarat", 531.

70 *GOW* 156; Levend, *Türk Edebiyatı Tarihi* I, 168, 303.

71 Levend, *Türk Edebiyatı Tarihi* I, 317-320.

Mecmuʿas with probably prosodic contents are:

- the *Camiʿu n-naẓa'ir* by an anonymous author; preserved in the manuscript Istanbul Üniversitesi Kütüphanesi T.Y. 2955; it is incomplete and begins with gazels rhyming in "b"; according to Fevziye Abdullah it was completed between 970 and 972,[72]
- another *Camiʿu n-naẓa'ir* compiled by an anonymous writer is preserved in the MS. Istanbul Üniversitesi Kütüphanesi T.Y. 1547,[73]
- the Mecmuʿa Revan 1972 and Millet Ali Emiri Efendi Manzum 674 quoted by E. Ambros and İ. Erünsal,[74]
- and the collection of royal gazels by Mehmed II, Bayezid II, Selim I and Süleyman brought together in the *Mecmuʿa-i eşʿar* in T.K.S. Y. 131[75].

The titles of these works have taken us to the seventeenth and eighteenth century. By that time it was felt that the poets of the early Ottoman ages had been sufficiently anthologized. Poetry could grow stale through repetition. New anthologies appeared which were collections of the best work of contemporaries.

Religious Anthologies

Not all anthologies were regarded as repositories of paradigms but many were collections of works of religious teaching and singing. ʿAruż was not all-important here; there was room for collections of poetry in the syllabic metre (national metre, *millî vezin*). An old collection of this kind is that compiled in turkophone Egypt by ʿAlī b. Ahmed b. Emīr ʿAlī. In it he collected Turkish mystical poems by ʿĀşık Paşa,[76] Kaygusuz Abdal, and Yunus Emre under the title *Mecmūʿa-i latīfe*, extant in the MS. Topkapı Sarayı Müzesi Kütüphanesi no. Koğuşlar 950.[77] It was dedicated to the Mamluk Sultan Kaytbay, who loved Sufi poetry and song, and who was also the recipient of the Turkish treatise on prosody mentioned above.

---

72 Ergin, "Melihi" in *TDED* II 1948, 61; Levend, Edeb. Tar. 169)

73 Levend, *Türk Edebiyatı Tarihi* I, 169.

74 Ambros, *Candid Penstrokes. The lyrics of Me'ali*, XX.

75 F.E. Karatay, *Topkapı Sarayı Müzesi Kütüphanesi Türkçe Yazmalar Kataloğu* I, Istanbul 1961, 266 no. 2701.

76 A. Zajączkowski, *Poezje Stroficzne ʿĀšïq-Paša*, Warsaw, 1967.

77 Karatay, *Türkçe Yazmalar Kataloğu* II, 88f., no. 2253; Müjgân Cunbur in *X. Türk Dil Kurultayında okunan Bilimsel Bildiriler 1963* (Ankara 1964), 23ff. especially p. 28; M. Akalın, "Kaygusuz Abdal'ın Gevher-nâmesi", *Edeb. Fak. Araştırma Dergisi, Ahmet Caferoğlu Özel Sayısı*, sayı 10, Ankara, 1979, 189-197.

The Anatolian Haccī Kemāl from Eğridir compiled in 1512 his *Cāmiʿü n-naẓā'ir*, which is preserved in the MS. İstanbul, Bayezit Devlet Library, Umumî 5782.[78] The compiler, to judge from his introduction, was concerned with various forms of religious, especially mystical poetry. In his preface Haccī Kemāl states that he brought together poems by 266 poets, including his own, as expressions of those poets who grew up inspired by God.[79] The three monorhyme poems mentioned above by Şeyyād Hamza in Haccı Kemal's collection have religious themes; they follow the kaside form of monorhyme in

-ām (I)
-ūn, rhyming with Turkish Un (II)
-ānı (III)

The *Çarhnāme*, a poem "which expounds the religious and mystical thoughts of a diwan poet" is included, as are ten gazels by Caʿfer Çelebi.[80]

The anonymous compiler of the anthology entitled *Cāmiʿü l-Meʿānī*, preserved in the Nuruosmaniye Library no. 4904, completed in Istanbul in 940/1533-34[81], explicitly speaks of his religious purpose. M. Ergin who examined the manuscript described the compiler as a fervent mystic, a man of good taste, equipped with a good knowledge of Persian and Turkish and their dialects, a calligrapher (the writing is beautiful taʿlik), and a "friendly and modest person". Whereas nazire collections often contain only a limited number of poems, the *Camiʿ ul-Meʿani* unites practically the collected works of a small number of poets, specifically treating religious subjects. The contents are in Persian and Turkish, mostly in poetry, with prose excerpts, by, among others, Kaygusuz, Kemal-i Ümmi, Nesimi, and Yunus Emre.[82] All these have been brought together for the sake of religion.

---

78 Fuat Köprülü, "Anatolische Dichter in der Seldschukenzeit. I. Şejjad Hamza", *Kőrösi Csoma Archivum* I/3 (June 1922), 184-188; Turkish version in *Türk Yurdu* 1340; "Anadolu metinleri, XIII. asır, 1. Şeyyad Hamza", *Türkiyat Mecmuası* VII-VIII (1940-1941), 95-101; M. Mansuroğlu, "Anadolu Türkçesi (XIII. Asır). Şeyyad Hamza'ya Ait Üç Manzume", *TDED* I (1946), 180-195; M. Ergin, "Câmi-ül-Meâni'deki Türkçe Şiirler", *TDED* III (1949), no. 3-4, 539-569; Levend, *Türk Edebiyatı Tarihi* I, 168.

79 MS. Bayezit Umumi Ktph., no. 5782, 1b.

80 Erünsal, *Life and Works of Tâcî-zâde Caʿfer Çelebi*, lxxxvii; G. Kut, "Mukhtarat", 531.

81 M. Ergin, "Câmi-ül-Meâni'deki Türkçe Şiirler", *TDED* III (1949), no. 3-4, 539-569; Levend, *Türk Edebiyatı Tarihi*, 170. Description: *İstanbul Kütüphaneleri Yazma Divanlar Kataloğu*, 1947, I, 6-7 on Yunus Emre. The MS Nuruosmaniye 4904 has often been quoted: Ergin, op. cit., 539-540.

82 Ergin, "Câmi'ü l-Meâni'deki Türkçe Şiirler", *TDED* III (1949), 541-544.

A *Mecmuʿa-i kelam-i ʿurefa-i billah* in the T.K.S., Y. 1821, announces mysticism as its priority; it includes ilahis by Yunus Emre.[83]

The Tezkires as Anthologies

The biographers of poets consistently give samples of verses at the conclusion of each notice. In their assessment of their own achievement and the work of colleagues the tezkire writers made anthologies of established poets, of poets as yet unestablished, or posthumous collections of minor poets. They combed mecmuʿas for couplets, and when such a couplet was part of a gazel or kaside, it often represented the matlaʿ which could be the best couplet of the poem. Sometimes entire gazels or a significant portion of a kaside or of a mesnevi might be recorded.[84] Misraʿs inserted within the narrative might serve to justify a point made by the biographer or to associate an event with a line of poetry once uttered by a famous poet.[85]

The tezkire genre was close to informal compilations of which the Ottomans, avid collectors, were fond.[86] Scrapbooks and ʿmemorabilia albums' (*cönk*)[87] were kept, and a poet from the East was called a ʿwalking scrapbook', *ayaklu cönk*.[88]

All of these collections exhibit a concern for tradition, and the material acquires significance when we differentiate between the purposes of the compilers which may be prescriptive and prosodic or directed towards religious performance. It is important to consider the suggestion which their appearance gives of the relation between compiler and user, allowing for a number of possibilities. The format is a pointer to a concern for practical issues[89]. The great cataloguing enterprises that gave us the lists of poets in anthologies of poetry[90] should now be

83 Karatay, *Türkçe Yazmalar Kataloğu* I, 268 no. 2705.

84 For a survey see Levend, *Türk Edebiyatı Tarihi*, I, 251-352. For tezkires as collections see C. Dilçin, "Divan Şiirinde Gazel", 127-131.

85 J. Stewart-Robinson, "The Ottoman Biographies of Poets", *JNES* 72, with other examples, such as the kitʿa, rubaʿi, muhammes, ta'rih, muʿamma, lugaz, naʿt, and sharkı; see also Harun Tolasa, "Şair tezkirelerinde örnek verme işlemi." *EÜSBFD* 1 (1980), 199-230.

86 Andrews, "Tezkere-i Şuʿara of Latifi", 19.

87 C.H. Fleischer, *Bureaucrat and Intellectual in the Ottoman Empire*, Princeton 1986, 251.

88 H. Sohrweide, "Dichter und Gelehrte aus dem Osten im osmanischen Reich (1453-1600), *Der Islam* 46 (1970), 273.

89 For a description see Gibb, *HOP* III, 203,

90 *TüYATOK* III 07, Istanbul 1983, 192-196, gives full lists of anthologies in the Elmalı Library.

followed by indexes of first lines[91] (for which Andreas Tietze pleaded years ago). Erünsal has pointed out that Caʿfer Çelebi quietly paid tribute to a line by Fuzuli.[92] Correspondences in rhyme[93], too, for which an example is given in Appendix I, may serve as demonstrable evidence of connectedness and may help us to orient our understanding of Turkish poetry.

Appendices

I Rhymes in three anthologies (Sayf's appendix to his *Gülistan* [s], ʿÖmer b. Mezid's *Mecmuʿatü n-naẓaʾir* [ö], Sultan Gawri's *Diwan* [g]) and in the *Diwan* by Taci-zade Caʿfer Çelebi [c]

-ā	108	c	r1	kas
-ā	117	c	m1	kas
-ā	11b	g	kas	
-ā	4b	g	kas	
-abdur	158-160	ö	h	
-ā beni	456	c	m1	
-ā beni	181-186	ö	remel	
-ā beni	462	c	r1	
-ā bir kepenek	297	c	r2	
-ā bize	26a	g		
-ā bu gice	410	c	r2	
-ā didiler	224	c	r2	
-ā gele	377	c	m11	
-ā ḥakkı	20b	g	münacat	
-ā kılan Allāhdur	22a	g		
-ā kılan kim	150-152	ö	h	
-ā köñül		sayf		
-ā mı gelür	219	c	r2	
-ā yine	60	c	r1	kas
-ā-yıʿīd	93	c	r1	kas
-āb	125	c	r1	kas

91 Mustafa Tatçı provided lists of first lines of poems by Yunus Emre in three collections extant in the manuscripts Berlin, Ms. or. oct. 2575 and Ms. or. oct. 2869, and Vienna, Mxt. 190.

92 Erünsal, *Life and Works of Tâcî-zâde Caʿfer Çelebi*, XCI-XCII.

93 Provided by Hüseyin Ayan in his doctoral dissertation on Nesimi, referred to in his "Seyyid Nesimi Hakkındaki Çalışmamız", *Ed. Fak. Araştırma Dergisi* (Erzurum 1971), 71.

-āb	205	c	r1	
-āb	482	c	r1	
-a benüm çok sevdügüm	341	c	r1	
-āb gibi	423	c	r2	
-āb iki	452	c	reci	
-āb olıcak	286	c	r2	
-āb olubdur	58b-59a	g		
-āb olur	222	c	m1	
-āb üstine	38	c	r1	kas
-āb-ı nāz	264	c	m1	
-ābda	383	c	r1	
-ābdan maḥẓūẓ	278	c	h1	
-āblar	218	c	r1	
-acuğı	437	c	m1	
-ād	135-137	ö	h	
-ād eyle	391	c	r2	
-ād eylemişsin eyleme	234-236	ö	remel	
-ād it ki gitdük üşde şehrüñden	373	c	h1	
-ād olmasun	199	ö	remel	
-āda gel	329	c	r1	
-ādan gelür	241-2	ö	remel	
-ādan gelürüz	27a	g		
-ādān	121	c	h1	kas
-adıla	84b	g		
-ādur	67-73	ö	h	
-ādur söylenür	238-9	ö	remel	
-āf	157-158	ö	h	
-āf	281	c	r1	
-aġ	280	c	r1	
-āġ ateş	129	c	h1	kas
-aġı	115-125	ö	h	
-aġ içinde	131-133	ö	h	
-aġ içinde	385	c	h3	
-aġa dahı	427	c	hafı	
-aġında dur dahı	60a-60b	g		
-aġum benüm	46a-47a	g		
-āh	399	c	müci	
-āh	381	c	m1	
-āh	213	c	m1	
-āh baña	197	c	müci	

-āh beni	415	c	r2	
-āh bilür	228	c	r2	
-āh egri	451	c	h1	
-āh eyler	253	c	r2	
-āhdur	239	c	r1	
-āhı	478	c	h2	
-āhı	431	c	h2	
-āhı sensedüm	232	ö	remel	
-āẖlar	245	c	r1	
-āhumdur benüm	335	c	r1	
-ak	54b-56a	g		
-a közleriñ		sayf		
-ak	289	c	m1	
-āk	295	c	h3	
-āk idelüm	343	c	r2	
-akı	52b-53a	g		
-ākī	425	c	h3	
-ākinden	365	c	r2	
-akınġa		sayf		
-āl	321	c	r1	
-āl	87a	g		
-āl	42	c	r1	kas
-āl	2b	g		kas
-āl olmak neden	361	c	r1	
-āl-i Mustafā	15b	g	kas	
-āle	44a-46a	g		
-āli	81a	g		
-āli Pīrīnüñ	307	c	r1	
-ālik	14a	g		kas
-ālum benüm	337	c	r1	
-ām	83	c	r1	kas
-ām aña	201	c	m1	
-ām üstine	401	c	r1	
-āme	484	c	haf1	
-āme	393	c	m2	
-āmeler	248	c	r1	
-āmet ancak	65b-66b	g	(Cem)	
-āmlara	404	c	r2	
-āmum var idi	438	c	r1	
-āmuz var bizüm	345	c	r1	

-ān	483	c	r1	
-ān	27	c	m1	kas
-ān	139	c	müc1	kas
-ān ağladı	436	c	r1	
-ān aña	199	c	r1	
-ān baña	196	c	r1	
-ān beni	447	c	r1	
-ān beni	454	c	r1	
-ān būse	396	c	h1	
-ān dahı	419	c	m1	
-ān degül	328	c	r1	
-ān dur	48a-49a	g		
-ān eglencesi	414	c	r1	
-ān elden gider	29b-31a	g		
-ān eyledi	446	c	r1	
-ān eylemek olmaz	67b	g		
-ān gerek	300	c	r1	
-ān gözlerüñle kaşlaruñ	242-3	ö	remel	
-ān her gice	407	c	r1	
-ān menzilidür	137-139	ö	h	
-ānı çeşmümüñ	160-170	ö	r	
-anı yok mı	133-135 ö	h		
-ān ider Halīl	61b	g		
-ān idersin	481	c	h3	
-ān idi	422	c	m1	
-ān idici	432	c	r2	
-ān ile bahş	209	c	r1	
-ān imiş bildük	299	c	müc1	
-ān itdi firāk	283	c	r1	
-ān körünür		sayf		
-ān Muhammed	12b	g	kas	
-ān oğurladı	68a	g		
-ān ola	198	c	m1	
-ān öldürür	257	c	rec1	
-ān olmadı	444	c	r1	
-ān olmasun	200	ö	remel	
-ān olmayan	362	c	r1	
-ān olsa şemʿ	279	c	r1	
-ān olsa gerek	293	c	r2	
-ān oynamak	187-193	ö	remel	

-ān şekil	322	c	r2	
-ān sizlere	57a-58a	g		
-ān tevbe kıl	23b	g	kas	
-ān-ı ʿışk	287	c	r1	
-ān-ı kerem	476	c	r2	
-ān-ı misk	97	c	m1	kas
-āna begcügezüm	332	c	haf1	
-āna getürme	411	c	h2	
-āna sıhhat yaraşur	236	c	reci1[94]	
-āna Mustafā	434	c	m1	
-āna yaraşur	I,168		Zati	
-ānam	340	c	h3	
-āndan bilürem sen de bilürsin	88-89		ö	h
-āndur	244	c	r2	
-āne	412	c	h1	
-āne	31b-34b	g		
-ānedür	242	c	r1	
-āneye	409	c	r1	
-āneyi	207-211	ö	remel	
-anı çeşmümüñ	160-171	ö	remel	
-anı çıkdı	74a	g		
-anı dürüst	208	c	r1	
-ānı	21-38	ö	h	
-ānı	463	c	r2	
-ānı	418	c	h1	
-ānı dur		sayf		
-ānı eylemez	265	c	m2	
-ānı kamer	256	c	r1	
-ānı kimdür dimezem	336	c	r1	
-ānı yine	394	c	r2	
-ānī		sayf		
-ānı Ahmed	155-156 ö	h		
-ānidüm	70a	g		
-ānıdur	133	c	r1	kas
-ānı gördüm	129-131	ö	h	
-ānın öp	203	c	r1	
-ānın yasdanur	230	c	r1	
-ānını	439	c	r1	

94 For this rhyme see below, sultana sıhhat yaraşur.

-ānlar içinde	378	c	h2	
-ānlık.dan	372	c	r2	
-anmaz mı	440	c	h1	
-ān murādı	154-155 ö	h		
-ānsuzdur ol	319	c	r1	
-ānum benüm	350	c	r1	
-ānum boynuña	395	c	r1	
-ānum sensedüm	233-4	ö	remel	
-ānum taññıyçün	50a-51a	g		
-ānum var imiş	273	c	r1	
-ānumdur benüm	348	c	r1	
-ānumuza	398	c	r2	
-anuñ	69a	g		
-ānuñ	78-81	ö	h	
-ānuñ senüñ	480	c	r1	
-ānuñ senüñ	292	c	r1	
-ar erür		sayf		
-ar hey	464	c	r1	
-ār	169	c	mücı	kas
-ār	249	c	r1	
-ār	72	c	r1	kas
-ār	250	c	m1	
-ār andan	369	c	h1	
-āra bakmaz	152-153	ö	h	
-ār ayruluğı	435	c	r2	
-ār dahı	450	c	r2	
-ār elden çıkar	226-228	ö	remel	
-ār elden gider	29a-b	g	r1[95]	
-ār eyledi	458	c	r1	
-ār eyler	233	c	h1	
-ār ider	254	c	r1	
-ār idi	453	c	r1	
-ār ile	392	c	r1	
-ār imişsin böyle bilmezdüm seni	433	c	r1	
-ār isteyen	357	c	r1	
-ār itsem gerek	110	c	r1	

95 For this rhyme see also Hatayi no. 69, Zati 288; Taşlıcalı Yahya. Cf. Andrews, *Poetry's Voice, Society's Song. Ottoman Lyric Poetry*, Seattle and London, 1985, 123-4; A.N. Tarlan, *Zatî Divanı*, I Istanbul 1967.

-ār kadeh	211	c	mücı	
-ār laʿl	317	c	mı	
-ār olduġı-çün	47	c	hafı	kas
-ār öldürür	248	ö	mütekārib	
-ār olmasun	194-199	ö	remel	
-ār olmasun kimse	413	c	hı	
-ār olubdur dōstlar	255	c	rı	
-ār sebz	267	c	mı	
-ār şud	36b	g		
-ārum ḫoş mıdur	244-5	ö	r	
-ār yok	290	c	rı	
-ār-ı Mustafā	10b	g		
-āra beñzetdüm	346	c	mücı	
-ārda	388	c	rı	
-ardan sakınub	204	c	r2	
-ārdan	220-223	ö	remel	
-ar dirler	48-53	ö	h	
-ārdur	473	c	rı	
-āreler	226	c	rı	
-āre ne	246-7	ö	r	
-ārı	461	c	hı	
-ārı benefşe	101	c	h2	kas
-ārından	86-88	ö	h	
-ārı olam	352	c	r2	
-ārı yüzinde	387	c	h2	
-ārını	449	c	rı	
-arını bilmez	82a	g		
-ārlıġı	421	c	rı	
-ār öldürür	248-9	ö	mütekarib	
-ārum hoş midür	244	ö	remel	
-ārum nicesin hoşca misin	359	c	r2	
-ārum tanrıyçün	49a-50a	g		
-ārum yok	285	c	mücı	
-ārunām senüñ	302	c	mı	
-āruñla	408	c	r2	
-āruñ elin	364	c	r2	
-āruñ ola	200	c	r2	
-āruñ senüñ	294	c	rı	
-as	485	c	h3	
-aş eylemez	25b	g		

-ās	270	c	r1	
-ās	275	c	müc1	
-āsı	142-145	ö	h	
-āsı çeşmümüñ	170-171	ö	r	
-ası çeşmümüñ	308	c	r1	
-āsı nedür	27b	g		
-āsı var	232	c	r1	
-āsın	18	c	h3	kas
-aşlar	171-181 ö	remel		
-aşlaruz biz	268	c	h2	
-aşmasun	368	c	m1	
-aşum benüm	356	c	r1	
-at	277	c	r1	
-āt	206	c	h3	
-ātı	7a	g	kas	
-atından	83b	g		
-ay göñül	326	c	r2	
-ay sakal	323	c	r2	
-āya	38-48	ö	h	
-āya kemer	225	c	r2	
-āya k.omazlar	231	c	h2	
-āya uġradum	338	c	r1	
-āye zülfüñ	298	c	h3	
-āyı kimseye	402	c	r1	
-āyile	74b	g		
-ayım		sayf		
-āyuñdur senüñ	314	c	r1	
-āż	276	c	r1	
-āz gül	186	c	r1	kas
-āz olsun begüm	349	c	r1	
-āz olur	252	c	r1	
-āza	405	c	h1	
-āza	125-125	ö	h	
-eb olmaz	269	c	h2	
-ebi	430	c	r2	
-ede	379	c	m1	
-edi	441	c	m1	
-ef	78a	g		
-ehi	428	c	r2	
el benüm ü etek senüñ	72b	g		

-elden	154	ö	h	
-elüm	331	c	r2	
-em	98-108	ö	h	
-em	82b	g		
-em degül	216-220	ö	remel	
-emdür	243	c	müc1	
-emdür	109-115	ö	h	
-emin	363	c	r1	
-emüñ	291	c	r2	
-en	66	c	r1	kas
-en	370	c	r1	
-en behey kāfir	220	c	haf	
-en durur	240	c	r1	
-en ölicek	315	c	r2	
-en tutar	238	c	m1	
-enc	210	c	r2	
-end ile	400	c	m1	
-enden	360	c	h2	
-enden cüdā	202	c	r1	
-endi	429	c	h2	
-eng	306	c	r1	
-engiçün	51a-52a	g		
-eni	460	c	r1	
-eni	417	c	r2	
-enüñ	313	c	r2	
-er	90-98	ö	h	
-er	241	c	r1	
-er	223	c	h3	
-er		sayf		
-er	22	c	r1	kas
-er bu gice	389	c	r2	
-er depredür	228-232	ö	remel	
-er devridür	235	c	r1	
-er döne döne	36b-38a	g		
-er düzer	236-238	ö	remel	
-er ey dost	207	c	h2	
-er kākül-i müşkīn-i dōst	78	c	r1	kas
-er kana kana	38b-39b	g		
-er lāle	151	c	müc1	kas
-er leẕīẕ	216	c	m1	

-er nergis	158	c	r2	kas
-er yana yana	39b-40a	g		
-er yanar	68b	g		
-er yazar	246	c	r1	
-ercük olur	71a-71b	g		
-erdedür	211-216	ö	remel	
-erden	81-86	ö	h	
-erden ayrıldum	333	c	müc1	
-erdi	426	c	h3	
-erdi anuñ	312	c	r1	
-eri		sayf		
-eri	442	c	r2	
-erlik	310	c	h1	
-erüñ	303	c	r2	
-eş	272	c	h2	
-eş oldı	420	c	r2	
-esi var	217	c	h2	
-estedür	227	c	r1	
-et ola	114	c	r2	kas
-et virüb durur	234	c	m1	
-et yegdür	261	c	r2	
-et yok	284	c	h1	
-ete	80a	g		
-eti	201-207	ö	remel	
-eti dervīşlerüñ	20	c	r2	kas
-etüm	339	c	r1	
-ey	455	c	h2	
-īb	245	ö	r	
-ībi	145-147	ö		
-īb	42b-43b, 79a	g		
-ide	382	c	r1	
-īh	212	c	müc1	
-ıkdur	229	c	h1	
-il	330	c	h1	
-īl	316	c	r2	
-ilsün	358	c	h2	
-īm	8b	g	kas	
-īm	165	c	r1	kas
-īm	40a-41b	g		
-īm üstine	384	c	r1	

-īn	367	c	r1
-īn eyler	247	c	r2
-ında tutar		sayf	
-īnesine	380	c	r2
-īni	459	c	h1
-īnüñ	304	c	h3
-ir	259	c	m2
-ir dahı	424	c	r1
-īr	75a	g	
-īr	260	c	h1
-īr	469	c	müc1
-īr eyledüñ	239-241	ö	remel
-īr eylemez	223-226	ö	remel
-īr eylemiş	271	c	r1
-īr olasın sen	366	c	h1
-īr olasın sen	42a	g	
-īrüñ senüñ	311	c	r1
-iş	274	c	r2
-īş itmedüñ	309	c	r1
-itmesün	371	c	r1
-itmez	266	c	m2
-i yüz	147-148	ö	h
-iyyeti	201	ö	remel
-mā	34b-36a	g	
-olıcak dostum	354	c	r1
sultāna sıhhat yaraşur		85b	g
-ū	376	c	h1
-ubdur	126-129	ö	h
-ūb olur	258	c	r1
-ūb olacakdur	63a	g	
-ūb olasın sen	41b, 73a	g	
-ūd	215	c	m1
-ūd ola	195	c	r1
-ūdur çāre ne	246-7	ö	remel
-ül	139-142	ö	h
-ül	318	c	h1
-ül	320	c	r1
-ül eylerem	334	c	r1
-ül gibi	445	c	r1
-ül hemīşe	140-150	ö	h

-ül şāh şāh	214	c	r1
-ū	53-63	ö	h
-ūlar	262	c	h1
-ūlar ile	386	c	r2
-ülüñ	301	c	r1
-ümden	153	ö	h
-ūm olaydum kāşkī	457	c	r1
-ūn eylemez	263	c	r1
-ūn ider	221	c	r
-ūn	374	c	r1
-ūn eyleme	390	c	r1
-ūn gibi	448	c	r1
-ūn olacakdur	62a, 64b	g	
-ūnumdan benüm	351	c	r1
-ūr (distich)		sayf	
-ūrī (öri)	73-77	ö	h
-ūr olacakdur	63b	g	
-ürdi	416	c	h2
-usı yok	282	c	r1
-ūsına	403	c	r1
-ūsından	375	c	r2
-ūza gele	406	c	r2
-ūze	397	c	r2
yavuz gözden yavuz dilden	63-66	ö	h

II ʿAruż Manuals

The series is opened by Kadi ʿAbdullāh from Divrigi, a judge in Cairo, who in 849/1445-6 composed his short mesnevi *Bahr-i dürer* which is extant in two manuscripts, Dublin T. 473[96] and Berlin Ms. or. oct. 3744, 153b-181a.[97] The work has been published by Tourkhan Gandjeï[98] and awaits detailed study. It consists of 210 verses composed in the hazac metre, and treats the technical terms of Arabo-Persian prosody, the metrical feet; 'faults';

96 Manuscript presented by the minister Yashbek min Mahdi (died in 1480) to the library of his Sultan, al-Malik al-Ashraf Sayf addin Kaytbay (ruled 1469-1496). V. Minorsky, *A Catalogue of the Turkish Manuscripts and Miniatures*, Dublin, 1958, 110-111.

97 Manuscript produced for the library of Sultan Kanısawh al-Gawri. M. Götz, *Türkische Handschriften Teil 2*, Wiesbaden 1968, 207 no. 304.

98 T. Gandjeï, "The Bahr-i dürer: an early Turkish treatise on prosody", *Studia turcologica memoriae Alexii Bombaci dicata*, Naples, 1982, 237-249.

the sixteen traditional metres, mentioning that Khalil b. Ahmad excluded the mutadārik[99], and explains the six circles containing sixteen metres, concentrating on those variants of the metres which were actually used in, or were congenial to Turkish poetry.[100]

Berlin Ms. or. oct. 3744, 144b-147a, is a short treatise by Ahmedi entitled *Risale fi l-ʿaruż*.[101]

Berlin Ms. or. oct. 3744, 147a-153a, is another *Risale-i ʿaruż*.[102]

Mir ʿAli Shir Nawaʾi's Chagatay Turkish *Mizan al-awzan*, preserved in the manuscript dated 933/1526-7 of his collected works Paris, Bibliothèque Nationale, Suppl. Turc 317,[103] makes use of the circles and discusses some specifically Eastern Turkish verse forms.[104] It was completed after 898/beg. 23 Oct. 1492 and dedicated to Sultan Husayn Mirza.

Zahir ad-Din Muhammad Babur's treatise on *ʿaruż* is preserved partially in a manuscript in Rampur as well as the manuscript Paris, Bibliothèque Nationale, Suppl. Turc 1308 which was published by I.V. Stebleva.[105] The treatise which appears not to bear any title (*Muhtasar*) was composed by Babur not earlier than 1523 and not later than 1525.[106] Babur, just as Nawaʾi, "illuminates the rules of the ʿaruż with examples from Turkic poetry" as well as specific Turkic poetic forms adjusted to some of the ʿaruż metres (for instance, tuyugh, qoshuq, türki). Babur adds considerably to the information provided by Mir ʿAli Shir Nawaʾi.

Dervish Mehmed Çelebi with the pen-name Lemʿī, Lāmiʿī's son, wrote a treatise on prosody entitled *Risale-i Bahrü l-evzān fī l-ʿarūz*[107] which is extant in the MS. Konya, Yusuf Ağa Library no. 139.

---

99 Verse 181. On Khalil b. Ahmad's refraining from mentioning the mutadārik see W.F.G.J. Stoetzer, *Theory and Practice in Arabic Metrics*, Leiden 1989, 81-83.

100 Gandjeï, "Treatise on prosody", 237.

101 Götz, *Türkische Handschriften Teil 2*, 192 no. 283.

102 Götz, *Türkische Handschriften Teil 2*, 194 no. 286.

103 E. Blochet, *Catalogue des manuscrits turcs*, Paris 1933, I, 309. For the Ms. St. Petersburg partially published by Samojlovič in 1926 see M. Fuad Köprülü, "La métrique ʿaruz dans la poésie turque", *PhTF* II, 266,

104 J. Eckmann in *PhTF* II, 350; M.E. Subtelny, "Mir ʿAli Shir Nawaʾi", *EI* VII, 1993, 91 no. VI.

105 E. Blochet, *Catalogue des manuscrits turcs*, II, Paris 1933, 229. I.V. Stebleva (ed.), Zachir ad-din Muchammad Babur. *Traktat ob ʿAruze. Faksimile rukopisi. Izdanie teksta, vstupitel'naja stat'ja i ukazateli*, Moscow 1972.

106 Stebleva, *Razvitie*, 40-43, with older literature (M.F. Köprülü, "Türk klasik edebiyatında hususi nazım şekilleri: Tuyug", in *Türkiyat Mecmuası* II; reprinted in the same author's *Türk dili ve edebiyatı hakkında araştırmalar*, Istanbul 1934.

107 Günay Kut Alpay, "Lamiʿi Chelebi and his Works", *JNES* 35 (1976), 74.

Metres and rhyme fill the first makale of the handbook on metrics and rhetoric which Mustafa b. Şaʿban, known as Sururi (d. 969/1561-2), composed in 956/1549 under the title *Bahrü l-maʿarif*; it is preserved in many manuscripts.[108]

Nutki's short *Risale-i ʿaruż* is preserved in the Berlin Ms. or oct. 3636, 59a-68b.[109]

ʿAli b. Hüseyn el-Amasi (end seventeenth century) wrote a *Risale-i ʿaruż* which is part of a collection of metrical works extant in the Berlin MS. or. oct. 3238, 46a-90b.[110]

An *ʿIlm-i ʿaruż*, probably a translation, is preserved in the Berlin MS. or. quart 1741, 212a-213b.[111]

One Derviş ʿAli Amidi's *Ahval-i bahir* is preserved in the Elmalı Library.[112]

Ravzatü l-evzan, Leiden, Cod. Or 451 (2)[113] is a Turkish poem on sixteen Arab and sixteem Persian metres.

III Titles of ʿAruż Manuals and Collections Cited

Bahr-i dürer, Dublin, Chester Beatty Library, T. 473; Berlin. Ms. or. oct. 3744, 153b-181a.

Bahrü l-evzān by Lemʿī, Dervish Mehmed Chelebi, Konya, Yusuf Ağa Library no. 139 (listed under the title *Risale-i Bahrü l-evzān fī l-ʿarūz*).

Bahrü l-maʿarif by Mustafa Sururi, completed in 1549, dedicated to Prince Mustafa. There are many MSS., I cite only Berlin Ms. or. oct. 2298, Vienna N.F. 35, Leiden Cod. Or. 451 (1) and Cod. Or. 2082.[114]

Cāmiʿü l-meʿānī, Istanbul, Nuruosmaniye 4904; completed in Istanbul in 940/1533-34.

Cāmiʿü n-neẓāʾir, Edirneli Naẓmī, Istanbul, Nuruosmaniye 4915[115].

Cāmiʿu n- neẓāʾir, Pervāne b. ʿAbdullāh, Istanbul, T.K.S., Bağdat Köşkü 406.

Cāmiʿü n-neẓāʾir, Eğridirli Haccī Kemāl, Bayezit Devlet Library, Umumî 5782; work dated 918/1512.

Camiʿu n-neẓāʾir, anonymous, Istanbul Üniversitesi Library, T.Y. 2955; completed between 970 and 972, purpose unspecified.

108 For a description of its contents see M. Götz, *Türkische Handschriften Teil* 2, 193 no. 284-285.

109 H. Sohrweide, *Türkische Handschriften (3)*, Wiesbaden 1974, 188 no. 224.

110 H. Sohrweide, *Türkische Handschriften* (5), Wiesbaden 1981, 188 no. 203.

111 H. Sohrweide, *Türkische Handschriften* (5), Wiesbaden 1981, 190 no. 205.

112 *TÜYATOK* II 07, 475 no. 1601.

113 Jan Schmidt, *Catalogue of Turkish Manuscripts in the Library of Leiden University*, vol. I, Leiden 2000, 117-118.

114 M. Götz, *Türkische Handschriften Teil* 2, 193 no. 284; Flügel I 208 no. 229; Jan Schmidt, *Catalogue of Turkish Manuscripts in the Library of Leiden University*, vol. II, Leiden 2002, 238-241 (Cod. Or. 2082).

115 Erünsal, *Life and Works of Tâcî-zâde Caʿfer Çelebi*, Bibliography, cxvii-cxix.

Dīwān-i Mevlānā es-Sulṭān el-Melik el-Eşref Kanısavh Gawrī, Staatsbibliothek zu Berlin Preußischer Kulturbesitz, Ms. or. oct. 3744, part 1.[116]

Gülistān bi t-Türkī, Leiden, Library of the University, Cod. or. 1553.

Mecmaʿu n- naẓā'ir, see Mecmūʿatü n-neẓā'ir (Edirneli Naẓmī).

Mecmūʿa-i laṭīfe, ʿAlī b. Ahmed b. Emīr ʿAlī, Koğuşlar 950.

Mecmūʿa-i neẓā'ir, Berlin Ms. or. oct. 3652, part 1; Götz.

Mecmūʿatü n-neẓā'ir, Edirneli Naẓmī, Istanbul, Topkapı Sarayı Müzesi Library Ahmed III 2644 (described by Karatay, TY 396 no. 3070).

[*Mecmuʿatü n-neẓā'ir*] by Edirneli Naẓmi, entitled *Naẓā'ir ü l-eşʿār* in the MS. Vienna, H.O. 142 (Flügel no. 693).

Mecmūʿatü n-neẓā'ir, Istanbul, Millet Library, Ali Emiri Manzum Eserler no. 674 (Ambros, Erünsal).

Mecmūʿatü n-neẓā'ir, Edirneli Naẓmī, Istanbul, Millet Ktp., Ali Emiri Manzum Eserler no. 683 (vol. I).

Mecmūʿatü n-neẓā'ir, Edirneli Naẓmī, Istanbul, Millet Library, Ali Emiri Manzum Eserler no. 684 (vol. II).

Mecmūʿatü n-neẓā'ir, Istanbul, Topkapı Sarayı, Revan no. 1972 (Ambros, Erünsal).

Mecmūʿatü n-neẓā'ir, Istanbul, Süleymaniye Library, Es'ad Efendi no. 3418 (Erünsal).

Mecmūʿatü n-neẓā'ir, Istanbul, Süleymaniye Library, Hasan Hüsnü Paşa no. 1031 (Erünsal).

Mecmūʿatü n-neẓā'ir, Edirneli Naẓmī, Istanbul, Nuruosmaniye 4222.

Mecmūʿatü n-neẓā'ir, ʿÖmer b. Mezīd, London, School of Oriental and African Studies, no. 27,689; work dated 840/1437, MS. undated.

Mecmūʿa-yı şuʿarā-yı kadīm Istanbul Üniversitesi Library, T.Y. 752 (Erünsal; purpose unspecified).

Mecmūʿatü n-neẓā'ir, Istanbul Üniversitesi Library, T.Y. 1547 (Erünsal; purpose unspecified).

Metāliʿü n-neẓā'ir, Hisālī of Budin (died 1062/1651), Istanbul, Nuruosmaniye 4252-4253; in two volumes, undated, autograph copy.[117]

Mizan al-awzan, Mir ʿAli Shir Nawa'i, preserved in seven manuscripts, headed by Istanbul Topkapı Sarayı, Revan 808, (dated 901-902/ 1500), and Paris, Bibliothèque Nationale, suppl. Turc 317.

H.O. 142, *Naẓa'irü l-eşʿār* = Edirneli Naẓmi's *Mecmuʿatü n-naẓa'ir* (Flügel no. 693).

Nuhbetü l-Asar li zeyl-i Zübdetü l-eşʿar, Belig, autograph dated Bursa, 1139, Istanbul Üniversitesi Library, T.Y. 1182.

Ravzatü l-evzan, Leiden, Cod. 451 (2) Warn., CCO I, no. CCXXXIV. Begin of a Turkish poetical work on metrics.

---

116 Götz, *Türkische Handschriften* 2, 207 no. 304.

117 G. Kut, "Mukhtarat", 531.

Risale fi l-ʿaruż, Ahmedi, Berlin Ms. or. oct. 3744 (144b-147a) = Götz 2 192 no. 283.

Risale-i ʿaruż, Berlin Ms. or. oct 3744, part 3[118].

Risale fi l-ʿaruż by ʿAbdullah = *Bahr-i dürer*, Berlin Ms. or. oct 3744, part 4.[119]

Risale-i Bahrü l-evzān fī l-ʿarūz, see *Bahrü l-evzān*.

Zübdetü l-Eşʿar by Kaf-zade Feyzullah Efendi (Fa'izi), preserved in the manuscripts Vienna H.O.141 (entitled *Zubdetü l-erbabü l-meʿarif*); Istanbul, T.K.S. Revan 837[120], Üniversite, T.Y. no. 1646, Süleymaniye, Esʿad Efendi no. 2726; Şehit Ali Paşa no. 1877, Hamidiye no. 1065; Nuruosmaniye, no. 3722, 3723; Millet, Emiri Manzum 1325.

Without title, Collection of poetry from the fifteenth and sixteenth century, Berlin Ms. or. oct. 3058.[121]

Zahir ad-Din Muhammad Babur's treatise on *ʿaruż*, Paris, Bibliothèque Nationale, Suppl. Turc 1308.

IV Manuscripts for comparison, by location

Berlin, Staatsbibliothek zu Berlin Preußischer Kulturbesitz, Ms. or. oct. 3744

144b-147a: *Diwan-i Mevlana es-Sultan el-Melik el-Esref Kanisavh Gawri*; Ahmedi's *Risale fi l-ʿaruż* = Götz 192 no. 283; *Risale-i ʿaruż* = Götz 194 no. 286.

Dublin, Chester Beatty Library, T 473, *Bahr-i dürer*.

Istanbul, Topkapı Sarayı Müzesi Library, Ahmed III 2644: Edirneli Nazmi, *Mecmūʿatü n-neẓāʾir*.

T.K.S. Bağdat Köşkü 406: Pervāne b. ʿAbdullāh, *Cāmiʿu n-neẓāʾir*.

T.K.S. Koğuşlar 950: ʿAlī b. Ahmed b. Emīr ʿAlī, *Mecmūʿa-i latīfe*.

T.K.S. Revan no. 1972: *Mecmūʿatü n-neẓāʾir*.

T.K.S. Revan 837, *Zübdetü l-Eşʿar* by Kaf-zade Feyzullah Efendi (Fa'izi).[122]

Süleymaniye Library, Es'ad Efendi no. 3418: *Mecmūʿatü n-neẓāʾir*, a mecmuʿa containing Turkish kasides (*Kasa'id-i Türkiye*) by famous poets of the fifteenth and sixteenth centuries (Erünsal, Lxxxviii f., bibl.).

Süleymaniye Library, Hasan Hüsnü Paşa no. 1031: *Mecmūʿatü n-neẓāʾir*.

Süleymaniye Library, Esʿad Efendi no. 2726: *Zübdetü l-Eşʿar* by Kaf-zade Feyzullah Efendi (Fa'izi).

Süleymaniye Library, Şehit Ali Paşa no. 1877: *Zübdetü l-Eşʿar* by Kaf-zade Feyzullah Efendi (Fa'izi).

---

118 Götz, *Türkische Handschriften* 2, 194 no. 286.

119 Short description by Götz, *Türkische Handschriften* 2, 192 no. 282.

120 F.E. Karatay, *Türkçe Yazmalar Kataloğu* I, 406 no. 1225. ʿOM II, 386.

121 Götz, *Türkische Handschriften* 2, 206 no. 303 with names of poets.

122 F.E. Karatay, *Türkçe Yazmalar Kataloğu* I, 406 no. 1225.

Süleymaniye Library, Hamidiye no. 1065: *Zübdetü l-Eşʿar* by Kaf-zade Feyzullah Efendi (Fa'izi).

Süleymaniye Library, Collection Nuri Arlasez no. 263: *Mecmūʿatü l-eşʿār*, Catalogue 1991, p. 19.

Nuruosmaniye no. 3722- 3723: *Zübdetü l-Eşʿar* by Kaf-zade Feyzullah Efendi (Fa'izi).

Nuruosmaniye no. 4222: Edirneli Nazmi, *Mecmūʿatü n-neẓā'ir.*

Nuruosmaniye no. 4252-4253: Hisālī of Budin (died 1062/1651) *Meṭāliʿü n-neẓā'ir* in two volumes.

Nuruosmaniye 4904: *Cāmiʿü l-Meʿānī*, completed in Istanbul in 940/1533-34.

Istanbul, Nuruosmaniye 4915: Edirneli Nazmi, *Cāmiʿü l-neẓā'ir.*

Millet Library, Ali Emiri Manzum Eserler no. 674: *Mecmūʿatü n-neẓā'ir.* Millet Library, Ali Emiri Manzum Eserler 683: Edirneli Nazmi, *Mecmūʿatü n-neẓā'ir* (vol. I).

Millet Library, Ali Emiri Manzum Eserler no. 684: Edirneli Nazmi, *Mecmūʿatü n-neẓā'ir* (vol. II).

Millet Library, Ali Emiri Manzum Eserler no. 685: *Şiir mecmuası.* Contains poems by poets of the fifteenth and sixteenth century, the Şehr-engiz by Mesihi from Pristina and the mesnevi ʿIşret-name or Saki-name by perhaps a different Mesihi in Eastern Turkish (Mine Mengi).[123]

Millet Library, Ali Emiri Manzum Eserler no. 1325: *Zübdetü l-Eşʿar* by Kaf-zade Feyzullah Efendi (Fa'izi)[124].

Istanbul Üniversitesi Library, T.Y. 752: *Mecmūʿa-yı şuʿarā-yı kadīm.*

Istanbul Üniversitesi Library, T.Y. 1182: Belig, *Nuhbetü l-Asar li zeyl-i Zübdetü l-eşʿar*, autograph dated 1139, Bursa.

Istanbul Üniversitesi Library, T.Y. 1547: *Mecmūʿatü n-neẓā'ir.*

Istanbul Üniversitesi Library, T.Y. 1646: *Zübdetü l-Eşʿar* by Kaf-zade Feyzullah Efendi (Fa'izi).

Istanbul Üniversitesi Library, T.Y. 2955: *Camiʿu n-neẓā'ir* by an anonymous, completed between 970 and 972.

Bayezit Devlet Library, Umumî 5782: Eğridirli Haccī Kemāl, *Cāmiʿü n-neẓā'ir*, work dated 918/1512.

Konya, Yusuf Ağa Library no. 139: Lemʿi, Mehmed Chelebi, *Risale-i Bahrü l-evzān fī l-ʿarūz.*

Leiden, Library of the University, Cod. or. 1553: *Gülistan bi t-Türki.*

Bahrü l-maʿarif by Mustafa b. Şaʿban, known as Sururi, Cod. Or. 451 (1) and Cod. Or. 2082.

Ravzatü l-evzan, Cod. Or. 451 (2).

---

123 M. Mengi, "The Fifteenth Century Ottoman Poet Mesîhî and His Works", *Erdem* 2 no. 5 (Ankara 1986), 357-372.

124 List of poets' names in Levend, *Türk Edebiyatı Tarihi* 1, 295-298.

London, British Library, Rieu 190a, *Zübdetü l-Eş'ar* by Kaf-zade Feyzullah Efendi (Fa'izi).

School of Oriental and African Studies, no. 27,689: 'Ömer b. Mezīd, *Mecmū'atü n-neẓā'ir*, work dated 840/1437, MS. undated.

Paris, Bibliothèque Nationale, Suppl. Turc 317, *Mizan al-awzan* by Mir 'Ali Shir Nawa'i.

Suppl. Turc 1308. Zahir ad-Din Muhammad Babur's treatise on *'aruż*.

Vienna

Österreichische Nationalbibliothek, H.O. 141, *Zübdet erbabü l-me'arif* by Kaf-zade Feyzullah Efendi (Fa'izi).

H.O. 142, *Neẓa'irü l-eş'ār* = Edirneli Nazmi's *Mecmu'atü n-naẓa'ir* (Flügel no. 693).

N.F. 35, *Bahrü l-ma'arif* by Mustafa Sururi.

CHAPTER 23

The Sultan's Prayer before Battle

One, but not the only end of Ottoman history writing was to entertain and to edify.[1] It is with the latter end in view that a selection of "prayers before battle" will be considered here. The range in time will be fixed by the "Chroniclers' narrative"[2] and Neşrī's *Cihān-nümā* recension completed between end 1486 and early 1493[3] on the one hand, and by Selānikī (on the battle of Egri) on the other. The field of choice within these dates has been reduced by the exclusion of important but (to me) inaccessible works. Subject to these limitations, I try to concentrate in the following pages on a variety of prayers before battle, and I venture to offer them as my contribution to the Festschrift for V.L. Ménage.

Descriptions of pitched battles[4] afforded occasions for elaborations on the theme of the petition-prayer (*hācet namāzı; salāt al-hāca*)[5] and 'supplication' (*tażarruʿ*) in passages where the sultan humbly turned to God for help. The linking of *tażarruʿ* with prayer and significant words (*günāh*) indicates that the writers who elaborated on this theme were undoubtedly thinking of humiliation and repentance in the religious sense. From Sinān Pasha's (died 1486) *Tażarruʿnāme*[6] and from later *tażarruʿnāmes*[7] it is evident that the word was associated with intense spiritual contemplation and self-examination. Another term that was

1 V.L. Ménage, "On the recensions of Uruj's 'History of the Ottomans', *BSOAS* 30 (1967), 314. I should like to thank C.H. Fleischer and A. Karamustafa of Washington University, St. Louis, for their comments on a draft of this article in May 1991, and for the great generosity with which Professor Fleischer put his library and numerous microfilms at my disposal.

2 V.L. Ménage, "Some notes on the *devshirme*", *BSOAS* 29 (1966), 72-73, with earlier literature.

3 Superbly and definitively analyzed by V.L. Ménage, *Neshrī's History of the Ottomans. The Sources and Development of the Text*, Oxford, 1964. For the edition by F.R. Unat and M.A. Köymen, *Kitâb-ı Cihan-Nümâ. Neşrî Tarihi*, Ankara, 1949-1957, Ménage's siglum *Ank* will be used here.

4 T. Majda has called attention to war imagery in his "Characteristics of Early Turkish Epic Style (13th-1st half of 15th century)", in *Problemy języków Azji i Afryki*, Warsaw 1987, 223-231.

5 Ömer Nasuhi Bilmen, *Büyük İslâm İlmihali*, Istanbul, 1986, 189-190; A.J. Wensinck, "*Salāt*", *EI First Edition*, vol. III: 104; cf. [Wensinck] in *Handwörterbuch des Islam*, Leiden 1941, p. 644 (*salāt al-hādja* "zur Erlangung heissersehnter Wünsche"; [Wensinck] "*Salāt*", *İslam Ansiklopedisi X* (1967), 122 (*dilek namāzı*); cf. G. Monnot "*Salāt al-khawf*", "the prayer of fear", *EI second ed.* VIII (1995), 945-935.

6 M. Tulum (ed.), *Tazarruʿname*, Istanbul, 1971. Sinān Pasha wrote his 'Book of Humiliation', which soon became a highly esteemed work of exemplary prose in Ottoman literature, after severe humiliations inflicted on him by Mehemmed II, and after his rehabilitation by Bāyezīd II.

7 Cf. M.Z. Pakalın, *Osmanlı Tarih Deyimleri ve Terimleri Sözlüğü* III, Istanbul, 1954, 427.

 | DOI 10.1163/9789004355767_024

used in this context was *münācāt*, "silent and fervent prayers, intimate conversations with God".

In treatments of this supplication theme by history writers we are faced with concepts of the highest value to the Ottomans.[8] We find a choice of references, explicit and implicit, to 'piety, faith in God' (*īmān*), 'compassion' (*merhamet*), 'breed' (*asl*),[9] 'purity of motive', 'psychic power' (*himmet*), 'honour' (decorum and fame; *nāmūs-i pādişāhī*), 'readiness to hold consultations as enjoined by God' (*meşveret*), 'justice' (*ʿadl u siyāset*), 'giving up of one's life as an offering', 'martyrdom for the faith'.

These Ottoman concepts are generally contrasted with the 'error, aberration' (*dalāl*) of the Christians, with their vain boasting, their lack of foresight and order, their arrogance, their greed for money, slaves, food and wine, their carousing and feasting on pork so familiar to the *ġazavātnāme* literature from 'pre-Ottoman', indeed Seljuk and Crusaders' days.

It is noteworthy, although outside the scope of this paper, that the Turkmens and the Anatolian princes in ʿĀşıkpaşazāde, Neşrī and others display a 'lack of breeding' (*bī-asl, harāmzāde*), an inferior quality (*nā-cins*), 'evil-thinking, rancour' (*bed-gümān*),[10] 'trickery' (*hīle*), an 'infidelity and treachery', a 'feebleness of faith' (*żaʿīf ül-īmān, çürük iʿtikād*), 'haughtiness' (*tekebbür*),[11] and a 'lack of sense' (*kusūr-i ʿakl*).[12] However legitimate their begs might have felt in reoccupying their territories in which they had been confirmed by Timur,[13] they had no right to wage an 'unholy war' against the Ottomans who, as true ghazis, were carrying on the *cihād*, the battle with the infidel being God's work.[14] The Chroniclers', ʿApz's, Neşrī's, and Saʿdeddīn's descriptions of the evils and devastations of war as having befallen the principalities and the Turkmens are, it should be observed,

8 For a discussion of values see J.R. Walsh, "The Historiography of Ottoman-Safavid Relations in the Sixteenth and Seventeenth Centuries", *Historians of the Middle East*, 197-210.

9 ʿApz particularly stresses the notion of breed; he repeatedly refers to the Ottoman genealogy, especially after the conquest of Constantinople.

10 The prince of Karaman is addressed as a retrograde (*müdbir*) and mischief-maker (*müfsid*), Neşrī, Ank 219.

11 Pervading ʿApz's and the other Chroniclers' chronicles is a suspicion and a resentment of the Karamanids, the other Anatolian Princes, and especially the Turkmen chieftains. Ġāzī Umur Beg of Aydın, an ally, was an exception.

12 M. Tulum (ed.), *Tursun Bey. Târîh-i Ebü'l-Feth*, Istanbul, 1977, 161.

13 On the status quo established by Timur see H. İnalcık, "Mehemmed I", in *EI* VI (1991), 973-978.

14 V.L. Ménage, "The Beginnings of Ottoman Historiography", in B. Lewis and P.M. Holt (ed.), *Historians of the Middle East*, London, 1962, 177-178; C. Imber, "The Ottoman Dynastic Myth", Turcica 19 (1987), 13.

part of the insistence that war was God's scourge for securing the order of the world (*nizām-i ʿālem*), that highest of Ottoman arguments. Defeat and despoiling, even the treacherous stratagems devised by Yörgüç Pasha, were the portion of people whose cause was unrighteous.

The main purpose of what follows is to sketch the concepts presented in the 'supplications' of Ottoman rulers before important battles with Christian enemies, in their soliloquies or inner dialogues, and to trace their relationship with the *ġazavātnāme* genre. Thus, from the focal point of Kosovo I, I shall move both forward and backward in time, reviewing supplication passages connected with some major pitched battles, especially Varna, and Kosovo II.

Neşrī's *tażarruʿ* of Kosovo I is one representative of a long line of literary 'supplications' which lies behind it and which was to continue.[15] The 'germ' of Neşrī's Kosovo I *tażarruʿ* does not seem to be in the poems preceding ʿApz's Kosovo I, but in ʿApz's, and Neşrī's own, rendering of the short prayer at Kosovo II, which must be taken up later. In Neşrī's revised version – he acknowledges "records" (not ʿApz) for his account of what happened on the eve of the battle Kosovo I occupies a central position.

Kosovo I 1389

This battle was the only instance where an Ottoman sultan was killed on a battlefield.[16] This fact and indeed the reign of Murād I was fit matter for an epic poem with the moral purpose of arousing admiration and encouraging imitation. Ahmedī, whose *Iskendernāme* Neşrī cites explicitly by title and by referring to the story of Alexander and the King of India,[17] had not done this for the first Kosovo battle, which had happened during his lifetime. For Neşrī the object of writing was, of course, not to compose an epic poem, but to extract from his sources material for history. But he did dramatize the narrative by using direct speech. Neşrī, who often changed ʿApz's verse[18] into prose, did not use the three poems by which ʿApz created a presentiment of the sultan's death and then described the situation before and after Kosovo I, including a ritual prayer on horseback per-

15 The theme of giving one's life as an offering was to reappear in the poetry of Shāh Ismāʿīl.

16 Alderson, Structure, 107. Prince Lazar I Hrebeljanović and King Tvrtko I also died. On the heroic epics commemorating Kosovo Polje see M. Braun, *Kosovo. Die Schlacht auf dem Amselfelde in geschichtlicher und epischer Überlieferung*, Leipzig 1937.

17 Ank 486, 283.

18 Ménage, "Beginnings", 175, and *Neshrī's History*, 17. For the practice of inserting poetry into prose see R. Dankoff, "The Lyric in the Romance: The Use of Ghazals in Persian and Turkish Masnavis", *JNES* 43 (1984), 9-25, esp. 23.

formed by the ghazis, and a prayer by the sultan.[19] Instead, he let himself be guided, as Ménage has shown, by a (no longer extant) source which was related to, but more elaborate than, the Oxford Anonymous[20]. This source enabled Neşrī to give, in his Kosovo I chapter, a full picture of Murād I as a heroic leader. The devotion and enthusiasm he inspires indeed are shown in the plot of Kosovo I which is in the following phases: Murād reaches Kratovo, the Serbian envoy taunts the sultan; a council is held; the Serbian envoy reports back to his prince; the sultan reaches Kruševac, two insolent Serbian envoys are beheaded; the Turks reach good flat ground and let the army rest, Murād and Bāyezīd view the huge enemy army, Murād is overcome by sadness and anxiety and humiliates himself before God; there is another council: the use of camels is discussed and rejected, Murād sums up the discussion; the infidels hold a drinking party. The morning; battle order, incitement and promises; ʿAlī Pasha performs the morning-prayer and takes *fāl* from the Koran; battle order of the Serbians, their recklessness. Sultan Murād I guides his men and is guided by the advice of his viziers and his son Bāyezīd (Prince Yaʿkūb, significantly, does not have a speaking part). By making Bāyezīd (I) a 'secondary hero' Neşrī stresses that his ascendance to the sultanate had been as anticipated as the death of the sultan, whose assassin is lurking among the slain. Neşrī's description of the morning of the battle is a grand elaboration on the theme 'dawn'. But the heart of the matter is the 'supplication' and self-sacrifice of Murād I on the eve and during the night before the battle, and this must be examined in detail.

The actual *tażarruʿs* at Kosovo I are in three phases, (i) Murād's immediate reaction after seeing the enemy, (ii) his summing-up of the war-council, (iii) mist and dust at nightfall, (iv) his performing the petition-prayer, (v) his spending the night in supplication. His concerns are, visibility; possible defeat; consciousness of his responsibility for the Muslims who are to die. His purity of motive; he enters the battlefield, not in search of slaves and booty[21], but in sole zeal for God's approval. He confesses to being a frail human being. He elects to die for the Muslims as a ransom for them. He sums up that God who made him a ghazi in the

19 F. Giese, *Die altosmanische Chronik des ʿĀšıkpašazāde*, Leipzig, 1929, 55-58. Cf. ʿApz ed. ʿAlī, 63.

20 Ménage, "Beginnings", 176; the same author's *Neshrī's History*, 13-14, 61, beginning chapter 45 = Ank 268; İnalcık, "Rise", 157.

21 An early ascetic, Sufi rejection of war conducted with the aim of gaining plunder has been noted in Ahmedī's *dīvān* by T. Kortantamer, *Leben und Weltbild des altosmanischen Dichters Ahmedī*, Freiburg, 1973, 236, and Colin Imber, "Ottoman Dynastic Myth", reprinted in *Studies in Ottoman History and Law*, Istanbul 1996, 295 ("Ahmadi ... deplored the popular practice and understanding of Holy War because its motive was plunder")..

first place is now asked to provide the martyrdom in the end. (vi) At dawn the mist vanishes as rain sets in. The military action begins.[22]

(ii) "It is recorded that when it became night and darkness descended upon the army, the night became extremely dark and the air was excessively thick with fog. At the same time a wind blew which choked the world with dust in such a way that it was impossible to tell a man from a horse[23]. (iii) Murād Han Ġāzī endured this until the wind abated, and then he performed a pure ablution and a petition-prayer consisting of two *rikʿat*. He placed his face on the earth and in that dark night he (iv) lamented until the following day and humbled himself before God the Almighty".

"He said: 'My God, my master, my lord! So many times have you accepted my prayer in your Presence and have not forsaken me. Accept my prayer once more: give us rain, and by pushing away this darkness and this dust make the world shining with light so that we can observe the army of the infidels and fight face to face". "O God, possessions and slaves are yours; you give them to whom you will, and I am an insignificant, incapable slave of yours. You know my thoughts and my secrets. You know that my intention is not to gain property and riches. I did not come here for male or female slaves. I only genuinely and sincerely desire your approval".

In the following passage Murād offers himself as ransom for the Muslims, with the 'stipulation' that these Believers shall not be killed at the hand of the infidels. "O Lord God, make me a victim sacrificed for these Muslims. Only do not let these Believers be defeated at the hands of the infidels and be destroyed. O God, do not make me the means of the killing of so many souls. Make them victorious and successful. I give my life for these as a sacrifice; only accept this. I am willing to give up my soul for the soldiers of Islam. Only do not show me the death of these Believers. God, make me a guest in your neighbourhood and sacrifice my soul for the souls of the Believers. You made me a ghazi in the beginning; provide the (bread of) martyrdom in the end'. When Sultan Murād Ġāzī had prayed in this manner, uncovering his head and putting his face to the ground, lifting up his hands, God – whose lauds be recited and who be extolled – answered his prayer.

---

22 Neşrī's *tażarruʿ* has undergone alteration in those parts which involve the self-sacrifice. In Mz (F. Taeschner, *Ǧihānnümā* I, Leipzig, 1951) the pleading with God is simpler; in Mn (F. Taeschner, *Ǧihānnümā* II, Leipzig, 1955) a 'stipulation' and a 'bargain', perhaps to prepare the audience for the death of the sultan and the Turkish victory, have been added.

23 It is difficult to imagine a dense fog simultaneous with a strong wind bringing dust. Neşrī's own more concise draft (of which Mz survived), which mentioned only a combination of excessive darkness with fog and dust, is more convincing and may be based on an observer's account. For a comparable situation in Persian romances see J. Scott Meisami, *Medieval Persian Court Poetry*, Princeton, 1987, 99.

In that very instant clouds enclosed the sky and a merciful rain inundated the face of the earth. And the fog, too, lifted from the army of Islam and settled down on the infidels..."

The Battle of Varna, 10 November 1444.

The "Chroniclers", the Anonymous Chronicles and Oruç, relate in some detail the battle of Varna, for which Murād II had to be recalled from his retreat in Manisa.[24] They may have consulted *ġazavāt-nāmes* as Halil İnalcık has suggested.[25] The death in battle of (Güyegü "Son-in-law") Karaca Beg, the Beglerbeg of Anatolia, is told; his troops and later the Rumelians flee, and Sultan Murād, finding himself almost alone, turns to God.

> He lifted his face to heaven, (performed very many supplications) and said, 'O God, give strength to the religion of Islam, and give victory and help out of consideration for the light of Muhammad Mustafā who is the noblest of beings, for the religion of the true light of Islam and for the light of Muhammad'. In this way he lamented. Even before the arrow of his prayer attained its target, God the Almighty fulfilled his prayer. By the blessings of the miracles of the Prophet, and the psychic power of the Men of the Unseen, by the blessing of the faith of the ghazis God gave him victory and sent an insinuation into the heart of the accursed king

(Władysław III of Poland) so that he challenged the sultan, out of pride and arrogance; his horse stumbled and he fell.[26] N. Atsız writes that the Chroniclers are mistaken in describing as a rout what was really a feigned retreat in the classical manner.[27] But 'Apz, too, reports that Karaca the governor of Anatolia was killed, and that the king broke the ranks of the janissaries by a cavalry charge, seeking single combat with the sultan. The Turks hamstrung his horse so that he fell down, and a soldier named (Koca) Hıżır then beheaded the king. This turned the

24 Ménage, "Beginnings", 172.

25 H. İnalcık, "Rise", 158-159; cf. the same author's *Fatih Devri Üzerinde Tetkikler ve Vesikalar* I, Ankara, 1954, 76, in which he mentions the *Ġazānāme-i Rūm* dedicated to Mehemmed II.

26 F. Giese, *Die altosmanischen anonymen Chroniken I. Text und Variantenverzeichnis*, Breslau, 1922, 69; with considerable variants; *II. Übersetzung*, Leipzig, 1925, 92-93; F. Babinger, *Die frühosmanischen Jahrbücher des Urudsch*, Hanover, 1925, 57, 119.

27 "It is clear, Atsız wrote, "that such a rout could not turn into victory by the sultan's prayer", Atsız, *Edirneli Oruç Beğ. Oruç Beğ Tarihi*, Istanbul, [1972], 95.

battle.[28] Faced with this choice of versions, Neşrī again turned to his source related to the Oxford Anonymous, which may have provided him with the following dramatic verbal exchange. When the Turkish ranks are broken, Murād II calls out to the governor of Anatolia "Karaca, the infidel has beaten us" (*Kāfir bizi sıdı Karaca*). The outcry does reflect panic on the sultan's part, but "Dayı" ("Uncle") Karaca, who is holding the sultan's horse,[29] keeps up his courage; the sultan's standard remains in its place as a rallying point, the drums are beaten and the criers call out their customary "Why do you flee – the infidel is beaten (*Kāfir sındı*)".[30]

Kosovo II 1448

ʿĀşıkpaşazāde who fought in the second battle of Kosovo, this "greatest *ġazā*", described Murād II – without squeamishness about booty and male and female slaves[31] – as praying before the military action. The phases are, (i) Murād views the enemy army at daybreak on Friday, (ii) he performs a petition-prayer, (iii) his supplication expresses a concern that his sins might be remembered and held against his men: "He dismounted, performed a petition- prayer of two *rikʿat*, touching the ground with his face. He spoke the supplication: 'O Lord, preserve thou this handful of the community of Muhammad... help them for the sake of the Prophet; do not make these men weak at the hands of the enemy because of my sins". He then mounted his horse (and attacked).[32] Neşrī follows him closely:

> "When Sultan Murād saw the army of the infidels, he immediately dismounted, touched the earth with his face, performed a petition-prayer (*hācet namazı*) of two *rikʿat* and entreated God – may he be exalted – 'Do not make this one squadron (*bölük*) of your poor believing slaves weak at

---

28 Giese, *Altosmanische Chronik des ʿĀšıkpašazāde*, 122, chapter 118.

29 In the thick of battle the Aga of the janissaries accused Karaca Beg of murdering Prince ʿAlāʾeddīn whose Dayı he was; he is sometimes confused with the Beglerbeg of Rumeli; İnalcık, *Fatih Üzerinde Tetkikler*, 60, 104.

30 Ank 650-652 = Ménage chapter Murād II, 37; The (salaried) *boz ünci* had the task to cry *kāfir sındı kaçdı*; cf. Ank 301; Ménage, *Neshrī's History*, 49.

31 Economic aspects of booty are discussed in Cemal Kafadar, "When Coins Turned into Drops of Dew and Bankers Became Robbers of Shadows: The Boundaries of Ottoman Economic Imagination at the End of the sixteenth century", PhD Thesis McGill University, Montreal, October 1986, 32 and 209, note 39.

32 Giese, *Altosmanische Chronik des ʿĀšıkpašazāde*, 124-125, chapter 120. ʿApz ed. ʿAlī, 135, has a different version.

> the hands of the infidels because of my many sins. God, preserve the community of the Friend out of regard for Him. And make them victorious and successful'. Then he lifted up his head, suspended the entreaty, at once pronounced the intention of *ġazā* and mounted his horse".[33]

Having the sultan express contrition at his "many sins" is not fortuitous; by this device both historians glance at his sudden abdication (a failure in duty) and at his being a seeker after pleasure (*'ayş ü nūş*). The Anonymous Chronicles and Oruç are silent on this point.

As chronicles and histories multiply in the sixteenth century, we notice a change of mood in descriptions of the rulers in battle. The first sultans of the Ottomans had been heroes. They died quietly: their soul flew away. Neşrī twice uses the phrase, "the phoenix of his soul flew up like an angel to his nest in paradise" to describe Murād I's and Mehemmed II's death. Mehemmed I died after an illness – *Allāh emrine ulaşdı*.[34] It was realized that Murād I's exploits were greater than those of other Turkish sultans; in Neşrī's words, "None of the padishahs of the house of 'Osman waged *ġazā* like this one". Murād II died after a warning by a dervish; he repented of his sins and his soul went to God.[35] As heroes the sultans had been exposed to anxiety. They had displayed humility and modesty. They had been vulnerable: helpers stood by them.[36] Being isolated, they entered into contact with the supernatural. Ertoġrul and Osman had their dreams. 'Osman spent a night in adoration of the Koran. 'Apz recorded Murād II's expression before a campaign that he would fight "with the grace of God and the miracles of the Prophet and the psychic power of the saints".[37] But as the leaders of a "small band" of ghazis were transfigured into Lords of the Conjunction, the prophetic voice of that invisible being the *hātif-i ġayb*[38] became their appropriate contact with the world above. Mehemmed II heard this voice before the battle with Uzun Hasan,[39] and so did Sultan Süleymān later.

If the *Tevārīh-i Āl-i 'Osmān* are one of the most enduringly popular of Ottoman chronicles, this is, in part, because each generation seems to find in their story what it needs. One updating is the *Süleymānnāme* by Hadīdī, a mesnevi in *hezec*,

33 Ank 664; Ménage chapter Murād II, 40.

34 Neşrī Ank. 550. On Orhan's death Ank 188, on Süleymān's Ank 487; on Mūsā's Ank 516.

35 Neşrī Ank 307, 680.

36 Murād II had been girded and assisted by the intercession of the saintly Emir Hazret of Bursa; Giese, *Chroniken*, 77-78.

37 Giese, *Altosmanische Chronik des 'Āšıkpašazāde*, 93 f. chapter 93 (campaign against Vlad Drakul).

38 T. Fahd "Hātif" *EI* III (1971), 271.

39 Tulum, *Tursun Bey*, 157.

completed in 1523, describing the history of the Ottomans down to the appointment of Ibrāhīm Pasha. Hadīdī wrote sultan's supplications before the first and the second Kosovo battle, but none before or during the battle of Varna.[40] Another updating, in a sense, of the *TA'O* story in the middle of the reign of Süleymān is the *Cāmiʿ ül-meknūnāt* by Mevlānā ʿĪsā, a mesnevi in two metres, completed in 1529/30 (first recension)[41] and in 1543 (second recension).[42] The author's major concerns – *ġazā*, booty, the end of the world – give the impression of reflecting contemporary feeling. ʿĪsā's mesnevi contains the prayer (*duʿā*) at Varna which by then had become traditional. In describing the same battle, ʿĪsā slips into legend: the Hıżır who had fought at Varna was the saint, not a plain janissary.[43] ʿĪsā's chapter on Mohács includes a *tażarruʿ* pronounced by Süleymān which does contain words of self-humiliation, doubts about the possibility of a Christian success, and the joy of becoming a martyr. While no one could accuse ʿĪsā of sophistication, the *Cihādnāme-i Sultān Süleymān*, composed shortly after 1529 by the poet Levhī, abounds in gazels, kasides and mesnevi pieces, and is full of images that are symbolic rather than documentary. Levhi's description of Süleymān's campaign in Hungary is introduced by poems describing 'spring'. At night the ruler turns to God in a poetical *münācāt*, humiliating himself before the judge of the needs of mankind, *kāżī l-hācāt*.[44]

A wealth of imaginative detail had been developed in the sixteenth century, when the *Ġazavāt-i Sultān Murād* was compiled. The single surviving manuscript combines the campaigns leading up to and finishing with the battle of Varna with the *Menākıbnāme* of Mahmūd Pasha. The editors have advanced arguments to the effect that it goes back to eyewitness accounts, and that it conforms to Christian records of the battle of Varna.[45] The description is in stages which furnish abundant material for our subject: a *münācāt* in verse is pronounced before

40 F. Babinger, *Die Geschichtsschreiber der Osmanen und ihre Werke*, Leipzig, 1927, 59-60; the MS British Museum Or. 12,896 is used by A. Uğur, *The Reign of Sultan Selīm I in the Light of the Selīm-nāme Literature*, Berlin, 1985, 19, 229-230. Another MS is Istanbul Üniversitesi Kütüphanesi, T.Y. 1268. I take this opportunity of thanking Professor Fleischer for the help he gave me with microfilms of this and other manuscripts.

41 MSS. Ankara, Türk Tarih Kurumu Y. 240 (Part 6), and Leiden, University Library, Or. 1448.

42 MSS. Istanbul Üniversitesi Kütüphanesi T.Y 2546 and T.Y. 3263. For this work as one of the sources of the *Künhü l-ahbār* see C.H. Fleischer, *Bureaucrat and Intellectual in the Ottoman Empire*, Princeton, 1985, 248 and 250, and for its eschatological aspects my "Sāhib-Kırān und Mahdī. No. 17 in this volume.

43 For Hıżır in Turkish lore see H. Özdemir, *Die altosmanischen Chroniken als Quelle zur türkischen Volkskunde*, Freiburg, 1975; Fleischer, *Bureaucrat and Intellectual*, 167.

44 MS. Istanbul, Topkapı Sarayı Müzesi Kütüphanesi, Hazine 1434. F.E. Karatay, *Topkapı Sarayı Müzesi Kütüphanesi Türkçe Yazmalar Kataloğu* I, Istanbul, 1961, 228 no. 694.

45 H. İnalcık and M. Oğuz (ed.), *Gazavât-ı Sultân Murâd b. Mehemmed Hân. İzladi ve Varna*

Murād II crosses the dangerous Straits (48); he incites his troops to battle, then at night he performs supererogatory (*navāfil*) prayers and recites poetry (57) till the morning; he exhorts his men again ('let me see if you are men or cowards'); the date is given (1 Receb 848). During the battle the King challenges Murād (62). Karaca, like a lion in battle, offers himself as a sacrifice; he pronounces a supplication and becomes a martyr together with his soldiers (63); the King then sees his chance to charge, but Şāhīn Pasha exhorts his soldiers "Now is the day, let me see you fight; you were born to be sacrificial rams", the cowards flee, the 'pig' Yanko (John Hunyadi) is hit by an arrow in the eye, he faints, the Padishah stands firm; he gives himself up to God (64). The battle lasts from noon till late into the afternoon, the Padishah is in distress, the janissaries are fleeing. Seeing this situation, the Padishah dismounts and pronounces a *münācāt* in verse. Then he takes a handful of earth and touches his breast with it, and after he has placed his hand on his forehead, he springs up like a lion, mounts his horse, takes his sword in hand; now the other troops come; they throw the King from his horse. On the following morning the sultan holds a prayer of thanks (67); there follows a poem about the 'object lesson' (*ʿibret*) provided by this battle, the description being summed up by the author's thanks to God (68) and his admonishment that supplication is necessary for Muslims... (71).

I regret being unable to include Kemālpaşazāde's accounts of Kosovo I, Varna[46], and Kosovo II.[47] His work occupies a central and connecting position between the *Tevārīh-i Āl-i ʿOsmān* and the 'Persianizing' histories.[48] The publication by A. Uğur of defter IX contains a prayer before the battle of Çaldıran in which Sultan Selīm does not appear; it is his soldiers who stay awake all night and present supplications (*tażarruʿ*) to the Creator.[49] Neither does Kemālpaşazāde mention, in his splendid description of the battle of Mohács, a sultan's *tażarruʿ*; indeed, the sultan did not actually conduct the battle; it was Ibrāhīm Pasha who

---

Savaşları (1443-1444) Üzerinde Anonim Gazavâtnâme, Ankara, 1978, 58 and notes p. 105 no. 39, esp. 108-109 note 42.

46 Cited in İnalcık, *Fatih Devri*, 60, 75.

47 Ş. Turan, *İbn Kemal: Tevârih-i Al-i Osman, VII. defter*, Ankara, 1957, and the same author's *İbn Kemal: Tevârih-i Al-i Osman, VII. defter (tenkidli transkripsiyon)*, Ankara, 1957. For the last part of the reign of Murad II, 847-855, only one manuscript, Paris, Suppl. turc 157, is known: V.L. Ménage, "MS Fatih 4205: An Autograph of Kemāl-Pashazāde's *Tevārīkh-i Āl-i ʿOthmān*, Book VII", *BSOAS* 23 (1960), 263-264.

48 For the *Ġazavāt-nāme* which Kemālpaşazāde incorporated into his seventh defter see İnalcık, "Rise", 163, 167; Ş. Turan, *İbn Kemal: Tevârih-i Al-i Osman, VII. defter (tenkidli transkripsiyon)*, Ankara, 1957, introduction.

49 A. Uğur, *Reign of Sultan Selīm I in the Light of the Selīm-nāme Literature*, 105, 383; based on the MS Süleymaniye, Veliyüddin Ef. 2447.

commanded the attacking troops.[50] Celālzāde Mustafā, Koca Nişāncı, describes how the citizens of Istanbul prayed for victory when the army left for Hungary, and how, in the plain of Mohács, Sultan Süleymān incited his troops to fight. Then the sultan lifted his hands to God, presented his needs (*hācāt*) and performed *tażarruʿ* and *münācāt*, and the people present, perhaps the angels in heaven, chanted *āmīn* in unison and shed tears (five *beyt* on duʿā).[51]

The proud *tażarruʿ* with which Hākī prefaces his *Süleymānnāme*, an epic account of Süleymān's campaign against Persia (Nakhçivan) completed in 1556/7, contains not one word of self-humiliation or doubt about the possibility of a Safavid success. On the contrary, his verses make proud assertions about the exalted position of his sultan.[52]

While Hoca Saʿdeddīn[53] writes in the easy-flowing and highly polished (linguistically Middle-Ottoman) "Persian-Ottoman" prose for which he has often been praised, it is noteworthy that, besides interweaving his concepts, he inserts mesnevi verse in Old Ottoman ('modernized' in the printed edition) invoking, without mentioning a source, the long prayers said in Ibn 'Alā's *Dānişmendnāme* of 1360/61, in which the hero and his friend Artuhi pronounce both *münācāt* and *tażarruʿ*[54] in verse. Saʿdeddīn's effort to achieve a special style merits separate study.[55] His *tażarruʿ* before Kosovo I (*Tāc* I, 119-120) is on themes with which he and his contemporaries were deeply concerned. Honour is foremost. His concerns are that the banners of Islam may bend, that a fall from glory to dishonour, casualties, even enemy occupation may occur; the immediate problem of 'dust' only comes fourth; his concerns are about the ruin of years of endeavour; his appeal to be a ransom points forward to Murād's death. "But the army-leading

50 Pavet de Courteille, *Histoire de la campagne de Mohacz par Kemal Pachazadeh*, Paris, 1959.

51 P. Kappert (ed.), *Geschichte Sultan Süleymān Kānūnīs von 1520 bis 1557*, Wiesbaden, 1981, 62, 63, 143b and 144b.

52 MS Topkapı Sarayı Müzesi Kütüphanesi, Revan 1289, Karatay, *Topkapı Sarayı Müzesi Kütüphanesi Türkçe Yazmalar Kataloğu* I, 220 no. 673; GOW 54, note 2.

53 His *Tāc üt-tevārīh* was begun under Selīm II and dedicated to Murād III in 1575. He died on 2 October 1599. On his indebtedness to Oruç see V.L. Ménage, "Another text of Uruç's Ottoman chronicle", *Der Islam* 47 (1967), 273-277. My "Khodja Efendi, Saʿd al-Din", EI V (1986), 27-28. Cited: Tac ut-tevarih, 2 vols., Istanbul 1279/ 1861. A nocturnal prayer which Saʿd ed-Din put into the mouth of ʿOsman was translated by Colin Imber: "Make the enemies of religion level with the dust; scatter the armies of the unbelievers. Make my sword the light on the road of religion; make it the guide to the mujāhids", Colin "The Ottoman Dynastic Myth", reprinted in *Studies in Ottoman History and Law*, Istanbul 1996, 310.

54 I. Mélikoff, *La Geste de Melik Dānişmend* II, Paris, 1960, 57-59, 106-107, 110-111, 152-153, 164-165, 188-189; 200.

55 Imber, "Ottoman Dynastic Myth", quotes from the long prayer, in verse, which Saʿdeddīn put into the mouth of ʿOsmān.

king became sad because of the great numbers of the enemy force, and his compassionate eyes became moist on behalf of the soldiers of Islam, especially as from the enemy side there blew a contrary wind, and the fear that the fact that the shield of dust filled that plain would make the eyes of the forces of Islam opaque and turbid became an additional burden. Consequently the sultan – performing his task – shed successive tears, which were the envy of tulips upon the countenance of entreaty, and in the darkness of the night he opened the hand of need (*hācet*), and he lifted a silent and fervent prayer to the court of the judge of the needs of mankind (*kāżī l-hācāt*) and said with earnest supplication (*tażarruʿ*) and misery and a flood of tears 'my God, you are the ruler who gives shelter to the people of the universe, and you are the one on whom hope is fixed for the commonalty of servants in palaces and in poverty, in hardship and in ease. Do not make the upright banners of Islam crooked in the hands of the despicable infidels, and [do not make] this weak slave ill-famed among mankind. Verse:

For the honour of the most honourable Friend, for the blood that flowed in Kerbela;
for the eye that weeps in the night of separation, for the face which is put down on the way of your love;
For the sad heart of the suffering, for their sigh which affects the soul;
Make, o Lord, your kindness a companion of the way; make your guarding an aid and protection for us;
Be the defender and helper of the Muslims. Keep the hand of the enemy away from us.
Do not look, o Lord, at our sin; grace with favour our heart-felt sigh.
Do not, o Lord, destroy the warriors for the faith. Do not make us the target of the enemy's arrow.
Protect our eyes from the dust of the battlefield. Guard the troops of Islam from danger.
Do not, o Lord, ruin with your wrath our endeavour and our exertion which have lasted so many years, and our good name in campaigns for Islam:
Do not ruin (them); do not make my face black among the people.
I will become a ransom (*fidā*) in the way of Islam; I will become the shield for the soldiers on the way of salvation.
Make me a martyr in the way of religion; make me fortunate in the hereafter.
Do not let the domain of Islam be trodden under foot, do not make it a resting-place of the race of error;
Your beneficence is great for the Muslims; I wish that it may reach completion'.

> With words of this kind and sorrowing he performed earnest supplication and entreating and spent that dark night in supplication and lamentation."

Mustafā ʿĀlī in his influential universal history, the *Künh ül-ahbār,*[56] recomposed the ritual prayer of two *rikʿat* and a *münācāt* before Kosovo I, eliminating its contents.[57]

For the Varna battle Hoca Saʿdeddīn wrote a *münācāt* (*Tāc* I 380-381), the spirit of which agrees with the *tażarruʿ* of the Anonymous Chronicles. In this battle both Saʿdeddīn and Mustafā ʿĀlī[58] mention only Koca Hıżır the janissary. On Kosovo II Saʿdeddīn is relatively short; he has no reason to go into the sultan's contrition, as he has spoken of sins earlier on. His *tażarruʿ* is in indirect speech (*Tāc* I 395:10): "While he requested a favourable opportunity and invoked God's help in battle, he lifted his prayers to the mirror-like face of the wished-for in order that the desired countenance might manifest itself. With supplication and humbling himself in prayer and in need he asked from the court of God the Absolute Actor that the soldiers of Islam be victorious. After praying in the heart in this way and presenting the exigencies he asked the Protector for aid, seeking his support and then mounted an ambling sorrel horse and becoming firm like a mountain in the middle of the troops whose orbit is victory and on the field of vengeance he made the fighters listen to, and inspired them by the Koranic "kill those who join other gods with God" (Sura 5:5).

As a statesman Hoca Saʿdeddīn had advised against beginning what came to be known as the Long War with Austria. But when the decision had been made he encouraged Mehemmed III to take the field in person, and to become, thirty years after Süleymān died on campaign, the first sultan to lead the army into Hungary again. He took with him the Standard of the Prophet, which had only recently been brought from Damascus.[59] Before Egri[60] the ʿulemāʾ said prayers (*duʿā*) and 'supplications' day and night – and the siege succeeded.[61] Mustafā

56 Fleischer, *Bureaucrat and Intellectual*, passim; on ʿĀlī's beginning and completion of the work p. 140 and 148.

57 ʿĀlī, *Künhü l-ahbār*, IV, 72-3, Vākıʿa 13.

58 ʿĀlī, *Künhü l-ahbār*, IV, 214.

59 Mehmet İpşirli (ed.), *Selânikî Mustafa Efendi. Târih-i Selânikî* II, Istanbul 1989, II, 611. A.H. de Groot, "Sandjak-i Sherif", *EI* IX (1997), 13-15.

60 Cf. Jan Schmidt, "The Egri-Campaign of 1596. Military History and the problem of sources", *Habsburgisch-osmanische Beziehungen. CIEPO Colloque Wien, 26.-30. Sept. 1983*, Vienna, sic: 1985, 125-144. Reissued in Jan Schmidt, *The Joys of Philology*, vol. I Istanbul 2002, 107-121.

61 İpşirli, *Târih-i Selânikî* II, 635.

Selānikī[62] describes this and the great battle in the plain of Mező-Keresztes (Haçova) Egri (Erlau campaign)on 25-26 October, 1596, when Christian forces overran the Ottoman infantry ranks. While the sultan lamented and cried "intercession o Prophet of God and o God, help" placing his forehead on the "Noble Mantle" (*hırka-i şerīf*) his excellency the Hoca Efendi Mevlānā Sa'deddīn strengthened him with eloquent words to stand firm with patience and perseverance",[63] and almost at the very moment of defeat, the battle was won.[64]

It is not easy briefly to summarize the common features and differences of the 'supplications' which we have discussed. Most of them were held at night; the ritual element, the prayer, was crucial. The sacrificial nature of the death of Murād I was not forgotten: Sultan Süleymān is credited by at least one author (Mevlānā 'Īsā) with a willingness to die as a martyr. The internal structure of the 'supplications' changed; so did their patterns of concepts, rhetoric and tone within the changing historical fabric. If 'Apz in his report on Kosovo II provides the short plot and the 'germ' of the *tażarru'*, Neşrī in his Kosovo I chapter may be said to have established the precedent for later passages sounding the note of epic heroism. Mustafā 'Ālī in his *Künh ül-ahbār* offers abridgement on a larger scale, while adding interesting reflections which are outside the scope of this paper. Sa'deddīn both relates back to the *Tevārīh-i Āl-i 'Osmān* and points forward to the other masters of Ottoman historiography. They all comment on Ottoman values.[65] A final consideration, in writing this paper, has been to suggest how useful it would be to avoid a sharp distinction between the documentary and the literary (of the genre of the *Battāl-nāme* and the *Dānişmend-nāme*).[66] In this the prayer before battle may be a fruitful line of enquiry.

---

62 On Selānikī as a historian see C.H. Fleischer, *Bureaucrat and Intellectual*, 130-131.

63 İpşirli, *Târih-i Selânikî* II, 641; Nurhan Atasoy, "Khırka-yı Sherīf", *EI* V (1986), 18-19.

64 C.H. Fleischer, *Bureaucrat and intellectual*, 169.

65 Their study may be extended, for example, by the sultans' promises to God (Bāyezīd I's *adak* before the battle of Nicopolis) or by their 'incitements to battle'.

66 İnalcık, "Rise", 156-157; Ménage, "Recensions of Uruj", 315. Cf. also G.L. Lewis, "The Utility of Ottoman Fethnames", *Historians of the Middle East*, 192-196.

CHAPTER 24

Re-reading the Story of the Religious "Fitna" of 1711

In Ramadan 1123/beginning 13 October 1711, Cairo witnessed a short-lived popular uprising. A religious student of Ottoman extraction preached in the mosque of Sultan Mu'ayyad against posthumous miracles of saints and the veneration of tombs. Nobody died, the magnificent tomb in the Mu'ayyadiya was left untouched, and the most sinister thing anyone actually witnessed was that some Turkish derwishes were beaten and "frightened away". Yet the affair caused enough consternation to merit the name of *fitna*. The story seems to retain its interest, as one would gather from several critical assessments which have appeared in the last decades.[1] There is, however, much in the "fitna" story that is far from clear.

In trying to appreciate the course of events and their meaning, one is hampered by what is, to all appearances, a rich but puzzling textual tradition. Before discussing the religious and political aspects of the uprising, it would therefore be desirable not merely to consider such factual matters as locations and persons involved, but also to deal fairly thoroughly with the more controversial problems of the nature and reliability of the sources. These problems are complex and cannot be treated here. Although the sources' many differences should put us on our guard, historians have amalgamated them all into one text; for such a full text readers may be referred to Peters' treatment of the story.

Textual Tradition

The primary source is Ibn al-Hallaq who wrote both in Arabic and in Turkish[2] (see appendix). There are a large number of verbal echoes in both his chronicles. The next Turkish chronicler is ʿAbdulkerim. Ahmad Çelebi known as Shalabi, another contemporary chronicler,[3] apparently knew no Turkish but had access to the Arabic work by Ibn al-Hallaq. Shalabi's deviations from Ibn

1 See article 6 in this volume; Peters 1987; Winter 1991; Behrens-Abouseif 1994; Peskes 1999. The following is based on the Cleveringa Lecture given at the Dutch-Flemish Institute at Cairo on 30 November 2000.

2 For an excellent description see Hathaway 1990, 54-56, 65.

3 Hathaway 1990, 67; Abd al-Rahim, introduction to his edition of Awdah.

 | DOI 10.1163/9789004355767_025

Hallaq include omissions and added material. The relation of the text by Yusuf al-Mallawani to the unpublished Arabic text by Ibn Hallaq has yet to be investigated. As the case stands at present, Mallawani is verbally very close to passages in the relevant sections of the Arabic Ibn Hallaq.

Past and Present Attitudes to the "Fitna"

The critical reaction to the religious uprising of 1711 begins in the chronicles. They exhibit a tendency to blacken the main character. "Preaching" in Ibn al-Hallaq becomes "inciting" already in ʿAbdulkerim. Ahmad Shalabi's account is full of shocked asides[4] and sneers against the preacher, his followers[5] and one of them in particular.[6] Ahmad Shalabi from the first takes sides between the Azhar shaykhs and the preacher, making the latter quickly and deservedly lose his case, and underlining the authority of the former. The insertion of four Azhar shaykhs' signatures early on in the narration is a striking demonstration of this.[7] The poem in which Hasan al-Hijazi wrote down his memories of the uprising accuses the preacher of inciting the military. Al-Jabarti, while incorporating Hijazi's text, reduced the matter to an Ottoman episode. Its obscurity lasted until the appearance, in 1831, of Joseph von Hammer's *History*, which mentioned "bold heretical views" (*kühne Ketzereyen*). Ignaz Goldziher linked the teachings of the "pious youth" to the monotheistic reaction preceding the true beginning of the Wahhabi movement. In the nineteen-fifties and sixties the preacher was praised as a "bold spirit" leading the first, pre-Wahhabi, reform movement in eighteenth-century Egypt.[8] Hijazi's and Shalabi's hostility surfaced again in the nineteen-eighties and nineties; the preacher was

4 Ahmad Shalabi relates, "I sat in the company of our teacher, Shaykh ʿAlî al-Taylûnî, talking about the fanaticism (*taʿassub*) of this errant band and their affection for this Muʿtazilite. Then the shaykh said: 'The person who has said: The first people to obey the Dajjâl are the inhabitants of Egypt has certainly spoken the truth.'"

5 The ambiguous reference to "Turks, who could not distinguish between a written *mim* and *nun*" has been interpreted as meaning "illiterate Turks", or "Turkish immigrants who spoke little Arabic", but the illiteracy falls to the ground if the phrase is understood as a sexual insult (see Schmidt, 15, note 22).

6 Ahmad Shalabi records that one follower (whose name and rank is given) urinated in the Mu'ayyad mosque. Peters 95.

7 Ahmad Shalabi is at pains to establish a *fatwa* signed by four shayhks, Khalifi and Diwi (Shafiʿite), Nafrawi (Malikite), and Sayyid Ali (Hanafite). Peters 96 and particularly 105.

8 Mahmud al-Sharqawi, H.A.R. Gibb and Harold Bowen, Bayard Dodgde, Gamal el-Din el-Shayyal, summarized in Flemming 1975.

charged with "radicalism and violence" and with "threatening ... public order".[9] The uprising itself, often held to be 'pre-Wahhabi' or 'proto-Wahhabi,' came to be seen as "a violent confrontation between neo-Hanbalis, or pre-Wahhabites, and Sufis and believers in Sufism." The preacher was drawing on the stock of ideas represented by Birgiwi, to whom we shall return. Historians seem to suppose the group to present not principles but interests – their ethnic group, their profession: "a struggle of Turk against Arab, a "revolt"[10] of a thousand "illiterate Turks",[11] "a gang of Turkish soldiers in Egypt in an "unsettled psychological mood".[12] Such claims must not be ignored, though the objection may be raised that the movement attacked Turkish derwishes and risked conflict with the Turkish government. The conclusion was drawn that the uprising was "without clear-cut ethnic lines."[13] Indeed, whereas the beaten dervishes seem to have been ethnic Turks,[14] the preacher's adherents may well have been locals of ambiguous identity. Bearing in mind that some fourteen thousand local Egyptians were inscribed on the rolls of the Ottoman regiments and drew their regiment's monthly stipend while enjoying the military's tax-exempt status,[15] it seems plausible to hold that the "Turks" referred to by Shalabi and others were local *ʿaskeri*s on the Sultan's payroll perceived, by extension, as "Turks."

Religious Issues

We may now return to the central religious figure of the uprising. His name is nowhere given. He was "a student of religion" (*sukhta, softa*); to his adherents he was the 'preacher' and later 'our shaykh.' It is worth stressing that he attacked certain Turkish brotherhoods and demanded the conversion of their tekkes into schools. The suggestion has been made that he belonged to the surplus of under-employed young men who formed a *softa* problem in Turkey but not in Egypt.[16] He was of Ottoman Turkish (Rumi) extraction, but instead of connecting him with the the Istanbul-based movement of the Qadızadeliler, a Syrian

9 Winter 159.
10 Behrens-Abouseif 103.
11 Peters 100; Winter 1992, 158.
12 Peters 111.
13 Winter 1992, 158.
14 "Turkish soldiers assaulted Egyptian derwishes", Peters 105.
15 As Jane Hathaway has shown, their being Egyptian did not disqualify them for membership in a regiment as "honorary soldiers." Hathaway, Qazdaglı, 14, with earlier literature.
16 Peters 100.

Naqshbandi background may be proposed. The fact that the Mamluk chiefs decide to have him sent to "his vilayet", and that he is indeed sent by ship to Syria, can be used as evidence that the preacher's province of origin was indeed Syria. Behind this argument lies the view that he came to Cairo to study and to teach, in Arabic; it is fair to conclude that the *Risala* by Birgiwi on which he based his teaching was *al-Tarîqa al-Muhammadiyya* by the prominent Hanafi scholar Muhammad al-Birgiwi (1522-1573), and that he found in Birgiwi a source of religious inspiration. This belief is given colour by the view that the famous Damascene Naqshbandi scholar ʿAbd al-Ghani al-Nabulusi (1641-1731)[17] is the author of a voluminous commentary of *al-Tarîqa al-Muhammadiyya*, identifying Birgiwi's sources, most of which were, as Radtke shows, Hanafite *fatwa* collections. Birgiwi was neither a neo-Hanbali nor an all-out opponent of sufism, but a scholar who strove to integrate mystical experience into the system of the sunna, while rejecting music and dance.[18] Any uncertainty as to the "essentially Hanbalite ideas of Ibn Taymiyya and Ibn Qayyim al-Djawziyya" [surviving] "in Hanafite Ottoman religious culture"[19] must therefore be regarded as part of the history of past attitudes to the uprising.

The starting-points for examining the religious aspects of the uprising are five in number:

i. From Thursday, 10 Ramadan 1123/22 October 1711, the Rumi student sat down to preach in the Mu'ayyad Mosque, just inside Zuwayla gate.[20] The circle of his companions soon expanded. First the Ayvan of al-Shafiʿi and then the main hall of the Mu'ayyad mosque were packed tight, but more people kept coming.
ii. The Turkish Ibn Hallaq, our main informant, adds that the student sat studying the *Risala* by Birgiwi together with his companions, and that he started preaching when people assembled. Another religious work to which the preacher referred was *al-Tabaqat al-kubra* by the Shafiʿite scholar ʿAbd al-Wahhab al-Shaʿrani (1492-1565). This book was used by

17 For al-Nabulusi and his Turkish disciples see Barbara Kellner-Heinkele 1990, 107-112; Peskes 1999, 149-50.

18 Radtke 2002, 29. I am indebted to B. Radtke, who allowed me to cite his article in preparation.

19 Peters 109.

20 He "did not sit down on the kursi as was the custom for preaching, but sat on the ground, and stayed liked this for fifty days," according to the unpublished Arabic Ibn Hallaq, which is here practically identical with the printed version published under the name of Yusuf al-Mallawani.

the preacher to refute al-Shaʿrani's views of posthumous miracles of saints.

iii. The preacher proclaimed six theses: (First) The miracles of the saints cease with their death. And what is narrated about their miracles after death is invalid. What is mentioned by al-Shaʿrani in his *Tabaqat* about some saints having access to the Well-Preserved Tablet is groundless. (Second) Not one of the prophets and saints has beheld the Well-Preserved Tablet. Even our Prophet has not beheld it – how then can one of the saints have beheld it! (Third) It is obligatory (*vajib*) to remove all the balls, candles and pieces of ornament from the abodes of saints. And burning candles, oil- and any other lamps is not only not permissible but prohibited (*haram*). And whoever kisses the thresholds of their shrines is an infidel (*kafir*). It is not permissible to build cupolas and ceilings above their graves; it is obligatory to pull them down. (Fourth) As for the *tekkes* that have been constructed to house a crowd of derwishes (*ıshıq*) – Gulshenī, Mevlevi, Bektashi and similar tekkes, their abolition is obligatory, as is the eviction of the derwishes living in them. Students of religious science (*talib-i ʿilm*) must take their places. (Fifth) It is prohibited to visit in congregations the tombs of Imam Shafiʿi and of others during the nights before Saturday in order to practice the recollection of God (*dhikr*) loudly and publicly (*cehrâne*). (Sixth) It is prohibited and idolatry that during the nights of Ramadan at the Iron Gate a band of ignoramuses *bir alay juhhal* shout and jump until midnight, saying that they practice the recollection of God. It is a duty of the judge and of others to stop them, for this belongs to the chapter of "forbid what is abominable". He who is able to prevent them and does not do so is a sinner." Here the preaching ended.

iv. The preacher's denouncement of the "shouting and jumping of ignoramuses" at Bab Zuwayla makes its impact on his listeners who immediately take sticks, head for the Gate, beat the *dhikr*-performers and allow nobody near the Gate for several nights ("sticks" in Ibn Hallaq become "swords and cudgels" in Shalabi's chronicle. Other inferences from his preaching – such as "cupolas should be torn down", or, "Gulshanis, Bektashis and Mevlevis should be evicted"[21] – are of minor force beside the rejection of the *dhikr*-performers.

v. Not all the audience is won over. Ibn Hallaq reports that "some men reached an agreement and went to the Azhar Mosque. They had a meeting with the religious scholars and presented the preacher's sayings to them and requested a *fatwa* as to how this was to be answered". They

21 Omitted by Ahmad Shalabi; Peters 103.

received a *fatwa*, which ran "(ad 1) The miracles of the saints are a reality (haqq). They do not end with death, because it is conceivable that they occur after death. Whoever says that the miracles of the saints end with death, is a Muʿtazilite";[22] (ad 2) "And it is not permissible to say that the prophets have not beheld the Well-Preserved Tablet. Especially to say this about our Prophet is an insult (*edebsizlik*)." "Correction [of the reprehensive] is necessary against whoever says this openly". "If he perseveres in his words and does not repent he will be killed". "(ad 4) It is not permissible to change the nature of the tekkes and to convert them into madrasas, for that is contrary to the founder's stipulation, and that is like [any other] decisive text in canon law." (Theses 3, 5 and 6 of the preacher were passed over). The ulama were thus signalling to the movement that (a) the preacher was a Muʿtazilite who did not believe in miracles; he had insulted the Prophet; he could be killed, and (b) that to convert tekkes into madrasas, contrary to the founder's stipulation, was against Divine Law.

vi. Meanwhile, at the Muʾayyadiyya, the preacher has ascended the pulpit; he reads the *fatwa* carefully and then addresses his audience: "You men! The Arab scholars of your province have given you a *fatwa* contrary to what I have told you, and have found it permissible to have me killed." The point has been made that the words "your ulama, *awlad al-Arab*", were deprecating or show a lack of respect.[23] But, for reasons to be discussed presently, it can be argued that he referred to the fact that two Arab shayks, one Shafiʿite and one Malikite, had signed, whereas the signature of the shaykh of his own Hanafi *madhhab*, Sayyid Ali al-Siwasi, a strict theologian,[24] was apparently absent. The preacher continued, "as matters are, I for my part shall have a debate with them in the presence of the Qadiʿasker". "Let me see in what way they have produced this legal opinion to have me killed." "If there is anybody among you who supports me, let him say so!" "They all answered: Yes we are with you!" He reminded them: "In the present situation our cause (*daʿva*) with these heretics is a religious cause. To assist in this is a great merit".

vii. The scene ending the preacher's public appearance is again located in the Muʾayyadiyya. The preacher says: "Community of Muhammad! In the

22 Referring to the Muʿtazilites' denial of saints performing miracles categorically, both during their lifetime and after their deaths. Peters 106; cf. De Jong/Radtke 4.

23 Peters 1987, 108; Winter 1992, 159.

24 Sayyid Ali was one of those who considered the use of coffee as haram. More details in Peters 105 note 52.

desire to bring the True Religion to victory be here tomorrow, all of you." "Know that anyone who acts in contradiction to this and fails to turn up will be a sinner! Be present, all of you. Let us be victorious and defeat those heretics and ignoramuses (*jahiller*)!"

Political Issues

Points which underline the political aspect and that highest of all Ottoman arguments, the avoidance of civil tumult, now come into play. When we encounter the preacher again, he is silent; his followers have taken over. The Chief Judge's formalities – his admission that the *fatwa* is invalid, his insistence that the court is closed – are angrily rejected by the followers. Their actions have already been described; it will suffice to quote some relevant lines here. The Qadi hides in his house; the deputy judge cannot escape; they turn on him. They force him to write a certificate according to their wishes and to sign it. This they take and leave the court. On the second day, a Tuesday, after performing the noon prayer, the preacher does not come out to preach as was his custom. "The people waited for him, but he did not come. They looked for him in his room and did not find him. They asked the students who answered that they did not know." Now they suspect that the Qadi may have warned him not to ascend the pulpit. They say: "Let us go to the Qadi together and ask him." They leave the mosque, saying: "Come with us whoever helps truth to victory." Along the way, they pick up those whom they meet in the covered bazar, so that they become a very large assembly of people. When they enter the court en masse, the Qadi and the others present are startled. This time the deputy judge escapes. Only the Judge remains. They surround him and ask "the Efendi: What did you do to our preacher? Was it you who prevented him from preaching? No, he answered, I know nothing about it. If you know nothing about it, get up, go with us to the Pasha and tell him to issue a ferman and to appoint an officer (agha) to summon Khalifi and Nafrawi." The adherents, some thousand men, now take the Chief Judge, make him mount, go up to the Viceroy's residence and hold a rally there protesting the delay in the debate. The preacher is by now silent and powerless.

His followers appear to have thought that such a debate – their quarrel is only with Khalifi and Nafrawi – would encourage other citizens to support his cause. There is no reason to suppose that what his followers hoped would have a seditious effect after the disastrous civil war, a real *fitna*, that had recently ravaged Cairo. The Viceroy, suspecting another sedition, asks the Mamluks to exercise their authority and enforce the peace appropriate to the Sultan's honour. Ibn Hallaq has the contents of the *tezkire* to the Mamluk Beys; If the intention of the impertinence (*edebsizlik*) of these people is not to cause another civil war (*fitne*), then the story of this preacher is a pretext. Their raiding the court, humiliating the Judge of the Sheriʿa, beating his man, their disrespect in having him mount and come here at an untimely hour and their attack on the imperial Diwan, all these are not their own deeds. There is somebody inciting them! If it is your intention again to foment a revolt (*fitna*), both of us, the Qadi and I, shall, before the Sultan's and our honour is injured, start and go to the Porte. There he ended his *tezkire*. The Mamluk Beys hold a meeting in which the note is read to the senior officers of the Corps. "When they had learnt this, they all said: We shall seek those who are the cause of this commotion and shall question them. He shall be punished regardless of the corps [in which he is inscribed], and the preacher shall be banished to his *vilayet*." One day later the preacher's men wait in vain for him. There will be no debate. There is nothing the preacher can do except shut himself up in the house of a friend. As for the others, "each of them tightened the *taylasan* which they wore on their heads and went into hiding."

The Agha of the Janissaries sends the chavushes into the Mu'ayyad Mosque to inspect the prayer cells.[25] The preacher is put on a ship leaving from Bulaq, departs for Syria via Damietta, and finally goes to Jerusalem.

There is an instance, occurring under Sultan Qaytbay, of a certain Shafiʿi scholar (Ibrahim al-Biqȃi, 1407-1480) who had shown open contempt for "ignorant derwishes." Al-Biqȃi had condemned [sufis] as heretics, and had generated a feuding in Mamluk Cairo that raged for over seven months. That crisis had been resolved through intervention by Sultan Qaytbay himself. It ended in public disgrace for al-Biqȃi,[26] who was sent to Damascus.[27] The fact that the Rumi preacher of 1711 was also sent (unmolested) to Syria suggests that official sensitivity might have been sharpened by this analogy. Of the followers some escaped, some were questioned; some were beaten and some were banished. It is hard to believe that this moderate result would have accrued to the congregation if they had been guilty of sedition. Why such resolute avoidance of violence? Is it because these people were local Arabophone *ʿaskeri*s on the payroll of the Sultan? People who had raided the court, humiliated the Qadi, beat his *tarjuman*, threatened to vandalize residences, but were not really violent: there was no rampage; nobody was killed. Sticks were used.

25 The order is to eject the students living there, Peters 98.

26 Homerin 24-247.

27 Homerin 247.

It may be fair to conclude from all this that three often interweaving themes make up the story: The preacher's commitment to Birgiwi's, and perhaps, by extension, Nabulusi's, teaching; his silence but not total defeat (some people were evicted from the cells);[28] the impulsive loyalty of his followers[29] who may very well have been locals perceived as "Turks", out-manoeuvred by the combined efforts of the governing Ottomans and Mamluk Beys; and finally, the relation of eighteenth-century Egyptian chronicles to one another, authors who were talking two different languages, not only Turkish and Arabic, but *ʿaskeri* and *reʿaya*; Sufi and anti-Sufi; and who were correcting and opposing each other.

Other characters, high in the hierarchy but subordinate in our story, appear with their names.[30] So do the religious dignitaries.[31]

Bibliography

Primary Narratives

ʿAbdülkerīm b. ʿAbdurraḥmān, *Taʾrīḫ-i Miṣr*, in Turkish, events down to 9 Ṣafer 1128/3 February 1716. MSS.

28 Ahmad Shalabi amplifies: cells were nailed up.

29 Ahmad Shalabi does acknowledge that "all the time they were as deluded as ever in their obedience to this Mutazilite and their deep attachment to him."

30 The highest-ranking Ottoman was Veli Pasha, the viceroy, a former Muhafiz of Chios who had arrived on Thursday, 27 Rajab 1123/10 September 1711, and Rasûlzâda, the Chief Judge. The Defterdar. The leading Shaykh al-balad was Ibrahim Bey Abû Shanab, who headed the Qasimi faction which emerged victorious out of the great fitna of that same summer. His competitor, the other Shaykh al-balad, was Qaytas (Ghitas) Bey, the boss of the recently-defeated Faqari faction. Even the name of a lower-ranking official is known: ʿAbduh, interpreter of the chief judge. The Janissary Agha, ʿAli Agha. ʿAbduh al-Diwi, head of the Shafiʿites at al-Azhar, was absent: he was in exile. He had defended the defeated party with a fatwa. His 'presence' was perhaps a slip of Ahmad Shalabi's. Peters 105 note 51.

31 Ahmad al-Nafrâwî (chief of the Malikite madhhab, 1631-1713). The al-Azhar election in 1709 led to the death by shooting of a number of people broke out between the followers of two shaykhs, al-Nafrawi and al-Qalini, over the post of Shaykh al-Azhar (Winter 1992, 120). Firearms were used and ten victims remained dead in the court of al-Azhar. The viceroy punished al-Nafrawi with house arrest and it seems that al-Qalini became Shaykh al-Azhar; he died on 18 Rajab 1123 (1 September 1711) and Nafrawi probably succeeded him then. For more details see Peters 105 note 49. Ahmad al-Khalifi (1649-1715), a prominent Shafiʿite scholar; Peters 105 note 50. Al-Sayyid Ali from Siwas in Turkey, a Hanafite shaykh (1661-1734). The name is supplied by Shalabi. More details in Peters 105 note 52. He travelled and taught in Turkey.

London, British Library, Add. 7878. (Winter 298).
Istanbul, Süleymaniye, Hacı Mahmut Efendi 4877 (Winter 298).
Istanbul, Süleymaniye Library, MS Hekimoğlu Ali Paşa 705.
Aḥmad Jalabī b. ʿAbd al-Ghanī, *Awḍaḥ al-ishārāt fī-man tawallā Misr al-Qāhira min al-wuzarā wa l-bāshāt*, introduced and edited by Fu'ād Muḥammad al-Māwī, Cairo 1977.
Aḥmad Shalabī b. ʿAbd al-Ghanī al-Miṣrī, *Awḍaḥ al-ishārāt fī-man tawallā Misr al-Qāhira min al-wuzarā wa l-bāshāt*, introduced and edited by ʿAbd al-Raḥīm ʿAbd al-Raḥmān ʿAbd al-Raḥīm, Cairo 1978.
Ahmed Pasha (Cezzâr), *Ottoman Egypt in the Eighteenth Century: The Niẓâmnâme-i Mısır of Cezzâr Aḥmed Pasha*, ed. and translated from the original Turkish, Stanford J. Shaw, Cambridge, MA, 1962, second printing, 1964.
Birgiwī, Muḥammad al-Birgiwī, *al-Ṭarīqa al-Muḥammadiyya*, ed. Mustafa l-Babi al-Halabi, 2nd pr. Cairo 1379.
Damurdashī, Aḥmad al-Damurdashī Katkhuda ʿAzaban, *Al-Damurdashi's Chronicle of Egypt, 1688-1737: al-Durra al-muṣāna fī akhbār al-kināna*, ed. and trans. ʿAbd al-Wahhab Bakr and Daniel Crecelius, Leiden, 1991.
Damurdashī, al-Amīr Aḥmad al-Damurdashī, *Kitāb al-durra al-muṣāna fī akhbār al-kināna fī akhbār mā waqiʿa bi-Miṣr...*, ed. ʿAbd al-Raḥīm ʿAbd al-Raḥmān ʿAbd al-Raḥīm, Cairo 1989 (Institut Français d'Archéologie).
Al-Ḥallāq, Muḥammad b. Yūsuf, *Tuḥfat al-aḥbāb bi-man malak Miṣr min al-mulūk wa n-nūwāb*, completed in 1128/beg. 27 December 1715. Unique MS: St. Petersburg, Academy of Sciences, call number B 1036. V. Rosen, *Les Manuscrits Arabes de l'Institut des Langues Orientales*, St. Petersburg 1877, 30 no. 58 (GAL II 198); A.I. Michajlova, *Katalog arabskich rukopisej Instituta narodov Azii*, part 3, *Istorija*, Moscow 1965, 134 no. 92, call number B 1036. Microfilm in the University Library, Leiden.
Al-Ḥallāq, Meḥmed b. Yūsuf, *Taʾrīḫ-i Mıṣr Qāhire*; in Turkish; six MSS:
1) Vienna, H.O. 40a, Österreichische Nationalbibliothek, fragment containing only the year 1122/beg. 3 March 1710.
2) Stockholm, Royal Library 75. Down to the year 1126/beg. 17 January 1714;
3) Istanbul University Library, T.Y. 628, carefully written MS, down to the year 1127/beg. 7 January 1715.
4) Vienna, Österreichische Nationalbibliothek, H.O. 40b; fragment from the year 1127/beg. 7 January 1715.
5) Paris, Bibliothèque nationale, Suppl. Turc 512, down to the year 1128/beg. 27 December 1715;
6) Vienna, Österreichische Nationalbibliothek, H.O. 37, down to the year 1130/beg. 5 December 1717.
[Ḥasan Pasha], *Kitāb-i tevārīḫ-i Miṣr-i Ḳāhire ḫaṭṭ-i Ḥasan Paşa*, MS. Istanbul, Süleymaniye Library, Hacı Mahmud Efendi 4877.

Ḥuseyn Efendî, *Ottoman Egypt in the Age of the French Revolution*, translated from the original Arabic with introduction and notes by Stanford J. Shaw, Cambridge, Mass. 1964.

Jabartī, ʿAbd al-Rahman b. Ḥasan al-Jabartī, *ʿAjāʾaib al-āthār fī l-tarājim al-akhbār*, 4 vols. Cairo (Bulaq), 1297/1888.; 7 vols. Cairo, 1958-1967.

Jabartī, ʿAbd al-Rahman b. Ḥasan al-Jabartī, trans. by Chefik Mansour Bey and others as *Merveilles biographiques et historiques ou Chroniques du Cheikh Abd el-Rahman el-Djabarti*, 9 volumes, Cairo, 1888-1896.

Mustafa ʿĀlī, *Mustafa Ali's Description of Cairo of 1599*, ed. and trans. Andreas Tietze, Vienna, 1975.

Shaʿranī, ʿAbd al-Wahhāb al-Shaʿranī, *al-Ṭabaqāt al-kubrā*, 2 vols., Cairo, n.d.

Shaʿranī, ʿAbd al-Wahhāb al-Shaʿranī, *Laṭāʾif al-minan*, 2 vols., Cairo, 1357/1938.

Shaʿranī, ʿAbd al-Wahhāb al-Shaʿranī, *Lawāqih al-anwār al-qudsiyya fī bayān al-ʿuhud al-Muḥammadiyya*, 2 vols., Cairo, 1381/1961.

Mallawani, Yūsuf al-Mallawānī Ibn al-Wakīl, *Tuḥfat al-aḥbāb bi-man malak Miṣr min al-muluk wa l-nuwwāb*, ed. Muhammad al-Shishtawi, Cairo 1419/1999 (based on Ms. 28 Taʾrīkh, Maktabat Rifāʿa al-Ṭahṭāwī at Sohag; microfilm: Mahad al-Makhtutat al-tabi li-Jamiʿat al-Duwal al-Arabiyya, Cairo: Tarikh 136).

Yūsuf Efendi, *Tarih-i Mısr*, Istanbul, Süleymaniye Library, MS Esad Efendi 2148.

Secondary Sources

ʿAbd al-Rahim ʿAbd al-Rahman ʿAbd al-Rahim, "Yusuf al-Mallawani's *Tuhfat al-Ahbab* and Ahmad Shalabi ibn ʿAbd al-Ghani's *Awdah al-isharat*, in Crecelius, Daniel (ed.), *Eighteenth Century Egypt. The Arabic Manuscript Sources*, Claremont, CA, 1990, 39-50.

Crabbs, Jack A., Jr., "Historiography and the Eighteenth-Century Milieu", in Crecelius, Daniel (ed.), *Eighteenth Century Egypt. The Arabic Manuscript Sources*, Claremont, CA, 1990, 9-24.

Crecelius, Daniel (ed.), *Eighteenth Century Egypt. The Arabic Manuscript Sources*, Claremont, CA, 1990.

Flemming, Barbara, "Šerīf, Sultan Ġavrī und die "Perser", *Der Islam* 45 (1969), 81-93.

Flemming, Barbara, "Die vorwahhabitische *fitna* im osmanischen Kairo 1711", *İsmail Hakkı Uzunçarşılı Armağanı*, Istanbul 1975, 55-65.

Flemming, Barbara, "Mısır Türk Tarihçiliği Hakkında Notlar", in H.D. Yıldız, E.Ş. Erdinç, K. Eraslan (ed.), *Istanbul Üniversitesi Edebiyat Fakültesi Türkiyat Enstitüsü. I. Milletlerarası Türkoloji Kongresi (1973). Tebliğler I. Türk Tarihi*, Istanbul 1979, 57-62.

Flemming, Barbara, "Drei türkische Chronisten im osmanischen Kairo", in I. Ševčenko en F.E. Sysyn (ed.), *Eucharisterion. Essays presented to Omeljan Pritsak on his Sixtieth Birthday. Harvard Ukrainian Studies* (Cambridge, MA) III/IV (1979-1980), 228-235.

Hagen, Gottfried, and Tilman Seidensticker, "Reinhard Schulzes Hypothese einer islamischen Aufklärung, *ZDMG* 148 (1998), 83-110.

Hammer, J. von, *Geschichte des Osmanischen Reiches*, VII, Pest 1831, 170; IX, Pest 1833, 194-196.

Hathaway, Jane, "Sultans, Pashas, *Taqwims*, and *Mühimmes*: A Reconsideration of Chronicle-writing in Eighteenth Century Ottoman Egypt", in Crecelius, Daniel (ed.), *Eighteenth Century Egypt. The Arabic Manuscript Sources*, Claremont, CA, 1990, 51-78.

Hathaway, Jane, *The politics of households in Ottoman Egypt. The rise of the Qazdağlıs*, Cambridge 1997.

Heyworth-Dunne, J., *An Introduction to the History of Education in Modern Egypt*, London, 1939.

Holt, P.M. (ed.), *Political and Social Change in Modern Egypt*, London, 1968.

Holt, P.M., "Ottoman Egypt (1517-1798): An Account of Arabic Historical Sources", in Holt, P.M. (ed.), *Political and Social Change in Modern Egypt*, London, 1968.

Homerin, Th. Emil, *From Arab Poet to Muslim Saint. Ibn al-Fāriḍ. His Verse, and His Shrine*, Columbia 1994.

Homerin, Th. Emil, "Sufis and their Detractors in Mamluk Egypt. A Survey of Protagonists and Institutional Settings", in F. de Jong & B. Radtke (ed.), *Islamic Mysticism Contested. Thirteen Centuries of Controversies & Polemics*, Leiden 1999, 225-247.

Kahle, P., "Zur Organisation der Derwischorden in Egypten". *Der Islam* 6 (1919 149-169.

Kellner-Heinkele, Barbara, "ʿAbd el-Ġanī and his Turkish disciples", in *Revue d'Histoire maghrébine* (Tunis) 17 (1990), 59-60, 107-112.

Kemper, Michael, *Sufis und Gelehrte in Tatarien und Baschkirien, 1789-1889. Der islamische Diskurs unter russischer Herrschaft*, Berlin 1998.

Lewis, Bernard, "The Ottoman archives as a source for the history of the Arab lands," *Journal of the Royal Asiatic Society* (1951), 139-155.

Macdonald, D.B., *The religious attitude to life in Islam*, Chicago 1909.

Meier, Fritz, *Essays on Islamic Piety and Mysticism*, translated by John O'Kane, with editorial assistance of Bernd Radtke, Leiden 1999.

Peskes, Esther, "The Wahhabiya and Sufism in the Eighteenth Century", in F. de Jong & B. Radtke (ed.), *Islamic Mysticism Contested. Thirteen Centuries of Controversies & Polemics*, Leiden 1999, 145-161.

Peters, "The Battered Dervishes of Bab Zuwayla. A Religious Riot in Eighteenth-Century Cairo", in Nehemiah Levtzion and John O. Voll (eds.), *Eighteenth-Century Renewal and Reform in Islam*, Syracuse 1987.

Radtke, Bernd, *Autochthone islamische Aufklärung im 18. Jahrhundert*, Utrecht 2000.

Radtke, Bernd, "Erleuchtung und Aufklärung: Islamische Mystik und europäischer Rationalismus", *Die Welt des Islams* 34 (1994), 48-66.

Radtke, Bernd, "Birgiwīs *Tarīqa muhammadiyya*. Einige Bemerkungen und Überlegungen", *Journal of Turkish Studies* 26/II (2002), pp. 159-174.

Rafeq, Abdul-Karim, "Syrian Manuscript Sources for the History of Eighteenth Century Ottoman Egypt", in Crecelius, Daniel (ed.), *Eighteenth Century Egypt. The Arabic Manuscript Sources*, Claremont, CA, 1990, 103-114.

Schmidt, Jan, "Sünbülzāde Vehbī's Şevḳ-Engīz, an Ottoman pornographic poem", *Turcica* XXV (1993), 9-37.

Schulze, R., "Islamische Aufklärung", *Die Welt des Islams* 36 (1996), 276-325.

Shaw, Stanford J., "Archival Sources for Ottoman History: The Archives of Turkey", *Journal of the American Oriental Society* 80 (1960), 1-12.

Shaw, S. J., *The Financial and Administrative Organization and Development of Ottoman Egypt, 1517-1798*, Princeton, 1962.

Shaw, Stanford J., "Turkish Source Materials for Egyptian History", in Holt, P.M. (ed.), *Political and Social Change in Modern Egypt*, London, 1968.

Shaw, St. J., "Other Turkish Sources", in Holt, P.M. (ed.), *Political and Social Change in Modern Egypt*, London, 1968.

Shoshan, Boaz, *Popular culture in medieval Cairo*, Cambridge 1993.

Şeker, Mehmet (ed.), *Imam Birgevi*, Ankara 1994.

Rosen, V., *Les Manuscrits Arabes de l'Institut des Langues Orientales*, St. Petersburg 1877.

Michajlova, A.I., *Katalog arabskich rukopisej Instituta narodov Azii*, part 3, *Istorija*, Moscow 1965.

Mojaddedi, Jawid A., "Legitimizing Sufism in al-Qushayrī's Risāla", *Studia Islamica* 90 (2000), 37-50.

Schlegell, B.R. von, *Principles of Sufism*, Berkeley 1990.

Thorning, H., "Beiträge zur Kenntnis des islamischen Vereinswesens auf Grund von Basṭ Madad et-Taufîq", *Türkische Bibliothek* ed. by G. Jacob and R. Tschudi, XVI [Berlin, 1913], 164ff.

Wensinck, A.J.-[C.E. Bosworth], "Lawḥ" in EI² vol. V (Leiden, 1986), 698.

Wensinck, A.J., *The Muslim Creed*, Cambridge 1932.

Winter, Michael, *Society and Religion in Early Ottoman Egypt: Studies in the Writings of ʿAbd al-Wahhāb al-Shaʿrānī*, New Brunswick, 1982.

Winter, Michael, *Egyptian Society Under Ottoman Rule 1517-1798*, London and New York, 1992.

Yıldırım, Ç.C., trans., *Tarikati Muhammediyye – İmamı Birgivi*, Istanbul 1981.

Zilfi, Madeleine, "The Kadizâdelis: Discordant Revivalism in Seventeenth-Century Istanbul", *Journal of Near Eastern Studies* XLV (1986), 251-269.

Zilfi, Madeline, *The politics of Piety: The Ottoman Ulema in the Postclassical Age (1600-1800)*, Minneapolis 1988.

CHAPTER 25

The Poem in the Chronicle: The Use of Poetry in Early Ottoman Historiography

It is a great honour to be invited to contribute to the volume dedicated to the memory of Aldo Gallotta. Like all Turkologists working on early Ottoman historical writing I am greatly indebted to him. His edition and systematic study of Murād's work opened up a new body of material. This may be justification, too, for touching on a specific aspect of early Ottoman history-writing.[1] This writing frequently alternated between realism and stylization, between reality and legend. Some authors had recourse to verse, and to an exchange of 'question and answer'. In this they resemble old Arabic histories in which the prose tale would describe occurrences in full detail, followed by poems which, while only vaguely mentioning what actually happened, would comment on the event. This ancient technique has been traced back to the beginnings of Islamic historiography and even beyond.[2] In fact, "the inclusion of scattered verses in a prose text is a well-nigh universal phenomenon"[3]. It is characteristic of Arabic, Persian[4] and Turkish *adab* literature. The perfect Persian example was Saʿdī's *Gulistān*, in which the anecdotes are told in prose and the poet's moralising reflections are mostly put into poetical fragments.[5]

Where this feature, the insertion of poetry, occurs in history writing, it invites direct comparison with the insertion of lyrics in the Turkish "romantic" tradition, which is considered to have culminated in Fużūlī's *Leylī ve Mecnūn*. The poet inserted ghazals with or without his pen-name (*maḫlaṣ*) or the indication "by the author" (*li-müʾellifihi* or *li-münşihi*) into his mesnevī (long poem consisting of rhymed couplets). Did the chronicler in turn insert mesnevīs,

1 In the following I have added references to take account of recent publications on the subject, which I discussed in July 1990, at the CIEPO meeting in Jerusalem.

2 I. Lichtenstadter, "History in Poetic Garb in Ancient Arabic Literature", in I. Ševčenko en F.E. Sysyn (eds.), *Eucharisterion. Essays presented to Omeljan Pritsak on his Sixtieth Birthday. Harvard Ukrainian Studies* III/IV (Cambridge, Mass., 1979-1980), Part 2, 559-568. For the function of poetry in the popular Arabic prose epic see U. Steinbach, *Dât al-Himma. Kulturgeschichtliche Untersuchungen zu einem arabischen Volksroman*, Wiesbaden, 1974.

3 R. Dankoff, "The lyric in the Romance. The Use of Ghazals in Persian and Turkish Masnavīs", *JNES* 43 (1984), 23.

4 "Conspicuous traits of the stylistic development of Persian prose are the interspersion of prose with poetical fragments". J.T.P. de Bruijn, "Iran", *EI* 2nd edition, 58.

5 J.T.P. de Bruijn, "Iran", 67.

 | DOI 10.1163/9789004355767_026

narrative or non-narrative, or even poetical fragments in his prose text? The actual situation may reflect different approaches of the respective authors. Our subject are prose works of history, that is prose for a "utilitarian" purpose; religious prose enriched by poetry such as the early Anatolian *Behcetü l-ḥadāyıḳ* or the fifteenth-century *Tażarruʿnāme* by Sinān Pasha[6] lies outside the scope of this paper.

What was the purpose of poetry in Ottoman historical prose writing? Few scholars have as yet pursued the question much beyond statements like "the theme afforded the writer full scope for his gifts". Ottomanists have hitherto been overwhelmingly, and justifiably, concerned with textual principles and the transmission of sources. It was admitted that poetry with its rhyme-words or epithets was less easily deformed by scribes,[7] but few of these inserted poems were thought to be of great literary merit; exercises on well-worn themes like the 'Ubi sunt?' theme were not thought to have great relevance for the study of historical events. Verses went unobserved by students, poems dwindled into lines of prose.[8]

For our purpose it is useful – in contrast to the usual chronological order – to make an unconventional broad distinction in Ottoman historical writing between long mesnevīs on the one hand, and prose compositions on the other. This writing in fact begins with a mesnevī. Ahmedī's *Dāstān-i Tevārīḫ-i mulūk-i Āl-i ʿOsmān*, dedicated to Emīr Süleymān at Edirne towards 1410, is a part of that poet's great didactic *Iskender-nāme*, in which the account on the Ottomans is a prophecy of what is going to happen after the time of Alexander and Aristotle.[9]

Let me mention in passing some Turkish and Persian works in the *Menāḳıb-nāme* and *Ġazavātnāme* tradition, written in the fifteenth and sixteenth century, such as the epic of Ġāzī Umur in Enverī's universal history, the *Düstūrnāme*, finished in 1465,[10] the Persian *Ġazānāme-i Rūm* by Kāshifī (around 1456),[11] the *Ġazavātnāme-i Miḫāl-oġlu ʿAlī Beg* by Sūzī Çelebi, 1795 *beyt* of straight-

6 A. Mertol Tulum, *Sinan Paşa. Tazarru'nâme*, Istanbul 1971.

7 V.L. Ménage, "The Beginnings of Ottoman Historiography", B. Lewis and P.M. Holt (eds.), *Historians of the Middle East*, London, 1962, reprinted 1964, 168.

8 See, for example, R.F. Kreutel, *Vom Hirtenzelt zur Hohen Pforte*, Graz-Vienna-Cologne 1959.

9 Published in facsimile by İsmail Ünver, *Ahmedî. Iskender-nâme. İnceleme – Tıpkıbasım*, Ankara, 1983. Cf. V.L. Ménage, "The Beginnings of Ottoman Historiography", 169.

10 Ménage, "Beginnings", 173.

11 Manuscript in the Library of the University of Istanbul, T.Y. 1388; A.S. Levend, *Türk Dilinde Gelişme ve Sadeleşme Evreleri*, Ankara 1972, 13; cf. İnalcık, "The Rise of Ottoman Historiography", *Historians of the Middle East*, 163.

forward mesnevī, apparently without lyrics.[12] The *Ḳuṭbnāme* by Firdevsī, too, on the naval expedition to Mytilene, is a straightforward mesnevī, as is the *Ġazavātnāme* by Safāyī on the exploits of Kemāl Re'īs. He wrote during Sultan Süleymān's reign, as did Mevlānā ʿĪsā, the author of the *Cāmiʿü l-meknūnāt*, which is again a prophecy, in the style of the *Iskender-nāme*, of what was going to happen after the time of that sultan. The long career of the Turkish corsair and Grand Admiral of the Ottoman fleet (abt. 1466 -1546)[13] was chronicled by his contemporary Seyyid Murād, whose *Ġazavāt-ı Ḫayr al-Dīn Paşa* sets him apart in that he made two complete versions, one a long mesnevī version in the Remel metre,[14] and the other the prose version (down to 1541) so extensively studied by Aldo Gallotta.[15]

In almost all these works the historical mesnevī has the same "austere and unrelieved quality" that Robert Dankoff found in the earlier epic and religious mesnevīs. An exception to this rule is Ḳıvāmī's *Fetḥnāme* on the Conqueror's *ġazā*s, a mesnevī containing monorhyme "lyrics".[16] The Old Ottoman of these works, I suggest, is the voice, not of simplicity, but of a genre.[17]

When we come to historical prose down to about 1600 A.D., the situation is more complicated. The heroic tales of *Dede Ḳorḳut* which employ a mixture of prose and a type of free verse are the subject of much ongoing research.[18] The *Dānişmend-nāme* (1360) is in prose with numerous verse insertions of varying length and both mesnevī and ghazal/kaside forms. The verses employ the *ʿarūż* metres.[19] Among the works which ought to be considered in this connection is the voluminous *Saltuḳ-nāme* in prose.[20] The *Baṭṭāl-nāme* (fourteenth cen-

12 Published by A.S. Levend in his *Gazavât-nâmeler ve Mihaloğlu Ali Bey'in Gazavât-Nâmesi*, Ankara 1956.

13 A. Gallotta, "Khayr al-Dīn (Khıπır) Pasha", *EI* second edition IV (1978), 1155-1158.

14 The *Ġazavāt* redaction in verse survived in one manuscript which is incomplete at the end; the text apparently covered the material down to 1541 as did the prose redaction.

15 "Le Ġazavāt di Ḫayreddīn Barbarossa", *Studi Magrebini* III (Naples 1970), 79-160. A. Gallotta, "Il 'Ġazavât-i Ḫayreddîn Paşa' Pars Secunda e la Spedizione in Francia di Ḫayreddîn Barbarossa (1543-1544)", C. Heywood en C. Imber (eds.), *Studies in Ottoman History in Honour of Professor V.L. Ménage*, Istanbul 1994, 11-90.

16 Published by F. Babinger, *Fetihnâme-i Sultan Mehmed*, Istanbul 1955.

17 Discussed in my "Notes on the {IsAr} future and its modal functions", B. Kellner-Heinkele en M. Stachowski (red.), *Laut- und Wortgeschichte der Türksprachen*, Wiesbaden 1995, 43-57.

18 Cf. C. Kafadar, *Between Two Worlds. The Construction of the Ottoman State*, Berkeley-Los Angeles-London, 1995, 177-178.

19 Dankoff, "The lyric in the romance", 22.

20 Ş.H. Akalın (ed.), *Saltuk-nâme* in 3 volumes, Ankara-Istanbul 1988-1990 (not seen); F. İz published the manuscript H. 1616 in the Topkapı Sarayı, Cambridge, Mass., 1986 (six volumes).

tury?) is a prose epic which contains lyric insertions.[21] The *Ġazavāt-i Murād b. Meḥemmed Ḫān*,[22] though mainly in prose, contains a few passages of verse, which convey religious feelings and the horror inspired by the carnage in the battle of Varna.[23]

After glancing at these heroic prose works it will be useful to divide the Ottoman histories into three groups; prose virtually without insertions; prose with insertions of narrative mesnevī; prose with all sorts of narrative and non-narrative insertions in mesnevī, ghazal, and other forms.

•••

Firstly, Neshrī's *Cihān-nümā*. This compilation (1485-1495), which has been called the best representative of early Ottoman historical writings, is practically without poetry.[24] The author[25] carefully removed the verses from his predecessor's (ʿĀshıḳpashazāde, 1484-85) work or paraphrased them into prose, smoothed down "questions and answers" into narrative, and toned down criticism.[26] After him Mustafā Selānīkī, a writer of small rhetorical pretensions who covered the events from 1563 to 1600,[27] wrote without poetry.

Secondly, there is a group of at least four Ottoman histories, in which narrative mesnevī passages have been incorporated. The anonymous *Tevārīḫ-i āl-i ʿOsmān* contain, next to prose folk-tales in the garb of the *menāḳıb*,[28] certain mesnevī passages, which were taken from the *Iskender-nāme* and, according to İnalcık, from a rhymed work, probably by Ḥamzavī.[29]

The *Ṭabaḳātü l-memālik* by Celālzāde Muṣṭafā Çelebi, a highly esteemed elaborate history of the reign of Sultan Süleymān to 1555, is written in *inshāʾ*, "middle" prose and everyday speech.[30] It contains mesnevīs in which the rhetorical devices of the author's prose are strikingly absent. One of them is a

21 Dankoff, "The lyric in the romance", 22, quotes from Kocatürk, 295. For ongoing editorial work by George Dedes see Kafadar, *Between Two Worlds*, 169 note 9.

22 Ed. Halil İnalcık and Mevclûd Oguz, *Gazavât-ı Sultân Murâd b. Mehemmed Hân*, Ankara 1978.

23 B. Flemming, "The Sultan's Prayer before Battle", See no. 23 in this volume.

24 V.L. Ménage, *Neshrî's History of the Ottomans. The Sources and Development of the Text*, London, 1964.

25 Perhaps a minor poet, of whose poetical talent Laṭīfī had a low opinion. He only has a short *kaside* in praise of Bāyezīd. Ménage, loc. cit., 1.

26 Ménage, "Beginnings", 175.

27 Klaus Schwarz (ed.), *Mustafâ Selânîkî. Târîh-i Selânîkî. Die Chronik des Selânîkî*, Freiburg 1970.

28 Cf. Hasan Özdemir, *Die altosmanischen Chroniken als Quelle zur türkischen Volkskunde*, Freiburg 1975.

29 H. İnalcık, "The Rise of Ottoman Historiography", 154.

30 P. Kappert (ed.), *Geschichte Sultan Süleymân Kânûnîs von 1520 bis 1557*, Wiesbaden, 1981,

şehrengīz on Amasya, signed with the author's *maḫlaṣ* Nişānī. Another story in mesnevī is situated at the mid-point of the narrative of Alḳās Mīrzā, the younger brother of Shāh Tahmāsp I who went over to the Ottomans, then tried to go back to the Safavids but was killed by the latter (1549). This story, with its religious, Shiʿite, overtones, puts emphasis on the double treason committed by the prince. The editor has pointed out that in this poetical insertion events are described not necessarily as they happened, but as they might or ought to have happened.[31]

An alternation between ornate prose and simple lucid mesnevī is equally observable in Ḫwāca Saʿdeddīn's *Tācü t-tevārīḫ*. Saʿdeddīn's mesnevī passages on the abdication of Murād II are reminiscent of Celālzāde's poetic treatment of events "as they might have happened".

Thirdly, at least five Turkish histories form a group in which the prose narrative is enriched by the insertion of poetical fragments. ʿĀshıḳpashazāde's well-known account of Ottoman history[32] constitutes a prose narrative interspersed by at least 203 poems, the creative possibilities of which have been explored by G. Procházka-Eisl.[33] Combining his poetry with direct speech, often questions and answers, the chronicler sometimes strips away the veneer of political convention, elucidating the darker strains of ordinary life.[34] Oruç b. ʿĀdil[35] is no less successful in his use of, among Koran quotations, many poems of his own and a poem of victory and thanksgiving composed in monorhyme by a commander in the field (Yaʿḳūb Pasha, Derviş Yaʿḳūb) which serves to enhance the victory over the Derencil Ban at Krbova.[36]

36-40, analyzed the prose style of the work, with earlier literature, especially Fahir İz' *Eski Türk Edebiyatında Nesir* I, Istanbul 1964.

31 P. Kappert, *Geschichte Sultan Süleymân Kânûnîs*, 23-26.

32 H. İnalcık, "How to Read ʿĀshık Pasha-Zāde's History", C. Heywood en C. Imber (eds.), *Studies in Ottoman History in Honour of Professor V.L. Ménage*, Istanbul 1994, 63-75,

33 G. Procházka-Eisl, "Die lyrischen Einschübe in der altosmanischen Chronik des Āşıkpaşazāde", *Osmanlı Araştırmaları* XV (1995), 93-122.

34 "Āšıḳpašazādes Blick auf Frauen", see no. 26 in this volume.

35 For this author see R.F. Kreutel, *Der fromme Sultan Bayezid. Die Geschichte seiner Herrschaft (1481-1512) nach den altosmanischen Chroniken des Oruç und des Anonymus Hanivaldanus*, Graz Wien Cologne 1978, 109, 172.

36 Trencsény Imre, the Hungarian Banus of Croatia, was defeated in 1493 by Yaʿkûb Pasha. The poem was translated and commented upon by R.F. Kreutel, *Der fromme Sultan Bayezid*, Graz Vienna Cologne, 1978, 71-72, 164; B. Moser, *Die Chronik des Ahmed Sinân Çelebi genannt Bihištî. Eine Quelle zur Geschichte des osmanischen Reiches unter Sultan Bâyezid II.*, Munich 1980, 144; Reindl, *Männer um Bayezid*, 350.

Tursun Beg's *Ta'rīḫ-i Ebū l-Feth*, begun in 1488,[37] is an original work based on the author's personal experiences. His Turkish prose is vigorous and has an attractive conversational quality. Tursun begins with an introduction which is a formal prologue in the manner of the great literary mesnevīs: praise to God, praise to the family of the Prophet, prayers, and a philosophical discussion of the function of the ruler. With this prologue, the stage is set for a history which is "sprinkled" with lyrical insertions in Arabic, Persian, and Turkish, *naẓm*, *mıṣrāʿ*, *beyt*, *ḳıṭʿa*, and some rather long pieces of mesnevī. What purpose did these poems serve? Did they only serve as evidence of Tursun Beg's skill in the poetic arts?[38] Are they a "hodgepodge of lyrics", strung together by the thread of the narrative?[39] Mertol Tulum has shown that sometimes the figures of speech escape from cliché into direct observation of natural objects, and he indicated that the verses may form a running commentary on the progress of the action, for example on Ottoman casualties in the war against the Mamluks. An example of Tursun's use of verse to highlight a crisis (Murād II has abdicated – the state is in danger – the administration of the empire is beyond the strength and knowledge of the young Mehmed II) are the following audacious lines addressed by the grand vizier "in Turkish" (*Türkīce*) to the retired sultan,

> Hey man, what a comical thing you have done,
> while your business was gold you made it silver,
> you brought a weaned calf of twelve
> put it in your place and made it a water buffalo.[40]

The poet Bihishtī, Ahmed Sinān Çelebi, wrote his *Tevārīḫ-i āl-i ʿOsmān* (covering the period 1389-1502) in ornate, *sacʿ*- rhyming *inshāʾ* prose. His insertions may be divided into quotations from the Koran and from "Ibn-i Rāvendī" on the one hand and mesnevī and ghazals, *naẓm* and *ḳıṭʿa* on the other, in Turkish and Persian, of the sophisticated kind used as vehicles for the concepts of romantic poetry. When Bihishtī celebrates the victory at Krbova he composes a long poem of his own, casting out Yaʿḳūb Beg's poem which he must have known from Oruç.[41]

37 The work has been published three times: (i) by Meḥmed ʿĀrif in the Supplement to the *TʿOEM* 1330 h., (ii) by A. Mertol Tulum, *Tursun Bey. Târîh-i Ebü'l-Feth*, Istanbul, 1977, and (iii) by H. İnalcık and Rhoads Murphey, Minneapolis/Chicago 1978.

38 H. İnalcık, "Tursun Beg, Historian of Mehmed the Conqueror's Time", *WZKM* 69 (1977), 55-71.

39 Dankoff, "The lyric in the romance", 9.

40 Tulum (ed.), *Tursun Bey. Târîh-i Ebü'l-Feth*, 35.

41 B. Moser, *Chronik des Ahmed Sinân Çelebi*, 27-31; 33-34.

Kemālpashazāde (writing around 1502) stands out as a great history writer. His *Tevārīḫ-i Āl-i ʿOsmān*, the largest and most important compilation of his time, is without doubt also an important literary work. He follows Oruç and, like Tursun, he uses the cosmopolitan poetic diction we have glanced at above, but also the colloquial resources of Turkish. The poetry in his work merits a special study. It is known that Kemālpashazāde quoted from Koran and Hadith, that he versified proverbial sayings,[42] that he inserted his own poems in Persian and Turkish and that he incorporated some verses from Oruç. He applied this form of citation (*tazmīn*) also to the *Ġazavāt-i Dāvūd Pasha* by Ḫayreddīn Çelebi at the end of his seventh volume.[43]

Muṣṭafā b. Aḥmed, known as ʿĀlī (1541-1600), was a historian and a literary man. Politics inspired his 'Essence of Histories', begun in 1592, which gives us the clue to where he got the flexible, passionate style that may be called unique. He did not invent the alternation between prose and poetry (hundreds of poems in Turkish, Persian, and Arabic),[44] but he invented the perfect use of speech rhythms to give force to his assertions.[45]

Since few of the historical works preceding ʿĀlī have been analyzed, it is too early to say anything about the distribution of the traditions of inserting narrative and non-narrative ("lyric") poems, either in the mesnevī form or in the form of ghazal and poetical fragments. Ottomanists have of course noticed that Kemālpashazāde, Celālzāde, Saʿdeddīn, ʿĀlī and their Turkish forerunners Bihishtī, Tursun Beg, and even Oruç, wrote almost in two dictions, ornate, artificial and Persian, and colloquial, natural and Turkish (with *orta nesir* in between)[46]. But it is clear that more efforts of scholarship are needed before we know fully what these authors, presumably with the sanction of contemporary readers, were aiming at with their poetry.

Enough has been said, I hope, though more examples could be quoted, to put it beyond doubt that it would be useful to establish the place of poetry in historical prose, and at the same time to re-establish a sense of connection between history and literature. It is a relatively uncharted subject. Quotations were accepted means of adding refinement or conducting a dispute. Pieces of

42 Ş. Turan's introduction to his *İbn-i Kemal. Tevârih-i Âl-i Osman I. Defter*. Ankara, 1970, 29. On proverbs in the anonymous chronicles see H. Özdemir, *Die altosmanischen Chroniken*, 9-39.

43 Cf. İnalcık, "The Rise of Ottoman Historiography", 163, 167; Ş. Turan, *İbn Kemal: Tevârih-i Al-i Osman, VII. defter (tenkidli transkripsiyon)*, Ankara, 1957, introduction.

44 J. Schmidt studied poetical intermezzi in *Pure Water for Thirsty Muslims. A Study of Muṣṭafā ʿĀlī of Gallipoli's Künhü l-Aḥbār*, Leiden 1992, 222-225.

45 For satire in ʿĀlī's poetry see A. Tietze, *Mustafâ ʿAlî's Description of Cairo of 1599*, Vienna, 1975, 20-21.

46 F. İz, *Eski Türk Edebiyatında Nesir* I, Istanbul 1964, introduction.

poetry are of importance for the historian because of their social uses; they were often intended to be sung; they could entertain friends and patrons; they gave the satisfactions that came from exercising craftsmanship and skill; they were a means of stating points of view towards incidents in the narrative, of providing a deeper insight into what had happened, to comment on the effects of war, to lament a bad world, to admonish audiences who also knew the romances. Where verses were eliminated and criticism was toned down we become aware of the thin line dividing public opinion and reasons of state.

CHAPTER 26

ʿĀşıḳpaşazāde's View of Women*

As is well known, the Chronicle of ʿĀşıḳpaşazāde sets forth the rise of the Ottomans in 156 chapters, which we will cite following Giese's edition[1] and according to the numbered subsections (§) in Ménage's studies.[2] The work, with its interspersed verses,[3] was often recited, especially to the accompaniment of the saz,[4] apparently for men (who are addressed as "brother" *aḫī* in §75, *ḳarındaş* §85, *ḳardaş* and "companion" *yoldaş* §51). But similarly it was also read, and with the words "you dear ones" *iy ʿazīzler* §26, "my darling(s)" *iy cānum*, and even *iy ḳarındaş* §19 and §29,[5] it was able to address itself to both sexes. Indeed, the female milieu, in which folkloric forms arose,[6] could even have its share in the productive literary devices employed in the chronicle.

We will not read ʿĀşıḳpaşazāde primarily as a source for society "as it really was" but as a work of literature in which female figures appear. A good portion of the early Ottoman state is here represented through its women: Turkish princely families in their wives and sisters, the Ottoman Turkish upper strata in kadi's spouses and wet-nurses, high-status dervishes in the Shaykh's daughter, the nomads in female cattle-drivers. The Greek high nobility appears before us in the Mistress of İznikmid (İzmit), the lower Greek nobility in castle damsels, the Greek lower classes in the women in the marketplace of Eskişehir, the Armenian country folk for whom their monks put in a good word, in the region

* Translated by John O'Kane.

1 Friedrich Giese (ed.) *Die altosmanische Chronik des ʿĀšıkpaşazāde* (Leipzig, 1929); Richard F. Kreutel (transl.) *Vom Hirtenzelt zur Hohen Pforte* (Graz, 1959). Cf. the editions of ʿĀlī Bey (İstanbul, 1332) and Çiftçioğlu Nihal Atsız, in *Osmanlı Tarihleri* 1 (İstanbul, 1949).

2 Victor L. Ménage, *Neshrī's History of the Ottomans: The Sources and Development of the Text* (London, 1964). With Ménage the abbreviation Ank will be used for Faik Reşat Unat and M. Altay Köymen (ed.), *Kitâb-ı Cihan-nümâ: Neşrî Tarihi* (Ankara, 1957).

3 An important lacuna, the verses that Kreutel left out of his translation, is filled by Gisela M. Eisl, "Die lyrischen Einschübe in der altosmanischen Chronik des ʿĀşıqpaşazāde"; M.A. thesis, Vienna 1988, a shortened version of which was published in *Osmanlı Araştırmaları* 15 (1995): pp. 93-122. I am especially grateful to Professor G.M. Procházka-Eisl for having sent me her works.

4 Eisl, "Lyrische Einschübe", p. 114.

5 Eisl, "Lyrische Einschübe", pp. 28, 40, 49, 93 in connection with §29 ḳ*arındaş* and §67 *ḳardaş*; cf. Redhouse "brother or sister".

6 Wolfram Eberhard and Pertev Naili Boratav, *Typen türkischer Volksmärchen* (Wiesbaden, 1953), Introduction; Pertev Naili Boratav, *Türkische Volksmärchen* (Berlin, 1967), pp. 335-37.

 | DOI 10.1163/9789004355767_027

around Erzincan. The Serbian royal house is represented by the spouse of Bāyezīd and a female ruler of Bosnia (§126), the Christian lands by "sweethearts" and "paramours", i.e. good-looking captives. As for the "sisters of Rūm", *bacıyan-ı Rūm*, the postulated fourth group of Rūm (*aḫī, abdāl, ġāzī*), regarding whom Republican Turkish literature has fabricated an attractive image, they are absent in ʿĀşıḳpaşazāde/Giese (though they go on resurfacing elsewhere, despite Köprülü's retraction).[7] In each of these cases the historical context must be touched upon, if only briefly, to the extent required for comprehension. In the interest of the theme of "women"[8], now and then it will be desirable to look a bit beyond the boundaries of this one chronicle.

ʿĀşıḳpaşazāde's chronicle, along with its fundamentally pro-Ottoman tendency,[9] displays certain inner contradictions. The attitude toward the nomads was still changeable and adapted itself to the interests of the moment. Slavery,[10] too, was apparently not completely uncontested. Approval of the taking of slaves could turn into rejection. ʿĀşıḳpaşazāde praises capturing booty,[11] mentions in §10 that in this case they "took no slaves" (*esīr almadılar*) but in the immediately following verse emphasizes: "With ʿOs̱mān everything revolved around banqueting (*ṭoy*) and battles for the faith (*ġuzāt*);[12] if one man took gold and silver, another took horses, and still another took girls that pleased him." On the other hand, in the verses in §29 ʿĀşıḳpaşazāde looks back to a bygone era when they (the Ottomans) carried on no trade in slaves. "They sold no slaves and they bought none either; there was no strife over slaves..."[13] Pure harmony with the Greeks prevailed, and yet deceit in war (*müdārā*) and

7 Speros Vryonis, Jr., *The Decline of Medieval Hellenism in Asia Minor and the Process of Islamization from the Eleventh through the Fifteenth Century* (Berkeley, Los Angeles, London, 1971), p. 363, cites ʿĀşıḳpaşazāde from ʿĀlī's edition; M. Fuad Köprülü, *Osmanlı İmparatorluğunun Kuruluşu* (Ankara, 1959), had at first assumed that the philologically untrustworthy term *bacılar* referred to Dulkadır female warriors. Cf. Cemal Kafadar, *Between Two Worlds: The Construction of the Ottoman State* (Berkeley, Los Angeles, London, 1995), p. 176, ftn. 94.

8 This being a contribution to the Festschrift Hans Georg Majer "Āşıḳpaşazādes Blick auf Frauen", Sabine Prätor & Christoph K. Neumann (eds.), *Frauen, Bilder und Gelehrte. Studien zu Gesellschaft und Künsten im Osmanischen Reich*, Istanbul, 2002, pp. 69-96.

9 Leslie Peirce, *The Imperial Harem: Women and Sovereignty in the Ottoman Empire* (New York, Oxford, 1993), p. 32, for this reason warns against viewing the chronicles as sources.

10 Cf. Bernard Lewis, *Race and Slavery in the Middle East: An Historical Enquiry* (New York, Oxford, 1990). See also my "Female Participation", no. 27 in this volume.

11 On the historical aspect of taking booty in general cf. Cemal Kafadar, *Between Two Worlds*, pp. 86-88.

12 "War and peace", *bazm u razm*; Eisl, "Lyrische Einschübe", p. 15.

13 Eisl, "Lyrische Einschübe", p. 47.

feigned trust[14] are described on both sides. To begin with the Germiyanids were more feared adversaries[15] than one wanted to admit later on. The forced resettlement of their own population is not accepted uncritically; fratricide is criticized by means of the stylistic device of dialogue.[16] The pure lineage of the Ottomans is contrasted with the "impure one" of the neighboring Anatolian princes.[17] The exclusively paternal principle of inheritance of the Ottomans, for which Leslie Peirce has collected the evidence with great meticulousness,[18] is set forth emphatically, though without completely renouncing a maternal line of the House of ʿO͟smān.[19] After the opening chapters in which women play a role, ʿĀşıḳpaşazāde has the tendency, from around the middle of the chronicle onwards, to present far fewer individual women (Neşrī continues the tendency, followed by Kemālpaşazāde, the mufti, who on the basis of his office, affirmed[20] the social ideal of separation of the sexes and as a historian energetically ousted women from early Ottoman history). But in the second half of the chronicle, in §136, we get the chance to see a royal woman once again.

As is customary in his literary genre, which is equally popular with the high and the low, ʿĀşıḳpaşazāde is out to educate his public, and this means in particular encouraging the less privileged to conform to their traditional role in family and society. Thus women as well could feel themselves addressed in the appeals for modesty, patient acceptance of what God has preordained, and in warnings against egotism and pride.[21] It would not have surprised them that ʿĀşıḳpaşazāde speaks of "human beings" (*ādem*)[22] as of men. Humanity goes on transmitting itself through a paternal line. "These human beings are all sons of a father" (*ḳamu bir ata oğlıdur bu ādem* §61).[23]

---

14 Kreutel, *Hirtenzelt*, pp. 32, 125; cf. Kafadar, *Between Two Worlds*, p. 126. On *müdārā* in the sense of "flattery, simulation, feigned friendship" see also §73, Eisl, "Lyrische Einschübe", p. 102.

15 Cf. Kafadar, *Between Two Worlds*, pp. 104, 112, 114.

16 On §67 cf. Procházka-Eisl, "Lyrische Einschübe", *Osmanlı Araştırmaları* 15 (1995): p. 110; on fratricide ibid., p. 119.

17 Cf. my "The Sultan's Prayer Before Battle", no. 23 in this volume.

18 Membership in the House of ʿO͟smān is inherited exclusively through the paternal line, aristocratic spouses have no sexual relations with the ruler, with amazing discipline sexual relations are limited to one child per concubine, and only the relationship of being the Sultan's mother ever raised a woman to real power. On these points cf. Peirce, *Harem*, Part 1.

19 Peirce, *Harem*, pp. 275-77.

20 Peirce, *Harem*, p. 269.

21 Eisl, "Lyrische Einschübe", p. xxvii.

22 In §36; cf. Eisl, "Lyrische Einschübe", p. 56.

23 Eisl, "Lyrische Einschübe", p. 39. Other examples in the same work: "The father gains no friend in his own son" (§75, Eisl, pp. 104-05); the father shows his son the way, and the

It is almost superfluous to point out that the environment in which ʿĀşıḳpaşazāde wrote was intimate with slavery. A complete household was made up of free persons and slaves. The more women a farmer could employ on his farm, the better matters stood for him economically.[24] The segregation of the sexes, which had already existed in the Byzantine state, was based on the availability of poorer women and female slaves. The latter, the non-Muslim female slave, stood on the lowest rung of the social ladder.[25] From the moment that a girl or a woman fell into captivity, her status was no longer defined by her family relationships but by the price she could fetch (if the *akıncıs* took many captives, as at Belgrade in §116, "a fine female slave" [*nefīs cāriye*] could be had "for a boot")[26] and later on by the household position she served in. A return to her parental home was out of the question. Her situation depended on her age, her physical strength and her appearance. The most beautiful could be passed on as a gift. Thus in §51 we see that good-looking virgins and boys are among the wedding gifts of Evrenoz; and in §152 Gedik Aḥmed Paşa gives the daughters and wives of the Genoese of Kaffa as gifts to the Sultan's men. Poets had female slaves bestowed on them.[27] In the day and age of ʿĀşıḳpaşazāde's chronicle, according to ʿĀşıḳ Çelebi, a certain Ṭūṭī ḳadın was given as a gift to the poet Aḥmed Paşa.[28]

ʿĀşıḳpaşazāde's terminology for describing persons of the female gender[29] corresponds to the distinction between sexually active and "post-sexual"

latter should take advice from his father (§23, Eisl, p. 39). Sons are a comfort to their father (§117).

24 Eberhard/Boratav, *Volksmärchen*, p. 25.

25 "The bottom of the social pile was, of course, the non-Muslim female slave", Bernard Lewis, *Political Language of Islam* (Chicago, London, 1988), p. 66.

26 In §116 ʿĀşıḳpaşazāde himself expresses satisfaction at the good price he received in Edirne for nine male and female slaves. Bihiştī was disappointed; cf. Brigitte Moser, *Die Chronik des Ahmed Sinân Çelebi, genannt Bihiştī* (München, 1980), p. 139; in Mytilene Tursun Beg acquired a boy, a girl and a *çetel*(?)-slave, according to M. Tulum (ed.), *Tursun Bey: Târîh-i Ebü l-Feth* (İstanbul, 1977), p. 120; Halil İnalcık and Rhoads Murphey, *The History of Mehmed the Conqueror by Tursun Beg* (Minneapolis, Chicago, 1978 [photocopy edition with "summary translation"]), p. 40 ("chattel slave").

27 Apaḳ, who became famous thanks to Niẓāmī, is dealt with by Johann Christoph Bürgel in "Die Frau als Person in der Epik Niẓāmīs", *Asiatische Studien* 42,1 (1988): pp. 127-44.

28 G.M. Meredith-Owens (ed.), *Meşāʿir üş-şuʿarā or Tezkere of ʿĀşıḳ Çelebi* (London, 1971), folio 36a. But both the title *ḳadın* that was conferred on her (cf. Peirce, *Harem*, p. 312, ftn. 74) as well as the "slipper money" that was allegedly paid to her (cf. Harold Bowen, "Bashmaḳlıḳ" in EI²) point to the sixteenth century.

29 The entire field is dealt with by Saadet Çagatay, "Die Bezeichnungen für Frau im Türkischen, I", *Ural-Altaische Jahrbücher* 35 (1963): pp. 158-63. For the folkloristic perspective in research on women, which above all has focused on their reproductive capacities,

(Peirce) women, which distinction in turn contributed to defining their social status. As in other literary works on early Ottoman history, at the top among women stands the worthy, respectable "dame", the "lady", as well as the "consort" (*ḫatun*, *ḫatun* [*kişi*]) or widow. They are matrons who may show themselves in public and who enjoy respect and greater freedom of movement.[30] ʿĀşıḳpaşazāde's interest in the maternal line of the Ottomans was not so pronounced that he was prepared to seek out the House of ʿO̱smān's eldest female blood-relations. They only lead a shadow existence until §12 where ʿO̱smān speaks of his mother,[31] his mother-in-law (*ḳayın anam*) and his spouse (*ḫatunum*). One was probably meant to feel that their names were not necessary. Everything spouse-like is summed up in ʿO̱smān's "spouse *par excellence*" (featured wife), Mal Ḫatun, whom ʿĀşıḳpaşazāde identifies as being the daughter of the charismatic Shaykh Edebali: ʿO̱smān marries her in §4 after the well-known prophetic dream, leaves her behind in §16 with her father in Bilecik (*ḫatunını atasıyla Bilecikde bile ḳodı*) and buries her with his own hand (*kendü eliyle defn eyledi*) in §28 where he expressly refers to her by name as Mal Ḫatun.[32]

After this, only the women of the ruling class who have some functional value for the literary aspect of his chronicle continue to appear in ʿĀşıḳpaşazāde. Thus he portrays no formal marriage ceremony involving Murād I,[33] but he does depict weddings with three high-ranking Turkish women, celebrations that are productive literary factors in that they offer colorful entertainment. Three chapters – §§50-52 – deal with the marriage in 1381 of the princess of Germiyan, the daughter of the famous Süleymān Şāh, with the young Bāyezīd.[34]

---

cf. Carola Lipp, "Frauenforschung" in *Grundriss der Volkskunde: Einführung in die Forschungsfelder der Europäischen Ethnologie*, ed. Rolf W. Brednich (Berlin, 1988), pp. 251-72; especially pp. 254-55.

30 Peirce, *Harem*, pp. 279-80.

31 Peirce assumes that ʿO̱smān issued from a formal marriage.

32 Historically matters were different. ʿO̱smān married the sheikh's daughter but her name wasn't Mal Ḫatun but Rābiʿa or Bālā. Mal Ḫatun was the daughter of a certain Umur or ʿÖmer Beg and, having outlived ʿO̱smān, was buried in the family tomb in Bursa. In this regard see Peirce, *Harem*, pp. 33-34 and 295, following İsmail Hakkı Uzunçarşılı, "Gazi Orhan Bey Vakfiyesi", *Belleten* 5 (1941): pp. 284-85.

33 That Bāyezīd I was the son of a certain Gülçiçek of Greek origin, who according to oral tradition had first been abducted for another harem and then married Murād, is not found in ʿĀşıḳpaşazāde. Peirce, *Harem*, pp. 36 and 296, following Kepecioğlu. Her tomb stood on its own in Bursa: Peirce, *Harem*, pp. 51-52 and 300, following Baykal.

34 Possibly the marriage with this descendant of powerful princes and charismatic sheikhs was not consummated because she was herself too charismatic: Peirce, *Harem*, pp. 40 and 297, following Çağatay Uluçay. According to another tradition, which even attributes to

And there are two celebrations in §94 for the daughter of Isfendiyāroğlu (Ḫadīce Ḥalīme) who married Murād II, the one arranged by her father, and a second one held in Bursa. Two similarly splendid celebrations for the Dulkadır princess (Sittī Ḫatun), who married Meḥmed II shortly before he became Sultan (for a second time), are described by ʿĀşıḳpaşazāde in §121 (her dowry was too small). Foreign spouses of royal blood are accorded no special consideration,[35] as is the case with the Byzantine Emperor's daughter, Theodora, who married Orḫan in 1346 and by way of exception bore children,[36] as well as Mara, the spouse of Murād II. Moreover, the social environment demanded a colorful personification of immorality in contrast with the old Turkish values, and for this the Serbian king's daughter, Maria Olivera Lazarević, the spouse of Bāyezīd I, was well suited. Bāyezīd received Olivera, the daughter of Lazar I Hrebelyanović and sister of the "Laz" Stephen Lazarević, as a "gift". The sexually robust woman – she satisfies all his desires[37] but remains a Christian – is blamed for having introduced wine-drinking at the court, against which ʿĀşıḳpaşazāde speaks out in §58 and §62. In §63 he places direct speech in her mouth – she asks that the Danube port of Semendria be given to her sister and gets her wish.[38] In this respect, aspects of a generally rather negative judgment of Bāyezīd are developed through her.[39]

Just as spouses of royal origin bore no children, their descent and building activities were not given attention. Recognition of female aristocratic blood, as Peirce puts it, would have compromised the integrity of the sultanate.[40] It was not marriage but the progenitor that determined the succession. A passage in Bihiştī, who wrote not long after ʿĀşıḳpaşazāde, indirectly confirms this. He

her a mother (!) named Muṭahhare, a granddaughter of Celāl ed-Dīn Rūmī, she was called Devletşāh.

35 After the rule of Murād II, the Sultans no longer concluded inter-dynastic marriages: Peirce, *Harem*, p. 275.

36 The daughter of John VI Kantakuzenos; Peirce, *Harem*, p. 41.

37 Kreutel performs a service to Ottoman polemic when he renders *ḳız* as "Giaur girl", whereas he translates *ḳız* in *Hirtenzelt*, p. 102, as "virgin".

38 Kreutel's doubt (*Hirtenzelt*, p. 279) about her speaking like this – he believes the Serbian king must have made the request – does not do justice to the function of women in the context of the chronicle.

39 Paul Wittek and Anthony D. Alderson, *The Structure of the Ottoman Dynasty* (Oxford, 1956) accept the perverting role of the Serb female. The question as to the causes of the Timur catastrophe is dealt with by Peirce, *Harem*, p. 32, and Kafadar, *Between Two Worlds*, pp. 106 and 111. Colin Imber, *Studies in Ottoman History and Law*, Istanbul 1996, pp. 297-298 ("influence of his Serbian wife, Olivera [and]... her corrupting influence".

40 Peirce, *Harem*, pp. 40-41.

notes on the occasion of the death of Matthias Corvinus (1492) that *Matyas Kīral* had left a son by the name of Imre (John Corvinus) whose mother had been a prostitute. "But with the Christians it is established that a child who was not (born) from a wife cannot become the ruler."[41] There are a few Muslim spouses of aristocratic descent who receive respectful attention in ʿĀşıḳpaşazāde: Paşa Kiriçe, the consort of the Germiyanid Yaʿḳūb in §94, who Murād II called *şāh ḫatun*, and Ṣāra Ḫatun, as well as the spouse of Uzun Ḥasan; they are exploited for their literary potential.

Matrons of royal descent negotiated peace treaties, as is several times reported in ʿĀşıḳpaşazāde.[42] In §116, the ruler of Karaman "sends" his wife (without her name being mentioned) as well as his vizier (whose name is mentioned) as ambassadors to Murād II in order to excuse himself for hostile actions. In §136 a non-Ottoman of royal descent, Ṣāra Ḫatun, the mother of Uzun Ḥasan, brings gifts to Meḥmed II whom she calls "son", and he confers on her the respectful title of "mother". He calls the Kurdish shaykh who is accompanying her "father". ʿĀşıḳpaşazāde even has her speak with the conqueror. Her unpretentious, straightforward speech is a master stroke of ʿĀşıḳpaşazāde. She accompanies the Sultan, is amazed at the arduous march through the mountains, and finally intercedes on behalf of the Emperor of Trebizond who is an uncle of her daughter-in-law.[43] "But regarding this matter the Sultan was silent." Instead, ʿĀşıḳpaşazāde has the Sultan describe what it means to be a *ġāzī*.

Then somewhat later – to cite another chronicler – Selçuk Ḫatun, a high-ranking matron and sister of the deceased Sultan Murād, negotiated with Bāyezīd II; the latter's brother, Prince Cem, had "sent" her – so writes Bihiştī.[44] However, even in cases where high-ranking women took on the role of advocate to obtain pardon or assistance, this must only have occurred as an assignment and under supervision.

An interesting interim episode is that in §30 involving "Yalakonya", a relative of the Emperor and consequently a member of the Byzantine high nobility. When her brother Kaloyan (Kaloyannes) has been killed in action, she assumes

41 Bihiştī (35v) reports that the Sultan was pleased to hear that the king's son was unsuitable and illegitimate; in Moser, *Bihiştī*, pp. 134-35, 144.

42 Peirce, *Harem*, p. 42, mentions the influence that Mara, the widow of Murād II, exerted on Meḥmed II's diplomacy.

43 Uzun Ḥasan had married Kyra Katerina Komnena, known as Despina Ḫatun, the daughter of the Emperor of Trebizond Kaloyannes who died in the year of the wedding 1458 and was succeeded on the throne by his brother David Komnenos. Walther Hinz, *Irans Aufstieg zum Nationalstaat im fünfzehnten Jahrhundert* (Berlin, Leipzig, 1936), pp. 39-41.

44 Moser, *Bihiştī*, p. 65.

an independent political role and is even given a long text to speak. As mistress of the castle of Nicomedia, she explains to her people in an original manner why they must surrender and she obtains for herself and her people freedom to withdraw from the city. She retreats during the night, having received upon request assurances of protection from molestation. She is allowed to have ships loaded in the harbor as she wishes. The charm of this inserted story consists in a certain tension between conformity to Ottoman usage and foreignness; she closely binds herself to her new environment but at the same time she contrasts herself with it ("the Turks", she says at this point, "call the castle Ḳoyunḥiṣār") and thus she lets another world – the Greek one – cast light into the world of the *ġāzīs*. Verses about a woman who has charge over herself and over others would be felt as disturbing. ʿĀşıḳpaşazāde instead weaves in reflections about transitoriness and false pretensions.

Women were the property of men. A female Türkmen in §99, whose husband has been killed, is *boş* "unowned, unprotected", i.e. "masterless".[45] The disciples of the bold Shaykh Bedr ed-Dīn expressly excluded their wives when they decided to share all their goods with one another. Ottoman scholarship with its judgmental opinions which, for example, seeks to give reasons for forced resettlements (*sürgün*) or approves of them,[46] has also been lenient in its treatment of slavery. It emphasizes as a positive aspect that slavery was for the most part not hereditary, that allegedly slaves were easily integrated,[47] and that a female slave could bear children and be set free by her master.[48] At the same time, however, scholarship has regretted that child-bearing concubines threatened the nuclear family, that they represented in fact dangerous rivals for the wife, who wished to be the only one to bear children to her husband.[49] In any case, the acceptance and interpretation of the Ottoman value system

45 On "herrenlos" cf. Luise F. Pusch, *Das Deutsche als Männersprache* (Frankfurt a.M., 1984), p. 155.

46 An example: Kreutel's commentary (*Hirtenzelt*, p. 281) on §77. The miserable nomadic lifestyle of a Tatar tribe is transformed to prosperity in Rumeli where the men can now abduct women and girls. Kreutel, along with Ömer Lütfi Barkan, emphasizes the advantages of the deportations.

47 Yvonne J. Seng, "Fugitives and Factotums: Slaves in Early Sixteenth-Century Istanbul", *JESHO* 39 (1996): pp. 136-69.

48 Leslie Peirce argues, with the harem of the Sultans in mind, that not only didn't the separation of the sexes hinder women from surmounting their subordinate role but actually contributed to the formation of a hierarchy of their own.

49 Cemal Kafadar, "Women in Seljuk and Ottoman Society up to the Mid-19th Century", in *9000 Years of the Anatolian Woman: 29 November 1993 – 28 February 1994, İstanbul Topkapı Sarayı Museum* (İstanbul, 1993), pp. 197-98.

should not preclude that those who, to adopt the view of Ruth Klūger,[50] belong to the gender of the slave women analyze motifs[51] and problems raised in statements of the texts.

In ʿĀşıḳpaşazāde's early chapters the woman is not only property, she also functions as a guardian of property. As such, especially in §3, ladies, walking beside the cattle during the nomadic migration, protected the group's property by depositing the Ottoman tribe's valuables before entering the summer pastures. As ʿĀşıḳpaşazāde emphasizes, in this way they promote harmony with the Greeks which, moreover, was the basis for economic exchange. "The infidels had great trust in them." The men (the Tekfur and ʿO̱smān) in §11 have not yet met one another in person (*illā furṣat bulunmazlar kim ḳarvayalar*). In §9 the role of women in guaranteeing protection is underlined: the Ottomans always maintained friendship with the lord of the castle of Bilecik; when they set out for the *yayla*, they left their valuables in Bilecik castle, and when they returned, they brought typical nomad gifts, "they did not, however, send them with men, *er kişi*, but with ladies, *ḫatunlar*". On the occasion of the lord of Bilecik Castle's marriage to the daughter of the lord of Yārḥiṣār castle, "the ladies who always did the herding" (*hemişe ileden*) again functioned as the escort of the cattle.[52] Having forced their way into the castle, the disguised Ottomans[53] killed the gatekeepers. After that we hear no more about female cattle-drivers.

"Seclusion", writes Peirce, "was not simply about gender; it was...also about status."[54] "Yalakonya" withdraws at night because she and her retinue in this way enjoy greater security. ʿO̱smān's remark that "our ladies (*ḫatunlarumuz*) are accustomed to the open countryside (*ṣaḥrāya ögrenmişler*) and Bilecik is a confined place (*dar yirdür*)" refers to the nomads' fear of the city.[55] In addition, women were not meant to come into eye-contact with strange men. This is what ʿO̱smān had in mind (§12),[56] first of all, when he has them move in the darkness of evening (*aḫşam ḳarañusında*), secondly, when he asks for a

50 Ruth Klüger, *Frauen lesen anders* (München, 1996), p. 85.

51 Her preoccupation with the modern Kazak novel stimulated Annemarie von Gabain to supplement her "sociological-philological" study of (male) Kazaks (published in *Acta Orientalia Hungarica* 11 [1960]) with a "subjective literary study" entitled "Ohnmacht und Macht der Kazakin" (in *Central Asiatic Journal* 25 [1981], pp. 54-65).

52 I differ from Kreutel, *Hirtenzelt*, p. 36: "und gab ihnen als Treiber lauter Frauen bei" (he assigned only women over them [the cattle] as cattle-drivers).

53 A fairy-tale motif; cf. the forty robbers in Eberhard/Boratav, *Volksmärchen*, p. 179, III variant 4.

54 Peirce, *Harem*, p. 271.

55 Eberhard/Boratav, *Volksmärchen*, p. 22.

56 The fact that they are men in disguise makes no difference for our argument.

separate campsite for them, "so that our ladies need not feel shame when they behold the local Tekfurs" (*ḫatunlarumuz ondağı tekfūrleri görüb utanmasunlar*).[57] "That is to say", ʿĀşıḳpaşazāde stresses, "they did not put their ladies on display" (*āşikāra getürmezler*). When calm prevails in a city as in Begpazarı in §115 (dealt with at greater length in Neşrī Ank 636, whose compiler embellishes the event with locally known details), the women go into the hammam. At the weddings involving Sultans highly respected women show themselves. ʿĀşıḳpaşazāde lists the matchmaking matrons and the bridesmaids (*düñür*) under the name of their husbands in §52 and §121; in §52 the bride is consigned to the care of the wet-nurse of the princely bridegroom (Bāyezīd), in §94 Isfendiyār's bride is consigned to Dadı Ḫatun, the wet-nurse of Sultan Meḥmed II.[58] Thus not only was the mother of a sultan retroactively ennobled by her son but so too was his wet-nurse.

Women of lower status, out of necessity, perform their tasks actively and visibly, and such is the case in §9 with the Greek women, wives of the infidels of Bilecik, who, in order to ply their trade, visit the marketplace of Eskişehir that had been pacified by the Ottomans. Considering how little of the everyday life of women is described, we learn, none the less, that ladies walked beside the cattle during the migration to higher pastures, and we know that the leather sacks full of cream, cheese, rugs and kilims that brought about peace were the work of their hands; that it was they who raised the lambs; and that they wore *ʿavret donı* and *baş bezleri* (§12). Acts of adaptation in the contacts with the Greek and Frankish communities – as a novelty, women cut their hair; men shave off their beards – are disapproved of in §31. When an *il* or tribe heads for the summer pastures of Emir Dağı (Neşrī Ank 636, following §115), the women and boys are in danger. Not only were the female slaves visible while they were engaged, as in Antiquity, in personal services and practicing crafts,[59] but they could be heard as musicians (in §118)[60] and as female singers.[61]

57 Kreutel, *Hirtenzelt*, p. 271, comments: "Der Türken Frauen schämen sich als Muslims, in der Öffentlichkeit sich unter die Christen zu mengen und sich von ihnen anstarren zu lassen." (The wives of the Turks feel ashamed to mix with the Christians in public and to let themselves be stared at by them.)

58 Cf. Peirce, *Harem*, p. 131, on the subject of Daye Khatun.

59 On the jobs they performed in public (pedlar, hairdresser, doctor, midwife, etc.) see Peirce, *Harem*, p. 271.

60 Kreutel translates *çalıcı ʿavretler* as "dancing women" (Tanzweiber), probably to convey the contempt expressed in the context.

61 Women have voices in order to sing or to speak (with eloquence and wit); in this regard cf. Fedwa Malti-Douglas, *Woman's Body, Woman's Word: Gender and Discourse in Arabo-Islamic Writing* (Princeton, 1991), pp. 35-39.

For a woman of an age to be sexually active and bear children a variety of terms are employed depending on the level of discourse. Quite general is *ʿavret* or *ʿavrat*;[62] *ḳız* is "girl, maiden", *ḳız oğlan* is "virgin"; cf. *ḳız oğlan cāriye* "virgin female slave" in §51; *gelin*, according to the context, means "bride"[63] or "daughter-in-law". In addition, there are terms based on family relationships such as *ana* "mother",[64] *ḳayın ana* "mother-in-law", *dul* "widow", *düñür* "relatives through marriage"; *ḫāla* "paternal aunt"; *ḥalāl ḫatun* "wife"; *ḳız* "daughter"; *ḳız ḳarındaşı* "sister". *Eş* too can mean "wife". Again according to the context, captured women can be called *esīr*, *cāriye* §22 and *ḳaravaş*, i.e. "female slave"; as well as *maḥbūb* "beloved",[65] or *nāzenīn* "girl" §22. In paired terms at times the man comes first, as in §10 *eri ve ʿavreti* "their (the infidels') men and women" and at times the woman: *ʿavret u eri* in §99 "(Turkmen) women and their men"; *ʿavret, oğlan* "women and boys" (see below); *dişi erkek* "female and male" in §121.[66] In the hammam "the women folk", *dişi ehli*, gather together. Girls and boys together is: *er ve ḳız oğlan* (§116). The subject folk, *reʿāyā*, have *ehl ū ʿiyāl* "wives and household" (thus Neşrī Ank 800); in §135 "married couples" low down on the social scale (Armenians) are designated *ḳoca ve ḳarı* or *ḳarılar ve ḳocalar*.

Orḫan's spouse *"par excellence"* (featured wife) and the mother of his children is Nilüfer (Lülüfer) in ʿĀşıḳpaşazāde. In §12 and §13 he describes how ʿOs̲mān abducts her as a nameless Greek noble during the preparations for her wedding and gives her to his son; in §13 ʿĀşıḳpaşazāde briefly mentions their wedding celebrations. She converts to Islam and gives proof of her piety through building works. ʿĀşıḳpaşazāde emphasizes that she gave birth to Murād I as well as Sūleymān Paşa. In the verses of §13 she is praised with the words: "This high-ranking lady has given birth to Sultan phoenixes" and in §13 her death and burial are mentioned.[67] Later on the activity of child-bearing will be withdrawn from view and the birth of a prince will be described along

62 Cf. *taze ʿavretler* "young women" and *iḫtiyār ḫatunlar* "elderly ladies" in Peirce, *Harem*, p. 280.

63 Pejorative *ʿarūs* ("bride") in the conceit: the [treacherous] old newly-wed, the world (*köhne nev-ʿarūs*), in §82; cf. Eisl, "Lyrische Einschübe", p. 113.

64 *ata vu anayı ġuṣṣalu ḳomak*: "to leave behind father and mother stricken with grief" (due to fratricide), §70; cf. Eisl, "Lyrische Einschübe", p. 99.

65 Cf. Eisl, "Lyrische Einschübe", p. 148.

66 Eisl, "Lyrische Einschübe", pp. 159-60.

67 Eisl, "Lyrische Einschübe", p. 21. Historical sources actually reveal that the abducted damsel of Yārḥiṣār castle was probably a certain Asporça. The historical Nilüfer – her name is a concubine's name – was presumably a later spouse or concubine and, as such, the mother of Murād I, but not of Süleymān. Süleymān's mother was possibly Orḫan's female cousin Efendi/Eftendize: Peirce, *Harem*, pp. 34-35.

the lines: "the bud of good fortune has blossomed in the rose garden."[68] Motherhood as a result of rape is treated in various ways by the chroniclers, depending on the level of the social conflict it presents. ʿĀşıḳpaşazāde gives his attention to the uncertain descent of children who have come into the world this way (see below). Tursun Beg twice raises the question of to what extent a free woman who has been violated by indecent elements can still be considered "chaste" (*maṣūn*).[69] In the folkloristic milieu of the *Kitāb-ı Dede Korkut* a shepherd meets a peri, desires her and sleeps with her: "*ṭamaʿ idüp cimāʿ eyledi.*"[70] There is no express mention of coercion. A shepherd, let it be noted, a figure out of the nomadic past. With allusion to ancient myths (in cases of intimacy with the gods the consequences were "honorable"), the fairy becomes pregnant with a special powerful creature, albeit one of evil nature: Tepegöz.[71]

In §94 ʿĀşıḳpaşazāde depicts how Murād II "gives away" his sisters. Only a few Ottoman princesses were married abroad. It was an undesirable giving away of power,[72] especially if a Sultan's daughter bore sons to a political adversary. Such was the case with İlaldı Ḫatun, the daughter of Meḥmed I who had six sons with the Karamanid, Tāc ed-Dīn İbrāhīm Beg (1423-64).[73] ʿĀşıḳpaşazāde employs an image from the repertoire of defamation in their regard. In §122 the act of giving birth is attributed to her husband, an enemy of the Ottomans: "The belly of Karamanoğlu İbrāhīm was slashed open, he bore bastard sons (*ḳarnı yarıldı ḥarāmzāde oğlanlar ḍoğurdı*); then "all the bastard sons that Karamanoğlu had borne fled and entered the belly of their mother"

68 Moser, *Bihiştī*, p. 91. Oruç states: "gebar die Prinzessin, die Tochter des Padischahs, die dem Sultan Ahmed vermählt war, einen Sohn..."; Richard F. Kreutel's translation in *Der fromme Sultan Bayezid: Die Geschichte seiner Herrschaft (1481-1512) nach den altosmanischen Chroniken des Oruç und des Anonymus Hanivaldanus* (Graz, Wien, Köln, 1978), p. 88.

69 Tulum, *Tursun Bey*, p. 107 and 154; İnalcık/Murphey, *Tursun Beg*, folio 90a.

70 Muharrem Ergin, *Dede Korkut Kitabı: Metin-Sözlük* (Ankara, 1964), p. 85; "He desired her and straightway violated her" (Geoffrey Lewis, *The Book of Dede Korkut*, [Zürich, 1958], p. 231). A full analysis: C.S. Mundy, "Polyphemus and Tepegöz", BSOAS 18 (1956): pp. 279-302; "I made its daughters and daughters-in-law dance on my white breast" *kızını gelinini aġ gögsümde oynatdum* (Rik Boeschoten, *Het boek van Dede Korkoet*, Amsterdam 2005, p. 206; Lewis p. 175); cg. also no. 28 in this volume.

71 A sentimental adaptation in verse was undertaken by Orhan Seyfi Orhon in 1919 with the title *Peri Kızı ile Çoban Hikayesi*: "The Fairy Girl and the Shepherd: A Turkish Ballad", transl. by A.L. MacFie and F. MacFie, *Asian Folklore Studies* 46 (1987): pp. 99-104.

72 Peirce, *Harem*, pp. 65-71, deals with the attitude toward marriage with regard to Ottoman princesses.

73 As is known, he gave preference to Isḥāḳ, the son of a female slave.

(*Karamanoğlu ḍoğurduğı ḥarāmzāde oğlanlar anaları ḳarnına girdiler*).[74] Already in §116 the more lowly Karamanid had reared up against the higher-ranking Meḥmed (entailing consequences described below) and in accordance with this "topsy-turvy world" he fails to conform to his natural destiny. The role change simultaneously draws away attention from the mother of his sons (§122 and §141). ʿĀşıḳpaşazāde further escalates the defamation in §131 (poem) from a child-bearing mammal to a bird, to a croaking crow that lives in the wild, causes damage and wanders about in rowdy crowds *karġa dernegi* (assemblage of fools or scoundrels). The accompanying poem, in one great sweep, denies noble rank to a series of Anatolian princes, adding: "Karamanoğlu has laid eggs and hatched crows, hot-headed, worthless gallow birds."[75]

With the amalgamation of women and property, as mentioned early on, we are face to face with the central problem affecting sexual relations. The assumption behind a literary treatment of the subject was mastery of the passions, as demanded in Islamic ethical literature, and disciplining one's desires. The freedom of movement of young women was regulated with the utmost strictness. But young men of a sexually aggressive age also had to be controlled. From the viewpoint of grown men, women and boys represented the group that gave rise to *fitne*. And the mobility of boys (beardless youths) and young men was also carefully watched over; boys had to be protected from the desires of men.[76] As already in the ancient Mediterranean world, about whose training and socio-cultural conditioning of masculinity we are well informed,[77] pederasty was tolerated, if with some uneasiness.[78] Hagiographical writings and biographies of poets contain rich materials on this subject. In the *şehrengīz*-genre that deals with "those who amorously inflame the city", poets introduce as the

---

74 Kreutel, in *Hirtenzelt*, p. 196, changes the target of the polemic: to the effect that "ihm ein rechtes Raubgesindel von Söhnen geboren worden sei" (sons were born to him who were no more than downright thieving riff-raff) and further on: "Da flohen die Räubersöhne..." (Then the thieving sons took to their heels). We are not concerned here with robbers but with the descent of the Karamanids, against whom ʿĀşıḳpaşazāde relentlessly engages in polemic.

75 Understood somewhat differently by Procházka-Eisl, "Lyrische Einschübe", p. 120. Cf. Edmund Leach, "Anthropological Aspects of Language: Animal Categories and Verbal Abuse", in *New Directions in the Study of Language*, ed. Eric H. Lenneberg (Cambridge, Mass., 1964), pp. 23-63. For this reference I am grateful to Dr. Léon Buskens of Leiden.

76 Cf. Peirce, *Harem*, p. 280.

77 Useful in this regard is David Cohen, "Consent and Sexual Relations in Classical Athens", in *Consent and Coercion to Sex and Marriage in Ancient and Medieval Societies*, ed. A.E. Laiou (Washington DC, Dumbarton Oaks, 1996), pp. 5-16.

78 Peirce, *Harem*, p. 280, ftn. 50. Cf. Jan Rypka, *Báqí als Ghazeldichter* (Prague, 1926), pp. 71-79.

"beloved" good-looking young people who exercise professions.[79] In the older chronicles "the religious scholars" are accused of adultery and pederasty.[80]

Control over women is expressed with particular verbs. In the language of the chronicles women are often "sent or dispatched"; *göndermek* is the verb frequently employed. They are "taken" in marriage. In war they are "apprehended", "taken possession of" (*dutmak*), as in §22. Tatars, for whom a lower stylistic level was thought to be appropriate, lie in wait in §77 for infidel girls "in order to grab them for themselves (to snatch, to get hold of)" (*kāfir ḳızın gözedür kim kapaydı*).[81] They are "pressed to the breast"; "used", "put in service" (*ḳul-lan-*); (see below).

In war, sexual coercion functioned as an instrument of power both outwardly and inwardly, i.e. *vis-à-vis* captured women of the enemy, as well as women of the home society. Just as four-fifths of history writing that survives from Antiquity describes armed conflicts,[82] war in ʿĀşıḳpaşazāde and similar chronicles takes up ample space. The old Ottoman chronicles, Oruç, Tursun Beg, ʿĀşıḳpaşazāde, and even the *Kitāb-ı Dede Korkut* with its idyllic scenes – in all these works the action is for the most part played out in war. Whereas in folklore women appear as comrades-in-arms,[83] such is not the case in the chronicles. At most, men disguise themselves in women's clothes as in §12. "From reading the ancient classics it is sufficiently well known how the heroes before Troy...raped the women of their enemies as a matter of course, just as the Romans raped the Sabine women they abducted. The same practice is current in any army you care to look at up to the present day."[84] For the women who were taken possession of by the strictly exogamous Ottomans, this meant that they served as victory trophies and found themselves used in a bond of marriage that was both ethnically and religiously exogamous, or as concubines. In the acquisition of women through raids and conquest, as Leslie Peirce

79 Edith Ambros, *Candid Penstrokes: The Lyrics of Meʾālī, an Ottoman Poet of the 16th Century* (Berlin, 1982), pp. 41-60. Michael Glünz, "Ṣāfīs Şahrangīz: Ein persisches Mathnawī über die schönen Berufsleute von Istanbul", *Asiatische Studien* 15,2 (1986): pp. 133 ff.; Walter Andrews, "The Sexual Intertext of Ottoman Literature: The Story of Me'âlî, Magistrate of Mihalich", *Edebiyat* 3 (1989): pp. 31-56. On the praise of good-looking boys in the *Sūrnāme* cf. Gisela Procházka-Eisl, *Das Sūrnāme-i Hümāyūn* (İstanbul, 1995), pp. 61-66.

80 Kafadar, *Between Two Worlds*, p. 111.

81 Eisl, "Lyrische Einschübe", p. 107.

82 Carola Meier-Seethaler, *Ursprünge und Befreiungen: Die sexistischen Wurzeln der Kultur* (Frankfurt a.M., 1992), p. 300.

83 Kafadar examines the value of *ġazavāt* literature as a source for the mood of early Ottoman times.

84 Meier-Seethaler, *Ursprünge und Befreiungen*, p. 269; Klüger, *Frauen lesen anders*, p. 85.

points out in reference to the *Dede Korkut Kitābı*, nomadic heritage and the Islamic practice of keeping female slaves as concubines overlap.[85] Stories about the abduction of girls are also suited to the *ġazavātnāme* genre.

During war, a woman's free consent on the basis of love does occur in ʿĀşıḳpaşazāde, quite explicitly, in fact, in §§26-27 in the case of the daughter of the Greek lord of the castle at Aydos. She converts to Islam and marries a Muslim. What is known about the event and how the way of looking at this episode changes has been studied by Hasan Özdemir.[86] I will therefore not spend time enumerating well-known motifs but will limit myself to the aspect of the young woman's consent. At a much later time, in the *Ġazavātnāme* of Sūzī Çelebi, the dream of a Wallachian prince's daughter functions as a foreshadowing of her love relationship with the hero.[87] Implicitly, of the two women that ʿĀşıḳpaşazāde most preferred, Mal Ḫatun and Nilüfer, the first is in agreement with her divinely ordained marriage. In the *Kitāb-ı Dede Korkut*, whose numerous figures of women and girls suggest a closer tie with female tradition, a girl falls in love with a good-looking man who arouses her desires. Thanks to this folkloristic work, we obtain surprising insights into aspects of emotional relations between the sexes and into the attitude toward nature[88] in a society – one based moreover on slavery – that was established upon an idealized, fairy-tale past.

After free consent, we come to abduction and coercion that was followed by accommodation. The early Ottoman chroniclers distinguish grades of coercion. Whether it has to do with individuals or small groups, what we would call coercion is represented as happy consent. ʿĀşıḳpaşazāde ends §12 with the acquisition for the Ottoman family of the second important woman, Nilüfer. Men disguised in women's clothes and hidden in bales of felt launch a surprise attack, ʿOs̱mān kills the bridegroom (the lord of Bilecik castle) and, the next morning, having stormed Yārḥiṣār, the castle of the bride's father, he captures the bride along with her father, and gives her to his son Orḫan. At least one expectation of the public had to be taken into consideration here. In order morally to guard against the charge of violating the rights of hospitality – after all ʿOs̱mān had abducted his "brother's" bride – the verses belonging to §11 had

85 Peirce, *Harem*, pp. 36-37.

86 Hasan Özdemir, *Die altosmanischen Chroniken als Quelle zur türkischen Volkskunde* (Freiburg, 1975).

87 See the article "Sūzī Çelebi" in *Lexikon des Mittelalters*, vol. VIII (München, Zürich, 1996), p. 340.

88 Considering which animals were most popular could provide us with insight into attitudes toward nature in the 15th and 16th centuries; cf. Mehmet Kaplan, "Dede Korkut Kitabında Hayvanlar", in *Fuad Köprülü Armağanı* (İstanbul, 1953), pp. 275-90.

announced that the Greek himself was planning attacks.[89] In case the public was awaiting elucidation about the reaction of the bride, §13 meets this expectation: her conversion to Islam, her sons, her building works, everything suggests her consent.

For those directly concerned, if they ended up in the zone of permissible, often collective, sexual violence, it made little difference whether this was based on nomadic practice or the Islamic concept of slave acquisition. What was perpetrated on women and boys on both sides in the 15th and 16th centuries were facts concerning which chroniclers had to take into consideration certain expectations of their public. The obvious literary aid was a shift in register which transformed the "abduction" into "seduction".

After the conquest of Nicaea (İznik) in §32, it was necessity that imposed the legal, mass marriages of the *ġāzīs* with the beautiful widows of the city's defenders who had fallen in battle or died of hunger. It became the task of the new masters once again to occupy the deserted city in which individual furnished houses remained standing. ʿĀşıḳpaşazāde describes in prose and verse how Orḫan gave the widows of İznik to the *ġāzīs* along with furnished houses, cash and valuables, and how the widows quickly came to feel comfortable (*üns*). Then he has the *ġāzīs* say in verse: "They speak Greek and flirt with us; it sounds as if they're plucking harps and playing the saz." The Greek women cast glances like gleaming arrows, they are redolent with musk, "these Greek sweethearts came forth swaying", they must be angels say the *ġāzīs*, transported by "the rosy cheeks" (*yanaġı gülgūn*), the "ruby lips" and "locks reeking of amber". Considered in the cold light of day, the long poem is nothing other than the depiction of a prevalent idea that the women, who are presumably hungry and wandering about in misery, are enjoying themselves. In brief, it is a poetic description of coercion followed by consent, contrived by a functional shift in style or rather a shift in register, namely from realistic prose to the imagery of poetry. The assumption that the poem is not by ʿĀşıḳpaşazāde himself[90] leaves out of consideration this shift in register which also appears at the end of §22 (transition from the prose text to lines of verse: *esīr-i ḫūb u nāzīk nāzenīnler* "charming captives and coy, flirtatious girls").[91] We have already signaled this

89 Cf. Eisl, "Lyrische Einschübe", p. 18. Kafadar, *Between Two Worlds*, pp. 40, 85 105, 124 and 129, offers further, in part self-contradictory, reasons for war.

90 Eisl, "Lyrische Einschübe", pp. xix and 54, judged that the verses were absolutely untypical for ʿĀşıḳpaşazāde ("ein für ʿApz absolut untypisches Gedicht") with a choice of words that we are not accustomed to from him.

91 Understood somewhat differently in Eisl, "Lyrische Einschübe", p. 33.

stylistic device[92] above (in connection with the Tatars) and we will meet with it again on occasions of coercion of large throngs of women.

In the *Dede Korkut Kitābı*, for instance, a pre-Ottoman hero boasts: "I made the daughters and the daughters-in-law [of the townsfolk of a seaport of infidels] dance upon my white chest" (*kızını gelinini aġ gögsümde oynatdum*). Here, by way of hinting, abduction and seduction are at play together. To this correspond the ever renewed repetitions in the chronicles of "pressing against the chest"[93] of girls and boys by the *ġāzīs*. The impression is given that, despite initial resistance, the experience is a pleasant one for those affected; here we are reminded of the myths of seduction about the Greek gods.[94] The topos of initially fighting back and resisting which then turns into seduction is found everywhere, from ancient Arabic poetry up to the German classical period;[95] I suspect its presence in two formulations in the *Book of Dede Korkut*: "There are beauties who scratch the eyes and win hearts (*göz ḳaḳuban göñül alan görklüsi olur*) and everyone "wants to kiss the neck of beauties who scratch the eyes and steal hearts" (*göz ḳaḳuban göñül alan görklüsinüñ boynı öpem*).[96] In §112 we encounter an erotic choice of words with a macaronic sprinkling of amorous phrases from South-Slavic, when at the siege of Belgrade the Serbian king is provoked: "Your sweethearts have come over to Islam, their beauty has become the mirror of Love."[97]

92 Cf. my "Bemerkungen zur türkischen Prosa vor der Tanẓīmat-Zeit", no. 4 in this volume, and my "Notes on the {IsAr} future and its modal functions", in *Laut- und Wortgeschichte der Türksprachen*, ed. Barbara Kellner-Heinkele and Mark Stachowski (Wiesbaden, 1995), pp. 43-57.

93 On *bağrına başmak* see examples of usage collected by Özdemir, *Altosmanische Chroniken*, p. 46, no. 57. In the later Divan literature the verb is *sīneye çekmek*; cf. Rypka, *Báqí*, pp. 109 and 118.

94 Mary R. Lefkowitz, "Seduction and Rape in Greek Myth", in *Sex and Marriage*, ed. Laiou, p. 17, cited above in ftn. 76; and see also Klüger, *Frauen lesen anders*, p. 86, for equivalent portrayals.

95 The First Hunter in Schiller's *Wallensteins Lager*, Scene 5: "Was haben die Herren vom Regiment/Sich um das niedliche Lärvchen gerissen" (How the gentlemen of the regiment have scrambled to get hold of that sweet baby face); and the Second Hunter in Scene 6: "Es sträubt sich – der Krieg hat kein Erbarmen – das Mägdlein in unsern sennigten Armen" (The maiden puts up a struggle – war has no mercy – in our sinewy arms). Cf. Ruth Klüger on Goethe in *Frauen lesen anders*, p. 87; see also Goethe's remark to Schiller on 25 July 1798, "denn dass ein Sultan ein Mädchen verschenkt, will wohl eigentlich nichts heißen" (after all, that a Sultan gives [someone] a girl as a gift, doesn't really mean anything).

96 Ergin, *Dede Korkut*, pp. 69-70; Hein, *Dede Korkut*, pp. 188-89; Lewis, *Dede Korkut*, p. 119.

97 Eisl, in "Lyrische Einschübe", p. 148, refers to earlier literature (Paul Wittek in *OLZ* 34 [1931], p. 707).

The collective frenzy of violence after the taking of the super fortress Constantinople had to be portrayed in a softer light. According to ʿĀşıḳpaşazāde's §123 "the *ġāzī*s [...] captured its people, killed their Tekfur and pressed their beloveds (feminine form, *maḥbūbelerini*) against their chest (*bağrılarına basdılar*). During the plundering that continued for days, Tursun Beg celebrates, in rhymed prose and Turkish-Arabic poetry, the beauty of the masses of boys and girls who were abducted. He brings to bear the complete inventory to do with beauty, the moon-faced boys who challenge the sun itself and the star-like girls with their "silver wrists" and their "dove-heels" (*gümiş bileklü gügercin topuḳlu*). "White roses flecked with blood" and "two unripe pomegranates on a silver tray" characterize the captive girls, as well as both "langorous" and "murderous" eyes (*gözi bīmār-veş illā ki ḳattāl*),[98] already referred to above.

In *cihād* and during *ġazā* as well, sexual coercion, i.e. rape, was perpetrated collectively and massively on non-Muslim slaves, both women and boys. In situations of violence they fell prey to abduction and "seduction". Here naive faith in one's own values and institutions could be shaken, and it was necessary to protect them. Naturally, as in the case of blinding,[99] a euphemistic verbal designation was required which the *dīvān*-literature was able to provide.

The *ġāzī*s behave "in a manly manner" to the infidel girls *and* boys whom they abducted from the houses of their fathers and mothers; the captives "seduce" them – outside their homes, and the abducted somehow give their consent, at least in part. After the conquest in 1550 of Moton (in the Morea), the *ġāzī*s found "most delightful, heart-enthralling Frankish boys and girls in their houses wearing gold-embroidered clothes like white-skinned Christian dolls overlaid with gold, and abducted them".[100] Or in ʿĀşīḳpaşazāde's §153: "For two months the *ġāzī*s roamed about in the land of Moldau (Ḳara Boğdan); there was an incredible plethora of booty, herds of horses and sheep, and the *ġāzī*s pressed their beautiful beloveds against their chest."[101] The number of such text passages saturated with metaphors runs into the dozens.

Confronted with the anxieties of men, ʿĀşıḳpaşazāde chooses various stylistic means. A man would appear to be the primary victim of disgrace if the enemy did something to his female relatives. There was everything to fear if a daughter, wife or mother fell into enemy hands: captivity entailed the utmost

98 Tulum, *Tursun Bey*, pp. 60-62. Tursun Beg's repertoire of erotic war metaphors that includes an infidel "rival (in love)" as a howling dog (he gives an eyewitness account of an event on the Sava in the year 1458, Tulum, p. 99) merits a separate study on its own.

99 "To open the eye of the heart", §72; "To apply iron cosmetic to the eyes", §117.

100 Kreutel, *Oruç*, p. 130.

101 Kreutel, translates (somewhat euphemistically) "zogen sie in die Arme" (drew them into their arms), *Hirtenzelt*, p. 262.

ignominy. The decision to retrieve a woman, an ancient motif (Helen), is formulated in such a way in the *Dede Korkut Kitābı* that Kazan wants to get back his mother lest the infidels carry out their threat to make her pregnant and have her bear a son. ʿĀşıḳpaşazāde resorts to this register in §132 when he has a Frankish lord of the castle express his fear that the *ġāzī*s could "press to their breast" the wives and daughters of Amasra. All metaphors have disappeared in §66 where compassion and sympathy for the Muslim man are appropriate. Following in the footsteps of Dede Korkut, ʿĀşıḳpaşazāde adds a poem in which he has the Muslim Ṭaharten (Muṭahharten), ruler of Erzincan and the nephew of Eretna, denounce, in sorrow and anger, the injustice done to him by Sultan Bāyezīd I: "I have no more peace in the world, for summer and winter I keep watch over the road. Son, daughter and my wife (*oġul ḳız ʿavretüm*) have been separated from me – am I meant to be pleased with this? ... Why do you expect friendship from this deed of yours? You have separated me from my beloved wife!" (*ayırasın beni sevdük eşümden*).[102]

As the cause of Meḥmed II's campaign in the Morea in 1460 ʿĀşıḳpaşazāde, at the beginning of §129, presents an episode, also taken over by Neşrī, which arises from a male sense of responsibility but corresponds as well to the expectations of a female public: A traveller who arrives in Patras sees how the infidels there make Muslim women (*ʿavret*) work for them and mistreat them violently. "You poor women, how have you ended up in the land of the Giaurs...?" "Alas, we are not the only ones! There are many like us! And what we must suffer only Allah knows and no one else!"[103] And they weep and lament. The traveller reports this to the Sultan in Edirne. Sultan Meḥmed II immediately raises the cry for holy war.

Other passages, devoid of metaphors and with strong expression, are to be found which treat non-*cihād*, i.e. war between Muslims. Danger was always present for women, even when it was not a question of special acts of revenge from the Ottoman point of view. "You should protect your honor and the honor of your women" (*ʿırżuñuzı ve ehl ü ʿiyālüñüz ʿırżıñı saḳlayasız*), writes the Ottoman commander to Isfendiyāroġlu İsmāʿīl Beg who is beleaguered in Sinope (and with whom, as ʿĀşıḳpaşazāde reports in §133, the Ottomans are going to reach an amicable understanding); nothing and no one can stand up

102 Eisl, "Lyrische Einschübe", p. 90. Regarding Timur's demand (1402) that all Muṭahharten's relatives whom Bāyezīd had carried off to Bursa be delivered to him, see Tilman Nagel, *Timur der Eroberer und die islamische Welt des späten Mittelalters* (München, 1993), p. 354.

103 "Deem not that God is unaware of what the evildoers work": Tursun Beg, in connection with extreme oppression (in Tokat), cites Koran 14:42. Tulum, *Tursun Bey*, p. 154.

to the Ottoman army; so what chance is there for the chastity of free women?[104] That is how Tursun Beg formulates it. ʿĀşıḳpaşazāde's way of presenting matters is that should the Ottomans be exceedingly provoked, their troops would lay hands on Muslim women. The aspects of this behavior that were not in conformity with the ideals of the Ottoman nature were at least in part blamed on foreign influences, especially on the infidels or those only recently converted ("renegades" in Western usage). In ʿĀşıḳpaşazāde's §116 news reaches the Sultan "that the Karamanids have broken their treaty and caused the women and children of the Muslims to be subjected to acts of violence in contradiction to the *şerīʿa.*" In a rage, Murād II musters the army of Islam, wisely adding all the infidel troops under his command in Rumeli, advances before Konya, and gives the city over to be plundered(!). The inhabitants of the principality of Karaman, no infidels but ethnic cousins, are subjected to horrific affliction; their women are violated. What was there to say now about the women who became pregnant as a result of this and were abandoned? "In that year there came into the world many boys and girls whose descent (*ḥaseb u neseb*) was unknown." The sentence attests to something like compassion. And thus, so ʿĀşıḳpaşazāde concludes the section, "the Karamanid İbrāhīm Beg was to blame that an Ottoman laid waste a Muslim land and perpetrated violence against Muslims: until that time no one had suffered violence at the hands of an Ottoman." This was injustice, oppression (*ẓulm*), committed by the Sultan, in fact rape as violation of male property rights, as if to say: "the Karamanid has had his womenfolk violated", but with one openly stated qualification: "He himself is to blame for not restraining the Turgut Turkmens", and one tacit reproach: infidel troops had been involved. In §135 when there is no immediate success under Meḥmed II in capturing the fortress of Ḳoylıḥiṣār, the Ottomans lay waste the surrounding countryside and in the process *ʿazab*s force their way into an Armenian village and come upon "many" Armenian husbands and wives (*Ermenī ḳocasını ve ḳarısını*)[105] against whom they commit dastardly outrages contrary to the *şerīʿa*. Interestingly, Armenian monks complain about these excesses to their former overlord Uzun Ḥasan.[106] ʿĀşıḳpaşazāde feels obliged, however, to voice criticism which, as frequently in his chronicle, he cloaks in

104 Tursun Beg himself, as secretary of the Divan, wrote the letter on the order of Maḥmūd Paşa; cf. Tulum, *Tursun Bey*, pp. 106-07; İnalcık/Murphey, *Tursun Beg*, p. 45. On the problem of chastity see ftn. 68 above. ʿĀşıḳpaşazāde sums up the letter differently.

105 Kreutel: "armenische Greise und Weiber" (Armenian greybeards and women); and a little later he has the Armenians themselves referring to "unseren Weibern und unseren alten Männern" (our women and our old men).

106 Presumably it was a known fact that Uzun Ḥasan had given assistance in the construction of two Armenian churches near Erzincan.

the form of a dialogue. Question: Is this appropriate behavior for the army of the House of ʿO̱smān? Answer: There are various units in the armed forces and in the case of these *ʿazab*s it is a matter of mere auxiliaries, mercenaries who are deployed against refractory peoples. But in the verses ʿĀşıḳpaşazāde reproaches the "unwashed" *ʿazab*s,[107] from whom the Ottoman commander-in-chief has distanced himself in §133. In §149 Muslims – Karamanids and Turkmens subordinate to the Aḳḳoyunlu – indecently assault the women and children of Muslims in Tokat contrary to the *şerīʿa* (*müslümanlaruñ ʿavretine ve oġlanına nā-meşrūʿ işler işlediler*). Neşrī (Ank 798) abbreviates at this point and makes no mention of women.

Oruç is lost for words when his sources inform him that Janissaries, that is to say new-Ottomans, indecently assaulted the wives and daughters of the Varsak Turkmens. It is simply impossible to recount. Here heinous crimes against the religious law have been committed ("may it have a good final outcome!"). The entire event could not, as on other occasions, be designated "war for the faith" but only as an "incident".[108] The victims of sexual violence are also reduced to being objects in the case where another new-Ottoman, Rūm Meḥmed Paşa, in ʿĀşīḳpaşazāde's §145 burned the local mosques and medreses in Larende and razed them to the ground. "He laid waste everything like the house of his father[109] and let the women and children be robbed and stripped naked" – ʿĀşıḳpaşazāde feels obliged to compose a sorrowful poem about the smoke of *ẓulm* that has engulfed the world.

Acts of violence which ran contrary to the *şerīʿa* constituted behavior like that of the infidels (*kāfirāne işler*).[110] Slaves were reduced to being mere objects that Muslim soldiers, on occasion, stole from their comrades. This was a frowned-upon act of violence. One can read about it in Oruç in a chapter on the glut and satiety that resulted as people were abducted in droves and prisoners froze to death. What happened in such a situation, by way of raids on prisoners of war within the army itself, is translated, interestingly, as "rapes" by Kreutel, following Oruç. The *ġāzī*s had taken many prisoners in Poland and were on their return march with them. Some people lay in ambush along the way and they stole the prisoners, murdering a part of them in the process. In the face of this horror, it appeared to the chronicler that rain, cold and hunger on the Danube (in all probability slaves froze to death as well) was a punish-

107 Eisl, "Lyrische Einschübe", p. 177; cf. Kreutel, *Hirtenzelt*, p. 322.

108 Kreutel, *Oruç*, p. 138.

109 "like the house of his father": perhaps this is a curse in the sense of: may the same occur to his father's family line.

110 Lewis, *Political Language of Islam*, p. 86.

ment sent from God.[111] In Anatolia, in time of great danger, the *reʿāyā* ran off in order to lead their families to safety. A reviser of Neşrī who was familiar with the locality in question interpolates a report in Ank 800 about such a case: before the great decisive batttle between Prince Muṣṭafā and the followers of Uzun Ḥasan (belongs in ʿĀşīḳpaşazāde's §149), the subject folk ran away and ascended as high up into the mountains as they could with their wives and families (*yollarından ayrılub ehl ü ʿiyāli birle yüce yüce ḍağlar başını özleyüb ḳaçdılar*).

In extreme cases of hopelessness, military activity, whether or not it had ever served to defend women and children, was suspended.[112] In §139 the "Tekfur" (here it is the Duke) of Midilli/Lesbos comes forth alone from his fortress in which he has left his son, daughter and wife, and surrenders.[113] The opposite is planned in ʿĀşīḳpaşazāde's §152: the Genoese defenders of the fortress Mengūp/Teodoro (in the Crimea), where many men (*ḫaylı ādemler*) from outside have taken refuge, want to defend themselves to the bitter end, for which purpose they first "wished to drive forth their wives and boys" (*ʿavretin oğlanın ṭaşra sürmek istediler*).[114] Men forcibly resettled in Istanbul successfully protested in §124 against the rent they were meant to pay for the "Giaur houses". "Many abandoned their wives and children and fled" – so writes ʿĀşīḳpaşazāde, which Neşrī (Ank 709) retains in his text almost verbatim. Tursun Beg describes how Bosnian mountain dwellers throw themselves to their death with wife and child so as not to fall into the hands of the Ottomans.[115] The last resort of men in a desperate situation, i.e. themselves killing their own wives and children, occurs in Oruç.[116]

It seems appropriate for a festschrift to conclude with a rescue attempt which in the end proves to be successful for the women. The inhabitants of the town Sivrihisar were beleaguered by the Karamanids in 1443 (the event, had ʿĀşıḳpaşazāde described it, would have been in §115). The starving townsfolk take counsel with the fortress commander and decide to evacuate their wives (*ʿavret*) and children (*oğlan*). They have all the maidens and brides (*ḳız, gelin*)

111 Kreutel, *Oruç*, p. 109. Unfortunately, Oruç is not available to me in the original text. Cf. also Joseph von Hammer, *Geschichte des osmanischen Reiches* (Pest, 1828), vol. II, p. 312.

112 Meier-Seethaler, *Ursprünge und Befreiungen*, p. 296.

113 Regarding the event (1462) see von Hammer, *Geschichte*, vol. II, pp. 69-70.

114 To drive them into the open (and abandon them to their fate). Misleadingly translated both by Hans Joachim Kißling, *Die Sprache des ʿĀşıḳpaşazāde* (Breslau, 1936), p. 37, "sie wollten Frauen und Kinder umsiedeln" and Kreutel, *Hirtenzelt*, p. 259, "und wollten sogar sein Weib und seinen Sohn ausweisen".

115 Tulum, *Tursun Bey*, p. 125.

116 Kreutel, *Oruç*, p. 130.

put on slippers, in which they are to march out of a certain city gate at midnight in the direction of Mudurnu; "one would then see what their destiny was." Placed at the head of their procession was a saintly old man by the name of ʿAlī Dede whom the narrator thinks very highly of. The old man's death by decapitation at the gate causes a miracle, the Karamanids repent of their intentions and depart in shame, and we hear nothing more about the evacuation. The story is endowed with hagiographical characteristics.[117]

A more precise, comparative reading of ʿĀşıḳpaşazāde shows that, during the course of the long development of his chronicle that came to completion under Bāyezīd II, various images of women emerge. Differences in the image of women led to differences of register in language. Some considerations to do with the public caused the author to introduce female motifs as productive factors in his work of literature. Having examined the function of such factors in the work, we feel confirmed in our view that ʿĀşıḳpaşazāde composed his chronicle with care and consciously deployed his stylistic resources – to a greater extent than scholars have granted him until now.[118]

Any danger that the Ottoman civilian population once had to fear from the Germiyan or from the Karamanids, during the Timur catastrophe, and finally in the wars against Uzun Hasan, belonged to the past at the time of the final redaction of the chronicle. For certain turns of events in war, a realistic description of which was deemed to be offensive to contemporaries, the repertoire of metaphor from *dīvān* literature was employed as carrier of the description. To represent feelings of Muslim men and women, especially suffering, dialogue and folklore were suitable. If when reading, it may seem that individual women gradually disappear from the chronicle because they are considered unnecessary and undesirable by the author ʿĀşıḳpaşazāde and his milieu, none the less in the second half of the work they continued their potential existence and, if it suited the composition, were able, in however sketchy a form, to be perceived by the public as free agents or passive sufferers.

117 Printed in Ank 639. Ménage, *Neshrī's History*, p. 49, has shown that the source of the episode is the Neşrī editor, ʿAlī b. ʿAbdullāh, who completed copying the MS A in 1561. On Sivrihisar and its townsfolk, considered to be the country bumpkins of Anatolia, as well as Ḫoca Naṣreddīn, see Boratav, *Türkische Volksmärchen*, p. 325.

118 Procházka-Eisl, "Lyrische Einschübe", p. 104.

CHAPTER 27

Female Participation in Earlier Islamic Mysticism (9th to 16th Century)*, **

1 Introduction

The aim of the present essay is to examine some hagiographical works with regard to the participation of women in earlier Islamic mysticism. The dominant opinion is that Sufism "more than strict orthodoxy... [offered] women a certain number of possibilities actively to take part in religious and social life",[1] and that "among Sufis, the Islamic mystics, women [enjoyed] far greater esteem than in orthodox Islam".[2] Man and woman, as the Koran teaches, are equal in the sphere of religion; women as well can advance along the path to salvation.[3] Disparagement and belittling of women was disallowed – in contrast to Christianity – because as Annemarie Schimmel emphasizes: "The Prophet's love of women, his numerous wives and his four daughters precluded any feeling of contempt of the feminine which one so often meets with among Christian monks."[4] But other viewpoints on the question have

* Translated by John O'Kane.

** This essay began in the aula of Leiden University where, on the 28th of November 1997, the author delivered in Dutch her final lecture that dealt with the above subject. Time limits made it necessary to leave out numerous considerations and details, and therefore plans were made for a later, more comprehensive German version of the essay. The manuscript was completed in March 1998 and only in February 2003 editorially prepared for publication, 93 (2003) in WZKM (see Bibliography). I must here thank several friends for their help, in particular Prof. Dr. J.T.P. de Bruijn, Dr. Sibylle Duda, Prof. Dr. Claus Peter Haase, the late Prof. Dr. Petra Kappert, Prof. Dr. Remke Kruk, Prof. Dr. Gisela Procházka-Eisl, Drs. Thijs Rault and Dr. Willem Stoetzer.

1 A. Schimmel, *Mystische Dimensionen des Islam. Die Geschichte des Sufismus*, Frankfurt a. M. and Leipzig 1995, pp. 614-15; (original English edition) *Mystical Dimensions of Islam*, The University of North Carolina Press, Chapel Hill, 1975.

2 Wiebke Walther, *Die Frau im Islam*, Leipzig 1980, 3rd revised edition, Leipzig 1997, the text appearing beneath illustration 6. In Michael W. Dols, *Majnūn: The Madman in Medieval Islamic Society. Edited by Diana E. Immisch*, Oxford 1992, p. 228, it is maintained that: "A far greater role in the orders was allowed for the participation of women than in orthodox Islam."

3 Harald Motzki, "Dann machte er daraus die beiden Geschlechter, das männliche and das weibliche... Die islamischen Wurzeln der islamischen Geschlechterrollen", in Jochen Martin and Renate Zoepfel (eds.), *Aufgaben, Rollen und Räume von Frau und Mann*, Freiburg/München 1989, pp. 623-24.

4 Schimmel, *Dimensionen*, p. 603.

 | DOI 10.1163/9789004355767_028

been expressed. Jamal J. Elias separated the earthly woman from a glorified, abstract femininity,[5] and Fedwa Malti-Douglas has spoken specifically of a current in mysticism and philosophy that is hostile to women.[6] The present attempt at stock-taking is predominantly based on the hagiographical compendium *Nafaḥāt al-uns* (*The Breaths of Intimacy*) by the Persian Jāmī which the Ottoman Turk, Lāmiʿī, translated and adapted. Thirty-four pious women are dealt with in *The Breaths of Intimacy* in a separate chapter, as if by way of recalling the separation of the domains of men and women. The women, as if in a large edifice with many rooms, are lodged in their own women's quarters or, to employ a different image, in their own neighborhood in the city with which Lāmiʿī compares his work. Thus an edifice or a city neighbourhood in which in Jāmī's time, however, no contemporary women lived. He ends his entries on women in the thirteenth century. Differing from him, his adaptor and continuer, Lāmiʿī, retains the canonized thirty-four but adds a recent woman from his own era (XII). In so doing, he adds the keystone in this edifice of hagiography whose foundations Arab compilers had laid and on which the classical Persian poet Jāmī continued to build[7] and which Lāmiʿī supplemented in Turkish in 1521 with his own treatment so that *The Breaths of Intimacy* deliberately establishes the points of contact between Turkish, Persian and Arab mysticism. The number of women in the hagiographical work is small, given that around six hundred *vitae* of male mystics stand over against thirty-four notices on saintly women. What does this say with regard to the participation of women? Let us look at the social position of female mystics and the polarity that existed between free women and female slaves, in particular female slave singers (II). To what extent were Islamic female mystics associated with the ideal women of Islam (III)? As already indicated, the hagiographers, in their accounts about saintly women,[8] chiefly make use of a narrative repertoire that had been preserved over centuries. It is indispensable to order this material chronologically, even though it is in a fragmentary state. For this purpose two

5 The female human being takes part in "a lesser capacity" than a man; abstract femininity symbolizes an ideal which all women should strive to attain; Jamal J. Elias, "Female and Feminine in Islamic Mysticism", *The Muslim World* 78 (1988), pp. 209-24. For a comprehensive treatment of the subject: Annemarie Schimmel, *Meine Seele ist eine Frau. Das Weibliche im Islam*, München 1995.

6 Fedwa Malti-Douglas, *Woman's Body, Woman's Word. Gender and Discourse in Arabo-Islamic Writing*, Princeton, N. J., 1991, p. 109, also cites literature representing the opposite standpoint.

7 On Jāmī's work and the Sufi biographies that were divided into classes (*ṭabaqāt*) and that he used as his sources, see Schimmel, *Dimensionen*, pp. 130-31.

8 Margaret Smith, *Rābiʿa the Mystic*, Cambridge 1928.

periods of Islamic mysticism present themselves. Firstly, the formative period which from the viewpoint of female mystics can be called the Rābiʿa period (IV, VIII), and secondly, the period of organized mysticism which in the framework of our inquiry we wish to call the post-Rābiʿa period (IX). In order to investigate the religious dreams of a charismatic spouse of a mystic we will reach beyond the confines of *The Breaths of Intimacy* (V). The history of the one-time female slave singer Tuḥfa (VI) presents a connection between female mystical experience and madness.[9] The relatively free interaction of female mystics with their husbands in the Rābiʿa period (VII) could not be maintained under organized Sufism. In this phase, which we have called the post-Rābiʿa period (IX), women appear to have been shut out and have become invisible. In the hagiographical tradition they are referred to, if at all, without names. This is the case both for pre-Mongol and post-Mongol times. After 1220, when Turkish and Mongol women migrated into Iran and Anatolia, hagiographical entries are meagre (X). The consequences of enslaving women during wartime are briefly dealt with here (XI), because the Turkish hagiographer Lāmiʿī devotes a remarkable notice to a female contemporary (XII). In anticipation, it may be maintained that women have always participated in Islamic mysticism under limiting restrictions, though these have varied in different circumstances.

II The Social Position of Women

As is known, women in Islamic society were divided into believing Muslims and infidel women. Wearing the veil and fasting distinguished Muslim women from non-Muslim women – those who were protected non-Muslim subjects[10] or prisoners of war. The veil up to the present time has been an important means of establishing distinctions. It could say something about age and the civil status of a woman. Women did not wear the veil in the private sphere. By means of the veil a Muslim woman could define certain situations as private or public. It offered a woman the possibility of expressing symbolically how she related or wished to relate to others. Thus in the presence of a male relative she could pointedly don the veil and thereby distance herself from the man in question. Conversely, by removing her veil in the presence of a man who was unrelated to her, she could set up a barrier to marriage, that is to say by con-

9 A subject that apparently has scarcely received attention in the domain of female Islamic mysticism. Female insanity is dealt with marginally in Dols, *Majnūn: The Madman in Medieval Islamic Society*.

10 In the Ottoman Empire these would be Jewish, Armenian and Greek women.

versing with him in an unconstrained manner. Only adults of the opposite sex for whom it was forbidden to marry were allowed to converse with one another and even to touch. A woman could bring about such a situation of unconstraint by removing her veil and thereby appealing to the man not to make sexual advances toward her.[11] It is reported about two of the female mystics who will be discussed here, Fāṭima (in VII) and Selīme (XII), that they wished to establish this unconstrained situation.

Women believers were either free or slaves. Women who were not well-off, and especially slave women, were visible due to their carrying out certain tasks.[12] Slave women stood lowest down on the social ladder.[13] Breast-feeding slave women served as wet-nurses and as such could be lent out by their master.[14] Within their class they were further subdivided. Lowest in status was the non-Muslim female slave. Above the ordinary slave women stood the female slaves who played music, performed dances and sang. Free virgins and young married women were fit for work but they had to be invisible to the outside world. "Pious morality did not look at all favorably on a woman leaving the house."[15] If a woman stepped over the boundary of her domain, she made herself, to a certain extent, invisible by means of the veil. Invisibility before the outside world especially characterized young, free women who were better-off; the higher her social rank, the more closed off a woman was.[16] Elderly women,

---

11 According to Marjo Buitelaar, "Kleed een rietstengel aan en je hebt een bruid" (roughly: "It's the clothes that make the man"), C. Huygens and F. Ros (eds.), *Dromen van het Paradijs. Islamitische kunst van het Museum voor Volkenkunde Rotterdam*, Rotterdam 1993, pp. 151-67, especially p. 161.

12 "Those with noble rank practice polygamy exclusively with slave women who are a man's bed fellows. The Caliphs of the 4th/10th century all have a female slave for a mother." Thus Adam Mez, *Die Renaissance des Islâms*, Heidelberg 1922, p. 343. On the strict application of this rule during the heyday of the Ottomans, see Leslie Peirce, *The Imperial Harem. Women and Sovereignty in the Ottoman Empire*, New York-Oxford 1993.

13 Cf. H. M[üller] in Klaus Kreiser and Rotraud Wielandt (eds.), *Lexikon der Islamischen Welt*, Stuttgart-Berlin-Köln 1992, pp. 258-60; on "the very unfavorable position" of the female slave see Motzki, "Dann machte er daraus die beiden Geschlechter", p. 619.

14 Tilman Nagel in Maria Haarmann (eds.), *Der Islam. Ein historisches Lesebuch*, München 1992, pp. 64-66.

15 Mez, *Renaissance des Islâms*, p. 341. By way of comparison: in fourteenth-century Siena a girl after the age of twelve was no longer allowed to leave her father's house; there one never met unmarried daughters outside the house; Roswitha Schneider, "Katharina von Siena als Mystikerin", in Peter Dinzelbacher and Dieter R. Bauer (eds.), *Frauenmystik im Mittelalter*, Ostfildern bei Stuttgart 1985, pp. 290 f.

16 Susanne Enderwitz, *Liebe als Beruf. Al-ʿAbbās Ibn al-Aḥnaf und das Ġazal*, Beirut 1995, p. 146.

on the other hand, could appear outside the house and accomplish tasks, tend the sick and, for instance, lead about an insane man on a chain. An elderly woman could get away with reproaching a tyrannical ruler.[17] Women cooked for men and children, washed clothes, kept the house clean, and did things of that kind. They were completely different from the female slave singers. But even their world of peaceful domestic joys, in the center of which stood the housefather who divided his love among his wives, was not secure. The author of the Arabic book of decent manners which we will be frequently citing, felt obliged to give warning. A man was not immune to the cunning of women;[18] they were capable of intrigues and inclined to write secret letters, even when they sat veiled and locked up behind a bolted door.[19] A man should not bestow his trust or his love on a free woman or a female slave. "For in this respect all women are equally unfaithful."[20] Preferably girls should not learn to write – "lecherous men" could possibly approach a woman who knows how to write, by means of love letters...[21] Both sexes were in danger because of their sexuality but the passionate nature of a woman which was imagined to be especially intense and her "unlimited desire" served as a pretext to declare that watching over her physical modesty with every possible means was the highest duty.[22] According to the unassailable definition of femininity established by men, the difference was maintained between the "bad" nature of real women and the purity of a few unattainable ideal women. Precisely because she differed so much from the "ordinary representatives of her sex", Rābiʿa is said to have contributed "to the formation of the image of the ideal pious woman who could then be praised in the most glowing descriptions".[23] (In this regard see III).

Here we examine more closely the female slave singer from the viewpoint of early mysticism. At great expense the musical slave girls were trained to sing, to recite and to play the lute. They assumed an important role in social life;

17 Schimmel, *Dimensionen*, p. 431.

18 On the subject of "female cunning and trickery" in which all negative aspects of female sexuality are encoded, cf. Malti-Douglas, *Woman's Body*, pp. 53-55.

19 Dieter Bellmann (translation and edition), *Ibn al-Washshāʾ. Das Buch des buntbestickten Kleides*, 3 vols., Leipzig and Weimar 1984, II, pp. 60-61.

20 Bellmann, II, p. 57.

21 Werner Ende, "Sollen Frauen schreiben lernen? Eine innerislamische Debatte und ihre Widerspiegelung in Al-Manār", in Dieter Bellmann (ed.), *Gedenkschrift Wolfgang Reuschel. Akten des III. Arabistischen Kolloquiums, Leipzig, 21.-22. November 1991*, Stuttgart 1994, especially pp. 51, 56.

22 Cf. Jonathan P. Berkey, "Circumcision circumscribed: Female excision and cultural accommodation in the Medieval Near East", *IJMES* 28 (1996), pp. 19-38.

23 Schimmel, *Dimensionen*, p. 503.

they were, after all, along with the other female slaves, the only women who were admitted to the company of men, in particular as courtesans.[24] Although there were notable examples of erudite free women, it can be said that "female slave singers were the only educated group in the female population".[25] Poetry dealing with worldly love was well known to them; one of the poems transmitted from Rābiʿa al-ʿAdawiyya has been identified as this type of worldly love poem.[26]

The selling price of a female slave singer was high because of her long and costly training, but subsequently she provided for her own sustenance and that of her owner as well. He received visits as well as presents, which at times could be taken to mean hard cash,[27] he enjoyed an abundance of different foods and drinks,[28] and he was accorded credit to take out loans.[29] Her singing and musical performance was meant to make men fall in love with the female slave. The profession for which she had received her training was that of a singer but her "business" was designated as "love".[30]

However, she was not a prostitute, although on occasion her owner definitely allowed acts of prostitution to take place. Were she to engage in such activities without his consent, she would be punished by him.[31] Firstly, her owner profited from such activities and, secondly, he was sometimes forced into it so as not to offend his male visitors. In connection with the first point, Ibn al-Washshāʾ (d. 936) remarks: "...it is claimed that a female singer only desires gifts and precious objects because she loves her master and cares about him, that for this reason she asks for small and large presents and is friendly and concerned...(but this is not true!)."[32] On the second point, Ibn al-Washshāʾ

24 Charles Pellat, "Ḳayna", *EI²* IV (1978), pp. 820-24. Malti-Douglas, *Woman's Body*, pp. 31-32, 36-37, 128, 171-72, emphasizes that female slave singers as courtesans, defined by their sexual status (virgin or not), made use of their wittiness as well as their voices.

25 Bellmann, III, p. 10.

26 G.J.H. van Gelder, "Rābiʿa's poem on the two kinds of love: a mystification?", in F. de Jong (ed.), *Verse and the fair sex, a collection of papers presented at the 15th Congress of the UEAI 1900*, Utrecht 1993, pp. 66-76.

27 Bellmann, II, p. 26.

28 Charles Pellat, *Arabische Geisteswelt. Ausgewählte und übersetzte Texte von al-Ǧāḥiẓ (777-869). Unter Zugrundelegung der arabischen Originaltexte aus dem Französischen übertragen von Walter W. Müller*, Zürich and Stuttgart 1967, p. 431.

29 Al-Jāḥiẓ/Pellat, pp. 431-32.

30 Bellmann, II, p. 149.

31 In a poem a love-smitten man wants to taste the saliva of the slave woman he loves. She refuses out of fear of punishment by her owner; Bellmann, II, p. 109. A female slave appeals to her owner to be lenient with his property; Bellmann, II, p. 149.

32 Bellmann, II, p. 23.

notes: "The master and owner of the female slave [is] interested in ... keeping [the lover] in a congenial mood. For he is determined that the lover should also show him appreciation in order to spend entire nights and days alone and undisturbed with his beloved."[33] Al-Jāḥiẓ mentions the possibility that a female slave may be bought from her owner by a love-smitten visitor so as to make legal his intimate contacts with her.[34] It can also happen that someone who owns several female slave singers goes off to a region where he is not known and hires them out.[35]

The female slave singer is described as beautiful, enchanting and provocative, in a well-known work by the witty man of letters, al-Jāḥiẓ,[36] and in the book on good manners by Ibn al-Washshā' – both authors being approximate contemporaries of Tuḥfa who will be discussed here and the mystic Sarī al-Saqaṭī (772-867). Her exterior was "elegant".[37] She was utterly beautiful.[38] She sang and played a musical instrument, her clothing was splendid, if somewhat conspicuous, she smelled of perfume, and she used nail polish.[39] At the same time, she is characterized as shameless. She spoke "openly of her desires". She raised toasts to gentlemen. She sent love letters and small gifts to her owner's visitors.[40] Her glances and smiles were both furtive and audacious. Her clothing deviated from that of respectable ladies and was lewd.[41] She was regarded as false and mendacious. Even when she was actually in love, which did happen, she lied: she put forward the illegal claim to be a free woman to make it possible for her lover "to possess" her without plunging himself into ruinous costs. Or she pretended to be ill and caused herself to be sold, thus making it possible for the man she loved to purchase her more cheaply.[42]

---

33 Bellmann, II, p. 24.

34 Al-Jāḥiẓ/Pellat, p. 422.

35 "Then there is no more remunerative occupation he can exercise than to go abroad with his female slave singers and to work as a procurer on their behalf. He only takes this (ignominy) upon himself because he is inflamed with passionate love for them. [Before that] he had been hindered from attaining his goal because of the supervision of their former masters, fear of their guards and the strictness of their isolation." Al-Jāḥiẓ/Pellat, p. 422.

36 Al-Jāḥiẓ/Pellat, pp. 422 ff. (Ch. xlv).

37 Bellmann, II, pp. 148 and 178.

38 Bellmann, II, pp. 119 and 146.

39 Bellman, II, p. 67.

40 Bellmann, II, pp. 158 and 178.

41 Bellmann, II, pp. 74-75.

42 Al-Jāḥiẓ/Pellat, pp. 427-29; this part of the text is taken over more extensively by Walther, *Frau im Islam*, p. 144. The case of an outstanding female slave singer, born around 815, who was purchased, conferred as a gift, set free in a legally unbinding manner and made into a concubine without her knowledge, is treated in the Maqāma "Shârija, Die Singsklavin"

The beautiful and desirable female slave appealed to several of the senses: the eye, the sense of smell, the sense of touch, and the ear.[43] Her playing an instrument (the lute, flute, guitar and tambourine) and her singing were pleasing to the ear. She continued her training with music and singing teachers.[44] By means of verses her trade was inscribed on the palm of her hand and on her forehead. Slave dealers wrote advertisements on her forehead (e.g. "Breath from the mouth makes one content").[45] That her owner wrote verses on her forehead with a tincture of musk is mentioned by Ibn al-Washshāʾ who cites al-Jāḥiẓ.[46] Erotic verses were written on her palms, her feet and on her sashes, footstraps, sandals, collars, headbands and skull-caps.[47] She herself wrote: love letters and verses on letter paper, musical instruments, and on drinking cups.[48]

She was surrounded by ambivalence. A house in which female slave singers performed was a place of eroticism – and of culture. These girls knew thousands of poems[49] – but the contents had to do with worldly love.[50] Love of good-looking girls was "no sin"[51] – Ibn al-Washshāʾ warned against pederasty[52] – but these artistic reciters were nothing other than decoys which drew men to the girls' owner. Consequently, they were represented as purveyors of hypocrisy and mendacity, prostitution and lewdness. Al-Jāḥiẓ did not fail to notice the contradictory situation, the dilemma of these young women. "How can the female slave singer be safe from seduction or how is it meant to be possible for

in Gernot Rotter, *Abu l-Faradsch. Und der Kalif beschenkte ihm reichlich. Auszüge aus dem "Buch der Lieder". Aus dem Arabischen übertragen*, Tübingen-Basel 1977, pp. 178-85.

43 Al-Jāḥiẓ/Pellat, p. 426.

44 "Moreover, she does not stop studying her profession and devoting herself to it by receiving instruction from singing masters whose lesson in music is purely love play and whose recital is an attempt at seduction. But she is forced to do this by her profession." Al-Jāḥiẓ/Pellat, p. 430.

45 Bellmann, II, pp. 174-75.

46 Bellmann, II, p. 178.

47 Bellmann, I, p. 170, and II, pp. 156 and 173-74.

48 Bellmann, II, pp. 181, 188.

49 They were songs that had as their exclusive object love, sensual desire, passion and that which al-Jāḥiẓ calls "adultery" and "pandering". The most capable female slave singers knew by heart upwards of four thousand songs containing two to four verses each.

50 "The verses she learns are such as only incidentally contain mention of God, inspire no fear of divine punishment and arouse no desire for reward in the hereafter..." Al-Jāḥiẓ/Pellat, p. 430.

51 In connection with this, Ibn al-Washshāʾ cites the poem of a "witty" Sufi "of good breeding"; Bellmann, II, p. 141. Love of a female slave is given preference in the world depicted by Susanne Enderwitz, *Liebe als Beruf*, p. 93.

52 Bellmann, II, pp. 30-31, and III, ftn. 73.

her to remain chaste, since she has appropriated passion unto herself, just as she learns the languages and manners of her surroundings, and, from her birth (sic) to the hour of her departure from the world, she lives in a milieu that impedes her from thinking of God because it only consists of pleasant entertainment and all kinds of festivities and vulgarities..."[53]

The men to whom she devoted herself al-Jāḥiẓ called "lechers and shameless people from whom there is not a serious word to be heard". Whereas al-Jāḥiẓ admitted that in exceptional cases genuine affection existed on the part of the female slave singer, Ibn al-Washshāʾ quite frankly impresses on his readers her mendacity and faithlessness. Genuine affection is completely foreign to her, she possesses no fidelity; fidelity is simply unknown to her. Ibn Washshāʾ levels no criticism at her visitors but he warns against her; she only devotes herself to "rich men" in order to wheedle "gifts" out of them, as long as there is still something to be had from them. She flirts with "young gentlemen" but does the same with ugly and impotent men. Ibn al-Washshāʾ advised his male readers to anticipate the faithlessness of female slaves, to turn away from them as quickly as possible, and on no account to become attached to one of them but to banish "the traitor" from their heart in haste. "At any rate female singers are false." But in fact "housewives" were not to be trusted either, they simply "had no opportunity for love!"[54] Sexual insatiability was imputed to the female slave singer: they demand several lovers at the same time and are not satisfied with a single beloved.[55]

From a present-day viewpoint, the young slave women represent uprooted human beings who had to learn everything anew, including languages and customs. The female slave singer was selected and trained for a role that from the outset was dishonorable and irreversible,[56] in (almost) every regard the opposite from the free woman who was kept under lock and key. Men wanted the female singer to be as she was; at the same time she was reproached for being the way she was. The vehemence, indeed the mockery at the expense of those targeted,[57] is not difficult to understand. The men of letters at least recognized

53 Al-Jāḥiẓ/Pellat, p. 430. Walther, *Frau im Islam*, p. 145, quotes further from this work.

54 Bellmann, II, pp. 21-22, 25, 62, 63 f., 144. Ibn Washshāʾ vehemently turns against the view expressed in a poem that female singers are more faithful than "honest wives": Bellmann, II, p. 23.

55 Bellmann, II, pp. 21 and 59.

56 "If a female slave singer wanted to set out on the right path, she wouldn't know what it is, and if she wished to live respectably, she wouldn't be capable of doing so" – according to al-Jāḥiẓ/Pellat, p. 431.

57 On this subject cf. Wiebke Walther, "From Women's Problems to Women as Images in Modern Iraqi Poetry", *Die Welt des Islams* 36 (1996), pp. 224-25; on poems of the Abbasid

why men belittled female slave singers, namely in order not to have to belittle themselves.

III Ideal Women

Which women were ideal women? Rābiʿa, after whom the next section is named, was very famous but was she really an exemplar, were there "thousands who resembled her",[58] or was she not rather a consoling image? The Sufis loved the Virgin Mary, to whom the Spirit of God had foretold the birth of the spiritual child Jesus.[59] In modern scholarly research little importance is given to Āmina, the mother of the Prophet.[60] Neither Margaret Smith and Annemarie Schimmel nor Wiebke Walther has devoted attention to her. She is given attention in Turkish religious iconography. Among the many miniatures of the Turkish *Siyer* from 1388, illustrated at the Ottoman court toward the end of the sixteenth century and whose text is based on Ibn Isḥāq and others, we encounter Āmina, the noblest woman of the Quraysh, married to ʿAbdullāh of the family of Hāshim who had a second wife besides Āmina. She receives from ʿAbdullāh one of the signs of prophethood, the divine light. According to Sunnī doctrine, this light, also called *nūr-i Muḥammadī*, was transmitted from one prophet to another, beginning with Adam, up until the Prophet Muhammad. The biographical tradition attributes to Āmina two dreams involving light which she beholds when she is pregnant with Muhammad. In one dream someone tells her: "You are pregnant with the lord of this people; say at his birth: 'I place him under the protection of the One and name him Muhammad.'" And at the moment of the birth, she dreams that a light goes forth from her, so powerful that it illuminates the castles of Syria.[61] One of the miniatures repre-

era in which female slave singers are ridiculed or defamed, ibid. p. 237.

58 Thus Syed Ameer Ali, *The Spirit of Islam*, London 1922, p. 229; quoted from W. Montgomery Watt in Waardenburg, *Islam. Norm, ideaal en werkelijkheid*, Weesp-Antwerpen 1984, p. 374, along with bibliography.

59 The Koranic stories about the Virgin Mary in surah III, verse 51 and surah XIX, verses 17 and 28, provide the basis for this; Schimmel, *Dimensionen*, p. 609. Annemarie Schimmel, *Jesus und Maria in der islamischen Mystik*, München 1996, pp. 142-58.

60 "The Prophet's widowed mother, Āmina, is a shadowy figure, for she died when her son was only six years old", Charis Waddy, *Women in Muslim History*, London and New York 1980, p. 10.

61 Tor Andrae, *Die person Muhammeds in lehre und glauben seiner gemeinde*, Stockholm 1918, pp. 30 f., with parallels in other religions; Toufic Fahd, *La Divination Arabe. Études religieuses, sociologiques et folkloriques sur le milieu natif de l'islam*, Leiden 1966, p. 261.

senting a pregnant Āmina portrays this light as an aureole. On the night of the birth Āmina is alone; angels help her. After giving birth, the mother[62] sits upright on a chair, now without the light of prophethood and therefore without the aureole. The face of the child is veiled. Āmina supports it, more out of reverence than as a gesture of affection. The child has no need of being supported, for although still small in size, he is the Prophet in his divine light, provided with an aureole. Āmina's face is also veiled. They are surrounded by objects that indicate a living-room with a prayer niche or a mosque. A lamp hangs in a room where Āmina, dressed in green, kneels alongside the small Prophet who is swathed in light and stretches forth his hand toward a bowl that angels offer him. Āmina holds up her open left hand, as well as her right one whose finger expresses amazement. Next the miniature painters paint the wet-nurse Ḥalīma who was entrusted with breast-feeding Muhammad. Āmina dies when the Prophet is six years old; her tomb is in Mecca. She is a significant link in the chain between the many male prophets from Adam onwards and the Prophet Muhammad. On the night of her giving birth she is raised up triumphantly and at the same time reduced to being the bearer of the light. She does not belong to the House of the Prophet (*ahl al-bayt*). She was not a mediator with access to divine authority. The reverence of the pious is accorded her wherever the Prophet's birthday is celebrated.

Much greater is the devotion which is felt for Fāṭima, the daughter of the Prophet; in Sunnī iconography she also bears the nimbus of the divine light;[63] her tomb is visited in Medina, chiefly by Shīʿites who apply to her the concept of *ʿiṣma* "sinlessness". It is not Āmina who appears as the mother of the believers but it is the Prophet's wives, from Khadīja, the first spouse and the first

62 Helga Möbius, "Mutter-Bilder. Die Göttermutter und ihr Sohn", in: Renate Möhrmann, *Verklärt, verkitscht, vergessen. Die Mutter als ästhetische Figur*, Stuttgart-Weimar 1996, pp. 21-38.

63 Volume IV of what is now known as the Dublin Manuscript of the *Ḍarīr*-cycle is more generous with haloes than the other volumes. Not only Fāṭima and her mother Khadīja, but other wives of the Prophet such as ʿĀʾisha and Umm Salama, are veiled and are even depicted with a halo: in any case their names – not always correctly – are found in the explanatory inscriptions in the miniatures. Cf. B. Flemming, "Religiöse Geschichte in der türkischen Ikonographie", in *Anatolica* 10 (1983), pp. 133-48. ʿĀʾisha and Umm Salama have been depicted with a wreath of flame: Basim Musallam, "Die Ordnung muslimischer Gesellschaften", in Francis Robinson (ed.), *Islamische Welt. Eine illustrierte Geschichte*, Frankfurt am Main/New York 1997, pp. 210-18, published a miniature from the Dublin Manuscript.

Muslim,[64] who is depicted with an aureole, up to the childless ʿĀʾisha, "the mother of the believers" *par excellence*, as well as the first transmitter of *ḥadīth*s.

Without a doubt motherly love belonged to the ideal image of the noble lady, as it did to the image of the ordinary wife. In contrast with this is the fact that the majority of the saintly women recorded in hagiography were childless. If the image of the ideal woman was modeled on Rābiʿa, then it was a matter of an abstract Rābiʿa: the embodiment of pure love for God.

IV Women of the Rābiʿa Period

Twenty-seven of the thirty-four women in *The Breaths of Intimacy* belong to the period we usually designate as the formative period of Islamic mysticism which preceded actual Sufism and extended from the eighth century to the year one thousand approximately. With reference to male mystics, this period is also called the period of self-education; the young mystic attached himself to one or more "masters of instruction". With reference to women, I name this time span the Rābiʿa period after the best-known Islamic female mystic. We may also include with her three female anchorites whose names, exact time of life, and actual words are not recorded, and who originate in the chronicle of Yāfiʿī. The social background or rank of such women is at first glance quite varied. Their status ranges from daughter of an emir and of notables to that of a simple peasant woman. All sorts of unnamed women appear as leading or marginal figures. Slave women, those with light as well as dark skin, are least likely to be mentioned by name. The only female singer and player of a musical instrument who we will be considering more closely bears the slave-name Tuḥfa "Gift". Twenty women in the Rābiʿa period are presented in *The Breaths of Intimacy* with their proper names, which should not be taken as a matter of course, and only seven appear without names. They are in relationships which, in the case of men, are usually referred to as *ṣuḥbat* "association" or "companionship". A woman attached herself to a male or female teacher in order to learn something about self-training and the meaning of sacred Traditions and technical terms.[65] Women like Rābiʿa, Rayḥāna, Shaʿwāna, Maryam, ʿAfīra and

64 Aflākī one time calls the wife of Mawlānā "a second Mary" and another time "the Khadīja of the age". John O'Kane (translator). *The Feats of the Knowers of God (Manāqeb al-ʿārefīn) by Shams al-Dīn Aḥmad-e Aflākī*, Leiden-Boston-Köln 2002, pp. 67 and 139.

65 Fritz Meier, "Qushayrīs Tartīb as-sulūk", in *Oriens* 16 (1963)/*Fritz Meier. Essays on Islamic Piety and Mysticism*, translated by John O'Kane, Leiden 1999, p. 93.

Muʿādha[66] were in contact with one another, served and helped each other and learned from one another. Due to the dignity that radiated from women like Shaʿwāna, who preached and recited with a beautiful voice and pleasant intonation before a mixed gathering, women of her kind acquired important influence, and her gatherings clearly caused less offense than they would in later times when segregation of the sexes had become more firmly rooted. In the legendary stories of the Rābiʿa period, even in the one that deals with the peculiar relationship of Kaʿb's daughter with her male slave,[67] emphasis is placed upon the woman's refusal to engage in a sensual love relationship with a man.

Celibacy prevails in the stories about women of the Rābiʿa period. Rābiʿa al-ʿAdawiyya (born 714 or 715 in Basra and allegedly died in 801) is the personality after whom we have named this period. Wondrous events from her legendary life as a celibate belong to the basic repertoire of anecdotes of early Islamic mysticism. These include that she was born unto poor, respectable parents and that when she once was outside the house, she was abducted and sold as a slave. Later she lived as a freed woman. It was characteristic of her former status as a female slave that she acted in service roles in which she was both visible and audible, not invisible and inaudible, as free women, especially those of child-bearing age, were obliged to be.

It is reported that in the European Middle Ages, Christian women who wished to devote themselves to God were quite prepared "even to live together chastely with men". They were not "man-haters" and even where they admitted having struggled against sexual desires, they did not reproach men as a group for difficulties they experienced. So Dinzelbacher informs us and continues: "This is in stark contrast to celibate men, one must add, who filled entire volumes with negative projections onto the opposite sex stemming from their

66 Elias, "Female and Feminine" recounts the stories following Jāmī and others; pp. 208-12, 211: Ufira. Almost the same remark about a woman becoming "a 'man' in the path of God" is noted in Bruce B. Lawrence, "Honoring women through sexual abstinence. Lessons from the Spiritual Practice of a Pre-Modern South Asian Sufi Master, Shaykh Nizam ad-din Awliya", in M.-E. Subtelny (ed.), *Annemarie Schimmel Festschrift. Journal of Turkish Studies* vol. 18 (1994), p. 156.

67 Fritz Meier, *Die schöne Mahsatī*, Wiesbaden 1963, pp. 29-31, indicates the passage in *The Breaths of Intimacy* where a woman's love is presented as mystical love. According to Meier's study (pp. 27-42), the basis for this is probably a Persian romance in which the unhappy love for a certain Bektaş on the part of the woman who composed poetry in Arabic is portrayed. The theme "bad woman with black slave" is dealt with by Malti-Douglas, *Woman's Body*, pp. 60-62.

own repressed sexuality."[68] Similarly, male Muslims, whether celibate or not, did not greet the first appearance of women in the realm of mysticism with enthusiasm. Abū Ḥafṣ al-Ḥaddād, a former blacksmith (d. circa 878/79),[69] stated that he had always found the remarks of women reprehensible (*makrūh*). Dhū'l-Nūn felt that there was something "debasing" or "disgraceful" about accepting anything from women.[70] All the same, the high-ranking wealthy female mystic, Umm 'Alī Fāṭima, by means of her dignity and courage, which in part at least may have been based on the status of her father, gained the respect of critical men. Two of these important women themselves chose their husbands: Fāṭima, a daughter of the emir of Balkh, caused Aḥmad b. Khiḍrūya to ask her father for her hand in marriage. Another man, Aḥmad b. Abī'l-Hawārī (d.844/45), was chosen in marriage by Rābiʿa bint Ismāʿīl who was likewise wealthy and who was known as Rābiʿa the Syrian. In both cases the hagiographers note that bachelors, to begin with, baulked at marrying. Incidentally, Rābiʿa bint Ismāʿīl, reportedly went on pressing Aḥmad b. Abī'l-Hawārī to marry her. But Aḥmad's spiritual teacher, Dārānī, had forbidden him to marry. It is reported in the *vita* of Dārānī that Aḥmad said to Rābiʿa: "Listen, I have no desire for women, because I am preoccupied with my religious state." She replied: "You listen, I am certainly more preoccupied with my state than you are with yours. I have no desire for men. But I have inherited three hundred thousand dinars from my husband. This is licit wealth and I wish to spend it on you and your brethren and through you become acquainted with the righteous so that they become a path to God." At this point, Aḥmad b. Abī'l-Hawārī again consulted with his teacher who, after some reflection, ordered: "Aḥmad, marry her! The woman is a Friend of God..."[71] The marriage did take place. *The Breaths of Intimacy* transmits that Aḥmad b. Abī'l-Hawārī loved her not as a wife but as a sister. Rābiʿa the Syrian then became famous for "states" that continually alternated between love and fear of God, which she expressed in verses. Jāmī and Lāmiʿī set great store by the report that with her higher vision she beheld the year of the Caliph Hārūn al-Rashīd's death on the underside of a bowl. She looked after her spouse and cooked for him while she went on praying. However, her husband, Aḥmad b. Abī'l-Hawārī, who as a bachelor had had no desire for women, then took a second wife, whereupon the disap-

68 Peter Dinzelbacher, *Mittelalterliche Frauenmystik*, Paderborn-München-Wien-Zürich 1993, p. 60.

69 He was famous as a representative of proper morals. Richard Gramlich, *Alte Vorbilder des Sufitums. Zweiter Teil: Scheiche des Ostens*, Wiesbaden 1996, p. 113.

70 Elias, "Female and Feminine", p. 213.

71 Richard Gramlich, "Abū Sulaymān ad-Dārānī", *Oriens* 33 (1992), p. 61.

pointed spouse Rābiʿa sought advice from her female mystic teacher and spiritual guide, Ḥakīma of Damascus. The latter already knew about the second wife and tried to help Rābiʿa get over the shock with a verse from the Koran.[72] That is the whole of it; the only further thing we learn is that on her way home Rābiʿa staggered to such a degree that she feared men on the street would think she was drunk.

The emir's daughter Fāṭima from Nishapur, the older wife of Aḥmad b. Khiḍrūya, was held to be a religious scholar. Being herself a transmitter of a Koran commentary,[73] she argued with like-minded important mystics such as Bāyazīd Bisṭāmī and Abū Ḥafṣ, debated with them and replied to their questions. After the death of her husband, she sold her lands and set out on the pilgrimage to Mecca where she remained and pursued studies for seven years. She passed away in her home city of Balkh.[74] Thus far the narrative corpus in *The Breaths of Intimacy* which has been filtered in many ways and at times condensed to the point of obscurity. Recognition of outstanding women depended on individual men. In a later phase, the theosophist and mystic Ibn al-ʿArabī would concede some space for the feminine.[75]

V The Charismatic Woman of Tirmidh

The contents of dreams could contribute to the construction of the male consciousness of mystics who (as for example Qushayrī[76]) saw no reason to grant a role in their writings to female dreams in a society in which "even the dream of a woman [was] less true than that of a man".[77] But since great importance was given to dreams, it seemed fairly reasonable for a mystic to expect recognition for himself in the dreams people in his surroundings had about him.

72 Koran 26:89: ["On the day when neither wealth nor sons shall profit,] except for him who comes to God with a pure heart" (Only he who brings a pure heart to God will be saved). Al-Jāḥiẓ cites the well-known justification, "that God has only allowed an individual man to have four wives and then after their death or divorce from them another four, and likewise as many female slaves as he wishes, so that the women in question will not be without spouses"; al-Jāḥiẓ/Pellat, p. 308.

73 See Gramlich, *Alte Vorbilder des Sufitums*, p. 96, ftn. 7.

74 Gramlich, *Alte Vorbilder des Sufitums*, p. 100, with a comprehensive bibliography.

75 Cf. Elias, "Female and Feminine", pp. 216-18.

76 Richard Gramlich, *Das Sendschreiben al-Qušayrīs über das Sufitum. Eingeleitet, übersetzt und kommentiert*, Wiesbaden 1986.

77 "[...] because they possess lesser intellectual capacities", as Schimmel, *Dimensionen*, p. 608, quotes from an authoritative *ḥadīth* collection.

Thanks to this state of affairs, the religious dreams of a woman, the mother of small children and wife of the scholar and theosophist Muḥammad b. ʿAlī, known as al-Ḥakīm al-Tirmidhī (circa 820-910),[78] (both contemporaries of the Traditionist Abū ʿĪsā al-Tirmidhī [825-92]),[79] came to be written down and preserved. This woman – with Bernd Radtke we will refer to her as the wife of Tirmidhī (Annemarie Schimmel calls her Umm ʿAbdallāh in her book review; see below) – not only received religious messages regarding the husband she revered but also beheld dreams that directly referred to her own person. This makes Tirmidhī's autobiography, also dubbed a spiritual "Itinerarium", which has been photomechanically edited and translated by Bernd Radtke into German and together with John O'Kane into English,[80] a precious source for the participation of women in mysticism.

Tirmidhī's wife, between circa 880 and 883 AD, beheld religious dreams which reveal her to be a woman endowed with charismatic gifts. Her husband wrote down these dreams in Arabic and partly in Persian. Tirmidhī, after pursuing studies in Basra and then making the pilgrimage to Mecca (around 860), had returned to his home city which was under the jurisdiction of Balkh. Once at home, he had subjected himself for a time to fasting, seclusion and various ascetic trials. After strict self-training and experiencing dreams which confirmed him in his high spiritual rank, Tirmidhī held gatherings with like-minded people and attracted disciples to himself. Adversaries and the envious accused him of heretical innovations. He was suspected of wishing to present himself as a prophet, was obliged to explain himself in Balkh before the local governor and was ordered not to speak about love of God. But then, as a result of "discord and rebellion", his enemies were driven out of the city; when they returned later, committed disciples had gathered around Tirmidhī and his reputation had become so firmly established that his opponents gave up.[81] Tirmidhī's

78 Yves Marquet, "al-Tirmidhī, Abū ʿAbd Allāh Muḥammad b. ʿAlī al-Ḥakīm", *EI* X (2000), p. 544, locates the year of his death between 318/936 and 320/938. But see Bernd Radtke, *Al-Ḥakīm at-Tirmiḏī. Ein islamischer Theosoph des 3./9. Jahrhunderts.* Freiburg 1980, pp. 16 ff.

79 G.H.A. Juynboll, "al-Tirmidhī, Abū ʿĪsā Muḥammad b. ʿĪsā b. Sawra", *EI* X (2000), p. 546.

80 *Badʾ shaʾn al-Ḥakīm at-Tirmidhī* "The Beginning of the Affair of Abū ʿAbdallāh Muḥammad al-Ḥakīm at-Tirmiḏī". Bernd Radtke, "Tirmiḏiana Minora I. Die Autobiografie des Theosophen von Tirmiḏī", *Oriens* 34 (1994), pp. 242-98. "The Beginning of the Affair" of Tirmidhī, almost one half of which consists of dream visions of his wife (and three of his disciples) fills nine folios (17 pages) of the Ankara University manuscript, İsmail Saib I 1571. B. Radtke and John O'Kane, *The Concept of Sainthood in Early Islamic Mysticism. Two works by Al-Ḥakīm Al-Tirmidhī. An annotated translation with introduction*, Richmond, Surrey, 1996.

81 Radtke, "Autobiografie", pp. 249 (10), 251 (14) and 252 (15).

autobiographical work covers this period of growing recognition and comfortable domestic life, and also contains dreams. Included among the manifest contents of his own dreams are references to his home city. The trading city and port of Tirmidh (Termez) on the northern bank of the Amu Darya was endowed with a market and several mosques, had a fortress and was surrounded by ruins, cemeteries, steppes and deserts. In his dreams, Tirmidhī wandered about inside buildings, domed edifices and tents, and in the cemetery. He reports that in past times when he imposed trials on himself, he wore shabby clothes, rode to the market on a donkey and accustomed himself to the barking of dogs in the alleyways. His wife – he speaks of her as *ahlī*, without giving her name – had beheld, from around 880 on in a time span of two to three years, a series of remarkable religious dreams which Tirmidhī wrote down because he considered them to be about himself and as a confirmation of his spiritual claim. The text says: "There continually came over me dreams (*al-ruʾyā*) on my wife's part, all of them shortly before morning. She had dream after dream, as if it was a question of a message (*risāla*). She did not have to interpret them because their sense was clear and their interpretation was obvious."[82] Tirmidhī's wife lived with her husband in a town house with a garden[83] where guests were sometimes entertained.[84] In the first recorded dream the wife is in the porch,[85] another time in their house in a large room[86] that contained a place of prayer and was furnished with bedsteads upholstered with silk. The couple slept in one bed and sometimes on the roof of the house.[87] Worries about her housekeeping duties pursue her even in her dreams. She has to entertain guests and keep the house clean; when an angel orders her to tell her husband: "Clean your house", she takes it personally and replies that she has children (sons, *awlād*)[88] and cannot keep the house clean. In response the

82 In "Autobiografie", p. 252 (16), Radtke translates: "Meine frau hatte fortwährend träume, die mich betrafen, alle kurz vor morgen", which is translated by Radtke and O'Kane in *Concept of Sainthood*, p. 24, as: "Then my wife had further dreams in which I appeared, all of them towards dawn."

83 Radtke, "Autobiografie", pp. 261 (26) and 263 (29).

84 Radtke, "Autobiografie", p. 256 (18).

85 Radtke, "Autobiografie", p. 251 (14).

86 Radtke, "Autobiografie", p. 254 (17).

87 Radtke, "Autobiografie", p. 256 (18). Cf. Koran 43:33, Motzki, "Dann machte er daraus die beiden Geschlechter", p. 608.

88 Radtke, "Autobiografie", p. 254 (16); cf. Harald Motzki, "Das Kind und seine Sozialisation in der islamischen Familie des Mittelalters", in Jochen Martin and August Nitschke (eds.), *Zur Sozialgeschichte der Kindheit*, Freiburg/München 1986, pp. 391-441.

angel explains he is not referring to urine but to the tongue.[89] He orders her to hold up the Koranic verse 21:47 as a warning to her husband who must still work on curbing his superfluous talk. The angel places a handful of myrtle in her hand. When she asks whether she should keep it for herself or give it to her husband, the angel replies: "This you have in common. You are both exactly in the same place." In the same dream she sees herself distinguished above her two female blood-relations, her sisters.[90]

In the manifest content of her dreams, moreover, Tirmidhī's wife displays her familiarity with gardening, grapes, date palms, bushels of fresh dates, aromatic herbs that are only green in summer and evergreen myrtle.[91] She dreams of gushing springs and pools of water. One time she dreams she is in a place she does not know, alongside a large pool full of limpid water. White grapes hang down over the pool and she and her sisters are eating some of them.[92] Another time she dreams that her husband took water from a brass vessel for his ablutions.[93] Like her husband she sees in a dream localities outside the city, among them a ravine and a cemetery; she sees all the way to Dāwūdābād and comes before the gate of a fortress and its place of prayer.[94] She beholds the feared Turks in a dream.[95]

She appears to be happy to belong to her husband's (*zawj*) spiritual, as well as his intimate, sphere of life. In a long dream she experiences mortal fears in his regard: when (in the dream she returns home in tears, she finds him unharmed: he is the first among the forty chosen, trustworthy men.[96] Three times the Prophet Muhammad[97] appears to her, on one occasion the Prophet

89 Radtke, "Autobiografie", p. 254 (16), comments: "Der traum ist eine botschaft für ihn, überflüssiges reden zu unterlassen" (The dream is a message for him to eliminate unnecessary talk).

90 Radtke, "Autobiografie", p. 254 (16): "Sie kommen dir nicht gleich und sind dir nicht ebenbürtig" (They are not on a par with you and are not your equal).

91 Radtke, "Autobiografie", p. 253 (16).

92 Radtke, "Autobiografie", pp. 252-53 (16).

93 Radtke, "Autobiografie", p. 260 (26).

94 Radtke, "Autobiografie", p. 257 (19), a dream from the 24th of Ramadan, and p. 260 (26).

95 Perhaps the Qarluq who had begun to contest the Samanids' dominance over the region.

96 Marquet, "al-Tirmidhī", p. 544: "In 269/883, a dream experienced by his wife confirmed that he had just acceded to the rank of the forty *ṣiddīḳ*s."

97 Radtke, "Autobiografie", pp. 248 and 265, points out that she could be certain that her dreams of the Prophet were experiences of reality because "Muḥammad says in the well-known canonical *ḥadīth* (*Concordance* II, p. 200): 'Whoever sees me in a dream sees me in reality.'"

ʿĪsā (Jesus) does so.[98] She dreams that while she is asleep in bed with her husband, the Prophet gets into the bed with them.[99] In the dream she is pleased by the visit of the Prophet to their conjugal home. She kisses his hand, and when she may wish for something, she asks for her inflamed eye to be cured. The Prophet then orders her to place her hand on her eye and after pronouncing the Muslim profession of faith, to add: "He gives life and causes death. The good is in His hands, and He has power over everything!" Thereupon she wakes up, pronounces these words and is immediately freed from her ailment.[100] Several times, from the first recorded dream onwards, an angel appears to her in the form of a young man with curly hair dressed in white clothes,[101] whose teeth shine like pearls when he smiles.[102] Later as well an angel presents himself in this form to the dreaming woman and when she questions him, he replies: "We travel about on the earth and reside in Jerusalem...and we visit God's worshippers."[103] What the angel transmits to her, he calls religious "exhortation" (*mawʿiẓa*). Another time, while dreaming she beholds a tall fruit-bearing date palm that reaches to Mecca; a green bird endowed with speech[104] flies upwards from branch to branch and when it perches on a dry branch, the branch becomes green, and so the bird continues until the top of the tree.[105] In a later dream she is told: "I have given you knowledge (*ʿilm*) of the first and the last things."[106] She delved into the knowledge of the names of God, whose names her husband had occupied himself with.[107] Every day a name was disclosed to her: "The light of the name shone on her heart and the interior of the name was revealed to her." Now she was no longer limited to her domesticity; instead she was admitted to the gathering of the mystics in the midst of whom

98 Radtke, "Autobiografie", p. 256 (18).

99 Radtke, "Autobiografie", p. 259 (24).

100 Radtke, "Autobiografie", pp. 259-60 (25).

101 Radtke, "Autobiografie", p. 251 (14).

102 Radtke, "Autobiografie", p. 254 (16). On the flashing of white teeth associated with smiling in the Arab imagination and the expecially radiant smile of the Prophet, cf. Ludwig Ammann, *Vorbild und Vernunft. Die Regelung von Lachen und Scherzen im mittelalterlichen Islam*, Hildesheim 1993, p. 59.

103 Radtke, "Autobiografie", p. 253 (16).

104 The Koranic promise that martyrs continue to live was made more concrete in *ḥadīths* through the idea that their spirits reside in Paradise in the form of green birds: T. Seidensticker, "Der Rūḥ der Toten", in E. Wagner and K. Röhrborn (eds.), *Kaşkūl. Festschrift... Gießen*, Wiesbaden 1989, p. 146. See the Traditionist Tirmidhī, *Sunan* V 231, 12 f.

105 Radtke, "Autobiografie", p. 255 (17).

106 Radtke, "Autobiografie", p. 264 (31).

107 Marquet, "al-Tirmidhī", p. 544: "As was later to be the practice of the Ashʿarīs, he accepted the condensing of the hundred names of Allah into ten attributes."

she recounted that God's name "The Kind One" had occurred to her. Thereupon, as her husband reports, she desired to hear sermons and "to demand from her (lower) soul (*nafs*) the fulfilment of its duties". Her last dream began with her receiving the inspiration: "Oh Light and Right Guidance of all things, it is You Whose light dispels the darkness!"[108] Five or six days later she was sitting in the garden. Then all the names of God became "luminous" for her; she dreamt that God gave her a seal or a seal-ring;[109] this, as she informed her husband, filled her with joy and zeal. On the next day she was told in Persian that she would be given three things: "'My magnificence, My awesomeness and My splendor.' And a light shone for me from above."[110] Two or three years later after her period of dreams, she beheld another dream, the only one which her husband dates, namely mid-morning on Saturday, ten days before the end of Dhū 'l-Qaʿda 269 (June 1st 883). Tirmidhī's spiritual itinerary breaks off when the charismatic apparitions of his wife reached a high point. Tirmidhī gives no information about the further course of his wife's life. Even as it stands, the process of her development as a mystic is extraordinary. Her statements in Persian (one whole dream is recorded in Persian) represent early evidence for the neo-Persian written language. Her situation resembles that of the lay visionaries of the High Middle Ages who reported their visions in the vernacular language which the recorder then translated into Latin.[111] To begin with, scholarship credited to Tirmidhī's account the dreams of his wife that bore his seal of approval and declared her to be "a medium", "a dream medium"[112] or "a simple housewife",[113] who was in the service of Tirmidhī's spiritual ascent.[114] More recently, however, she has been recognized as "an active female mystic" *in her own right*.[115] Tirmidhī's wife, one of the very few women in the early Middle Ages whose visions have been transmitted to us, occupies a place

108 Radtke, "Autobiografie", p. 263 (29).

109 Radtke, "Autobiografie", p. 269 (29). Radtke and O'Kane, *Concept of Sainthood*, p. 35, connect this with Tirmidhī's claim to be the last and the highest holy man, "the seal of Friendship with God" (*khatm al-walāya*).

110 Radtke, "Autobiografie", p. 264 (30).

111 Peter Dinzelbacher, *Mittelalterliche Visionsliteratur. Eine Anthologie*, Darmstadt 1989, p. 20.

112 Radtke, "Autobiografie", p. 251 (14): "...tritt die frau Tirmiˇdī als traummedium zum erstenmal auf" (...for the first time Tirmidhī's wife appears as a medium for dreams).

113 "...the simple young Persian housewife", Annemarie Schimmel, review of Radtke and O'Kane, *Concept of Sainthood*, in Journal of Islamic Studies (January 1999), pp. 59-60.

114 Radtke, "Autobiografie", p. 265.

115 Radtke and O'Kane, *Concept of Sainthood*, p. 9; cf. also pp. 2, 26 and 27.

within the community of saints of all epochs who were endowed with visionary gifts.[116]

VI Madness – Tuḥfa

Exceptional psychic states that could be induced through an ascetic manner of life were already considered a sign of sanctity in the early phase of Islamic mysticism. As such, along with religious rank, they could entail an important elevation of status for the woman concerned, namely legal freedom. Rābiʿa al-ʿAdawiyya, according to her *vita*, was set free by her owner because of her sanctity. In *The Breaths of Intimacy*, the female slave singer Tuḥfa is set free when a mystic who recognizes her sanctity intervenes on her behalf and wishes to purchase her freedom. At the same time, the story of this female slave singer and musician makes it clear what risks a slave ran if she refused nourishment, continually wept and gave up sleep: she might be considered holy but she could also die as happened at a gathering when a moving sermon on love caused the death of another female mystic along with other persons. A woman who wept incessantly could go blind; she could be declared insane and carted off to the madhouse with her hands and feet in chains. This is what happened to the female slave singer Tuḥfa. The place where it occurred is not named; it was probably Baghdad. Where Tuḥfa was born was irrelevant. As a young female slave, she had lodging, food to eat, and an elite training as a female slave singer. But she could no longer bear her life and smashed her instrument. Her flight into dialogue with God gave the impression that she had lost her mind. After she had spent a year weeping without food and without sleep, her owner delivered her to the madhouse in chains as if deranged but as beautifully turned out as when he had purchased her. He justified his action by maintaining that as a female slave singer in whom he had invested much money, she had failed and damaged him financially. For her part, she experienced the life of coquetry and seductive provocation as godless. She loved no human being (men sounded her out on this). She could now only imagine love as love of God. In the fasting and sleeplessness which she voluntarily imposed upon herself lay her self-affirmation. Her condition akin to madness – she let out cries and succumbed to fainting-spells – rendered her inviolable; her honor was now based on her nearness to God. It was her duty to give up her role as a

116 Cf. Tore Nyberg "Birgitta von Schweden – Die aktive Gottesschau", in Peter Dinzelbacher and Dieter R. Bauer (eds.), *Frauenmystik im Mittelalter*, Ostfildern bei Stuttgart 1985, pp. 275-89.

prostitute. As a pious Muslim, Sarī Saqaṭī[117] had to concede this to her. He broke out in tears at the sight of her. Four men spontaneously endeavored to set Tuḥfa free: the highly reputed but no longer well-off Sarī, the rich man, the director of the hospital, and her owner. Her emancipation occurred as if by a miracle. The first thing Tuḥfa did once she was free was to change her clothes. Elegance was the hallmark of the female slave singer. The patched frock was appropriate for a free woman. Her weeping disappointed Sarī. He attempted to console her in a good-natured way. But she no longer replied and withdrew to a place where she would be entirely safe from eroticism.[118] The three men guessed her destination and set out for Mecca. In a truly ghostly fashion Tuḥfa wandered about Mecca like a sexless phantom. She was undernourished and exhausted; after all, she had fasted for a whole year. But she was of sound mind, she recognized Sarī, though he did not recognize her. She still went on reciting poetry. The man who had at first been delighted by her outer appearance became a listener. In her texts, which she had not composed herself but had learned by heart, she found consolation. The first-person narrator, looking back on her sinful life, thinks she is afraid because of what "she had perpetrated earlier". Whether her poems were to do with worldly love or were religious, certainly the form itself, speech in verse, was a means for her to keep up her psychic strength.[119] Sarī could not refrain from asking what benefit she had got by cutting herself off from the world. When she heard that her former owner was nearby, she uttered a short prayer and died. Two of the men died. Sarī survived and became the first-person narrator of the miracle of how she was set free from slavery.[120] Thus Tuḥfa, who followed the way of self-annihilation, lost her life on the path of God (see the translation in XIV).

117 Sarī al-Saqaṭī, Abū'l Ḥasan, born in Baghdad as the son of an old-clothes dealer, was a rich whole-sale merchant who set out on the mystic path, travelled far and wide, and then came back to Baghdad in 833 where he became an important teacher. B. Reinert, "Sarī al-Saḳaṭī" in *EI* IX (1997), pp. 56-59.

118 In Mecca she was safe from molestation. In Ibn Washshā' a young female slave singer, engaged in circumambulating the Kaʿba, defends herself in verse against the charge of lacking proper reverence and modesty: "In truth, pure virgins are elevated above all shadow of a doubt! Like gazelles that the law, with no doubt, forbids to hunt round about Mecca. Speaking maliciously out of sheer habit, one takes them to be whores and maintains that Islam alone holds them back from the vice of prostitution!" Bellmann, I, p. 130.

119 Ruth Klüger, *Weiter leben. Eine Jugend*, Göttingen 1992, pp. 123-24, 127.

120 The question as to whether Sarī really heard the poems from her like this, or whether they were quotations from well-known poems in the style of Arabic *belles-lettres*, must be left to the Arabists to decide.

VII Relations with Men

The ascetic female mystics of the Rābiʿa period were certainly not "man-haters". On the other hand, of the married female mystics who lived in this period, not only Rābiʿa but others as well suffered under polygamy (in fact polygyny). The corpus of early Traditions already reports on jealousy in the harem of the Prophet,[121] just as the early *vitae* of female mystics hint at the suffering of women whose husbands married an additional wife. Ibn al-ʿArabī informs us of a measure to stop a husband from doing so by telekinesis (see IX). It is reported about one of the women of piety, Umm Ḥassān, that she turned down a marriage proposal.

Only two of the early female mystics appear before us as mothers. One of them, Fiḍḍa, asked her husband to slaughter their only sheep since extreme poverty presented no excuse for not entertaining a guest with everything one had to offer;[122] but she requested that her husband slaughter the sheep out of sight of their little boys because otherwise the children would weep. God rewarded the sacrifice of the couple by sending down to them a sheep that yielded honey and milk.

The other mother in *The Breaths of Intimacy* refused to believe what her mystic guide, Sarī Saqaṭī, told her: that her son, whom his teacher had sent to the mill-pond, had drowned. The teacher sent someone to Shaykh Sarī and informed him of what had happened. Sarī, as to whose kind and helpful character the previous chapter testifies, accompanied the teacher to the mother. "They went there together. Shaykh Sarī began by speaking about patience. Then he spoke about acceptance. The woman asked: 'Oh master, why are you speaking like this?' Sarī replied: 'Your son has drowned in the pond.' She said: 'My son?' He: 'Yes.' The woman said: 'Believe me, God the Sublime certainly hasn't done this.' Shaykh Sarī once more began to speak about acceptance. The woman said: 'Get up and come with me!' They stood up and went with her to the stream. She asked: 'Where did my son drown?' They said: 'Here.' She called out: 'Muḥammad!' Her son replied: 'Here I am, mother.' At that the mother plunged into the water, grasped her son's hand and brought him home."

Sarī Saqaṭī asked his disciple, Junayd, what the meaning of this was. The latter replied: "This is a woman who accepts everything that God has laid upon her. Such a person assumes nothing will happen to her that she hasn't been

121 Walther, *Frau im Islam*, p. 76.

122 Geert Jan van Gelder, "Eten, etiquette en ethiek: voedsel in de klassiek-Arabische literatuur", in Marjo Buitelaar and G.J. van Gelder, *Eet van de goede dingen! Culinaire culturen in het Midden-Oosten en de Islam*, Bussum 1995, pp. 59-79.

informed of in advance. Since she hadn't been informed of the death of her son, she resolutely dismissed it out of hand, saying: 'God the Sublime has absolutely not done this.'"

Only by way of hints do Muslim female mystics now and then give expression to their superiority over male theologians, a superiority based on experience and piety. *The Breaths of Intimacy* does disclose between the lines the occasional disapproval voiced by mystically gifted women toward their male colleagues. Such was the case when Ḥakīma of Damascus shook her head at the male mystic who took two wives; or when the pious mother did not believe her spiritual guide who told her that her son had drowned. A pious woman who in the wintry cold weather prepared a meal of bread and milk for the mystic Nūrī, which he picked up with soot-blackened fingers, thought to herself: "Oh God, how dirty are your holy men!" The mystic in question read her thoughts, of course, and punished her so that she felt ashamed and sought forgiveness.

We should here look more closely at a criticism Fāṭima of Nishapur levelled against the great mystic Bāyazīd Bisṭāmī, as it involves the function of the veil referred to earlier (11). The emir's daughter renounced all contact with the world and lived in retirement with Aḥmad b. Khiḍrūya whom she had chosen herself as husband. When he one day visited Bāyazīd Bisṭāmī, she accompanied him, and when she saw Bāyazīd, she removed her veil and talked to him without embarrassment. Her husband – he too married a second younger wife[123] – was upset by this and reproached her for it. She replied: "[I am doing this] because you are my natural spouse, while he is my spiritual friend; through you I attain my (sensual) desires but through him I attain God. The proof is that he has no need of my company, whereas you do." She continued to treat Bāyazīd with the same unselfconsciousness until one day he noticed her henna-stained hands and asked her why she colored them with henna. She replied: "Oh Bāyazīd, as long as you didn't see my hands and my henna, our being together (*ṣuḥbat*) was free of embarrassment but now, since your eye has taken them in, my being together with you is forbidden by religious prescription."[124] This dignified rebuke[125] spoken by the woman did no harm to the high

123 Her name, Ḥakīma-i Zāhida, is given by Richard Gramlich, *Alte Vorbilder des Sufitums*, p. 100.

124 Reynold A. Nicholson, *The Kashf al-Maḥjúb. The oldest Persian Treatise on Súfism, by...al-Hujwírí*, Leiden-London 1911, pp. 110 f.; cf. the text of ʿAṭṭār in Reynold A. Nicholson, *The Tadhkiratu'l-Awliyá ("Memoirs of the Saints") of Muḥammad Ibn Ibráhím Farídu'ddín ʿAṭṭār*, London/Leiden 1905-1907, I, p. 289.

125 Curiously, scholars excuse the faux pas of the man and put the blame on "the world" (or implicitly on the woman?); Schimmel, *Dimensions*, p. 427: "From that moment onward

esteem Bāyazīd had for her; on the contrary, he went as far as to say: "Whoever wishes to see a man disguised in women's clothes, let him look at Fāṭima!"[126]

The male Sufi, by self-mortification and going without food, refused to give himself over to his worldly surroundings. Primarily, this great endeavor meant fighting against the lower ego, the recalcitrant soul (*nafs*), which was feminine. With the aim of maintaining continual ritual purity, ascetic men avoided everything "that gave the slightest impression of the forbidden and the impure",[127] a scrupulosity that could easily degenerate into fastidious exaggeration, especially in connection with anything concerning contact with persons of the female sex. So much for the men. As for the women who travelled the path to God, at least those among them who resembled Rābiʿa, they endeavored in their own way to be radical in their avoidance of impurity. By fasting they could free themselves from their own female body, the seat of everything wicked. Domination of the desires meant subjection of the feminine within themselves.[128] To be wholly taken up with love of God was also attractive in the sense that it implied an enhancement of the status of the feminine. A very good, serious, highly moral pious woman was "like a man".[129] Through her self-effacement – to the extent of her physical non-existence – a woman could escape from having a different nature. Here arises the phantasm of a woman being the copy of male concepts.[130] Jāmī cites the Arabic saying: "The sun need not feel shame because it's feminine (grammatically), nor is it to the

free spiritual conversation was no longer possible between the two mystics, for 'the world' had interfered." She says the same thing in *Dimensionen*, p. 606: "Von da an war keine freie mystische Unterhaltung zwischen den beiden Heiligen mehr möglich, weil 'die Welt' dazwischengetreten war." Schimmel is followed by Elias, "Female and Feminine", p. 213: "...this world had encroached upon the transcendent perfection of their relationship."

126 Gramlich, *Alte Vorbilder des Sufitums*, p. 102.

127 J.T.P. de Bruijn, "Vroomheid en mystiek", in Jacques Waardenburg (ed.), *Islam. Norm, ideaal en werkelijkheid*, Weesp-Antwerpen 1984, p. 196.

128 Menstruation stops; cf. Elias, "Female and Feminine", p. 211. On the overall subject cf. Christina von Braun, "Das Kloster im Kopf. Weibliches Fasten von mittelalterlicher Askese zu moderner Anorexie", in Karin Flaake and Vera King (eds.), *Weibliche Adoleszenz. Zur Sozialisation junger Frauen*, Frankurt/New York, 2nd edition 1993, pp. 213-30.

129 In biographical dictionaries one finds sections under the heading "Women Who Attained the Status of Men". Elias, "Female and Feminine", p. 211. Almost the same remark about a woman becoming "a 'man' in the path of God" is noted in Bruce B. Lawrence, "Honoring women through sexual abstinence. Lessons from the Spiritual Practice of a Pre-Modern South Asian Sufi Master, Shaykh Nizam ad-din Awliya," in M.-E. Subtelny (ed.), *Annemarie Schimmel Festschrift, Journal of Turkish Studies* vol. 18 (1994), p. 156.

130 Cf. Möbius, "Mutter-Bilder. Die Göttermutter und ihr Sohn", pp. 21-38.

moon's credit that it's masculine."[131] These are verses which, as part of a panegyric on behalf of a manly prince, are already found in an elegiac poem by al-Mutanabbī (born in Kufa 915) on the death of the mother of his prince.[132] Jāmī, whom Lāmiʿī follows in Turkish translation, could already hark back to the topos of the exceptional woman's superiority which at a later date Turkish poet colleagues of his would take over (see XIII below).

In order to dominate instinctive drives and passions special acts of willpower would be called for on the part of women, namely sobriety, moderation and a capacity for fasting. With regard to the latter, women were meant to be less naturally inclined than men (the reverse of what one finds in Christian tradition). Ascetic Muslim women intensified these acts of willpower and virtues by over-achievement: moderation in eating became renunciation of food, indeed years of doing without nourishment; sleeping for short intervals became renunciation of sleep, remaining permanently awake. Eyes were not simply lowered in modesty but were permanently directed to the ground, for up to forty years; no more glances were raised to the sky at all. These women were not merely serious but tears constantly gushed forth from their eyes. The three female anchorites (in Yāfiʿī) briefly referred to above imposed constraints on their freedom of movement (by remaining on a column).

Male Sufis attempted to counteract the spread of extreme fasting among women. The female ascetics were advised that they should eat and drink and sleep more. Someone asked a female ascetic who was thin and pale whether he should fetch a doctor. Other women who were constantly weeping and shedding tears were warned that they could go blind; regret was expressed at the visible effects of sleeplessness that they displayed. Little boys threw stones at a supposed female heretic who was actually a holy woman.

VIII Characterization of the Rābʿia Period

One may justifiably maintain that an unmarried woman who became an ascetic and a mystic was permitted to claim the right to a contemplative life for herself. Dignity and high reputation characterized the small group around Rābiʿa, as well as other such women. Aided by their memory, which could be

131 A. Schimmel translates the Arabic poem quoted by Jāmī (*Dimensions*, p. 620).

132 Sayf al-Dawla of Aleppo; cf. *Dīwān Abī ṭ-Ṭayyib al-Mutanabbī*, ed. Friedrich Dieterici, Berlin 1861, p. 393; cf. A.J. Arberry, *Poems of al-Mutanabbi: a Selection with introduction*. ʿĀbidī, Jāmī's editor, refers to the passage on p. 926 of his edition.

well developed or even excellently trained,[133] women were transmitters of Traditions from the Prophet. They held their own gatherings that were called *ṣuḥbat* and *majlis*, and they participated in mixed gathering of others. Like men, they gave lectures to do with mystical experiences; they uttered wise sayings, proclaimed rules to follow in life, they learned much poetry and also formulated much in verse themselves, spoke and sang. It was an advantage for women of the Rābiʿa period that the men of early Islam also had an actual aversion to writing, that generally speaking oral performance was given preference and learning Traditions by heart was more highly valued than writing them down.[134] All in all, the time span that I refer to as the Rābiʿa period, i.e. the period before the mystical brotherhoods, by means of its ascetic culture offered women an alternative so that, in small circles of like-minded persons, if needs be as unmarried female outsiders, they could exercise control over their life themselves. Apparently, these women did not feel hindered from practising solidarity among themselves, whereas the early male ascetics, with their strict renunciation and their supererogatory pious actions, anxiously had their own individual salvation in mind.[135] And the duty to undertake the pilgrimage to Mecca offered an opportunity to travel, overland or on the sea, not only for free men but for free women as well, if they had the financial means to do so. Well-off women[136] took the opportunity to visit the holy sites of Mecca and Medina, several times if it was possible, and might reside there for a period of time.[137] This was the era during which the male theologians developed the doctrinal systems of Islam.

---

133 Adam Mez supposes that around 912 "women put forward claims to higher professions. ...There were female theologians whose lectures were eagerly attended and female preachers. Karīma in Mecca was famous; she had succeeded in learning the whole of Bukhâri's *Sahih* in five days." Mez, *Renaissance*, p. 343.

134 Michael Cook, "The Opponents of the Writing of Tradition in Early Islam", *Arabica* XLIV (1997), pp. 438-530.

135 Schimmel, *Dimensionen*, p. 324.

136 Holy men could accomplish the pilgrimage on behalf of women, persons with no means, and the sick.

137 Pious "longer-term residence" also had its drawbacks; cf. Fritz Meier, "Zum Vorrang des Glaubens und des guten Denkens vor dem Wahrheitseifer bei den Muslimen", *Oriens* 32 (1990), pp. 28-29/"The Priority of Faith and Thinking Well of Others over a Concern for Truth among Muslims", *Fritz Meier. Essays on Islamic Piety and Mysticism.* Translated by John O'Kane, Leiden 1999, p. 622.

IX The Post-Rābiʿa Period

The time from the 11th century is known as the phase of the rise of the mystical brotherhoods, the institutionalization of mysticism as Sufism. At that time the shift began from the "master of instruction" of the early period to the "master of training", indeed to the master of spiritual exercises who also had the power to apply punishment.[138] With the establishment of the first "rules of orders" for male mystics, the Sufis or dervishes, a change becomes apparent affecting the autonomous religious life of asceticism of women mystics. In order to draw close to the overriding goal in male communities, the breaking and taming of the lower soul (the *nafs*), rules of behavior were worked out[139] which had as their first premise the exclusion of women from liturgical gatherings or from "retreats" (withdrawals in seclusion) of the male dervishes. "Man", that is to say the young mystic, "must renounce the world, should not possess anything and must know the prescriptions of God... Then he must be permanently in a state of ritual purity with regard to his person and his clothing."[140] One of the three things which posed a danger for the Sufi was contact with women.[141] The sexuality of women was a danger but marital relations with them were recommended.[142] The early mystic Hujwīrī discusses the pros and cons of marriage; he is inclined toward celibacy which he feels Sufism is actually based upon. For him the introduction of marriage, from a man's perspective, is an adverse development; after all, it is unimaginable that a Sufi would find a wife who did not cause him distraction.[143]

At least as drastic was the change from the perspective of women with a mystical temperament, i.e. those with charismatic gifts. They necessarily had to come into conflict with the masters who offered training for men, a conflict for which there were only two solutions: either a female attitude of refusal with all the risks it entailed or acceptance of marriage. There are still some sporadic reports from the post-Rābiʿa period concerning the first solution: a female preacher of penitence in Baghdad, Maymūna bint Sakūla (died 1002) "with a sweet tongue for preaching" was an ascetic and once said: "As of today I have

138 Meier, "Qušayrī", pp. 2-3/*Essays*, O'Kane, pp. 94-95.

139 Schimmel, *Dimensionen*, p. 330.

140 Meier, "Qušayrī", p. 29/*Essays*, O'Kane, p. 122.

141 Cf. Monika Gronke, *Derwische im Vorhof der Macht*, Stuttgart 1993, p. 95, ftn. 169, with earlier literature (the other two things were sitting with people of a different nature and keeping company with young men).

142 A relevant *ḥadīth* is examined by Malti-Douglas, *Woman's Body*, pp. 52-53.

143 Reynold A. Nicholson, *The Kashf al-Maḥjúb. The oldest Persian Treatise on Súfism, by ... al-Hujwírí*, Leiden-London 1911, p. 361. Cf. Elias, "Female and Feminine", pp. 214-15.

worn this robe of mine for forty-seven years without it ever becoming torn; moreover, it was my mother who spun it for me. A dress in which no sin is committed against God never tears."[144] Women of the lowest social classes, and Rābiʿa was among their number, had borne themselves, for all their asceticism, with a certain easy informality in the sense that they were "visible" and "audible". Women of better-off families were denied this kind of informality. A woman belonged in the house. Street, market and fountain belonged to the lower orders, to work, trade and business, i.e. to men. Free women visiting the marketplace were taken as a sign of decline in moral standards, indeed as a portent signaling the end of the world. Cemeteries and shrines were frequented in order to pray for children,[145] and the weekly visit to the bath was another recognized outing for free women who could pass time there and exchange news.[146]

Thus at a time when Christian female mysticism was nearing its heyday,[147] in the Islamic world a shift took place that was unfavorable to women. A certain religious behavior and lived experience, namely that of a pragmatic mysticism that had been experienced and developed early on in the domain of women, was taken up in the domain of the male dervish orders which in principle however would not, it must be repeated, admit any women. Within the framework of our essay we wish to call this span of time, from the 11th century on, the post-Rābiʿa period.

After the strictest ascetic practices in their youth, shaykhs[148] married, and so female participation in mysticism could come about because a woman was the daughter, mother or spouse of a mystic. Such individual cases, as we have seen, had already occurred in the Rābiʿa period but in the age that followed this acquired a more exemplary character. A good example for the early post-Rābiʿa period is once again a Fāṭima (d.1087), once again from Nishapur. She was the daughter of the mystic teacher Abū ʿAlī al-Daqqāq (d. 1015) and married his disciple, the famous Khorasanian theologian and mystic al-Qushayrī (986-1072) with whom she resided in Nishapur.[149] "She was renowned for her piety

144 Mez, *Renaissance*, p. 320, from Ibn Taghrībirdī.

145 Schimmel, *Dimensionen*, pp. 339 and 345.

146 H. Gr[otzfeld], "Bad", in Kreiser/Wielandt, *Lexikon der Islamischen Welt.*

147 Cf. Donald Weinstein and Rudolph M. Bell, *Saints & Society. The Two Worlds of Western Christendom, 1000-1700*, Chicago 1982, pp. 220-22; in their view the era of female saints began in the 13th century; the percentage of women remained high into the 14th and 15th centuries and then dropped off sharply in the 16th century.

148 ʿAbd al-Qādir Gīlānī (1088-1166), the strict preacher and prototype of sanctity, had forty-nine sons; cf. Schimmel, *Dimensionen*, pp. 350-51.

149 Heinz Halm, "al-Ḳushayrī", *EI*² V (1986), p. 526.

and learning; she was also a highly esteemed transmitter of Traditions from the Prophet."[150] Her husband al-Qushayrī was one of the shaykhs of training. As such, he addressed himself in his Sufi text-book and the short specialized work attributed to him, *Gradation in Travelling on the Path to God,* exclusively to male novices, young mystics, young brethren and students. Whether his wife actively participated in mysticism is not known. He left behind, it is said, six sons and "several daughters" (all by his wife Fāṭima?). It is characteristic for the reports about the post-Rābiʿa period in *The Breaths of Intimacy* that the women mentioned are, for the most part, not mystics. Moreover, the section of the book that covers this period is considerably shorter than the one dealing with the Rābiʿa period and contains incidents, not *vitae*; not twenty-seven but seven women, of whom three remain unnamed and three are female slaves. As an example of such incidents, let us mention that of an unnamed "wise" lady who filled the provision containers of an impoverished landowner. Free women appear as relatives of Sufis: on hand are an aunt of the celebrated Shaykh ʿAbd al-Qādir Gīlānī and the unnamed sister of a preacher. The only striking personality is an elderly woman of dazzling beauty, Fāṭima bint al-Muthannā of Cordova with whom Ibn al-ʿArabī studied and about whom he writes lovingly and with admiration, in contrast to Tirmidhī, whose writing he comments on.[151] Referring to her as "mother", an unnamed woman turns to her for help. The woman's husband has set out from the city on his way to marry an additional wife. This Fāṭima has the capacity to make the first surah of the Koran, the *Fātiḥa,* move like an object by her spiritual power (telekinesis). She sends the *Fātiḥa* after the husband, he is literally obstructed and gives up his intention of marrying a second wife.[152]

Occasionally the sisters of a shaykh go with him on the pilgrimage to Mecca; someone is mentioned as having a son-in-law and so must have a daughter, but no names are given. The use of "non-Arabic" became more common and gradually came to be justified with a clearer conscience. "Behind the curtain" women in the post-Rābiʿa period, the time of the dervish orders, could teach sacred Traditions.[153] They could learn from men with whom they were permitted to have contact and, if the situation were to arise, transmit to them their own mystical experiences (dreams, visions). The path of this kind of study and

---

150 Schimmel, *Dimensionen*, p. 605.

151 Radtke, "Autobiografie", p. 265, draws attention to the contrast between Ibn al-ʿArabī and Tirmidhī as far as the prominence given to the role of women, with a reference to Schimmel, *Dimensionen*, pp. 611 f.

152 Cf. also Elias, "Female and Feminine", pp. 215-16.

153 Malti-Douglas, *Woman's Body*, p. 33.

teaching, even if it was merely oral, could only be pursued by women from the social classes for whom manual work was not a constraint and who enjoyed sufficient leisure. Daughters and granddaughters of religious scholars could acquire forms of knowledge that were based on memory and oral transmission. A systematic theological education in the theological colleges (*madrasa*),[154] which were first founded in Khorasan, then in Baghdad and later in other Islamic lands, in Turkish Anatolia and Istanbul, was of course closed to women. In Mecca resided both male and female religious scholars and mystics. A young woman of Mecca, whose ancestors had migrated there from Persia in the early days of Islam, in 1201/02 met "the Greatest Shaykh" Ibn al-ʿArabī who fell in love with her and years later, in memory of this love, wrote a poem to which he then added a mystical commentary.[155] He praised her for her erudition and her literary talent.

What was written in Arabic enjoyed greater prestige than a work in "the popular vernaculars" Persian (as with Tirmidhī's wife) and Turkish. The non-Arabic speaking female mystics, as was only natural, expressed themselves chiefly in their own language. A certain learned Arabic-speaking woman had all sorts of advantages – she does not appear in *The Breaths of Intimacy* – namely the highly educated Egyptian Umm Hāniʾ, who taught Traditions, visited Mecca thirteen times and each time continued her studies there.[156] Her activity does not seem to have resulted in written works. The fact that she wept when hearing the names of God and the Prophet, that she fasted and prayed during the night, connects her with the women of the previous age. She was only a little older than Jāmī who, as we have mentioned, writes significantly less about the period of organized Sufism than about the first ascetic, individualistic period; this is true with regard to men as well as women. Ibn al-ʿArabī's female teacher is an exception; otherwise no women mystics who act with autonomy any longer appear in *The Breaths of Intimacy*.

Again, shaykhs married and were intermarried and interrrelated with one another and with the secular authorities. This means that daughters were offered in marriage. Already the old mystic Dārānī had been married but he

154 Gail Minault, "Women's Education: Better Women and Better Muslims", in Nicole Grandin and Marc Gaborieau (eds.), *Madrasa. La Transmission du savoir dans le monde musulman*, Paris 1997, pp. 158-67, is not available to me.

155 Reynold A. Nicholson, *The Tarjumán al-Ashwáq, A Collection of Mystical Odes by Muḥyiddín Ibn al-ʿArabí*, London 1911; cf. Schimmel, *Dimensionen*, p. 376; Elias, "Female and Feminine", p. 215.

156 Musallam, "Ordnung muslimischer Gesellschaften", pp. 210-18, cites many female religious scholars, chiefly experts on *ḥadīth*, in Mamluk Egypt and Syria whose lives were recorded by al-Sakhāwī.

emphasized that the last thing he intended was "to seek security in a woman", and that he also did not want children; they were good for nothing...[157] In the same way, Jalāl al-Dīn Rūmī's father, Bahā'-i Walad (he wrote circa 1206-10), felt that his own being married posed a dilemma between concern for his children and concern for his inner religious life. His wives – he was married to several women – experienced sensual feelings for Bahā' who attached a religious, even a mystical, component to the sexual act and gave expression to his sense of well-being among his wives.[158] Shaykh Ibrāhīm Zāhid Gīlānī (d. 1301) had two wives; he married a fourteen-year-old.[159]

The old hostile view of the mystics toward everything feminine was maintained. A woman was the cause of the first calamity which befell Adam in Paradise,[160] as well as the first conflict on earth (between Cain and Abel).[161] Now misogynous remarks of the mystics were directed against "the abominable wives".[162] Married life with them was endured, as it were, as a sort of ascetic struggle.

x Turkish and Mongol Women

Looked at from the standpoint of women, the post-Rābiʿa period falls into two phases, the first of which extends from roughly the year one thousand up to the Mongol invasion. The second phase began in Iran from 1221, when Mongol and

157 Gramlich, "Dārānī". Ḥātim al-Aṣamm (d. 851-52), one of the early Sufis, had four wives and nine children; putting his trust in God, he showed no concern for his daily sustenance; cf. Gramlich, *Alte Vorbilder des Sufitums*, p. 65.

158 Fritz Meier, *Bahā'-i Walad. Grundzüge seines lebens und seiner Mystik*, Leiden 1989, pp. 19, 50, 251, 346-47, 350, 355; Aflākī, who began writing in 1318, informs us about Mawlānā's family life in Konya, including the treatment of slaves and favorite foods; cf. O'Kane, *Feats of the Knowers of God (Manāqeb al-ʿārefīn)*, pp. 279-80.

159 Gronke, *Derwische*, p. 250.

160 In the Koran Eve shares the guilt with Adam; later she receives the blame: Malti-Douglas, *Woman's Body*, pp. 45-46 and 91.

161 Reynold A. Nicholson, *The Kashf al-Maḥjúb. The oldest Persian Treatise on Súfism, by...al-Hujwírí*, Leiden-London 1911, p. 364.

162 Schimmel, *Dimensionen*, p. 606, mentions "a saucy, ill-bred or all too garrulous wife". Heinz Halm recounts in *Der Islam, Lesebuch*, p. 58: "A pious religious scholar, married to a woman who is a real hell-cat, conceives of his lot as a trial; when she bickers with him because he spent the night with a serving girl, a slave, his students advise him to divorce and even volunteer to take it upon themselves to pay back the dowry. But he rejects this easy solution out of sheer altruism because he fears 'some other Muslim could be punished with her'."

Turkish women, under pressure of large-scale migrations caused by war, entered the stage. The history of the great upheaval which brought with it the integration of these women into the culture of both Sunnī- and Shīʿite-oriented Islam, still remains to be written. Tribal women who enjoyed considerable freedom, did not wear the veil and were often good horsewomen,[163] had to get accustomed to the constraints to which Islamic law and practice subjected them.[164] The position of women among the Mongols was infinitely freer than among the Arabs, with far less separation of the sexes. The fact that tribal women danced along with men during the mystical "hearing" (*samāʿ*) appeared to conservative Muslim men to be the summit of "licentiousness" (*ibāḥa*). The conflict these women found themselves in is only known to us from Muslim sources which were written, naturally, by men. These authors stood aghast before "an ungodly way of life, unrestrained by Islamic religious law", a world which "was full of heretical innovation".[165] Even after the secular rulers had long since become Muslims,[166] Shaykh Ṣafī from Ardabil (d. 1334; the Sunnī founder of the the Ṣafawiyya dervish order) saw himself surrounded by just such "a decline in moral standards that was spreading throughout the country". He was never satisfied in his passionate fight against all the freedoms of the immigrant Mongol and Turkish women. Against their "carryings-on" he upheld a strict separation of the sexes in the name of Islam and, with a downright apprehensive scrupulousness, he kept women at bay, except for his own wives. Even the first lady of Persia had to put up with humiliating treatment at his hands. Baghdād Khātūn[167] bore the title "Female Sovereign" (Khudāvandigār) and was the daughter of a high-ranking emir and from 1327 to 1335 she was married in her second marriage with the ruler Abū Saʿīd. When she accompanied her husband and his vizier on a visit to Shaykh Ṣafī in Ardabil, with her spouse's consent she entered the room where Shaykh Ṣafī was seated with important male guests during a banquet. The shaykh changed his seat so he could turn his back toward her. When the ruler asked him to fulfill her wish and provide her with a morsel to eat, he had no choice in the matter but he offered

163 N. Tomiche, "al-Marʾa. 1. In the Arab world", *EI* VI (1991), pp. 466-72; J. Chelhod, "al-Marʾa 2. The Arab woman in customary law and practice", *EI*² VI (1991), pp. 472-85.

164 B. Spuler, *Die Mongolen in Iran. Politik, Verwaltung und Kultur der Ilchanzeit 1220-1320*, 3rd revised edition, Berlin 1968, p. 395; A.K.S. Lambton, "al-Marʾa. 3. In Persia. a. Before 1900", *EI*² VI (1991), pp. 481-85.

165 Gronke, *Derwische*, pp. 82-83, 126 f., 258.

166 On the entry of the Īlkhāns into Islam, its Sunnī and Shīʿite forms as well as mysticism, cf. Tilman Nagel, *Timur der Eroberer und die islamische Welt des späten Mittelalters*, München 1993, pp. 70-87.

167 R.M. Savory, "Baghdād Khātūn", *EI*² I (1960), pp. 980 f.

the morsel with his left (impure) hand behind his back to be passed on to Baghdād Khātūn. Asked to explain his offensive behavior, he declared that God had forbidden looking at the wife (of another man).[168] The daughter of the Īlkhān Gaykhātū, whose name was Qutluġ Mulk (d. 1338), was said to have attached herself to Shaykh Ṣafī as a disciple. What is interesting for us is that she is supposed to have experienced visions which she informed him of by letter.[169] The shaykh and his sons personified a new power: an intelligent male dervishdom oriented toward politics which, released from asceticism and spiritual reveries, lived for the here and now[170] and, in the midst of power and honor, sought its happiness in possessions and the accumulation of goods of this world, estates and properties.[171] This dervishdom devoted itself energetically to imposing discipline on all the women who were still "free-wheeling" and roaming about. A young woman who had laughed at Shaykh Ṣafī became incurably ill; once they learned about the cause, i.e. her laughter, people gave up looking after her.[172]

In principle, the presence of women was unwelcome in the dervish orders; at most their participation was tolerated as disciples. Allowing them to join in gatherings was viewed as criminal heresy, in milder cases as breaches of etiquette which aided and abetted *fitna*. *Fitna*, signifying revolt, turmoil and agitation, found its embodiment in young women and beardless youths. That is what Lāmiʿī means when, by way of criticizing the Bektashīs, he says: They "have thrown off the yoke of Islamic law from their necks and were grazing in the meadow of lawlessness."[173] None the less, female membership in this controversial group has been maintained up to the present day. And the Khalwatiyya also admitted women. Lāmiʿī remonstrates with them gently in *The Breaths of Intimacy* with some reservation, though his position is clear: "Nowadays the Khalwatiyya is criticized; it is condemned in view of its faults. This is impolite and smacks of fanaticism, and the rejection of the path of the

168 Hanna Sohrweide, "Der Sieg der Safaviden in Persien und seine Rückwirkungen auf die Schiiten Anatoliens im 16. Jahrhundert", *Der Islam* 41 (1965), p. 108. For her part, the princess tested the shaykh by sending him two young women dressed as men; Gronke, *Derwische*, p. 133.

169 Gronke, *Derwische*, p. 126.

170 Monika Gronke refers to Shaykh Ṣafī, with his considerable wealth and worldly-oriented activity, as the embodiment of an ideal Muslim and an "exemplary ascetic": Gronke, *Derwische*, pp. 258, 259, 261, 269. His son followed in his father's footsteps, ibid. p. 270.

171 Gronke, *Derwische*, pp. 139, 150, 152, 214 f., 217, 276. On other shaykhs who were pious landowners, cf. Schimmel, *Dimensionen*, p. 336.

172 Gronke, *Derwische*, p. 86.

173 Cf. my "Glimpses", no. 20 in this volume.

shaykhs provokes the wrath of God... It should be said that 'in our time cases of changing from one order to another and falsifying ascetic exercises has increased'. For in order to attract more disciples they have had recourse to admitting women and boys. They allow women to participate in their 'spiritual retreats' and bring youths to their gatherings."[174]

Again, women joined the extreme Shīʿite Qızılbaş-Ṣafawiyya developed by Shaykh Junayd.[175] The manner of their daily life and experience – in part they still belonged to nomadic tribes – seriously clashed with Muslim tradition, was an "innovation" and, as such, so contrary to the moral concepts of Sunnī Muslims that it provoked the most severe countermeasures. That women got together in the evening with men to perform ceremonies caused the Ottoman authorities to harbor the worst suspicions and to mete out dreadful punishments. In the background loomed the Ottoman ruler's wariness with regard to pretenders to the throne, as well as false prophets who called themselves the Mahdī and gathered around them peasants and nomads. Finally, it scarcely needs to be pointed out that during the suppression of the revolt of Badr al-Dīn and Börklüce masses of women were killed. As was the case with their men, women too were spied upon. They were banned and declared outlaws.[176]

Despite all this, were there women in the post-Rābiʿa period who remained unmarried in order to devote themselves to mysticism? Did childless women hold gatherings? Apparently yes, otherwise Taqī al-Dīn al-Ḥiṣnī (1351-1426), an adversary of celibacy among men, would not have reproached women "for having chosen a celibate life for their own comfort and convenience. They were incited to this by Satan who spoke to such women as follows: 'You are a pious woman who is occupied with God and if you do not marry, then you will be free from the business of children; you can go out of the house, your possessions will steadily increase, and your worshipping God will be your livelihood.'" And this sort of woman, adds the author, then also receives further "help from other women worshippers of God who have been corrupted by Satan".[177] This undisguised disapproval certainly refers to women like those who "in the late Middle Ages were able to come together 'in convents' in order to pursue the mystic path or generally speaking to lead a religious life".[178] On the other hand,

174 On the admission of female novices into a branch of the later Khalwatiyya, cf. Bernd Radtke, Seán O'Fahey and John O'Kane, "Two Sufi Treatises of Aḥmad ibn Idrīs", *Oriens* 35 (1996), p. 155.

175 Sohrweide, "Sieg", pp. 189-90, as well as p. 107, ftn. 77; Gronke, *Derwische*, p. 258.

176 Sohrweide, "Sieg", pp. 122, 148, 165, 187.

177 Quoted in Margaret Smith, *Rābiʿa the Mystic*, Cambridge 1928.

178 Schimmel, *Dimensionen*, p. 615.

it is difficult to imagine that an abandoned "convent" in which outcast women "could remain until they found the opportunity to remarry" would have been a place of female mysticism rather than merely an emergency accommodation.

For the late Middle Ages, when the great period of female mysticism in the Christian world had already waned, in Egypt "convents" for Muslim women with abbesses called *shaykha* are mentioned. However, a great deal more philological research regarding women's "participation"[179] would be required before one could determine whether there had been a female mystical current comparable to Christian mysticism in the High Middle Ages, distinguished by its own way of life, an intense religiosity and an accumulation of charismatic experiences.[180] In our chief hagiographical source, *The Breaths of Intimacy*, there is scarcely any such evidence to be detected for the post-Rābiʿa period. The tendencies which excluded women prevailed into the time when our authors Jāmī and Lāmiʿī lived, i.e. into the fifteenth and sixteenth centuries.

Granted that women endowed with religious zeal may have been active in provisional lodgings – Zaytūna, an elderly female mystic lived in the ruins of a Christian monastery; the unmarried Tunisian holy woman, ʿĀʾisha al-Manūbiyya, settled into a caravanserai which the religious scholars did not approve of – we read nothing about spiritual work by women living in communally shared premises which is what the Christian convents were.

Certainly, from the earliest age a Muslim girl learned to treat the Koran with reverence. Free women, who remained at home under strict control, could learn to read. And well-off women were active as benefactresses of Sufis, in particular after the establishment of hospices of the dervish orders.[181] However, in order not to give rise to *fitna*, which ran counter to the spiritual calling of men, no woman was allowed to enter their domain, for instance to do washing for the dervishes, to cook or to invite them home for dinner. On the other hand, if this did happen, the women had to be of an advanced age, such as they are described in many of the *vitae*. Young female slaves were brought up as Muslims. Far from their homes and their people, they had to unlearn their own language and customs. They then had to learn – which could take years – the idioms of the women and men of their new surroundings, i.e. Turkish, in the Ottoman Empire; there as well, in the fifteenth and sixteenth centuries,

179 Peter Dinzelbacher, "Rollenverweigerung, religiöser Aufbruch und mystisches Erleben mittelalterlicher Frauen", in Peter Dinzelbacher and Dieter R. Bauer (eds.), *Religiöse Frauenbewegung und mystische Frömmigkeit im Mittelalter*, Köln-Wien 1988, pp. 1.58.

180 Dinzelbacher, *Mittelalterliche Frauenmystik*, p. 31.

181 Schimmel, *Dimensionen*, p. 616.

musical female slaves were still trained in singing, recitation and playing instruments.[182]

Slave women who were concubines were perceived as a threat by married women. "Women", according to the Ottoman author ʿĀlī in the sixteenth century, "are dominated by fleshly lusts because of their nature...they sit their whole life long locked up like in a prison and cannot take part in soldiering or carry out administrative tasks, they face great risks in childbirth... The greatest fault of a woman is that she does not tolerate other wives or female slaves around her, even though this is allowed by religious law."[183]

XI Enslavement

As an eye-witness for the transition of free women into a state of slavery as a result of war, let us cite Hans Dernschwam (1494-before 1568), a widely travelled man, who acted as a representative of Anton Fugger (1493-1560). In the spring of 1553, Dernschwam, who was almost sixty, with three horses and a coachman at his own expense joined the embassy of King Ferdinand I to the Ottoman court, followed the legation which under Ogier Ghislen van Busbecq (1522-92)[184] went on to the Anatolian city of Amasya, and then returned with them by the same route to Vienna where they arrived on the 11th of August 1555. On the way back from Amasya to Vienna, he travelled through Bulgaria in July 1555 and noted:

> (How female slaves were being transported along with good-looking boys): "We encountered Turks with captured Hungarian people, women, children and good-looking boys..."[185]

182 Yvonne J. Seng, "Fugitives and Factotums: Slaves in Early Sixteenth-Century İstanbul", *JESHO* 39 (1996), pp. 136-69; and cf. Ch. Pellat, "Ḳayna", *EI*² IV (1978), p. 822: "The *ḳiyān*, far away from their native land, express their nostalgia."

183 Jan Schmidt, "Muṣṭafā ʿĀlī van Gallipoli, een Ottomaans historicus over zijn eigen tijd", *MOI Publicatie* 12, Nijmegen 1984, p. 73.

184 Z.R.W.M. von Martels, *Augerius Gislenius Busbequius. Leven en werk van de keizerlijke gezant aan het hof van Süleyman de Grote*, Groningen 1989.

185 Babinger, Franz (ed.), *Hans Dernschwam's Tagebuch einer Reise nach Konstantinopel und Kleinasien (1553/55)*, München and Leipzig 1923.

XII Selīme

As much as the Turkish mystic Lāmiʿī admired his Persian model Jāmī, being a man of letters he independently shaped the *vitae* of the Anatolian mystics and added several. Remarkably, he also expanded what had become the canonical repertoire of thirty-four pious women, which came to a close in the 13th century, by adding a female contemporary with whose presentation he concluded his work on *The Breaths of Intimacy*. The text which he devotes to Selīme, a singular female mystic, is as follows in translation: Selīme, God sanctify her secret. Ḫvāca Muḥammad Qāsim, who was the great-grandson of the venerable Ḫvāca ʿUbaydullāh Samarqandī, God sanctify his secret, related: "I purchased a seven-year-old slave girl together with her mother. The girl's name was Selīme. From the time of her childhood she experienced spiritual inspirations. She was with me for about seven years. I never once observed that religious indifference came over her, not even for the space of a single breath. Most of the time she wept. People accused her of being insane. And she was bound to me in a perfect bond and didn't hide her state from me. And when I conversed with someone outside, she would recount all of it and reported the very words that had been exchanged. And she was continually engaged in struggle [against the lower self]. If I wanted to know something, I would ask her about it while she was asleep. She would give a detailed answer. None the less, she would go on sleeping in this state and when she woke up, she would excuse herself, saying: 'Oh master, you know my madness and still you sit by me so often!' One day I wanted to set her free. She refused, beseeching me earnestly. I said: 'I want to marry you!' She said: 'Do not cast me under a veil of separation out of love and kindness.' I asked: 'How could you fall under a veil of separation?' She replied: 'I have a perfect love of you in God, and not for the space of a breath is this love separated from me. From the moment you set me free, you would become a stranger for me and someone I'm not allowed to have contact with. And if suddenly you would marry me, at that moment my love would become love for someone I'm not allowed to have contact with, and I would fall into separation from God.' One day she came out of the bathhouse. I saw that she was weeping profusely and I asked: 'What's the matter with you?', and I pressed her, saying: 'Answer me!' She said: 'Today there was a large crowd of people in the bathhouse. As often as I looked, at no moment did I see that anyone was with God. I saw them all as prisoners of religious indifference. That's why I'm crying.' She died when she was fourteen years old. God sanctify her secret!"

Selīme's place of origin is unknown. A woman could become a slave by being descended from slaves or as a non-Muslim who is not covered by a treaty of protection and is taken prisoner in war. That she belonged in the second category is more likely during that time of great Ottoman conquests. The slave markets after victory registered unprecedented records of sales along with a corresponding drop in prices. I will only mention the example of the conquest of Negroponte (Euboea, Agriboz), where in 1470 such an amount of booty was conquered in the way of "speaking property (*māl nāṭiq*)" and "dumb property (*māl ṣāmit*)", girls and boys, that it was like an ocean.[186] Before the seven-year-old was purchased by the high-ranking Naqshbandī Qāsim[187] along with her mother,[188] she had therefore already experienced war, capture and several changes of place. That the battlefield or the conquered fortress after the fighting had stopped could be a place of orgiastic ecstasy, is reported by the Ottoman chronicles in euphemistic language.[189] The adolescent Selīme strikes us as being an over-excited, abused child. Her hearing is hypersensitive.[190] She has an attachment to her master who in a friendly way, in the style of the old Sufi masters, makes use of her *firāsa*, her gifts of clairvoyance or telepathy. She tries to maintain this intimacy. When he informs her that he wants to set her free, she protests in tears.[191] Presumably she lived in Bursa, Lāmiʿī's city. She was lucky: in another household or in a silk factory her ultimate consolation, her preoccupation with God, would most likely have been denied her. She fulfills

186 M. Tulum (ed.), *Tursun Bey. Târîh-i Ebü l-Feth*, Istanbul 1977, p. 148; H. İnalcık and Rhoads Murphey, *The History of Mehmed the Conqueror by Tursun Beg*, Minneapolis & Chicago 1978 (photomechanical edition with "summary translation"), p. 58; and cf. M. Plessner, "Māl", *EI* VI (1991), p. 205.

187 Ḫvāca Muḥammad Qāsim, to whom Lāmiʿī spoke, was a great-grandson of ʿUbaydullāh Aḥrār (d. 1490) who ruled in Samarqand since 1457; Qāsim's father ʿAbd al-Hādī had settled in Ottoman territory.

188 In the 19th century when female slaves were imported from the Caucasus, "those who had children...were bought as wet-nurses with their child. Their child was then given for money to another wet-nurse and raised [by her]. It was then considered...to be a foster-sister [of the child of the master and mistress]. A foster-child of this kind had privileges and a [higher] position. Although it was a slave, there was virtually no one who would think of selling it"; Börte Sagaster, *Im Harem von Istanbul. Osmanisch-türkische Frauenkultur im 19. Jahrhundert*, Rissen 1989, p. 156; and cf. J. Chelhod, "Raḍāʿ. 2. In Arabian society", in *EI*² VIII (1995), p. 362.

189 Dealt with here in no. 26.

190 On 5 January 1996, Susanne Meyer reported in the weekly *Die Zeit* about child victims of the war in the former Yugoslavia. A girl who had experienced a "selection" in Vukovar suffered from anxious states, wept continually and was frightened by voices in her head.

191 A master can take his female slave as a concubine but only marries her after having set her free. A slave woman who bears a child to her master – the child is free – can no longer be sold or transferred and is set free at the death of her master.

the duty of ritual purity by visiting the bathhouse. But in this place of female relaxation she is unable to endure because what she hears there, talk and perhaps laughter, is religious indifference; she cannot support it and comes back in tears. She suffers under the sins of "the world", of other people, and breaks down her body through continual fasting, sleeplessness and prayer. She does not join those who had been set free like Rābiʿa al-ʿAdawiyya who went on living, or like Tuḥfa who perished as a free woman. It meant little to her to be "accused" of insanity. Because she would lose the privileges of her "madness" and of her position as a slave by being set free, she renounces the elevation in status. She dies at the age of fourteen. With her *vita* reported by her owner, thus comes to a close this examination of female participation in Sufism during the post-Rābiʿa period: as wife, daughter, mother, or female slave of a mystic.

XIII Epilogue

The supposition that women enjoyed greater esteem in Islamic mysticism than in non-Sufi circles cannot, generally speaking, be justified on the basis of the sources we have referred to here. Unfortunately, we will probably never be able to approach the Islamic female mystics through such a multitude of texts as we possess in the case of Christian female mysticism.[192] Nevertheless, B. Radtke, through the example of what has been handed down concerning Tirmidhī's wife, has shown how much can be achieved by philological research into sources. It is not easy to remain unmoved by the dreams of this charismatically gifted woman. A search among the collected manuscript materials for letters and for diaries of pious Muslim women still remains to be done (perhaps the visionary letters of Qutluġ Khātūn will be found). When Lāmiʿī's Ottoman contemporary, the unmarried *dīvān*-poetess Mihrī Khātūn (d. 1512), wrote verses defending women, her male colleagues seized the opportunity to resort once again to the old Arabic saying about the feminine sun and the masculine moon.[193] For women who had the capacity to read and write the way was open to keeping a diary. Sufism of the seventeenth century is illuminated by the religious experiences of Asya Khātūn from Skopje (Üsküp) whose dream

192 Dinzelbacher, *Mittelalterliche Frauenmystik*.

193 E.J.W. Gibb, *A History of Ottoman Poetry*, II, London 1902 (reprint 1965), pp. 123-35. On the poetess, see Th. Menzel-E.G. Ambros, "Mihrī Khātūn", *EI* VII (1993), pp. 23-24.

diaries Cemal Kafadar has brought to light and edited.[194] Ottoman women of the nineteenth and twentieth century belonged to mystical orders.[195] With the gradual modernization of society, autonomous voices of women came to be heard along with the voices of the one-sided male worldview. The Ottoman harem moved into a palace furnished in European style, Ottoman harem life was modernized,[196] and slavery came to be a theme treated in literature[197] and was gradually abolished.[198] It was now a question of slowly bringing about change in family structures, methods of education and deep-rooted feelings of self-assessment.[199]

XIV Appendix: Tuḥfa

Translation of the literary version of Tuḥfa's story which ultimately goes back to the Arabic chronicle of Yāfiʿī:[200]

Tuḥfa, God sanctify her secret. Sarī Saqaṭī, God sanctify his secret, related: "One night I couldn't sleep. I felt a strange agitation and restlessness, so much so that I neglected the night-time prayers. After performing the morning prayers, I went outside and walked around everywhere I thought I might shake off my restlessness but it didn't do any good. Finally, I went to the hospital in order to feel fear and penitence at the sight of those in misery. When I entered the hospital, my heart opened and my breast

194 Cemal Kafadar, *Rüya Mektupları. Asiye Hatun. Giriş, çevrimyazı, sadeleştirme*, Istanbul 1994.

195 Elias, "Female and Feminine", p. 222.

196 Börte Sagaster published the memoirs of the Ottoman musician and poetess Leylā Saz (1850-1936) about the Sultan's harem. This was up to the late 1850s the sole institution in the Ottoman Empire in which women received a systematic education. Here newspapers were read and the piano was played: *Im Harem von Istanbul. Osmanisch-türkische Frauenkultur im 19. Jahrhundert*, Rissen 1989.

197 Börte Sagaster, *"Herren" und "Sklaven". Der Wandel im Sklavenbild türkischer Literaten in der Spätzeit des Osmanischen Reiches*, Wiesbaden 1997.

198 Ehud R. Toledano, *The Ottoman Slave Trade and its Suppression: 1840-1890*, Princeton (New Jersey) 1982.

199 Ruth Klüger, *Frauen lesen anders*, München 1996, p. 229.

200 ʿAbdullāh b. Asʿad al-Yāfiʿī, *Rawḍ al-rayāḥīn fī ḥikāyāt al-ṣāliḥīn*, Cairo, no date; the Persian translation of Hishmat Muʾayyad, edited by Darvīsh ʿAlī Buzjānī, *Rawḍat al-riyāḥīn*, Teheran 1365/1986, is not available to me. Virginia Vacca has translated some selections from the *Rawḍ al-rayāḥīn, Abdallàh al-Yàfi'i. Il Giardino dei fiori Odorosi. Racconti scelti*, Rome 1965; cf. J.G. Gerbranda, "De bespreking van mysticae bij Lāmiʿī en Cāmī", M.A. thesis, Leiden University, August 1997.

expanded.[201] Suddenly, I saw a female slave, especially fresh and pure, and wearing splendid clothes. From her a marvelous scent wafted over me. She had a beautiful appearance and was of delightful beauty. Her hands and feet were in chains. When she saw me, her eyes filled with tears, and she sang a series of verses. I asked the director of the hospital who this was. He said: 'It's a slave girl who has gone mad. Her master put her in chains [and brought her here] so she would get better.' When she heard the director of the hospital speak this way, she emitted a sob from her throat; then she began to sing these verses (Arabic):

'You people, I am not possessed but
I am intoxicated, while my heart remains sober.
You've chained my hands, though I've done no misdeed
other than that I strive for His love and openly admit it.
I am snared in love of a beloved
whose gate I don't wish to depart from.
People, what you call my saintliness is my ruin,
and what you call my ruin is my saintliness.
Anyone who loves the Lord of lords
and chooses Him, meets with no blame.'

Her utterances caused me pain and plunged me into grief and weeping. When she beheld the tears in my eyes, she said: 'Oh Sarī, you only experience this outburst of tears because you have heard this. But if you were to come to know Him with true knowledge, what your state would be like then!' After that she lost consciousness for a long while. When she returned to her senses, I exclaimed: 'Oh slave!' She said: 'At your service, Sarī!' I asked: 'How do you know who I am?' She said: 'Since I've come to know Him, I've never been left without knowledge.' I said: 'I hear you speak of love. Who is it you love?' She replied: 'I love Him Who has made known to me His favors and has bestowed gifts on us. He is close to souls and hears those who make requests.'

I asked: 'Who locked you up in here?' She said: 'Oh Sarī, the malevolent have given each other assistance.' She then let out such a cry that I thought life was leaving her body. After that she again recited some verses which accorded with her situation. I said to the director of the hospital: 'Release her immediately!' This he did. I said to her: 'Go wherever you wish.' She said: 'Oh Sarī, where should I go? He Who is the beloved of my

201 Cf. Hellmut Ritter, *Das Meer der seele. Mensch, welt und Gott in den geschichten des Farīduddīn ʿAṭṭār*, Leiden 1955, pp. 170 and 229 where Sufis are mentioned who visit the madhouse or hospital to experience penitence by gazing at the sick and all the misery. English translation by John O'Kane: *The Ocean of the Soul. Man, the World and God in the Stories of Farīd al-Dīn ʿAṭṭār*, Leiden-Boston 2003, pp. 176-77 and 239.

heart has made me a slave of one of His slaves. If my owner agrees, I will go, if not, I will endure with patience.' By God, she was smarter than me. Suddenly, her owner entered the hospital. He greeted me and showed me much respect. I said: 'Instead of showing me all this politeness, it would be better to treat this slave woman with respect. What is the reason that you had her locked up?' He replied: 'There are many reasons for it. She has lost her mind. She doesn't eat, doesn't drink, doesn't sleep and won't let me fall asleep. She is given to much reflection and much weeping. And as matters stand, she is everything I own. I spent my whole fortune and purchased her for twenty thousand dirhams. I hoped to make profit from her because she has reached perfection in her art.' I asked what her art was. He said: 'She is a singer.' I asked: 'How long has the illness gone on?' He: 'She's had it for a year.' I: 'How did it begin?' He said: 'She took her lute in her hand and sang these verses:

> "Truly, my whole life long I've broken no vow.
> And after experiencing serenity I've betrayed no love.
> I've filled my flanks and my heart with ecstasy.
> How should I have enjoyment or forget and find peace?
> Oh You, besides Whom I have no master,
> I see that You've left me a slave among the people."

Thereupon she stood up, broke her lute and began to weep. I suspected her of being in love with someone; then it became clear there was no trace of that. I asked her: "Is this how your situation is?" With tormented spirit and faltering tongue, she sang:

> "God spoke to me from within my heart,
> while His warning to me was on my tongue.
> He brought me close to Him after I'd been far away,
> because God chose me and selected me.
> I responded to that to which I was called,
> voluntarily obedient unto Him Who called me.
> I felt fear because of what I'd perpetrated earlier.
> But love arrived and set me free from fear."'

Now I (Sarī) said to the slave girl's owner: 'You should know that I will take upon myself the price for the slave girl – I even want to pay still more.' He cried out: 'Oh you poor man! How can you pay her price? After all, you're a dervish!' I said: 'Don't be hasty. Wait here while I go and fetch the money for her.' Then I went off weeping. By God, I had nothing, not even a fraction of her selling price. I brooded throughout the long night and raised up supplications. I couldn't close my eyes and went on beseeching: 'Oh my Guardian, You know everything about me, what is open and what is hidden. I have placed my trust in Your kindness. Do not bring me to destruction!'

Suddenly, someone knocked at the door. I asked: 'Who is it?' A person replied: 'One of the lovers.' I opened the door and beheld a man with four slaves and he had a wax candle with him. He said: 'Master, may I come in?' I: 'Enter.' Once he was inside, I asked him who he was. He said: 'I am Aḥmad b. Muthannā. This night a heavenly voice called to me in a dream: "Take five purses of gold and deliver them to Sarī and confer on him the joy of purchasing Tuḥfa. For We hold Tuḥfa in special favor." As soon as I heard this, I prostrated myself to offer God thanks for the kindness He had shown me.' Sarī recounts: 'The rest of the night I sat [with the money] and waited for morning. When I had performed the morning prayers, I went out. I took him [Aḥmad b. Muthannā] by the hand and brought him to the hospital. The director was already on the look-out, gazing to the left and right. When he saw me, he said: 'Welcome! Come in. Truly, Tuḥfa enjoys proximity and esteem with God the Sublime. Last night a secret voice called to me (verse): "She has My attention which is not without special favor. She has drawn near and then ascended to all the mystical states."'

When Tuḥfa saw us, her eyes filled with tears. She prayed in a whisper: 'You have made me famous among the people.' At the same moment that we were sitting there, Tuḥfa's owner rushed in weeping. I said: 'Don't weep. I have brought the sum you asked for with an addition of five thousand pieces of silver.' He: 'By God, no!' I: 'With an addition of ten thousand pieces of silver.' He said: 'By God, no!' I said: 'Then with an additional sum amounting to the sum you [originally] paid for her.' He said: 'Even if you gave me the whole world, I wouldn't accept it because Tuḥfa, as God is my witness, is free.' I: 'What does this mean?' He replied: 'Master, last night I was rebuked. Bear witness that I have renounced my entire fortune and taken refuge with God. (Arabic:) My God, be guarantor for my livelihood and be friendly regarding my daily sustenance.' I (Sarī) turned around and looked at Ibn Muthannā. He was also weeping. I asked: 'Why are you weeping?' He said: 'It seems God the Sublime isn't pleased with me concerning that to which he called me. But God the Sublime gave me orders that Tuḥfa should be set free with my wealth. And now my wealth has played no role in setting her free. It seems as if in this matter God isn't pleased with me. Bear witness that I've given my entire wealth as alms in all sincerity.'[202]

I said: 'Amazing! What a great blessing Tuḥfa confers on everyone!'

At that, Tuḥfa stood up. She took off the splendid clothes she was wearing and dressed herself in a robe made entirely from patches sewn together. Weeping, she went outside. I exclaimed: 'God the Sublime has brought about your release. Why then this weeping?' She replied with the following poem:

'I fled away from Him unto Him
and I wept in fear of Him over His absence.

202 Cf. the formula *khāliṣ al-fuʾād* "with pure heart" in Karl Jahn, *Türkische Freilassungserklärungen des 18. Jahrhunderts (1703-1776)*, Naples 1963, pp. 15, 59 and 61.

And by Him I swear He is what I seek,
while I have always been in His presence
so as to acquire and obtain what I hoped with Him.'

Then we went outside, and as much as we looked for Tuḥfa, we couldn't find her. We set out for the Kaʿba. Ibn Muthannā died along the way, and I travelled to Mecca in the company of Tuḥfa's owner. At the time that we were performing the sacred circumambulation, we heard the voice of a wounded person. From an injured heart the person exclaimed (poem):

'Whoever loves God is a sick person in the world
whose illness drags on and whose cure is his illness.
The Protector gives him of His love to drink in a cup
and He quenches his thirst when He gives him to drink.
He is ecstatic in love of Him, ascends to Him
and wishes for no beloved other than Him.
Thus whoever boasts of his love for Him
swoons in love of Him until he beholds Him.'

I went before the wounded person who, upon seeing me, said: 'Oh Sarī!' I said: 'At your service. Who are you – God have mercy on you – ?' She replied: 'There is no god but God! After having once known me, [now] you don't recognize me. I am Tuḥfa.' She had become like a ghost. I said: 'Oh Tuḥfa, what benefit did you get after you chose to be isolated from people?' She said: 'God the Sublime bestowed on me intimacy in His proximity and shyness toward everything other than Him.' 'Ibn Muthannā died on the way here', I said. She said: 'God the Sublime sanctify his secret! God bestowed so many miracles on him such as no eye has ever beheld before. In Paradise he will be my neighbor.' I said: 'Your master who set you free has accompanied me.' She uttered a concealed prayer. Then she collapsed against the Kaʿba and gave up the ghost. When her master came and heard that she had died, he fell down over her. I wept and shook him but saw that he too had given up the ghost.

I looked after their corpses, wrapped them in a shroud and buried them. God the Sublime sanctify their secret!"

Bibliography

I

ʿĀbidī, Maḥmūd (ed.), *Nūr ad-Dīn Jāmī. Nafaḥāt al-uns min ḥaḍarāt al-Ḳuds*, Teheran 1370/1991.

Babinger, Franz (ed.), *Hans Dernschwam's Tagebuch einer Reise nach Konstantinopel und Kleinasien (1553/55)*, München and Leipzig 1923.

Lāmiʿī, *Fütūḥ ül-müdschāhidīn li-tervīḥi l-ḳulūbi l-müšāhidīn* (*Terdscheme-i Nafaḥātü l-üns*), Istanbul 1289/1872.

Radtke, Bernd, „Tirmiḏiana Minora I. Die Autobiografie des Theosophen von Tirmiḏ", *Oriens* 34 (1994), 242-298.

II

Ammann, Ludwig, *Vorbild und Vernunft. Die Regelung von Lachen und Scherzen im mittelalterlichen Islam*, Hildesheim, Zürich, New York 1993.

Bellmann, Dieter (ed. and transl.), *Ibn al-Waššāʾ. Das Buch des buntbestickten Kleides*, 3 Bde., Leipzig and Weimar 1984.

Berkey, Jonathan P., "Circumcision circumscribed: Female excision and cultural accommodation in the Medieval Near East", *IJMES* 28 (1996), 19-38.

Braun, Christina von, "Das Kloster im Kopf. Weibliches Fasten von mittelalterlicher Askese zu moderner Anorexie", in Karin Flaake, Vera King (eds.), *Weibliche Adoleszenz. Zur Sozialisation junger Frauen*, Frankfurt/New York 2. ed. 1993.

Cook, Michael, "The Opponents of the Writing of Tradition in Early Islam", *Arabica* XLIV (1997), 438-530.

Dinzelbacher, Peter, "Rollenverweigerung, religiöser Aufbruch und mystisches Erleben mittelalterlicher Frauen", in Peter Dinzelbacher and Dieter R. Bauer (eds.), *Religiöse Frauenbewegung und mystische Frömmigkeit im Mittelalter*, Köln-Wien 1988, 1-58.

Dinzelbacher, Peter, *Mittelalterliche Frauenmystik*, Paderborn-München-Wien-Zürich 1993.

Elias, Jamal J., "Female and Feminine in Islamic Mysticism", *The Muslim World* 78 (1988), 209-224.

Ende, Werner, "Sollen Frauen schreiben lernen? Eine innerislamische Debatte und ihre Widerspiegelung in Al-Manār", in Dieter Bellmann (ed.), *Gedenkschrift Wolfgang Reuschel. Akten des III. Arabistischen Kolloquiums, Leipzig, 21.-22. November 1991*, Stuttgart 1994.

Gelder, Geert Jan van, "Rābi`a's poem on the two kinds of love: a mystification?", in F. de Jong (ed.), *Verse and the fair sex, a collection of papers presented at the 15th Congress of the UEAI 1990*, Utrecht 1993, 66-76.

Gramlich, Richard, *Alte Vorbilder des Sufitums. Zweiter Teil: Scheiche des Ostens*, Wiesbaden 1996.

Gramlich, Richard, „Abū Sulaymān ad-Dārānī", *Oriens* 33 (1992), 22-85.

Gronke, Monika, *Derwische im Vorhof der Macht. Sozial- und Wirtschaftsgeschichte Nordwestirans im 13. und 14. Jahrhundert*, Stuttgart 1993.

Haarmann, Maria (ed.), *Der Islam. Ein historisches Lesebuch*, München 1992.

Kafadar, Cemal, "Women in Seljuk and Ottoman Society up to the Mid-19th Century, in *9000 Years of the Anatolian Woman, 29 November 1993 – 28 February 1994, Istanbul Topkapı Sarayı Museum*, Istanbul.

Kafadar, Cemal, *Rüya Mektupları. Asiye Hatun. Giriş, çevrimyazı, sadeleştirme*, Istanbul 1994.

Klüger, Ruth, *Weiter leben. Eine Jugend*, Göttingen 1992.

Klüger, Ruth, *Frauen lesen anders*, München 1996.

Kruk, Remke, "Clipped Wings: Medieval Arabic Adaptations of the Amazon Myth", *Harvard Middle Eastern and Islamic Review* I (1994), 132-151.

Kruk, Remke, "Ibn Baṭṭūṭa: Travel, Family Life, and Chronology. How seriously do we take a father?", *al-Qanṭara* XVI (1995), 369-384.

Lawrence, Bruce B., "Honoring women through sexual abstinence. Lessons from the Spiritual Practice of a Pre-Modern South Asian Sufi Master, Shaykh Nizam ad-din Awliya", in M.-E. Subtelny (ed.), *Annemarie Schimmel Festschrift. Journal of Turkish Studies* vol. 18 (1994), pp. 149-161.

Lewis, Bernard, *Race and Slavery in the Middle East. An Historical Enquiry*, New York-Oxford 1990.

Malti-Douglas, Fedwa, *Woman's Body. Woman's Word. Gender and Discourse in Arabo-Islamic Writing*, Princeton, N.J., 1991.

Mansur, Fatma, "Turkish Women in the Ottoman Empire: The Classical Age" in Lois Beck und Nikki Keddie (eds.), *Women in the Muslim World*, Cambridge, Mass., 1978, 229-244.

Meier, Fritz, *Die schöne Mahsatī*, Wiesbaden 1963.

Meier, Fritz, *Bahā'-i Walad. Grundzüge seines lebens und seiner mystik*, Leiden 1989.

Möbius, Helga, „Mutter-Bilder. Die Göttermutter und ihr Sohn", in: Renate Möhrmann, *Verklärt, verkitscht, vergessen. Die Mutter als ästhetische Figur*, Stuttgart–Weimar 1996, 21-38.

Motzki, Harald, „'Dann machte er daraus die beiden Geschlechter'...", in Jochen Martin und Renate Zoepfel (eds.), *Aufgaben, Rollen und Räume von Mann und Frau*, Freiburg and München 1989, 607-641.

Peirce, Leslie P., *The Imperial Harem. Women and Sovereignty in the Ottoman Empire*, New York-Oxford 1993.

Pellat, Charles, *Arabische Geisteswelt. Ausgewählte und übersetzte Texte von al-Ǧāḥiẓ (777-869). Unter Zugrundelegung der arabischen Originaltexte aus dem Französischen übertragen von Walter W. Müller*, Zürich and Stuttgart 1967.

Radtke, Bernd und John O'Kane, *The Concept of Sainthood in Early Islamic Mysticism. Two works by Al-Ḥakīm Al-Tirmidhī. An annotated translation with introduction*, Richmond, Surrey, 1996.

Radtke, Bernd, Seán O'Fahey und John O'Kane, "Two Sufi Treatises of Aḥmad ibn Idrīs", *Oriens* 35 (1996).

Sagaster, Börte, *Im Harem von Istanbul. Osmanisch-türkische Frauenkultur im 19. Jahrhundert*, Rissen 1989.

Sagaster, Börte, *"Herren" und „Sklaven". Der Wandel im Sklavenbild türkischer Literaten in der Spätzeit des Osmanischen Reiches*, Wiesbaden 1997.

Schimmel, Annemarie, *Mystische Dimensionen des Islam. Die Geschichte des Sufismus*, Frankfurt a.M. and Leipzig 1995.

Schimmel, Annemarie, *Meine Seele ist eine Frau. Das Weibliche im Islam*, München 1995.

Schimmel, Annemarie, *Jesus und Maria in der islamischen Mystik*, München 1996.

Seng, Yvonne J., "Fugitives and Factotums: Slaves in Early Sixteenth-Century İstanbul", *JESHO* 39 (1996), 136-169.

Smith, Margaret, *Rabi'a the Mystic*, Cambridge 1928.

Spellberg, D.A., "Writing the Unwritten Life of the Islamic Eve: Menstruation and the Demonization of Motherhood", *IJMES* 28 (August 1996), 305-324.

Toledano, Ehud R., *The Ottoman Slave Trade and its Suppression: 1840-1890*, Princeton (New Jersey) 1982.

Utas, B. (ed.), *Women in Islamic Societies. Social attitudes and historical perspectives*, Kopenhagen 1983, reprint 1988.

Walther, Wiebke, *Die Frau im Islam*, Leipzig 1980, 3rd. revised edition, Leipzig 1997.

Walther, Wiebke, "From Women's Problems to Women as Images in Modern Iraqi Poetry", *Die Welt des Islams* 36 (1996), 237-241.

CHAPTER 28

Goethe and Diez in the year 1790*

Introduction

It is my intention[1] to take a critical look at the early years of our field of study, in particular at Heinrich Friedrich von Diez (1751-1817), one of the men who advised Goethe in matters concerning Turkish literature. By way of preparing the ground, I would like to draw attention to some things that Goethe und Diez, who never actually met, have in common. In the middle section of the present essay I will deal with the experiences of Goethe and Diez in the crucial year 1790. The third section will be devoted to Diez' contribution to Turcology.

I

First some of what they have in common. Goethe as well as Diez was brought up as Protestants. Goethe's Latin teacher in Frankfurt was a Turk.[2] Both were men of the German Enlightenment.[3] Both had studied the works of Baruch Spinoza (1632-1677); in his book on Spinoza Diez attributed the spirit of Christ to "Turks and heathens."[4]

Both men belonged to Freemasonry which was then a new, but already prohibited, phenomenon in Germany.[5] Diez had entered the apprentice grade at

---

* Translated by John O'Kane.

1 Based on a paper read on the opening day of the Fourth Conference of German Turcologists in Hamburg on March 15, 1999. By far the most illuminating account of Diez's involvement in the *West-östlicher Divan* is that by Mommsen 1961. While working on her book, Katharina Mommsen corresponded with Wolfgang Lentz to whose teaching I owe my first acquaintance with Goethe's relations with Hammer and Diez. With this I wish to pay tribute to Mommsen and Lentz.

2 The Latin teacher, one of eight private tutors, "Was a Turk, captured after his father had been killed in battle, and brought up as a Christian: a student of theology, he eventually became deputy head master of the city's grammar school (his discipline was poor)". Boyle 1991, p. 54.

3 That Goethe retained in essence the spirit of the German idealistic continuation of European Enlightenment has been demonstrated by Mayer 1974, p. 122, and Mayer 1999, pp. 91-92.

4 Diez 1783, 32-33: "Therefore Turks and heathens possess the spirit of Christ, because they worship God in the service of justice and charity, whatsoever their belief about Mahomet or other things may be." For Goethe's professed discipleship of Spinoza see Boyle 1991, pp. 278, 383-384.

5 Boyle 1991, p. 274.

 | DOI 10.1163/9789004355767_029

the age of nineteen; Goethe was initiated as a Fellow at the age of thirty-two.[6] Freemasonry was extra-territorial; the secret societies created free spaces, refuge and patronage[7] in the absolutist state.[8] In Turkey Diez was told about the "deceitful legend about Freemasonry" by an acquaintance.[9]

Both men were collectors. There is no need here to list Goethe's collections. Diez collected Latin classics; he was one of the greatest bibliophiles of the eighteenth century and built up a formidable collection of oriental manuscripts from Turkey.

Goethe was a licentiate of law; Diez was a law clerk (Referendar) and chancellor, before he became chargé d'affaires and subsequently an envoy. Both were ennobled,[10] Goethe was full privy councillor (Geheimer Rat) and Diez would become, at the end of 1790, a privy legation councillor. Both were unmarried – Goethe was the father of a son, August Vulpius, born December 1789 by Christiane Vulpius.

Goethe was a European celebrity. Diez was not, but he was a scholar of wide learning,[11] and he exemplified – next to Friedrich August Wolf und Johann Gottlieb Fichte – the *Typus* of dominant figures of the eighteenth century, figures that were characterized by an immense self-esteem. Both belonged to the generation into whose life the French Revolution came when they were mature men and women. With mention of the year 1790 a political context is suggested which is quite different from the so-called "Goethezeit" of decades later, when Diez at times acted as an advisor to Goethe.

Goethe's life, i.e. the period from 1749 to 1832, is usually divided into two halves with the year 1790 taken as a watershed.[12] This division also suggests itself for the life of Heinrich Friedrich von Diez who was two years younger. I will now attempt to describe that particular watershed year.

---

6 Goethe became a Master in 1782. He "joined the order within the order, the Illuminists, in February 1783", Boyle 1991, p. 173.

7 Diez was a Protégé of the Prussian State Councillor (Staatsrat), Christian K.W. von Dohm (1751-1820).

8 On the anonymously published brochure Diez 1772 another anonymous author – presumably Goethe – wrote that same year an ironical review in the *Frankfurter Gelehrten Anzeigen*; cf. Mommsen 1961, p. 4, fn. 2.

9 This was Yazıcı Ahmed Efendi, mentioned in Diez 1813, pp. 504 f. – Diez 1815, p. 472, describes his acquaintance as a former pasha of two horse tails who collected coins and tinkered with pocket-watches. On Freemasonry in the Ottoman Empire see J.M. Landau, "Farmāsūniyya", EI2 Suppl. Leiden 2004, pp. 296-297.

10 Goethe in 1782 (imperial patent of nobility; cf. Boyle 1991, p. 342); Diez in 1786 (Prussian patent of nobility).

11 Mommsen 1961, p. 4.

12 Boyle 1991 deals with Goethe's biography up to July 1790. Boyle 2000 begins in 1790 with Goethe's return from Italy on 19 June 1790.

II

The year 1790 belonged to the last years of the *Ancien Régime*.[13] Both men played their role in different theatres of action. At the beginning of the year Goethe was in Weimar and Venice. Diez spent the first half of the year in Istanbul. From there[14] he had followed one of the most disastrous campaigns in Ottoman history (1789) from which the armies of Selīm III had scarcely recovered. The boundaries of the Ottoman Empire had in the meantime shifted, in present-day terminology, from the Ukraine to Moldavia and Romania, in fact even to within the vicinity of Bulgaria. By the terms of the Küçük Kaynarca treaty, the Sultan had renounced Muslim territory in the Crimea. In 1783 Russia had annexed the Crimea. In 1788 Oczakow (Özü) fell to the Russians under Potemkin.[15]

The Sublime Porte had a "bulwark" in Prussia. Her "envoy extraordinary" was Heinrich Friedrich von Diez, a tall man with an imposing presence, in his middle thirties,[16] whom the aged Frederick the Great, after a curious audience, had appointed as chargé d'affaires and briefed.

Diez, the son of a merchant, was trained as a jurist after a youth which included first-rate university studies in Halle. Equipped with a knowledge of languages, he then learned French and Turkish as well. Since 1772 he was a writer by dint of his profession. As a chancellor he had filled hundreds of pages in the registers of his Magdeburg chancellery, and brought order to old materials. In Istanbul sending dispatches became his daily practice. He promoted trade[17] and endeavoured successfully to win the trust of Turkish ministers; with the Western ambassadors, senior in rank, he got on less well.[18]

---

13 On the initial appeal of the ideas of the French Revolution in the Ottoman Empire see Lewis 1961, pp. 53-59. For early reactions in Germany see Boyle 1999, pp. 589-591.

14 Diez was recalled in 1790. In many publications (also my own), the erroneous date 1791 is given. Appointed on 17 March 1784, Diez had arrived in Constantinople on 16 July 1784.

15 Daniel Nikolaus Chodowiecki's drawings on the occasion of the fall of Oczakow are reproduced in Sievenich and Budde 1989, pp. 272-273.

16 A pastel portrait, painted on cardboard, made in Berlin in 1791, is reproduced in Mommsen 1961. For "envoy extraordinary" see Shaw 1971, pp.41 ff.

17 According to his own statement, in 1785 he had set up a Prussian consulate in Moldavia and Wallachia (see his manuscript Diez A.4.0.129). On Moldavia and Wallachia, Ottoman provinces occupied by the Russian army, 'principalities', see Lieven 2009, p. 71. Incidentally, in 1806 Joseph von Hammer (on whom more presently) was sent to Jassy as Austrian agent (consul-general) in Moldavia.

18 In the Ottoman ranking system he was not an ambassador (*büyük elçi, ambassadeur*), but initially chargé d'affaires (*maṣlahat-güzār*) and then envoy (*orta elçi, envoyé*); Karamuk 1975, p. 111 citing Lewis 1965. Choiseul-Gouffier 1752-1817 left for Turkey in 1784, Berkes 1964, p. 64.

His office was not an easy one. The Porte pressed him to make unambiguous declarations regarding the much-vaunted Prussian friendship.[19] On February 9th 1789, he had assurances by word of mouth coaxed out of him to the effect that Prussia would attack Austria and bring about the return of the Crimea from Russia. This was what his instructions said at times, but they were unclear, contradictory and changeable.[20] Moreover, at the Sublime Porte people always knew everything; they were aware of his instructions which on one occasion were downright stolen from him. So now, in January 1790, Diez used his remaining freedom of movement and, urged on by his government, brought about an offensive alliance with the Sublime Porte, but according to the Porte's formulation.[21] This meant that Prussia agreed to declare war against Russia and Austria.

However, in the words of Shaw, "Berlin declined to come through with that, and sacrificed its envoy instead." Instead of approval Diez received a sharp reproach. He had got King Frederick William into an awkward situation from which he could only retract himself by recalling Diez (this had already been under discussion in December 1789). How could Prussia possibly commit herself to wage war on Russia as well as Austria with the added impossible goal of winning back the Crimea for Turkey? For all that, Diez had succeeded in setting a long term of five months for ratification. His government took advantage of this.

Diez, at the age of thirty-nine, felt his dismissal painfully. For six full years he had maintained a permanent residence in Istanbul, four of which as an envoy. He embarked on a Dutch merchantman[22] which would convey him and a young companion, Tahir Bey, to Hamburg via Gibraltar.

On May 20th 1790 he was still writing from Istanbul: "I had my farewell audience with tears from the ministers, embarked the day before yesterday and am leaving later today under sail for Hamburg. Just now I receive the sad news that "Çorbacı" – the subordinate commander of his red-cloaked janissary escort[23] – "has died out of grief at my departure."

19 Karamuk 1975, p. 160.

20 Karamuk 1975, pp. 183 and 186.

21 Shaw 1971, p. 46; Karamuk 1975, p. 186.

22 Presumably the "De Ester en Dirk" arriving from Messina under Captain Cornelis Clay. Nanninga 1966, p. 1421. I am indebted to Dr. Jan Schmidt of The Hague for this reference.

23 Diez mentioned a guard of honor which the Porte had given him since the time of Selīm. On the janissary escort (against the occasional wrath of a mob) see Aksan, p. 121. For the office, see Gibb and Bowen 1950, pp. 319-322.

Turkish friends who were sincerely saddened took their leave on board. They all agreed: "Never before have we here had an envoy like him."[24] On May 23rd he embarked, in September he was in Hamburg and thereafter in Berlin. In this early summer of 1790, Goethe found himself at a centre of events. The Prussian army – it was still Frederick II's army with its janissary music and crack Guards regiments Gendarmes and Garde du Corps – had been advancing into Silesia since June 1790 in order to attack Austria in Bohemia. In this way Frederick William II appeared to be demonstrating to the Porte his fidelity to an alliance,[25] which he had in fact not yet ratified.

There was definitely talk of a *campaign*. "All Europe braced itself for war".[26] Goethe was quartered in the camp with Duke Carl August who as a Prussian major-general commanded an elite brigade made up from Gendarmes (in Zirlau and Oelse) and Gardes du Corps (in Gräben near Striegau). Goethe knew that the campaign was a threatening gesture: *I wish that this large demonstration of a warlike intention may turn out to be for the greater good of Germany and Europe* – so he wrote, still from Weimar, to the Duke on July 1st 1790. The political Goethe had written earlier: *Since essentially the purpose of war can only be peace, it is surely fitting for a warrior if he is able to make and preserve peace without war.*[27] In fact, Prussian, Austrian and other European plenipotentiaries would negotiate peace in the small Silesian weavers' town of Reichenbach (Dzierzoniów) in the summer of 1790.[28]

In Istanbul, where Diez's Prusso-Ottoman treaty had a tremendous effect,[29] the ratification of this pact was awaited with impatience. But Frederick William II stalled as long as he could and only ratified it at the latest possible moment, on June 20th in the camp at Schönwalde. He knew through his spy in the Ottoman camp near Vidin[30] – Yusuf Pasha had moved north from there –

24 In contravention of etiquette, Selīm III ordered a note of appreciation to be included in the Recreditive; he received the stamp of approval, "*man sei mit ihm vollkommen zufrieden gewesen*". Zinkeisen 1859, p. 758.

25 Karamuk 1975, p. 195.

26 Shaw 1971, p. 50.

27 The letter sent to the Duke in Berlin and dated January 17th [1790] is cited in Boyle 1991, p. 742. Goethe had lived through Frederick the Great's intervention in the Bavarian War of Succession which had brought about peace, and on that occasion he had visited Berlin with Duke Carl August from May 10th to June 1st 1778. Boyle 1991, pp. 300-301; Boyle 1995, pp. 345-346.

28 For the Treaty of Reichenbach 1790 see Shaw 1971, pp. 51ff.; Karamuk 1975, pp. 196-199; Boyle 2000, pp. 5, 10, 77-78.

29 Shaw 1971, p. 47.

30 A secret negotiator of the king, Colonel von Götze, arrived in Istanbul at the beginning of August 1788 (Karamuk 1975, p. 175). In February 1790 he had already announced his presence

that the Turkish army was on the point of being disbanded for the summer. In the meantime, on July 17th 1790 the Convention of Reichenbach was signed. Austria and Prussia came to an agreement: Austria would end its war against the Ottoman Empire, and Prussia would not attack Austria.

Now two documents must be delivered to the Sultan: the Prusso-Ottoman alliance which had finally been ratified, and the Convention of Reichenbach. An elaborate charade was enacted so that the first document travelled as slowly as possible, whereas the second was transmitted at lightning speed. The Prusso-Ottoman alliance document was entrusted to a mere military courier (*Feldjäger*) named Möhring, who moved slowly and pretended to fall sick in Venice. By contrast, a high-ranking officer (Colonel Count de Lusi) speedily conveyed the news of the Reichenbach agreements to the Turkish headquarters near Vidin and set about initiating an armistice.[31] On August 7, 1790 the Prussian ratification finally arrived in Istanbul. On August 18 the new Prussian envoy Major von Knobelsdorf came, the bombshell of Reichenbach fell[32] and touched off a furor.

In the meantime, Goethe with all of official Prussia, had moved to Breslau, the Silesian capital, where he would reside for several weeks in August and September 1790. *One does not yet know*, he wrote on August 12th 1790, *how and when the campaign will end. It is said that it still depends on the declaration of the Russians.* He had been told that a courier was *expected any moment from Petersburg*. But the Russians would have nothing to do with Reichenbach and carried on waging their war, albeit suffering "from Potemkin's annual spring lethargy."[33]

A warm understanding immediately arose between Goethe and Kaspar Friedrich von Schuckmann (1755-1834), a promising state official and young widower in whose house Goethe met Henriette Eleonore Augusta, Baroness von Lüttwitz (1769-1799). He was clearly strongly, if briefly, attracted to the cultivated young noblewoman who reciprocated his feelings. He intended to marry Henriette von Lüttwitz, but was refused by her father. Henriette's younger brother brought the story to public notice,[34] but only the passing of

in the Turkish headquarters in Vidin where he had arrived from Istanbul. In July 1790 he reported from the camp of the Ottoman commander-in chief Yūsuf Paşa near Vidin.

31 Shaw 1971, p. 51-53.

32 Shaw 1971, p. 55. Karamuk 1975, pp. 200-202.

33 Shaw 1971, p. 52. For Goethe's role in Duke Carl August's policy at the time see Boyle 1991, pp. 641-642, and Boyle 2000, pp. 77-78.

34 Lüttwitz 1835. In 1791 Henriette von Lüttwitz married Kaspar Friedrich von Schuckmann and moved to Bayreuth with him in 1795. Their daughter Marianne (later von Pannwitz) was born in 1796. Henriette met Giacomo Casanova (1725-1798) and corresponded with

many years has permitted an assessment of this little-known event in Goethe's life.[35] Nicholas Boyle pointed to a *passing sentimental attachment to a titled lady, soon to become Schuckmann's second wife.*[36] Goethe was to remain in friendly contact with Schuckmann throughout the latter's career in the "Prussian machine in which he eventually rose to the rank of minister."[37]

Goethe's forty-first birthday was near. On 26 August, with a hundred thalers travel money, Goethe ondertook a journey into the county of Glatz. Goethe climbed the Heuscheuer[38] where a Prussian officer was inspecting the Karlsberg fortress.[39] On 28 August, a Saturday, he arrived at Wünschelburg in the vicinity of the country seat of the Lüttwitz family at Mittelsteine,[40] which had just been renovated after military use. He may have spent his birthday as a guest of the family. The significant poem which Boyle missed[41] was not lacking: indeed, a strophic poem commemorates his Breslau love.[42] Goethe spent two days at Landeshut; on 30 and 31 August he made a flying visit to Bohemia and then returned to Breslau.

---

him, confessing to agonizing loneliness and anxiety. "Henriette von Schuckmann", http:/de.wikipedia.org/wik/Henriette_von_Schuckmann, accessed 2-4-2013.

35 Reference may be made to Lüttwitz 1835; Hoffmann 1889, Lengersdorff 1965, Conrady 1985, Ziolko 1992. Piontek (1925-2003) 1993, Wilpert 1998, Boyle 1999, p. 111, and Boyle 2000, p. 84. I delivered a paper outlining "Goethes Aufenthalt in Schlesien 1790. Die Wasserscheide" on 25 June 1999 at the "Goethes geistiges Europa" Congress held at the Goethe-Museum Düsseldorf. Unpublished manuscript.

36 Boyle 2000, p. 84, citing Grumach iii 358-9. In Holger Fliessbach's German translation (*flüchtige, sentimentale Bindung an eine adlige Dame, die wenig später Schuckmanns zweite Frau wurde*) her name is disclosed in the index: "*Schuckmann, H.E.A.* (*geb. von Lüttwitz*)", Boyle 1999, p. 111. For the year 1788 Boyle had noted that "the implication of [...] episodes is that Goethe did not as yet consider his liaison with Christiana to be permanent and that he was beginning to look around for a titled young lady to marry..." Boyle 1991, pp. 550, 580; Boyle 1995, pp. 636, 672.

37 Boyle 2000, p. 80.

38 "The most distinctive peak of the region" (Boyle 2000, p. 83). According to Hoffmann, Goethe on his birthday, immediately after arrival at Wünschelburg, climbed the Heuscheuer plateau. Ziolko, *Schlesische Reise*, 35.

39 Weczerka, *Stätten*, p. 574.

40 Lengersdorff, p. 185. Goetze stayed at an inn.

41 "On this occasion, however, the guiding genius deserted him and no poem or special episode presented itself." Boyle 2000, p. 83.

42 *Ach wir sind zur Qual gebohren* ... The poem survived in Goethe's notebook and was published, but was pointedly excluded from the canonical text editions. Ziolko, *Schlesische Reise*, pp. 35 and 64; Piontek 1993.

On 3 September 1790, Goethe, Duke Carl August of Weimar and the inspector-general of the Silesian mines, Count Frederick William von Reden (1752-1815), set out from Breslau to visit the industrial installations of Prussian Upper Silesia. Count Reden had studied in England and had arranged for the acquisition in 1786 of a steam engine of the Newcomen/Watt type. The travellers inspected the Friedrichsgrube where the lead (needed for ordnance) and silver deposits of Tarnowitz (Tarnowskie Góry) were mined and water was pumped out of the pits with the assistance of two "fire machines." Goethe sketched the basic principles of the steam engine in his notebook. These belonged to the first steam engines operating on the European continent. In his carriage, Goethe noted down in his notebook a distich destined for the guest book of the community of mining engineers (*Knappschaft*), praising their work and encouraging them:

> Fern von gebildeten Menschen am Ende des Reiches wer hilft euch
> Schätze finden und sie glücklich zu bringen ans Licht?
> Nur Verstand und Redlichkeit helfen; es führen die beiden
> Schlüssel zu jeglichem Schatz welchen die Erde verwahrt.

Goethe's world was the Holy Roman Empire of the German Nation: he had travelled to its southern periphery in Agrigento, Sicily,[43] and now stood at its eastern periphery. The Polish state was disappearing into neighbouring empires. After its first partition in 1772 its eastern part was reduced to a borderland region of the Russian Empire. The Prussian "campaign" against Austria of June 1790 being called off, the travellers crossed into Galicia[44] which Austria had newly acquired and which was yet to become a crown land of the Habsburg Empire. They drove along the River Vistula to Cracow (Kraków), at approximately 50°4 ' N 19°56 ' E the easternmost point in all of Goethe's travels. In Cracow the party stayed for three days.[45] The name of Scheidt, director of a mineralogical collection, appears in the notebook. The party went to the old salt mines of Wieliczka to be led round in the weird white caves of what was then the richest salt mine of the Habsburg Monarchy. On 8 September a flying visit to Częstochowa and a return via places with coking-ovens (sketched in the notebook) ended this half-secret journey.

43 Boyle 1991, p. 475. Lieven 2002, p. 161.

44 Rothe 1998, p. 42, ignores the political context.

45 A plaque commemorates his stay in a hotel on the ancient market-place <http://www.peter-rathay.de/Goethe-in-Schlesien.html> access 8.9.2011. Boyle 2000, p. 83f. – In 1795, after the third Polish partition, Austria was to create the combined crown land Galicia and Bukowina (with Lemberg/Lwow as capital); Lieven 2002, pp. 272-273.

Back in Breslau, Goethe finished his poem for the *Knappschaft* and gave it to Count Reden. The poem was inserted into the Tarnowitz guest book and read with mixed feelings. Goethe was in Breslau for the third time. Now the pendulum swung to the negative side; the Lüttwitz family had refused him. Breslau was "noisy, dirty, stinking", waiting was tedious.

Goethe had recourse to a device which had helped him before to find clarity and relief; he rode off to an unannounced destination (seven days between 12 and 18 September 1790). A short notice *Riesengebirge. über die Schneekupp nach Breslau d. 15. Sept* leaves no doubt that his destination was the highest mountain ridge dividing Silesia and Bohemia. He climbed the Schneekoppe, Mt. Snežka, altitude 1603 metres, at night in full moon of 15 September. Resting on hay in the lodge below, he climbed the top at 5. a.m. and had a fine view of the Bohemian heartland. Now the desired poem presented itself:

> In der Dämmrung des Morgens den höchsten Gipfel erklimmen,
> Lang den Boten des Tags schauen den freundlichen Stern,
> Ungeduldig den Blick der Himmelsfürstin erwarten –
> Wonne des Jünglings wie oft hast du mich nächtig geweckt.

With the concluding lines

> Nun erscheint ihr mir, Boten des Tags, ihr himmlischen Augen
> Meiner Geliebten, und stets kommt mir die Sonne zu früh,

this poem, on two leaves in his Silesian notebook, marks the turning point of the year 1790, Goethe's definitive bond with Weimar and Christiane Vulpius. Goethe himself announced this by publishing this "northern" poem among his Venetian Epigrams.

And then he must wait again in Breslau; the Sultan's courier seemed endlessly delayed. Goethe's waiting in the hustle of Breslau has historical source value in so far as it documents the agitation with which official Prussia anticipated the Ottoman reaction to Reichenbach. Finally, on September 17th 1790 a courier arrived from the Ottoman camp with the acceptance of the armistice. Only then did the King leave Breslau and was Goethe, too, allowed to depart. Goethe travelled via Warmbrunn, climbed the Schneekoppe (again), and went on to Dresden where he arrived on 25 September 1790. On September 19th 1790 the armistice was signed in Giurgevo (Jerköi, Giurgiu) in Wallachia.[46]

No Ottoman official was present either in Reichenbach or Breslau. It was in accordance with proud Ottoman tradition that the Sultan received envoys and

46 Shaw 1971, p. 47.

provided their board and lodgings. It was Reichenbach in particular that made it clear to Selīm III that he needed resident embassies in the European capitals (the first was opened in London in 1793). But for now, in November 1790, he despatched a special envoy of the old kind to Berlin, Ahmed ʿAzmī Efendi,[47] who was to remind Prussia of its commitment as an ally to declare war on Russia, since the Crimea must by all accounts be reconquered.

A European war had been averted. In Sistowa (Svistov, Turkish Ziştovi), where a peace conference was convened, the negotiators arrived in the late fall of 1790 but would need time until the 4th of August 1791 until the peace between Austria and the Ottoman Empire could be signed.[48] These matters disappeared from Goethe's field of vision. He immersed himself in the comparative anatomy of animals and had his *Venezianische Epigramme* published; the 94th of which, written in Silesia, was his confession of love for Christiane Vulpius.

Out of office, Heinrich Friedrich von Diez complained in November-December 1790 about considerable financial troubles and difficulties. Then his government had second thoughts: the treaty was not so bad really; and they thanked Diez – by forgiving him.

In five ways Diez had profited from his diplomatic mission: he came to know the world from his post in Istanbul; he acquired a sound knowledge of the Turkish language and country; he enlarged his manuscript collection. He acquired important manuscripts from the Palace.[49] He became acquainted with Turks and came to love them;[50] he received the title "von" and a generous pension,[51] in addition to the character of a Prussian privy legation councillor. With this rank he was sent into retirement.

---

47 His appearance in Berlin is documented in the "Berlin Costume Book" from the library of the Prussian King Frederick William II, Staatsbibliothek zu Berlin, which was on loan in the exhibition *Im Lichte des Halbmonds. Das Abendland und der türkische Orient*, Dresden and Bonn 1995-1996, pp. 276-278, No. 352.

48 Karamuk 1975, pp. 200-204.

49 Diez 1811a, p. 39. After Selīm III's accession to the throne, harem ladies who had served his predecessor were transferred to the Old Palace; they were able to generate some income not only from handiwork (Peirce 1993, pp. 122-124, 139), but also by selling their books through the intermediacy of a harem official.

50 He had had audiences with two sultans: Abdülhamid I. and Selim III, whose portrait of 1789 he owned (it is lost). Among the company he kept was Yazıcı Ahmed Efendi, mentioned in fn. 7. Another acquaintance was Numan Bey, whose nephew accompanied Diez to Berlin. He knew the *Kapudan Pascha Ghazi Hasan Pascha* (mentioned in the introductory passages, dated 1802, to Diez 1811b, p. 242). Diez' Turkish teacher was a certain Ibrahim Efendi.

51 In Hamberger/Meusel 1796 (presumably information from Diez himself) it is reported that he lived "as a private person without office" on his estate at Philippsthal near Potsdam. Babinger 1913, p. 93, reports that in addition Diez possessed a sizeable personal fortune said

Though formally retired,[52] he continued to actively assist the government by looking after Ottoman diplomats in Berlin. I will say a few words about these diplomats before I consider, in my third and final section, Diez's contribution to Turcology.

The special envoy, Ahmed ʿAzmī Efendi, who arrived via Breslau,[53] was met by Diez who undertook negotiations with him;[54] ʿAzmi stayed eleven months until the middle of January 1792.[55] He had been in Berlin before in the company of his brother-in-law Ahmed Resmi Efendi (1708-1783).[56] Now it was Azmi Efendi who was active in pursuing diplomacy; he composed an envoy's report which concludes with a description of Prussia – a Potemkin-style Prussia, where the people lived in peace and were happy to pay taxes, where there was no mention of the serfs' misery and their longing for freedom. This reveals to what extent ʿAzmī Efendi's report was written for a Turkish public which he wished to win over to contemporary Ottoman ideas of reform.[57]

ʿAlī ʿAzīz Efendi, the first permanent ambassador at the Prussian court,[58] arrived in Berlin at the beginning of June 1797[59] and after initial difficulties to do with protocol[60] was not active diplomatically. He and Diez exchanged notes in Turkish on philosophic and scientific matters.[61] ʿAzīz Efendi translated ori-

to have been acquired in Constantinople especially by issuing Prussian passports and commercial letters (Handelsbriefe) which were highly sought after at the time.

52 "No employment in the service of the state elsewhere", Zinkeisen 1859, p. 763.

53 Ziolko 1994, p. 24, has traced the engraving of the envoy that the Breslau copper engraver Endler made at that time. Schwarz provides a commentary in Sievenich and Budde 1989, pp. 803-805, on the engraving (published ibidem, p. 271), which documents the reception of Ahmed ʿAzmī Efendi by the King of Prussia.

54 At that time Diez received in Berlin two letters of Mehmed Raşid Efendi: see Diez A.40.129.

55 Karamuk 1975, p. 205. Schwarz 1989, p. 805, summarizes the contents of the king's correspondence with the sultan.

56 Aksan, pp. 70 ff.; on Ahmed Resmi's illness and death, see Aksan p. 184.

57 Findley 1980, pp. 118-119; especially pp. 372-373 with additional bibliography; and cf. Findley 1995.

58 *Iqāmet elçisi.* To begin with Moralı ʿAli Efendi was appointed to Berlin, but he was reassigned to Paris. The position in Berlin was then meant to be taken up by Naʾili Mehmed Efendi, Secretary of the Artillery Corps. When the latter could not fill the post due to illness, ʿAli ʿAziz Efendi was appointed. Shaw 1971, p. 188, cites Kuran 1968.

59 Zinkeisen 1863, pp. 18 and 55.

60 He was received only as envoy, whereas the honors of an ambassador were due to him. The episode which is not dealt with in Zinkeisen is depicted at length in the Ottoman historians; cf. Cevdet 1877, pp. 232f., 240f.; cf. also the description in Karal 1946, pp. 167 f.

61 "But while he [Ali Aziz Efendi] demonstrated some interest in these matters, his replies showed [that he had] no idea whatsoever about experimental science and the rational

ental fairy-tales from French, became all the while more independent and wrote "Fantasy Pieces" (*Muḥayyelāt*),[62] for which he is famous today. On 29 October 1798 he suddenly died in Berlin and was buried there.[63]

III

Diez's spiritual change from being a freethinker to a strict Lutheran[64] goes back to the turning point of 1790. He became a prelate in the Pomeranian fortified city of Kolberg (now Kołobrzeg). As an author he added his title of prelate to that of privy councillor to a legation. Now instead of dispatches his Turkish manuscripts lay before him. In politically insecure times he reaped the benefits of his Istanbul years in writings which for the time being, during the years of the Napoleonic wars, remained unpublished.

After the battle of Jena and Auerstädt on 4 October 1806 and the destruction of the Prussian army, Napoleon controlled Germany. The closure of the University of Halle, the plundering of Weimar, the siege of Kolberg (March to July 1807), from where Diez moved to Berlin, Prussia's survival after losing half her territory and population,[65] the liberation of Berlin by Russian forces on 4 March 1813 – Reichenbach coming to prominence again as allied headquarters against Napoleon[66] – all these were political dates in the midst of which, that is to say between 1806 and 1813/15[67] – an extraordinary literary and journalistic creativity flourished in general and also in the field of Oriental Studies.

---

philosophy developed in the West since the Enlightenment." Shaw 1971, p. 451 note 37, citing Kuran 1963, pp. 37, 45-58.

62 "One solitary exception to the general lack of interest in Western literature" (Lewis 1961, p. 53). In 1948 Andreas Tietze published a brilliant study of the work (Tietze 1948). On the sojourn of Turkish ambassadors cf. Höpp 1996 (unavailable for this research).

63 Frederick William III (1797-1840) ordered the burial of the deceased envoy according to Islamic rites on a plot donated by the crown; in 1804 and later more members of the Ottoman embassy were buried here. In 1866 the burial plot was relocated to Neukölln and became the first Muslim cemetery on German soil. Boer Harkötter, pp. 3-4.

64 As Babinger 1913, p. 95, put it, Diez became "after his return from the East (*Morgenland*) and especially ... in Berlin a zealous representative of Lutheran doctrine."

65 Her Polish provinces became a new small state, the so-called Duchy of Warsaw (Lieven 2009, p. 51), of which Cracow, regained in 1809 by Prince Poniatowski, formed a part.

66 For ten weeks in June 1813 "European top-level diplomacy was concentrated on the small area between Napoleon's headquarters at Dresden, allied headquarters at Reichenbach in south-western Silesia, ... and the Bohemian capital, Prague, where the peace conference took place." Lieven 2009, pp. 356-357.

67 On the liberation of Berlin and the 1813 spring campaign Lieven 2009, pp. 298 and 303.

Diez was now in his fifties and had been living in Berlin since 1807.[68] Diez' retirement home was a house in the "pleasantest park of Berlin" on the Spree, Stralauer Viertel, Mühlenstrasse 49. He emphasized his love of things Oriental by having a Turkish, Persian, and Chinese room and by wearing oriental vestments. He was a hospitable host who kept open table after the fashion of an envoy. He was a friend of Goethe's friends Friedrich August Wolf and Wilhelm von Humboldt; he met intellectual and social celebrities in his home[69] and from 1815 on exchanged letters with Goethe.

There is, perhaps, no better example of the final days of the Old Regime than that of H.F. von Diez. Just as at the time jurists and historians along with philologists were active in scholarly fields other than their own, Diez had published philosophical essays and occasionally written on Cicero.[70] Now he published matters Turkish, translated from the Turkish, presented discoveries, instigated debates and did not shrink from confrontation and violent statement. His *Denkwürdigkeiten Asiens* inspired enormous controversy. Goethe drew from Diez's works "fresh eastern air" *frische östliche Luft* for the *West-östlicher Diwan*.[71]

Diez's collaboration on Joseph von Hammer's *Fundgruben des Orients* that began to appear in Vienna in 1809[72] was short-lived and stood under an inauspicious star. He contributed one poem that criticized its day and age[73] and a text by Kemalpaşazade which he himself wished to withdraw.[74] It was, to

68 On 27 October 1806, Napoleon made a solemn entrance into the city, accompanied by his marshals Davout and Augereau. Henri Beyle, better known as Stendhal (1783-1842), entered Berlin in Napoleon's entourage. The generals Jean Rapp, Pierre-Augustin Hulin and Henri Jacques Guilleaume Clarke served as governors of the French garrison.

69 For all essentials see Mommsen 1961, pp. 2-4 and passim.

70 In Hamberger/Meusel 1806 Diez (always written Dietz) is presented as a philosophical writer. The rules he followed when undertaking translations he had set down thirty years earlier in his preface to his Cicero translation (Diez 1780).

71 Wurm 1971, p. 101 footnote 6 and p. 184 no. 156, showed that Goethe occupied himself with Diez (Hezārfenn, Tenqīh-i Mulūk) for his *Paralipomena*.

72 Frontispiece in Golz 1999, p. 184. The six volumes (Vienna 1809-1818) were preserved in the library of the Duchess Anna Amalia in Weimar. Golz 1999, p. 262.

73 Criticizing D.-D. Cardonne (see below, footnote 91), Diez published a poem in which a certain Üveysī laments the lawless carryings-on of the inhabitants of Istanbul under Murad IV: *Fundgruben* I, pp. 249-274. Gibb 1904, pp. 210-218, translated the remarkable poem once again and edited it in 1909. Heyd 1973, p. 157, still wondered whether the famous Veysī was actually the poem's author.

74 *Fundgruben* I pp. 397-399. Kemalpaşazade ("What is Man?").

begin with, the choice of his contributions that unleashed the storm between him and Hammer, the greatest historian of the Ottoman Empire.[75]

Joseph von Hammer-Purgstall[76] was born at Graz on 9 June 1774, fifteen years before the French Revolution. Entering the Austrian diplomatic service in 1796, he was appointed in 1799 to a position in the Austrian embassy in Constantinople, and in this capacity took part in the expedition against the French in Egypt and later went to England. A friend of (Admiral Sir) Sidney Smith (1764-1840), he was a political liberal, feeling kindred to everything "English." In the year 1809, when Napoleon captured Vienna, Hammer had been left in Vienna (his superior Count Stadion and the Court Chancellery having retired to Ofen), where after the capitulation he defended the manuscript holdings of the imperial library against Napoleon's rapacious commissioner.[77] Hammer's unyielding spirit of opposition against bureaucratic absolutism made the new Austrian foreign minister, Prince Clemens Metternich (1771-1859), decide that he was "too good" for a diplomatic career. With his friend Count Wenceslaus Rzewuski Hammer founded the *Mines de l'Orient* or *Fundgruben des Orients*, that remarkable token of European scholarly history. Passionately campaigning for the foundation of the Imperial Austrian Academy of Sciences in Vienna which was finally established by Imperial Patent on 14 May 1847, Hammer became its first president and gave the inaugural address on 2 February of the revolution year 1848. When the ennobled *Hofrat* and baron Hammer-Purgstall died in Vienna on 23 November 1856, Goethe, Heinrich Friedrich von Diez and Hālet Efendi were dead.[78]

75 Mommsen 1961 does greater justice to Diez in her more subtle treatment than does Fück 1955, p. 161. Solbrig 1973 deals with the conflict from the viewpoint of Hammer.

76 Fück 1955, pp. 158-166.

77 For the story of the abduction of the manuscripts to Paris see Ferdinand Menčik "Die Wegführung der Handschriften aus der Hofbibliothek durch die Franzosen im Jahre 1809" (*Jahrbuch der kunsthistorischen Sammlung des A.H. Kaiserhauses* XXVII. 1910, pp. IVff.) and Othmar Doublier "Die Wiener Hofbibliothek in Kriegsgefahr" (*Zentralblatt für Bibliothekswesen*, Jahrgang LIII, pp. 46 ff. www.zeno.org/Kulturgeschichte/M/Hammer-Purgstall,+Joseph access 3.9.2011.

78 H.W. Duda, "Joseph Freiherr von Hammer-Purgstall. Diplomat, Orientalist, Schöpfer und erster Präsident der österreichischen Akademie der Wissenschaften", Graz 1978, pp. 14-17. (Veröffentlichungen der Hammer-Purgstall-Gesellschaft Nr. VI). H. Jansky, "Hammer-Purgstall – Historiker und Begründer der österreichischen Akademie der Wissenschaften", ibid. pp. 18-21. Andreas Tietze contributed a personal account in *Morgenlaendisches Kleeblatt ... aufgelesen durch Joseph von Hammer, Vienna 1819,* facsimile edition Vienna 1991. A portrait of Hammer from the Goethe-Nationalmuseum is in Golz 1999, p. 224.

Goethe, the "amateur" in his theory on colour, followed the feud raging between Hammer and Diez with the greatest interest and showed sympathy for Diez's situation which he perceived as similar to his own. It is worth adding that the polemic with Hammer,[79] for all its acrimony, was by no means unique. Contemporaries could remember even more embittered polemical writings: for example, the lashes with which the Homeric scholar Friedrich August Wolf had castigated Herder,[80] or the combats of the literary critic and publisher Friedrich Nicolai (1733-1811),[81] who, incidentally, had met the first Turkish envoy in Berlin, Resmī Ahmed Efendi, and had published the translation of this envoy's report along with a preface by himself.[82] Given this interest, it was not strange that Nicolai undertook the distribution, in 1811, of three works by Diez.

Accustomed to setting forth his learned views without much technical jargon, Diez produced a translation, with commentary, of a Turkish history of the Russo-Ottoman war 1768 to 1774[83]– note the work's proximity to recent events! – and a small book by Lalezari on growing tulips; of great interest to Goethe were his two publications on mirrors for princes.[84] In his *Denkwürdigkeiten von Asien* that were planned to be in several volumes, two of which were published, he presented what appeared to him to be the most important of his manu-

79 Hammer, who conducted other bitter feuds as well in the *Fundgruben*, recalled in that work in 1818 the late "vituperative" Diez ("schmähsüchtigen Angedenkens") and reproached his errors in Hammer 1832, pp. 331 and passim.

80 Bernays 1868 describes them (1795 "Prolegomena to Homer"). Another ferocious polemicist was the Homer translator J. Heinrich Voss, a writer of pastoral idylls.

81 Reich-Ranicki 1996, pp. 32-52, acknowledges Nicolai as "the founder of our literary life."

82 [Hammer] 1809. On the identity of the translator, see Babinger 1927, p. 311. Concerning a certain learned man mentioned by Nicolai "who for a long time resided in the East" and had contributed explanatory comments: the person in question could well be Diez, as Schwarz 1989, p. 806, suspected.

83 Diez 1813 is the translation, with comments, of Resmi Ahmed Efendi, *Hulaset ül-iʿtibar*, see Aksan 1995 p. 221-223. This was the only responsible critique of what was at the time the penultimate Russo-Turkish war, with an analysis of the causes of Turkey's defeat, urging the need for reform (Berkes 57f.).

84 Diez 1811b and c. Frontispiece and pages from the "Book of Kabus" *Buch des Kabus oder Lehren des persischen Königs Kjekjawus für seinen Sohn Ghilan Schach.* Diez 1811b, pp. 38-239 and 385 in the Goethe-Nationalmuseum and in the Anna Amalia Library in Weimar are reproduced in Golz 1999, p.190 (frontispiece) and p. 300-302. Goethe's rough draft of a poem paying homage to Diez in the Goethe and Schiller Archive is reproduced in Golz 1999, p. 282-283. Goethe borrowed the Kabus volume from the Weimar library in January and May 1815 and read in it often; later he received a copy from the author for his own library (Golz 199, p. 190).

script treasures.[85] Goethe received a copy from Diez on 23 December 1815, wrote a letter of thanks and according to his diary perused it in January 1816.[86] In July 1815 Goethe consulted Diez for a manuscript copy in the Weimar library.[87]

A hundred years later a twenty-two-year old Orientalist – a Turcologist[88] – judged this publication activity to be "estimable" attempts at popularizing the "knowledge of languages, customs and traditions of the East," in other words, producing "popular scholarship" which in the German-speaking world still carries with it negative connotations. Diez did reserve recognition, the young scholar wrote in 1913, because Goethe owed him thanks for "ample stimulation in his eastern studies", but when it came to advancing the field of Oriental Studies, he (Diez) had lacked the scholarly tools.[89]

For all these somewhat patronizing attitudes,[90] it should not be forgotten to what extent Diez' work was state-of-the-art in what was yet to become Turcology. That is to say, with regard to Oriental Studies at that time Paris,[91] soaring above Vienna,[92] had risen to solitary heights. Berlin had the Prussian Academy of Sciences, in which Diez became an honorary member in 1814; Goethe was an external member, Hammer was a corresponding member. The University of Berlin, that world-famous research institution, was established

85 Diez 1811 and 1815b; cf. Mommsen 1961, p. 2. Excerpts from the *Denkwürdigkeiten* are in the Goethe and Schiller Archive in Weimar, photograph Golz 1999 p. 178-179. The book, Diez 1811, was kept in Weimar in the library of the Duchess Anna Amalia; photographs of pages 254, 268, 174-175, 271-273, 466-467 of Diez 1811 vol. I in Golz 1999, p. 293-299 and p. 176. Frontispiece and leather binding in Golz 199, p. 188-189.

86 Photograph of frontispiece and page 371 in Golz 1999, pp. 188 and 263.

87 Rührdanz 1999, p. 105 and 111, note 64.

88 On Franz Babinger (1891-1967) cf. Killy 1995; Hanisch 1995; Kröner 1983 and Grimm 1998.

89 Babinger 1913, pp. 95 and 99.

90 Repeated by Bosse 1999 who mentioned publications "des Berliner Amateur-Orientalisten Heinrich Friedrich von Diez," pp. 115, 120, 127-128. For a more nuanced opinion see Boeschoten 2005, pp. 243-244.

91 Thanks to Antoine Silvestre de Sacy (1758-1838) France took the lead in the field of Oriental Studies. At the École spéciale des langues orientales vivantes (which was called this way since 1790; it had evolved out of the institute for *jeunes de langue* founded in 1669) Ottoman and Chagatai Turkish were taught. D.-D. Cardonne (1720-1783) held a chair for Turkish and Persian.

92 Both France and Austria trained *Sprachknaben* (*jeunes de langue, dil oğlanı*). The French, the oldest allies of the Ottomans, had their interpreters' school in Istanbul. In Vienna the Empress Maria Theresia in 1753 founded the Imperial and Royal Oriental Academy for the training of consular officials. Hammer of course was an alumnus.

in 1810.[93] One may mention in passing that there was not yet an independent field of German studies (Germanistik) either; its contours were just emerging.[94]

Diez was, to repeat the point, a scholar with a broad education. In the first place, he collected Turkish manuscripts and described them in his own hand in a catalogue which Wilhelm Pertsch, a user of the catalogue, accords rather sparing praise: "Though somewhat verbose, it is none-the-less very good, having been produced with diligence, conscientiousness and expert knowledge."[95]

It would be wrong to be dismissive of Diez's expert knowledge or of his working equipment. Among his grammars and dictionaries not only did he use both editions of the best dictionary of the time by Meninski,[96] but in the four volumes of the second edition, Vienna 1786, the "New Meninski",[97] he had added in the margins and on separate sheets of papers many thousand words, definitions and phrases which he had drawn "in part from living knowledge of the languages [one of them the Nogay language], and in part from numerous manuscripts".[98] Not every scholar had such a living "knowledge of language."[99]

Diez is the discoverer and first investigator of the national epic of the Turks and Azerbaijanis, the *Kitāb-ı Dede Korkut*.[100] This has been specifically acknowledged by Ettore Rossi and Geoffrey Lewis. He investigated the eighth of the twelve stories, the one about Depegöz. He made a carefully detailed comparison of the Turkish version with the Homeric story about the giant Polyphemus and came to the conclusion that the Turkish version represented

93 Grafton 2006.

94 "Des Knaben Wunderhorn" appeared in 1805/08 and the "Kinder- und Hausmärchen" of the brothers Grimm were published in 1812/15. Around the same time the first critical edition of the *Nibelungenlied* appeared.

95 Wilhelm Pertsch (1832-1899), originally a Sanskritist, was librarian in Gotha from 1855 and compiled, in addition to the Gotha Catalogue, Pertsch 1898.

96 Meninski 1680. On Franz Mesgnien de Meninski (1623-1698), see Fück 1955, p. 93. The printing-press with Arabic type which Meninski founded in Vienna was destroyed during the second Turkish siege. Meninski's Grammar had appeared in 1677. Cf. Babinger 1919, p. 116. Diez 1811a, p. 57, speaks of "the splendid Meninski. No one can value his service more highly than I do because in his way he has made the impossible possible."

97 Joseph von Hammer, who had been a collaborator on the "New Meninski", helped rescuing its copies in the depot during the French siege and bombardment of Vienna in 1809.

98 Thus Diez in his last will and testament cited in Balcke 1928, p. 193.

99 Regarding the tensions between "practical researchers" and "armchair scholars" in Arabic studies cf. Fück 1955.

100 Rossi 1952; Ergin, 1964; Lewis, 1974; cf. Hein 1958; Boeschoten 2005; See my No. 26 in this volume.

the legend's original form.[101] The next step was made by Wilhelm Grimm in a celebrated study published in 1857, "Die Sage vom Polyphem", *Abhandlungen der Königlichen Akademie der Wissenschaften*, Berlin 1857.

Already in his Istanbul days Diez had taken an interest in the manuscripts of the Bible translation in middle-Ottoman that had been promoted by Jan Amos Komenský (Comenius) and carried out in Istanbul under the supervision of Levinus Warner, resident of the States General since 1655.[102] Early in 1814, in a letter to Dr. Pinkerton of the Bible Society, Diez declared himself ready to prepare the Leiden manuscript for publication. From the end of 1814 to the last days of his life this self-imposed task kept him engaged at his desk;[103] only out of friendship did he put in time to undertake a Nasreddin Hoca translation for Goethe, an act of self-abnegation which the latter acknowledged with special gratitude.

From 1816 Diez suffered from weak eyesight and gout. After severe illness he died on April 7th 1817. Friedrich August Wolf wrote a moving obituary to him in *Die Vossische Zeitung*. In the person of Jean Daniel Kieffer, professor at the Collège de France, was found a Turcologist[104] who was prepared to publish the Leiden Turkish Bible in Paris for the English Bible Society which actually came about between 1819 and 1827.[105]

In his will Diez bequeathed his books and manuscripts to the Prussian Royal Library (Königliche Bibliothek),[106] whose holdings of oriental manuscripts

---

101 Diez 1815c. An analysis and history of the relevant scholarship was given in Mundy 1956. As Mommsen 1951, pp. 238-240, showed, Goethe was struck by analogies between Tepegöz and Timur and even with Napoleon... In the *West-östlicher Diwan* the book Timur was meant to tell about the figure and violence of a demonic world-destroyer.

102 See Malcolm 2007a, and my "Turkish Bible Manuscripts", No. 15 in this volume.

103 He received help from the young F.A.G. Tholuck who later became a famous Old Testament scholar; cf. Babinger 1913, p. 98. Diez died when four books of the Pentateuch had been revised, copied and prepared for the press; further details are found in Cooper 1901.

104 Jean Daniel Kieffer (born in Strassburg, died in Paris 1832), one of the *jeunes de langue*, was active in Constantinople in 1796 at the French embassy as secretary and translator for his teacher, the French chargé d'affaires Pierre Ruffin, subsequently one of France's leading orientalists. With the outbreak of war both men were thrown into prison and spent three years in the dismal confinement of Yedikule (Shaw 1971, p. 192). They were freed in 1803. Kieffer occupied Ruffin's chair of Turkish at the Collège de France, while the latter continued in his office as chargé d'affaires in Istanbul. Upon the death of Ruffin, Kieffer was appointed professor; cf. Cooper 1901, p. 12; Malcolm 2007, p. 360.

105 More details are found in Cooper 1901 and Malcolm 2007, p. 360.

106 As Diez had changed his original intention and bequeathed his cash assets not to his brother but to the charity fund of the Berlin Cathedral, his family – in vain – contested the validity of the will in a seven years' lawsuit on the grounds that Diez, due to mental and physical

thereby doubled. Whether Diez was an "amateur" or not, there is no doubt that he was a notable connoisseur of Persian and Turkish miniature painting and calligraphy. His collection became the cornerstone of the Persian and Turkish miniature holdings of the Prussian Royal Library. These begin with the rare fourteenth-century paintings from Tabriz and Herat in Diez A. Fol. 70, 71 and 72. Diez bequeathed four albums of royal provenance[107], a splendid Kāşifī *Raużat aş-şuhadā'* from the Sultan's library, one manuscript from Timurid Herat (Diez A. Fol. 7, No. 4), and other manuscripts from Safawid Tabriz (No. 14) and Shiraz (Diez A. fol. 3 and 1, Nos. 24 and 26).[108]

Interestingly, two important albums of royal provenance found their way from Diez to the British Library. "A later set of costume paintings in two albums, also in the British Museum [1974-6-17-012[1] and [2]) was a gift from the Sultan Abdülhamid I (d. 1789) to General (sic) Diez, Prussian ambassador at Istanbul. These paintings are of the high quality to be expected in such a gift. In all there are two hundred and twenty-five paintings of the costumes, equipment and emblems of the Sultan and of the ministers, officials and servants, from the Grand Vizier to the lowliest cook, including eunuchs, women officials and servants of the Harem..."[109]

Diez's own works are no longer easily accessible; for this reason later scholarship has treated him unfairly sometimes.[110] To elucidate in its complexity the social and scientific process by which Turcology has come to be an independent academic discipline is still an ongoing task. And this includes the occasional alienation and an ill-feeling between "practical Ottoman studies" (Osmanistik) and "general Turcology" ("Allgemeinturkologie"); between "amateurs" and "professionals". Remember that Hammer named himself a true amateur. As for the achievement of Heinrich Friedrich von Diez, it should not be passed over in haste. On the contrary, it should be appreciated as a part of the complex process that led to the emergence of the present-day field of scholarship in Turkish.

---

weakness, was not fit to draw up a valid last will and testament; on this subject Balcke 1928, p. 190f. Solbrig 1973, fn. on page 28, mistakenly maintains that Diez was "finally, due to his confused state of mind, certified by his relatives as being incapable of managing his affairs."

107 Described by M.Ş. İpşiroğlu 1964.

108 Stchoukine 1971, No. 84, pl. 11, 51, 52.

109 Nora M. Titley, *Persian Miniature Painting and its influence on the Art of Turkey and India. The British Library Collections*, London 1983, p. 158 note 34.

110 Thus Babinger 1927, p. 153, and Flemming 1968 where, without taking account of Gibb 1904, Diez's "Ermahnung an Islambol" is taken to be a translation of the *Vāqi'anāme* also known as *Ḫābnāme* (see above fn. 82).

Bibliography

Aksan, Virginia H. 1995: *An Ottoman Statesman in War and Peace. Ahmed Resmi Efendi 1700-1783*, Leiden-New York-Köln.

Andreas, Willy 1959: "Carl August und Goethe in Schlesien (1790)", *Ostdeutsche Wissenschaft* 6 (1959), 158-170.

Babinger, Franz 1913: "Ein orientalistischer Berater Goethes: Heinrich Friedrich von Diez", *Goethe-Jahrbuch* 34.

Babinger, Franz 1919: "Die türkischen Studien in Europa bis zum Auftreten Josef von Hammer-Purgstalls", *Die Welt des Islams* 7.

Babinger, Franz 1927: *Die Geschichtsschreiber der Osmanen und ihre Werke*, Leipzig.

Balcke, Curt 1928: "Heinrich Friedrich von Diez und sein Vermächtnis in der Preussischen Staatsbibliothek". In: Abb, Gustav 1928 (ed.): *Von Büchern und Bibliotheken. Abschiedsgabe Ernst Kühnert*. Berlin, 187-200.

Baumgart, Wolfgang 1940: *Goethe in Schlesien*, Breslau.

Berkes, Niyazi 1964: *The Development of Secularism in Turkey*, Montreal.

Bernays, Michael 1868: *Goethes Briefe an Friedrich August Wolf*, Berlin.

Beydilli, Kemal 1984: *1790 Osmanlı-Prusya ittifakı. Meydana gelişi – tahlili – tatbiki*, Istanbul.

Beydilli, Kemal 1985: *Büyük Friedrich ve Osmanlılar. XVIII. yüzyılda Osmanlı-Prusya münasebetleri*, Istanbul.

Böer, Ingeborg, Ruth Haerkötter and Petra Kappert 2002: *Türken in Berlin 1871-1945*, Berlin.

Boeschoten 2005: Rik Boeschoten, *Het Boek van Dede Korkoet*, Amsterdam.

Boyle, Nicholas 1991: *Goethe: The Poet and the Age. Volume I. The Poetry of Desire* (*1749-1790*). Oxford.

Boyle, Nicholas 1995: *Goethe. Der Dichter in seiner Zeit. Band I 1749-1790. Aus dem Englischen übersetzt von Holger Fliessbach*, Munich.

Boyle, Nicholas 1999: *Goethe. Der Dichter in seiner Zeit. Band II 1791-1803. Aus dem Englischen übersetzt von Holger Fliessbach*, Munich.

Boyle, Nicholas 2000: *Goethe: The Poet and the Age. Volume Two. Revolution and Renunciation* (*1790-1803*). Oxford.

Cevdet 1877: *Cevdet Paşa Ta'rīhi* 1294/1877-1878: VI, Istanbul.

Conrady, Karl Otto 1985: *Goethe. Leben und Werk*, 2 volumes, Königstein, Taunus.

Cooper, A.A. 1901: *The Story of the* (*Osmanlı*) *Turkish Version with a brief account of related versions*, London.

Diez, Heinrich Friedrich 1772: *Vortheile geheimer Gesellschaften für die Welt, von einem Unzertrennlichen in der A*[*micitia*] (published anonymously).

Diez, Heinrich Friedrich 1780: *Cicero's erstes Buch Tuskulanischer Untersuchungen von der Verachtung des Todes*, Magdeburg and Leipzig.

Diez, Heinrich Friedrich 1783: *Benedikt von Spinoza nach Leben und Lehren*, Dessau and Leipzig.

Diez, Heinrich Friedrich von 1811a: *Denkwürdigkeiten von Asien in Künsten und Wissenschaften, Sitten, Gebräuchen und Alterthümern, Religion und Regierungsverfassung aus Handschriften und eigenen Erfahrungen gesammelt... Erster Theil.* Berlin.

Diez, Heinrich Friedrich von 1811b: *Buch des Kabus oder Lehren des persischen Königs Kjekjawus für seinen Sohn Ghilan Schach. Ein Werk für alle Zeitalter aus dem Türkisch-Persisch-Arabischen übersetzt und durch Abhandlungen und Anmerkungen erläutert ...* Berlin.

Diez, Heinrich Friedrich von 1811c: *Ueber Inhalt und Vortrag, Entstehung und Schicksale des königlichen Buchs, eines Werks von der Regierungskunst; als Ankündigung einer Uebersetzung, nebst Probe aus dem Türkisch-Persisch-Arabischen des Waassi Aly Dschelebi ...* Berlin.

Diez, Heinrich Friedrich von 1813: *Wesentliche Betrachtungen oder Geschichte des Krieges zwischen den Osmanen und Russen in den Jahren 1768 bis 1774 von Resmi Achmed Efendi aus dem Türkischen übersetzt und durch Anmerkungen erläutert ...* Halle and Berlin.

Diez, Heinrich Friedrich von 1815a: *Der neuentdeckte oghuzische Cyklop verglichen mit dem Homerischen.* Halle and Berlin. (Offprint of part of 1815b).

Diez, Heinrich Friedrich von 1815b: *Denkwürdigkeiten von Asien in Künsten und Wissenschaften, Sitten, Gebräuchen und Alterthümern, Religion und Regierungsverfassung aus Handschriften und eigenen Erfahrungen gesammelt ... Zweyter Theil.* Berlin and Halle.

Diez, Heinrich Friedrich von 1815c: *Wage der Blumen oder Anweisung zum Tulpen- und Narcissen-Bau aus dem Türkischen des Scheich Muhammed Lalézari.* Halle and Berlin.

Ergin, Muharrem 1964: *Dede Korkut Kitabı. Metin-Sözlük*, Ankara.

Findley, Carter V. 1995: "Ebu Bekir Ratib's Vienna Embassy Narrative: Discovering Austria or Propagandizing for Reform in Istanbul?", *WZKM* 85, 41-80.

Findley, Carter V. 1980: *Bureaucratic Reform in the Ottoman Empire. The Sublime Porte, 1789-1922*, Princeton, New Jersey.

Flemming, Barbara 1968: *Türkische Handschriften. Teil 1*, Wiesbaden (VOHD XIII,1).

Flemming, Barbara 1986: "Zwei türkische Bibelhandschriften in Leiden als mittelosmanische Sprachdenkmäler", *WZKM* 76 (1986), 111-118.

Friedenthal, Richard 1963: *Goethe. Sein Leben und seine Zeit*, Munich.

Fück, Johann 1955: *Die arabischen Studien in Europa bis in den Anfang des 20. Jahrhunderts*, Leipzig.

Gibb, E.J.W. 1904: *A History of Ottoman Poetry*, Vol. III, ed. Edward G. Browne, London.

Gibb, E.J.W. 1909: *A History of Ottoman Poetry*, Vol. VI, ed. Edward G. Browne, London.

Gibb, H.A.R., and Harold Bowen 1950, *Islamic society and the West*, Vol. One, part I., London.

Golz, Jochen 1999 (ed.), *Goethes Morgenlandfahrten. West-östliche Begegnungen*, Frankfurt am Main.

Golz, Jochen, and Gothe, Rosalinde 1999: *Goethe. Venezianische Epigramme*, Frankfurt am Main and Leipzig.

Gonnella, Julia, Friederike Weis, Christoph Rauch (eds.), *The Diez Albums, Contexts and Contents*, Leiden 2016.

Grafton, Anthony 2006: "The nutty professors. The history of academic charisma", *The New Yorker*, October 23, 2006, 82-87.

Grimm, Gerhard 1998: "Franz Babinger (1891-1967). Ein lebensgeschichtlicher Essay", *Die Welt des Islams* 38, 286-333.

Grumach, Renate (ed.) 1977: *Goethe. Begegnungen und Gespräche. Begründet von Ernst Grumach und Renate Grumach, Band III 1786-1792*, Berlin-New York.

Hamberger/Meusel 1796: *Das gelehrte Deutschland ... Angefangen von G.Chr. Hamberger. Fortgesetzt von Joh. Georg Meusel. 2ter Bd., 5. Ausgabe.* Lemgo.

Hamberger/Meusel 1806: *Das gelehrte Deutschland ... Bd. 12, mit Klassifikation der Teutschen Schriftsteller nach den Wissenschaften*). Lemgo.

[Hammer, Joseph von] 1809: *Des Türkischen Gesandten Resmi Ahmet Efendi Gesandtschaftliche Berichte von seinen Gesandtschaften in Wien im Jahre 1757, und in Berlin im Jahre 1763. Aus dem türkischen Originale übersetzt.* Berlin and Stettin.

Hammer, Joseph von 1809-1818: *Fundgruben des Orients, bearbeitet durch eine Gesellschaft von Liebhabern*. 6 Bände. Vienna.

Hammer, J. von 1819: *Morgenlaendisches Kleeblatt*. 1819, reprint 1981 with biography by Andreas Tietze.

Hammer, J. von 1832: *Geschichte des osmanischen Reiches. Band VIII*. Pest.

Hanisch, Ludmila Hanisch 1995: "Akzentverschiebung – Zur Geschichte der Semitistik und Islamwissenschaft während des "Dritten Reichs", in *Berichte zur Wissenschaftsgeschichte* 18, 217-226.

Hein, Joachim 1958: *Das Buch des Dede Korkut*, Zürich.

Heyd, Uriel 1973: *Studies in Old Ottoman Criminal Law. Edited by V.L. Ménage*. Oxford 1973.

Höpp, Gerhard (ed.) 1996: *Fremde Erfahrungen. Asiaten und Afrikaner in Deutschland, Österreich und in der Schweiz bis 1945*, Berlin.

Hoffmann, Adalbert 1898: Adalbert Hoffmann 1889: *Goethe in Breslau und Oberschlesien und seine Werbung um Henriette von Lüttwitz. Neue Beiträge zu Goethe's Lebensgeschichte*, Oppeln and Leipzig.

İpşiroğlu, M.Ş. 1964: *Saray-Alben. Diez'sche Klebebände aus den Berliner Sammlungen. Beschreibung und stilkritische Anmerkungen*, Wiesbaden (VOHD VIII).

Karal, Enver Ziya Karal 1946: *Selim III'ün Hatt-ı Humâyunları* II, Ankara.

Karamuk, Gümeç 1975: *Ahmed Azmi Efendis Gesandtschaftsbericht als Zeugnis des osmanischen Machtverfalls und der beginnenden Reformära unter Selim III.*, Bern.

Kuran, Ercüment 1963: "Osmanlı daimî elçisi Ali Aziz Efendi'nin Alman Şarkiyatçısı Friedrich von Diez ile Berlin'de İlmî ve Felsefî muhaberatı, 1797", *Belleten* XXVII, 45-58.

Kuran, Ercüment Kuran 1968: *Avrupa'da Osmanlı İkamet Elçiliklerinin Kuruluşu ve İlk Siyasi Faâliyetleri, 1793-1821*, Ankara.

Lengersdorff, Irma Margarete 1965: "Eine Heiratsabsicht Goethes aus dem Jahre 1790", *Goethe. N.F. des Jahrbuchs der Goethe-Gesellschaft*, Weimar 1965, 175-192.

Lewis, Bernard 1965: "Elçi", *Encyclopaedia of Islam* II, 694.

Lewis, Geoffrey 1974: *The Book of Dede Korkut*, Harmondsworth.

Lieven, Dominic 2002: *Empire. The Russian Empire and Its Rivals*, London.

Lieven, Dominic 2009: *Russia against Napoleon. The Battle for Europe, 1807 to 1814*, London. Penguin Books 2010.

Lüttwitz, Ernst Freiherr von 1835: *Biographie des Königl. preussischen Staatsministers Freiherrn von Schuckmann*, Leipzig.

Malcolm, Noel 2007a: "Comenius, Boyle, Oldenburg, and the Translation of the Bible into Turkish", *Church History and Religious Culture* 87 (2007), 327-362.

Malcolm, Noel 2007b: "Comenius, the Conversion of the Turks, and the Muslim-Christian Debate on the Corruption of Scripture", *Church History and Religious Culture* 87 (2007), 477-508.

Mayer, Hans 1999: *Goethe. Herausgegeben von Inge Jens*. Frankfurt am Main.

Mayer, Hans 1974: *Goethe. Ein Versuch über den Erfolg*, Frankfurt am Main.

Meninski 1677: *Linguarum orientalium, turcicae, arabicae, persicae institutiones seu grammatica turcica*. Vienna.

Meninski, Franciscus A. Mesgnien 1680: *Thesaurus linguarum orientalium, Turcicae, Arabicae, Persicae, continens nimirum Lexicon Turcico-Arabico-Persicum et Grammaticam Turcicam*. 3 volumes Vienna.

Meninski 1780 [-1802]: *Lecicon Arabico-Persico-Turcicum*, ed. Bernhard von Jenisch and other alumni of the Oriental Academy. 3 volumes Vienna.

Mommsen, Katharina 1961: *Goethe und Diez. Quellenuntersuchungen zu Gedichten der Divan-Epoche*, Berlin; reprint Bern 1998.

Mundy, C.S. 1956: "Polyphemus and Tepegöz", in BSOAS XVIII, 279-302.

Nanninga, J.G. 1966: *Bronnen tot de geschiedenis van den Levantschen handel IV (1765-1826)*, 2. volume, Den Haag.

Neudecker, Hannah 1994: *The Turkish Bible Translation by Yaḥya bin 'Ishak, also called Ḫaki* (1659), Leiden.

Neudecker, Hannah 1997: "An Ottoman palace revolution witnessed by a court musician", *DS-NELL*, pp. 163-192.

Peirce, Leslie P. 1993: *The Imperial Harem. Women and Sovereignty in the Ottoman Empire*. New York and Oxford.

Pertsch, Wilhelm 1889: *Verzeichniss der türkischen Handschriften*, Berlin (Die Handschriften-Verzeichnisse der Königlichen Bibliothek zu Berlin, vol. VI).

Piontek, Heinz 1993: *Goethe unterwegs in Schlesien. Fast ein Roman*, 2nd edition Würzburg.

Pröhl, Karl 1986: *Die Bedeutung preußischer Politik in den Phasen der orientalischen Frage. Ein Beitrag zur Entwicklung deutsch-türkischer Beziehungen von 1606-1871*, Frankfurt a.M.

Reich-Ranicki, Marcel 1996: *Die Anwälte der Literatur*, Munich.

Rossi, Ettore 1952: *Il `Kitab-ı Dede-Qorqut*, Vatican City.

Rothe, Wolfgang 1998: *Der politische Goethe. Dichter und Staatsdiener im deutschen Spätabsolutismus*, Göttingen.

Roxburgh, David J. 1995: "Heinrich Friedrich von Diez and his Eponymous Albums: MSS. Diez.a. Fols. 70-74", *Muqarnas* 12, 112-136.

Rührdanz, Karin, "Illustrationen zu Rašīd al-Dīn's Ta'rīh-i Mubārak-i Gāzānī in den Berliner Diez-Alben", in Denise Aigle (ed.), *L'Iran face à la domination mongole*, Teheran 1997, pp. 295-306.

Rührdanz, Karin 1999: "Orientalische Handschriften in der Herzogin Anna Amalia Bibliothek", 97-111. In: Jochen Golz (ed.), *Goethes Morgenlandfahrten. West-östliche Begegnungen*, Frankfurt am Main.

Schwarz, Klaus 1989: "Vom Krieg zum Frieden. Berlin, das Kurfürstentum Brandenburg, das Reich und die Türken". In: Sievenich, Gereon & Budde, Hendrik (ed.) 1989, *Europa und der Orient 800-1900*. Berlin, 245-278.

Shaw, Stanford J. 1971: *Between Old and New. The Ottoman Empire under Sultan Selim III 1789-1807*, Cambridge, Massachusetts.

Sievenich, Gereon and Budde, Hendrik (ed.) 1989: *Europa und der Orient 800-1900*. Berlin.

Solbrig, Ingeborg H. 1973: *Hammer-Purgstall und Goethe. "Dem Zaubermeister das Werkzeug"*, Bern and Frankfurt am Main.

Stchoukine, Ivan, B. Flemming, P. Luft and H. Sohrweide 1971: *Illuminierte islamische Handschriften*, Wiesbaden (VOHD XVI).

Steiger, Robert 1982: *Goethes Leben von Tag zu Tag. Eine dokumentarische Chronik*. Zurich and Munich.

Tietze, Andreas 1948: "`Azîz Efendis Muhayyelât", *Oriens* I, 248-329.

Tornius, Valerian 1926: *Goethes Leben von Wilhelm Bode. 1790-1794. Vereinsamung*, Berlin.

Unseld, Siegfried 1991: *Goethe und seine Verleger*, Frankfurt a.M. and Leipzig.

Urzidil, Johannes 1981: *Goethe in Böhmen*, Zürich and Munich 1962; third edition.

Volz, G.B. 1907: "Eine türkische Gesandtschaft am Hofe Friedrichs des Großen im Winter 1763/64", *Hohenzollern-Jahrbuch*.

Vrolijk, Arnoud and Jan Schmidt, Karin Scheper 2012: *Turcksche boucken. The Oriental collection of Levinus Warner, Dutch diplomat in seventeenth-century Istanbul*, [The Hague].

Weczerka, Hugo (ed.) 1977: *Schlesien (Handbuch der historischen Stätten)*, Stuttgart.

Wilpert, Gero von 1998: *Goethe-Lexikon*, Stuttgart.

Wurm, Heidrun 1971: *Der osmanische Historiker Hüseyn b. Ğaʿfer, genannt Hezārfenn, und die Istanbuler Gesellschaft in der zweiten Hälfte des 17. Jahrhunderts*, Freiburg.

Zarncke, Friedrich 1884: *Goethes Notizbuch von der schlesischen Reise im Jahre 1790*, Leipzig.

Zinkeisen, Johann Wilhelm 1857: *Geschichte des osmanischen Reiches in Europa, Fünfter Theil*, Hamburg and Gotha.

Zinkeisen, Johann Wilhelm 1859: *Sechster Theil. Umschwung ... (von 1774) im Jahre 1802* Gotha.

Zinkeisen, Johann Wilhelm 1863: *Geschichte des osmanischen Reiches in Europa, Siebenther Theil*. Gotha.

Ziolko, Karl-Heinz 1992: *Goethes Schlesische Reise*. Munich.

Ziolko, Karl-Heinz 1994: *Friedrich Gottlob Endler. Ein schlesischer Kupferstecher der Goethezeit*. Munich.

CHAPTER 29

On the Çırçıp: Yesterday and Today*

On Wednesday, the 7th of February 2007, in the *ilçe* Ceylanpınar of Şanlıurfa Province an accident took place in which ten for the most part young persons drowned in the "Çırpı". Much sympathy was expressed in the media. Alevis in particular recalled Dede Garkın who had lived at this spot where the old caravan route from Aleppo to Mosul crossed over the Çırçıp. And here as well was situated the battlefield on which in 1516 the incorporation of the region of Diyarbekir into the Ottoman Empire was sealed. Today this is where Highway 400, known as a new "Silk Route", goes on to Iran and Iraq.

1 The Çırçıps

The river name Çırçıp (Djurdjib)[1] designates at least three larger streams and water courses which, instead of flowing in a single riverbed, draw a network of wadis (*dere yatağı*) from the mountain rises southward through the plain where they are conveyed to a valley that today constitutes the headwaters of the Western Khabur, the only perennially flowing tributary of the Euphrates in Upper Mesopotamia. In the summer these are wadis with little water; in the winter, however, they contain great volumes of water and are transformed into torrential rivers.

The most important of the Çırçıps, the Great Çırçıp (on different maps: Büyük Çırçıp, Büyükcircipsuyu, Djurdjub, Curcup Deresi, Syr. Jarjab), arises in the *ilçe* Viranşehir on the southern slope of the 1938-meters-high Karaca Dağ, an extinct volcano, that like a headland looks down on the plain. The surface of its summit is a flat grassland surrounded by jagged basalt rocks.[2] Its slopes stretch a great distance south; on them at the end of the 1980s, amid stony meadows, green watered fields flourished where – as in Ottoman times –

* Translated by John O'Kane.

1 In Carl Ritter (*Die Erdkunde im Verhältniss zur Natur und zur Geschichte des Menschen, oder allgemeine vergleichende Geographie. Die Erdkunde von Asien. Band VII. Zweite Abtheilung. Das Stufenland des Euphrat- und Tigrissystems.* Berlin 1844, p. 255), the Çırçıp is recorded (mistakenly) as the western Dschagschak or Djachdjack.

2 Sinclair, T.A.: *Eastern Turkey: An Architectural and Archaeological Survey*, Vol. IV, London 1990, pp. 177-78.

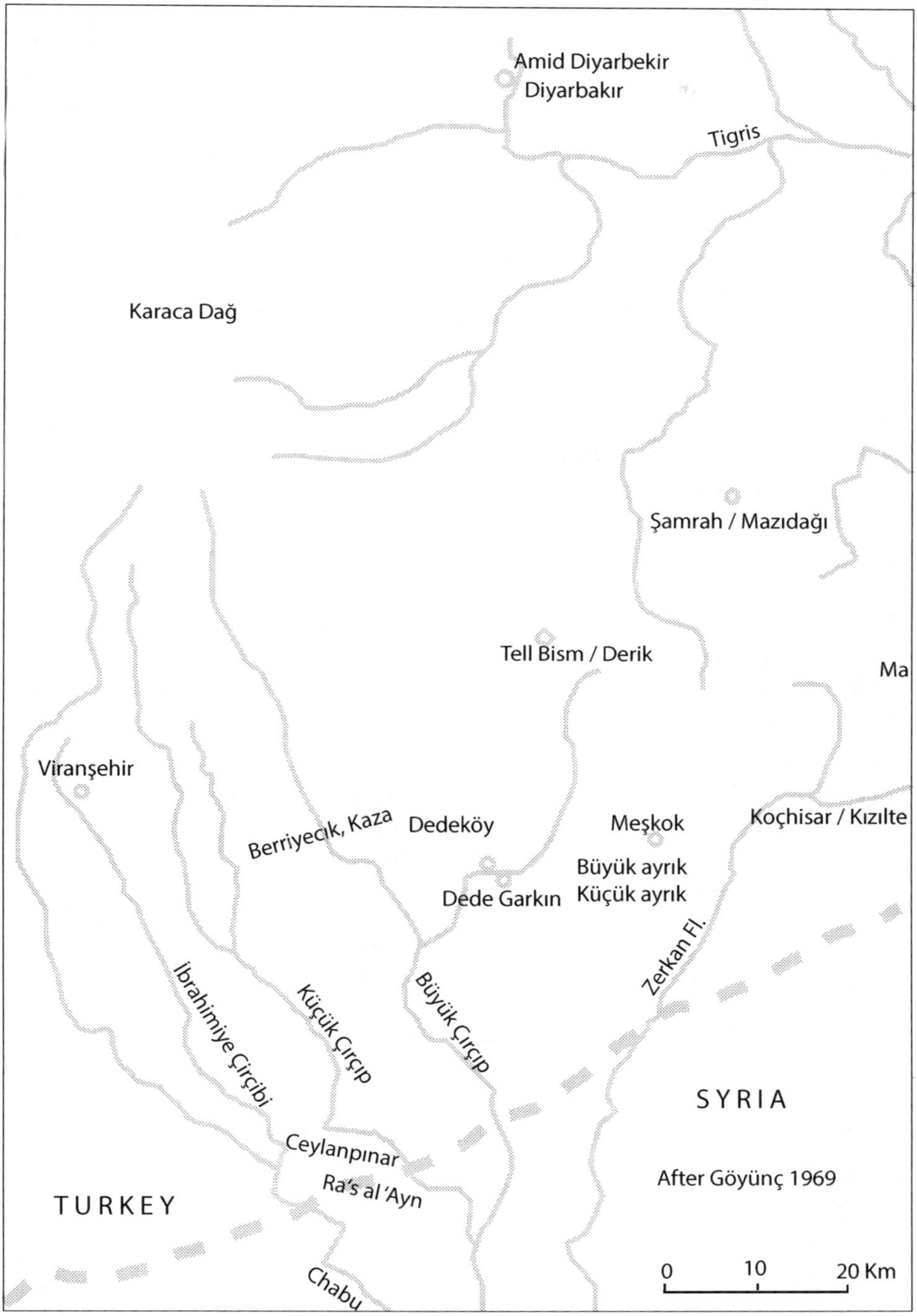
Amid Diyarbekir
Diyarbakır
Tigris
Karaca Dağ
Şamrah / Mazıdağı
Tell Bism / Derik
Ma
Viranşehir
Berriyecik, Kaza
Dedeköy
Meşkok
Koçhisar / Kızılte
Büyük ayrık
Küçük ayrık
Dede Garkın
Zerkan Fl.
İbrahimiye Çirçibi
Küçük Çırçıp
Büyük Çırçıp
SYRIA
Ceylanpınar
Ra's al 'Ayn
After Göyünç 1969
TURKEY
Chabu
0
10
20 Km

MAP 1

mountain rice was cultivated.[3] From the 1158-meters-high Kaletepesi (Kel Tepesi?) emerges another Çırçıp, the İbrahimiye Çirçibi or Arslanbaba Deresi. From the Gözelem Tepe (447 m) descends the Beşmağaralar Deresi which is perhaps the Djirdjib Abu Daradj that Max von Oppenheim described as at first flowing southward through a deep carved-out valley and then, due to a barrier of rock, swerving in a right angle to be redirected eastward. A small Çırçıp, Küçük Çırçıp, appears to flow still further to the south-west toward Ra's al-ʿAyn.[4]

The Çırçıps flow chiefly toward the south. In a valley, where hundreds of springs arise, in the present-day *ilçe* Ceylanpınar, the Büyük Çırçıp leaves the national territory of Turkey at a border village that had earlier been named after the river (Büyükçırçıp; now Yeşiltepe and Aydoğdu), near the train station Gürpınar. After its entry into the national territory of the Arab Republic of Syria, the Çırçıp, which is now called Jarjab, flows on further through part of the Mesopotamian plain. South of Ra's al-ʿAyn, near as-Safih, it flows into the Great (Western) Khabur from the left.

2 Two Caravan Routes from Urfa to Diyarbekir

There were two west-to-east routes for caravans and armies that went from Aleppo to the east.[5] The northern one ran around the volcanic mass of the Karaca Dağ[6] to Siverek. At the beginning of the 20th century this road, the forerunner of the present-day Highway 360, was only used to a limited extent by motor vehicles because it was strewn with basalt rocks. To the left, stretched the desolate fields of broken and disintegrating lava; to the right, climbed ter-

3 Göyünç, Nejat & Hütteroth, Wolf-Dieter: *Land an der Grenze. Osmanische Verwaltung im heutigen türkisch- syrischen Grenzgebiet im 16. Jahrhundert*, İstanbul 1997, pp. 37, 51 and 115, with illustrations 9 and 10. The authors travelled in the region in 1988 and 1991.

4 This impression is conveyed by modern tourist maps. The position of the riverbeds in the 1960s can be seen on the map in Nejat Göyünç *XVI. Yüzyılda Mardin Sancağı*, İstanbul 1969. On the other hand, it seems as if Göyünç and Hütteroth 1997 consciously avoid using the name Çırçıp. The earlier literature on "the 'Wadi al-Djirdjib' which has not much water in it" is found in Honigmann, E: "Ra's al-ʿAyn or ʿAyn Warda" in: *EI* VIII (1995), p. 434.

5 Both routes are shown on Map II in Tavernier, Jean- Baptiste: *Les six voyages de Turquie et de Perse*, with introduction and commentary by Yerasimos, Stéphane: Introduction et notes, Paris 1981, I; Map 2 in Bruinessen, Martin van & Boeschoten, Hendrik: *Evliya Çelebi in Diyarbekir*, Leiden-Cologne 1988.

6 Sinclair, T.A.: *Eastern Turkey: An Architectural and Archaeological Survey*, Vol. III, London 1989, pp. 408-09; Bruinessen, Martin van: "The Ottoman Conquest of Diyarbekir", in Bruinessen, Martin van & Boeschoten, Hendrik: 1988, pp. 36-37.

race upon terrace up the mountain from where the lava had flowed down.[7] From Siverek the road continued to the traffic hub Kara Amid (Diyarbekir, Diyarbakır) with branches in the direction of Bitlis or to al-Cazira (Cizre) in the direction of Mosul.[8]

The older, southern route made use of the Roman or Byzantine highway which went from Edessa (Ruha, Urfa, Şanlıurfa) through the Tektek Dağ via Viranşehir over bridges[9] to the former Dunyasir (Koçhisar, Kızıltepe),[10] Nisibis (Nusaybin), al-Cazira and Mosul.

3 Dede Garkın, Türkmens, Alevilik5

At one of the bridges on the southern highway, at the point where it crossed the Çırçıp, there once stood the Sufi lodge (*zaviye*) of a Türkmen shaykh by the name of Dede Garkın. Of fundamental importance for our knowledge of his *vita* are hagiographical reports, one of which stems from Elvan Çelebi in 1358-59.[11] The dates of the shaykh's birth and death remain unknown. What can be said is that Dede Garkın was a disciple of Abu l-Vafa Tac al-ʿArifin (d. 501/1107), an Iraqi Sufi of partly Kurdish descent, and that he entered the region with the Iraqi Türkmens who from the 11th century immigrated into what was then Byzantine but later became Seljuq Upper Mesopotamia.[12]

It is possible that Dede Garkın is not his actual name but that of his Oguz tribe, the Karkın. The Karkın (Garkın, Karkun, Kargun) joined with the Aleppo Türkmens who gradually divided into a sedentary group and a group of nomads.[13] Dede Garkın, also called Ulu Garkın, was influential because of his

---

7 Wigram, W.A.: *The cradle of mankind. Life in Eastern Kurdistan*, London 1922, 2nd edition, p. 13.

8 A good sketch of the stages of the road Urfa – Diyarbekir – Cizre is found in Niebuhr, Carsten: *Reisebeschreibung nach Arabien und den umliegenden Ländern*, Copenhagen 1778; reprint of the editions of 1774-78 (Copenhagen) and 1837 (Hamburg) with added preface by Dietmar Henze, Graz 1968.

9 Göyünç, Nejat & Hütteroth, Wolf-Dieter: 1997, p. 53, were shown remains of bridges from earlier times.

10 Ritter, Carl: 1844, pp. 366 and 373; Göyünç, Nejat & Hütteroth, Wolf-Dieter: 1997, pp. 41 and 130; Groot, A.H. de: "Kočhisar IV", in: *EI* V (1986), p. 248.

11 Erünal, İsmail E. & Ocak,. Ahmet Yaşar (eds.): *Menâkibu'l-Kudsiyye Fî Menâsibi'l-Unsiyye*, Ankara 1995, pp. xl-xlii.

12 Woods, John E.: *The Aqquyunlu. Clan, Confederation, Empire*, Minneapolis and Chicago 1976, pp. 40 and 237, ftns. 11 and 12.

13 Sümer, Faruk: *Oğuzlar (Türkmenler)*, Ankara 1972, 2nd edition, pp. 312-14; on the list of Karkın villages (pp. 439-40) in Iskilib (Sancak Çorum) are Dere-i Karkın and Karkın -Dere.

asceticism and his fear of God; his teachings won him numerous adherents; the latter wore distinctive buckskin caps. The *dede* won the approval of the Turkish prince of the region, referred to by Elvan Çelebi as "sultan" – there were several of them in Upper Mesopotamia at the beginning of the 12th century[14] – and the prince donated seventeen villages to him. As shaykh of the Vefaiyye, Dede Garkın was regarded during his lifetime as a guarantor of orthodoxy. His preaching and performing miracles resulted in a popular religious movement. One of his "four hundred" *halife*s was the ascetic shaykh of the Türkmens, Baba Ilyas. By the latter presenting himself as a "Messenger of God" (*Resulullah*) his entry into the Muslim heterodoxy of Anatolia was completed.[15] And Baba Ilyas' disciple was Baba Ishak who originated from Syria and led the great Baba'i revolt which shook the Seljuq state in 1240.[16]

Up to now the places where Dede Garkın lived are thought to have been Ablustain/Elbistan and Maraş, but he could also have chosen his residence along the southern caravan route, that still flourished in his day, and been buried there. After the upheavals caused by the Mongols, the Confederation of the Akkoyunlu had its central region in Diyarbekir.[17] Today the memory of Dede Garkın's activity still lives on in the area of the Çırçıp, and likewise a Shaykh İbrahim is named as his *halife* whose place of origin is supposed to have been İbrahimiye, not far from the Çırçıp.

The religious movement kindled by Dede Garkın and others like him found its ecstatic continuation in the Kızılbaş-Safawiya. Its leaders became saints of the Alevilik, that "religious syncretism" which under the influence of the Kızılbaş-Safawiya would lead to the formation of a new heterodox current of faith.[18] The Safawid Cunayd, who would transform the Safawid order into the

---

Is Dede Karkın meant? In 1766 Carsten Niebuhr learned from his friend Dr. Patrick Russell in Aleppo of a tribe "Dede Garkın" with a thousand tents in the region of Aintab (Gaziantep).

14 Felix, Wolfgang: *Byzanz und die islamische Welt im früheren 11. Jahrhundert*, Vienna 1981, pp. 131-82; Sinclair, T.A.: 1990, IV, pp. 31 f.

15 Sümer, Faruk: op. cit.; Ocak, Ahmet Yaşar: *Osmanlı İmparatorluğunda Marjinal Sûfîlik: Kalenderiler*, Ankara 1992, p. 64. In *Turcica* 31 (1999), pp. 549-53, Martin van Bruinessen gives an overview of the broad field of research on heterodox Islam in Anatolia in his book review of Mélikoff, Irène: *Hadji Bektach: un mythe et ses avatars*, Leiden 1998.

16 Karamustafa, Ahmet T.: "Early Sufism in Eastern Anatolia", in: Lewisohn, Leonard (ed.): *Classical Persian Sufism: from its Origins to Rumi*, London/New York 1993, pp. 175-83, with earlier literature.

17 Sinclair, T.A.: 1989, III, pp. 385-405.

18 Kehl-Bodrogi, Krisztina & Kellner-Heinkele, Barbara & Otter-Beaujean, A.: *Alevism in Turkey and comparable syncretistic religious communities in the Near East*, Leiden 1997.

heterodox Shi'ite Kızılbaş movement supported by Türkmen tribes, resided – around 1456 – for three years in Diyarbekir. When Cunayd's grandson, Shah İsmail, annexed Diyarbekir in 1507/08 and installed Muhammad Khan Ustaclu as governor, remnants of the Akkoyunlu Confederation, Turkish and Kurdish tribes,[19] both partially belonging to the Boz Ulus, were living relatively undisturbed on Karaca Dağ.[20] Still in 1526 three shaykhs were registered for tax purposes in the village Dede Garkın.[21]

Shah İsmail endeavoured to incorporate in his empire regions outside Iran where he had followers. This in turn drove Kurdish princes into the arms of the Ottoman Sultan who promised them autonomy.[22] When Sultan Selim had destroyed Shah İsmail's army at Çaldıran (on 23 August 1514), the latter turned over the Safawid province of Diyarbekir to his brother-in-law Kara Khan Ustaclu, the brother of Muhammad Khan Ustaclu who had died in the battle. In order to defend what remained of the province, he laid siege to Amid whose inhabitants had gone over to the Ottoman Sultan. In the summer of 1515, Selim I conferred on Bıyıklı Mehmed Paşa,[23] the *Beglerbegi* (Governor-General) of Erzerum, the task of relieving the siege of Amid.[24] In fact, Kara Khan had to

19 Sümer, Faruk: 1972, pp. 175-77. The appearance together of Türkmen and Kurdish tribes in Seljuk Anatolia has been known for a long time; cf. Flemming, Barbara: *Landschaftsgeschichte von Pamphylien* [...] *im Spätmittelalter*, Wiesbaden 1964, pp. 41-43; İnalcık, Halil: "The Yürüks: Their Origins, Expansion and Economic Role", in: *The Middle East and the Balkans under the Ottoman Empire*, Bloomington 1993, p. 97; and Bruinessen, Martin van: "'Aslını ınkar eden haramzadedır!' The Debate on the Ethnic Identity of the Kurdish Alevi", in: Kehl-Bodrogi, Krisztina & Kellner-Heinkele, Barbara & Otter-Beaujean, A.: 1997, p. 9.

20 Bruinessen, Martin van: "The Ottoman Conquest of Diyarbekir", in: Bruinessen, Martin van & Boeschoten, Hendrik: *Evliya Çelebi in Diyarbekir*, Leiden-Cologne 1988, pp. 27-28, 35 and 41.

21 Göyünç, Nejat: 1969, p. 61. The *zaviye*, which was shown to Göyünç as a *ziyaret*, should be thought of as a lodge of the shaykhs; see here below ftn. 69. It could be a pious establishment from the Akkoyunlu period, such as the few that Göyünç describes for Mardin (1969, pp. 119-22).

22 Allouche, Adel: *The Origins and Development of the Ottoman-Safavid Conflict*, Berlin 1983, pp. 90-99; Bruinessen, Martin van: 1988, pp. 13-28.

23 Bacqué-Grammont, Jean-Louis: *Les Ottomans, les Safavides et leurs voisins. Contributions à l'histoire des relations internationales dans l'orient islamique de 1514 à 1524*, İstanbul 1987, pp. 157 and 162-63; Idem: "Mehmed Pasha, Bıyıklı", in: *EI2* VI (1991), pp. 992-93. According to Faruk Sümer, he was an Akkoyunlu Turk: *Safevî Devletinin Kuruluşu ve Gelişmesinde Anadolu Türklerinin Rolü* (*Şah İsmail ile Halefleri ve Andolu Türkleri*), Ankara 1976, p. 39.

24 İlhan, M. Mehdi: "Bıyıklı Mehmed Paşa'nın Doğu Anadolu'daki Askeri Faaliyetleri", in: *IX. Türk Tarih Kongresi. Ankara 21-25 Eylül 1981, Kongreye Sunulan Bildiriler*, II. Cilt, Ankara 1988, pp. 807-18; Bruinessen, Martin van: 1988, p. 16.

abandon the siege of Amid in mid-September 1515. He marched south to join forces with groups of Türkmens of Diyarbekir at Birecik. However, Bıyıklı Mehmed cut off his route.

4 The Battle between Koçhisar and Dede Garkın

On Rabiʿ II 922/May 1516 – in the plain between [Eski] Koçhisar and Dede Garkın (also called Karkın or Karghandede) on the southern caravan route – the battle took place in which the Safawid troops were defeated by the Ottoman-Kurdish army.

The Safawid army, one of the best that Shah İsmail still had, with little infantry and no artillery, depended entirely on the Kızılbaş-Türkmen tribal cavalry. Among them was a Türkmen tribe with whom the sister of Shah İsmail and her whole female entourage, dressed in cavalrymen's clothes, are said to have fought. Kara Khan Ustaclu divided his troops into two groups. His right wing was to attack the Kurdish cavalry, his left wing was to attack the Ottoman right, avoiding completely the Janissaries and the artillery.

Bıyıklı Mehmed Paşa stood in the middle with two thousand Janissaries and his cannons. His right wing was made up of the cavalry of fief-holders from Anadolu and Karaman. The Kurdish princes and their tribal armies, which the Kurdish statesman Idris Bidlisi had supplied him with, were positioned on his left wing where they played a decisive role.[25]

The Kızılbaş army was almost entirely annihilated. Its remnants dispersed, most of them into the plain toward Sincar. The Safawids Kara Khan and his generals Turmış Khan and Husayn Khan Şamlu fell in battle. İsmail's sister managed to flee via Tell Afar to Mosul and from there to Kirkuk and Tabriz.[26]

After the battle of Dede Garkın/Koçhisar, a few of Diyarbekir's fortresses still remained in the hands of the Kızılbaş, in particular Ruha/Urfa which was quickly conquered.[27] The immediate consequence of the battle, however, was the capture of Amid. Bıyıklı Mehmed Paşa, who occupied the city in September 1516, became the *Beglerbegi*, Governor- General, on November 5th. The Kurdish allies were richly rewarded; consideration was shown for their Shafiʿite school of jurisprudence.[28]

---

25 Bruinessen, Martin van: 1988, p. 16, with bibliography.

26 Hammer, Joseph von: *Geschichte des osmanischen Reiches*, II, Pest 1828, p. 446, following Italian historians and authors of reports; for details concerning the vattle see Göyünç, Nejat: 1969, pp. 25-28, 32, 34, and 42.

27 Bacqué-Grammont, Jean-Louis: 1987, pp. 166 and 322, and ftn. 651 on p. 200.

28 Bruinessen, Martin van: 1988, p. 16. In the Paşa-Sancak there were even three Kurdish princes: ibid., p. 25, ftn. 14.

The Battle of Eski Koçhisar has its place in history.[29] From a distance, the Ottoman-Safawid confrontation appeared to be a "Turkish-Iranian" conflict.[30] Nationalistic Turkish historiography saw "the unity of *Turkey* as assured" due to the victory.[31] The "victory of the *sunna* of Anatolia over the Shiʿa of Iran" was emphasized: at Çaldıran the foundation was laid, at Eski Koçhisar the roof was set in place.[32] The wide-spread declaration and interpretation of a specifically Kurdish loyalty to the *sunna*, on closer consideration, goes back in fact to Idris Bidlisi who had negotiated the alliance of leading Kurdish families with the Ottoman Sultans. In the meantime, it has been pointed out that not all Kurdish tribes that were incorporated into the Ottoman Empire were firm Sunnis.[33] Similarly, it is clear that they were not all followers of the extreme Shiʿite pro-Safawid Kızılbaş.[34] Whoever wished to avoid being pursued like the latter was well advised to behave loyally to the Sultan.[35]

5 The Passage of Armies along the Northern Route

Despite the losses in human life that persecutions of the Kızılbaş entailed, Selim I was able to accomplish his military goals: his troops had scarcely defeated the Safawid army at Dede Garkın and Koçhisar, when in August 1516 they fought the decisive battle against the Mamluks which made possible the Ottoman entry into Cairo on January 1517.

---

29 Joseph von Hammer (1828, p. 461) recalled with regard to the Roman Empire: "...(the) rule of Osman in the Near East was only firmly established by means of extending the borders to the Tigris and Euphrates. The Roman Empire as well believed that its rule in Asia was not sufficiently wide and secure until its legions stood on the shores of the Euphrates. Only the latter, not the Tigris, forms the natural boundary of water that holds out the best promise for the two great empires that border upon one another in hostility..."

30 "The bloody battle decided in favor of the Turks; the defeated Persians [...] took to flight in the broad plain of Sinjar and on the roads to Mosul and Kerkuk." So wrote C. Ritter following Hammer, Joseph von: 1828, pp. 146-47.

31 Sümer, Faruk: 1976, p. 40.

32 Danişmend, İsmail Hami: *İzahlı Osmanlı Tarihi Kronolojisi* 2, İstanbul 1971, 23.

33 Bruinessen, Martin van: 1997, p. 8; Idem: 1988, pp. 14-15. A survey, published by the newspaper *Milliyet* on 21 and 22 March 2007, found that 22 percent of the 11,445,000 Kurds in Turkey today describe themselves as Alevis.

34 Halil İnalcık (1993, pp. 100 f.) distinguishes "Kızılbaş" as a designation for pro-Safawid Türkmens from the designation "Yürük" or simply "Türkmen".

35 Sohrweide, Hanna: "Der Sieg der Safaviden in Persien und seine Rückwirkungen auf die Schiiten Anatoliens im 16. Jahrhundert", in: *Der Islam* 41 (1965), pp. 95-223; Sümer, Faruk: 1976; Gölpınarlı, A.: "Kızılbaş", in *IA* VI (1955), pp. 789-95.

The northern route via the north edge of Karaca Dağ became a *via militaris* under Sultan Süleyman: he made use of it several times for large troop movements. Of the first two marches stage-by-stage descriptions have been preserved. On the way back from the first Persian campaign "against the two Iraqs" Süleyman came to Amid in October 1535, took up residence there for twenty days and celebrated the Feast of the Sacrifice with his troops.[36] The continuation of his march in the direction of Aleppo, more or less following the present-day road Diyarbakır-Siverek, was documented by Nasuh Matrakçı in the illustrated *Menazil-i Sefer-i ʿIrakeyn*. The army marched along the volcano's northern slopes which are strewn with basalt blocks. As the 15th stage, Nasuh drew "from nature" Kızıldepe on the slope of Karaca Dağ (*Karacadağ zeylinde Kızıldepe*) as a red bulging mountain ridge. Having marched over Karaca Dağ, the army crossed the Akbiñar River; then after passing by Kocagöz depesi, the Cüllab River was forded east of Urfa.[37]

In 1548, on his second Persian campaign, Sultan Süleyman came from Van to Amid. Once again Bayram was celebrated and they settled into winter quarters: the troops from Rumeli camped in Mardin and those from Anadolu in Urfa. And again Nasuh Matrakçı documented the continuation of the march, indeed in somewhat fuller detail: they marched north of Karaca Dağ to Ruha/Urfa where they arrived on 14 December 1548.[38]

In 1549, the Sultan marched from Aleppo across the Euphrates. Since he had fallen ill in Elmalu, in July 1549 he allowed himself a period of rest on the *yayla* of Karaca Dağ which offered good grazing for horses and camels. According to Evliya Çelebi, he had a spring named Hamrevat led from Karaca Dağ through a subterranean conduit into the castle of Amid.[39] From there at the beginning of October 1549 he moved to the plain named Cülek or Çülek near Amid and then disbanded the army in Aintab.[40]

---

36 Kappert, Petra: *Geschichte Sultan Süleyman Kanunis von 1520 bis 1557 oder Tabakat ül-Memalik ve Derecat ül-Mesalik von Celalzade Mustafa genannt Koca Nişancı*, Wiesbaden 1981, p. 77.

37 Yurdaydın, Hüseyin G.: *Nasuhü's Silahi (Matrakçı). Beyan-i Menazil-i Sefer-i Irakeyn-i Sultan Süleyman Han*, Ankara 1976, pp. 108-09, fol. 104a below, pp. 104 above and 104b below; op. cit. xxi, 41: *görülerek yapılmışlardır*. On the river Collab (Colab) cf. Sümer, Faruk: 1976, p. 193. Evliya Çelebi was in Culab in 1646. On Cellab in Urfa see İlhan, Mehdi M.: "Urfa and its environs in 1560s", Wiesbaden 2001, p. 7:

38 Yurdaydın, Hüseyin G. (1976, pp. 172-73) has edited the two itineraries together, the one of 1535 with illustrations and the one of 1548 without illustrations.

39 Bruinessen, Martin van &Boeschoten, Hendrik: 1988, pp. 146-47.

40 Kappert, Petra: 1981, pp. 406b–507a and 409a(?); Danişmend, Ismail Hami: 1971, p. 262.

The fourth march to Diyarbekir of the Sultan, who was affected by illness and old age, was overshadowed by the execution of Prince Mustafa suspected of rebellion,[41] and because of which unrest arose in the army. The Sultan marched from the winter quarters at Aleppo via Birecik – Ruha/Urfa – and once more via the halting-station Kızıldepe (May 1554), i.e. again via the northern slope of Karaca Dağ. On 15 May 1554 outside Amid, due to the vacillation of the soldiers, the Sultan was forced to convene a solemn war-Divan on the parade grounds located by the Tigris (*ordugah Çülek*). In so doing, he succeeded in getting the officers of the Janissaries individually to swear oaths of allegiance to him.[42] After eight days, the march resumed which in the summer of 1554 would lead to Süleyman declaring war against Shah Tahmasp and finally to the peace agreement of Amasya on 29 May 1555.[43]

In the south-east, Selim I had conquered the Dulġadır principality and the area of Diyarbekir. In Diyarbekir the first census was carried out in 1518 and the second one in 1540. To begin with, the rural population put up a resistance in the turbulent eastern provinces that were greatly agitated by influences emanating from Persia.[44] One could only speak of "internal security" after deportations, and after revolts, tribal insurrections and, not least, religious disturbances had been suppressed with the utmost severity in terrible battles.[45]

The border *vilayet* Diyarbekir was at times sealed off from Persia. Such was the case in 1559 when the governor of the province was set in action against Prince Bayezid who had abandoned his residence Amasya and fled with his troops to Shah Tahmasp. In July 1562 Prince Bayezid was handed over and put to death. The summary punishment of his followers, the Yevimlü, only further reinforced the ranks of the discontent; the central government was not successful in suppressing unrest throughout the country. Rather, such unrest would lead to the Celali uprisings that we will mention and which also did not spare Diyarbekir.[46]

---

41 Kappert, Petra: *Die osmanischen Prinzen und ihre Residenz Amasya im 15. und 16. Jahrhundert*, Istanbul 1976; Veinstein, G.: "Süleyman", in *EI* IX (1997), p. 836.

42 Kappert, Petra: 1981, pp. 96 and 448a. On Divans held during campaigns: ibid., pp. 31 f.; Danişmend, İsmail Hami: 1971, p. 288.

43 Hammer, Joseph von: 1828, pp. 321-22 and 326; Veinstein, G.: *EI* IX (1997), p. 836.

44 Yınanç, Refet & Elibüyük, Mesut: *Maraş Tahrir Defteri (1563)*, I, Ankara 1988, xxviii-xxix.

45 See my "Sahib-Qıran and Mahdī (No. 17 in this volume). Göyünç and Hütteroth (Istanbul 1997, p. 124) are too confident in their assumption that in the period of Kanuni Süleyman [...] the power of the Ottoman Empire manifestly grew along with internal security"; cf. Veinstein, G.: *EI* IX (1997), pp. 832-36.

46 Turan, Şerafettin: *Kanunî'nin oğlu Şehzâde Bayezid Vak'ası*, Ankara 1961, p. 173; Kappert, Petra: 1976, pp. 146-47 and 151 ff.

6 Taxation on the Southern Caravan Route 1564-1766

In 1564, two years after the last revolt of the local princes, the Ottoman administration once again had the tax revenues registered that were to be collected from the province of Diyarbekir on behalf of the Sultan and the *timar*-holders.[47]

The *Beglerbegi*, i.e. the finance director, was supposed to deliver to the capital the *irsaliye*, the central government's share of the taxes, in the form of cash or natural produce. In the large border province Diyarbekir, for which the term *eyalet* was used from 1591,[48] the *Beglerbegi* or Governor-General held back a considerable part of the taxes. When he favored his own followers in conferring *timars*,[49] the central government intervened and ordered an examination of all the titles of *timar*- holders in the eastern provinces. At the time of his appointment in 1585, the new Governor-General had to pledge that for each of the next three years he would pay 20,000 gold pieces into the central treasury.[50] Evliya Çelebi, who spent a few weeks in Diyarbekir in April and May 1655, reports on the financial bureaucracy of the province.

The villages of Viranşehir, Dede Garkın, Meşkuk and Koçhisar lay along the caravan route at approximately equal distances from one another on the edge of the volcanic slopes of Karacadağ and in the alluvial plain. With the help of the Diyarbekir *Defter* of 1564, edited by Göyünç and Hütteroth, and the accounts of the travellers Jean-Baptiste Tavernier (March 1644) and Carsten Niebuhr (spring 1766), with regard to these villages the following picture can be obtained.

The soil allowed the cultivation of wheat and barley; the rivers drove watermills. The obligations of the peasants and the nomads vis-à-vis their feudal landlords were set forth in the Register of 1564. On produce most of them paid a levy of one- fifth; only Koçhisar and Dede Karkın paid a reduced levy of one-seventh. Having the greatest capacity to pay was the most highly populated Nestorian village Meşkuk with 404 persons liable to pay tax.[51] In second place

47 On the earlier registers see Bruinessen, Martin van: 1988, pp. 38-41; İlhan, Mehdi M.: 2001, p. 15.

48 İnalcık, Halil: "Eyalet," in: *EI* II (1965), pp. 721-24.

49 Fekete, L.: *Die Siyaqat-Schrift in der türkischen Finanzverwaltung*, Budapest 1955, p. 104 (on the right to confer *timars* of up to 4999 *akçes* per year); ibid., pp. 740 and 771 (on *irsaliye*).

50 The *defterdar* had embezzled the *irsaliye* and bribed the incumbent *Beglerbegi*. Fleischer, Cornell H.: *Bureaucrat and Intellectual in the Ottoman Empire*, Princeton 1986, pp. 104-05.

51 On Meşkuk Köyü see Göyünç, Nejat: 1969, pp. 69 and 153. Today two villages are found here in the *ilçe* Kızıltepe of the province Mardin: Büyük ayrik and Küçük ayrik; cf. KöyKöy Türkiye Yol Atlası 2004, p. 203 A1. Göyünç, Nejat: 1969, p. 60, knew of a Büyük ayrik that

came Dede Karkın. Although with its 183 persons liable for taxation it had fewer tax-payers than Koçhisar, its farmers paid more taxes for wheat than the latter. In third place came Koçhisar (present-day Kızıltepe), and only then in fourth place came Viranşehir which in its tax payments was far behind Koçhisar.

Looking from west to east, in the *nahiye* Viranşehir lay Davudi Garbi, a *timar* with seven persons liable for tax. It was the westernmost village in the *kaza*. Viranşehir itself (Constantina, Tela, Antoniopolis, Maximilianopolis),[52] *ze'amet* of the *Sancakbeg* and seat of the *na'ib* of the *nahiye*, at the time mostly a field of ruins and Christian graves, had only 33 persons liable for tax on wheat, barley, rice, vegetable gardens and cotton; in addition there were charges for winter fields and hay, as well as for a water-mill (on the Çırçıp?).

Dede Karkın (Garkın, Dadacardin), being *hass* property of the Sultan, was located in the *sancak* or *kaza* Berriyecik in the *nahiye* of Tell Bism. The peasants, sedentary Türkmens of the Karkın tribe,[53] as we mentioned, paid more tax on wheat than did Koçhisar; they operated a water-mill and in particular a dyeing works that was taxed 15,120 *akçes*, both these activities indicating that at the time there was a greater volume of water in the Çırçıp which was crossed by a bridge at this point. In 1644, the village (formerly *un gros bourg*) lay in ruins. Only the very long and very well-constructed stone bridge still remained on which one crossed over a river that "was quite wide when it overflowed its banks". Having become cave-dwellers, the local people offered hens, butter and cheeses to travellers who passed through the area.

Near to Dede Garkın, the meadows Aġca Mescid, Aġce Koru, Ġibal and Kuyucak as well as Ceviz Yeri (a cultivable field, *mezra'a*) and the Dögerlü, a Türkmen clan who like the Karkın belonged to the Bozok and grazed their livestock by Bogan, were taxed a flat rate and fields were allocated to them as *timars*. Kethudalar, to the north of Dede Garkın, counted seven persons liable to taxation, while Yeñice had nine: both were tiny villages that paid tax on wheat and grain.

Presumably, Kurb al-Mā was located on the caravan route in the *nahiye* Dinabi (on the Çırçıp?), being *hass* property of the Sultan with nine households and yet 197 inhabitants who paid tax on wheat and barley.

When the caravan came to the *nahiye* Sahra-yi Mardin, it had reached the *sancak* or *kaza* of Mardin. On the edge of the volcanic plateau was situated the

was still Christian in 1960 and a Muslim Meşkuk-i ayrik; Göyünç, Nejat: 1969, p. 69 (Meşkuk-i arab, Küçükmeşkuk).

52 Dealt with in detail in Sinclair, T.A.: 1990, IV, pp. 191-93.

53 On the Karkın see Section 3. above.

village Meşkuk or Meşkok (*Cara* in Tavernier),[54] Meşkinan, present-day Büyük ayrik, *hass* property of the Sultan. Here 404 persons liable to taxation paid the full levy on wheat, barley, vegetable gardens and water- mills. The total population came to 1340 people. The "tax paid by non-Muslims" (*ispence* or *cizye*?) amounted to 10,000. In 1644, a caravanserai was on hand. At the time the local Nestorians, who possessed a shabby church of their own,[55] were subjects of a few Turkish families.

Another village Karkın, a *timar*, was located near Meşkuk. There 15 persons liable to taxation paid tax on wheat and barley.

The plain before Koçhisar, where so decisive a battle had taken place in 1516, was a twenty-mile-long battle-field.

Koçhisar/Dunaysir (Cousasar in Tavernier; Kodsje hissâr, Gunasser or Dunasser in Niebuhr) was crown property of the Sultan with 202 persons liable to taxation. The total population consisted of 712 persons – the register ignored the "non- Muslims" – and they paid the lower-rate levy on wheat, barley, vegetable gardens, cotton and honey, and once again on a water- mill. In 1644, it was a rather large village without a caravanserai where one came across Armenian and Nestorian Christians who held separate religious services in their own language. The Nestorians, after every service, kept both their old Bibles in the "Chaldean" language in a cupboard (*coffre*) under the ground. Of three large monasteries, two were destroyed except for their church towers, and the third was transformed into a mosque. According to Niebuhr, in 1766 Koçhisar was the residence of a *Sancakbeg* under the Voivode of Mardin.[56]

The Register of 1564 recorded "non-Muslims" without specifying their religious ... denominations or ethnicity,[57] i.e. Nestorian and Armenian Christians who led a shadow existence, as well as Kurds recognizable by their names, Bektashis (a Bektaş-i Büzürg to the north of Tell Bism) presumably Alevite Türkmens (Dede Karkın), and unmistakable Kızılbaş in the mountainous

54 Tavernier, Jean-Baptiste: 1981, II, pp. 247-48.

55 The "Nestorians" of this region considered themselves to belong to the Eastern Church and not to the Roman Church, toward which at the time they still adopted a sceptical attitude. Cf. Frazee, Charles A.: *Catholics and Sultans. The church and the Ottoman Empire 1453-1923*, Cambridge 1983, pp. 142-44; Sinclair, T.A.: 1989, III, p. 222.

56 The archive material has been appraised in Göyünç, Nejat: 1969, pp. 61-69 and 153, as well as in Göyünç, Nejat & Hütteroth, Wolf-Dieter: 1997, pp. 55, 114-15, 137, 192, 200 and 204. The numbers (of the documents concerned?) are P1 and P35 (Dede Garkın), M1, M31, M52, M92, M134, M150-51. Tavernier, Jean-Baptiste: 1981, II, pp. 247-48; Niebuhr, Carsten: 1778, II, pp. 366-67 (see ftn. 8).

57 Göyünç, Nejat & Hütteroth, Wolf-Dieter: 1997, p. 127; Bruinessen, Martin van: *Turcica* 31 (1999), pp. 558-60.

district of Mardin.[58] The Ottoman provincial authorities, as well as the *timar*-holders, were obligated to register and pursue the pro-Safawid Kızılbaş.[59] What followed were arrests, prosecutions before the courts and condemnation of the Kızılbaş as traitors and heretics, along with semi- voluntary or forced resettlement and flight across the borders. This may be the explanation for why Dede Karkın was deserted in 1644. The Kızılbaş in the 16th century tended to flee into Persia. Later, pressure from the Celali revolt and the reprisals of the government caused the population to emigrate and flee to West-Anatolia.[60]

The authorities exempted from taxes the caravanserais that still existed but levied road tolls (*bac*) on subjects and foreigners. Thus in Koçhisar tolls were paid in order to go to Diyarbekir. Two and a half piasters had to be paid for mule and horse loads.[61] Where Tavernier observes that Sultan Murad IV on his way through in 1638 had a stretch of the road repaired and a bridge built, Niebuhr notes that a castle built at that time had been destroyed by 1766. It was no longer possible to maintain security in the face of the attacks of the nomads, who resisted the government's attempts at settling them, and in the face of the pressure of Bedouin attacks.[62]

7 Viranşehir and Kızıltepe on the present-day "Silk Route"

Today Sections 26 and 27 of Highway 400 connect Şanlıurfa with Viranşehir, passing through the GAP agricultural complex beneath Tektek Dağı. The ring canal around the Urfa-Harran plain, whose agriculture is in the midst of being transformed by the gigantic irrigation project GAP (Güneydoğu Anadolu Projesi), in the south-east runs parallel to the national border up to near Mardin.[63] In the face of systematic renaming – since 1956 in the Turkish Republic appropriation of the region has been carried out by the *Ad Değiştirme*

---

58 In the hilly plateau of the mountainous region of Mardin, *Kuh-i Mardin*, Kurdish clan members with Kızılbaş names (Mehmed b. Şahkulı ve gayri, Pir Zeyd ve Şahkulı, Şahkulı b. Şemseddin, Şah kulı and a Kılbaş (sic) keth., tax-payer to a Milli chief) had placed themselves under the protection of the nomad prince, Mahmud Beg.

59 Sohrweide, Hanna: 1965, pp. 192-95.

60 Sümer, Faruk: 1972, pp. 186-89; Griswold, William J.: *The Great Anatolian Rebellion 1000-1020/1591-1611*, Berlin 1983; İnalcık, Halil: 1993, pp. 107 and 128, ftn. 46; following Sümer, Faruk and Woods, J.

61 Tavernier, Jean-Baptiste: 1981, II, p. 253.

62 Sinclair, T.A.: 1989, III, p. 409: the route had become too unsafe in the 18th and 19th centuries.

63 Hütteroth, Wolf-Dieter & Höhfeld, Volker: *Türkei*, Darmstadt 2002, p. 225, with map.

İhtisas Komisyonu[64] – it is interesting how long the names of villages and bodies of water retained an echo of bygone times; until 1928, as indicated in *Köylerimiz*, village names such as İbrahimi maintained themselves in the *merkez nihayesi* of Viranşehir,[65] as did still another İbrahimi, a Bekdaşı, Maşkok sagir and kebir, and many others.

The (three) Çırçıps, along with the Khabur and abundant subterranean water reserves, belong to the GAP region. For the area of the two Çırçıps in the border administrative district Ceylanpınar the regulation of landed property was brought about in 1990 under the direction of GAP *Bölge Kalkınma İdaresi Başkanlığı*. Through courses villagers can acquire a diploma of a master of irrigation (*Sulama Ustası*); the mechanization of agriculture is being pushed forward.

The National Highway 400 (E 90, earlier E 24) is part of the *Türkiye Transit Karayolu*. It goes to Cizre where Highway 430 heads its way via Silopi through the border station *Habur Sınır Kapısı* and on into Iraq. Passing Şırnak, Hakkâri and Yüksekova, National Highway 400 continues to Esendere, the border crossing into Iran (Urmia).

Today Viranşehir (in the province of Şanlıurfa) and Kızıltepe (in the province of Mardin) are located along the 400. The distance between the two district-cities only comes to 75 km, in today's time about an hour and a half by car.

On this stretch of the road, a short way behind Viranşehir and Eser, at the beginning of March 2003 work was begun on a bridge suitable for heavy military equipment. Apparently, the river basin of the Büyük Çırçıp was meant to be crossed. It was the time when preparations were being made for the strategic deployment of *Task Force Iron Horse* (called *Demir At* in the Turkish press) of the Fourth Mechanized Infantry Division of the US Army. Advance parties were busy piling up supplies, the so-called *Iron Mountain* of the division, along Highway 400. Their transport ships were anchored in the Bay of Iskenderun and the Bay of Mersin. But shortly before *Operation Iraqi Freedom* was about to be launched from within Turkey, the landing of the Fourth Infantry Division was cancelled after the Turkish National Assembly gave a no-vote to the relevant government proposition.[66]

---

64 Öktem, Kerem: *Creating the Turk's Homeland: Modernization, Nationalism and Geography in the late 19th and 20th Centuries*, under: <http://www.ksg.harvard.edu/kokkalis/GSW5/oktem.pdf> (accessed on 27/11/2007).

65 [Dahiliye Vakâleti]: *Köylerimiz'in Adları*, İstanbul 1928, pp. 354 f.; cf. also Göyünç, Nejat & Hütteroth, Wolf-Dieter: 1997, pp. 37-41.

66 Girdner, Eddie J.: "Pre-emptive War: The Case of Iraq", in: *Perceptions. Journal of Inter-*

At Viranşehir the north-south connecting road 905 branches off for Ceylanpınar. Three miles before Ceylanpınar lies the settlement Evrenpaşa Köyü. It was built at the instigation of President Kenan Evren in 1986 for 1800 Özbeks who had lost their home in northern Afghanistan after the invasion of the Soviet troops (December 1974).[67] The road runs through an immense plain along the huge estates of the Ceylanpınar Farm founded in 1943 (*Ceylanpınar Tarım İşletmesi*) which extends up to the border with Syria. The farm belongs to TİGEM, the General Direction of Farms (*Tarım İşletmeleri Genel Müdürlüğü*). With Ceylanpınar and the farms in Pınar, Beyazkule and Gümüşsuyu, it constitutes the largest government-owned property in Turkey and is the biggest employer in the region. On the other hand, since the 1980s the number of workers it employs has dropped from 4500 to 1235. In place of workers with secure jobs, day-labourers have been introduced who are employed by subcontractors (*taşeron*). In the case of a dairy farm of the TİGEM run by a subcontractor, the employees are young women and children without job security. Hundreds of them are driven to work on TİGEM estates from a radius of many kilometres. Until recently trucks served as a means of transport on whose open load area there was room for seventy to eighty persons in good weather. Since the road accident of February 2007, small buses provide transportation.

On the above-mentioned unfortunate day, the 7th of February, during rainy weather a heavy goods vehicle built in 1973 with license plate 63 SE 107 was conveying on its open load area only forty-three young women and children to their work at a TİGEM plant that processes sheep's milk. Having arrived at the fenced-in, guarded site, the chauffeur attempted to cross the damaged bridge over the "Çırpı" which was swollen from the previous night's rain. The bridge collapsed, the truck fell into the river and turned over on its side. Forty-one people fell from the truck's load area into the water. Thirty-three persons who had clung onto the body of the truck were dragged to land by the local people who rushed to the spot and made use of inflated truck inner tubes and ropes. The chauffeur, after having saved several persons, was himself swept away by the current and drowned along with his wife and other young women and children. Who was to blame for the death of these ten persons? The chauffeur, who had negligently disregarded a warning before the bridge, was dead. The

national Affairs, IX, No. 4, Ankara 2004-2005, pp. 12-13. On the event and the redirection of the Fourth Infantry Division to Kuwait: Philipps, David L.: *Losing Iraq. Inside the Postwar Reconstruction Fiasco*, New York 2005, pp. 113-20.

67 Salk, Gundula: "Die türksprachigen Afghanistanflüchtlinge in der Türkei", in: *Materialia Turcica* 17 (1996), pp. 69-71 and 76; cf. www.sanliurfa.com/vl/index.php (access on 4/12/2007); www.sanliurfa.gov.tr/valilik/ceylancografya.html (access on 4/12/2007).

subcontractor could refute the reproaches aimed at him: he had put up a warning before the damaged bridge. A major reproach was levelled against child labour, the low wages of the milkmaids and the lack of insurance. Due to this situation, which was problematic for a government enterprise, the particular form of "privatization" and transference to a subcontractor (*taşeronlaştırma*) were held responsible.[68] Schoolchildren also suffer during the winter floods despite some regulatory adjustments. When the Çırçıp swells and becomes a wide and deep stream, children of the village Yukarı Karataş, who must go to school, take off their shoes and wade through the rushing ice-cold Çırçıp Deresi. In the summer, however, the inhabitants take pleasure in their Çırçıp; in the dry riverbed or wadi (*dere*) they hold picnics.

Highway 400 crosses the boundary of the *vilayet* Mardin eleven kilometres above Dedeköy.[69] Near Dedeköy an Alevi- *ocak* named Şeyh İbrahimli (Şıhlı) is recorded with its centre in the village Merzime.[70]

On Section 28 of Highway 400 is located Kocatepe, a *bucak* of the *ilçe* Derik. The district city Derik (earlier Tell Bism) lies 19 km above the 400. The present-day district city Mazıdağı (earlier Şamrah) lies to the north of Derik.

Kızıltepe (earlier Koçhisar/Dunaysir) since 1975 is located on Highway 400, the new "İpek Yolu". This link with the overland traffic – all the way into Iraq – has helped the district city enjoy quick growth. To the darker chapters of recent history belongs the story of the shooting of the twelve-year-old schoolboy Uğur Kaymaz together with his father, the truck driver Ahmet Kaymaz, on 21 November 2004 by security forces (they were acquitted on 18 April 2007 by a court in Eskişehir).

---

68 Günçıkan, Berat: "TİGEM' in Çocuk İşçileri", in: *Cumhuriyet*, 27 April 2007; Idem: "Kâr Hırsına Kurban Edilen 'TİGEM'ın Çocukları", under: www.gundemcocuk.org/index (access on 4/12/2007); cf, Özmen, Kemal: Özelleştirme, Kayıt Dışı, İş Cinayeti: 9 Ölü, BİA Haber Merkezi, Şanlıurfa-İstanbul, 8/02/2007, under: www.bianet.org/kategori/cocuk/91592/ozellestirme-kayit-disiis- cinayeti-9-olu (access on 4/12/2007).

69 At the edge of the village Dede Köy that counted 50 to 60 souls and was located on the Büyük Çırçıp (*ilçe* Viranşehir in the province Şanlıurfa), Nejat Göyünç, in the 1960s, saw the remains of the lodge of Dede Karkın ; he also found the foundations of the piers of the long bridge over the Büyük Çırçıp. Cf. Göyünç, Nejat: 1969, pp. 25, 42, 61, 76 and 79. The village lies on the border of the province. That the historical remains are located on the eastern bank, i.e. in the *ilçe* Derik of Mardin Province, is clear from *Köy Köy Türkiye Yol Atlası*, 6th edition, İstanbul 2004, p. 202 C2 and Index ("Şanlı Urfa/Derik").

70 Hamza Aksüt cites (see footnote 73 below) an unpublished, undated dissertation by M. Salih Erpolat (*Diyarbakır Beylerbeyliğindeki Yer İsimleri*); Göyünç, Nejat: "XVI. Yüzyılda Mardin Sancağı", in: *Alevi Forumu: Arguvan Alevileri*(?); Hamza Aksüt in *Yol*, excerpt from 3 February 2004, p. 45. Further information below in ftn. 73.

8 Prospects: Eyalet or Vilayet?

The province of Diyarbekir, as mentioned, was an *eyalet* in the Ottoman Empire, that is to say, the largest administrative unit under a *beglerbegi* (governor-general). In the administration of provinces the old system and its ever-present administrative boundaries are maintained.[71] Even institutions that are active beyond the *vilayet* level such as, for example, GAP, *Devlet Su İşleri* or the railroad and road construction departments effect little change in the system. In the present-day centrally organized and integrated State the governors (*vali*) and the heads of districts (*kaymakam*) are appointed by the Minister of the Interior and have been carefully trained as administrative officials who represent the government and the ministers. The powers of the elected mayors (*belediye başkanı*) are limited; thus the mayor of Ceylanpınar complained that he was concerned for the surviving dependents of the Çırçıp disaster but that he was left on his own "because of the party he belonged to".[72]

Since the 1980s, politics on the highest level has been preoccupied with large-scale provincial reform; there has been talk of eight *eyalets* (Ankara, İstanbul, İzmir, Adana, Erzurum, Diyarbakır, Eskişehir, Trabzon). On 1 March 2007, the seventh president, Kenan Evren, who had been living in retirement since 1989, spoke out in *Sabah* in favour of *eyalets*, i.e. regional *valiliks* (*bölge valilikleri*). To be sure, he added, he was thinking of the distant future; at best in twenty to fifty years' time an *eyalet* system could be introduced.

For the time being, the riverbed of the Çırçıp separates the provinces Şanlıurfa (administrative number 63) and Mardin (47) – on the one side the *ilçe* of Viranşehir (Urfa), on the other the *ilçe* of Derik (Mardin). The bridge of Dede Garkın still exists, though in a ruined state; even the modest remains of a *türbe* are still preserved and continue up until today to attract pious Kurds who revere the site as the tomb of Şirin Dede.[73]

---

71 Findley, Carter V.: *Bureaucratic Reform in the Ottoman Empire. The Sublime Porte, 1789-1922*, Princeton 1980, pp. 309-13. Findley deals with the Young Turk *General Law on Provincial Administration* of 26 March 1913 which today still provides the basic framework for the administration of the provinces. Cf. also Göyünç, Nejat & Hütteroth, Wolf-Dieter: 1997, p. 42.

72 Günçikan, Berat: "TİGEM'in Çocuk İşçileri", in: *Cumhuriyet*, 27/04/2007.

73 Cf. Aksüt, Hamza (www.aleviyol.com/forum), who visited the *türbe* in 2003. Aksüt, Hamza: *Anadolu Aleviliginin Sosyal ve Coğrafi Kökenleri*, Ankara 2002 (not available to me); Aksüt, Hamza: *Mezopotamya'dan Anadolu'ya. Alevi Erenlerin İlk Savaşı (1240)*, under: www.aleviforum.com/showthread/php?t=8453 (accessed on 27/11/2007); Yalçın, Alemdar &Yılmaz, Hacı: *Kargın Ocaklı Boyu ile ilgili yeni belgeler*, under: www.hbektas.gazi.edu.tr/portal/html/modules.php? (dated 14/04/2006; accessed on 27/11/2007).

Bibliography

Aksüt, Hamza, *Anadolu Aleviliğinin Sosyal ve Coğrafi Kökenleri*, Ankaa 2002 (not accessible).

Aksüt, Hamza, *Mezopotamya'dan Anadolu'ya. Alevi Erenlerin İlk Savaşı (1240)* <http://www.aleviforum.com/showthread/php?t=8453> (access 27 November 2007).

Allouche, Adel, *The Origins and Development of the Ottoman-Safavid Conflict*, Berlin 1983.

Bacqué-Grammont, Jean-Louis, *Les Ottomans, les Safavides et leurs voisins. Contribution à l'histoire des relations internationales dans l'orient islamique de 1514 à 1524*, Istanbul 1987.

Bacqué-Grammont, Jean-Louis, "Mehmed Pasha, Bıyıklı", *EI2* VI (1991), pp. 992-993.

Bacqué-Grammont, Jean-Louis, *Les Ottomans, les Safavides et leurs voisins. Contribution à l'histoire des relations internationales dans l'orient islamique de 1514 à 1524*, Istanbul 1987.

Bruinessen, Martin van, & Boeschoten, Hendrik, *Evliya Çelebi in Diyarbekir*, Leiden-Köln 1988.

Bruinessen, Martin van, "The Ottoman Conquest of Diyarbekir", in M. van Bruinessen und H. Boeschoten, *Evliya Çelebi in Diyarbekir*, Leiden-Köln 1988, pp. 13-28.

Bruinessen, Martin van, "'Aslını inkar eden haramzadedır!' The Debate on the Ethnic Identity of the Kurdish Alevi", in K. Kehl-Bodrogi, B. Kellner-Heinkele und A. Otter-Beaujean, *Alevism in Turkey and comparable syncretistic religious communities in the Near East*, Leiden 1997, pp. 8-15.

Bruinessen, Martin van, review of Irène Mélikoff, *Hadji Bektach: un mythe et ses avatars*, Leiden 1998, in *Turcica* 31 (1999), pp. 549-553.

[Dahiliye Vekaleti], *Köylerimiz*, Istanbul 1928.

Danişmend, İsmail Hami, *İzahlı Osmanlı Tarihi Kronolojisi 2*, Istanbul 1971.

Erünsal, İsmaiL E., and Ahmet Yaşar Ocak (eds.), *Menâkıbu'l Kudsiyye Fî Menâsıbi'l-Ünsiyye*, Ankara 1995.

Fekete, L., *Die Siyaqat-Schrift in der türkischen Finanzverwaltung*, Budapest 1955.

Felix, Wolfgang, *Byzanz und die islamische Welt im früheren 11. Jahrhundert*, Vienna 1981.

Findley, Carter V., *Bureaucratic Reform in the Ottoman Empire. The Sublime Porte, 1789-1922*, Princeton 1980.

Fleischer, Cornell H., *Bureaucrat and Intellectual in the Ottoman Empire*, Princeton 1986.

Flemming, B., *Landschaftsgeschichte von Pamphylien, Pisidien und Lykien im Spätmittelalter*, Wiesbaden 1964.

Flemming, B., "Sahib-Kıran und Mahdi: Türkische Endzeiterwartungen im ersten Jahrzehnt der Regierung Süleymans, in: Kara, Györgyi, *Between the Danube and the Caucasus*, Budapest 1987, pp. 43-62.

Frazee, Charles A., *Catholics and Sultans. The church and the Ottoman Empire 1453-1923*, Cambridge 1983.

Girdner, Eddie J., "Pre-emptive War: The Case of Iraq", *Perceptions. Journal of International Affairs*, Vol IX No. 4, Winter 2004-2005, pp. 5-30.

Gölpinarli, A., "Kızılbaş" in *İA* VI (1955), pp. 789-795.

Göyünç, Nejat, *XVI. Yüzyılda Mardin Sancağı*, Istanbul 1969, 2nd ed. Ankara 1991.

Göyünç, Nejat, "Onaltıncı Yüzyılın İlk Yarısında Diyarbekir", *İÜEF Tarih Dergisi* XXIII (1973), pp. 26-34.

Göyünç, Nejat, and Wolf-Dieter Hütteroth, *Land an der Grenze. Osmanische Verwaltung im heutigen türkisch-syrischen Grenzgebiet im 16. Jahrhundert*, Istanbul 1997.

Griswold, William J., *The Great Anatolian Rebellion 1000-1020/1591-1611*, Berlin 1983.

Groot, A.H. de, "Kočhisar IV" in *EI* V (1986), p. 248.

Günçikan, Berat, *Kâr Hırsına Kurban Edilen 'TİGEM Çocukları'* <http//:www.gundemcocuk.org/index> (access 4 December 2007).

Hammer, Joseph von, *Geschichte des osmanischen Reiches*. Zweyter Band. Pest 1828.

Honigmann, E., "Ra's al-`Ayn or `Ayn Warda", *EI* VIII (1995), pp. 433-435.

Hütteroth, Wolf-Dieter, and Volker Höhfeld, *Türkei. Wissenschaftliche Länderkunden*, Darmstadt 2002.

İçişler BakanliğI İller Müdürlüğü, *Köylerimiz*, Ankara 1969.

İlhan, M. Mehdi, "Bıyıklı Mehmed Paşa'nın Doğu Anadolu'daki Askeri Faaliyetleri", *IX. Türk Tarih Kongresi. Ankara 21-25 Eylül 1981, Kongreye Sunulan Bildiriler II. Cilt*, Ankara 1988, pp. 807-818.

İlhan, M. Mehdi, "Urfa and its environs in the 1560", *Archivum Ottomanicum* 19, Wiesbaden 2001, pp. 5-68.

İnalcik, Halil, "Eyalet", *EI* II (1965), pp. 721-724.

İnalcik, Halil, "The Yürüks: Their Origins. Expansion and Economic Role", in *The Middle East and the Balkans under the Ottoman Empire*, Bloomington 1993, pp. 97-136.

Kappert, Petra, *Die osmanischen Prinzen und ihre Residenz Amasya im 15. und 16. Jahrhundert*, Istanbul 1976.

Kappert, Petra, *Geschichte Sultan Süleyman Kanunis von 1520 bis 1557 oder Tabakat ül-Memalik ve Derecat ül-Mesalik von Celalzade Mustafa genannt Koca Nişancı*, Wiesbaden 1981.

Karamustafa, Ahmet T., "Early Sufism in Eastern Anatolia", Leonard Lewisohn (ed.), *Classical Persian Sufism: from its Origins to Rumi*, London/New York 1993, pp. 175-198.

Karamustafa, Ahmet T., *God's Unruly Friends. Dervish Groups in the Islamic Later Middle Period, 1200-1550*, Salt Lake City 1994.

Kehl-Bodrogi, Krisztina, B. Kellner-Heinkele und A. Otter-Beaujean, *Alevism in Turkey and comparable syncretistic religious communities in the Near East*, Leiden 1997.

Köy Köy Türkiye. Yol Atlası, 1/400.000, 4th ed., Istanbul 2004.

Niebuhr, Carsten, *Reisebeschreibung nach Arabien und den umliegenden Ländern, Kopenhagen 1778, um ein Vorwort von Dietmar Henze vermehrter Nachdruck der Ausgaben Kopenhagen 1774-78 und Hamburg 1837*, Graz 1968.

Ocak, Ahmet Yaşar, *Osmanlı İmparatorluğunda Marjinal Sûfîlik: Kalenderiler*, Ankara 1992.

Öktem, Kerem, *Creating the Turk's Homeland: Modernization, Nationalism and Geography in the late 19th and 20th Centuries* <http//www.ksg.harvard.edu/kokkalis/GSW/oktem.pdf>, access 27-1-2007.

Özmen, Kemal, "Özelleştirme, Kayıt Dışı, İş Cınayeti: 9 Ölü", *BİA Haber Merkezi*, Şanlıurfa-Istanbul, 8 February 2007, www.bianet.org/bianet/kategori/cocuk/91592/ozellestirme-kayit-disi-is-cinayetu-9-olu, access 4 December 2007.

Phillips, David L., *Losing Iraq. Inside the Postwar Reconstruction Fiasco*, New York 2005.

Ritter, Carl, *Die Erdkunde im Verhältniss zur Natur und zur Geschichte des Menschen, oder allgemeine vergleichende Geographie. Die Erdkunde von Asien. Band VII. Zweite Abtheilung. Das Stufenland des Euphrat- und Tigrissystems*, Berlin 1844.

Salk, Gundula, "Die türksprachigen Afghanistanflüchtlinge in der Türkei", *MATERIALIA TURCICA* 17 (1996), pp. 61-76.

Sinclair, T.A., *Eastern Turkey: An Architectural and Archaeological Survey. Vol. III*, London 1989.

Sinclair, T.A., *Eastern Turkey: An Architectural and Archaeological Survey. Vol. IV*, London 1990.

Sohrweide, Hanna, "Der Sieg der Safaviden in Persien und seine Rückwirkungen auf die Schiiten Anatoliens im 16. Jahrhundert", *Der Islam* 41 (1965), pp. 95-223.

Sümer, Faruk, *Oğuzlar (Türkmenler)*, 2nd ed. Ankara 1972.

Sümer, Faruk, *Safevî Devletinin Kuruluşu ve Gelişmesinde Anadolu Türklerinin Rolü (Şah İsmail ile Halefleri ve Anadolu Türkleri)*, Ankara 1976.

Turan, Şerafettin, *Kanunî'nin oğlu Şehzâde Bayezid Vak'ası*, Ankara 1961.

Veinstein, G., "Süleyman", *EI* IX (1997), pp. 836-842.

Wigram, W.A., *The cradle of mankind. Life in Eastern Kurdistan. Second ed.*, London 1922.

Woods, John E., *The Aqquyunlu. Clan, Confederation, Empire*, Minneapolis and Chicago 1976.

Yalçin, Alemdar & Hacı Yılmaz, *Kargın Ocaklı Boyu ile ilgili yeni belgeler*, www.hbektas.gazi.edu.tr/portal/htm/modules.php? dated 14-4-2006, access 27 November 2007.

Yerasimos, Stéphane (ed.), *Jean-Baptiste Tavernier. Les six voyages de Turquie et de Perse*, Introduction et notes, 2 vols. Paris 1981.

Yinanç, Refat and Mesut Elibüyük, *Maraş Tahrir Defteri (1563) I*, Ankara 1988.

Yurdaydin, Hüseyin G., *Nasuhü's Silahi (Matrakçı). Beyan-ı Menazil-i Sefer-i İrakeyn-i Sultan Süleyman Han*, Ankara 1976.

Publications

Books

1. *Landschaftsgeschichte von Pamphylien, Pisidien und Lykien im Spätmittelalter*, Wiesbaden 1964. 160 pp. (Abhandlungen für die Kunde des Morgenlandes XXXV,1).

Translation into Turkish, by Hüseyin Bağçeci, forthcoming.

2. *Türkische Handschriften. Teil 1*, Wiesbaden 1968. 392 pp., 10 ill. (Verzeichnis der orientalischen Handschriften in Deutschland, XIII,1).
3. With I. Stchoukine, P. Luft, H. Sohrweide, *Illuminierte islamische Handschriften*, Wiesbaden 1971. 340 pp., 12+42 ill. (Verzeichnis der orientalischen Handschriften in Deutschland, XVI).
4. *Faḫrī Ḫusrev u Šīrīn. Eine türkische Dichtung von 1367*, Wiesbaden 1974. 486 pp., facs. (Verzeichnis der orientalischen Handschriften in Deutschland, Suppl. 15).
5. *Die Sprachen der türkischen Dichter*, Leiden 1977.
6. With Jan Schmidt, *The Diary of Karl Süssheim (1878-1947). Orientalist between Munich and Istanbul*, Stuttgart 2002 (Verzeichnis der orientalischen Handschriften in Deutschland, Supplementband 32).

Ed., with J.-L. Bacqué-Grammont, M. Gökberk, İ. Ortaylı; G. Schubert (red.), *Türkische Miszellen. Robert Anhegger Festschrift*, Istanbul 1987.
Ed., with J.J. Witkam en J.T.P. de Bruijn, *Manuscripts of the Middle East* 3, Leiden 1989.

Articles

1. "Faḫrī Ḫusrev u Šīrīn vom Jahre 1367. Eine vergessene türkische Dichtung aus der Emiratszeit", *Zeitschrift der Deutschen Morgenländischen Gesellschaft* 115 (1965), pp. 36-64.
2. "Türkische Handschriften der Staatsbibliothek", *Forschungen und Fortschritte der Katalogisierung der orientalischen Handschriften in Deutschland* (Forschungsbericht 10 der Deutschen Forschungsgemeinschaft), Wiesbaden 1966, pp. 1-9.
3. "Ein alter Irrtum bei der chronologischen Einordnung des Tarǧumān turkī wa `aǧamī wa muġalī", *Der Islam* 44 (1968), pp. 226-229.
4. "Bemerkungen zum neuen türkischen Taschenwörterbuch", *Ural-Altaische Jahrbücher* 40 (1968), pp. 247-249.

5. "Šerīf, Sultan Ğavrī und die "Perser", *Der Islam* 45 (1969), pp. 81-93.
6. "Zwei türkische Herren von Avlona", *Der Islam* 45 (1969), pp. 310-316.
7. "Ičil (Ičel)", Encyclopaedia of Islam IV (1971), pp. 1006-1007.
8. "Zum Tode von Ananiasz Zajączkowski", *Ural-Altaische Jahrbücher* 43 (1971), p. 122.
9. "Bemerkungen zur türkischen Prosa vor der Tanzimat-Zeit", *Der Islam* 50 (1973), pp. 157-167.
10. "Karachaniden", "Kleinasiatische Begliks", "Türkei", *Lexikon der islamischen Welt*, Stuttgart 1974.
11. "Ein Gazel von Ḥasan oğlu (Unbekannte Gedichte im Divan von Sultan Gavrī)", with Turkish translation, *I. Türk Dili Bilimsel Kurultayına Sunulan Bildiriler 1972*, Ankara 1975, pp. 331-341.
12. "Die vorwahhabitische *fitna* im osmanischen Kairo 1711", *İsmail Hakkı Uzunçarşılı Armağanı*, Istanbul 1975, pp. 55-65.
13. "Neuere wissenschaftliche Arbeiten und Forschungsvorhaben zur Sprache, Geschichte und Kultur der vorosmanischen und osmanischen Türkei in der Bundesrepublik Deutschland" *Turcica* V (1975), pp. 131-147.
14. "Aus den Nachtgesprächen Sultan Ğaurīs", in H. Franke e.a. (ed.), *Folia rara Wolfgang Voigt LXV. diem natalem celebranti ab amicis et catalogorum codicum orientalium conscribendorum collegis dedicata*, Wiesbaden 1976, pp. 22-28.
15. "Die Hamburger Handschrift von Yûsuf Meddâhs Varka und Gülşâh", in Gy. Kaldy-Nagy (ed.), *Hungaro-Turcica. Studies in honour of Julius Németh*, Budapest 1976, pp. 267-276.
16. "Ḥālet Efendis zweite Audienz bei Napoleon", in *Rocznik Orientalistyczny* 37 (1976), pp. 129-136.
17. "Zum Stand der mamluk-türkischen Forschung", in W. Voigt (ed.), *Zeitschrift der Deutschen Morgenländischen Gesellschaft. Supplement III,2. XIX. Deutscher Orientalistentag 1975*, Wiesbaden 1977, pp. 1156-1164.
18. "Hamburg, 5.-10. IX. 1976. Comité d'Etudes Pré-Ottomanes et Ottomanes. 2. Internationale Arbeitstagung für vorosmanische und osmanische Studien", *Turcica* 9 (1977), pp. 265-270.
19. "Literary Activities in Mamluk Halls and Barracks", in M. Rosen-Ayalon (ed.), *Studies in Memory of Gaston Wiet*, Jerusalem 1977, pp. 249-260.
20. "Isparta", in *Encyclopaedia of Islam* IV (1978), pp. 210-211.
21. "Anadolu Beylikleri", in *İslam Ansiklopedisi* 129. *cüz* (Istanbul 1978), pp. 280-286.
22. "Karl Süßheim 1878-1947", in *Der Islam* 56 (1979), pp. 1-8.
23. "Mısır Türk Tarihçiliği Hakkında Notlar", in H.D. Yıldız, E.İ. Erdinç, K. Eraslan (eds.), *Istanbul Üniversitesi Edebiyat Fakültesi Türkiyat Enstitüsü. I. Milletlerarası Türkoloji Kongresi (1973). Tebliğler I. Türk Tarihi*, Istanbul 1979, pp. 57-62.
24. "Beylikler Devrinin Bir Romantik Mesnevisi: Fahrî'nin Husrev u Şîrîn'i", in H.D. Yıldız, E.S. Erinç, K. Eraslan (eds.), *Istanbul Üniversitesi Edebiyat Fakültesi*

Türkiyat Enstitüsü. I. Milletlerarası Türkoloji Kongresi (1973). Tebliğler II. Türk Dili ve Edebiyatı, Istanbul 1979, pp. 325- 329.

25. "Drei türkische Chronisten im osmanischen Kairo", in I. Ševčenko and F.E. Sysyn (eds.), *Eucharisterion. Essays presented to Omeljan Pritsak on his Sixtieth Birthday. Harvard Ukrainian Studies* (Cambridge, Mass.) III/IV (1979-1980), pp. 228-235.
26. "Ahmedi", Aydın ogullari", "Aqsarayi", Bešir Celebi", in *Lexikon des Mittelalters* I, Munich and Zürich 1980, pp. 232, 1313, 2064.
27. "Adalet Ağaoğlu. Meine Lebensgeschichte" (Translation), in *Akzente. Zeitschrift für Literatur* 27/6 (1980), pp. 503-517.
28. "Cem", "Dede Qorqut", "Ebu l-ghazi", "Evliya Celebi", "Fuzuli", "Ghalib Dede", "Gülşehri", "Hatayi", "Hüseyin Bayqara", *Moderne Encyclopedie van de Wereldliteratuur*, Haarlem-Antwerpen, II-IV, 1980.
29. "Literatur im Zeichen des Alphabetwechsels", in *Anatolica* 8 (1981), pp. 133-157.
30. "Der Erzähler Erdal Öz", in K. Röhrborn and H.W. Brands (eds.), *Scholia. Beiträge zur Turkologie und Zentralasienkunde Annemarie von Gabain zum 80. Geburtstag dargebracht*, Wiesbaden 1981, pp. 55-63.
31. "Der Ǧāmiʿ ül-meknūnāt. Eine Quelle ʿĀlīs aus der Zeit Sultan Süleymāns", in H.R. Römer and A. Noth (ed.), *Studien zur Geschichte und Kultur des Vorderen Orients. Festschrift für Bertold Spuler zum siebzigsten Geburtstag*, Leiden 1981, pp. 79-92.
32. "Het einde der tijden bij de Turken in de 16de eeuw", in E. de Moor (ed.), *De taal van de islam. Opstellen over arabische, turkse en afghaanse cultuur. Midden Oosten en Islampublicatie* 7, Nijmegen 1981, pp. 91-107.
33. "Turkse discussies omtrent het christendom", in Sj. van Koningsveld (ed.), *Historische betrekkingen tussen moslims en christenen. Midden Oosten en Islampublicatie* 9, Haarlem 1982, pp. 113-126.
34. "Kadi Burhaneddin", "Karacaoglan", "Kemal Tahir", "Lamii", "Mahmud al-Kashgari", "Mehmed Akif", "Mesihi", "Nazim Hikmet", "Necati Beg", "Necatigil", "Nesimi", "Nesin", *Moderne Encyclopedie van de Wereldliteratuur*, V, VI.
35. "Religiöse Geschichte in der türkischen Ikonographie", in *Anatolica* 10 (1983), pp. 133-148.
36. "Osmanische Chronistik", in *Lexikon des Mittelalters* II, Munich and Zürich: Artemis 1983, pp. 2027-2028.
37. "Orhan Seyfi Orhon", "Ören", "Öz", "Pazarkaya", "Pir Sultan Abdal", "Sabit", "Sadettin", "Savaşçı", "Şeyhi", "Seyyid Battal Gazi", "Sinan Paşa", *Moderne Encyclopedie van de Wereldliteratuur* VII, VIII, 1983.
38. "Das Osmanenreich zwischen 1300 und 1789", in R. Kurzrock (ed.), *Die islamische Welt* I, Berlin: Colloquium Verlag 1984, pp. 62-72.
39. "Zur türkischen Literatur", in R. Kurzrock (ed.), *Die islamische Welt* II, Berlin 1984, pp. 97-105.

40. "Soysal", "Süleyman Celebi", "Süreya", "Tamer", "Tarancı", "Turkse literatuur, algemeen, pre-islamitische periode", "Turkse literatuur in Anatolie tot 1500", "Osmaanse literatuur 1500-1600", "De periode na 1945: proza", "Turkse literatuur buiten Turkije", "Turkse literatuur in West- en Centraal-Azie", "Uyar", "Veysel", "Yahya", "Yalçın", "Yunus Emre", "Yusuf Has Hacib", "Zati", *Moderne Encyclopedie van de Wereldliteratuur* IX, X, 1984.
41. "Habsburgisch-osmanische Beziehungen", *Travaux et Recherches en Turquie* 2 (1984), pp. 273-274.
42. "Literarisierung der Geschichtsschreibung am Beispiel der Gazavatnames (Resümee)", *Zeitschrift der Deutschen Morgenländischen Gesellschaft. Supplement VI. XXII. Deutscher Orientalistentag vom 21. bis 25. März 1983 in Tübingen* (1985), pp. 355-356.
43. "Literatur und Gesellschaft im osmanischen Reich", B. Kellner-Heinkele (ed.), *Türkische Kunst und Kultur aus osmanischer Zeit*, Recklinghausen 1985, pp. 92-104.
44. "Khodja Efendi, Saʿd al-Din", *Encyclopaedia of Islam* V, Leiden 1986, pp. 27-28.
45. "Ḳiṣṣa in older Turkish literature", *Encyclopaedia of Islam* V, Leiden 1986, p. 194.
46. "Lāmiʿī", *Encyclopaedia of Islam* V, Leiden 1986, pp. 649-651.
47. "Madjnūn Laylā in Turkish literature", in *Encyclopaedia of Islam* V, Leiden 1986, pp. 1105-1106.
48. "Turkse dichters en hun patroons in de vijftiende en zestiende eeuw", J.T.P. de Bruijn, W.L. Idema and F.P. van Oostrom (eds.), *Dichter en hof. Verkenningen in veertien culturen*, Utrecht 1986, pp. 167-181.
49. "Zwei türkische Bibelhandschriften in Leiden als mittelosmanische Sprachdenkmäler", Claudia Römer (red.), *Wiener Zeitschrift für die Kunde des Morgenlandes. Festschrift Andreas Tietze zum 70. Geburtstag gewidmet von seinen Freunden und Schülern*, 76 (1986), pp. 111-118.
50. "Hanna Sohrweide. 1919-1984", *Der Islam* 63 (1986), pp. 1-4.
51. "Dursun Beg", "Enveri", *Lexikon des Mittelalters* III, Munich and Zürich 1986, pp. 1484-1485, 2020.
52. "Wolfgang Voigt (1911-1982) and the cataloguing of Oriental manuscripts", *Manuscripts of the Middle East* I (1986), pp. 103-104.
53. "Romantische Auswanderer im Reich ʿAbdülhamids", G. Schubert (red.), *Türkische Miszellen. Robert Anhegger Festschrift*, Istanbul 1987, pp. 131-143.
54. "Ṣāḥib-Ḳirān und Mahdī. Türkische Endzeiterwartungen im ersten Jahrzehnt der Regierung Süleymāns", György Kara (ed.), *Between the Danube and the Caucasus*, Budapest 1987, pp. 43-62.
55. "Political genealogies in the sixteenth century", *Osmanlı Araştırmaları. Journal of Ottoman Studies* VII-VII (1988), pp. 123-137.
56. "Fahri", *Lexikon des Mittelalters* IV, 1988, p. 233.
57. "Gazavatname-i Sultan Murad", *Lexikon des Mittelalters* IV, 1988, p. 1151.

58. "Geschichtskalender", *Lexikon des Mittelalters* IV, 1988, pp. 1382-1382.
59. "Prognostika und Geschichte", *IX. Türk Tarih Kongresi. Ankara 1981. Kongreye Sunulan Bildiriler* II, Ankara 1988, pp. 745-751.
60. "From archetype to oral tradition: Editing Persian and Turkish literary texts", *Manuscripts of the Middle East* 3, Leiden 1989, pp. 7-11.
61. "Marthiya in Turkish literature", *Encyclopaedia of Islam*, 1989, pp. 609-610.
62. "Mathnawī in Turkish", *Encyclopaedia of Islam*, 1989, pp. 835-837.
63. "Historiographie, osmanischer Bereich", *Lexikon des Mittelalters* V, 1990, p. 54.
64. "Bertold Spuler (5.12.1911-6.3.1990)", *Newsletter. Union européenne des arabisants et islamisants* 2 (Spring 1990), pp. 2-3.
65. "Ibn Bībī", *Lexikon des Mittelalters* V (April 1990), p. 314.
66. "Idrīs-i Bidlīsī", *Lexikon des Mittelalters* V (April 1990), p. 327.
67. "Kemālpaşazāde", *Lexikon des Mittelalters* V (November 1990), p. 1101.
68. "Kemāl, Sarīğa", *Lexikon des Mittelalters* V (November 1990), p. 1101.
69. "Die türkische Qaside", W. Heinrichs (ed.), *Neues Handbuch der Literaturwissenschaft. Band 5. Orientalisches Mittelalter*, Wiesbaden 1990, pp. 258-264.
70. "Das türkische Gasel", W. Heinrichs (ed.), *Neues Handbuch der Literaturwissenschaft. Band 5. Orientalisches Mittelalter*, Wiesbaden 1990, pp. 278-283.
71. "Türkische Epik", W. Heinrichs (ed.), *Neues Handbuch der Literaturwissenschaft. Band 5. Orientalisches Mittelalter*, Wiesbaden 1990, pp. 319-325.
72. "Das Verhältnis von Hoch- und Volksliteratur im Türkischen", W. Heinrichs (ed.), *Neues Handbuch der Literaturwissenschaft. Band 5. Orientalisches Mittelalter*, Wiesbaden 1990, pp. 475-483.
73. "A Sixteenth-Century Turkish Apology for Islam: the *Gurbetname-i Sultan Cem*", *Byzantinische Forschungen* XVI (Amsterdam 1991), pp. 105-121.
74. "Das Studium der Turkologie in Leiden", I. Baldauf, K. Kreiser, S. Tezcan (eds.), *Türkische Sprachen und Literaturen. Materialien der ersten deutschen Turkologen-Konferenz Bamberg, 3.6. Juli 1987*, Wiesbaden 1991, pp. 113-121.
75. "Nešri", *Lexikon des Mittelalters* VI (1992), p. 1098.
76. "Turkse religieuze miniaturen en albumbladen", C. Huygens en F. Ros (ed.), *Dromen van het Paradijs. Islamitische kunst van het Museum voor Volkenkunde Rotterdam*, Rotterdam 1993, pp. 86-95.
77. "The Reign of Murad II: A Survey (I)", *Anatolica* XX (1994), pp. 249-267.
78. "Mevlana ʿIsâ's view of Ottoman Hungary", *VII. CIÉPO Sempozyumu*, Ankara 1994.
79. "Glimpses of Turkish Saints: Another Look at Lāmiʿī and Ottoman Biographers", M.E. Subtelny (ed.), *Annemarie Schimmel Festschrift. Essays presented to Annemarie Schimmel on the occasion of her retirement from Harvard University, Journal of Turkish Studies* 18, Harvard University 1994, pp. 59-73.
80. "Public Opinion under Sultan Süleymân", H. İnalcık and C. Kafadar (eds.), *Süleymân the Second and His Time*, Istanbul 1994, pp. 49-57.

81. "Notes on ʿArūẓ in Turkish Collections", B. Utas and L. Johanson (eds.), *Arabic prosody and its Applications in Muslim Poetry*, Uppsala 1994, pp. 61-80 (Swedish Research Institute in Istanbul, Transactions Vol. 5).
82. "The Sultan's Prayer Before Battle", C. Heywood and C. Imber (eds.), *Studies in Ottoman History in Honour of Professor V.L. Ménage*, Istanbul 1994, pp. 63-75.
83. "Šeyḫī, Yūsuf Sinān", *Lexikon des Mittelalters* VII, Munich 1995, pp. 1820-1821.
84. "Notes on the {IsAr} future and its modal functions", B. Kellner-Heinkele en M. Stachowski (red.), *Laut- und Wortgeschichte der Türksprachen*, Wiesbaden 1995, pp. 43-57.
85. "Mevlānā ʿĪsā on Bektashis", in A. Popovic an G. Veinstein (eds.), *Bektachiyya. Études sur l'ordre mystique des Bektachis et les groupes relevant de Hadji Bektach*, Istanbul [1995/6], pp. 159-163.
86. "Šükrullāh b. Šihāb ed-Dīn", *Lexikon des Mittelalters* VIII, Munich 1996, p. 298.
87. "Sūzī Çelebi", *Lexikon des Mittelalters* VII, Munich 1996, p. 340.
88. "'Die Türken sind die klügsten Leute': Türkisches bei Theodor Fontane", *Zeitschrift für Türkeistudien (ZfTS)* 11 (1998), pp. 55-74.
89. "Mystiek in Turks Anatolië met bijzondere aandacht voor Lâmi'î's *Terjeme-i Nafaḥât*", Marjo Buitelaar and Johan ter Haar (eds.), *Mystiek: het andere gezicht van de islam*, Bussum 1999, pp. 18-34.
90. "Ṭas̲h̲köprüzāde 2. ʿIsām al-Dīn Aḥmad b. Muṣṭafā b. K̲h̲alīl, Abu 'l-K̲h̲ayr", *Encyclopaedia of Islam* X (1999), pp. 351-352.
91. "Turks. 3. Turkish Literature of the Golden Horde and of the Mamlūks", *Encyclopaedia of Islam* X (2000), pp. 716-718.
92. "Yūsuf and Zulaykhā in Turkish literature", *Encyclopaedia of Islam* XI (2001), p. 362.
93. "Re-reading the Story of the Religious "Fitna" of 1711", Ingeborg Hauenschild, Claus Schönig and Peter Zieme (eds.), *Scripta Ottomanica et Res Altaicae. Festschrift für Barbara Kellner-Heinkele zu ihrem 60. Geburtstag*, Wiesbaden 2002, pp. 79-93.
94. "'Āşıkpaşazādes Blick auf Frauen", Sabine Prätor & Christoph K. Neumann (eds.), *Frauen, Bilder und Gelehrte. Studien zu Gesellschaft und Künsten im Osmanischen Reich. Festschrift Hans Georg Majer*, Istanbul 2002, pp. 69-96.
95. "The poem in the chronicle: The use of poetry in early Ottoman historiography", Ugo Marazzi (ed.), *Turcica et Islamica. Studi in memoria di Aldo Gallotta*, Naples 2003, pp. 175-184.
96. "Teilhabe von Frauen an der älteren islamischen Mystik (9. bis 16. Jahrhundert)". *WZKM* 93 (2003), pp. 35-94.
97. "Old Anatolian Turkish poetry in its relationship to the Persian tradition", Lars Johanson and Christiane Bulut (eds.), *Turkic-Iranian Contact Areas*, Wiesbaden 2006, pp. 49-68.
98. "Goethe und Diez im Jahre 1790", Hendrik Fenz and P. Kappert (eds.), *Turkologie für das 21. Jahrhundert – Herausforderung zwischen Tradition und Moderne,*

Wiesbaden 2007 (Veröffentlichungen der Societas Uralo-Altaica, Band 70), pp. 129-148.

99. "Am Çırçıp: Einst und jetzt", Hendrik Fenz (ed.), *Strukturelle Zwänge – Persönliche Freiheiten. Osmanen, Türken, Muslime: Reflexionen zu gesellschaftlichen Umbrüchen. Gedenkband zu Ehren Petra Kapperts*, Berlin/New York 2009, pp. 145-167.

100. "Der Preis der Lyrik. Förderung, Auszeichnung, Opfer", in Börte Sagaster, Karin Schweißgut, Barbara Kellner-Heinkele, Claus Schönig (eds.), *Hoşsohbet. Erika Glassen zu Ehren*, Würzburg 2011, pp. 37-56

101. "Mensch und Natur an der Südostgrenze der Türkei", Brigitte Heuer, Barbara Kellner-Heinkele, Claus Schönig (eds.), *"Die Wunder der Schöpfung. Mensch und Natur in der türksprachigen Welt"*, Würzburg 2012, pp. 259-270.

102. "Fakhrī", *Encyclopaedia of Islam* 3rd edition, 2012.

103. "Aus den kalifornischen Jahren: Andreas Tietze an der UCLA", *Archivum Ottomanicum* 30, Wiesbaden 2013, pp. 5-30.

Unsigned: "Fożūlī, Moḥammad", in *Encyclopaedia Iranica*.

Translations of Scholarly articles

1. Mecdut Mansuroğlu, "Das geschlossene e im karachanidischen Türkisch", *Ural-Altaische Jahrbücher* 29 (1957), pp. 215-223.
2. (with Hanna Sohrweide) Claude Cahen, "Zur Geschichte der städtischen Gesellschaft im islamischen Orient des Mittelalters", *Saeculum* IX (1958), pp. 59-76.
3. Reşid Rahmeti Arat, "Zu einer Schriftmusterhandschrift", *Ural-Altaische Jahrbücher* 33 (1961), pp. 205-217.

Book Reviews

1. X. de Planhol, *De la plaine pamphylienne aux lacs pisidiens*, Paris 1958, *Oriens* 13-14 (1960-61), pp. 424-425.
2. I. Melikoff, *La Geste de Melik Danişmend*, Paris 1960, *Journal of the American Oriental Society* 82 (1962), pp. 391-393.
3. *Belleten* 23 (1959), *Oriens* 15 (1962), pp. 426-429.
4. 14 short notices in *Ural-Altaische Jahrbücher* 34 (1962).
5. F. Köprülü, *Osmanlı Devleti'nin Kuruluşu*, Ankara 1959, *Oriens* 16 (1963), pp. 300-301.
6. *Belleten* 24 (1960), *Oriens* 17 (1964), pp. 223-226.

7. S. Mardin, *The Genesis of Young Ottoman Thought*, Princeton 1962, *Der Islam* 42 (1965), pp. 110-112.
8. B.D. Papoulia, *Ursprung und Wesen der 'Knabenlese' im osmanischen Reich*, Munich 1963, *Byzantinische Zeitschrift* 38 (1965), pp. 122-124.
9. F. Kochwasser (red.), *Zeitschrift für Kulturaustausch. Türkei-Nummer*, Stuttgart 1962, *Der Islam* 40 (1965), pp. 271-272.
10. A. Zajączkowski, *Poemat iranski Ḫusrev-u-Šīrīn w wersji osmansko-tureckiej Seyhi*, Warsaw 1963, *Der Islam* 42 (1966), pp. 290-291.
11. 22 short notices in *Ural-Altaische Jahrbücher* 36 (1966).
12. J. Blaškovič, *Arabische, türkische und persische Handschriften der Universitätsbibliothek zu Bratislava*, Bratislava 1961, *Oriens* 18-19 (1967), pp. 495-497.
13. K. Steuerwald, *Untersuchungen zur türkischen Sprache der Gegenwart I-II*, Berlin 1964, *Der Islam* 43 (1967), pp. 226-229.
14. T.W. Arnold, *Painting in Islam*, second edition New York 1965, *Der Islam* 43 (1967), pp. 203-204.
15. A. Hoghoughi, *Catalogue critique des manuscrits persans de la Bibliotheque Nationale et Universitaire de Strasbourg*, Strasbourg 1964, *Der Islam* 43 (1967), pp. 211-213.
16. O. Spies and B. Emircan, *Türkischer Sprachführer*, Bonn 1966, *Der Islam* 44 (1968), pp. 308-309.
17. R.M. Meriç, *Mimar Sinan Hayatı, Eseri I*, Ankara 1965, *Der Islam* 44 (1968), pp. 308-309.
18. H.E. Mayer, *Geschichte der Kreuzzüge*, Stuttgart 1965, *Der Islam* 44 (1968), pp. 272-273.
19. 11 short notices in *Ural-Altaische Jahrbücher* 40 (1968).
20. Y. Pazarkaya and H. Mader, *Orhan Veli Kanık. Poesie. Türkisch-deutsch*, Frankfurt 1966, *Die Welt der Literatur*, Hamburg, 29 February 1968.
21. P. Schreiner, *Studien zu den Braxea xronika*, Munich 1967, *Zeitschrift der Deutschen Morgenländischen Gesellschaft* 118 (1968), pp. 374-375.
22. A. Zajączkowski, *Turecka wersja Šāh-name z Egiptu Mameluckiego*, Warsaw 1965, *Der Islam* 45 (1969), pp. 174-177.
23. F. Taeschner, *Geschichte der arabischen Welt*, Stuttgart 1964, *Der Islam* 46 (1970), p. 135.
24. H. Hilgenberg, H. Staudinger, E. Wagner, *Unsere Geschichte – unsere Welt, I-III, Munich 1963-1964*, *Der Islam* 46 (1970), pp. 212-215.
25. A. Zajączkowski, *La Chronique des Steppes Kiptchak- Tevarih-i Deşt-i Qipcaq-du XVIIIe siecle*, Warsaw 1966, *Der Islam* 46 (1970), pp. 202-203.
26. A.B.M. Habibullah, *Descriptive Catalogue of the Persian, Urdu and Arabic Manuscripts in the Dacca University Library I*, Dacca 1966, *Der Islam* 46 (1970), p. 190.

27. H.J. Kissling (ed.), *Ušāqīzāde's Lebensbeschreibungen berühmter Gelehrter und Gottesmänner des osmanischen Reiches im 17. Jahrhundert*, Wiesbaden 1965, *Der Islam* 46 (1970), pp. 181-183.
28. H.J. Kissling (ed.), *Der See-Atlas des Sejjid Nuh*, part 1, Munich 1966, *Der Islam* 46 (1970), p. 191.
29. G. Doerfer, *Türkische und mongolische Elemente im Neupersischen unter besonderer Berücksichtigung neupersischer Geschichtsquellen*, II-III, Wiesbaden 1965-1967, *Der Islam* 46 (1970), pp. 166-170.
30. İ. Kerkük (ed.), *Kerkük üzerine söylenmis şiirler*, Ankara 1963, *Der Islam* 46 (1970), p. 201.
31. A. Ateş, *Şehriyar ve Haydar Baba'ya Selam*, Ankara 1964, *Der Islam* 46 (1970), p. 202.
32. A. von Gabain, *Das uigurische Königreich von Chotscho 850-1250*, Berlin 1961, *Oriens* 21-22 (1971), pp. 526-528.
33. R.F. Kreutel, *Osmanisch-Türkische Chrestomathie*, Wiesbaden 1965, *Der Islam* 48 (1971), p. 171.
34. P.T. Suzuki, *West European Research on Modern Turkey, Newsletters 1970*, *Der Islam* 48 (1971), p. 169.
35. 13 short notices in *Ural-Altaische Jahrbücher* 43 (1971).
36. U. Heyd, *Revival of Islam in Modern Turkey. Lecture delivered March 28, 1968*, Jerusalem 1968, *Der Islam* 49 (1972), pp. 147-148.
37. K. Jahn, *Türkische Freilassungserklärungen des 18. Jahrhunderts (1702-1776)*, Napels 1963, *Der Islam* 49 (1972), pp. 358-359.
38. *Leylā and Mejnūn by Fuzūlī. Translated from the Turkish by Sofi Huri, with a history of the poem, notes, and bibliography by Alessio Bombaci*, London 1970, *Der Islam* 49 (1972), pp. 356-358.
39. G. Doerfer, *Türkische Lehnwörter im Tadschikischen*, Wiesbaden 1967, *Der Islam* 49 (1972), pp. 364-365.
40. A. Zajączkowski, *Poezje Stroficzne 'Asiq-Pasa*, Warsaw 1967, *Ural-Altaische Jahrbücher* 45 (1973), pp. 308-309.
41. S. Vryonis, Jr., *The Decline of Medieval Hellenism in Asia Minor and the Process of Islamization from the Eleventh through the Fifteenth Century*, Berkeley-Los Angeles-London 1971, *Zeitschrift der Deutschen Morgenländischen Gesellschaft* 124 (1974), pp. 165-171.
42. G.S. Harris, *Troubled Alliance. Turkish-American problems in historical perspective, 1945-1971*, Washington D.C. 1972, *Der Islam* 51 (1974), p. 185.
43. S. Tekin, *Die Kapitel über die Bewußtseinslehre im uigurischen Goldglanzsutra (IX und X), bearbeitet von K. Röhrborn und P. Schulz*, Wiesbaden 1971, *Der Islam* 51 (1974), pp. 188-189.
44. F. Mansur, *Bodrum. A Town in the Aegean*, Leiden 1972, *Orientalistische Literaturzeitung* 70 (1975), pp. 490-492.

45. T. Kortantamer, *Leben und Weltbild des altosmanischen Dichters Ahmedi unter besonderer Berücksichtigung seines Diwans*, Freiburg i. Br. 1973, *Der Islam* 52 (1975), pp. 188-190.
46. K. Steuerwald, *Türkisch-Deutsches Wörterbuch. Türkce-Almanca Sözlük*, Wiesbaden 1972, *Ural-Altaische Jahrbücher* 47 (1975), pp. 231-234.
47. M.N. Hacıeminoglu, *Kutb'un Husrev ü Şirin'i ve Dil Hususiyetleri*, Istanbul 1968, *Ural-Altaische Jahrbücher* 48 (1976).
48. L. Ligeti (ed.), *Researches in Altaic Languages*, Budapest 1975, *Der Islam* 54 (1977), pp. 172-174.
49. J. Eckmann, *Middle Turkic Glosses of the Rylands Interlinear Koran Translation*, Budapest 1976, *Die Welt des Islams* 18 (1978), pp. 125-126.
50. J. Kayaloff, *The battle of Sardarabad*, 1973, *Orientalistische Literaturzeitung* 73 (1978), p. 71.
51. G. Schäfer, *Die Gül Camii in Istanbul*, 1973, *Orientalistische Literaturzeitung* 73 (1978), p. 70.
52. P. Benedict, *Ula. An Anatolian Town*, Leiden 1974, *Orientalistische Literaturzeitung* 74 (1979), pp. 158-159.
53. A.J.E. Bodrogligeti, *Halis' Story of Ibrahim. A Central Asian Islamic Work in Late Chagatay Turkic*, Leiden 1975, *Bibliotheca Orientalis* 36 (1979), pp. 393-394.
54. G.M. Smith, *Yusuf-i Meddah. Varqa ve Gülšāh. A Fourteenth Century Anatolian Turkish Mesnevi*, Leiden 1976, *Die Welt des Islams* 20 (1980), pp. 127-128.
55. E. Prokosch, *Krieg und Sieg in Ungarn. Die Ungarnfeldzüge des Großwesirs Köprülüzade Fazil Ahmed Pascha 1663 und 1664*, Graz-Vienna-Cologne 1976, *Die Welt des Orients* 11 (1980), pp. 183-184.
56. K. Binswanger, *Untersuchungen zum Status der Nichtmuslime im Osmanischen Reich des 16. Jahrhunderts*, Munich 1977, *Der Islam* 57 (1980), pp. 390-392.
57. P. Schreiner, *Die byzantinischen Kleinchroniken, I-II*, Vienna 1975-1977, ZDMG 130 (1980), pp. 587-588.
58. W.G. Andrews, *An Introduction to Ottoman Poetry*, Minneapolis and Chicago 1976, *Orientalistische Literaturzeitung* 76 (1981), pp. 384-385.
59. M. And, *Turkish miniature painting*, 1978, *Orientalistische Literaturzeitung* 76 (1981), pp. 486-487.
60. M. And, *Magic in Istanbul*, 1978, *Orientalistische Literaturzeitung* 76 (1981), pp. 575-577.
61. A. Tietze, *The Turkish Shadow Theater and the Puppet Collection of the L. A. Mayer Memorial Foundation*, Berlin 1977, *Orientalistische Literaturzeitung* 77 (1982), pp. 64-65.
62. M. Götz, *Türkische Handschriften. Verzeichnis der orientalischen Handschriften in Deutschland XIII,4*, Wiesbaden 1979, WZKM 74 (1982), pp. 280-282.

63. E. Prokosch, *Studien zur Grammatik des Osmanisch-Türkischen unter besonderer Berücksichtigung des Vulgärosmanisch-Türkischen*, Freiburg 1980, *Der Islam* 59 (1982), pp. 372-374.
64. W.F. Weiker, *The Modernization of Turkey. From Ataturk to the Present Day*, New York/London 1981, *Tijdschrift voor Geschiedenis* 95 (1982), p. 303.
65. J.C. Bürgel, *Nizami. Chosrau und Schirin*, Zürich 1980, *Persica* 11 (1984), pp. 149-150.
66. W. Eberhard, *China und seine westlichen Nachbarn*, Darmstadt 1978, *Persica* 11 (1984), pp. 150-151.
67. W. Hale, *The political and economic development of modern Turkey*, London 1982, *Tijdschrift voor Geschiedenis* 97 (1984), pp. 141-142.
68. C.A. Frazee, *Catholics and sultans. The church and the Ottoman Empire 1453-1923*, London and Cambridge 1983, *Tijdschrift voor Geschiedenis* 97 (1984), pp. 238-239.
69. H. Reindl, *Männer um Bayezid. Eine prosopographische Studie*, Berlin 1983, *Der Islam* 63 (1986), pp. 172-173.
70. B. Moser, *Die Chronik des Ahmed Sinan Celebi genannt Bihištī*, Munich 1980, *Der Islam* 63 (1986), pp. 173-175.
71. A.C. Schaendlinger with Claudia Römer, *Die Schreiben Süleymans des Prächtigen an Karl V., Ferdinand I. und Maximilian II.*, Vienna 1983, *Der Islam* 63 (1986), pp. 175-176.
72. H.G. Majer (ed.), *Das osmanische "Registerbuch der Beschwerden" (Šikāyet Defteri) vom Jahre 1675*, Vienna 1984, *Journal of the Economic and Social History of the Orient* 29 (1986), pp. 218-220.
73. G. Heiss and G. Klingenstein (ed.), *Das Osmanische Reich und Europa 1683 bis 1789: Konflikt, Entspannung und Austausch*, *Tijdschrift voor Geschiedenis* 99 (1986), pp. 274-275.
74. K. Nehring, *Adam Freiherrn zu Herbersteins Gesandtschaftsreise nach Konstantinopel. Ein Beitrag zum Frieden von Zsitvatorok*, Munich 1983, and A. Wenner, *Tagebuch der kaiserlichen Gesandtschaft nach Konstantinopel 1616-1618*, Munich 1984, K. Nehring, *Iter Constantinopolitanum*, Munich 1984, *Die Welt des Islams* 26 (1986), pp. 226-227.
75. W. Felix, *Byzanz und die islamische Welt im früheren 11. Jahrhundert*, *Die Welt des Islams* 26 (1986), p. 199.
76. *The Union Catalogue of Manuscripts in Turkey: Türkiye Yazmaları Toplu Kataloğu* (TÜYATOK), *Manuscripts of the Middle East* I (1986), pp. 109-110.
77. C. Woodhead, *Ta'liki-zade's sehname-i hümayun. A history of the Ottoman campaign into Hungary 1593-96*, Berlin 1983, *Wiener Zeitschrift für die Kunde des Morgenlandes* 77 (1987), pp. 276-279.
78. D. Duda, *Islamische Handschriften I. Persische Handschriften*, Vienna 1983, *Bibliotheca Orientalis* XLIII (1986), pp. 237-239.

79. K.-D. Grothusen (ed.), *Südosteuropa-Handbuch Band IV. Türkei*, Göttingen 1985, *Tijdschrift voor Geschiedenis* 100 (1987), pp. 81-82.

80. J.L. Bacharach, *A Middle East Studies Handbook*, Cambridge/London 1984, *Tijdschrift voor Geschiedenis* 100 (1987), pp. 82-83.

81. Milan Adamović, *Kelile ü Dimne. Türkische Handschrift T189 der Forschungsbibliothek Gotha*, Hildesheim-Zürich-New York 1994, *Wiener Zeitschrift für die Kunde des Morgenlandes* 87 (1997), pp. 368-370.

Commemorative Volume

J. Schmidt (ed.), *Essays in Honour of Barbara Flemming, Journal of Turkish Studies* 26/I-II, Harvard University 2002.

In the Press

Hanna Sohrweide, unter Mitarbeit von Barbara Flemming, Jan Schmidt and Tobias Völker, *Türkische Handschriften der Staats- und Universitätsbibliothek Hamburg und der Staatsbibliothek zu Berlin – Preussisscher Kulturbesitz* (VOHD XIII, 7).

Index

Abbasids 205
abdāl 267, 272, 353
ʿAbd al-Ghanī al-Nabulūsī 334
ʿAbd al-Latīf, Mamluk court functionary 49
ʿAbd al-Qādir b. Ibrāhīm ad-Dimashqī 11
ʿAbd al-Qādir Gilani 403 ftn., 404
ʿAbd al-Rahmān al-Gabartī (*see* al-Jabartī) 78-79, 85-87
ʿAbdalwahhāb ʿAzzām 91, 106, 116
ʿAbd al-Wahhāb al-Shaʿrānī 82 ftn., 334
ʿAbdī Paşa, Ottoman governor 140, 145
abdication 281, 324, 348
ʿAbdulhamīd I, sultan 432 ftn., 441
ʿAbdulhamīd II, sultan 45, 132-133, 138, 149, 157-163, 190-200-201
ʿAbdulkerim b. Abdurrahman 81, 83, 86-87, 145-147, 331
ʿAbdullāh 384 Hāshim family
ʿAbdullah Cevdet 133
ʿAbdullah Ilāhī (*see* Ilāhī) 262-263, 272
ʿAbdulmecid (poet) 293
ʿAbdurrahīm Mısırlıoglu 261
ʿAbdurrahīm Muhibb Efendi (Muhibb Efendi) 11, 39-40, 104
ʿAbdurrahman Cāmī (*see* Jāmī) 257-258
Abdülaziz, printer 162
Abdülhak Hamit (Tarhan) 160, 162, 166
Abkhazian 88
Ablustain/Elbistan 452
abnāʾ al-ʿAjam 48, 50
Abraham 230, 236-237, 247
Abū ʿAlī al-Daqqāq 403
Abū l-Fadl Muhammad al-Aʿraj 110
Abu l-Ghāzī Bahādur Khan 232
Abū Hafs al-Haddād 388-389
Abū ʿIsā al-Tirmidhī 390
Abū Ishāq Kāzerūnī 207
Abū Ishāq, sons of 207, 236
Abū l-Layth as-Samarqandī 113
Abū l-Vafā Tāc al-ʿĀrifīn 451
Abū Yazīd al-Balkhī 244
Abū Saʿīd, Ilkhan 407
Abulja Khan 230
ʿacam, *see* ajam 120
Adam 214, 250, 384-385, 406
Adıvar, Halide Edip 156-158, 167
Adıvar, Abdülhak Adnan 10
ʿAdnī, Mahmud Pasha 89, 294
Afghanistan 463
Afira 386
Aflakī 1 ftn., 254, 271
Agca Mescid 459
Agrigento, Sicily 430
ahl al-bayt 385
Ahmad, seal of prophets 246
Ahmad al-Budayrī 144
Ahmad al-Khalīfī 83, 337
Ahmad an-Nafrawī 83, 337
Ahmad as-Sivasī, Sihabeddin
Ahmad b. Abī l-Hawārī 388
Ahmad b. ʿAli al-Fayyūmī 110
Ahmad b. Hasan at-Tuluni al-Miʿmar 110
Ahmad b. Khidrūya 388-389, 3984
Ahmad b. Muthanna 418
Ahmad b. Zunbul ar-Rammāl 144
Ahmed I, Ottoman sultan 182
Ahmed III, Ottoman sultan 140, 182
Ahmed b. ʿAbdullah, king 210
Ahmed ʿAzmī Efendi 432-433
Ahmed Beg, Evrenosoghlu 264
Ahmed Bukharī 263
Ahmed Cevdet 271
Ahmed Chelebi, Shalabi 331-332
Ahmed b. Hemdem 65
Ahmed Faqīh 255
Ahmed Khvāca as-Sarayi 293
Ahmed Midhat 167
Ahmed Paşa, Ottoman poet 89, 129, 294, 355
Ahmed Paşa, governor of Egypt 217
Ahmed Paşa, governor of Egypt (1689-1691) 80
Ahmed Resmī Efendi 433
Ahmed Vefiq Pasha 269
Ahmed-i Dāʿī 33
Ahmedī 6-7, 29, 33, 175-176, 234, 282, 288-289, 293-294, 311, 319, 345
Ahmet Haşim 160, 162, 166
Ahmet Rāsim 152, 166
Ahvāl-ı qiyāmet 209-210
Aintab 456

ʿĀʾisha 386
ʿĀʾisha al-Manūbiyya 410
ʿajam 48, 50, 91, 120
ʿAjamī, al-Şanqajī 49
Aka Gündüz 159-160
Akbiñar River 456
ʿĀkif Paşa 62 ftn.
Akıncı 282, 284, 355
Akkā, Acre 102
Akkoyunlu, *see* Aqqoyunlu
Aksaray 263
aktarmak 164, 168
al Raschid family 197
ʿAlā ed-devle 218-219
alafranga society 158
Alaman 179, 221, 278
ʿalāmet, portent 171, 209, 216, 222-223, 282, 403
Alanos 26
Alans and Wallachs 26
Aleppo 13, 47-49, 57, 76, 173, 262, 400 ftn. 448, 450, 456-457
Aleppo Turkmens 451
Alevilik 452
Alevi ocak 464
Alevi Turkmens 460
Alexander the Great 221, 234-235, 319, 345
Alexandria (Egypt) 40-41
Algiers 279
ʿĀlī, *see also* Mustafa b. Ahmed 66, 68 170-171, 173, 411
ʿAlī Efendi, Seyyid, Moralı 104
ʿAlī (Qıssa-i Yusuf) 255
ʿAlī ʿAzīz Efendi 65, 71, 433
ʿAlī b. Abī Tālib 233
ʿAlī b. Ahmad b. Amīr ʿAlī 109, probably identical with
ʿAlī b. Ahmed b. Emīr ʿAlī 296
ʿAlī Beg, Albert Bobovski 184-189
ʿAlī Beg b. Şehsuvar 117
ʿAlī Çelebi (d. 1543) 64
ʿAlī Dede of Sivrihisar 374
ʿAlī Emirī 56, 77
ʿAlī al-Khalvetī 262-263
ʿAlī Nūrī Bey (Dilmeç) 190-191, 194, 198-201
ʿAlī Pasha (Kosovo I) 320
ʿAlids 209
Alpay, Şahin 190
Alphabet Commission 150
Alqās Mirza 348
Altındağ 42
Amasra 370
Amasya 257, 261, 263-264, 280, 348, 411; peace of 457
Ambros, Edith 290
Amid, Kara Amid, Diyarbakr 48, 56, 107, 451, 453-454, 456-457
Āmina 384-385
Amu Darya 391
Anadolu 454, 456
Anadoluculuk 43
Anatolia, *see* Rūm 7, 51, 29, 32-34, 37, 107-108, 117, 120, 130, 157, 178, 203, 205, 209, 211, 218-219, 226-227, 234, 253, 263, 274-275, 279, 286, 288, 284, 322-323, 373, 377, 405, 452, 455, 461
Anatolian principalities 274, 318, 354, 364
Andrews, Walter G. Jr. 271, 289-292
Andronikos II Palaiologos 26
angels 385, 391-393
Ankara 263
anthologies, prosodic 292-296
anthologies, religious 296-298
Anti-Christ 204
Antioch 252
Apulia 279
al-Aqfahsī 110
Aq Shemseddin, Ak Sheykh 260, 262-264
Aqhisari, Sheykh 283
Aqkerman 176
Aqqoyunlu 48, 54, 120, 228-229, 263, 372, 452-53
Aqsarayī Karīmaddīn 254
aqtāb 280, 283
Arabic 117-120, 120, 126
al-Arbaʿīn, barracks 112
Ardabīl 217, 407
ʿĀrif Çelebi, Fethullāh 70
arılaştırmak 168
Aristotle 280, 283, 345
Armenian from Damascus 185
Armenian monks 371
Armenian 88, 117-118, 188, 194, 197, 240, 352, 362, 371, 460
Armistice (Mütareke) 158, 163
Arnd, Friedrich 190-191, 193
Arnd, Mrs. 192-194, 197
Arnd-Kürenberg 191

Artin Efendi 194
Artuhi 327
ʿarūz manuals 310-312
Arzan ar-Rum 108
asfar yellow 236
Asfaraʾinī 73, 75
ʿĀşıq Çelebi 64, 66-67, 70, 117-118, 266-267, 269, 273, 355
ʿAshıq Pasha 55, 254, 260, 271-272, 288, 296
ʿAshıqpashazade (ʿApz) 176, 207, 318-319, 322-324, 347-348, 352-374
al-Ashrafiya, barracks 112-113
ʿĀsim 68
al-Asmāʾī 92
Asya Khatun 414
Atatürk 9, 40-41, 43, 136, 149, 152
Atatürk Law 43
Atay, Falih Rıfkı 153, 168
Atebetü l-hakaʾik 288
Atsız, Nihal 322
ʿAttār, Farīdaddīn 8
Austerlitz (1805) 104
Austria, Austrians 100, 132, 211, 284, 426-428, 430, 432
Austria, Long War with 329
Awad, Mohammad see Moh. Awad 56
awlād an-nās 105
awlād al-ʿArab 336
Ayās 280
Ayas al-Mahmudi al-Maliki az-Zahiri 113
Ayas Pasha, grand vizier 280
Ayasolug (Ephesus, Selçuk) 2-3, 29, 51
Aydın 93
Aydınoglu Cunayd 27, 29
Aydınoglu ʿIsa Beg 25
Aydınoğlu Muhammed Beg 25
Aydınoğulları 1-2, 9, 13-14, 27, 37
Aydos Castle 366
ʿazabs 371-372
Āzer 247, 252
Azerbayjan 90, 103
Azeri Turkish 118, 127
al-Azhar 78-79, 81, 83-85, 87, 140-141, 332, 335
Azharites 85
ʿAzīz Efendi *see* ʿAlī ʿAzīz Efendi
ʿAzīz b. Ardashīr Astarabadī 254
ʿAzīz-i Mısr 54
ʿAzize Melek Hatun 3
ʿAzmī Efendi 432-433
Baba Ishāq, Rasūl Allāh 206, 254, 452
Baba Ilyās 253, 255, 452
Babāʾī revolt 452
Babinger, Franz 35, 135, 173, 243
Babur, Zahir ad-Din Muhammad 311
bacılar, bacıyān 353
Badraddīn Mahmūd *see* Bedreddīn
Badraddīn al-ʿAynī 107
Baghdad 47-48, 134, 263, 395, 405
Baghdad campaign 279
Baghdad Khatun 407-408
Baghdad railway 191
al-Baguri 87
Bahaʾaddin Naqshband 257, 262
Bahaʾi Walad 406
Bahadur b. Sayfaddin al-Baytar 4
Bahira 246
Bahr-i dürer 310
Bahram 23-24
Bahrü l-maʿārif 312
Balı Beg 218
Balıkesri 263
Balkh 389-390
banishment 86, 157, 160, 338, 383
Banu l-Asfar 232
Banū Ishāq, Arabs 206-207
bānzāde 220
Bāqī 295
Baraq Baba 255
Barbier de Meynard 269
Barquq, Mamluk Sultan 50 ftn., 108
Barsbay min Tuman Bay 112
Barsbay, Sultan 108
Basra 390
Battāl-nāme 330, 346
al-Baydāvī 5
Bāyezīd I Yıldırım 28, 88, 228, 255, 263, 266, 275, 320, 356-358, 361, 370, 374
Bāyezīd, Prince 457
Bāyezīd, Prince (Bayezid II) 261
Bāyezīd II 69, 88, 169, 171, 176, 203, 213, 228, 258-259, 261, 276, 280, 283
Bāyezīd Bīstāmī 398-399
Bayreuth 192
Bediüzzamān Said Nursi 154
Bedouin 461
Bedreddīn of Samāvna, Sheykh 206, 208, 254-255, 275, 359, 409
Beglerbegi 458, 465

Begpazarı 361
Behcetül-hada'iq 344
Behram Cubin 23, 29, 31, 51
Bektashis 81-82, 255, 264, 268, 335, 408, 460
Bektimur ar-Ramadani, Mamluk 113
Belgrade 180, 203, 216-218, 220, 259, 278, 282, 355, 368
Belig, Seyyid Ismail 295
Benī Asfar 180, 221 sic Asfar!
Berdibek, Mamluk 113
Berkes, Niyazi 149
Berlin 426-427, 433-434, 438
Berriyecik 459
Beshīr 249
Beşmağaralar Deresi 450
Beyazkule 463
Bezirci, A. 166
Bible translation 283, 440
Bihishtī 169, 349, 357-358
bilād al-ʿAjam 48
Bilecik 356, 360-361, 366
Birecik 454, 457
Birgi (Pyrgion) 1-3, 26
Birgili Mehmed Efendi 81, 86, 140, 333-334, 339
Birgiwī *see* Birgili
Birkan, Abdullah 167
Birkat al-Hajj 111
Birnbaum, E. 36 ftn.
Bitlis 451
Bıyıklı Mehmed Paşa 453-454
Bobovius, Albert, s. Ali Beg Bobovski 184
Bodrogligeti, A. 293
Bohemia 220, 427, 429, 431
Bolu 266, 268
Bombaci, Alessio 61 ftn., 63
Bonaparte, Emperor of France, *see* Napoleon
booty 320, 324-325, 353, 369
Boratav, Pertev Naili 64, 163
Bosnia 353, 373
Bosphorus 200-201
Bostān 37
Bowen, Harold 79
Boyle, Nicholas 429
Boz Ulus 453
Bozdağ (Mt. Tmolos) 2
Bozoq 219, 459
Bozoqlu 218, 281
Böhlau al Raschid Bey, Hermann 197
Böhlau, Helene 190-194, 192-194, 196-197, 201-201
Böhlau, Hermann 190, 192
Börklüce Mustafa 29, 206, 409
Breaths of Intimacy 376 and passim
Breslau 428-431, 433
Brune, Marie-Anne, French general 96
Buda 278, 283
Bukhara 262
Bukharī, Shemseddin 272
Bulaq 85, 142, 338
Bulgaria 411, 425
Bursa 255, 259, 263, 268, 357, 413
Bursalı M. Tahir 55-56, 144, 173
Busbecq, Ogier Ghislen van 411
Büyük ayrik 460
Byzantine Emperor 124
Byzantium 26, 178, 181, 205-206, 355, 357-358

Caʿfer Çelebi 290, 294-295, 297
Caesar 234-235
Cain and Abel 406
Cairo 4-5, 48, 50, 56, 78, 80-81, 92, 105, 108, 140-144, 203, 310, 331, 334, 337-338, 455
Caliphate 42, 44, 229, supreme Caliphate 276
Calvinist 241
Cāmiʿü l-meʿānī 297
Cāmiʿ ül-meknunat 171, 207, 212, 214, 216, 222, 224-225, 277-284, 325, 346
Cāmiʿu n-neza'ir 294-295
Canpolat, Mustafa 292-293
Carl August, Duke of Weimar 427, 430
Catalans 125
Catholics 212, 240-241
al-Cazira 45a
cefr 210, 277, 283
Celāl, shaykh 204
Celāl of Bozoq 209
Celālī uprisings 211, 219, 457, 461
Celalzade Mustafa 70, 118, 327, 347
Cem, Ottoman Prince 51, 53, 89, 239-240, 243-245, 247-250, 261, 275, 358
Cemşid u Hurşid 289
Cevat Şakir Kabaağaçlı 157
Ceylanpınar 448, 450, 462-463, 465
Cezzār Ahmed Paşa 102
Chagatay 129-130
Charles II of Sweden 191

Charles V (Qarloz) of Habsburg 178, 180, 221, 224-225, 279
Chelebi Khalifa 258, 261, 264, 275
Chiusa, South Tyrol 198
Chosroes Parvīz 124
CHP Congress 156
Chroniclers' narrative 317, 322
Cicero 435
cihād 318
Cihādnāme-i Sultan Süleymān 325
al-Cili Şaydala 5
Circassia 88
Circassian Mamluks 108, 123
Cizre 451, 462
cizye 242
clairvoyance 413
Comenius, John Amos 183, 185-186, 212 ftn., 440
Commission for Great Turkish Writers and Poets 164
Constantinople 205, 207-208, 215, 229, 236, 239, 249, 369
Constitution, Second Turkish (1908) 134
Coptic scribe 142
Corfu 100-102, 279
Corvinus, John 358
Corvinus, Matthias 358
cönk 298
Cracow (Kraków) 242, 430
Crimea 229, 425-426, 432
Crimean Khans 231-232
Croatia, Croats 179
Crusades 205, 318
Cunayd *see* Junayd
Cülek, Çülek 456
Cüllāb River 456
Cyprus 211
Czechs 179, 216
Częstochowa 430
Çaldıran 326, 453, 455
Çarhname 297
Çırçıp River(s) 448, 450, 452, 459, 464-465
Çırçıp(s) 462
Çirpi "çirpi" 438, 463
Çorbacı 426

dābbat al-arz 210
ad-Daccāl 204, 207, 209-210, 223-224
Dadı Hatun 361
Dajjāl (Dadjjāl) *see* Daccāl 236, 265 ftn.
Damascus 204, 262, 389, 398
Damietta 85, 338
Daniel tradition 204-205, 212
Danishmendids 275
Danişmend, İsmail Hami 166, 182, 243
Dānişmendnāme 125, 179, 180, 182, 327, 346
Dankoff, Robert 289, 346
Danube 357, 372
dar ül-harb 239
Dar ül-Islam 276
Dārānī 388, 405
Dardanelles 201
ad-Darīr, Mustafa b. 'Ömer 108, 385 ftn.
Davudi Garbi 459
Davul newspaper 198-200
Dawudabad 392
ad-Dayrī 52-53, 108
Debreli Hüseyin Efendi 132
Dede Garkın/Karkın 448, 451-455, 458-462, 465
Dede Korkut 228, 346, 439
Dede Korkut Kitabı 363, 365-366, 368, 370
Dedeköy 464
Demotika (Dimetoka) 281
demür qapu 80
Depegöz, Tepegöz 363, 439
dépot légal 165
Derencil Ban 179, 348
Dergâh 156
Derik (Tell Bism, Mardin) 464, 465
Dernschwam, Hans 411
Derviş Çelebi 242
Derviş, Suat 164 ftn.
dervīşane 52, 294
Dervish Mehmed Chelebi 311
Devereux, R. 122
Devlet Su İşleri 465
Dhū l-Nūn 388
Dhūlqadir Turkmens 108, 117, 219
Dhū l-qarnayn 234-235
Dib Takuy 230, 236
Dib Yabghu 230
Diez, Heinr. Friedr. von 423-441
Directorate of Religious Affairs 153, 252
Diyarbakır 148, 451, 465
Diyarbekir 448, 451-454, 457-458, 461
Djingiz Khan 231-233
Djingizid Khans 226, 228, 231-232

Djoçi 231
Dodge, Bayard 79
Dögerlü, Turkmens 459
dream 177, 262, 275, 324, 356, 366, 377, 384, 389-394, 404, 414, 418
Dresden 431
Dreyfus affair 159
Duda, H.W. 149 ftn.
Duhayşa 91
Dulgadır principality 457
Dürder, Baha 167
Düstūrnāme 125, 288, 346

earthquake 175, 215, 278
East Middle Turkish 127
Ebced 154
Ebussuud 233, 279
Eckmann, János 57, 77
edā'-i türkī 67
Edebali, Shaykh 356
Edebiyat Fakültesi, Istanbul 136
Edebiyat-ı Cedide 157, 159
Edirne 265, 294, 345, 370
Edirneli Mecdī 256
Edom 236
Egri, Eger, Erlau 317, 329-330
Egridir 297
Egypt 5, 13, 16, 30, 40, 47-52, 54, 73, 76-80, 86, 92-94, 105, 107-108, 116, 118, 139, 144-147, 160 (exile), 217, 270, 278, 294, 296, 332-333, 410
Egyptian campaign, Bonaparte's 101-103, 436
Egyptians 333
Elias, Jamal J. 376
Elmalı, Elmalu 287, 298 ftn., 456
Elvan Çelebi 289, 451-452
Elvan, Sheykh, Pasha 254, 257
Elvan Shirazi 271
Emir Sultan 255
Emir Süleymān 345
Emir Dağı 371
Emirates, Anatolian 33, 241, 274
Emperor of the Romans 235
Emperor of Russia 232
Emperor of France, Napoleon 102, 104
Emperor, Çasār 218
Encyclopaedia of Islam 134, 136
England 96, 101, 103
Enis Avni 159
Enverī 288, 345
Eretna 370
Ergin, Muharrem 290, 297
Ertoghrul 177, 230, 236, 324
Erünsal, İsmail E. 290, 299
Erzerum 453
Erzi, Adnan Sadık 174
Erzincan 352, 370
Erzurum 219
Esau, ʿĪsū 207, 236-238
Esenbay min Sudun, Mamluk 113
Esendal, Memduh Şevket 157
Esendere 462
Eshref oghulları 227
Eshrefoghlu Rūmī 255, 274
Eshrefoghlu, ruler 274
Eskişehir 352, 361
Esztergom, Gran 279, 284
Euphrates River 448, 456
Evliya Çelebi 165 ftn., 252, 456, 458
Evren, Kenan, seventh President 463, 465
Evrenos Beg, Evrenoz 264, 355
Evrenpaşa Köyü 463
eyalet 458, 465
eyalets, eight 465
Eyyūbī 44, 55-56

Fa'izi 295
Fadl Allah Rashid al-Dīn 227
Fadl Allah b. Ruzbihan Khunjī 231, 234, 235
Fahr addīn ʿIrāqī 253
Fahr addīn ʿIsā Beg 6, 9, 14
Fakhr al-Dīn al-Rāzī 247
Fahreddin Yaʿqub b. Muhammed, Fahri 11, 34, 51
Fahri 14-15, 31, 37, 289
Fani 286
Faqiri 68 ftn.
Faridaddin ʿAttār 8
Faruk Nafiz (Çamlıbel) 160
Fatiha 404
Fātima 378, 386
Fatima, daughter of the Prophet 233
Fatima bint al-Muthanna of Cordova 404
Fatima from Nishapur 389, 398, 403
Fātima of Balkh 388
Fayyumi 114
Fazlullah b. Ruzbihan 47 ftn.
Fecr-i Âti 157
female slave singer 379, 382-383, 385-386

female slave 380-383, 387, 404, 410
Ferdinand I, Feravuş 178, 220, 279, 411
Ferheng-name-i Sa'di Tercemesi 9, 29, 288
Fethullāh 'Ārif Çelebi 70
Fevziye Abdullah 296
Fichte, Joh. Gottlieb 424
Fidda 397
Filibe 177, 219
Final Judgment 211
Final Hour 205, 210, 282
Fındıqlılı Mehmed 66
Findley, Carter V. 167
firāsa 413
Firdawsī 24, 29, 55, 124
Firdevsī, Kutbname 346
Firiste-oğlu 4
First Turkish Publication Congress 163
fitna 331, 337-338, 364, 408, 410
Fleischer, Cornell 170, 172, 226
forty chosen men 392
Fourth Mechanized Infantry Divison, US Army 462
Foy, Karl (1856-1907) 132
France 96, 100, 181, 222, 279
Franchini, Antoine 97-99, 102
Franks 1, 26, 38-39, 89, 125, 223, 370
Frederick II, the Great 425, 427
Frederick William II 426-427
freed woman 387
Freemasonry 423-424
French Revolution 424, 436
Friedrichsgrube 430
Friend of God 388
frontier state 276
Fuzūlī 289, 299, 344

Gabriel 248
Galata 194, 240
Galen 5
žālib Efendi 97
Galicia 430
Gallipoli 265, 283
Gallotta, Aldo 344, 346
Gamal el-din el-Shayyal 79, 86
Gandjeï, Tourkhan 310
ganīmet *see* booty 282
GAP Güneydoğu Anadolu Projesi 461-462, 465
Garīb-nāme 288
Garkın 459
Gavrī (Ghawrī), Mamluk Sultan 48-57, 73, 76-77, 88-91, 93, 95, 294
Gaykhatu, Ilkhan 408
gazā 276, 283, 324, 369-370
gazavāt 176, 214, 284
Gazavat-i Davud Pasha 350
Gazavat-i Murad b. Muhd. Han 325, 347
gazavatname 220, 239, 278, 284, 345, 366
gazi 276, 318, 321, 353, 359, 367, 369, 372
Gazi Mustafa Kemal s. Mustafa Kemal 152, 162
Gedik Ahmed Paşa 355
Gelibolu 283
Gem *see* Cem
Gennadius II Scholarius 241
Genoese 373, 374
George Kastriota 179
Georgievits, Bartholomeus 242
German Enlightenment 423
Germany, Germans 216, 218, 278
Germiyan 7, 9, 16
Germiyan, princess of 354, 356, 374
Gevrelü Uzun Musliheddin 261
Geyiklü Baba 260
al-Ghawrī 106, 109-111, 115
Ghazan, Mahmūd, Ilkhan 22, 254
Ghaznawid 227
Giaurs 370, 373
Gibb, H.A.R. 79
Gibb, E.J.W. 47, 60, 63-64, 68, 256, 268-269, 272
Giese, Friedrich 173, 353
Giray (Kerey) 231
Giurgevo (Jerköi, Giurgiu), Wallachia 431
Glatz 429
Goeje, M.J. de 173
Goethe, Joh. Wolfg. von 192, 195-196, 368 ftn., 423-424, 427-431, 435-436
Gog and Magog 179, 205, 210, 230, 234-235
Golden Horde 30, 37, 229, 231, 293
Goldziher, Ignaz 78, 332
Golius, Jacobus183, 185-186
Gospel, Authentic 246, 248, 252
gospels, five 246
Gök Alp 236
Götz, Manfred 36 ftn., 57 ftn.

Göyünç, Hütteroth 458
Gözelem Tepe 450
Grand Master of Order of Knights 217
Great Conjunction 206
Greek Orthodox Church 240, 251
Greek women 361-362
Greeks 353, 360, 366-367
green birds 393
Hrebelyanović, Lazar I 357
Grimm, Wilhelm 440
Grothe, Hugo 134
Gulistan 123
Gurbetnāme 239-243, 247, 251
Guttstadt, Corry 138
guzat 353
Gül ü Husrev 289
Gülhane Military Academy 40
Gülistan bi t-Turki 292
Gülsehri, Seyh Ahmed 18
Gülşeniye 90, 77, 80
Gülshehrī 254, 288
Gülsheni 82, 270, 272, 335
Gümüşsuyu 463
Gün Khan 227
Gündüz Alp 230
Güns Kösek 222, 279
Gürpınar 450

Haarmann, Ulrich 106 ftn.
Habib al-Umari 261, 263-264
Habīb en-Nejjār 252
Habsburg Empire 183, 430
Habur Sınır Kapısı 462
Haccī ʿAlihan b. Muhammed 2
Haccī Bayram 260-263, 272
Haccī Bektash Veli 219, 255, 258, 260, 264-266, 268-269, 271
Haccī Kemāl from Egridir 297
Haccī Halīfa, *see* Kātib Çelebi
Haccī Pasha 4-5, 7, 9, 10, 16
hācet namazı 317
Haçova 330
Hadayik as-sihr 287
Hadīce Halīme, Isfendiyar 357
Hadīdī 325
Hādimü l-haremeyn 276
Hādim Süleymān Paşa 55 ftn.
hadiths 67, 109-110, 120, 127, 180-181, 205-208, 236-237, 350, 386
hafīf 289
Hagia Sophia 239
Hague, The 199
Hākī, Süleymānnāme 327
Hākī, Yahya b. Ishaq 184-185, 187-189
Hakīm, al-Hakīm al-Tirmidhī 390
Hakīma of Damascus 389, 398
Hakkari 462
Hālet Efendi, Mehmed Saʿīd 96-97, 101-102, 104
Haleti 295
Halide Edip, *see* Adıvar 156-158, 167
Halikarnas Balıkçısı 157
Halīma 385
Halit Fahri (Ozansoy) 166
Halit Ziya (Uşaklıgil) 157, 167
Halk Kütüphanesi 162
Halle University 425, 434
Halvetiye 77, 93 *see* Khalvetiye
Hamburg 426-427
Hamdullah Suphi (Tanrıöver) 162
Hamid b. Musa al-Kayserī 260
Hamid ili 277
hammam, bathhouse 361-362, 403, 412, 414
Hammer-Purgstall, Joseph v. 80, 87, 139-140, 172-173, 269, 332, 435-438, 441
Hamrevat 456
Hamza Beg 6
Hamza, Molla 173
Hamza ash-Sharafi 110
Hamzavī 33, 347
Hamzevi, Ahmedī's brother 172-173
Hanafite 334, 336
Hanbalite 334
Harf Devrimi, İnkılabı 148
Harname 289
Hartmann, Martin 132, 134
Harun al-Rashid, Caliph 92, 388
Hasan Beg, Nishancı 261
Hasan Çelebi 64, 68
Hasan b. Husayn b. Ahmad b. at-Tuluni 110
Hasan b. Mahmūd Bayatī 51 ftn.
Hasanoğlı Asfara'ini 73-75, 90, 293
Hāshim 175, 384
hāss u ʿāmm 69
Hat Law 149
hātif-i gayb 324
al-Hawsh, barracks 112
Hayat 156

Haydar Çelebi 243
Hayreddin Barbarossa 222, 279, 346
Hayreddin Chelebi 350
Hayriye Hanım 200
Hayriye bint Ayad 191
hazac, hezec 51, 286-290, 293, 310
Hebbel, Friedrich 191
Heine, Heinrich 195
Helen motif 370
Herat 88, 130, 232, 262, 441
Herder, Joh. Gottfried 437
Herzl, Theodor 190, 200-201
Heuscheuer Mt. 429
Hezārfenn 186
Hijāz 210
al-Hijāzī, Hasan 78, 87, 332
Hindliler Tekkesi, Aksaray 195
Hırka-i sherīf 330
Hisali of Budin 295
Hızır 223, 325
Hizr Beg, Aydınoğlu 9
Hizr b. ʿAlī, Haccī Paşa 4
Hizr b. al-Hattab (Hacci Pasa) 4
Hoca Mesʿud 16, 33, 35, 287-288
Holt, P.M. 16, 139, 143
Holy Roman Emperor, Çasar 178
Holy Roman Empire 430
Holy War 214, 274, 276, 281
Hommel, Fritz 135
Hormuzd 23
hospital 4, 396, 415-416, 418
housefather 379
housewife 383, 394
al-Hujwirī 402
Humboldt, Wilhelm von 435
Hungarian campaign, third 278
Hungarian campaign, first 216
Hungarian campaign, second 216-217
Hungary 178, 180, 216-218, 241, 279, 282, 284, 325, 329
Hurşid-name 289
Husayn Bayqara 88, 92, 123
Husayn Khan Şamlu 454
Husayn Mirza, Sultan 311
Husayn Şarīf, Hanafī shaykh 53, 91
Huseyn b. Hasan 47, 51, 93
Husayn b. Hasan b. Muhd. al-Husayni Serif? 90
Husayn b. Muhd. al-Husayni, Şerīf 90
Husayn b. Muhammad al-Husaynī 49, 91-93, 106
Husayn b. Pir Hajji Abu Bakr 108
Husrev u Sirin 51
Husrev u Şīrīn by Şeyhī 289
Hünkar Sheykh 261
Hürriyet ve Iʿtilaf 41
Hüseyin b. Hasan Muhammed el-Huseyni el-Hanefi, Şerīf 47, 50-51
Hüseyin Cahit (Yalçın) 157
Hüseyin Hüsameddin (Yasar) 154
Hüseyin Kâzim Kadri 165 ftn.
Hüseyin Paşa, Giritli, Grand Admiral (1789-1792) 102
Hüseyin Rahmi (Gürpınar) 159, 167
Hvarezmī 4, 293
Hwaca Muhammad Qasim 412, 413 note
Hwaca ʿUbaydullah Samarqandī 412

ibāha 265, 269, 407
Ibn ʿAbd al-Wahhāb 86
Ibn Aja 55
Ibn ʿAlā 330
Ibn al-ʿArabī 135, 253, 389, 397, 404-405
Ibn al-Baytar 8
Ibn ad-Dawādārī 106, 107 ftn.
Ibn Battuta 3, 7
Ibn Bībī 35
Ibn Daniyal 106 ftn.
Ibn Firiste 4
Ibn al-Hallāq 80-81, 83, 86-87, 331-332, 338, 334
Ibn Iyās 48-50, 52-53, 56, 95
Ibn Kemal, *see* Kemālpaşazade 69, 71
Ibn Melek 2, 4, 5
Ibn Muhannā 128
Ibn Muthannā 418-419
Ibn al-Nizam 132-133
Ibn Nubata 119
Ibn Qayyim al-Jawziyya 334
Ibn Sīnā 5
Ibn Tagrībirdi 54 ftn., 105 ftn.
Ibn Taymiyya 86, 334
Ibn al-Washshā' 380-383
İbnülemin Mahmud Kemal İnal 154, 167, 173, 213, 277
Ibrahim Bahadur of Aydın 27

Ibrahim Beg, Defterdar 142
Ibrahim Beg 85 ftn.
Ibrahim al-Biqā'ī 338 correct ā
Ibrahim Gülşenī 80, 90, 93, 270, 272
Ibrahim, al-Hvāja al-Samarqandī 49
Ibrahim as-Sarrāf 263
Ibrahim Paşa, Damad (1726) 296
Ibrahim Paşa, grand vizier 175, 218-219, 222, 280, 325-326
Ibrahim Tannūrī 260
Ibrahim Zahid Gilani 406
Ibrahimi 462
Ibrahimiye 452
Ibrahimli, Şeyh 464
iʿjāz 246 ftn.
Idris Bidlisī 170-171, 237, 454-455
ihtiyarāt, preferable actions 177
Ilāhī, ʿAbdullah, Sheykh 254, 258, 262-264, 272
İlaldı Hatun 363
Ilkhans 127, 206, 227
Ilyās 223
Imam Shāfiʿī 82
İnalcık, Halil 65, 226, 243, 282, 322
İncil 246
Independence War 161
Independence Courts 148
India 5, 101, 103, 124, 221, 319
Indian 117-118
Indian cloister, Aksaray 195
Innocent VIII, Pope 243, 245
İnönü, İsmet 41, 43, 149 ftn.
inşā 66, 69, 71
İpek yolu 464
Iqbal, Muhammad 133
Iraq 107, 448, 456, 462, 464
Iraq, Persian 47
Iron Gate, Cairo 80, 83, 335
irsaliye 458
ʿĪsā, Prophet, Jesus 204, 212-213, 217, 223, 393
ʿĪsā Beg of Aydın 3-4, 6-7, 9, 11, 14, 19-20, 25, 27
Isaac, patriarch 236-237
Isfendiyaroğlu İsmāʿil Beg 370
Isfendiyāroğlu 357, 361
Ishāq, sons of 207
Ishāqīye 207
Ishtibzāde Ahmed 283
Iskendernāme 176, 214, 234, 282, 288, 345-347
Iskenderun, Bay of 462
Iskilip 264
İslam Ansiklopedisi 137
ʿisma, sinlessness 385
Ismāʿīl, Shah 50, 88, 217, 225, 229, 233, 284, 453-454
Ismāʿīl b. Qāsim al-Hanafī 109
Ismāʿīl Sā'ib Efendi 132
İsmail Habib (Sevük) 152
Israel, children of 250
Isrāfīl 210
Istanbul, Qostantiniye 103, 175, 195, 262, 274, 278, 327, 377
Istefanaki 97
İstiklal Mahkemeleri 148
Istolni Belgrad 279
ʿIsū, Esau 236-238
ışıklar, dervishes 219
Işk-nāme 289, 319
Italy, Bonaparte's Kingdom of 104
Ittihād ve Teraqqī 40
İz, Fahir 62-63, 65
İzmir 159, 465
İznik, Nicaea 367
Iznikmid (İzmit, Nikomedia) 352
ʿIzz ad-Dīn Asfara'ini 90
ʿIzz ad-Dīn b. Gānim al-Vāʿiz 6
ʿIzz ad-Dīn Qılıç Arslan 205

al-Jabartī 78-79, 85-87, 332
Jacob, patriarch 236-238
Jacobite, Monophysite 240, 249
Jaʿfar as-sadiq 280, 283
al-Jahiz 381-383
Jalāl ad-Din Rumi 288
Jāmī, ʿAbdurrahman 257, 260, 262, 376, 388, 399-400, 405, 410
Jami, Nafahat al-uns 258
Janberdi Ghazzālī 216
Janissaries 141-142, 177, 322, 338, 372, 454, 457
Janmar(d) min Özdemür 112
Japheth 207, 227, 229-232, 236-237
Japhetid 238
Jaqmaq, Sultan 106, 109, 115
Jarjab 450

Jarring, Gunnar 190
jealousy 397
Jem, Ottoman Prince, *see* Cem
Jena/Auerstädt 434
Jerusalem 85, 338, 393
Jesus 179, 208, 224, 244, 248-250, 384, 393
Jewish scholar, Paul 248
Jews 236, 240, 250
John the Baptist 250
John, evangelist 246
John Zápolya, Yanoş 178, 220
Jong, P. de 173
Junayd of Aydın 27, 29
Junayd, Shaykh (1429-1447) 48, 397, 409, 452-453

Kaʿb 387
Kaʿba 419
Kadi ʿAbdullah from Divrigi 310
Kadi Burhaneddin *see* Qadı Burhāneddīn
Kadir, A. 168
Kaffa 355
Kafzade Feyzullah Efendi (Fa'izi) 295
Kalenders *see* Qalender
Kaletepesi 450
Kaloyannes, Emperor of Trebizond 358
Kansu, Ceyhun Atuf 166
Kanuni 279
Kaplan, Mehmet 25, 166
Kara Khan 230
Kara Khan Ustaclu 453-454
Kara Boğdan 369
Karaca Beg güyegü 322-323
Karaca Dağ 448, 450, 456-458
Karakhanid 128
Karakhanid literature 286-287
Karakoyunlu *see* Qaraqoyunlu
Karaman 228, 255, 261, 274-275, 358. 371. 454
Karamanids 371-374
Karamanoğlu İbrahim 363-364, 371
Karaosmanoğlu, Yakup Kadri 157-158, 162, 167
Karatay, F.E. 111
Karkın Turkmens 459
Karkın 451
Kars 155
al-Kaşgarī 77 *see* Mahmūd al-Kāşgarī
Kāshifī, Rauzat al-shuhada 345, 441
Kātib Celebi 38, 66, 68, 144, 172, 251
Kaygusuz Abdal 296-297
Kayı Khan 237
Kayı, tribe 227-228
Kaymaz, Uğur 464
Kayser-i Rūm 235
Kayseri 263-264
Kaytbay, al-Malik al-Ashraf Sayfaddin, *see* Qaytbay
Kazan 370
Kazwini 287
Kemāl Re'is 346
Kemāl-i Ümmī 297
Kemalism 42
Kemalpaşazade 34, 62, 69, 169, 211, 230, 237, 257-260, 264, 326, 350, 34, 435
Kepecioglu 283
Kerbelā 217, 284, 328
Kerman 258
Khabur River, Western, Great 448, 450, 462
Khadīja 385
khalīfa 229
Khalīfī 337
Khalil b. Ahmad 311
Khalvetiye 277, 280, 284, 408, 409 ftn.
Khalwati order 258, 263-264
Khidr 234
Khorasan 73, 262-263, 274, 405
Khwandamīr 232
Khwarazmī 285, 293
Khwarezmian Turkish 75, 292
Khwarizmshahs 227
Kieffer, Jean Daniel 440
Kili 176
Kınalızade Hasan Çelebi 273
Kingdom of Peace 204-205, 211
Kınık tribe 227
Kipchak-Khwarazmian Turkish 107
Kirkuk 454
Kırşehir 204, 264, 271
Kissling, Hans Joachim 135
Kitāb-ı Dede Korkut 439
Kıvāmī *see* Qıvāmī
Kızılbaş *see* Qızılbaş
Kızıldepe 456-457
Kızıltepe (Koçhisar, Dunaysir) 459, 461-462, 464
Knappschaft 430-431

Knobelsdorf, von 428
Koca Hızır, janissary 322, 329
Kocagöz depesi 456
Kocatepe 464
Koçhisar 454-455, 458-461
Kolberg 434
Koman, M. Mesut 38, 136
Komensky, Jan Amos 440
Konewi, Sadreddin 253, 271
Konya 263, 371
Konya People's House 38, 136
Koran 93, 151, 153, 194, 241, 246, 324, 389, 392, 410
Korkud 228
Korkut Ata 228
Kosovo I (1389) 319-320, 325, 327, 329
Kosovo II (1448) 319, 323, 325, 329
Kostantinīye 207
Koylıhisār 371
Koyunhisār 359
Koyunluoğlu, İzzet 38
Kömürciyan, Eremiya Çelebi 188
Köprülü, M. Fuat 207, 353
Kösek, Güns, Köszeg 222, 279
Kratovo 320
Kraus, Fritz Rudolf 135
Krbova 348-349
Kreutel, Richard F. 372
Kruşevac 320
Kufa 210
Kumkapı, Armenian neighborhood 194, 197
Kurdish allies 454-455
Kurdish princes 453-454
Kurds, Kurdish 88, 117-118, 121-123, 158, 460-465
Kut, Güney 269
Kutadgu Bilig 288
Küçük Kaynarca treaty 425
Küçük Saʿid Pasha (1838-1914) 135
Kütahya River, Porsuk 265, 269

Lalezari 437
Lamiʿi 64, 256, 258-261, 263-264, 269-270, 272, 274-275, 376-377, 388, 400, 408, 410
Landeshut 429
Language Commission 158
Laranda, Larende 263, 372
Last Emperor 224
Last Judgment 209
Lāt, Menāt, ʿUzza 180, 218
Latifi 68, 270, 272-273, 286, 294
Latin Church 251
Lausanne 41
lawh mahfuz 82, 84-85, 87, Well-Preserved Tablet
laylat al-qadr 89
Lazarević, Maria Olivera 357
Lazarević, Stephen, "Laz" 357
Lemʿī 311
Lenz, Max 135
Lepanto 211
Lessing, Theodor 197
Levend, Agah Sırrı 39, 61-62, 64
Levhī 325
Lewis, Geoffrey 439
Leyla ve Mecnun 289
light, divine 384-385
light of Muhammad 322
lineage 226, 229, 231, 233, 237, 354
London 42, 134, 432
Lord of the Conjunction 221, 279, 324
Louis II of Hungary 178, 216
Luke, evangelist 246
Lusi, de, Count 428
Lutfi Pasha 279
Luther, Lutheran 192, 212 ftn., 241, 434
Lüttwitz, Henriette von 428-429, 431
Lvov, Lemberg 184

Macedonia 262, 264
madhouse 395, 415-416
madness 377, 395
madrasa 405
Maghrebī 262-263
Magrib 222
Māhān 177
Mahdī 171, 181-182, 204-204, 206, 209-210, 223, 277-278, 280, 283, 409
Mahmūd of Ghazna 20, 27, 55, 280
Mahmūd Gulistani 293
Mahmūd al-Kāşgarī 73, 77, 127-128, 227, 230, 234, 236, 285
Mahmūd aş-Şarqawi 78
Mahmūd Pasha 261
Mahmūd Pasha, Menākıbname 325
Mahmūd Shabistarī 271

majalis 92, 95
majlis 401
Mal Hatun 356, 366
malāhida 266
malāhim 214
Malatya 49
al-Malik al-Mu'ayyad aş-Şayh al-Mahmudi 80
Malikite 336
Malmö 200
Malti-Douglas, Fedwa 376-377
Mamluk chiefs of Cairo 85, 334
Mamluk state 7, 74 and passim
Mamluk glossaries 128
Mamluks 130, 203, 205, 226, 278, 286, 349, 455
Mango, Andrew 41
Manisa 322
Mansur b. Yusuf al-Maliki al-Ashrafi 113
Manūchehrī 128
Manuel II Komnenos 206, 241
Mar Ya'kūb 248
Maraş 452
march-lord 264
marches (uc) 1, 227, 229
Mardin 456, 459-462, 464-465
Mark, evangelist 246
martyrdom 318, 321
Mary, Virgin 246, 248
Maryam 386
masters of instruction 386, 402
masters of training 402, 404
Maşkok 462
Matariya near Cairo 53
Matthew, evangelist 246
maw'iza, exhortation 393
Maymuna bint Sakula 402
Mazıdağı (Şamrah) 464
Me'ālī 288, 290, 294
Mecca 160, 180, 209, 252, 385, 389-390, 393, 396, 401, 404-405, 419
Mecdī, Hada'iq ash-Shaqa'iq 268
Mecdī, Edirneli 256, 269
Mecmū'a-i kelam-i urefa-i billah 298
Mecmū'a-i latīfe 296
Mecmu'atü n-neza'ir 292-293
Medical Military Academy 40, 43
Medina 49, 210, 385, 401
Mehmed, Ishkname 289
Mehmed b. Yusuf el-Hallaq 140, 143-147
Mehmed I 324, 363
Mehmed II, Fatih 229, 234-235, 241, 257, 263, 275, 324, 349, 357, 361, 364, 370-371
Mehmed III, sultan 210, 329
Mehmed IV, Ottoman sultan 39, 184
Mehmed Akif (Ersoy) 43, 160
Mehmed Arif 243
Mehmet Emin (Yurdakul) 160, 163
Mehmed Giray II 232
Mehmed Paşa, el-Hacc 146
Mehmed Sa'īd Halet Efendi 96
Mehmet Rauf 159
melāhim 176, 277
Melamiye 284
melheme 210
Melkā 248
Melkites 251
Memet Fuat (Bengü) 167
Men of the Unseen 322
Ménage, V.L. 114 ftn., 174, 317, 320
Menakıbu l-Kudsiyye fi Menasibi l-Ünsiyye 289
Mengüp/Theodoro, Crimean fortress 373
Meninski, Franz Mesgnien de M. 439
Menteşe 4-5
Mersin, Bay of 462
Merzime 464
Meş'ale magazine 156, 161
Mes'ud b. Ahmed, Hoca Mes'ud 8-9, 18, 29
Mes'ud, Qul Mes'ud 8-9
Meşkuk 458, 460
Meşrutiyet 2, 149, 158, 163, 167
Metāli'ü n-neza'ir 295
Metternich, Clemens 436
Mevlana Celaladdin Rumi, *see* Jalal ad-Dīn 253, 270, 271
Mevlana 'Imād Mevlevī 293
Mevlānā 'Īsā 171-172, 181, 213-216, 218, 221, 225, 277-282, 325, 330, 346
Mevlana Ishāq 293
Mevlana Kazi Muhsin 293
Mevlana Shirazi 270
Mevleviye 1, 3, 81, 82, 335
Mezö-Keresztes, Haçova 330
Michael IX Byzantine co-emperor 26
Middle Arabic 119

Midilli/Lesbos 355 ftn. 26., 373
Mihri Khatun 414
Milas 4
millennium 211
Millî Şair 160
Millî Edebiyat 157
Ministry of Education 163-164
Mir ʿAlī Şīr Nawa'i 311
Mizan al-awzan 311
Mohács 179-180, 203, 216, 218, 278, 282, 284, 325-327
Mohammed Awad 56, 91, 93, 106-107 ftn.
Moldau 369
Moldavia 279, 425
Moltke, Helmuth von 193
Mongol women 407
Mongols 227, 274, 452
Monophysites 240
Montesqieu 42
Mordtmann, J.H. 35-36, 173, 268-269
Morea 259, 369-370
Morgenstern, David 131
Morkaya, Burhan Cahit 159
Mosaic Law 246
Moscovite Empire 179
Moscow 101
Mosul 448, 451, 454
Moton 176, 369
Mu'ayyad Mosque 52-53, 78, 80-81, 85-87, 90-91, 111, 140, 334, 336-338
Mu'ayyad Shaykh, Mamluk Sultan 52, 55, 106
Mu'ayyadīya, shaykh of the 53, 56
Muʿadha 387
Muʿcam 287
Mubarizeddin Muhammed Beg b. Aydin 2, 7-8, 10-11, 25
müdārā "feigned friendship" 354 ftn. 14
Mudurnu 374
Muhammad, the Prophet 175, 208-247, 250-252, 280, 322-323, 385-393, 397
Muhammad Khan Ustaclu 453
Muhammad Parsā 257
Muhammad al-Qudsī al-Şarīf 55
Muhammad b. ʿAbd al-Wahhab 79
Muhammad b. Ahmad al-Hasani al-Farnawi al-mukattib 109
Muhammad b. Ahmad al-Mahalli 111
Muhammad b. ʿAli, al-Hakīm al-Tirmidhī 390
Muhammad b. Hasan at-Tayyibi al-Azhari 109
Muhammad b. Muhammad b. al-Mudarris 3
Muhammad b. Muhammad b. ʿAli 109
Muhammad b. Yusuf al-Hallaq 80-81
Muhayyelāt 434
Muhibb Efendi 11, 39-40, 104
"Mühlbacher" 267
Muhyiddin 4,7
Muhyiddin, Kadi 283
Muhyiddin, Sheykh 261
münacat 318, 325-326
Mundji Bey 199
Munich 198
Münif Paşa 191, 193, 196
Münir Bey 199
Muqattam 81
Murad, Seyyid 344, 346
Murad Beg, Miralay 214, 224, 283
Murad I 29, 266, 319-321, 324, 327, 330, 356, 358, 362
Murad II abdication 349
Murad II 29-33, 37, 51, 228-233, 265, 271, 293, 322-326, 348, 356-358, 363, 371
Murad IV, Sultan 461
mürids 273
Musa of Aydın 27, 29
Musa al-Kazim 233
Mustafa, Prince 281, 283, 373, 457
Mustafa b. ʿOmar ad-Darir 108
Mustafa b. Celal Qoca Nişancı 70
Mustafa Kemal 41, 148-149, 151-152, 154, 156, *see also* Atatürk
Mustafa b. Ahmed, Ālī 170-172, 182, 213, 232, 237-238, 269, 273, 275, 277, 284, 329, 350
al-Mustajadda, barracks 113
Mutahharten 370
mutakarib 288
al-Mutanabbī 400
Mütareke 158, 167
Mutawalli/Qutb 80
Muʿtazilites 83, 84-85, 336
Muzaffaraddin b. Abdalvahid b. Sulayman al-Garbi 3
Mytilene 346

Naʿīmā 68
Nābī, Yūsuf 39

Nabulusi 338
Nafahat al-uns by Jāmī 376
Nafahat al-uns, translation 257-258, 263, 268, 270
Nafrawī 337
Nagy de Harsányi, Jakob 186
Nagyvárad (Grosswardein, Oradea Mare) 242
Nahit Sırrı (Örik) 159
Nakhchivan327
Nakşbendi *see* Naqshbendi 268, 270, 334
Nakūra, Mt. 252
Naples 245
Napoleon 39-40, 96-101, 434, 436
Naqshband Khvaca Bahaaddin 257
Naqshbandi Qasim 413
Nasīmīya 50
Nasiraddin Muhammad b. Jaqmaq 116
Nasiraddin Muhammad b. Qıjıq 48, 93
Nasreddin Hoca 440
Nastūr 248
Nasuh Matrakçı 456
Nawa'ī 76 ftn., 117, 122, 126, 129, 270, 311
Nazarenes, Nasārā 244
Nâzım Hikmet (Ran) 161-162
nazīre collections 297
Nazmi Mehmed Celebi 294
Necatigil, Behçet 257
Necīb Asim 173
Necip Fazıl (Kısakürek) 161
Negroponte, Euboea, Agriboz 413
Nemçe 179
neo-Hanbalis 333-334
Nergisī 60, 65
Neşātī 130
Neşrī 169, 171, 213, 230, 235, 237, 352-374
Neşrī's Cihānnümā 317-320, 323-324
Nesīmī, Seyyid ʿImādeddīn 47, 50, 75 ftn., 76, 255, 272, 297
Nesimīye 50
Nestorians 240, 249, 458, 460
Nestorius 248
Nibelungen 191-192
Nicaea (İznik) 244, 367
Nicene Creed 249
Nicolai, Friedrich 437
Nicomedia 359
Niebuhr, Carsten 458, 460-461
Niksar 182
Nile River 93
Nilüfer (Lülüfer) 362, 366
Nishānī 348
Nishapur 403
nizām-i ʿālem 319
Nizami, Anatolian poet 89
Nizami 11, 14, 17-19, 22-24, 29, 31-32, 37, 51, 289
Noah 207, 230-231
Noring, Knut Gustaf 190-191
Nuhbetü l-Asar li Zeyli-i Zübdetü l-eşʿār 2
Nur, Dr Rıza 40
nur-i Ahmed, light of the Propet 214, 278
Nūr-i Muhammadī 384-385
Nuremberg Laws 135
Nūrī 398
Nutuk, Speech, of Mustafa Kemal 156

O'Kane, John 390
Oczakow, Özü 425
Ofen (Buda) 203, 216, 220, 225, 436
Ögedei 231
Oghuz 207, 226-230
Oghuz tribes 234
Oghuz, son of Jem 228
Oguz/Türkmen 75, 128
Ohannes Aga 194
Olivera, daughter of Lazar 357
Omar Efendi 194
Omar al Raschid 190, 193, 195-196, 197-198
ʿOmar b. al-Farīd 105 ftn.
ʿOmar b. Muhammad b. Ahmad al-Hanafi 111
ʿÖmer b. Mezīd 292-294, 299
ʿÖmer Ruşenī 93
Ömer Seyfettin 158, 167
Operation Iraqi Freedom 462
Oppenheim, Max von 45-452
Order of Knights of St. John 178
ordugah Çülek 457
Orhan Seyfi (Orhon) 160, 162, 363 ftn.
Orhan 357, 362, 366
Orkhan, sultan 177, 260, 271
orta nesir 350
Oruç b. ʿAdil 169, 176, 348-350, 365, 372-374
Osman, House of 71, 228, 324
Osman 281, 324, 353, 356-360, 362, 366
Osman Aga 187-188
Osmancık 264

Osmanlı Müellifleri (OM) 51
Ossetic 88
Otranto 179
Ottoman Empire 96, 101, 103 and passim
Ottoman Turkish 150, 154
Oxford Anonymus 169, 236, 320, 323
Ozansoy, Halit Fahri 166
Özbeks, *see* Uzbeks 463
Özdemir, Hasan 366
Özdemir min Inal, Grand Amir 115 ftn.
Özkırımlı, A. 166

Pahlavī 124
Palestine 200
Pamuk, Orhan 155
Pamukkale 15
Pantokrator foundation 262
Pan-Turkism 42-43
Paraclete 246-247
Paris 41, 44, 96-98, 104, 132, 161, 195, 199, 438, 440
Pasha Chelebi 264
Paşa Kiriçe 358
Patras 370
Paul the apostle 247
Peirce, Leslie 354, 357
pencik 282
Pera 197
Persia 405, 407, 457, 461
Persian 117-124, 126-127
Persian campaigns 456
Pertsch, Wilhelm 35-36, 45, 439
Pervāne b. ʿAbdullāh 295
Pest 278
Peters, Ruud 331
petition-prayer 317, 320-321, 323
Peyami Safa 159
Phanariots 98 ftn.
Pınar 463
Pinkerton, Bible Society 440
Pir Ali 283
plague 92, 175, 180, 203, 215, 278
Poland 179, 322, 372, partitions of 430
Poles 216
polygamy, polygyny 397
Pope 178-179, 181, 222-223, 243-245, 251, 279
Porsuk River 265
Porte, Sublime 39, 96, 104, 119, 186, 200, 228, 231, 239, 334, 338, 425-427
Portugal 179
post-Rābiʿa period 377, 402-404, 406, 409-410, 414
Potemkin, Grigorii Aleksandrovich (general) 425, 428, 433
pre-Wahhabi 79, 332-333
Pressburg, Treaty of 104
Procházka-Eisl, Gisela 348
prostitute 358, 380, 382, 396
Protestants 183, 194, 241, 251, 423
Prussia 132, 425-434
Pseudo-Rūhī, Oxford Anonymous 236
Pur-i Hasan 73, 90

Qadabirdi min Hayrbek, Mamluk 112
Qadiʿasker 336
Qadi Burhaneddin 75 ftn., 254-255, 290
Qadızade 86
Qadızadeliler 86, 333
Qāf mountain 279
qa'ime 96, 142
Qalender, rebel 204, 208, 219, 255, 268
Qalender-Şah b. Bektaş 210
Qanısavh al-Gavrī (Qanısawh al-Ghawrī) 30, 57, 74, 79, 80, 88, 112, 123, 294
Qaraja 112, 114
Qaraqoyunlu 48, 108, 229
Qarluq 392 ftn.
Qāsim Paşa (Güzelce?) 219
Qaysunizade 110
Qaytas Beg 85 ftn.
Qaytbay, sultan 51, 53, 76, 89-90, 108-109, 111-112, 114-115, 294, 296, 310 ftn., 338
Qazvīnī 119
Qazwini, Muhammad 133
Qıjıqoğlu, Qıjıqzāde 48-49, 95
Qıvāmī 35, 170, 206, 346
qızıl elma 208
Qızılbaş 48, 118 ftn., 178, 203-204, 209, 217, 219, 242, 281, 284, 455, 460-461
Qızılbaş army 454
Qızılbaş-Safavīya 204, 409, 452-453
Qızılbaş-Turkmen 451
Qoca Nişancı 70, 170
Qoçi Beg 66
Qostantiniye, Istanbul 175, 207, 216
Qul Mesʿud 8-9
Quraysh 237, 384
Qushayrī 386 ftn., 389, 403-404

Qutb 30, 285
Qutluğ Mulk 408
Qutluğ Khatun 414

Rabiʿa 379, 384, 386, 399, 400, 403
Rābiʿa al-ʿAdawiyya 380, 387, 395, 414
Rābiʿa period 386-387
Rābiʿa bint Ismaʿil 388-389
Rābiʿa the Syrian 388
Radtke, Bernd 334, 390, 414
ramal 288
Ra's al-ʿAyn 450
Rashīd al-Dīn 227, 230, 232
Rashīd ad-Dīn Vatvat 6, 287
Rāşid 68
ar-Rawandī 133
Rayhāna 386
reʿaya 240, 373, 280
Reca'izade Mahmud Ekrem 65 ftn.
Reden, Frederick William von 430-431
Refik Halit (Karay) 157
Reichenbach (Dzierzoniów) 427-428, 431-434
reml, geomancy 277, 283
Republic, French, until 1804 104
Reşat Nuri (Güntekin) 156, 158-159, 163
Rescher, Oskar 256, 258
Resimli Ay 156, 162
Resmī Ahmed Efendi 433, 437
Reventlow, Franziska Gräfin zu 197
Rhodes 178-180, 203, 216-217, 278, 282
rhyme 290-291
rhymes in anthologies 299-310
Riesengebirge 431
Rīm, Rome 181
Risāla (Birgiwī) 334
Risale-i ʿaruz 294
Risale-i Bahrü l-evzan fi l-ʿaruz 311
Risaletü n-Nushiyye 288
Rıza Nur 40-41, 43-45, 154
Rıza Tevfik (Bölükbaşı) 160
Romania 425
Rome 236, 245, 251
Rome, the First, in Italy 179, 181, 205, 208, 210, 222-223, 237
Rome, the Second 237
Rome, fall of 211
Rome, primacy of 251
Rossi, Ettore 439
Rotterdam 198-199
Ruffin, Pierre Jean Marie 97, 101, 440 ftn.
Ruha/Urfa 54, 76, 454, 456-457
Ruhi al-Mamluk (Qaraja) 114
Rūhī Edrenevi 169, 213, 216, 228
Rūm 67, 79, 175, 204-205, 215, 221, 235-236
Rūm, Anatolia 255, 262, 265, 271
Rūm, fall of 181
Rūm, people of 238
Rūm, province of Amasya 255, 261
Rūm, sheykhs of 255, 260
Rūm, throne of 217
Rūm dili, Greek 125
Rūm Mehmed Paşa 372
Rūm Seljuks 228
Rumeli, Rumelia 274, 371, 456
Rūmī, Calal addin 248, 253
Rūmī, Ottoman Turkish 333
Rūmī, Mathnawī 272
Rūmī al-jins 49
Rumilik 271
Rús, Ukrainians 179, 216
Rusheni, Ömer Dede 263, 270, 272
Russia 96, 101-103, 179, 191, 217-218, 425-426, 430, 432, 434
Russo-Ottoman war 437
Rzewuski, Wenceslaus 436

Saʿdaddīn Farghānī 253
Saʿdeddin, Hvaca 66, 70 ftn., 71 ftn., 170, 237, 269, 318, 327, 329-330, 348
Saʿdī's Bustan 9, 288
Saʿdī's Gulistan 73, 344
Sabbath 248
Sabine women 365
Sabuncuoglu Şerefeddin 10
Sacco di Roma, Sack of Rome 179, 181, 223, 284
Sachsen-Weimar, Grand Duke of 191-192
sadeleştirilmek 168
Sādiqī Beg 130
al-Safadī 55-56
Safavids 48, 90, 107, 121, 127, 130, 233, 279, 281-282, 327, 348, 453-455
Safavīya, Shiʿite 48, 209
Safāyī 346
Safī al-Dīn, Shaykh, from Ardabil 233, 406, 408
Safih, as-Safih 450

Sağlam, Osman Ferid 174, 212, 277
Sahib-qırān 179, 181-182, 203, 221, 224-225, 279, 281
sahib-qiranī 181, 223
Sahn-i saman 262
Sahra-yi Mardin 459
Said Nursi 154
Saint-Cloud, castle 98
Sakarya River 265-266, 268-269
as-Sakhāwī 111
Salmān the Persian 246, 252
Saltuq-name 346
samāʿ 407
Samarqand 88, 130, 262, 413 ftn.
Samarqandi, Şamsaddin Muhammad 5, 412
Samavna 208
Sanqaşī 49
Santabay ash-Sharifi 110, 112 ftn., 114
Sāra Hatun 358
Sarī al-Saqatī 381, 396-397, 415-418
Sassanians 124
Sayf-i Ferghanī 254
Sayf-i Sarayī 73, 292-293, 299
Sayyid Ali al-Siwasī 336
saz 285, 352, 367
Schefer, Charles 133
Schimmel, Annemarie 375, 384, 390
Schmidt, Jan 37, 138, 170, 172
Schneekoppe, Mt. Sneñka 431
Scholem, Gerschom 135
Schönwalde 427
Schuckmann, Kaspar Friedr. von 428-429
Schwabing, Munich 197
Script Revolution 148, 150
Sehī Beg 269-270, 273, 294
Selaniki, Mustafa 317, 330, 347
Selçuk Hatun 358
Seljuks 35, 227, 237, 241, 274-275, 318, 452
Selīm I 49, 80, 117, 123, 171-178, 203, 235, 257, 261, 276, 278, 280-281, 326, 453, 455, 457
Selīm III, Ottoman sultan 97-100, 425, 432
Selīme 378, 412-413
Semendria 357
Sencer, İsmail Sa'ib 132
Serbian King 357, 368
Serbs 320
Sertel, M. Zekeriya 155 ftn.
Server Bedi, Peyami Safa 159
Servet-i fünun 157, 159-160
Seydişehir 274
Seyrekzade Mehmet ʿAsim 295
Seyyid Ahmed el-Bukhari 261
Seyyid ʿAlī Efendi 97
Seyyid Loqman 283
Seyyidī ʿAlīzade 123
Shad Bek min Özdemir 112
Shafiʿī, Imam 81-82, 334-335, 338
Shāfiʿite 336
Shah of Persia 203, 209, 233
Shāhin Pasha 326
Shahnāma Firdawsī 124
Shāhnāme in Turkish 108
Shalabi 331-333, 335
Shams-i Tabrizi 253
Shamsaddīn Muhammad b. Mahmud b. Khalil Ibn Ajā 111
Shaqā'iq 255-257, 266, 269
al-Shaʿrānī 335
Sharīf Husayn b. Hasan 108-110
Shaʿwāna 386-387
Shaw, Stanford 139, 143, 146, 426
Shaybanī Khan Uzbek 88, 231, 234
Shaykh of Mu'ayyad mosque 91
Shaykh Husayn 50
Shaykh al-balad 85 ftn.
Shaykh Safī 121
Shaykh of Sufis, Mu'ayyadiya 80, 90, 108
Shayyal, El-Shayyal 79, 86
Shehinshah, Ottoman prince 261
Shem 207, 236
Shemʿūn Safā, apostle Peter 252
Sheykh Bayezid 272
Sheykh Chelebi 264
Sheykh Hamid 263
Sheykh Ilahi *see* Ilāhī
Sheykh Rūshenī, Ömer Dede 270, 272
Sheykh Vefā 258, 272
Shihābaddin Ahmad al-Fayyumi 112
Shihabaddin Ahmad as-Sivasī 4
Shiʿism 229
Shiʿite 284, 348, 385
Shiʿites, extreme 209, 409, 455
Shiraz 108, 271, 441
Silesia 427-432
Silk Route 448, 461
Silopi 462

Simav in Germiyan 263
Sinān Paşa 56, 64, 317, 345
Sincar 454
sinlessness ʿisma 385
Sinop, Sinope 10, 40-41, 44, 370
Sipahsalar, Faridun b. Ahmad 254
Siracaddin Urmavi 5
Siryaqaws 111
Sistowa (Sivstov, Ziştivu) 432
Sivas 151, 263
Siver Bey 194
Siverek 450-451, 456
Sivrihisar 373, 374 ftn.
Siyer *see* Darīr 385
Skoplje Üsküp 414
slave dealers, markets 282, 353, 382, 413
slaves, female 321, 323, 355, 359, 360-362, 366, 369, 373, 377-383, 386-388, 395-396, 404, 410-412, 414, 416-417
slavery 2, 282, 318, 320-321, 353, 355, 359, 366-367, 372, 387, 396, 411, 415
Smith, Margaret 384
Smith, Admiral Sir Sidney 436
Society for Union and Progress 10
Sohrweide, Hanna 36 ftn.
Solaqzade 172
Soviet Russia 41, 148, 161, 463
Spain 39, 178-181, 221-223
Spinoza, Baruch 423
spirit of God 384
Spree River 435
Spuler, Bertold 135
St. Petersburg 428
Stadion, Johann Philipp, Count 436
Standard of the Prophet 329
steam engine 430
Stebleva, I.V. 311
Stockholm 200
Stoerck, Anton von (1731-1803) 136
Straits (Dardanelles) 326
Striedl, Hans 135-136
Strousberg, Bethel Henry 191, 200
Stuhlweissenburg 279
Suat Derviş 164 ftn.
Sufi 13, 50, 52, 80, 106, 206, 253-254, 257, 260, 262, 268, 270, 272-273, 296, 333, 339, 375, 384, 399-400, 402, 404, 410, 451
Sufism 85, 272, 258, 272, 375, 377, 386, 402, 414
Sufi orders 86, 105
suhbat, companionship 386, 398-401
sukhta, softa 333
Sultan Şah Hatun 2
Sultan Husayn Mirza 311
Sultan Veled 1, 254, 271, 288-289
as-Sunbuliya, barracks 113
Sunnis, Ottoman 209, 224, 284
supplication 317-320, 322-323, 325-330, 417
sūrnāme 39
Sururi 312
al-Suyūtī, Jalāl ad-dīn 92, 211
Sūzī Chelebi 180, 345, 366
Süheyl u Nevbahar 288, 290
Süleyman Çelebi 255, 272, 288
Süleyman, Emir, Ottoman 176, 214
Süleymān Paşa, Ottoman 362
Süleymān Shah 230
Süleymanshah, Aydınoğlu 2, 27
Süleyman Şāh of Germiyan 356
Süleyman, sultan 53, 70, 81, 118 ftn., 119, 180-183, 203, 208, 212-213, 216-217, 221, 224-230, 232, 245, 257, 259, 270, 273, 276-289, 324, 327-330, 346-347, 456-457
Süleymannāme by Hadīdī 324
sürgün forced settlement 359
Süssheim collection 35-36, 39, 137
Süssheim, Karl 11, 36, 131
Süssheim, Max 131, 135
Syria 47-50, 76, 85, 101, 103, 107-108, 111, 116, 118, 157, 226, 262, 278, 334, 338, 384, 452
Syria, Arab Republic 450, 463
Syrmia, Plain 218, 281
Székesfehérvár 279
Şāh Hatun 358
Şahin, shaykh 93
Şāhīn Qandī 185
Şahnama 47, 50-51, 88, 93
Şahnama, Turkish 47-48, 90
Şahqulı 204, 209
Şams-i Kays 287
Şanizade ʿAtaʾullah (d. 1826) 136
Şanlıurfa 448, 451, 461-462, 465
al-Şanqajī 49
Şarafaddīn Yunus al-ʿĀdilī 49
aş-Şaʿrānī 86, 335
Şaʿrāwī 82
Şarīf Husayn (Şerīf) 47, 52
aş-Şarqawī 79

Şaybanī Khan 88
Şayh ʿIzzeddin Pur-i Hasan Asfara'ini 73, 76
şehīd 180-181, 217
Şemseddīn Muhammed b. Mahmūd, Ibn Aja 55
Şemsettin Sāmī 166
Şerif 30, 47-57, 90, 93-95
Şerīfī 56
Şerīfī-yi Amidī 56
Şeyhī, Yusuf Sinan 30-31, 33-34, 37, 272-273, 289
Şeyhoglu Mustafa 9, 16-17, 29, 33, 289
Şeyyād Hamza 255, 286, 288, 297
Şirin Dede 465
Şırnak 462
Şükrī, Kurd 117-118, 121, 123, 127, 209
Şükûfe Nihal 159

Tabaristan 210
al-Tabbāh 57
Tabrīz 93, 107, 118, 258, 263, 270, 272, 441-442, 454
Tācī Beg 261
Taci-zade Caʿfer Celebi 64, 261, 290, 299
Taeschner, Franz 60, 68
Taharten 370
Tahiroglu, Khalvetī sheykh 264
Tahmasb I 279, 348, 457
tahrīf 246
Tajik 121
Takrir-i Sükûn 148, 151, 156, 160
Talʿat Pasha 134
Talhis al-balaga 287
Talleyrand, Prince Charles Maurice 97-98
Talu, Ercüment Ekrem 159
Tanpınar, Ahmet Hamdi 154, 160
Tanrıdağ 42
Tanzimat Period 60, 63, 135, 160, 163
Tapduk Emre 255, 265-266, 268-269
Taqī al-Dīn al-Hisnī 409
Tarīqa Muhammadīya 334
Tarnowitz (Tarnowskie Góry) 430-431
Tarsus 49
Task Force Iron Horse 462
taşeron, taşeronlaştırma 463-464
Taşköprüzade Ahmed 121, 255-258, 265-266, 269, 273-275
Taşlıcalı Yahya 291
Tata 279
Tatar Khans 228
Tatars 365, 368
Tavernier, Jean-Baptiste 458, 460-461
taylasan 338
Tayyarzade Ahmed Ata 269
tazarruʿ 317, 320, 325, 327-330
Tazarruʿname 64, 317, 345
TBMM National Assembly 462
Tears of Anatolia 254
Teke ili 204
Tekfur 360-361, 369, 373
telekinesis 397, 404
telegraph 39, 201
telepathy, firāsa 413
Tell Afar 454
Tell Bism 459-460,464
Temennā'ī 273
Temür, Mamluk 113
Tenibek min Tashbek 112
Tepegöz, Depegöz 363, 439
Testa family 172-174
Testa, Baron de 194
Tevarih-i Al-i ʿOsman, TʿAO 176, 182, 207, 324, 326
Tevfik Fikret 160, 166, 168
tezkire (biographies) 67, 269-271, 273, 295, 298
Theodora 357
Thermopylae 125
Tholuck, F.A.G. 440 ftn.
Tietze, Andreas 65, 71
TİGEM 463
Tigris 449, 457
Timur 27, 29, 226-228, 232, 262, 274, 318, 374
Timurids 88, 92, 108, 123, 226, 229, 231, 441
Timurtaş, shaykh 93
Tire 2, 4, 28
Tirmidh, Termez 391
Tirmidhī, Muhammad b. ʿAlī 390-391, 394, 404
Tirmidhī, wife of 390-392, 394, 405, 414
Togay Timur 231
Toğlı Hoca 293
Tokat 264, 372
Torah 250
toy, banqueting 353
Transylvania 179, 186, 220

Trebizond 125, 151
Trebizond, Emperor of 358
Trencsény Imre 179
Troy 365
Tuhfa 377, 381, 386, 395-396, 414-419
Tulum, Mertol 349
Tumanbay, last Mamluk sultan 80
Tunis 222, 279
Turābī 273
Turgut Turkmens 371
Turkism 42
Turkish women 356, 407
Turkmen dynasties 226-227
Turkmen tribes 229, 233, 318, 453-454, 459-460
Turkmens, province of 264-266, 269
Turkomans 1, 13, 47
Turks 392
Turmış Khan 454
Tursun Beg 169, 235, 349-350, 363, 365, 369, 371, 373
Tursun Fakih 288
Tūsī 258, 262
Tūtī Kadın 355
Tutmacı 33, 298
Türk 236
türkçeleştirmek 167-168
Türkiye Bibliyografyası 165
Türkmen 107, 128, 318, 359, 362, 371-372, 451-452
Türkmenlik 19
Tütengil, Cavit Orhan 42-43
Tütünsüz Ahmed Rızvān 176

Ubaydullah Ahrar 257, 261-262, 413 ftn.
uc, western marches 1
Uğur, A. 326
Ukraine 41, 425
Uljay (Abulja, Bulja) 230
Ulu ʿĀrif Çelebi 1
Uludağ, Süleyman 259
Umm ʿAbdallah 390
Umm ʿAlī Fātima 388
Umm Hāni' 405
Umm Hassan 387
Umm Salama 385 ftn.
Umur Beg of Aydın 3, 8, 11, 26-27, 125, 345
Umur II of Aydın 27, 29
Unitarian 241
Upper Mesopotamia 448
Upper Silesia 430
Urfa 450, 454, 456-457, 461, 465
Urmia 462
Uzbeks 231, 262
Uzluk, Feridun Nafız 135-136
Uzun, Fahri 166
Uzun Hasan 93, 120, 229, 324, 358, 371, 373-374
Ünver, İsmail 287

Vahīd-i Tabrizī 294
Vakit 156, 158, 167
Van 456
Varadin (Peterwardein) 218
Vardar valley 264
Vardar Yenicesi (Giannitsa) 264
Varna (1444) 179, 319, 322, 325, 329, 347
Varqa ve Gülşah 29, 288
Varsak Turkmens 372
Vefā'iyye 452
Velī Paşa 84
Venice 425, 428
Vesiletü n-necāt (Mevlid) 255, 288
Veysī 60, 65, 435 ftn.
Vidin 427-428
Vienna 44, 132, 200, 411, 435-436, 438
Vienna (1904) 200
Vienna (1529) 174, 181, 203, 212, 216, 219-222, 278-279, 283
Viranşehir (Constantina) 448, 451, 458-459, 461-463, 465
Virgin Mary 384
Vistula River 430
Voss, Richard 192-193, 198
Vulpius, Christiane 424, 431-432

Wagner, Richard 192
Wahhabi movement 78, 87, 140, 332-333
Wallachian princess 366
Walsh, John R. 12, 29, 32, 61 ftn., 68
Walther, Wiebke 384
al-Wāqidī 55 fn., 111
Warmbrunn 431
Warner, Levinus 183-184, 186, 440
Wedekind, Frank 200
Weimar 190-191, 196, 425, 427, 431, 434, 438

Weinreich, Uriel 122, 126
Well-Preserved Tablet, lawh mahfuz 335-336
Wiet, Gaston 111, 147
Wilhelm II 199-200
Wittek, Paul 207, 226
Wladyslaw III of Poland 322
Wolf, Friedr. August 424, 435, 437, 440
woman of Tirmidh 389
women, Jewish, Armenian, Greek 361, 377 ftn.
women, free Muslim 377-378
Woods, John E. 226
World War, First 134, 160

Ya'cūc ve Ma'cūc 217
Yāfi'ī 386, 400, 415
Yahşı Beg 2
Yahya b. Ishaq, s. Hākī
Yahya Kemal (Beyatlı) 160
Yahyā b. al-Tāj 56 ftn.
Yalakonya 358, 360
Ya'qub II of Germiyan 33, 358
Ya'qūb Beg 348-349
Ya'qūb, Prince 320
Ya'qub Shah of Arzanjan 108
Yārhisār castle 360, 366
Yasa of Djingiz 226
Yasawī 255
Yashbek min Mahdi 53-54, 76, 90, 108-109, 111, 310 ftn.
Yashbek's Dome 53-54, 108, 111
Yayla 360
Yazıcı Salahaddīn 213 ftn.
Yazıcıoghlu Ahmed Bīcān 265 ftn.
Yazıcıoghlu Alī 35, 228
Yazıcıoglu brothers 265
Yazıcızade Mehmed 260, 272
Yedi Meşale 161
Yedikule 197, 440 ftn.
Yenice (Vardar) 264
Yesari, Mahmut 159
Yesevī 255
yevimlü 457
Yıldız Palace 200
Yörgüç Pasha 319
Young Turks 134, 198
Young Turk Revolution 133, 149, 157, 201
Yukarı Karataş 464
Yūnus Emre 254-255, 258, 260, 265-269, 288, 296-298
Yūsuf al-Mallawani 332
Yūsuf b. Muhammad an-Nuri 6
Yūsuf Meddah 29, 33, 288
Yūsuf Nabi 39
Yūsuf Pasha (1790) 427
Yusuf Ziya (Ortaç) 160-161
Yücel, Hasan-Ali (1897-1960) 136, 160 ftn., 164 ftn.
Yüksekova 462
Yüksel, Sedit 166

Zahir ad-Dīn Muhammad Babur 311
Zajaczkowski, Ananiasz 57, 77
az-Zamahşarī 91
zaviye 81, 451
Zaytūna 410
Zedlitz, Christoph von 220
Zeyrek Mosque 262
Zihni Mehmed, Berberzade 144
az-Zimam, Zimamiya, barracks 112, 115
zimmī 241
Ziya Gökalp 42
Zola, Emile 159
Zübdetü l-eş'ār 295
Zürcher, E.J. 156 ftn.
Zuwayla Gate, Cairo, Iron gate 52, 80, 83, 334-335

Printed in the United States
By Bookmasters